MAIN PROBLEMS IN
AMERICAN HISTORY

THE DORSEY SERIES IN AMERICAN HISTORY

Main Problems in American History

_____Volume Two

Edited by

HOWARD H. QUINT
MILTON CANTOR
DEAN ALBERTSON

All of the University of Massachusetts

Third Edition ● 1972
THE DORSEY PRESS   *Homewood, Illinois   60430*
IRWIN-DORSEY LIMITED   *Georgetown, Ontario*

Third Edition

First Printing, March 1972

Library of Congress Catalog Card No. 75–185443
Printed in the United States of America

To the memory of our friends and colleagues

NORMAN FURNISS

FRANCIS B. SIMKINS

ARTHUR W. THOMPSON

Preface

We have designed this two-volume work, the collaborative effort of 34 scholars, primarily for use in college survey courses in American history. It does not replace textbooks customarily used to impart basic information to the student. Nor does it serve as a substitute for the reading of historical literature. Its function rather is to acquaint students with historical problems that are directly related to the general context of a survey course yet highly significant in themselves.

These problems, we believe, are particularly well adapted for use in small discussion sections of large lecture courses, inasmuch as they offer both a focus and a direction to such class meetings. As instructors and students well know, such sessions are frequently a chore for the former and a bore to the latter. And the reasons are not hard to discover: either the law of diminishing returns is defied by a review of the week's work, or a brave but futile effort is made to discuss documentary readings, assigned with little or no relationship to an understood frame of reference. In recent years, efforts have been made to have students read articles giving conflicting interpretations of historical events in the hope that they will see the exciting clashes of issues which make history the fascinating discipline that it is. But often such articles, appearing in scholarly journals and written for specialists, have a strong historiographical emphasis. They may confuse more than enlighten freshmen and sophomores.

We have attempted to write, each in his own way, an interpretive essay which will serve as a point of departure for a challenging class discussion. We do not claim to have said the final word on any subject; we have sought only to open up problems for further probing. Doubtless many instructors and students will take issue with our analyses or interpretations; their independent reactions should generate the intellectual interplay that must be at the very heart of any really satisfactory class discussion. We have made no effort to shape the essays to any particular pattern or to prevent the various writers from stepping on each other's scholarly toes, or at times from traversing the same historical ground.

Appended to each essay is a small number of documents which have a direct relationship to points raised in the essays. In this way, documents which by themselves might be dull and insignificant become alive and meaningful. This method of presentation helps the students understand how the historian makes use of primary source materials in arriving at conclusions and in writing history. Whenever possible, the contributors have selected documents which have not been overworked in source books and consequently will be reasonably fresh for students and instructors alike.

In again revising *Main Problems of American History* we have eliminated a few of the problems appearing in the last edition and have added six new ones. Nearly all of the remaining problems have been revised, some substantially and others very little, in response to suggestions by those who previously have taught from these volumes.

February 1972

HOWARD H. QUINT
MILTON CANTOR
DEAN ALBERTSON

Contents

18 Reconstruction: The Nation's Unfinished Business

HENRY F. BEDFORD
Phillips Exeter Academy

Reconstruction, Abraham Lincoln remarked as he received the news of Appomattox, "is fraught with great difficulty." The President's victory speech soberly emphasized the uncertain future, not the triumphant past; unlike many Americans, he had never expected military victory alone to restore the Union. He lacked specific solutions to the tangled political, economic, and social problems that lay ahead, but he was at least aware that the war had not solved them. In the dozen years after Lincoln's death, the northern effort to reconstruct the South subtly evolved into a national effort to secure sectional harmony. The nation's black population paid the price of reunion. And the dilemmas Lincoln had foreseen endured, like the granite in the monuments Americans of both sections erected to the dead.

There are no monuments to Reconstruction, for nations do not memorialize failures. Reconstruction just ended; it was not completed. If the South rejoined the Democratic Party and became once more a participant in the national political process, regional peculiarities have ever since set the section off from national politics. While diligent Southerners of both races slowly rebuilt their agrarian economy, industry rapidly transformed the rest of the country and created problems and opportunities that the South

did not wholly share. Finally, emancipation was only the essential first step toward equitable race relations. Postwar generations never finished the journey.

Statesmen of the time discussed Reconstruction as a legal and constitutional question. Were southern states entitled to constitutional rights as if they had never rebelled? Or were they, as Thaddeus Stevens claimed, "conquered provinces," subject to the unlimited power of Congress over federal territories? Was Reconstruction the President's prerogative, for his power to pardon was certainly relevant; or was it, instead, the responsibility of Congress, which must consent before the South would again be represented in the national legislature? Could Congress demand the ratification of a constitutional amendment as a condition for readmission? Could a state that was unqualified to participate in Congress legally ratify any amendment?

The Constitution held no final answers to these questions, as those who posed them knew. Yet the apparently trivial constitutional controversy masked a basic dispute over policy. Defenders of the South claimed the protection of continuous statehood to preserve what remained of the old way of life. Advocates of racial justice, by contrast, argued that the seceded states had abandoned the protection of the Constitution when they shirked the responsibilities of membership in a federal union.

Lincoln knew that Reconstruction was much more than a legal nicety. He dismissed the prolonged discussion of the legality of secession as "a merely pernicious abstraction." Lincoln thought Reconstruction could be accomplished "without deciding or even considering" whether the Confederacy had been outside the Union. Lincoln stressed agreement, not dispute: "We all agree that the seceeded States, so called, are out of their proper practical relation with the Union; and that the sole object of the government . . . is to again get them into that proper practical relation."

Many Republicans thought Lincoln's political conception of Reconstruction too narrow. These critics, called Radicals, wanted to punish the South and to create a new pattern of southern life. In place of ruined or neglected plantations, Radicals saw economically independent farmers of both races tilling their own small farms. Where illiteracy and discrimination had been decreed, they hoped to establish schools and toleration. They proposed to educate, or coerce, the South toward racial equality and to finish building that "more perfect Union" that the Constitutional Convention had begun.

Not all Republicans were radical, and not all Radicals accepted the whole program for remolding the South that such leaders as Charles Sumner and Thaddeus Stevens championed. Stevens proposed to confiscate all southern land except individual holdings of less than 200 acres. He suggested that some of this land be granted to Negroes to assure their economic independence. The rest, Stevens said, should be sold to reduce the national debt, to establish a fund for Union soldiers or their widows and children, and to replace northern property destroyed during the war. For if the South paid no reparation, northern taxpayers would, in effect, subsidize the defeated enemy by bearing the war's indirect costs. That situation, Stevens charged, was absurd.

Stern, unforgiving Thaddeus Stevens may have been right. Without economic security, black freedom was not firmly based; peonage and slavery have much in common. Yet, the radicalism of most of Stevens' Republican colleagues stopped at the confiscation of slaveholders' human property and did not extend to their plantations. Congress gave no farms to Negroes, but it did, at least temporarily, support and protect them in their transition from slavery to freedom.

The Freedmen's Bureau, established about a month before the end of the war, was the congressional instrument. In the confusion immediately after Appomattox, the bureau fed refugees of both races and helped them to relocate. It also secured jobs for freedmen and supervised their employment to prevent the concealed reestablishment of slavery. The agency established and maintained schools and hospitals, in both of which the South was deficient. And it attempted to protect the Negroes' legal equality and to prevent social discrimination.

The Freedmen's Bureau did not function equally well in all places. Some agents were corrupt; some abused the trust of Negroes; some developed the political possibilities inherent in the bureau to promote their own careers. Indeed, no part of Radical Reconstruction was free of political overtones. Thaddeus Stevens, forthright as usual, declared that any program must "secure perpetual ascendancy to the party of the union. . . ." The Thirteenth Amendment, Stevens pointed out, abolished the former practice of counting a slave as three-fifths of a person; as a result, the South once readmitted would be entitled to more Congressmen than had represented the section before the war. More Congressmen meant more electoral votes, thus endangering Republican control of the White House, for Democrats could fuse their northern minority with the South to create a national majority.

Stevens was probably honest in his conviction that the Republic could not be entrusted to "whitewashed rebels." But his motives may have been less disinterested than he acknowledged, and some Republicans certainly hoped to use Reconstruction to serve themselves. Stevens, for instance, owned a southern Pennsylvania iron mine that Confederates had extensively damaged; his interest in compensating northern propertyholders for wartime destruction may have arisen from his own losses. Like other ironmasters, Stevens was also a confirmed advocate of the protective tariff; protection seemed to depend on continued Republican supremacy, for Democrats had traditionally opposed the policy. The Pennsylvanian strove for Negro suffrage not only as a result of egalitarian conviction, but also because he wanted to perpetuate Republicanism with the support of black voters.

As Stevens' motives were mixed, so too were those of other Republicans. Through dominance of the Democratic party before the war, the South had prevented enactment of the comprehensive program that Republicans had finally completed. The fortuitous secession of the Confederacy had certainly hastened passage of protective tariffs, the national banking system, the Homestead Act, and federal grants to transcontinental railroads. Postwar Democrats were still hostile to part of this program. Furthermore, they were flirting with various forms of economic heresy, such as the notion that national bonds should be redeemed in the inflated greenbacks with which they had often been purchased, instead of in gold as the bond promised. Northern businessmen, whose opinions weighed heavily with Republican politicians, preferred fiscal orthodoxy. And the North glimpsed the promise of industrial plenty; it seemed no time for economic experimentation.

The South was equally unready for social and political experimentation in the form of Radical Reconstruction, and perhaps Abraham Lincoln agreed. A deadlock between Congress and the President seemed possible when Lincoln pocket vetoed the Wade-Davis bill, the first Radical attempt to punish and re-shape the South. Once a staunch Whig, Lincoln may have hoped to gain support for gradual change from the same coalition of moderates in both sections that had sustained his old party. Some Radicals so mistrusted the President that they welcomed Johnson's succession. For Andrew Johnson seemed to have nothing in common with those substantial Southerners whom Lincoln hoped might become the pillars of a southern Republican Party. But to the surprised dismay of the Radicals, the self-made man from Tennessee, who had never acted like a Southerner during the war, appeared ready to join the Confederacy after Appomattox.

For in 1865, Johnson used his power to pardon almost without limit. While Radicals fumed because Congress was in impotent recess, Johnson encouraged amnestied Southerners to establish new constitutions, hold elections, and complete Reconstruction before Congress resumed in December. He insisted that the South ratify the 13th Amendment, repudiate the Confederate debt, and repeal ordinances of secession. White Southerners hastened to adopt Johnson's terms, which were surely among the most generous ever imposed on a defeated foe. Although the President withheld political rights from a few prominent former Confederates, voters all over the South chose many of the men who had led them out of the Union to lead them back in. Mississippi and South Carolina elected Confederate generals as governors; Georgia chose the Confederacy's vice president, Alexander Stephens, for the Senate of the United States. Neither the southern voter nor Andrew Johnson made any tactful gesture to quiet mounting northern suspicion that a costly victory was being cheaply given away.

Negroes and others who had added equality to such war aims as freedom and union thought Johnson's terms too generous. For example, a group of black Virginians pointed out that Johnson's plan permitted former Confederates, who were organizing and dominating the state government, to suppress both black and white supporters of the Union. The President had left them, these Negroes complained, "entirely at the mercy of . . . unconverted rebels," and they appealed for "an *equal chance* with the white *traitors*" whom the President had pardoned. Without the protection of the ballot and federal arms to enforce equal rights, the Blacks expected their former masters would make freedom "more intolerable" than slavery.

Those whom Johnson pardoned did indeed try to preserve as much of the prewar social order as possible. Most white southerners had believed slavery essential to the region's civilization; they still believed that legal freedom could never make their former slaves the equal of any white man. So the black codes that southern legislatures adopted to replace slave codes made only grudging concessions to the freedmen.

These black codes allowed the Negro a family. They permitted one black to marry another and made black parents legally responsible for their children. Most statutes also defined the legal rights of freedmen, and they often made blacks the legal equals of whites in the courtroom, though in some states blacks could not testify against whites.

Equality ceased with these provisions. Apprenticeship regulations bounded the economic and social freedom of young Negroes; courts were to order the apprenticeship of unemployed young freedmen and give preference to their former masters, an arrangement that often differed little from slavery. Vagrancy regulations and laws forbidding disorderly conduct gave enforcement officers wide discretion and similarly restricted the social and economic life of black adults. Any Mississippi Negro who could not pay the poll tax or who lacked regular employment was guilty of vagrancy. Those convicted could be leased to employers who would pay fines and costs; former masters were again to have preference, and again the result might be only technically distinguishable from bondage. Even if the Negro avoided these statutes, other laws kept him out of the white community. For instance, the only black passengers permitted in first-class railroad cars in Mississippi were maids, who were allowed to wait on their white mistresses.

But the South's version of Reconstruction was incomplete without the approval of Congress, where reaction to the black codes was prompt and hostile. Even Republican moderates were unconvinced that the governments Johnson had approved represented loyal, reformed, and contrite Southerners. Radicals denounced Johnson's work as a sham and urged Congress to undertake genuine Reconstruction. Rebels had proudly reestablished " 'the white man's Government,' " Thaddeus Stevens reported, and Congress ought resolutely to prove that such governments were entirely unacceptable components of the federal Republic. Demagogues, including "some high in authority," he continued with a barbed reference to the President, had appealed to the "lowest prejudices of the ignorant" to maintain the dominance of southern whites. Stevens held that the white race had "no exclusive right forever to rule this nation," nor did he shrink from the conclusion: This nation, he said, must not be " 'the white man's Government,' " but rather "the Government of all men alike. . . ."

Stevens was still ahead of his party. Most northern states did not yet permit blacks to vote, and most Republicans were not yet ready to demand equal political rights for the freedmen. But northern Republicans did insist on more change than Johnson had secured. Congress sent the southern legislators home in December 1865 and established congressional terms for reunion in two bills and a proposed constitutional amendment. The President vetoed both bills and joined those who opposed the amendment. His intransigence blighted any hope for a compromise program. For moderate Republicans, forced to choose between Stevens's radicalism and the unreconstructed governments Johnson had endorsed, chose radicalism. Andrew Johnson's political ineptitude and the adamant refusal of white Southerners to concede Negroes more than technical emancipation drove the Republican Party to Thaddeus Stevens and military Reconstruction.

Moderates began with a bill to prolong the life of the Freedmen's Bureau and to give it a quasi-judicial authority over disputes arising from discrimination or denial of civil rights. The bill deprived state courts of jurisdiction in such cases and specifically contradicted southern black codes by making punishable the sort of discrimination they permitted. Though the bill's sponsors thought they had secured the President's approval, Johnson vetoed the measure. The bureau, he held, had grown out of the war's emergency and was based on the constitutional grant of power for war, which Congress could not legitimately invoke in peace. Once ordinary institutions, including civil courts, were reestablished, the bureau should disband.

Congress could not immediately override Johnson's veto, and moderates tried again to resolve the impasse with the Civil Rights bill of 1866. This measure officially made Negroes American citizens, thus overturning the *Dred Scott* decision, and guaranteed "the full and equal benefit of all laws ... for the security of person or property" to all citizens. Federal courts were to have jurisdiction over cases in which citizens had been deprived of equal rights. The bill received the support of every House Republican and all but three Republican senators. And Andrew Johnson vetoed it because it infringed on the reserved powers of the states.

Congress overrode that veto, and for good measure it salvaged the Freedmen's Bureau bill and also passed it over Johnson's veto. To preserve its handiwork, Congress then framed the constitutional amendment that eventually became the 14th. Johnson could not prevent the submission of the amendment to the states, but his hostility encouraged southern states to block ratification temporarily. Tennessee, the President's own state, ratified the amendment and was rewarded by full restoration to the Union. Other Southerners rejected the amendment and waited.

They waited too long, for the price of readmission went up. Andrew Johnson took his cause to the country in the congressional election of 1866. His performance on the stump struck the public as undignified, and his tour was as inept as his performance in the White House. Voters sent to Washington a new Congress with enough Radical votes to overwhelm the President.

Radicals lost no time. Congress took the initiative on Reconstruction and asserted its control over the rest of the government as well. The presidential authority to command the army was abridged by a requirement that all orders be issued through the Army Chief of Staff Ulysses S. Grant, who could not be removed or reassigned without the Senate's consent. The Tenure of Office Act required the Senate's approval for removal of any official for whom senatorial confirmation was necessary; Radicals hoped thereby to protect members of Johnson's Cabinet, particularly Secretary of War Edwin Stanton, who opposed the President's program. (Control of the Army was crucial to the Radicals because they expected to develop a plan of military reconstruction.) Congress took steps to eliminate involuntary congressional recesses and limited the power of the Supreme Court to decide cases that might invalidate congressional programs.

Andrew Johnson was not intimidated. He vetoed the Reconstruction Act and those supplemental measures Congress later added to make the program comprehensive. Since Congress promptly overrode them, his vetoes were futile. By these acts, Congress combined 10 states into five military districts and subordinated state governments to military commanders. The governments and constitutions Johnson had approved in 1865 were discarded, and new constitutions granting Negro suffrage and guaranteeing racial equality were required. This legislation unquestionably mocked the traditional rights of states, as both Johnson and the South claimed. Radicals, however, had minimal interest in the constitutional pretenses of the defeated section and counted the doctrine of states' rights an unmourned casualty of the Civil War.

And they set out to make the Presidency an unmourned casualty of Reconstruction. For though the resolution of the House impeached Andrew Johnson, the target at which many Radicals aimed was the office itself. The charge against Johnson specified 11 offenses, most of which arose from the President's attempt to remove Stanton from the Cabinet. But, Thaddeus Stevens confessed, he for one did not impeach the President for any particular offense, or even for all of them together. Stevens wanted to remove Johnson for his political mistakes, not for his moral or legal lapses. Impeachment, Stevens believed, was simply the only available method of ridding the nation of the President's wretched judgment.

The House debated all of Andrew Johnson's alleged crimes: his partiality toward the South, his public disrespect of Congress and its leadership, his undignified inauguration as Vice President, his baselessly rumored complicity in Lincoln's assassination, and his deliberate violations of the Tenure of Office Act. The President was acquitted partly because the Senate found the bill of particulars too flimsy a basis for so unprecedented a step. He was also acquitted because a few senators chose to support the independence of the executive branch rather than establish a precedent that might lead to a ministry responsible to the legislature, as is a parliamentary cabinet. The margin in the Senate was slim; Johnson survived by one vote. Thirty-five Republicans voted to

convict; 12 Democrats and 7 Republicans found for the President. With the roll calls in the Senate, Washington ceased to be the main forum for debate over Reconstruction. The President was isolated; Congress had done its part. At last Reconstruction was to take place in the South.

Americans since the 1870s have harshly judged the process. Black Reconstruction, so the story goes, was an undignified, corrupt, expensive, regrettable social experiment from which enlightened white conservatives freed the South in 1877. The freedmen, their often venal northern allies the carpetbaggers, and a few unprincipled southern white scalawags looted southern treasuries, discredited themselves, and demonstrated the political incapacity of the black population. Most white Americans have complacently believed that return to white control preserved the section from bankruptcy and barbarism.

The belief, like most stereotypes, has a factual basis. Reconstruction did bring unprecedented taxes to the southern states; not all the money was honestly spent. Negroes did not universally resist financial temptation, nor were they always dignified and wise in their legislative deliberations. Illustrative statistics abound. Florida spent more for printing in 1869 than her entire state government had cost in 1860. Sometimes, bookkeeping was so casual that even a state legislature could not calculate the state debt. According to one estimate, the South Carolina debt tripled in three years, while another figure indicated that it had increased nearly six times. South Carolina also maintained at public expense a luxurious restaurant and bar that impartially dispensed imported delicacies to legislators of both races.

But the term Black Reconstruction is misleading, and the usual view of the process that the phrase describes is inaccurate. Only in South Carolina did blacks ever control the legislature—and only in one house of it at that. They held high office elsewhere in the South—Mississippi sent two blacks to the Senate of the United States—but they were by no means so dominant as the term Black Reconstruction implied. White politicians, to be sure, had to have black support to succeed, but the simplistic picture of black rule is incorrect.

Nor is the image of corrupt extravagance entirely justified. Rebuilding after a war is always expensive, and taxpayers always resent the bill. Further, Reconstruction governments not only had to restore public buildings and services; they also had to furnish new facilities and services that had been inadequate in most of the South. In many southern states, for example, public education for either race dates from these legislatures. Often for the first time states also accepted limited responsibility for the welfare of the indigent and sick.

The notorious corruption of Reconstruction frequently came from ambitious schemes to bring new life to the southern economy and to break the region's dependence on agriculture by introducing railroads and industry. Only the state commanded enough credit to entice the railroads that seemed the indispensable foundation of prosperity. Southern states issued bonds to finance railroad construction, but the proceeds sometimes vanished before the track was laid. Fraud in the development of the American rail network, however, was not peculiar to the South; as had happened elsewhere, public funds were converted to private use, and politicians pocketed fees that might more candidly have been called bribes. Nor were corrupted legislatures confined to the South in the post-Civil War era. The peculation of southern legislators was trifling by comparison with the simultaneous scandals of the Grant administration.

And not all corrupt Southerners were black. Some Negro politicians were bribed and some misused public funds, though no individual stole so much as the white treasurer of Mississippi embezzled immediately after the state was supposedly saved from irresponsible blacks. And for every purchased politician, there must have been a buyer. The fast-buck promoters of railroads and industry were whites, not blacks, few of whom were enriched by the plunder they were said to have secured from public treasuries.

Few blacks, indeed, were able to find even a legitimate source of wealth. Their lack of property reinforced provisions in the black codes that limited mobility. Any freedman who could not prove steady employment had to have a license authorizing some other arrangement. The contract that proved employment often specified annual wage payments, a practice that forced employees into debt for what was consumed while earning the first year's wage. And if a black left his employer before the contract expired, he forfeited wages earned earlier in the year.

Wages were ordinarily paid with a portion of the crop, for the war-shattered southern economy lacked local capital to renew agricultural production. Forced to rebuild their farms on credit, impoverished landowners hired impoverished farmers to work the land, and both looked for a big harvest to pay bills and interest already charged at the local store. If a profit resulted, it was probably too small to carry either owner or laborer through the subsequent season, and so the cycle began once more.

When the laborer was black, as he often was, contract and credit effectively replaced the restrictions of slavery. For without economic independence, Negroes lacked the means to sustain constitutional equality. Usually, a threat to turn him off the land or to stop his credit at the store was enough to make a Negro docile. Often, an unfulfilled contract or an unpaid debt legally required him to remain on a plot of land that had already proved unprofitable. When he resisted economic leverage and legal restraint, the Ku Klux Klan and its imitators perfected direct and brutal means of reminding him of his inferiority. So credit, statute, and terror evolved as new ways to return the Negro as nearly as possible to his old bondage. Constitutional amendments were unenforced in some areas, even before federal troops retired. As blacks were intimidated, whites passed laws to keep their former slaves from the polls and from the company of their former masters. Formal segregation and constitutional disfranchisement were natural sequels in another generation.

Black Reconstruction depended on a benevolent national administration that would keep troops in the South until whites could be won to toleration or blacks could secure their own equality. Bayonets are perhaps an unlikely method of securing equality; in any case, the northern voter and, hence, the national government, tired of the task too soon. And the use of military means for democratic ends is only one of the ambiguities that plague those who would understand and evaluate Reconstruction, for the period is replete with dilemmas of ends and means. White southerners wanted to preserve what they could of their customary way of life: some, in the process, were deceitful; some were cruel; most were unyielding on the central issue of white supremacy. Blacks wanted to become free Americans, and in the attempt some were foolish and some corrupt, but most were humbly patient. Radicals wanted to reconstruct the South: most of them expected to assure continued Republican hegemony; some expected to get rich; others intended to secure racial justice.

The tragedy of Reconstruction is that so little was permanently accomplished. White Southerners took refuge in a sentimentalized past. Blacks displayed more patience and more humility and in the end were the principal victims of the tragedy. Radicals died, and their party found laissez-faire a more congenial ideology than racial equality.

SUGGESTED READINGS

BEALE, HOWARD K. *The Critical Year*. New York: Harcourt, Brace & Co., 1930.

BELZ, HERMAN. *Reconstructing the Union: Theory and Policy during the Civil War.*
Ithaca, N.Y.: Cornell University Press, 1969.

DONALD, DAVID. *Charles Sumner and the Rights of Man.* New York: Alfred A. Knopf, 1970.

——. *The Politics of Reconstruction, 1863–1867.* Baton Rouge: Louisiana State University Press, 1965.

DUBOIS, W. E. BURGHARDT. *Black Reconstruction.* New York: Russell & Russell, 1935.

DUNNING, WILLIAM A. *Reconstruction: Political and Economic.* New York: Harper & Bros., 1907.

FLEMING, WALTER L. (ed.). *Documentary History of Reconstruction.* Gloucester, Mass.: Peter Smith, 1960.

FRANKLIN, JOHN HOPE. *Reconstruction.* Chicago: University of Chicago Press, 1962.

MCFEELEY, WILLIAM S. *Yankee Stephfather: General O. O. Howard and the Freedmen.* New Haven, Conn.: Yale University Press, 1968.

MCKITRICK, ERIC. *Andrew Johnson and Reconstruction.* Chicago: University of Chicago Press, 1960.

NOLEN, CLAUDE H. *The Negro's Image in the South: The Anatomy of White Supremacy.* Lexington: University of Kentucky Press, 1967.

PATRICK, REMBERT W. *The Reconstruction of the Nation.* New York: Oxford University Press, 1967.

ROSE, WILLIE LEE. *Rehearsal for Reconstruction.* New York: Bobbs-Merrill Co., 1964.

SEFTON, JAMES E. *The United States Army and Reconstruction, 1865–1877.* Baton Rouge: Louisiana State University Press, 1967.

STAMPP, KENNETH M. *The Era of Reconstruction, 1865–1877.* New York: Alfred A. Knopf, 1965.

TREFOUSSE, HANS L. *The Radical Republicans: Lincoln's Vanguard for Racial Justice.* New York: Alfred A. Knopf, 1969.

WILLIAMSON, JOEL. *After Slavery: The Negro in South Carolina during Reconstruction.* Chapel Hill: University of North Carolina Press, 1965.

WOODWARD, C. VANN. *Reunion and Reaction.* Boston: Little, Brown & Co., 1951.

The Legal Basis for Reconstruction*

The Civil Rights Act of 1866 and the Reconstruction amendments to the Constitution were intended to require legal equality as Reconstruction began. The Civil Rights Act of 1875, which the Supreme Court of the United States subsequently declared unconstitutional, was a futile attempt to extend equality to public accommodations.

THE AMENDMENTS

ARTICLE XIII [proposed 1 Feb. 1865; declared ratified 18 Dec. 1865]

Section 1. Neither slavery nor involuntary servitude, except as a punishment for crime whereof the party shall have been duly convicted, shall exist within the United States, or any place subject to their jurisdiction.

ARTICLE XIV [proposed 16 June 1866; declared ratified 28 July 1868]

Section 1. All persons born or naturalized in the United States, and subject to the jurisdiction thereof, are citizens of the United States and of the State wherein they reside. No State shall make or enforce any law which shall abridge the privileges or immunities of citizens of the United States; nor shall any State deprive any person of life, liberty, or property, without due process of law; nor deny to any person within its jurisdiction the equal protection of the laws.

Section 2. Representatives shall be apportioned among the several States according to their respective numbers, counting the whole number of persons in each State, excluding Indians not taxed. But when the right to vote at any election for the choice of electors for President and Vice President of the United States, Rep-

resentatives in Congress, the Executive and Judicial officers of a State, or the members of the Legislature thereof, is denied to any of the male inhabitants of such State, being twenty-one years of age, and citizens of the United States, or in any way abridged, except for participation in rebellion, or other crime, the basis of representation therein shall be reduced in the proportion which the number of such male citizens shall bear to the whole number of male citizens twenty-one years of age in such States.

Section 3. No person shall be a Senator or Representative in Congress, or elector of President and Vice President, or hold any office, civil or military, under the United States, or under any State, who, having previously taken an oath, as a member of Congress, or as an officer of the United States, or as a member of any State legislature, or as an executive or judicial officer of any State, to support the Constitution of the United States, shall have engaged in insurrection or rebellion against the same, or given aid and comfort to the enemies thereof. But Congress may by a vote of two-thirds of each House, remove such disability.

Section 4. The validity of the public debt of the United States authorized by law, including debts incurred for payment of pensions and bounties for services in suppressing insurrection or rebellion, shall not be questioned. But neither the United States nor any state shall assume or pay any debt or obligation incurred in aid of insurrection or rebellion against the United States, or any claim for the loss or emancipation of any slave; but all such debts, obligations, and claims shall be held illegal and void.

Section 5. The Congress shall have power to enforce, by appropriate legislation, the provisions of this article.

ARTICLE XV [proposed 27 Feb. 1869; declared ratified 30 Mar. 1870]

Section 1. The right of citizens of the United States to vote shall not be denied or abridged by the United States or by any

---

*Source: Civil Rights Acts from *U.S. Statutes at Large*, Vol. XIV, p. 27 ff.; Vol. XVIII, p. 335 ff.

State on account of race, color, or previous condition of servitude.

Section 2. The Congress shall have power to enforce this article by appropriate legislation.

THE CIVIL RIGHTS ACT OF 1866

Be it enacted, . . . That all persons born in the United States and not subject to any foreign power, excluding Indians not taxed, are hereby declared to be citizens of the United States; and such citizens, of every race and color, without regard to any previous condition of slavery or involuntary servitude, except as a punishment for crime whereof the party shall have been duly convicted, shall have the same right, in every State and Territory in the United States, to make and enforce contracts, to sue, be parties, and give evidence, to inherit, purchase, lease, sell, hold, and convey real and personal property, and to full and equal benefit of all laws and proceedings for the security of person and property, as is enjoyed by white citizens, and shall be subject to like punishment, pains and penalties, and to none other, any law, statute, ordinance, regulation, or custom, to the contrary notwithstanding.

Sec. 2. . . . Any person who, under color of any law, statute, ordinance, regulation, or custom, shall subject, or cause to be subjected, any inhabitant of any State or Territory to the deprivation of any right secured or protected by this act, or to different punishment, pains, or penalties on account of such person having at any time been held in a condition of slavery or involuntary servitude, except as a punishment for crime whereof the party shall have been duly convicted, or by reason of his color or race, than is prescribed for the punishment of white persons, shall be deemed guilty of a misdemeanor, and, on conviction, shall be punished by fine not exceeding one thousand dollars, or imprisonment not exceeding one year, or both, in the discretion of the court.

Sec. 3. . . . The district courts of the United States . . . shall have, exclusively of the courts of the several States, cognizance of all crimes and offenses committed against the provisions of this act, and also, concurrently with the circuit courts of the United States, of all causes, civil and criminal, affecting persons who are denied or cannot enforce in the courts or judicial tribunals of the State or locality where they may be any of the rights secured to them by the first section of this act; and if any suit or prosecution, civil or criminal, has been or shall be commenced in any State court, against any such person, for any cause whatsoever, or against any officer, civil or military, or other person, for any arrest or imprisonment, trespasses, or wrongs done or committed by virtue or under color of authority derived from this act or the act establishing a Bureau for the relief of Freedmen and Refugees, and all acts amendatory thereof, or for refusing to do any act upon the ground that it would be inconsistent with this act, such defendant shall have the right to remove such cause for trial to the proper district or circuit court. . . .

Sec. 4. . . . The district attorneys, marshals, and deputy marshals of the United States, the commissioners appointed by the circuit and territorial courts of the United States, with powers of arresting, imprisoning or bailing offenders against the laws of the United States, the officers and agents of the Freedmen's Bureau, and every other officer who may be specially empowered by the President of the United States, shall be, and they are hereby, specially authorized and required, . . . to institute proceedings against all and every person who shall violate the provisions of this act, and cause him or them to be arrested and imprisoned, or bailed, as the case may be, for trial before such court of the United States or territorial court as by this act has cognizance of the offense. And with a view to affording reasonable protection to all persons in their constitutional rights of equality before the law, without distinction of race or color, or previous condition of slavery or involuntary servitude, except as a punishment for crime, whereof the party shall have been duly convicted, and to the prompt discharge of the duties of this act, it shall be the duty of the circuit courts of the United States, and the superior courts of the Territories of the United States, from time to time, to increase the number of commissioners, so as to afford a speedy and convenient means for the arrest and examination of persons charged with a violation of this act; and such commissioners are hereby authorized and required to exercise and discharge all the powers and duties conferred on them by this act, and the same duties with regard to offenses created by this act, as they are authorized by law to exercise with regard to other offenses against the laws of the United States.

THE CIVIL RIGHTS ACT OF 1875

Whereas it is essential to just government we recognize the equality of all men before the law, and hold that it is the duty of government in its dealings with the people to mete out equal and exact justice to all, of whatever nativity, race, color, or persuasion, religious or political; and it being the appropriate object of legislation to enact great fundamental principles into law: Therefore,

Be it enacted, That all persons within the jurisdiction of the United States shall be entitled to the full and equal enjoyment of the accommodations, advantages, facilities, and privileges of inns, public conveyances on land or water, theaters, and other places of public amusement; subject only to the conditions and limitations established by law, and applicable alike to citizens of every race and color, regardless of any previous condition of servitude.

SEC. 2. That any person who shall violate the foregoing section by denying to any citizen, except for reasons by law applicable to citizens of every race and color, and regardless of any previous condition of servitude, the full enjoyment of any of the accommodations, advantages, facilities, or privileges in said section enumerated, or by aiding or inciting such denial, shall, for every such offense, forfeit and pay the sum of five hundred dollars to the person aggrieved thereby, . . . and shall also, for every such offense, be deemed guilty of a misdemeanor, and, upon conviction thereof, shall be fined not less than five hundred nor more than one thousand dollars, or shall be imprisoned not less than thirty days nor more than one year. . . .

SEC. 3. That the district and circuit courts of the United States shall have, exclusively of the courts of the several States, cognizance of all crimes and offenses against, and violations of, the provisions of this act . . .

SEC. 4. That no citizen possessing all other qualifications which are or may be prescribed by law shall be disqualified for service as grand or petit juror in any court of the United States, or of any State, on account of race, color, or previous condition of servitude; and any officer or other person charged with any duty in the selection or summoning of jurors who shall exclude or fail to summon any citizen for the cause aforesaid shall, on conviction thereof, be deemed guilty of a misdemeanor, and be fined not more than five thousand dollars. . . .

DOCUMENT 18.2

Black Codes*

After Appomattox, the southern states conceded military defeat and acknowledged legal emancipation. But the black codes that were enacted throughout much of the Confederacy in the year following Lee's surrender derived from the statutes

*Source: W. L. Fleming (ed.), *Documentary History of Reconstruction*, Vol. I (Cleveland: Arthur H. Clark Co., 1906), pp. 279–93.

and customs of slavery. The first selection below is the police regulations of a Louisiana parish; the second is Mississippi's vagrancy statute; third is the provision for legal equality enacted in North Carolina.

LOCAL REGULATIONS
IN LOUISIANA (1865)

Whereas it was formerly made the duty of the police jury to make suitable regulations for the police of slaves within the limits of the parish; and whereas slaves have become emancipated by the action of the ruling powers; and whereas it is necessary for public order, as well as for the comfort and correct deportment of said freedmen, that suitable regulations should be established for their government in their changed condition, the following ordinances are adopted with the approval of the United States military authorities commanding in said parish, viz:

SEC. 1. *Be it ordained by the policy jury of the parish of St. Landry,* That no negro shall be allowed to pass within the limits of said parish without special permit in writing from his employer. Whoever shall violate this provision shall pay a fine of two dollars and fifty cents, or in default thereof shall be forced to work four days on the public road, or suffer corporeal punishment as provided hereinafter.

SEC. 2. . . . Every negro who shall be found absent from the residence of his employer after ten o'clock at night, without a written permit from his employer, shall pay a fine of five dollars, or in default thereof, shall be compelled to work five days on the public road, or suffer corporeal punishment as hereinafter provided.

SEC. 3. . . . No negro shall be permitted to rent or keep a house within said parish. Any negro violating this provision shall be immediately ejected and compelled to find an employer; and any person who shall rent, or give the use of any house to any negro, in violation of this section, shall pay a fine of five dollars for each offence.

SEC. 4. . . . Every negro is required to be in the regular service of some white person, or former owner, who shall be held responsible for the conduct of said negro. But said employer or former owner may permit said negro to hire his own time by special permission in writing, which permission shall not extend over seven days at any one time. . . .

SEC. 5. . . . No public meetings or congregations of negroes shall be allowed within said parish after sunset, but such public meetings and congregations may be held between the hours of sunrise and sunset, by the special permission in writing of the captain of patrol, within whose beat such meetings shall take place. This prohibition, however, is not to prevent negroes from attending the usual church services, conducted by white ministers and priests. . . .

SEC. 6. . . . No negro shall be permitted to preach, exhort, or otherwise declaim to congregations of colored people, without a special permission in writing from the president of the police jury. . . .

SEC. 7. . . . No negro who is not in the military service shall be allowed to carry fire-arms, or any kind of weapons, within the parish, without the special written permission of his employers, approved and indorsed by the nearest and most convenient chief of patrol. Any one violating the provisions of this section shall forfeit his weapons and pay a fine of five dollars, or in default of the payment of said fine, shall be forced to work five days on the public road, or suffer corporeal punishment as hereinafter provided.

SEC. 8. . . . No negro shall sell, barter, or exchange any articles of merchandise or traffic within said parish without the special written permission of his employer, specifying the article of sale, barter or traffic. . . .

SEC. 9. . . . Any negro found drunk, within the said parish shall pay a fine of five dollars, or in default thereof work five days on the public road, or suffer corporeal punishment as hereinafter provided.

Sec. 11. . . . It shall be the duty of every citizen to act as a police officer for the detection of offences and the apprehension of offenders, who shall be immediately handed over to the proper captain or chief of patrol. . . .

Sec. 14. . . . The corporeal punishment provided for in the foregoing sections shall consist in confining the body of the offender within a barrel placed over his or her shoulders, in the manner practiced in the army, such confinement not to continue longer than twelve hours, and for such time within the aforesaid limit as shall be fixed by the captain or chief of patrol who inflicts the penalty.

MISSISSIPPI VAGRANCY STATUTE (1865)

Sec. 1. . . . *Be it enacted*, etc., . . . That all rogues and vagabonds, idle and dissipated persons, beggars, jugglers, or persons practicing unlawful games or plays, runaways, common drunkards, common night-walkers, pilferers, lewd wanton, or lascivious persons, in speech or behavior, common railers and brawlers, persons who neglect their calling or employment, misspend what they earn, or do not provide for the support of themselves or their families, or dependants, and all other idle and disorderly persons, including all who neglect all lawful business, habitually misspend their time by frequenting houses of ill-fame, gaming-houses, or tippling shops, shall be deemed and considered vagrants, under the provisions of this act, and upon conviction thereof shall be fined not exceeding one hundred dollars, with all accruing costs, and be imprisoned, at the discretion of the court, not exceeding ten days.

Sec. 2. . . . All freedmen, free negroes and mulattoes in this State, over the age of eighteen years, found on the second Monday in January, 1866, or thereafter, with no lawful employment or business, or found unlawfully assembling themselves together, either in the day or night time, and all white persons so assembling themselves with freedmen, free negroes or mulattoes, or usually associating with freedmen, free negroes or mulattoes, on terms of equality, or living in adultery or fornication with a freed woman, free negro or mulatto, shall be deemed vagrants, and on conviction thereof shall be fined in a sum not exceeding, in the case of a freedman, free negro, or mulatto, fifty dollars, and a white man two hundred dollars, and imprisoned at the discretion of the court, the free negro not exceeding ten days, and the white man not exceeding six months.

· · · · ·

Sec. 5. . . . in case any freedman, free negro or mulatto shall fail for five days after the imposition of any fine or forfeiture upon him or her for violation of any of the provisions of this act to pay the same, that it shall be, and is hereby, made the duty of the sheriff of the proper county to hire out said freedman, free negro or mulatto, to any person who will, for the shortest period of service, pay said fine and forfeiture and all costs: *Provided*, A preference shall be given to the employer, if there be one, in which case the employer shall be entitled to deduct and retain the amount so paid from the wages of such freedman, free negro or mulatto, then due or to become due; and in case said freedman, free negro, or mulatto cannot be hired out, he or she may be dealt with as a pauper.

Sec. 6. . . . The same duties and liabilities existing among white persons of this State shall attach to freedmen, free negroes or mulattoes, to support their indigent families and all colored paupers; and that in order to secure a support for such indigent freedmen, free negroes, or mulattoes, it shall be lawful and is hereby made the duty of the county police of each county in this State, to levy a poll or capitation tax on each and every freedman, free negro, or mulatto, between the ages of eighteen and sixty years, not to exceed the sum of one dollar annually to each person so taxed, which tax, when collected, shall be paid into the county treasurer's hands, and constitute a fund to be called the Freedmen's Pauper Fund, which shall be applied by the commissioners of the poor for the maintenance of the poor of the freedmen, free negroes, and mulattoes of this State, under such regulations as may be established by the boards of county police in the respective counties of this State.

Sec. 7.... If any freedman, free negro, or mulatto shall fail or refuse to pay any tax levied according to the provisions of the sixth section of this act, it shall be *prima facie* evidence of vagrancy, and it shall be the duty of the sheriff to arrest such freedman, free negro, or mulatto or such person refusing or neglecting to pay such tax, and proceed at once to hire for the shortest time such delinquent tax-payer to any one who will pay the said tax, with accruing costs, giving preference to the employer, if there be one.

CIVIL RIGHTS IN NORTH CAROLINA (1866)

Sec. 1. *Be it enacted by the General Assembly of the State of North Carolina, ..* That negroes and their issue, even where one ancestor in each succeeding generation to the fourth inclusive is white, shall be deemed persons of color.

. . . . .

Sec. 3.... Persons of color shall be entitled to all the privileges of white persons in the mode of prosecuting, defending, continuing, removing and transferring their suits at law and in equity; and likewise to the same mode of trial by jury, and all the privileges appertaining thereto... And in all proceedings in equity by or against them, their answer shall have the same force and effect in all respects as the answer of white persons.

Sec. 4.... In all cases of apprenticeship of persons of color, ... the master shall be bound to discharge the same duties to them as to white apprentices....*Provided always*, That in the binding out of apprentices of color, the former masters of such apprentices, when they shall be regarded as suitable persons by the court, shall be entitled to have such apprentices bound to them, in preference to other persons....

Sec. 5.... In all cases where men and women, both or one of them were lately slaves and are now emancipated, now cohabit together in the relation of husband and wife, the parties shall be deemed to have been lawfully married as man and wife.

. . . . .

Sec. 7.... All contracts between any persons whatever, whereof one or more of them shall be a person of color, for the sale or purchase of any horse, mule, ass, jennet, neat cattle, hog, sheep or goat, whatever may be the value of such articles, and all contracts between such persons for any other article or articles of property whatever of the value of ten dollars or more; and all contracts executed or executory between such persons for the payment of money of the value of ten dollars or more, shall be void as to all persons whatever, unless the same be put in writing and signed by the vendors or debtors, and witnessed by a white person who can read and write.

. . . . .

Sec. 9.... Persons of color not otherwise incompetent shall be capable of bearing evidence in all controversies at law and in equity, where the rights of persons or property of persons of color shall be put in issue, and would be concluded by the judgment or decree of court; and also in pleas of the State, where the violence, fraud, or injury alleged shall be charged to have been done by or to persons of color. In all other civil and criminal cases such evidence shall be deemed inadmissible, unless by consent of the parties of record: *Provided*, That this section shall not go into effect until jurisdiction in matters relating to freedmen shall be fully committed to the courts of this State: *Provided, further,* That no person shall be deemed incompetent to bear testimony in such cases because of being a party to the record or in interest.

· · · · ·

Sec. 11.... Any person of color convicted by due course of law of an assault with an attempt to commit rape upon the body of a white female, shall suffer death.

Sec. 12.... The criminal laws of the State embracing and affecting a white person are hereby extended to persons of color, except where it is otherwise provided in this act, and whenever they shall be convicted of any act made criminal, if committed by a white person, they shall be punished in like manner, except in such cases where other and different punishment may be prescribed or allowed by this act....

DOCUMENT 18.3
Protest—Black and White*

Frederick Douglass, an escaped slave and an eloquent abolitionist, urged the nation not to stop with emancipation. As the selection below illustrates, reconstruction to him means racial justice.

Whether the tremendous war so heroically fought and so victoriously ended shall pass into history a miserable failure, barren of permanent results,—a scandalous and shocking waste of blood and treasure, ... or whether, on the other hand, we shall, as the rightful reward of victory over treason, have a solid nation, entirely delivered from all contradictions and social antagonisms, based upon loyalty, liberty, and equality, must be determined one way or the other by the present session of Congress. The last session really did nothing which can be considered final as to these questions. The Civil Rights Bill and the Freedmen's Bureau Bill and the proposed constitutional amendments, ... do not reach the difficulty, and cannot, unless the whole structure of the government is changed from a government by States to

*Source: "Reconstruction," *Atlantic Monthly*, Vol. 18 (December 1866, pp. 761–65.

something like a despotic central government, with power to control even the municipal regulations of States, and to make them conform to its own despotic will. While there remains such an idea as the right of each State to control its own local affairs,—an idea, by the way, more deeply rooted in the minds of men of all sections of the country than perhaps any one other political idea,—no general assertion of human rights can be of any practical value. To change the character of the government at this point is neither possible nor desirable. All that is necessary to be done is to make the government consistent with itself, and render the rights of the States compatible with the sacred rights of human nature.

The arm of the Federal government is long, but it is far too short to protect the rights of individuals in the interior of distant States. They must have the power to protect themselves, or they will go unprotected, spite of all the laws the Federal government can put upon the national statute-book.

Slavery, like all other great systems of wrong, founded in the depths of human selfishness, and existing for ages, has not neglected its own conservation. It has steadily exerted an influence upon all around it favorable to its own continuance. And to-day it is so strong that it could exist, not only without law, but even against law. Custom, manners, morals, religion, are all on its side everywhere in the South; and when you add the ignorance and servility of the ex-slave to the intelligence and accustomed authority of the master, you have the conditions, not out of which slavery will again grow, but under which it is impossible for the Federal government to wholly destroy it, unless the Federal government be armed with despotic power, to blot out State authority, and to station a Federal officer at every cross-road. This, of course, cannot be done, and ought not even if it could. The true way and the easiest way is to make our government entirely consistent with itself, and give to every loyal citizen the elective franchise,—a right and power which will be ever present, and will form a wall of fire for his protection.

... to this grand work of national regeneration and entire purification Congress must now address itself, with full purpose that the work shall this time be thoroughly done. The deadly upas, root and branch, leaf and fibre, body and sap, must be utterly destroyed. The country is evidently not in a condition to listen patiently to pleas for postponement, however plausible, nor will it permit the responsibility to be shifted to other shoulders. Authority and power are here commensurate with the duty imposed. . . .

If time was at first needed, Congress has now had time. . . . Whether its members look at the origin, the progress, the termination of the war, or at the mockery of a peace now existing, they will find only one unbroken chain of argument in favor of a radical policy of reconstruction. For the omissions of the last session, some excuses may be allowed. A treacherous President stood in the way; and it can be easily seen how reluctant good men might be to admit an apostasy which involved so much of baseness and ingratitude. It was natural that they should seek to save him by bending to him even when he leaned to the side of error. But all is changed now. Congress knows now that it must go on without his aid, and even against his machinations. The advantage of the present session over the last is immense. Where that investigated, this has the facts. Where that walked by faith, this may walk by sight. Where that halted, this must go forward, and where that failed, this must succeed, giving the country whole measures where that gave us half-measures, merely as a means of saving the elections in a few doubtful districts. . . .

Without attempting to settle here the metaphysical and somewhat theological question ... whether once in the Union means always in the Union ... it is obvious to common sense that the rebellious States stand to-day, in point of law, precisely where they stood when, exhausted, beaten, conquered, they fell powerless at the feet of Federal authority. Their State governments were overthrown, and the lives and property of the leaders of the Rebellion were forfeited. In reconstructing the institutions of these shattered and overthrown States, Congress should begin with a clean slate, and make clean work of it. Let there be no hesitation. It would be a cowardly deference to a defeated and treacherous President, if any account were made of the illegitimate, one-sided, sham governments hurried into existence for a malign purpose in the absence of Congress. These pretended governments, which were never submitted to the people, and from participation in which four millions of the loyal people were excluded by Presidential order, should now be treated according to their true character, as shams and impositions, and supplanted by true and legitimate governments, in the formation of which loyal men, black and white, shall participate.

... The people ... demand such a reconstruction as shall put an end to the present anarchical state of things in the late rebellious States,—where frightful murders and wholesale massacres are perpetrated in the very presence of Federal soldiers. This horrible business they require shall cease. They want a reconstruction such as will protect loyal men, black and white, in their persons and property; such a one as will cause Northern industry, Northern capital, and Northern civilization to flow into the South, and make a man from New England as much at home in Carolina as elsewhere in the Republic. No Chinese wall can now be tolerated. The South must be opened to the light of law and liberty, and this session of Congress is relied upon to accomplish this important work.

DOCUMENT 18.4
The Vision of One Radical

Whatever his motives, and regardless of Presidents and lesser obstacles, Thaddeus Stevens meant to punish the South for its war and to force white society to begin immediate restitution for the ancient wrong of bondage.

THE SOUTH MUST BE PUNISHED (1865)°

Unless the rebel States, before admission, should be made republican in spirit, and placed under the guardianship of loyal men, all our blood and treasure will have been spent in vain. I waive now the question of punishment which, if we are wise, will still be inflicted by moderate confiscations.... Impartial suffrage, both in electing the delegates and ratifying their proceedings, is now the fixed rule. There is more reason why colored voters should be admitted in the rebel States than in the Territories. In the States they form the great mass of the loyal men. Possibly with their aid loyal governments may be established in most of those States. Without it all are sure to be ruled by traitors; and loyal men, black and white, will be oppressed, exiled, or murdered. There are several good reasons for the passage of this bill. In the first place, it is just. I am now confining my argument to negro suffrage in the rebel States. Have not loyal blacks quite as good a right to choose rulers and make laws as rebel whites? In the second place, it is a necessity in order to protect the loyal white men in the seceded States. The white Union men are in a great minority in each of those States. With them the blacks would act in a body; and it is believed that in each of said States, except one, the two united would form a majority, control the States, and protect themselves. Now they are the victims of daily murder....

°Source: *Congressional Globe*, January 3, 1867, p. 252.

Another good reason is, it would insure the ascendency of the Union party.... I believe ... that on the continued ascendency of that party depends the safety of this great nation. If impartial suffrage is excluded in the rebel States, then every one of them is sure to send a solid rebel representative delegation to Congress, and cast a solid rebel electoral vote. They, with their kindred Copperheads of the North, would always elect the President and control Congress. While slavery sat upon her defiant throne, and insulted and intimidated the trembling North, the South frequently divided on questions of policy between Whigs and Democrats, and gave victory alternately to the sections. Now, you must divide them between loyalists, without regard to color, and disloyalists, or you will be the perpetual vassals of the free-trade, irritated, revengeful South.... I am for negro suffrage in every rebel State. If it be just, it should not be denied; if it be necessary, it should be adopted; if it be a punishment to traitors, they deserve it.

THE SOUTH MUST PAY (1867)°

Whereas it is due to justice, as an example to future times, that some proper punishment should be inflicted on the people who constituted the "confederate States of America," both because they, declaring an unjust war against the United States for the purpose of destroying republican liberty and permanently establishing slavery, as well as for the cruel and barbarous manner in which they conducted said war, in violation of all the laws of civilized warfare, and also to compel them to make some compensation for the damages and expenditures caused by said war: Therefore,

Be it enacted ... That all the public lands belonging to the ten States that formed the government of the so-called "confederate States of America" shall be

----

°Source: *Congressional Globe*, March 19, 1867, p. 203.

forfeited by said States and become forthwith vested in the United States.

Sec. 2. . . . The President shall forthwith proceed to cause the seizure of such of the property belonging to the belligerent enemy as is deemed forfeited by the act of July 17, A. D. 1862, and hold and appropriate the same an enemy's property, and to proceed to condemnation with the already seized.

Sec. 3. . . . In lieu of the proceeding to condemn the property thus seized as enemy's property, as is provided by the act of July 17, A. D. 1862, two commissions or more, as by him may be deemed necessary, shall be appointed by the President for each of the said "confederate States," to consist of three persons each, one of whom shall be an officer of the late or present Army, and two shall be civilians, neither of whom shall be citizens of the State for which he shall be appointed; the said commissions shall proceed to adjudicate and condemn the property aforesaid, under such forms and proceedings as shall be prescribed by the Attorney General of the United States, whereupon the title to said property shall become vested in the United States.

Sec. 4. . . . Out of the lands thus seized and confiscated the slaves who have been liberated by the operations of the war and the amendment to the Constitution or otherwise, who resided in said "confederate States" on the 4th day of March, A. D. 1861, or since, shall have distributed to them as follows, namely: to each male person who is the head of a family, forty acres; to each adult male, whether the head of a family or not, forty acres; to each widow who is the head of a family, forty acres—to be held by them in fee simple, but to be inalienable for the next ten years after they become seized thereof. . . . At the end of ten years the absolute title to said homesteads shall be conveyed to said owners or to the heirs of such as are then dead.

Sec. 5. . . . Out of the balance of the property thus seized and confiscated there shall be raised, in the manner hereinafter provided, a sum equal to fifty dollars, for each homestead, to be applied by the trustees hereinafter mentioned toward the erection of buildings on the said homesteads for the use of said slaves; and the further sum of $500,000,000, which shall be appropriated as follows, to-wit: $200,000,000 shall be invested in United States six per cent. securities; and the interest thereof shall be semi-annually added to the pensions allowed by law to the pensioners who have become so by reason of the late war; $300,000,000, or so much thereof as may be needed, shall be appropriated to pay damages done to loyal citizens by the civil or military operations of the government lately called the "confederate States of America."

Sec. 6. . . . In order that just discrimination may be made, the property of no one shall be seized whose whole estate on the 4th day of March, A. D. 1865, was not worth more than $5,000, to be valued by the said commission, unless he shall have voluntarily become an officer or employee in the military or civil service of "the Confederate States of America," or in the civil or military service of some one of said States, and in enforcing all confiscations the sum or value of $5,000 in real or personal property shall be left or assigned to the delinquent. . . .

DOCUMENT 18.5
Terror—Black and White*

The Ku Klux Klan and its imitators intimidated Negroes in order to keep them from demanding the rights allowed by law. Whites who befriended or aided freedmen were liable to the same harassing that Negroes received. The first narrative below is that of a South Carolina Negro, Elias Hill, a crippled Baptist preacher; the sec-

*Source: *Report of the Joint Select Committee to Inquire into the Condition of Affairs in the Late Insurrectionary States*, Vol. I (Washington, D.C., 1872), pp. 44–46, 78–79.

ond is that of a Scot, Cornelius McBride, who taught school in Mississippi.

ELIAS HILL'S TESTIMONY

On the night of the 5th of last May, after I had heard a great deal of what they had done in that neighborhood, they came. It was between 12 and 1 o'clock at night when I was awakened and heard the dogs barking, and something walking, very much like horses. As I had often laid awake listening for such persons, for they had been all through the neighborhood, and disturbed all men and many women, I supposed that it was them. They came in a very rapid manner, and I could hardly tell whether it was the sound of horses or men. At last they came to my brother's door, which is in the same yard, and broke open the door and attacked his wife, and I heard her screaming and mourning. I could not understand what they said, for they were talking in an outlandish and un-natural tone, which I had heard they gen-erally used at a negro's house. I heard them knocking around in her house. I was lying in my little cabin in the yard. At last I heard them have her in the yard. She was crying, and the Ku-Klux were whip-ping her to make her tell where I lived. I heard her say, "Yon is his house." She has told me since that they first asked who had taken me out of her house. They said, "Where's Elias?" She said, "He doesn't stay here; yon is his house." They were then in the yard, and I had heard them strike her five or six licks when I heard her say this. Some one then hit my door. It flew open. One ran in the house, and stop-ping about the middle of the house, which is a small cabin, he turned around, as it seemed to me as I lay there awake, and said, "Who's here?" Then I knew they would take me, and I answered, "I am here." He shouted for joy, as it seemed, "Here he is! Here he is! We have found him!" and he threw the bed-clothes off of me and caught me by one arm, while another man took me by the other and they carried me into the yard between the houses, my brother's and mine, and put me on the ground beside a boy. The first thing they asked me was, "Who did that burning? Who burned our houses?"—gin-houses, dwelling-houses and such. Some had been burned in the neighborhood. I told them it was not me; I could not burn houses; it was unreasonable to ask me. Then they hit me with their fists, and said I did it, I ordered it. They went on asking me didn't I tell the black men to ravish all the white women. No, I answered them. They struck me again with their fists on my breast. . . . Two of them went into the house. My sister says that as quick as they went into the house they struck the clock at the foot of the bed. I heard it shatter. One of the four around me called out, "Don't break any private property, gentle-men, if you please; we have got him we came for, and that's all we want." I did not hear them break anything else. They staid in there a good while hunting about and then came out and asked me for a lamp. I told them there was a lamp somewhere. They said "Where?" I was so confused I said I could not tell exactly. They caught my leg—you see what it is—and pulled me over the yard, and then left me there knowing I could not walk nor crawl, and all six went into the house. I was chilled with the cold lying in the yard at that time of night, for it was near 1 o'clock, and they had talked and beat me and so on until half an hour had passed since they first approached. After they had staid in the house for a considerable time, they came back to where I lay and asked if I wasn't afraid at all. They pointed pistols at me all around my head once or twice, as if they were going to shoot me, telling me they were going to kill me; wasn't I ready to die, and willing to die? Didn't I preach? That they came to kill me—all the time pointing pistols at me. This second time they came out of the house, after plun-dering the house, searching for letters, they came at me with these pistols, and asked if I was ready to die. I told them that I was not exactly ready; that I would rather live; that I hoped they would not kill me that time. They said they would; I had better prepare. One caught me by the leg and hurt me, for my leg for forty years has been drawn each year, more and more year by year, and I made moan when it hurt so. One said "G——d d——n it, hush!" He had a horsewhip, and he told me to pull up my shirt, and he hit me. He told me at every lick, "Hold up your shirt." I made a moan every time he cut with the horsewhip. I reckon he struck me eight cuts right on the hip bone; it was almost the only place he could hit my body, my legs are so short—all my limbs drawn up and withered away with pain. I saw one of them standing over me or by me motion to them to quit. They all had disguises on. I then thought they would not kill me. One of them then took a strap, and buckled it around my neck and said, "Let's take him to the river and drown him." "What course is the river?" they asked me. I told them east. Then one of them went feeling about, as if he was looking for something, and said, "I don't see no east! Where is the d——d thing?" as if he did not understand what I meant. After pulling the strap around my neck, he took it off and gave me a lick on my hip where he had struck me with the horsewhip. . . . He said I would now have to die. I was somewhat afraid, but one said not to kill me. They said "Look here! Will you put a card in the paper next week like June Moore and Sol Hill?" They had been prevailed on to put a card in the paper to renounce all republicanism and never vote. I said, "If I had the money to pay the expense, I could." They said I could borrow, and gave me another lick. They asked me, "Will you quit preaching?" I told them I did not know. I said that to save my life. They said I must stop that republican paper that was coming to Clay Hill. It has been only a few weeks since it stopped. The republican weekly paper was then coming to me from Charleston. It came to my name. They said I must stop it, quit preaching, and put a card in the newspaper renouncing republicanism, and they would not kill me; but if I did not they would come back the next week and kill me. With that one of them went into the house where my brother and my sister-in-law lived, and brought her to pick me up. As she stooped down to pick me up one of them struck her, and as she was carrying me into the house another struck her with a strap. She carried me into the house and laid me on the bed. Then they gathered around and told me to pray for them. I tried to pray. They said, "Don't you pray against Ku-Klux, but pray that God may forgive Ku-Klux. Don't pray against us. Pray that God may bless and save us." I was so chilled with cold lying out of doors so long and in such pain I could not speak to pray, but I tried to, and they said that would do very well, and all went out of the house. . . .

CORNELIUS McBRIDE'S TESTIMONY

. . . I had several warnings, in the shape of several school-houses being burned there; but inasmuch as I was on good terms with the people in the neighborhood where I was teaching, I did not apprehend any difficulty. There was a school-house burned down not far off from where I lived; Mr. Burt Moore was teaching the school there, and they threatened his life if he did not stop teaching. At Houston several teachers of colored schools were attacked; one of them told me that they ordered him to leave in three days or they would take his life. His wife was about to be confined, but he had to leave. But I did not fear any difficulty for myself, inasmuch as I had opened the school there with the consent of the white people in the neighborhood. During the last week in March some of my scholars told me they had heard that the Ku-Klux were out after me, but I did not pay any attention to it. I boarded with Mr. Thomas Johnson, an old gentleman; he was then in Alabama, and I was alone in the big house, and I had no arms in the house.

There were some colored people living in cabins in the yard, but there was no one with me in Mr. Johnson's house. Between 12 and 1 o'clock on Thursday night, in the last week of March, a body of men came to the house, burst in the doors and windows, and presented their rifles at me. I asked them, "What are you all coming here this time of night for, making this row?" The leader of the party said, "You God damned Yankee, come out here." Well, I realized my position at once; I knew it was a matter of life and death; I did not believe those men came there merely to whip me and then leave me, as they did colored men; I thought they meant to kill me, and I made up my mind to make an effort to escape. There were two men standing at the window with their rifles presented at me; I leaped out of the window, right between those two men. . . . I . . . ran to the house of a colored man in the yard, where there was a double-barreled gun; I was determined to get that, if I could, and defend myself. I had no time to wait for the colored woman to open the door, but I just burst right in. While I was running down the yard, they fired at me a number of times, crying out, "God damn you, stop, or we will blow your God damned brains out." . . .

While I was in the cabin trying to find the gun, these men came in before I could find it. There were two rooms in the house of the colored man, and I went into one of them and tried to hide. They came in and searched for me and got me. The colored people prayed to them, "O, don't hurt Mr. Mac; for God's sake let him alone." They said, "Don't make that noise; keep quiet; we will not hurt you; hold your tongues." They took me out of the house and across the yard; I asked them in what way I had injured them to justify that attack on me. They cursed me, told me to stop talking, struck me in the side with their bowie-knives that had their scabbards on, and with the but-ends of their pistols. They took me scarcely a quarter of a mile from the house, to a field near the road, and told me to take off my shirt, which I refused to do. Then one fellow struck me on the head with a pistol, cut my head, and knocked me down and then pulled off my shirt. . . .

Two of them then held me down, and one of them took a bundle of black-gum switches. I did not know what they were then, but one of the colored people told me the next day that they had picked up some thirty, and that they were black-gum . . . a peculiar kind of stick, which stings and raises the flesh when it hits. One of them took the bundle of switches and commenced to whip me. They said they were going to give me a hundred each. I do not know how many men there were; I counted only five around me, but I believe there were more than a dozen there. They agreed to give me a hundred lashes each. One man gave me a hundred, and then handed the bundle of switches to another, who gave me about seventy-five. He said he had given me seventy-five when I escaped from them. I asked them while they were whipping me what I had done to merit that treatment. They said I wanted to make these niggers equal to the white men; that this was a white man's country. They said, "God damn you! Don't you know this is a white man's country?" I said, "The white people in the neighborhood are satisfied with my conduct and the manner I have been conducting the school here. They have shown it by selecting me to take charge of their Sunday-school." They said, "Yes, God damn you, that is the worst feature in it, having a nigger teacher to teach the white school on Sunday!" I was fighting them all the time as well as I could—kicking at them and doing what I could—for the torture was horrible. I thought they would kill me any way when they got through whipping me, and I begged them to shoot me. One of them came up to me with his pistol and asked me if I wanted to be shot. I said, "Yes; I can't stand this." The leader of the party said, "Shooting is too good for this fellow. We will hang him when we get through whipping him." I saw a rope hanging from a limb of a tree by the side of the road. There was only one man standing between me and the fence of the plantation. I observed that, and I tried to gain his attention, for I was determined to make an effort to escape. They threatened to hang me, or to tie me. I hardly know what they said. I thought they were going to hang me. I got the attention of this man for a moment. He was standing between me and the fence, and had two pistols. I asked him whether they would let me off if I would promise to leave in the morning. All this time they were whipping me, but I managed to partly raise myself. I was half way up, on my hand and knee; I made a spring and made for this man, and struck at him as hard as I could. I do not know what part of his body I struck. I know he disappeared; I do not know where he went. The way was then clear to the fence, and I leaped the fence. . . . I went to the house of a neighbor there, Mr. Walser, and remained there during the rest of the night. Mr. Walser of course sympathized with me; he was my near neighbor and my friend. He said, "My God! Has it come to this now, that no man is safe, when you are attacked?" . . . The next day I taught my school as usual. They had threatened me while they were whipping me that if I held the examination I had advertised— they spoke something about the examination, and said they were preparing me for examination in another way. Some colored people brought me word that if I held that examination the Ku-Klux would come again and kill me that time sure; but I held my examination the following Monday notwithstanding the threats. I went there with a gun over my shoulder, and several people came there and brought their guns, and I held the examination. That night several white men and some colored men and myself laid out in the woods expecting that the Ku-Klux would come.

DOCUMENT 18.6

The Return of White Supremacy*

Even before federal troops left the region, southern whites began to substitute political organization for overt terror in their attempt to end Reconstruction. The excerpts from newspapers below come from Mississippi, Alabama, and Georgia; the political resolutions were adopted by most county Democratic organizations in Alabama. Together the readings reflect the region's determination to maintain white supremacy.

A MISSISSIPPI EDITORIAL (1875)

The republican journals of the North made a great mistake in regarding the present campaign in Mississippi in the light of a political contest. It is something more earnest and holy than that—it is, so far as the white people and land-owners are concerned, a battle for the control of their own domestic affairs; a struggle to regain a mastery that has been ruthlessly torn from them by selfish white schemers and adventurers, through the instrumentality of an ignorant horde of another race which has been as putty in their hands, molded to our detriment and ruin.

The present contest is rather a revolution than a political campaign—it is the rebellion, if you see fit to apply that term, of a down-trodden people against an absolutism imposed by their own hirelings, and by the grace of God we will cast it off next November, or cast off the willfully and maliciously ignorant tools who eat our bread, live in our houses, attend the schools that we support, come to us for aid and succor in their hour of need, and yet are deaf to our appeals when we entreat them to assist us in throwing off a galling yoke that has been borne until further endurance is but the basest of cowardice. . . .

*Source: W. L. Fleming (ed.), *Documentary History of Reconstruction*, Vol. II (Cleveland: Arthur H. Clark Co., 1906), pp. 387–95.

We favor a continuance of the canvass upon the broad and liberal basis that has heretofore characterized it; that is, we favor appealing to the negro by everything good and holy to forsake his idols and unite with us in ridding the State of a way that we despise; but at the same time that we extend the olive-branch and plead for alliance and amity, we should not hesitate to use the great and all-powerful weapon that is in our control; we should not falter in the pledge to ourselves and our neighbors to discharge from our employ and our friendship forever, every laborer who persists in the diabolical war that has been waged against the white man and his interests ever since the negro has been a voter.

LETTER TO AN
ALABAMA NEWSPAPER (1874)

. . . Is not the battle to be fought this fall one of common interest, and how dares any man either to go into the enemy's camp or seek to lay his burden upon the shoulders of another? . . . Is it not the time when the 80,000 white voters of Alabama should march as men with one banner and one voice? . . . Men, now, who walk out . . . between the two contending parties, begging quarters from friend and foe, are verily independents, (!) and deserve first to be shot down. Such independent men as these are seeking, through cowardly apprehensions, to make themselves the nucleus of the disaffected elements of the two parties, and thereby secure a position through cunning which they do not have the manliness to win upon principle. They are reaching out their arms to gather with one from the black fold and with the other the white. Perfectly independent; independent of race, color, and previous condition; independent of organization; independent of the history of consequences and results; independent of everything and everybody except office and the love of self. . . .

The protege of radicalism, these inde-pendents, the spawn of corruption or poverty, or passion, or ignorance, come forth as leaders of the ignorant or deluded blacks, to attack and plunder for avarice, and defile and deflower for passion. There may be no God to avenge the South, but there is a devil to punish independents without priestly benediction, and Alabama will witness the ceremony. . . .

Satan hath been in the democratic camp, and, taking these independents from guard-duty, led them up into the mountains and showed them the kingdoms of radicalism, his silver and gold, storehouses and bacon, and all these promised to give if they would fall down and worship him; and they worshiped him, throwing down the altars of their fathers and trampling them under their feet. . . .

Hard is life; but life cursed by passion, cursed by infidelity, cursed by ignorance and prejudice, by treason to race and country; cursed by ingratitude; yea cursed by the bite of radicalism, is a Gethsemane of crucifixion whose agony is without a language. . . .

All of the good . . . men of Alabama are for the white man's party. Outcasts, liberals, liars, hand cuffers, and traitors to blood are for the negro party. Decide where you will place yourself in November.

A GEORGIA EDITOR ASKS
FOR "BRUTE FORCE" (1874)

Let there be White Leagues formed in in every town, village and hamlet of the South, and let us organize for the great struggle which seems inevitable. The radicalism of the republican party must be met by the radicalism of white men. We have no war to make against the United Sates Government, but against the republican party our hate must be unquenchable, our war interminable and merciless. Fast fleeting away is the day of wordy protests and idle appeals to the magnanimity of the republican party. By brute force they are endeavoring to force us into acquiescence to their hideous programme. We have submitted long enough to indignities, and it is time to meet brute-force with brute-force. . . . It will not do to wait till radicalism has fettered us to the car of social equality before we make an effort to resist it. The signing of the [Civil Rights] bill will be a declaration of war against the southern whites. It is our duty to ourselves, it is our duty to our children, it is our duty to the white race whose prowess subdued the wilderness of this continent, whose civilization filled it with cities and towns and villages, whose mind gave it power and grandeur, and whose labor imparted to it prosperity, and whose love made peace and happiness dwell within its homes, to take the gage of battle the moment it is thrown down. If the white democrats of the North are men, they will not stand idly by and see us borne down by northern radicals and half-barbarous negroes. But no matter what they may do, it is time for us to organize. We have been temporizing long enough. Let northern radicals understand that military supervision of southern elections and the civil-rights bill mean war, that war means bloodshed, and that we are terribly in earnest, and even they, fanatical as they are, may retrace their steps before it is too late.

RESOLUTIONS OF
ALABAMA DEMOCRATS (1874)

Whereas the republican party of Alabama, for years past, has distinctly made and tendered to the people of this State an open, square issue of race; and

Whereas the tendencies of the doctrines, teaching and practices of said party, as more recently illustrated and evidenced by the passage by the United States Senate of what is known as the civil-rights bill, are to the effect that the negro, by reason of his emancipation, is elevated to,

and ought of right to enjoy, social as well as political equality; and

Whereas the white people of the South have sedulously endeavored to prevent this issue of race, and in various ways sought to escape and avoid the said issue, well knowing the direful consequences that would follow it; and

Whereas the white people of the South have hitherto forborne, and hoped to escape the consequences thus hurled defiantly into their faces by the poor negroes, at the instance of the thieving crew known as carpetbaggers, and the more contemptible and infamous gang known as scalawags, who, in full view of this issue, have, for the sake of plunder, power, and spoils, sided with the aforesaid deluded negroes, regardless of the hateful and direful consequences to ensue from the passage of said odious civil-rights bill, which is the culmination of all radical diabolism.

Therefore, we respectfully suggest to our county convention for consideration the following resolutions:

Resolved, That we, the people . . . , for the protection of our dearest and most sacred interests, our homes, our honor, the purity and integrity of our race, and to conserve the peace and tranquillity of the country, accept the issue of race thus defiantly tendered and forced upon us, notwithstanding our determination and repeated efforts to avoid it; and further

Resolved, That nothing is left to the white man's party but social ostracism of all those who act, sympathize or side with the negro party, or who support or advocate the odious, unjust, and unreasonable measure known as the civil rights bill; and that from henceforth we will hold all such persons as enemies of our race, and we will not in the future have intercourse with them in any of the social relations of life.

19 The Impact of Industrialization on American Society

SIGMUND DIAMOND
Columbia University

In the early summer of 1853 the yacht *North Star*, bearing on board the most renowned American businessman of the day, Commodore Cornelius Vanderbilt, steamed into the port of London during the course of a world cruise. The reputation of the Commodore, less towering than it was to become, was already something to conjure with; and the London press, even as it greeted him, attempted to extract from the story of his life something of value for its readers. Why did Vanderbilt have such high prestige in the United States, the *London Daily News* pondered, and produced the answer to its own query:

America . . . is the great arena in which the individual energies of man, uncramped by oppressive social institutions, or absurd social traditions, have full play, and arrive at gigantic development. . . .

It is the tendency of American institutions to foster the general welfare, and to permit the unchecked powers of the highly gifted to occupy a place in the general framework of society which they can obtain nowhere else. The great feature to be noted in America is that all its citizens have full permission to run the race in which Mr. Vanderbilt has gained such immense prizes. In other countries, on the contrary, they are trammelled by a thousand restrictions. . . .

Your men of rank here—your makers of millions for themselves and tens of millions for the country—too often spend their time, their intellect, their labor, in order that they may be able to take rank among a class of men who occupy their present position in virtue of what was done for them by some broad-shouldered adventurer, who, fortunately for them, lived eight hundred years ago in Normandy. . . . Here is the great difference between the two countries. In England a man is too apt to be ashamed of having made his own fortune, unless he has done so in one of the few roads which the aristocracy condescend to travel—the bar, the church, or the army.

It is time that the *millionaire* should cease to be ashamed of having made his own fortune. It is time that *parvenu* should be looked on as a word of honor. It is time that the middle classes should take the place which is their own, in the world which they have made. The middle classes have made the modern world. The Montmorencis, the Percys, the Howards, made the past world—and they had their reward. Let them give place to better men.

We do not have to accept the correctness of the newspaper's diagnosis to be convinced of the validity of the condition it was describing—that even so titanic a businessman as Vanderbilt was not regarded in the same way by people throughout the world, that the special characteristics of the cultural traditions and social structure of each country affect the degree to which it is possible for a country to produce a Vanderbilt and the way in which he will be esteemed.

But, of course, not even participation in the same cultural tradition or membership in the same society is enough to guarantee uniformity of outlook. So it was that even to his own countrymen Cornelius Vanderbilt was the object of assessments so diverse as to suggest that their authors could not have been speaking of the same person. To the boards of directors of the railroads with which he had been associated, Vanderbilt had "stood as the nation's foremost representative of public enterprise and material progress." A "true man, a sincere friend, a devoted husband and father, a liberal employer, an extraordinary genius of affairs, and a citizen of high public spirit," his career had been a dazzling success.

Beginning in an humble position, with apparently little scope of action and small promise of opportunity, he rose, by his genius, his indomitable energy, and his clear forecast, to the control of vast enterprises. . . . In a period of crafty devices for sinister ends, he taught the way of success through legitimate means. . . . As a citizen, he was true to the honor and welfare of his country. . . . If his patriotism was thus substantial, his philanthropy was equally generous and effective.

But to the editor of the *Nation,* E. L. Godkin—certainly no enemy of the social order—the same Vanderbilt was

a man who never served the country at large, nor the State, nor the city, in any public office; nor ever spent the time which is money in advancing the cause of any charity; nor in promoting education, which the self-made man may despise; nor in fostering the arts, which can always wait.

He was, in short, the

lineal successor of the medieval baron that we read about, who may have been illiterate indeed; and who was not humanitarian; and not finished in his morals; and not, for his manners, the delight of the refined society of his neighborhood; nor yet beloved by his dependents; but who knew how to take advantage of lines of travel, who had a keen eye for roads, and had the heart and hand to levy contributions on all who passed his way.

The correctness of the perception of the

London Daily News—that the absence of feudal-aristocratic traditions in the United States as compared with England accounts for the higher prestige of the parvenu in the former country—must not blind us to the fact that even within the United States the career of the businessman was susceptible of diametrically different verdicts. The same Vanderbilt who to his associates—and to many others—was a man of "high public spirit," was to Godkin—and to many others—an authentic robber baron, though in the wrong time and in the wrong place, swooping down from his mountain fastness to levy tribute on unprotected travelers.

Clearly, then, the status of the businessman in American society, high though it was in comparison with other societies, was not exactly unchallenged. And even among those who accorded the businessman their highest praise, there was a discernible—and in the years to come a momentous—disagreement as to what in fact was responsible for the high status he had achieved in his society. For Vanderbilt's corporate associates, his "glittering success" was not "due to any early adventitious advantages. He was essentially the creator, not the creature, of the circumstances which he molded to his purposes." But only 20 years later, Vanderbilt's longtime friend and colleague, United States Senator Chauncey M. Depew, speaking at the unveiling of a statue of his associate at Vanderbilt University, was somewhat less certain about the sources of Vanderbilt's success. True, he "neither asked nor gave quarter. . . . He was not the creation of luck nor chance nor circumstances." But was he entirely the architect of his own fortunes? Was there not something in his surroundings that contributed to his success? Senator Depew thought that there was.

The American Commonwealth is built upon the individual. It recognizes neither classes nor masses. . . . We have thus become a nation of self-made men. We live under just and equal laws and all avenues for a career are open. . . . Freedom of opportunity and preservation of the results of forecast, industry, thrift and honesty have made the United States the most prosperous and wealthy country in the world. Commodore Vanderbilt is a conspicuous example of the products and possibilities of our free and elastic conditions. . . . The same country, the same laws, the same open avenues, the same opportunities which he had before him are equally before every man.

What was the real object of the orator's praise—the qualities of the man which lifted him above his surroundings, or the "free and elastic conditions" of American society which placed no obstacles in the way of Vanderbilt's—or anyone's—rise to success? And did he neglect to point out that a large percentage of the self-made men had indeed risen not from the bottom but rather from the middle and top rungs of the economic ladder as a result of their happy accident of birth?

Illustrated in even this mere handful of quotations is a series of significant questions. What assurance has the great American man of business had that the community would elevate him to the position of distinction to which he aspired? What changes have taken place in the status of the businessman in American society, and what changes have occurred in the explanations that have been offered to account for his status? What inferences about American social thought—and about American society—may be drawn from the fact that the career of the successful businessman, which at one time is pointed to as a testimonial to the good qualities a man must have in order to overcome obstacles, is at another time pointed to as a testimonial to the good qualities of a society which puts no obstacles in the way of achieving business success? What are the functions and practices that the community associates with the status of the businessman, and how have these been evaluated differently over time and by different groups at the same point of time?

Such questions would be of importance in understanding a society at any time and

at any place, but certain developments in the history of the United States in the decades following the Civil War conspired to make them of crucial importance. For it was in those decades that a new society—an industrial society—was being formed; and in its formation—which involved the uprooting of millions of people, the learning of new ideas and habits and routines, the lifting of new groups to power and the suppression of the once powerful—the businessman stepped out into the limelight as the most powerful of the movers and shakers of his age.

In the changes that transformed American society, nothing was left untouched—the relation of citizens to their government and of groups of people to each other, the churches and the schools, the family; but behind these changes, emphasizing the crucial importance of the role of the businessman, lay a new method of production and distribution, based on factory and machine, with an increasingly refined technology that made use of ever-larger supplies of capital and specialized labor and of new modes of organizing and disciplining human energies. Land and people alike were being remade, as industrialization and urbanization changed the face of the landscape and forced millions of migrants from rural American and rural Europe to learn the techniques and disciplines of an industrial society.

A few statistics are enough to reveal the magnitude of the changes that took place. In 1870, mining and manufacturing together contributed only 14 percent to the national income, while agriculture contributed 20 percent. At the end of the century the contribution of agriculture had slipped to 16 percent and was matched exactly by the contribution of finance, while the contribution of mining and manufacturing rose to 21 percent. Steam-propelled machinery stood at the very center of the processes of industrialization, and the United States was producing the fuel that machinery needed. Coal production, which amounted to 14,610,042 tons in

1860, rose to a staggering 513,525,477 tons in 1914. In 1870, 2,346,142 horsepower was used in American manufacturing; in 1900, 11,300,081 was used. In 1900 the United States, the world's largest producer of food and raw materials, had become as well the world's leading manufacturer. But the statistics of economic growth do not fully summarize all the changes involved in the processes of industrialization. For untold millions, industrialization meant to be ripped loose from the places and from the ideas that earlier had been counted on to provide social stability. Between 1870 and 1900, total population in the United States, stimulated by both a high birth rate and massive immigration, nearly doubled—from 40 million to 76 million—but the increase was not evenly distributed throughout the country or throughout the economy; some regions and some occupations grew far more rapidly than others. Not quite 60 percent of the American labor force worked on farms in 1860, but only 37 percent did so in 1900; only 26 percent worked in transportation and industry in 1860, but 46 percent did so in 1900. The farm, the small New England town, the middle western river entrepôt were everywhere being shoved aside by the population centers more characteristic of the new stage of economic development that had been reached— the mill town, the coal town, the steel town, and, above all, the great metropolitan city.

For it was the great city, that most characteristic product of industrial society, that grew most spectacularly in the years following the close of the Civil War. In 1860, only one sixth of the American people lived in urban areas; in 1900, one third. During that same 40-year period the population of the nation's great cities grew more than twice as fast as that of the nation as a whole. New York, Chicago, and Philadelphia were, by the end of the century, true metropolises, each with well over a million people and each already showing that striking combination of

wonder and squalor that was to become the hallmark of the 20th-century city. As early as 1890, four out of every five persons in the commonwealth of Massachusetts were living in towns; rural Massachusetts, having largely disappeared from the census returns, continued to live on mainly in the realms of nostalgia and the poetic imagination.

In the midst of such movement and change, nothing remained settled, not even the moral and intellectual standards that for so long had provided the criteria for measuring the value of institutions and ideas. The sturdy yeoman was now a hayseed; the independent artisan was now a factory hand; David Harum had become a captain of industry; the center of affairs had shifted from the small-town counting-house to the polished boardroom of a bank in New York or Chicago. To swim with the wave of economic change meant choosing a different career and living in a different place; it meant being reeducated, learning new skills and new ideas; it meant rejecting much of what one had been taught to regard as standard and value. And even those who fought to preserve the old had to come to grips with the forces that were making their world obsolete. To swim with the tide or against the tide of economic change seemed to make little difference. Economic change was providing the environment in which, increasingly, most men lived out their lives; and in the creation of that new environment the decisions of businessmen—affecting the lives of millions of their countrymen—bulked ever larger.

Driving this change forward was a revolution that began in transportation and communication and then spread quickly to production and distribution. Between 1870 and 1900, railroad mileage increased from 30,000 to 193,000; as early as 1887, nearly 33,000 towns in the United States were being served by the railroad network. Merchants in Boston, Baltimore, New York, Philadelphia, and dozens of inland towns—eager to tap the distant markets brought within their reach by the development of cheap transportation—were stimulated to mobilize the capital and organize the skills needed to lay down the railroad network. Sometimes their hopes proved illusory, sometimes realistic, but in any case their decision to move ahead with the development of the railroad was the major economic stimulus of the post-Civil War period.

For one thing, railroad construction itself provided a direct and powerful stimulus to industrial production. As early as the 1880s, the railroads employed a labor force of more than 200,000; they provided, therefore, an enormous market for the products of stone quarries, lumber mills, and iron factories and for the excess capital of both foreign and domestic investors. Most important, of course, was the stimulus the railroad gave to the growth of the iron and steel industry. By linking the sections of the country more closely, the railroad made it possible to bring together more efficiently and cheaply the elements of industrial production. The railroad first created the demand for locomotives, rolling stock, bridges, and rails, and then provided the means for satisfying that demand—a fast, cheap, sure way of bringing iron ore to coal. Indeed, so insatiable was the demand of the railroad for steel that the steel industry transformed itself technologically to meet that demand. Rolling mills and blast furnaces using coke could outproduce the old charcoal-fueled ovens at the rate of 10 to 1. No longer were scarce supplies of expensive charcoal permitted to set limits on the size of furnaces and, therefore, on the amount they could produce; fed on unlimited supplies of cheap coal from western Pennsylvania, the size of the furnaces—stimulated by the voracious appetite of the railroad—increased steadily. Blast furnaces which shortly before the Civil War were producing at an average rate of 40 tons per day were producing at a daily average rate of 400 tons as the century drew to a close. Steel production—140,000

tons in 1873 and 500,000 tons in 1877—reached 2.5 million tons in 1886. By the end of the century the Carnegie Steel Company alone was producing about four fifths as much steel as the entire British steel industry.

But the railroad stimulated the economy in still another way—by creating the great national market that made mass production possible. Local businessmen who dominated regional markets now faced serious competition from products manufactured in distant factories and hauled to every market cheaply by the railroad. Businessmen, encouraged now by the greater size of their markets, increased their production in order to take advantage of lower costs and experimented with the development of lower-cost production methods. Stimulated to reduce costs to lower and lower levels so as to capture wider and wider markets, the steel industry brought down the price of rails from $160 per ton to $17 per ton in the 23 years between 1875 and 1898. Other industries felt the same stimulating effects of the growing market made possible by cheap transportation. Well before the assembly line, bringing down production costs, had been introduced in the automobile industry by Henry Ford, it was being widely used in the textile industry, in meat-packing, in canning, and in flour-milling.

Changes in technology—as in the case of mass production—were of great importance indeed, but by themselves they would not have succeeded in boosting the level of production to the point that it in fact reached. Changes in organization were also required.

First, of course, came changes in the organization of work in the factory. Standardization of parts, which long had been practiced in the Connecticut gun industry, spread to other industries—sewing machines and clocks, for example—and eventually into the standardization of the final assembly of all sorts of products. Nor was the drive for rationalization restricted to the workshop. Accounting and auditing departments, the sales division, and the head office were closely scrutinized and subjected to increasingly rigorous methods of supervision in an attempt to cut costs by providing standardized methods of procedure. Organization—the social structure of the firm—was seen to be a variable that, like land, labor, and capital, influenced the level of costs and productivity; and fundamental changes were made in traditional methods of assigning tasks in shop and office, supervising the activities of the labor force, determining the proper relation between supervisory and production personnel, and fixing the locus of authority for the performance of particular functions within the firm.

The factory was rationalized and organized, the office was rationalized and organized—and so was industry itself. To compete successfully for markets required the utilization of the latest techniques of science and technology to reduce costs to competitive levels. The very costs of modernization, however, were so great that only when factories operated at or near capacity could economies of production be achieved. But to operate at such levels would cause prices to fall. Every glimmer of hope for potential new markets—the establishment of a new railroad line, a new wave of immigration, the growth of a city, the opening of new territory, the enactment of a new tariff—was desperately grasped and was followed by a frenzy of expansion, only to be followed in turn by idle plant and equipment when the new markets had been saturated. Like the ruthless competition between industrial rivals, the ability of industry to achieve economies of production only when operating at capacity tended to drive down prices and, therefore, to threaten the security of even the most efficient producers. To escape from this cruel dilemma became an overriding concern of American businessmen toward the turn of the century, and led them into a search for "order," the most important outcome of which was the discovery of the importance of organization of the market.

First came efforts to organize the market by introducing changes within the structure of a single firm. Andrew Carnegie, for example, was already the dominant producer in the basic iron and steel industry when, in the 1880s, he began to reach out into all branches of the industry —into coalfields, railroads, and coking plants, into the Michigan and Mesabi iron ranges, into ore ships on the Great Lakes and ports to handle them. Even so, he could not free himself from the threat of combinations in the steel-consuming industries that were strong enough to affect his prices. In 1900, he announced plans that would carry combination a long step forward—his own entry into the manufacture of steel wire, tubes, and similar products—and was dissuaded from attempting to realize them by the offer of J. P. Morgan to buy him out for $450 million. Ultimately, it was Morgan himself who attempted to bring order into the industry in the way forecast by Carnegie—through the organization of the United States Steel Corporation, the world's first billion-dollar company.

Organizational efforts to curtail competition and create stability could not, however, in the very nature of the case, be confined to the level of the single firm. In the effort to create intercompany agreements, it was the railroad that pioneered, primarily because it had been the railroad that first felt the effects of unbridled competition. Direct mergers carried out under the auspices of the banking houses that financed the consolidations were attempted, and so were "traffic associations," formed to fix rates and share traffic among competing lines. But railroads were more vulnerable than other industries to some measure of government regulation, and railroad entrepreneurs were not given a free hand to solve their competitive problems in the way in which they would have preferred. Eventually, government regulation was required; but even so, by 1900 the vast national railroad network had been so shaken down that only six large systems controlled 95 percent of the mileage. Where the railroads led, other industries were quick to follow.

As early as the 1870s, "pools" were formed to divide territorial markets, fix production quotas, and set prices; but these "gentlemen's agreements"—generally formed during the despair that prevailed at the bottom of a business depression—could not withstand the tendency of their own members to cheat or to defect during the optimism that prevailed when the business cycle turned upward, when there was promise of new killings to be made. John D. Rockefeller's Standard Oil Company was the first spectacular example of an even more effective form of business organization—the trust. The shareholders of a number of competing firms turned over their voting stock to "trustees" in return for nonvoting, interest-bearing certificates; the small group of trustees could then fix pricing and marketing policies for all of the once-competing companies within the trust. But this, too, proved only an interim form of organization. Held to be in violation of the law, it was soon replaced, with the help of agreeable state legislatures which provided the necessary enabling legislation, by the holding company, a single firm which controlled the operations of several subordinate units by holding a controlling interest in them.

In the center of the apparatus whose decisions produced a far-flung network of relationships from which virtually no one was excluded, which affected the lives and the livelihoods of all, was the businessman. The making of those decisions involved the late 19th-century businessman in activities that would have been utterly foreign to his forebears. At an earlier time the successful businessman had had to concern himself only with costs and prices; other factors could be taken for granted. At an earlier time, but no longer —for now even costs and prices depended upon such variables as the programs of political parties, the temper of the legislature, the attitude of labor and its degree of organization, the state of public opinion— all of them variables over which the businessman did not have full and complete control. Yet, if he was to operate in the climate of security which he found necessary for the successful prosecution of his affairs, more and more of his environment had to be brought within his purview and made susceptible to his influence. The businessman was, then, increasingly powerful; but he was also, by virtue of the way in which every area of the social environment impinged upon him, increasingly vulnerable as well.

Were his flamboyance and his self-consciousness the result of his own awareness of his power and vulnerability? Whether they were or not, the fact is that the businessman of the late 19th century stepped out front and center with an éclat that his forebears had never exhibited. For one thing, the great man of business had become far more numerous than ever before. When Moses Yale Beach, owner of the *New York Sun,* had compiled a list of the richest merchants of New York City in 1845, he found only 21 millionaires. In 1892 the *New York Tribune* counted more than 4,000 millionaires in the United States. The businessman-millionaire had, moreover, become far more visible to his fellow-citizens; the great scale of his business activities, his forays into politics, his heroic appetites in the fields of entertainment and culture made of him a figure rarely if ever out of sight in the comings and goings of his time and place. As the light fell upon him, it was seen that he sat at the center of the web of influence that penetrated into every section of the country. His decisions helped shape the environment in which all Americans had to live; and, increasingly, that environment began to rub harder and more irritatingly against large numbers of people. Small wonder, then, that the businessman became a subject of analysis and discussion, an object for emulation or for scorn.

With the passage of time the businessman tended increasingly to become, for both defenders and critics, a symbol of an entire social order. His critics came to interpret his misdeeds less as the expression of his idiosyncratic nature than as the inevitable consequences of a society gone wrong; his defenders, therefore, of necessity had to become defenders of the social order as well. In the first quarter of the 19th century, when the social order needed no defense, and when all that needed to be expalined was why each person held the position that he did within that society, the success of the great businessman was expressed as a tribute to him who had the stuff to get ahead. In the last quarter of the 19th century, when the social order stood very much in need of defense, the success of the businessman—by now accepted by both friend and foe as a symbol of that order—was expressed as a tribute to a social order which showered its blessings equally upon all. But 1899 was the year of the death of Horatio Alger, Jr., and 1900 was the year of the birth of the United States Steel Corporation; and the cult of success—if it ever was an accurate description of American social reality—was certainly no longer that. In a society made up increasingly of overlapping organizations, the idea of individual success as the victory of character over circumstances continued to live on, but it was less the reflection of a living reality than it was a technique by which the millions who made up the labor force could be motivated to accept the discipline of a capitalist industrial society.

SUGGESTED READINGS

BALTZELL, E. DIGBY. *Aristocracy and Caste in America.* New York: Random House, 1964.

CAWELTI, JOHN G. *Apostles of the Self-Made Man.* Chicago: University of Chicago Press, 1965.

CHANDLER, ALFRED D. *Strategy and Structure: Chapters in the History of the Industrial Enterprise.* Cambridge, Mass.: M.I.T. Press, 1962.

COCHRAN, THOMAS C. *The American Business System.* Cambridge, Mass.: Harvard University Press, 1959.

COLE, ARTHUR H. *Business Enterprise in Its Social Setting.* Cambridge, Mass.: Harvard University Press, 1959.

DIAMOND, SIGMUND. *The Reputation of the American Businessman.* Cambridge, Mass.: Harvard University Press, 1955; New York: Harper & Row, Colophon Books, 1966.

——— . (ed.). *The Nation Transformed.* New York: George Braziller, Inc., 1963.

——— . "John D. Rockefeller and the Historians." In *Philosophy, Science, and Method: Essays in Honor of Ernest Nagel,* edited by Sidney Morgenbesser, et al. New York: St. Martin's Press, Inc., 1969.

FINE, SIDNEY. *Laissez Faire and the General-Welfare State: A Study of Conflict in American Thought, 1865–1901.* Ann Arbor: University of Michigan Press, 1956.

GINGER, RAY. *Age of Excess: The United States from 1877 to 1914.* New York: Macmillan Co., 1965.

HAYS, SAMUEL P. *The Response to Industrialism.* Chicago: University of Chicago Press, 1957.

JOSEPHSON, MATTHEW. *The Robber Barons.* New York: Harcourt, Brace & Co., 1934.

KIRKLAND, EDWARD CHASE. *Dream and Thought in the Business Community, 1860–1900.* Ithaca, N.Y.: Cornell University Press, 1956.

——— . *Industry Comes of Age.* New York: Holt, Rinehart & Winston, 1961.

LYNN, KENNETH. *The Dream of Success: A Study of the Modern American Literary Imagination.* Boston: Little, Brown & Co., 1955.

MILLER, WILLIAM (ed.). *Men in Business.* Cambridge, Mass.: Harvard University Press, 1962.

RAUCHER, ALAN R. *Public Relations and Business, 1900–1929.* Baltimore: Johns Hopkins Press, 1968.

RISCHIN, MOSES (ed.). *The American Gospel of Success.* Chicago: Quadrangle Books, Inc., 1965.

SUTTON, FRANCIS X., et al. *The American Business Creed.* Cambridge, Mass.: Harvard University Press, 1956.

TEBBEL, JOHN. *From Rags to Riches: Horatio Alger, Jr., and the American Dream.* New York: Macmillan Co., 1963.

WEIBE, ROBERT. *Business and Reform: A Study of the Progressive Movement.* Cambridge, Mass.: Harvard University Press, 1962.

Weiss, Richard. *The American Myth of Success*. New York: Basic Books, 1969.

Wyllie, Irvin G. *The Self-Made Man in America: The Myth of Rags to Riches*. New Brunswick, N.J.: Rutgers University Press, 1954.

DOCUMENT 19.1

What the Social Classes Owe to Each Other*

Tough-minded William Graham Sumner, who left the ministry of the Episcopal Church to become an academic sociologist, strongly opposed resort to political action as a means of achieving social and economic amelioration. Contrariwise, he provided moral and intellectual justification for the possessors of wealth.

I have before me a newspaper slip on which a writer expresses the opinion that no one should be allowed to possess more than one million dollars' worth of property. Alongside of it is another slip, on which another writer expresses the opinion that the limit should be five millions. I do not know what the comparative wealth of the two writers is, but it is interesting to notice that there is a wide margin between their ideas of how rich they would allow their fellow-citizens to become, and of the point at which they ("the State," of course) would step in to rob a man of his earnings. These two writers only represent a great deal of crude thinking and declaiming which is in fashion. I have never known a man of ordinary common-sense who did not urge upon his sons, from earliest childhood, doctrines of economy and the practice of accumulation. A good father believes that he does wisely to encourage enterprise, productive skill, prudent self-denial, and judicious expenditure on the part of his son. The object is to teach the boy to accumulate capi-

tal. If, however, the boy should read many of the diatribes against "the rich" which are afloat in our literature; if he should read or hear some of the current discussion about "capital"; and if, with the ingenuousness of youth, he should take these productions at their literal sense, instead of discounting them, as his father does, he would be forced to believe that he was on the path of infamy when he was earning and saving capital. It is worth while to consider which we mean or what we mean. Is it wicked to be rich? Is it mean to be a capitalist? If the question is one of degree only, and it is right to be rich up to a certain point and wrong to be richer, how shall we find the point? Certainly, for practical purposes, we ought to define the point nearer than between one and five millions of dollars.

There is an old ecclesiastical prejudice in favor of the poor and against the rich. In days when men acted by ecclesiastical rules these prejudices produced waste of capital, and helped mightily to replunge Europe into barbarism. The prejudices are not yet dead, but they survive in our society as ludicrous contradictions and inconsistencies. One thing must be granted to the rich: they are good-natured. Perhaps they do not recognize themselves, for a rich man is even harder to define than a poor one. It is not uncommon to hear a clergyman utter from the pulpit all the old prejudice in favor of the poor and against the rich, while asking the rich to do something for the poor; and the rich comply, without apparently having their feelings hurt at all by the invidious comparison. We all agree that he is a good member of society who works his way up from poverty to wealth, but as soon as he has worked his way up we begin to regard him with suspicion, as a dangerous member of society. A newspaper starts the silly fallacy that "the rich are rich because the poor are industrious," and it is copied from one end of the country to the other as if it were a brilliant apothegm. "Capital" is denounced by writers and speakers who

*Source: William Graham Sumner, *What the Social Classes Owe to Each Other* (New York: Harper & Bros., 1883), pp. 43–57.

have never taken the trouble to find out what capital is, and who use the word in two or three different senses in as many, pages. Labor organizations are formed, not to employ combined effort for a common object, but to indulge in declamation and denunciation, and especially to furnish an easy living to some officers who do not want to work. People who have rejected dogmatic religion, and retained only a residuum of religious sentimentalism, find a special field in the discussion of the rights of the poor and the duties of the rich. We have denunciations of banks, corporations, and monopolies, which denunciations encourage only helpless rage and animosity, because they are not controlled by any definitions or limitations, or by any distinctions between what is indispensably necessary and what is abuse, between what is established in the order of nature and what is legislative error. Think, for instance, of a journal which makes it its special business to denounce monopolies, yet favors a protective tariff, and has not a word to say against trades-unions or patents! Think of public teachers who say that the farmer is ruined by the cost of transportation, when they mean that he cannot make any profits because his farm is too far from the market, and who denounce the railroad because it does not correct for the farmer, at the expense of its stockholders, the disadvantage which lies in the physical situation of the farm! Think of that construction of this situation which attributes all the trouble to the greed of "moneyed corporations"! Think of the piles of rubbish that one has read about corners, and watering stocks, and selling futures!

Undoubtedly, there are, in connection with each of these things, cases of fraud, swindling, and other financial crimes; that is to say, the greed and selfishness of men are perpetual. They put on new phases, they adjust themselves to new forms of business, and constantly devise new methods of fraud and robbery, just as burglars devise new artifices to circumvent every new precaution of the lock-makers. The criminal law needs to be improved to meet new forms of crime, but to denounce financial devices which are useful and legitimate because use is made of them for fraud, is ridiculous and unworthy of the age in which we live. Fifty years ago good old English Tories used to denounce all joint-stock companies in the same way, and for similar reasons.

All the denunciations and declamations which have been referred to are made in the interest of "the poor man." His name never ceases to echo in the halls of legislation, and he is the excuse and reason for all the acts which are passed. He is never forgotten in poetry, sermon, or essay. His interest is invoked to defend every doubtful procedure and every questionable institution. Yet where is he? Who is he? Who ever saw him? When did he ever get the benefit of any of the numberless efforts in his behalf? When, rather, was his name and interest ever invoked, when, upon examination, it did not plainly appear that somebody else was to win— somebody who was far too "smart" ever to be poor, far too lazy ever to be rich by industry and economy?

A great deal is said about the unearned increment from land, especially with a view to the large gains of landlords in old countries. The unearned increment from land has indeed made the position of an English landowner, for the last two hundred years, the most fortunate that any class of mortals ever has enjoyed; but the present moment, when the rent of agricultural land in England is declining under the competition of American land, is not well chosen for attacking the old advantage. Furthermore, the unearned increment from land appears in the United States as a gain to the first comers, who have here laid the foundations of a new State. Since the land is a monopoly, the unearned increment lies in the law of Nature. Then the only question is, Who shall have it?—the man who has the ownership by prescription, or some or all others? It is a beneficent incident of the ownership of land that a pioneer who reduces it to use, and helps to lay the foundations of a new State, finds a profit in the increasing value of land as the new State grows up. It would be unjust to take that profit away from him, or from any successor to whom he has sold it. Moreover, there is an unearned increment on capital and on labor, due to the presence, around the capitalist and the laborer, of a great, industrious, and prosperous society. A tax on land and a succession or probate duty on capital might be perfectly justified by these facts. Unquestionably capital accumulates with a rapidity which follows in some high series the security, good government, peaceful order of the State in which it is employed; and if the State steps in, on the death of the holder, to claim a share of the inheritance, such a claim may be fully justified. The laborer likewise gains by carrying on his labor in a strong, highly civilized, and well-governed State far more than he could gain with equal industry on the frontier or in the midst of anarchy. He gains greater remuneration for his services, and he also shares in the enjoyment of all that accumulated capital of a wealthy community which is public or semi-public in its nature.

It is often said that the earth belongs to the race, as if raw land was a boon, or gift. Raw land is only a *chance* to prosecute the struggle for existence, and the man who tries to earn a living by the subjugation of raw land makes that attempt under the most unfavorable conditions, for land can be brought into use only by great hardship and exertion. The boon, or gift, would be to get some land after somebody else had made it fit for use. Any one in the world to-day can have raw land by going to it; but there are millions who would regard it simply as "transportation for life," if they were forced to go and live on new land and get their living out of it. Private ownership of land is only division of labor. If it is true in any sense that we all own the soil

in common, the best use we can make of our undivided interests is to vest them all gratuitously (just as we now do) in any who will assume the function of directly treating the soil, while the rest of us take other shares in the social organization. The reason is, because in this way we all get more than we would if each one owned some land and used it directly. Supply and demand now determine the distribution of population between the direct use of land and other pursuits; and if the total profits and chance of land-culture were reduced by taking all the "unearned increment" in taxes, there would simply be a redistribution of industry until the profits of land-culture, less taxes and without chances from increasing value, were equal to the profits of other pursuits under exemption from taxation.

It is remarkable that jealousy of individual property in land often goes along with very exaggerated doctrines of tribal or national property in land. We are told that John, James, and William ought not to possess part of the earth's surface because it belongs to all men; but it is held that Egyptians, Nicaraguans, or Indians have such right to the territory which they occupy, that they may bar the avenues of commerce and civilization if they choose, and that it is wrong to override their prejudices or expropriate their land. The truth is, that the notion that the race own the earth has practical meaning only for the latter class of cases.

The great gains of a great capitalist in a modern state must be put under the head of wages of superintendence. Any one who believes that any great enterprise of an industrial character can be started without labor must have little experience of life. Let any one try to get a railroad built, or to start a factory and win reputation for its products, or to start a school and win a reputation for it, or to found a newspaper and make it a success, or to start any other enterprise, and he will find what obstacles must be overcome, what risks must be taken, what perseverance and courage are required, what foresight and sagacity are necessary. Especially in a new country, where many tasks are waiting, where resources are strained to the utmost all the time, the judgment, courage, and perseverance required to organize new enterprises and carry them to success are sometimes heroic. Persons who possess the necessary qualifications obtain great rewards. They ought to do so. It is foolish to rail at them. Then, again, the ability to organize and conduct industrial, commercial, or financial enterprises is rare; the great captains of industry are as rare as great generals. The great weakness of all co-operative enterprises is in the matter of supervision. Men of routine or men who can do what they are told are not hard to find; but men who can think and plan and tell the routine men what to do are very rare. They are paid in proportion to the supply and demand of them.

If Mr. A. T. Stewart made a great fortune by collecting and bringing dry-goods to the people of the United States, he did so because he understood how to do that thing better than any other man of his generation. He proved it, because he carried the business through commercial crises and war, and kept increasing its dimensions. If, when he died, he left no competent successor, the business must break up, and pass into new organization in the hands of other men. Some have said that Mr. Stewart made his fortune out of those who worked for him or with him. But would those persons have been able to come together, organize themselves, and earn what they did earn without him? Not at all. They would have been comparatively helpless. He and they together formed a great system of factories, stores, transportation, under his guidance and judgment. It was for the benefit of all; but he contributed to it what no one else was able to contribute—the one guiding mind which made the whole thing possible. In no sense whatever does a man who accumulates a fortune by legitimate industry exploit his employés, or make his capital

"out of" anybody else. The wealth which he wins would not be but for him.

The aggregation of large fortunes is not at all a thing to be regretted. On the contrary, it is a necessary condition of many forms of social advance. If we should set a limit to the accumulation of wealth, we should say to our most valuable producers, "We do not want you to do us the services which you best understand how to perform, beyond a certain point." It would be like killing off our generals in war. A great deal is said, in the cant of a certain school, about "ethical views of wealth," and we are told that some day men will be found to such public spirit that, after they have accumulated a few millions, they will be willing to go on and labor simply for the pleasure of paying the taxes of their fellow-citizens. Possibly this is true. It is a prophecy. It is as impossible to deny it as it is silly to affirm it. For if a time ever comes when there are men of this kind, the men of that age will arrange their affairs accordingly. There are no such men now, and those of us who live now cannot arrange our affairs by what men will be a hundred generations hence.

There is every indication that we are to see new developments of the power of aggregated capital to serve civilization, and that the new developments will be made right here in America. Joint-stock companies are yet in their infancy, and incorporated capital, instead of being a thing which can be overturned, is a thing which is becoming more and more indispensable. I shall have something to say [subsequently].... about the necessary checks and guarantees, in a political point of view, which must be established. Economically speaking, aggregated capital will be more and more essential to the performance of our social tasks. Furthermore, it seems to me certain that all aggregated capital will fall more and more under personal control. Each great company will be known as controlled by one master mind. The reason for this lies in the great superiority of personal management over management by boards and committees. This tendency is in the public interest, for it is in the direction of more satisfactory responsibility. The great hinderance to the development of this continent has lain in the lack of capital. The capital which we have had has been wasted by division and dissipation, and by injudicious applications. The waste of capital, in proportion to the total capital, in this country between 1800 and 1850, in the attempts which were made to establish means of communication and transportation, was enormous. The waste was chiefly due to ignorance and bad management, especially to State control of public works. We are to see the development of the country pushed forward at an unprecedented rate by an aggregation of capital, and a systematic application of it under the direction of competent men. This development will be for the benefit of all, and it will enable each one of us, in his measure and way, to increase his wealth. We may each of us go ahead to do so, and we have every reason to rejoice in each other's prosperity. There ought to be no laws to guarantee property against the folly of its possessors. In the absence of such laws, capital inherited by a spendthrift will be squandered and re-accumulated in the hands of men who are fit and competent to hold it. So it should be, and under such a state of things there is no reason to desire to limit the property which any man may acquire.

DOCUMENT 19.2
Dives and Lazarus*

James Baird Weaver (1833–1912), emerged from the Civil War as brigadier general, and in the decades that followed became a principal spokesman for those Middle Westerners who demanded currency reform and government control of

*Source: James Baird Weaver, *A Call to Action* (Des Moines, Iowa Printing Co., 1892), pp. 362–78.

corporate monopolies, especially the railroads. Weaver, a Greenbacker, was the presidential candidate of the Peoples Party in 1892. His descriptions of the excesses of the wealthy and the plight of the poor were typical of the social criticism of American reformers at the turn of the century.

If the master builders of our civilization one hundred years ago had been told that at the end of a single century, American society would present such melancholy contrasts of wealth and poverty, of individual happiness and widespread infelicity as are to be found to-day throughout the Republic, the person making the unwelcome prediction whould [sic] have been looked upon as a misanthropist, and his loyalty to Democratic institutions would have been seriously called in question. Our federal machine, with its delicate inter-lace work of National, State and municipal supervision, each intended to secure perfect individual equality, was expected to captivate the world by its operation and insure domestic contentment and personal security to a degree never before realized by mankind.

But there is a vast difference between the generation which made the heroic struggle for Self-government in colonial days, and the third generation which is now engaged in a mad rush for wealth. The first took its stand upon the inalienable rights of man and made a fight which shook the world. But the leading spirits of the latter are entrenched behind class laws and revel in special privileges. It will require another revolution to overthrow them. That revolution is upon us even now.

Two representative characters—Dives and Lazarus—always make their appearance side by side in disturbing contrast just before the tragic stage of revolution is reached. They were present at the overthrow of ancient civilizations; the hungry multitude stood outside the gates when Belshazzar's impious feast was spread; they were both at the cave of Adullam when the scepter was about to depart from the tyrant Saul to the hands of the youthful David; they stood side by side when Alaric thundered at the gates of Rome; they confronted one another in the fiery tempest of the French revolution and they are sullenly face to face in our own country to-day. We will devote a few pages to the delineation of these forces as they appear in our civilization at the present period.

SOCIAL EXTRAVAGANCE

In the year 1884, as we are told by Ward McAllister, in his book entitled "Society as I Found It," a wealthy gentleman gave a banquet at Delmonico's at which the moderate number of seventy-two guests, ladies and gentlemen, were entertained. The gentleman giving the banquet had unexpectedly received from the Treasury of the United States a rebate of $10,000 for duties which had been exacted from him through some alleged misconception of the law. He resolved to spend the entire sum in giving a single dinner which should excel any private entertainment ever given in New York. He consulted Charles Delmonico, who engaged to carry out his wishes. The table was constructed with a miniature lake in the center thirty feet in length, enclosed by a network of golden wire which reached to the ceiling, forming a great cage. Four immense swans were secured from one of the parks and placed in this lake. High banks of flowers of every hue surrounded the lake and covered the entire table, leaving barely enough room for the plates and wine glasses. The room was festooned with flowers in every direction. Miniature mountains and valleys with carpets of flowers made vocal with sparking rivulets, met the eye on every hand. Golden cages filled with sweet singing birds hung from the ceiling and added their enchantment to the gorgeous spectacle. Soft, sweet music swept in from adjoining rooms, and all that art, wealth and imagination could do was done to make the scene one of unexampled beauty. And then the feast! All the dishes which ingenuity could invent or the history of past extravagance suggest, were spread before the guests. The oldest and costliest wines known to the trade flowed like the water that leaped down the cascades in the banqueting hall. The guests were wild with exultation and delight and tarried far into the night. But in a few brief hours the romanticism had passed, the carousel was broken, and the revelers were face to face with the responsibilities which none of us can evade. The fool and his money had parted.

SILVER, GOLD AND DIAMOND DINNERS

Some time after the "swan dinner" was given, three of the swell leaders of New York society planned to give each a handsome entertainment which should set all New York talking. Each instructed the head of the celebrated *cafe* to spare no expense and to make his dinner the best of the three. So magnificent were these entertainments that Lorenzo Delmonico designated them as the silver, gold and diamond dinners. Each had peculiarities which distinguised it from the others. At one of them each lady found snugly concealed in her napkin a gold bracelet with the monogram of Jerome Park in the center in chased gold.

DIAMOND VESTURE

At one of the stated receptions given at the Executive Mansion during the first session of the Forty-ninth Congress, there appeared among the throng of exquisitely attired guests, the wife of a noted New York millionaire. She was accompanied by two trusted attendants, handsomely dressed in citizens' garb, who remained constantly with her, but slightly to the rear so as to keep perfect watch over her drapery. As she swept through the hall with her train and into the great east room, her raiment glistened until it almost seemed that a celestial constellation had descended from the skies to attend this reception. Her vesture was studded with a vast number of diamonds and other precious stones, valued above one million dollars! The climax of absurdity was reached and the utmost height of folly scaled. Does the reader for a moment think that the circle of wealthy snobs to which this lady belongs has any regard to republican institutions? On the contrary, every sensible person knows that they are the bitter foes to every democratic impulse, and their extreme wealth enables them to make their hostility aggressive and effective.

Prince Astor's Wedding

In the year 1890, young Astor, a scion of the celebrated family which has so long been prominent in New York financial circles, was married. Both the groom and the bride represented millions of wealth and the wedding was an imposing and gorgeous affair. Twenty-five thousand dollars were expended on the day's ceremony. The presents were valued at $2,000,000, and the couple and their attendants and a number of friends, immediately departed on an expensive yachting cruise which was to cost them $10,000 a month to maintain. In speaking of these nuptials the *Christian Union* said: "When we read this we are reminded of Thackeray's description of the extravagance of the Prince Regent during the Napoleonic wars. 'If he had been a manufacturing town, or a populous rural district, or an army of 5,000 men, he would not have cost more. The nation gave him more money, and more and more. The sum is past counting.'"

Looked at soberly, the sums lavished upon our American commoners are as disgraceful to our institutions as were the squanderings of the Prince Regent to those of England. If the scandal is less it is because the disastrous concentration of hereditary wealth has as yet awakened less serious thought among us than the disastrous concentration of hereditary power had awakened in England. In the case of the Astors, quite as much as of the

Prince Regent, the enormous sums expended are the gift of the Nation, obtained without compensating service on the part of the recipients. The burden upon the labor of the country is as great.

A Sportsman's Dinner

Early in the present year, 1891, a well-known New York State Senator gave a notable banquet in honor of two distinguished citizens of that State, both of whom are prominently mentioned in connection with the nomination for the Presidency of the United States. The following description of the table and decorations appeared in the daily press at the time:

The library is upon the second floor of the club house, known for years to residents of this city as the Stewart Mansion. It is a large room, grandly furnished, and just the place for a dinner of this limited proportion. The table has been especially constructed for the occasion, and it is said that for two days a landscape gardener and a florist were employed in decorating it. A glance at it made this appreciable. Most of those present were ardent sportsmen, and to this instinct the table appealed in the strongest measure. It looked like an immense marsh, just the place for fowl, and up from the waters of the small lakes which dotted the view, four live diamond-backed terrapins shot up their heads every now and again and winked slyly at the guests. Cattail, ferns, grass and wild flowers hid the banks of the lakes, and amid this greenery stuffed wild waterfowl hidden, as if in the attempt to escape the guns of the sportsman. In the center of the pool lay the gnarled stump of an immense oak, and imbedded in this was a nest containing an egg for each of the guests.

The Banker's Banquet

The following editorial appeared in the Kansas City *Times,* August 30, 1889:

The contract for serving the banquet for the convention of the American Banker's Association was yesterday awarded to C. M. Hill, of the Midland Hotel. There were sixty competitors. The price is such as to insure one of the finest banquets ever served in this country. No expense will be spared to make the affair a grand success, even aside from the *menu.* The banquet will be given in the

Priests of Pallas' Temple, at Seventh and Lydia. It will be necessary to build and furnish an annex, where the cooking can be done for 1,500 covers. The preparations seem to take into contemplation a great flow of wine, as there will be six thousand wine glasses and about forty wine servers. There will be in all nearly three hundred waiters. It is estimated that the entire cost of the banquet will be from $15,000 to $20,000. Mr. Hill anticipates some difficulty in securing efficient waiters, and with this particular object in view, will make a trip to New York and Chicago.

This impious feast which took place in the very heart of the mortgage-ridden and debt-cursed West, was the most shocking and brazen exhibition of wanton extravagance and bad morals combined, which the laboring millions of America were ever called upon to behold. What a travesty upon common sense and the ordinary instinct of self-preservation to intrust the finances of a great Nation and the welfare of labor to the hands of such men.

This carousal was but history repeating itself. It is not necessary in our day that an armless hand shall come out of the darkness and write the decree of Heaven upon the wall of the palace while the drunken carousal is being held, as in the time of Belshazzar; nor does it now require an expert Hebrew prophet, like Daniel, to disclose to the King that the sword is about to enter, and that a greater than Darius is thundering at the gates of Babylon, commissioned from on high to restore the stolen treasures of the temple, and to transfer the kingdom to another. Belshazzar and his courtiers were not first-class scholars, nor were they close students of passing events. Tyrants, and those who carouse and forget the poor rarely are. They could neither read the writing nor tell what it signified, and so they called in an expert—a man of simple habits —who preferred to mourn in captivity rather than to share in the robbery of his race or to enjoy the favor of the King. The writing in our day is in plain English, and the children of the captivity and all, except the drunken worshippers of mammon, can interpret its meaning without difficulty.

At the Rich Man's Gate

About the time these princely entertainments were given, and in the same year with some of them, one of the metropolitan journals caused a careful canvass to be made of the unemployed of that city. The number was found to be *one hundred and fifty thousand persons who were daily unsuccessfully seeking work within the city limits of New York*. Another one hundred and fifty thousand earn less than sixty cents per day. Thousands of these are poor girls who work from eleven to sixteen hours per day.

In the year 1890, over twenty-three thousand families, numbering about one hundred thousand people, were forcibly evicted in New York City owing to their inability to pay rent, and one-tenth of all who died in that city during the year were buried in the Potters Field.

In the *Arena* for June, 1891, will be found a description of tenement house horrors, by Mr. B. O. Flower. He has done a valuable service to humanity by laying before the world the result of his investigations. After describing a family whose head was unable to find work, Mr. Flower says:

. . . This poor woman supports her husband, her two children and herself, by making pants at twelve cents a pair. No rest, no surcease, a perpetual grind from early dawn, often till far into the night; and what is more appalling, outraged nature has rebelled; the long months of semi-starvation and lack of sleep have brought on rheumatism, which has settled in the joints of her fingers, so that every stich means a throb of pain. The afternoon we called she was completing an enormous pair of custom-made pants of very fine blue cloth, for one of the largest clothing houses in the city. The suit would probably bring sixty or sixty-five dollars, yet her employer graciously informed his poor white slave that as the garment was so large he would give her an *extra cent*. Thirteen cents for fine custom-made pants, manufactured for a wealthy firm, which repeatedly asserts that its clothing is not made in tenement houses!

Thus with one of the most painful diseases enthroned in that part of the body which must move incessantly from dawn till midnight, with two small dependent children and a husband powerless to help her, this poor woman struggles bravely, confronted ever by a nameless dread of impending misfortune. Eviction, sickness, starvation—such are the ever present spectres, while every year marks the steady encroachment of disease and the lowering of the register of vitality. Moreover, from the window of her soul falls the light of no star athwart the pathway of life.

In another tenement, Mr. Flower found a poor widow with three children, making pants at twelve cents a pair. One of the children had been engaged, since she was two and one-half years old, in overcasting the long seams of the garmets, made by her mother! In the attic of another tenement a widow was found weeping and working by the side of a cradle where lay a sick child, whose large luminous eyes shone with almost phosphorescent brilliancy from great cavernous sockets, as they wandered from one to another, with a wistful, soul-querying gaze. Its forehead was large and prominent, so much so that looking at the upper part of the head one would little imagine the terrible emaciation of the body, which was little more than skin and bones, and the sight of which spoke more eloquently than words of the ravages of slow starvation and wasting disease. The woman was weeping because she had been notified that if one week's rent was not paid on Saturday she would be evicted, which meant death to her child who was suffering from a rupture, and for whom she was unable to purchase a truss.

The making at home of clothing, cigars, etc., in New York and Brooklyn is paid at prices on which no women could live were there not other workers in the family. Some of their occupations involved great risks to girls, such as the loss of joints, of fingers, of the hand, or sometimes of the whole arm.

One of the official statisticians says upon this subject: "The tenement house system of work and the large influx of foreign immigration in New York City affected women workers more than any other class of laborers. The moral condition of the working women is influenced for evil by the tenement house home in a way too vast for discussion here. One noteworthy cause of immorality is the taking of men as lodgers for the sake of extra income. Another is the long distance girls are compelled to traverse after dark, especially on leaving stores which remain open till ten or eleven o'clock on Saturday night. Another is the working of friendless young women in the metropolis, where they live without home restraint, suffering every conceivable discomfort, subject to long periods of idleness, which they often enter upon with an empty purse. And yet, the truest heroism of life and conduct may be found here beneath rags and dirt. As far as ventilation is concerned, a regulated work-shop is the exception. The average room is either stuffy and close, or hot and close, and even where windows abound they are seldom opened. Toilet facilities are generally scant and inadequate, a hundred workers being dependent sometimes on a closet or sink, and that, too, often out of order."

There are many factories in the rooms of which from one hundred to two hundred women and men are packed like sardines in a box, with little or no ventilation, troubled by the inconveniences of steam, smoke, darkness, and all sorts of stenches intensified by heat. In many cases no provisions exist for escaping the danger of fire and other disasters. There are industries in which the rooms are constantly filled with dust, causing dangerous diseases of the organs of respiration. Rheumatism is caused by dampness in laundries, dyeing and meat packing establishments, canneries, etc. Rattling machinery has caused many women to become hard of hearing; excessive heat affects their entire system, and in food factories salt and spices give them asthma and bronchitis. Thousands of women who run sewing machines or are compelled to stand all day die of consumption and other diseases. The moral conditions of the shops vary with the nature of the occupation, the character of the foremen or forewomen, and the interest the proprietor takes in his employes. Wherever the sexes work together indiscriminately great laxity obtains, and in many an instance the employers openly declare that so long as their work is done they do not inquire or care how bad the girls may be.

Considering the cost of living, wages are little, if any, higher in New York than in other cities.

In some shops week workers are locked out for the half day if late, or docked for every minute of time lost, an extra fine being often added. Fining for bad work is general. The shop rules are stringent in most cases, and in certain industries wages are reduced by charges for machine rent, cotton, repairs, etc., to an extent not obtaining elsewhere. The seamstresses constitute the poorest class and a regular system of fraud is practiced upon these defenceless creatures. For instance: A standing advertisement is kept in the papers asking for girls to do tailor sewing. When one applies she is told that it will take her several weeks to learn, but that good wages will afterwards be paid. The girl accepts and goes to work, and after four or five weeks demands pay. Then she is told she is not satisfactory and cannot be employed. Thus many hundreds of poor girls not only give their labor for nothing but supply their own machines to the fraudulent factory, thereby saving the bosses a considerable outlay.

The boarding houses where working women are compelled to live have for the most part bare and filthy floors, broken or blackened window panes and rickety furniture. Meager meals of ill-selected and ill-cooked food, the sights, sounds and smells of the filthy surroundings—these constitute the home comforts provided by these cheap boarding and lodging houses. Two girls are sometimes crowded into a little hall chamber, carpetless and fireless; three, and even four share a larger room without comfort or convenience. The dining room is often the family kitchen, living room and laundry. The sleeping rooms are so cold in winter that failing utterly to keep warm until the hour for retiring, the girls are allured by the warmth and brightness of the dance houses and saloons, where they must of necessity, meet undesirable and unsafe acquaintances.

LAZARUS AT BOSTON

The Rev. Walter J. Swaffield, of the Baptist Bethel, Boston, relates in the *Arena* for February 1891 the following facts which came under his personal observation while visiting the poor of his parish:

On the fifth floor of an over-crowded tenement house in the north end of Boston, a sick man, wife and six children were found huddled together in two dingy, smoky rooms, neither of them larger than 8x8, for which they had to pay one dollar and a half per week. The only means of support they had was the uncertain revenue derived by the woman for making pants. She could seldom earn more than two dollars and a quarter per week, leaving but seventy-five cents with which to clothe and support the family. For six years that woman had worn the same dress, while the children had but one or a part of one garment apiece.

Another family of seven persons, invalid husband, wife and five children were crowded in a room hardly large enough for two persons. All the furniture in the room was an old borrowed stove, one broken chair, and a broken bedstead, no cooking utensils. The children had scarcely a rag on them, and for their dinner was eating sliced raw potatoes. They had not tasted bread for three days, nor meat for weeks. One week after our visit, another child was born into the family, only to die of starvation and cold for the poor mother had no nourishment to give it, no fuel nor fire for two days, and was dependent upon the kindness of a widow in the next room for a warm place beside her fire.

In another house was an American family of six persons living in two rooms rented at one dollar and a half a week. The man out of work, not a morsel of food in the place, no fuel or fire, the only articles of furniture being a stove, a small truck, a dry goods box, and on the floor in the corner of the room a heap of seaweed which was their only bed. It had been gathered from the beach the day before.

Not far from this family was found another room full of poor and suffering ones without food or fire, in the depth of winter. The four eldest children huddled together in bed at noontime to keep each other warm, while the hungry and crying baby was blue with cold in the bosom of its starving mother.

A widow, left with five little children has to support herself and family, and pay one dollar and a half per week rent for two small rooms. Her only hope is in securing pants enough to make at fourteen cents a pair. In order to keep body and soul together she must teach the two little girls "Constance" and "Maggie," aged five and three how to sew, and thus do their part in keeping the wolf from the door. These two babies work early and late, the five-year-old seamstress overcasting the long seams of four pairs of pants a day, and the three-three-old dot [sic] managing to overcast two pairs. They handle the needle like professionals. Mother and two daughters together thus earn from two dollars and a quarter to two dollars and a half a week, after paying rent having but a single dollar left to feed and clothe the whole family.

The time of my visit was near the dinner hour, but all the preparation for the principal meal of the day was the stirring of corn meal into boiling water.

At Chicago

In the latter part of the year 1891, a committee from a Chicago Trade and Labor Assembly, at the request of a body of striking cloakmakers, made an investigation of the condition of that class of workers in the city. They were accompanied by an officer of the City Health Department, the City Attorney and artists and reporters of the local press. They found that thirteen thousand persons were engaged in the manufacture of clothing in Chicago, over one-half of whom were females. In order to reduce the cost of production the firms engaged in the manufacture of clothing have adopted the European Sweating System, which is in brief, as follows: The material for garments is cut to size and shape and delivered by the large firms to individual contractors known as sweaters, who relieve the firm of all other care or expense, taking the goods to what are known as sweating dens, usually located in the poorest neighborhoods of the great city. These sweaters are employed by the most opulent firms. The committee visited a large number of these dens, nearly all of which were dwelling houses which served as living and sleeping rooms for the sweater's family and the employes. In one room ten feet by forty, they found thirty-nine young girls, twelve children between ten and twelve years of age, eleven men and the sweater and his wife. The room and all the surroundings were filthy in the extreme. The rates of wages were of course very low, and yet the fear of discharge rendered it impossible to obtain satisfactory information. The committee found two thousand one hundred children at work in these dismal places who were under age and employed in violation of existing laws against child labor. Sanitary laws were also overriden in all of these miserable abodes. We take the following from the report of the committee:

The condition of the places visited was horrible. Overcrowding, long hours and low pay were the rule. Girls ten years old were found to be working ten and twelve hours a day for 80 cents per week. Ten girls were found, none over ten years old, who worked sixteen hours a day for from 75 cents to $1.20 per week. In a De Koven street den were found a half dozen men working eighteen hours a day for from $4 to $9 per week. At 168 Maxwell street were found ten men that worked sixteen hours a day each and received $6.50 to $9 per week. In the same place were six girls working from two to fourteen hours a day whose weekly pay averaged $3. One child was found in a house that worked for 75 cents per week. At 455 South Canal street a girl was found who declined to tell what she received fearing she would be discharged, and discharge meant starvation. At 69 Judd street the wages of the men were found to be from $5 to $9 per week, and one child there received $1 per week. The women worked fourteen hours a day. The product of this shop was sold to Marshall Field & Co. At 151 Peoria street, is a cloak-finishing establishment. Here the women receive one and one-half cents each for finishing cloaks. One woman was found on the street with a bundle of cloaks she had finished. She said that by hard work she finished twenty cloaks a day and earned thirty cents. This supported herself and two babies. The place 258 Division street was by far the worst visited. Eleven men worked twelve hours a day and received $5 to $9.50 per week. Twelve children here worked twelve hours for 75 cents per week. The place was terribly crowded, there being no water or light.

And yet in the face of these glaring conditions, which are common in all of our populous cities, empty headed political charlatans still vex the public with their puerile rant about protection for American labor.

Dives in His Palace

At the close of the year of our Lord 1891, while the Christian world was celebrating the lowly birth in the manger at Bethlehem, and while the wretched sweaters of Chicago were bending their aching backs in their dismal prisons, a wealthy merchant of that city moved into his resplendent mansion which had just been finished for his reception. He celebrated the event with a week of festivity. One of the local papers gave the following description of this palace:

It is located on Michigan boulevard and Thirty-fourth street, and has been in the course of construction for nearly two years. Among its principal features is an immense ball-room, which includes a completely fitted stage, a complete barber shop, a music room, which is divided by Mexican onyx columns from a conservatory, and one of the finest private libraries in the country. On the floor of the drawing room is a large aubixon rug, woven in one piece, the cost of which alone was upwards of ten thousand dollars. The floor of the large reception room is of Italian marble mosaic, and one of its attractive features is an old moorish fireplace. The dining room walls are finished in old tapestry of almost fabulous value. The bath rooms are white marble and onyx, the main one having an onyx wainscoting five feet in height, and above this a frescoing of pond lily design. There are study rooms for the youthful members of the family, while the apartments that have been reserved for guests would al-

most compare with the descriptions that have been handed down of portions of the interior of Solomon's temple.

Outer Darkness

The following dispatch from London concerning the recent Westphalia strike, is enough to shock the sensibilities of christendom and fill the world with mourning:

London, April 28, 1891.—A Berlin dispatch says that the severe measures of depression in Westphalia have had their effect and the strikers are thoroughly cowed. Many of their families are in a starving condition and expected remittances from Belgium and England have not arrived. The strikers are not permitted to hold meetings and if a few are seen gathering they are at once scattered by the police. Consequently they have little opportunity to arrange for common action.

And Has It Come to Us So Soon

About the close of the recent Jackson Park World's Fair strike, we clipped from the columns of one of the Chicago dailies the following local editorial. Speaking of the poor strikers the paper said:

The outlook discouraged them. None had any great supply of money and few had places to sleep. The outlook was altogether discouraging, and was made even more so by the action of the police, who broke up the picket lines as fast as they were formed, and even refused to allow them to congregate in any numbers.

About 9 o'clock in the morning a hundred or so weary strikers were stretched in the sun on the prairie near Parkside endeavoring to get some sleep, when word was passed for a meeting at Sixty-seventh street and Stony Island avenue. By 9:30 o'clock two hundred men had congregated there and Dr. Willoughby, the owner of the lot, objected. He notified the police that he did not want any trespassing on his premises, and Lieut. Rehm and a squad of ten officers were dispatched to the scene. He ordered the strikers to disperse, but they failed to obey with alacrity, and the police had to drive them off. There was some slight resistance, and several heads suffered in consequence from contact with policemen's batons.

We trust the brief pages of this chapter

may suffice to call the attention of the reader to the ghastly condition of American society and to remind him of the imperative call which is made upon him as an individual to do all in his power to arrest the alarming tendencies of our times. In the opinion of the writer, unless the people of America shall immediately take political matters into their own hands, the contrasts suggested in this chapter portend a tragic future. The millionaire and the pauper cannot, in this country, long dwell together in peace, and it is idle to attempt to patch up a truce between them. Enlightened self respect and a quickened sense of justice are impelling the multitude to demand an interpretation of the anomalous spectacle, constantly presented before their eyes, of a world filled with plenty and yet multitudes of people suffering for all that goes to make life desirable. They are calling to know why idleness should dwell in luxury and those who toil in want; and they are inquiring why one-half of God's children should be deprived of homes upon a planet which is large enough for all. The world will find a solution for these insufferable afflictions in the glorious era but just ahead. Even now the twilight discloses the outlines of a generous inheritance for all and we hear the chirping of sweet birds making ready to welcome with melody and gladness the advent of the full orbed day.

DOCUMENT 19.3
The Road to Business Success*

Andrew Carnegie (1835–1919) was not only the nation's most articulate spokesman of the cult of success and the ideas of which it was composed; he was himself the very epitome of that cult. In innumerable articles, and in such books as *Triumphant*

---

*Source: Andrew Carnegie, "The Road to Business Success," an address to the students of Curry Commercial College, Pittsburgh, June 23, 1885, in *The Empire of Business* (New York: Doubleday, Page & Co., 1902), pp. 3–18.

Democracy and *The Gospel of Wealth*, he held up the image of the self-made man and set forth the social philosophy of a society built upon competition and emulation.

It is well that young men should begin at the beginning and occupy the most subordinate positions. Many of the leading businessmen of Pittsburgh had a serious responsibility thrust upon them at the very threshold of their career. They were introduced to the broom, and spent the first hours of their business lives sweeping out the office. I notice we have janitors and janitresses now in offices, and our young men unfortunately miss that salutary branch of a business education. But if by chance the professional sweeper is absent any morning, the boy who has the genius of the future partner in him will not hesitate to try his hand at the broom. The other day a fond fashionable mother in Michigan asked a young man whether he had ever seen a young lady sweep in a room so grandly as her Priscilla. He said no, he never had, and the mother was gratified beyond measure, but then said he, after a pause, "What I should like to see her do is sweep out a room." It does not hurt the newest comer to sweep out the office if necessary. I was one of those sweepers myself, and who do you suppose were my fellow sweepers? David McCargo, now superintendent of the Alleghany Valley Railroad; Robert Pitcairn, superintendent of the Pennsylvania Railroad, and Mr. Moreland, City Attorney. We all took turns, two each morning did the sweeping; and now I remember Davie was so proud of his clean white shirt bosom that he used to spread over it an old silk bandana handkerchief which he kept for the purpose, and we other boys thought he was putting on airs. So he was. None of us had a silk handkerchief.

Assuming that you have all obtained employment and are fairly started, my advice to you is "aim high." I would not give a fig for the young man who does not already see himself the partner or the head of an important firm. Do not rest content for a moment in your thoughts as head clerk, or foreman, or general manager in any concern, no matter how extensive. Say to yourself, "My place is at the top." *Be king in your dreams....*

And here is the prime condition of success, the great secret: concentrate your energy, thought, and capital exclusively upon the business in which you are engaged. Having begun in one line, resolve to fight it out on that line, to lead in it; adopt every improvement, have the best machinery, and know the most about it.

The concerns which fail are those which have scattered their capital, which means that they have scattered their brains also. They have investments in this, or that, or the other, here, there, and everywhere. "Don't put all your eggs in one basket" is all wrong. I tell you "put all your eggs in one basket, and then watch that basket." Look round you and take notice; men who do that do not often fail. It is easy to watch and carry the one basket. It is trying to carry too many baskets that breaks most eggs in this country. He who carries three baskets must put one on his head, which is apt to tumble and trip him up. One fault of the American business man is lack of concentration.

To summarize what I have said: Aim for the highest; never enter a barroom; do not touch liquor, or if at all only at meals; never speculate; never indorse beyond your surplus cash fund; make the firm's interest yours; break orders always to save owners; concentrate; put all your eggs in one basket, and watch that basket; expenditure always within revenue; lastly, be not impatient, for, as Emerson says, "no one can cheat you out of ultimate success but yourselves."

I congratulate poor young men upon being born to that ancient and honourable degree which renders it necessary that they should devote themselves to hard work. A basketful of bonds is the heaviest basket a young man ever had to carry. He generally gets to staggering under it. We have in this city creditable instances of such young men, who have pressed to the front rank of our best and most useful citizens. These deserve great credit. But the vast majority of the sons of rich men are unable to resist the temptations to which wealth subjects them, and sink to unworthy lives. I would almost as soon leave a young man a curse, as burden him with the almighty dollar. It is not from this class you have rivalry to fear. The partner's sons will not trouble you much, but look out that some boys poorer, much poorer than yourselves, whose parents cannot afford to give them the advantages of a course in this institute, advantages which should give you a decided lead in the race—look out that such boys do not challenge you at the post and pass you at the grand stand. Look out for the boy who has to plunge into work direct from the common school and who begins by sweeping out the office. He is the probable dark horse that you had better watch.

DOCUMENT 19.4
Poor Little Stephen Girard*

The young men who listened to Carnegie and believed him did not all become presidents of their companies as a result, but no doubt most of them were encouraged to work harder. But what would have been the effect on behavior, especially on labor discipline, of those who listened to the cynical Mark Twain?

The man lived in Philadelphia who, when young and poor, entered a bank, and says he: "Please, sir, don't you want a boy?" And the stately personage said: "No, little boy, I don't want a little boy." The little boy, whose heart was too full for utterance, chewing a piece of licorice stick he had bought with a cent stolen from his good and pious aunt, with sobs plainly

---

*Source: Mark Twain, "Poor Little Stephen Girard," in Anna Randall-Diehl (ed.), *Carleton's Popular Readings* (New York, 1879), pp. 183–84.

audible, and with great globules of water rolling down his cheeks, glided silently down the marble steps of the bank. Bending his noble form, the bank man dodged behind a door, for he thought the little boy was going to shy a stone at him. But the little boy picked up something, and stuck it in his poor but ragged jacket. "Come here, little boy," and the little boy did come here; and the bank man said: "Lo, what pickest thou up?" And he answered and replied: "A pin." And the bank man said: "Little boy, are you good?" and he said he was. And the bank man said: "How do you vote?—excuse me, do you go to Sunday school?" and he said he did. Then the bank man took down a pen made of pure gold, and flowing with pure ink, and he wrote on a piece of paper, "St. Peter;" and he asked the little boy what it stood for, and he said "Salt Peter." Then the bankman said it meant "Saint Peter." The little boy said: "Oh!"

Then the bank man took the little boy to his bosom, and the little boy said, "Oh!" again, for he squeezed him. Then the bank man took the little boy into partnership, and gave him half the profits and all the capital, and he married the bank man's daughter, and now all he has is all his, and all his own too.

My uncle told me this story, and I spent six weeks in picking up pins in front of a bank. I expected the bank man would call me in and say: "Little boy, are you good?" and I was going to say "Yes"; and when he asked my what "St. John" stood for, I was going to say "Salt John." But the bank man wasn't anxious to have a partner, and I guess the daughter was a son, for one day says he to me: "Little boy, what's that you're picking up?" Says I, awful meekly, "Pins." Says he: "Let's see 'em." And he took 'em, and I took off my cap, all ready to go in the bank, and become a partner, and marry his daughter. But I didn't get an invitation. He said: "Those pins belong to the bank, and if I catch you hanging around here any more I'll set the dog on you!" Then I left, and the mean old fellow kept the pins. Such is life as I find it.

DOCUMENT 19.5
The Science of Railways: Organization and Forces*

An important element in the kind of social discipline sought by American owners and managers at the end of the 19th century was the cultivation of the "proper" attitude toward corporate executives. Here one of their spokesmen discusses how to maintain efficiency and order within the railroad, and sets forth one of the roles of the executive.

Subordination is a cardinal principle of organized labor—subordination to the employer, subordination to each other according to rank and natural precedence. It is based upon a just conception of the rights of men in their relation to property. All men, however, are entitled to justice and humane treatment.

The discipline of corporate forces is as absolute as that of a man of war. Obedience to superior authority is unqualified. It is, however, the privilege and duty of every subordinate in emergencies, when an order is given, to make such suggestions as the circumstances of the case demand. Here his responsibility ends, except in criminal cases.

An order once given, must be obeyed. Absolutism such as this involves grave responsibilities. It presupposes skill, accurate knowledge and appreciation.

In the administrative department of carriers lack of discipline breeds insubordination, idleness and extravagance. It engenders kindred evils in the operating department, with the added element of danger.

It is necessary that the forces of a railroad should possess *esprit de corps*, coupled with interest, intelligence and courage that no event can deaden or divert.

---

*Source: Marshall M. Kirkman, *The Science of Railways: Organization and Forces*, Vol. I (5th ed.; New York and Chicago: World Railway Publishing Co., 1896), pp. 69–70, 170–75.

While the discipline of corporate life is as absolute as that of an army, there is this difference between them: army life destroys the individuality of all below the rank of officer; corporate life intensifies the personality of subordinates by recognition and promotion. Everyone knows that promotion will follow intelligence, faithfulness and industry. The officers of railroads are drawn from the ranks. It is therefore for the interests of such corporations to build up the intelligence and morale of subordinates; to strengthen the force by careful selection and cultivation. Individuals should be taught to think and act for themselves in all cases where discretion can safely be allowed. They will thus be taught self reliance, and the exercise of prudence and good judgment. . . .

In general, that form of organization is best for corporate property that enforces the most minute responsibility and offers the greatest encouragement to those who work for it; that enables a company to know the measure of faithfulness and capacity of its servants; that rewards the trustworthy and takes cognizance of the derelict. . . .

It is probable that many labor associations have, at the bottom, a belief that the employer does not properly regard the interests of his employe. This belief is false. But in order to dispel it and in doing so break up such combinations as are subversive of the employe's interest, railways must actively interest themselves in the concerns of those who work for them. Their interests are jeopardized, not because they have been disregardful but because their employes believed they have. This erroneous impression the owner must correct if he would not have foreign and unfriendly agents meddling in his affairs. There are two ways in which corporations may and do manifest their interest in those who work for them. In America it is done by kindly treatment, the payment of high wages, continued service, promotion, and by making the employe self reliant and independent. In many countries wages are unavoidably low, and so corporations eke out their efforts by small annuities and distress funds, and by special interest in the sicknesses, discomforts and forebodings of those who work for them.

The vicissitudes of corporate service require a paternal form of government. The owner must be the father. Failure to recognize this will aggravate the growth of unfriendly labor associations. . . .

In general, employes are safer in the hands of the employer than in those of anyone else. His interest is permanent, material and fatherly.

The conception of the employer by those who work for him must be broad and charitable. Nothing is attainable without this. Employes must not be quick to believe they are treated unjustly, are overlooked or forgotten. They must be governed by reason. They must accept the conditions of life as they are. They must go ahead sturdily and cheerfully, believing that if they comprehend their business and are active in the discharge of it, their services will be recognized. They must also appreciate this truth, that those who are preferred are, on the whole, worthy of it. That while there are exceptions to the rule, they are unworthy of regard. Disappointed men, instead of repining, must seek by renewed zeal and attachment the recognition they desire. They must not seek, in such emergencies, through combinations, or otherwise, to force what they cannot peaceably attain. . . .

Unflagging industry and continual study is the only road to preferment. All others are makeshift, temporary and incomplete. When men do not progress as fast as they think they should, let them work and study the harder; do more and better work. There is no other road to preferment. . . .

DOCUMENT 19.6

Plutocracy's Bastiles: Or Why the Republic Is Becoming an Armed Camp*

While advocates of management prerogatives used the analogy with military organizations to legitimize the executive's authority, some critics of society saw in the activities of men of great wealth a potent source of the militarization of the United States. To muckraking editor B. O. Flower, men of great wealth were prepared to dig themselves in to defend their property. To the businessman, articles such as Flower's were proof that the society which had so long protected him was under attack.

For years conditions were such that the people did not appreciate the danger which threatened them, through the rapid rise of a plutocracy based on special privileges. But at last there came a day when they could no longer be blinded by Fourth of July orations or appeals to partisan prejudice. They found their houses being mortgaged and sold for debts they contracted in order to clothe and educate their children properly. Their employers and landlords were living in comparative luxury, while the great gamblers of Wall Street and the manipulators of trusts and monopolies were becoming multimillionnaires. This made them think for themselves. A thinking man makes a poor slave, and general dissatisfaction ensued, while increasing hard times in a nation mar-

---

*Source: B. O. Flower, "Plutocracy's Bastiles: Or Why the Republic Is Becoming an Armed Camp," *Arena*, Vol. X (1894), pp. 601–21.

vellously rich in money's worth increased the social discontent. . . .

This alarmed plutocracy. It felt that the time had come for action, and it has acted and is acting. In a republic corruption may flourish for a time, but unless there exists a powerful military organization, ready to obey the tools of corruption and enforce laws enacted for the benefit of a special class, a reaction will sooner or later take place and the corruptionists will be swept from power by the people. . . . Hence it is always to the military arm that an oppressive government, of whatever character, looks for a continuance of power. And for this reason every true patriot and lover of the republic should discourage the war spirit and seek to check the speed of the military tendency which plutocracy is so energetically fostering at the present time. . . .

The multiplication of armories is perilous for a republic, and doubly so where organized wealth has gained the power it sways in America. But it is indeed difficult to consider anything more contrary to the spirit of republican institutions than permitting the rich men of great centres of wealth to lavish their money upon armories. Who is so blind that he cannot see that the men who furnished the million dollars for the Seventh Regiment, and those who are paying for the three or four hundred thousand dollar Boston armory, would expect the regiments thus beholden to them to see as they saw, in case starving industry should be pitted against idle wealth, or in the case the industrial millions overthrow the money changers in the temples of legislation with their ballots and plutocracy beholds the intelligence of a great republic prepared to assert the cause of justice for all the people?

20 Affirmation and Anxiety: The American Puritan Ethos in the Late 19th Century

A. S. EISENSTADT
Brooklyn College

Like nearly all durable systems of religious belief, Puritanism was more than the sum of its doctrinal parts. It was also an ethos—which may be defined as a set of habits and attitudes unique to the culture in question. The Puritan ethos, then, was that body of characteristics and distinguishing attitudes held by its adherents. But by the 1800s, if not earlier, this cluster of values and ideals which defines an ethos had stained the *entire* fabric of our national life, serving most Americans as an instrument for perceiving the world around them and for guiding their actions within it. The ethos became, in effect, an American philosophy, a distillate of American ideas, a creed for achievement, a standard of loyalty, an American mythology. Even more, indeed, it was an ideology which bore upon men with the persuasion of a powerful faith. By their adherence to it, tribes of immigrants, abandoning other lands and other mores, merged into a larger nation. Crèvecoeur's American, this new man, and his millions of successors were more than freeholders, they were converts to a faith that stamped American life and thought with its distinctive seal.

The roots of this Puritan ethos were deep-struck and tenacious; and the ethos itself, it follows, was hardly limited to the 17th century and to Puritan's greatest decades. Indeed, the ethos stubbornly resisted the pressures of time. But the newer problems of American life, so apparent in the late 19th century, resulted in severe questioning and the Puritan ethos, in order to be viable, had to be redefined.

To say this, of course, is to pose a series of challenging questions. First of all, what do we mean by the American Puritan ethos? What were its substance and significance? What were its component ideals? And what was the other side of the Puritan ethos? To what extent was it an ideology of anxiety and fear no less than of hope and affirmation? What was its earlier history, and what were the dynamics of its evolution? How and why did each of its principal components come under reconsideration during the late 19th century, and in sum how was the ethos redefined?

The Puritan ethos itself was a union of four principal ideals:
1. The entrepreneurial.
2. The democratic-egalitarian.
3. The village-town.
4. The reformational.

The first ideal, the entrepreneurial, stressed the need for men to have a vocation which ultimately could bring great success. Industry and energy mattered more than anything else. American life offered men a career open to talents. To succeed, one had to make it on one's own: American heroes were a race of self-made men.

The democratic-egalitarian ideal held that men were born equal, that democracy was the soundest and generally the most advantageous form of human polity, that aristocracy was venal and pernicious, and that the people, over a period of time, were the best judge of society's interests.

The village-town ideal represented the localization of the Puritan ethos, setting it down, as it were, in an environment in which it could thrive. The village-town was a community of known individuals, sharing with each other a common fund of ideas.

The reformational ideal urged that institutions could be perverted and therefore had constantly to be kept pure. By its terms, the American was properly a planter and a supplanter, a creator and a recreator. As Emerson saw so clearly, he was always revising his whole social structure, beginning his world anew. He did it with an invocation of the divine spirit and the higher law. He was a spiritual contractor, building new edifices, improving old ones. Understandably, then, the proper business of America was the business of reform.

The Puritan ethos stressed possibility and affirmation. It joined John Calvin's injunction to do God's will in the world to John Locke's precept that man, having a vast capacity to learn and grow, could change the world to the measure of his own strivings and hopes. It emphasized man's potentiality for achievement. By its terms, to work was to pray. It was notably positive in that the desire for individual success was the prime article of faith. Aspiration, ambition, mobility, risk-taking: these were commendable American traits for the American to have. To find, one must seek. To succeed, one must venture. In sum, the American Puritan ethos ex-pressed the goal of a society consecrated to promoting the welfare of its individual members.

But the Puritan ethos had perforce another side. It stood ultimately on the shaky, shifting ground of anxiety. Fears of failure fringed the vision of success. If America was promises, it could also be the denial and frustration of promises. Belief could readily turn into disbelief. And for all the positive qualities that sustained the belief, despair was the other side of hope; incapacity was the counterpart to ability; uncertainty pushed aside conviction; and pessimism often prevailed over optimism.

The writing of American history has, regrettably, been far too little concerned with anxiety as a factor in the making of our society. Too many American historians have centered their attention on the positive side of their country's democratic faith, on the optimistic and affirmative aspects of our national myth. In George Bancroft, Providence guides our fortunate course; in Frederick Jackson Turner, the frontier makes our world safe for democracy; in Charles A. Beard, the hidden tale of economic advantage being gained by the few is really the progressive historian's first step in making it available to the many—in insisting, that is, that the terms of the myth be met. The darker side of the Puritan ethos, which Alexis de Tocqueville so well perceived, yet awaits its historian.

The American past, however, should not be seen only as a success story but rather as the account of the degree of success Americans could achieve. The question has always been whether and how far an ideal of entrepreneurship could be pursued, whether equality and democracy could be preserved, whether the interpersonal relationships of the village-town could be sustained and the larger sense kept alive that men could change their institutions to attain their ideals.

Where conditions were favorable, the optimistic aspect of the Puritan ethos could be both confirmed and maintained.

For the greater part of American experience, from the 17th through the early 19th centuries, conditions were indeed favorable. The implantation of the institutions and ideas of Puritan England amidst the fabulous natural resources of the New World not only created the Puritan ethos but also gave it a continuing vitality. This is not to say that it ruled American minds without interruption or that its terms were never challenged. Still for some two centuries, this ethos largely dominated.

But after the Civil War, during the grim decades of the late 19th century, changing circumstances began to impinge heavily upon the Puritan ethos and to impede its realization. The new age brought in its train a multitude of new institutions and conditions, so significantly different from the old ones as to challenge their continuance, indeed their survival. The sudden advent of big industry was the most obvious aspect of a larger historical phenomenon which included, among other things, the growth of great cities, the inpouring of millions of immigrants, and the expansion of the American empire.

Actualities restricted the operation of the Puritan ethos and prevented the realization of its ideals. Ambition had a lesser field in which to play. Success was much harder to grasp. The ethos showed its bleak side. Failure and the fear of failure rose as awesome challengers to affirmation and optimism.

Men who live by creeds also perish by them. Not that Americans were unable to accept the newer realities which confronted them: rather they could not tolerate the possibility that their creed was invalid. The ethos by which they had construed and shaped their world seemed belied by facts. Realities and fantasies, which Americans had hitherto so marvellously matched, no longer had a plausible connection. On the contrary, Americans in the process were driven hard into both sides of the Puritan ethos, the affirmative and the negative. On the one hand, they proclaimed more passionately and zealously than ever the validity of its basic ideals. But on the other, they looked at its ideals with doubt and fear, with the deep anxiety of men who were on the verge of losing faith, their most valuable possession.

Hard times, then, drove a deep wedge between the two contrapuntal aspects of the Puritan ethos: the affirmation of belief and its denial. Every article of the American faith had its counter article. Belief and doubt, great hope and great hopelessness, were locked into frightful combat.

The entrepreneurial ideal was never more loudly proclaimed and never more vehemently denounced than in these post-Civil War years. Teachers of the school of success and of the idea of the self-made man were legion. Scores of manuals proclaimed the gospel of hard work, good character, perseverance, frugality, sobriety, and the rest of the noble virtues by which one could climb the ladder of worldly success. But no fewer challenged the very soundness of the gospel itself. The great tracts of social reform questioned the feasibility of individual entrepreneurship, and the age was teeming with proposals for reconstructing American society—Socialist, Single Tax, Populist, Utopian, Christian Socialist, Social Gospel, and so on.

The democratic-egalitarian ideal was widely propagated and warmly espoused. Raucous Fourth of July celebrations were fitting occasions for commemorating the ideal as well as the country dedicated to its attainment. Patriotism was the great refuge of citizens in doubt, and the stronger the doubts, the warmer grew the patriotism. The Centennial Exhibition at Philadelphia in 1876 and the World's Columbian Exposition of 1893 at Chicago were proud testimonials to the achievements of the land of democracy and equality.

Counterparts to advertisements for the land of the free and equal and the home of the democrats were denunciations of those who seemed to be perverting democracy's institutions, undermining the rule of the people, and subjecting the republic to the rule of elitist interests and oligarchical views. It seemed clear that there was corruption in high places and low, indeed that the republic's foundations were being sapped. Newspapers carried remarkable disclosures of the dark workings of bosses, machines, and rings. There was a widespread, if not a paranoid, apprehension that the practice of open ways and public (and therefore honest) statements was being destroyed by secret deals and private (and therefore dishonest) arrangements.

Such apprehension had basis in fact. But fears exaggerated fact and inflamed suspicion. The age of exploitation was also the age of the great phobia and rampant nativism, of fears of conspiracy by the few against the people. With millions of new immigrants streaming into the United States (alien people who did not know its tongue or its political institutions), with men in key offices—municipal, state, and national—selling public franchises for private gain, with bitter struggles between capital and labor bloodying the land in a kind of new and dreadful civil war, the fear spread that the republican center could not hold. In sum, converting the democratic-egalitarian ideal into a cult of zealous patriotism—something quite different from what existed for over two centuries—was one side of the nation's response to the newer conditions of American life. The other was an apprehensive belief that the ideal and the republic were being destroyed by wicked and sinister men.

Every civilization, as it experienced the growth of great urban centers, has fashioned some form of the agrarian myth. According to myth, life on the farm and in the village nurtured the growth of all the civic virtues: hard work, devotion to one's family, patriotism, probity, manliness. Life in the city eroded these virtues. The city bred crime, irresponsibility, profligacy, immorality, disloyalty, venality. This agrarian myth had a particular currency in the Western world during the middle and late 19th century, and nowhere more vitally than in the United States. From 1860 to 1900, American urban population quadrupled, New York—symbol of the urban phenomenon—grew from a city of 800,000 persons to one of three and a half million, and the rural population of the United States declined from 80 percent of the total to 60 percent.

The contrast of village-town to city seemed to be one not merely of civic virtue to civic vice but, more significantly, of a known, intimate set of interpersonal relations to one that was unknown, impersonal, distant, and ultimately threatening. The anxiety that seized Americans on so many other grounds and that took so many other forms became particularly vivid when they beheld the city. Perhaps the most important social tract of the 1880s, Josiah Strong's *Our Country*, saw the city as the "storm center" of American civilization, the prime locus of all that was imperiling American life. Indeed, to the Reverend Strong and his generation, the city represented the greatest threat to the American Puritan ethos. The protest movements of the late 19th century were essentially those of rural America against urban America. The village-town ideal seemed to be everywhere under attack by forces that were beyond both control and comprehension.

In a highly perceptive study entitled *The Search for Order, 1877–1920* (1967), Robert H. Wiebe has suggested that during the latter decades of the 19th century the island communities of America lost their autonomy as well as control over the lives of their members. "Innumerable townsmen," says Wiebe, "continued to assume that they could harness the forces of the world to the destiny of their community. That confidence, the system's final foundation, largely disappeared during the eighties and nineties in the course of a dramatic struggle to defend the independence of the community." As the newer realities augured the end of the village-town, the ideal itself became a flag of men's loyalties, indeed of the stalwartness of their defense of the only world they had ever known. The horrendous side of that ideal was the specter of city life. And both the celebration of the village-town and the denunciation of the city reflected men's anxieties as they sensed that the values and virtues of an earlier America were vanishing before their very eyes.

The reformational ideal was in many ways the heart of the Puritan ethos. It conjoined, as we have earlier noted, the righteous activism of the one to the liberal, expansive social philosophy of the other. America served as a unique ground for the growth of the liberal ideology, one in which the absence of a profound historical antithesis produced a distinctive kind of development. Reformation became reform: a radical, one-time social alteration became a perennial way of life. Americans regarded themselves as revolutionaries by tradition, reformers committed to keeping the past alive.

Reform was thus an ongoing feature of American life, a device whereby the differences between newer realities and older premises could be resolved. Where the differences were not great, as in the later colonial and early national periods, effecting the resolution was not difficult. But during the late 19th century, differences between the realities and the premises of national life became almost unbridgeably wide. A people of ideology, Americans could neither remove the differences nor fully comprehend them. They sought above all to restore that union of ideals and actualities by which they had hitherto conducted their affairs. This indeed was the underlying theme of the major reform movements of the age. If the voices of the reformers were frantic, their message was unmistakably clear. They wished to bring back the idyllic republic they had been born into, the wonderful past they were sure they had lived. And they wished to purge the republic of the recent and evil innovations that were per-

verting its institutions almost beyond redemption.

Entrepreneurship, equality, democracy, the village-town: these were the tenets of the American Puritan ethos, and these had to be proclaimed, espoused, and defended. Their defense, moreover, was religious in character: not formally religious, to be sure, but of that quality with which they had invested all of their secular life. The protest literature of the day speaks the almost Biblical construction which that generation emphasized. Certainly, this was a time for Christ to come to cleanse out and redeem the kind of Chicago that all America had become, for men to follow in His steps, for all to see again that Christ was more than anything else a reformer, a social, indeed for some a socialistic, Messiah. The essential nature of American reform during these decades is improperly understood if one does not realize that the social reformers were Christian and that the Christian reformers were social.

In proposing the single tax as the way to end poverty and speed progress, Henry George, probably the most important social reformer of his age, felt certain that he could discern the future. "It is the culmination of Christianity—the City of God on earth, with its walls of jasper and its gates of pearl! It is the reign of the Prince of Peace!" George was but one of a host of men who preached Christian reformation and who denounced Christian corruption. Sodom and Gomorrah lay all around them, not merely cities of the plain but (as William Jennings Bryan would put it with the confidence of a subscriber to the village-town ideal) plainly cities. As defenders of the Puritan ethos saw it, a thoroughgoing moral reform was essential to bring the City of God to replace the cankered city that America had become.

In the late 19th century, then, there had arisen a fearful tension between established American values and the newer conditions of American life. The anxiety which beset large groups of Americans, particularly those whom the newer conditions had victimized or uprooted, drove them to a double response to each of the ideals of the ethos: They fervently embraced and proclaimed the ideal, and they no less fervently declaimed against those whom they feared were perverting it.

The tension between the ethos and the actuality, the ideal and the real could not be indefinitely sustained. The differences between them had to be closed. The Puritan ethos had to be redefined in order to permit its accommodation to the changed conditions of American life. It had to be translated into more modern terms.

Accordingly, national and local legislation began to protect not only entrepreneurs but also the wage earners who aspired to entrepreneurship or could not hope to achieve it. The ideal was more than defended, it was underwritten. The democratic-egalitarian ideal was widely proclaimed during the early decades of the 20th century, and much of progressive legislation—Congressional, state, and municipal—was devoted to infusing a new vigor into it. The progressives believed that disclosure and democracy, giving the people the facts and making it possible for them to participate in the political process, would revive honesty and purity in American life. If the belief was more honored by rhetoric than by realization, it was not for want of an attempt to honor it both ways.

The village-town ideal was translated into city terms, with the sense that all would be well if the virtues of the one could be used to cleanse out the vices of the other. And from what historians have told us, this is precisely what the progressive movement sought to do. The reformational ideal was given a new life, and the promise of renovation and readjustment that each of the successive administrations of the 20th century offered the electorate—a Square Deal, New Freedom, New Era, New Deal, Fair Deal, New Frontiers, Great Society, and New Federalism—showed that the ideal of perennial reformation had a continuing vitality in American life.

Where does the American Puritan ethos stand in our own age? What has become of each of its component ideals? How do these ideals express the actualities of American life? How far do we affirm the ethos, how far are we apprehensive about its being threatened or subverted? What factors would help explain the one construction of the ethos or the other? It is fair enough, too, in our study of American history, that we consider the substance and significance of the Puritan ethos at each phase of its evolution. We should certainly wish to know how it related to the real conditions of the time, how it differed from the Puritan ethos of a former age, and what were the circumstances that created the difference.

The American Puritan ethos is, then, the principal construct of our values, the pivot of our social ideas. It constitutes the very essence both of the American ideology and the American myth.

SUGGESTED READINGS

Bryce, James. *The American Commonwealth*. 2 vol. New York: Macmillan Co., 1888.

Commager, Henry Steele. *The American Mind: An Interpretation of American Thought and Character Since the 1880s.* New Haven, Conn.: Yale University Press, 1950.

Fine, Sidney. *Laissez Faire and the General-Welfare State: A Study of Conflict in American Thought, 1865–1901.* Ann Arbor: University of Michigan Press, 1956.

Ginger, Ray. *Age of Excess: The United States from 1877 to 1914.* New York: Macmillan Co., 1965.

Hays, Samuel P. *The Response to Industrialism, 1885–1914.* Chicago: University of Chicago Press, 1957.

Higham, John. *Strangers in the Land: Patterns of American Nativism, 1860–1925.* New Brunswick: Rutgers University Press, 1955.

HOFSTADTER, RICHARD. *The Age of Reform: From Bryan to F.D.R.* New York: Alfred A. Knopf, 1955.

MAY, HENRY F. *Protestant Churches and Industrial America.* New York: Harper, 1949.

NIEBUHR, REINHOLD. *The Irony of American History.* New York: Charles Scribner's Sons, 1952.

SPROAT, JOHN G. *"The Best Men": Liberal Reformers in the Gilded Age.* New York: Oxford University Press, 1968.

WIEBE, ROBERT H. *The Search for Order, 1877–1920.* New York: Hill and Wang, 1967.

WYLLIE, IRVIN G. *The Self-Made Man in America: The Myth of Rags to Riches.* New Brunswick, N.J.: Rutgers University Press, 1954.

DOCUMENT 20.1

Entrepreneurship: The Ideal Presented*

In *The American* (1877), one of his very first novels, Henry James addressed himself to the theme that was to distinguish all of his work: the contrasting character and values of Americans and Europeans. His hero, whom he pointedly named Christopher Newman, personifies the American entrepreneurial ideal. While James is everywhere conscious of the limitations of the ideal, he presents it here the way Americans regarded it—as a constructive component of their quest for a better world for themselves.

... Newman had come out of the war with a brevet of brigadier-general, an honour which in this case—without invidious comparisons—had lighted upon shoulders amply competent to bear it. But though he could manage a fight, when need was, Newman heartily disliked the business; his four years in the army had left him with an angry, bitter sense of the waste of precious things—life and time and

money and "smartness" and the early freshness of purpose; and he had addressed himself to the pursuits of peace with passionate zest and energy. He was of course as penniless when he plucked off his shoulder-straps as when he put them on, and the only capital at his disposal was his dogged resolution and his lively perception of ends and means. Exertion and action were as natural to him as respiration; a more completely healthy mortal had never trod the elastic soil of the West. His experience, moreover, was as wide as his capacity; when he was fourteen years old, necessity had taken him by his slim young shoulders and pushed him into the street, to earn that night's supper. He had not earned it; but he had earned the next night's, and afterwards, whenever he had had none, it was because he had gone without it to use the money for something else, a keener pleasure or a finer profit. He had turned his hand, with his brain in it, to many things; he had been enterprising, in an eminent sense of the term; he had been adventurous and even reckless, and he had known bitter failure as well as brilliant success; but he was a born experimentalist, and he had always found something to enjoy in the pressure of necessity, even when it was as irritating as the haircloth shirt of the mediaeval monk. At one time failure seemed inexorably his portion; ill-luck became his bed-fellow, and whatever he touched he turned, not to gold, but to ashes. His most vivid conception of a supernatural element in the world's affairs had come to him once when this pertinacity of misfortune was at its climax; there seemed to him something stronger in life than his own will. But the mysterious something could only be the devil, and he was accordingly seized with an intense personal enmity to this impertinent force. He had known what it was to have utterly exhausted his credit, to be unable to raise a dollar, and to find himself at nightfall in a strange city, without a penny to mitigate its strangeness. It was under these circumstances that he made his en-

*Source: Henry James, *The American* (1877; reprint ed., Boston: Houghton Nifflin Co., 1907), pp. 25–27.

trance into San Francisco, the scene, subsequently, of his happiest strokes of fortune. If he did not, like Dr. Franklin in Philadelphia, march along the street munching a penny loaf, it was only because he had not the penny loaf necessary to the performance. In his darkest days he had had but one simple, practical impulse —the desire, as he would have phrased it, to see the thing through. He did so at last, buffeted his way into smooth waters, and made money largely. It must be admitted, rather nakedly, that Christopher Newman's sole aim in life had been to make money; what he had been placed in the world for was, to his own perception, simply to wrest a fortune, the bigger the better, from defiant opportunity. This idea completely filled his horizon and satisfied his imagination. Upon the uses of money, upon what one might do with a life into which one had succeeded in injecting the golden stream, he had up to his thirty-fifth year very scantily reflected. Life had been for him an open game, and he had played for high stakes. He had won at last and carried off his winnings. . . .

DOCUMENT 20.2

Entrepreneurship: The Ideal Perverted.*

The entrepreneurial ideal could be thwarted by big business, above all by the trusts, which, as contemporary Americans regarded them, destroyed competition and snuffed out smaller business. Or else, those who subscribed to the ideal could be corrupted by money. Jacob Dryfoos, a central character in William Dean Howells's greatest novel, *A Hazard of New Fortunes* (1890), exemplifies this second possibility in the perversion of the entrepreneurial ideal. Starting out as a Pennsylvania Dutch

*Source: William Dean Howells, *A Hazard of New Fortunes* (1890; reprint ed., New York: Bantam Books, 1960), pp. 221–24.

farmer, Dryfoos became wealthy when oil was discovered on his land. Howells described the decline of Dryfoos as a "moral deterioration" due to "a bewildering change of ideals... I am not very proud when I realize that such a man and his experience are the ideal and ambition of most Americans."

There had been a time in his life when other things besides his money seemed admirable to him. He had once respected himself for the hard-headed, practical common sense which first gave him standing among his country neighbors; which made him supervisor, school trustee, justice of the peace, county commissioner, secretary of the Moffitt County Agricultural Society. In those days he had served the public with disinterested zeal and proud ability; he used to write to the *Lake Shore Farmer* on agricultural topics; he took part in opposing, through the Moffitt papers, the legislative waste of the people's money; on the question of selling a local canal to the railroad company, which killed that fine old State work, and let the dry ditch grow up to grass, he might have gone to the Legislature, but he contented himself with defeating the Moffitt member who had voted for the job. If he opposed some measures for the general good, like high schools and school libraries, it was because he lacked perspective, in his intense individualism, and suspected all expense of being spendthrift. He believed in good district schools, and he had a fondness, crude but genuine, for some kinds of reading—history, and forensics of an elementary sort.

With his good head for figures he doubted doctors and despised preachers; he thought lawyers were all rascals, but he respected them for their ability; he was not himself litigious, but he enjoyed the intellectual encounters of a difficult lawsuit, and he often attended a sitting of the fall term of court, when he went to town, for the pleasure of hearing the speeches. He was a good citizen, . . .

His moral decay began with his perception of the opportunity of making money quickly and abundantly, which offered itself to him after he sold his farm. He awoke to it slowly, from a desolation in which he tasted the last bitter of homesickness, the utter misery of idleness and listlessness. When he broke down and cried for the hard-working, wholesome life he had lost, he was near the end of this season of despair, but he was also near the end of what was best in himself. He devolved upon a meaner ideal than that of conservative good citizenship, which had been his chief moral experience: the money he had already made without effort and without merit bred its unholy self-love in him; he began to honor money, especially money that had been won suddenly and in large sums; for money that had been earned painfully, slowly, and in little amounts, he had only pity and contempt. The poison of that ambition to go somewhere and be somebody which the local speculators had instilled into him began to work in the vanity which had succeeded his somewhat scornful self-respect; he rejected Europe as the proper field for his expansion; he rejected Washington; he preferred New York, whither the men who have made money and do not yet know that money has made them, all instinctively turn. He came where he could watch his money breed more money, and bring greater increase of its kind in an hour of luck than the toil of hundreds of men could earn in a year. He called it speculation, stocks, the Street; and his pride, his faith in himself, mounted with his luck. He expected, when he had sated his greed, to begin to spend, and he had formulated an intention to build a great house, to add another to the palaces of the country-bred millionaires who have come to adorn the great city. In the meantime he made little account of the things that occupied his children, except to fret at the ungrateful indifference of his son to the interests that could alone make a man of him. He did not know

whether his daughters were in society or not; with people coming and going in the house he would have supposed they must be so, no matter who the people were. . . . He never met a superior himself except now and then a man of twenty or thirty millions to his one or two, and then he felt his soul creep within him, without a sense of social inferiority: it was a question of financial inferiority; and though Dryfoos's soul bowed itself and crawled, it was with a gambler's admiration of wonderful luck. Other men said these many-millioned millionaires were smart, and got their money by sharp practices to which lesser men could not attain; but Dryfoos believed that he could compass the same ends, by the same means, with the same chances; he respected their money, not them.

DOCUMENT 20.3

Democracy and Equality: The Ideal Proclaimed*

Andrew Carnegie's *Triumphant Democracy* (1886) was the Scottish-born industrialist's paean to American institutions, which he most favorably contrasted with European institutions, and particularly those of England. Whether or not the democratic-egalitarian ideal was actually practiced in the United States he did not in any way question. In the following excerpt. Carnegie explains the great attraction the ideal held for those who came to settle in the United States.

The generosity, shall I not say the incredible generosity, with which the Republic has dealt with these people met its reward. They are won to her side by being offered for their *subject*ship the boon of citizenship. For denial of equal privileges at home, the new land meets them with perfect equality, saying, be not only with

---

*Source: Andrew Carnegie, *Triumphant Democracy* (New York: Charles Scribner's Sons, 1886), pp. 18–19.

us, but be of us. They reach the shores of the Republic *subjects* (insulting word), and she makes them citizens; serfs, and she makes them men, and their children she takes gently by the hand and leads to the public schools which she has founded for her own children, and gives them, without money and without price, a good primary education as the most precious gift which even she has, in her bountiful hand, to bestow upon human beings. This is Democracy's "gift of welcome" to the new comer. The poor immigrant can not help growing up passionately fond of his new home and, alas, with many bitter thoughts of the old land which has defrauded him of the rights of man, and thus the threatened danger is averted—the homogeneity of the people secured.

The unity of the American people is further powerfully promoted by the foundation upon which the political structure rests, the equality of the citizen. There is not one shred of privilege to be met with anywhere in all the laws. One man's right is every man's right. The flag is the guarantor and symbol of equality. The people are not emasculated by being made to feel that their own country decrees their inferiority, and holds them unworthy of privileges accorded to others. No ranks, no titles, no hereditary dignities, and therefore no classes. Suffrage is universal, and votes are of equal weight. Representatives are paid, and political life and usefulness thereby thrown open to all. Thus there is brought about a community of interests and aims which a Briton, accustomed to monarchical and aristocratic institutions, dividing the people into classes with separate interests, aims, thoughts, and feelings, can only with difficulty understand.

DOCUMENT 20.4
Democracy and Equality: The Ideal Reclaimed*

If Andrew Carnegie was sure that the democratic-egalitarian ideal had been realized, the socialist reformers who flocked to the Bellamy Nationalist movement in the 1890s were no less sure that the ideal had been subverted. The following excerpts from Bellamy's magazine, *The New Nation,* tells us what they wanted.

The New Nation

Why a New Nation? Why will not the old one do?

These are some of the reasons why it will not do: In the old nation, the system by which the work of life is carried on is a sort of perpetual warfare, a struggle, literally, to the death, between men and men. It is a system by which the contestants are forced to waste in fighting more effort than they have left for work. The sordid and bitter nature of the struggle so hardens, for the most part, the relations of men to their fellows that in the domestic circle alone do they find exercise for the better, tenderer and more generous elements of their nature.

Another reason why the old nation will not do, is, that in it the people are divided, against nature, into classes: one very small class being the wealthy; another and much larger class being composed of those who maintain with difficulty a condition of tolerable comfort constantly shadowed by apprehension of its loss; with, finally, a vastly greater and quite preponderating class of very poor, who have no dependence even for bare existence save a wage which is uncertain from day to day.

In the old nation, moreover, half the people—the women, are dependent upon the personal favor of the other half,—the men, for the means of support; no other alternative being left them but to seek a

*Source: *The New Nation,* Vol. I (January 31, 1891), pp. 10-11 and (July 18, 1891), pp. 389–90.

beggarly pittance as workers in a labor market already overcrowded by men. In this old nation, the women are, indeed, as a sex, far worse off than the men; for, while the rich man is at least independent, the rich woman, while more luxuriously cared for, is as dependent for support on her husband's favor as the wife of the poorest laborer. Meanwhile, a great many women openly, and no one can tell how many secretly, unable to find men who will support them on more honorable terms, are compelled to secure their livelihood by the sale of their bodies, while a multitude of others are constrained to accept loveless marriage bonds.

In this old nation, a million strong men are even now vainly crying out for work to do, though the world needs so much more work done. Meanwhile, though the fathers and husbands can find no work, there is plenty always for the little children, who flock, in piteous armies, through the chilling mists of winter dawns into the factories.

In this old nation, not only does wealth devour poverty, but wealth devours wealth, and, year by year, the assets of the nation pass more and more swiftly and completely into the hands of a few score individuals out of 65,000,000 people.

In this old nation, year by year, the natural wealth of the land, the heritage of the people, is being wasted by the recklessness of individual greed. The forests are ravaged, the fisheries of river and sea destroyed, the fertility of the soil exhausted.

In this old nation, under a vain form of free political institutions, the inequalities of wealth and the irresistible influence of money upon a people devoured by want, is making nominally republican institutions a machine more convenient even than despotism for the purposes of plutocracy and plunder.

These are a few of the reasons why the old nation will not do. A few of the reasons why men are looking and longing for The New Nation:—

In The New Nation, work will not be warfare, but fraternal co-operation toward a store in which all will share. Human effort, no longer wasted by battle and cross-purposes, will create an abundance previously impossible.

More important far, the conditions of labor under the plan of fraternal co-operation will tend as strongly to stimulate fraternal sentiments and affectionate relations among the workers as the present conditions tend to repress them. The kindly side of men will no longer be known only to their wives and children.

In The New Nation, there will be neither rich nor poor; all will be equal partners in the product of the national industrial organization.

In The New Nation, the dependence of one sex upon another for livelihood, which now poisons love and gives lust its opportunity, will be forever at an end. As equal and independent partners in the product of the nation, women will have attained an economical enfranchisement, without which no political device could help them. Prostitution will be a forgotten horror.

In The New Nation, there will be no unemployed. All will be enabled and required to do their part according to their gifts, save only those whom age, sickness or infirmity has exempted; and these, no longer as now trodden under foot, will be served and guarded as tenderly as are the wounded in battle by their comrades.

In The New Nation, the children will be cherished as precious jewels, inestimable pledges of the divine love to men. Though mother and father forsake them, the nation will take them up.

In The New Nation, education will be equal and universal, and will cover the entire period of life during which it is now enjoyed by the most favored classes.

In The New Nation, the wasting of the people's heritage will cease, the forests will be re-planted, the rivers and seas repopulated, and fertility restored to exhausted lands. The natural resources of the country will be cared for and preserved as a common estate, and one to which the living have title only as trustees for the unborn.

In The New Nation, the debauching influence of wealth being banished, and the people raised to a real equality by equal education and resources, a true democratic and popular government will become possible as it never was before. For the first time in history the world will behold a true republic, rounded, full-orbed, complete,—a republic, social, industrial, political.

These will be some of the characteristics of The New Nation, to the advancement of which, till it shall have utterly replaced and supplanted the old nation, this paper is pledged.

The Root of the Present Social Discontent

A common argument used by the opponents of the radical industrial reformation ... is that the condition of the working classes in this country is better than it was a generation or so ago. This, it is argued, ought to be enough to satisfy reasonable workingmen and teach them contentment. As we have often before remarked, this sort of logic entirely misses the point of the industrial reform agitation. It does not turn on the question whether the lot of men is better or worse than it once was, but whether it is as satisfactory as it might be made under entirely new conditions. The workers of the world have at last reached the point of believing and declaring that the best the world can be made to yield is none too good for them.

But waiving the general demurrer to this line of argument, let us inquire what the facts really are as to the conditions of labor in New England fifty years ago as compared with the present day. It is an unquestionable fact that the hours of labor in the mills which now in Massachusetts have been reduced to 10, were then 12 and even 13, the operatives going to work in the morning on empty stomachs, having an intermission for breakfast, and keeping up their toil till after dark. It is also a fact that the tenements for operatives are generally better now than then, and that operatives are as a rule much better clothed and proportionally better paid. What is true in these respects of the relative condition of the factory operatives 50 years ago, and now, is also true of workers in general. The conditions of life in all respects were harder, ruder and more toilsome then than now.

How then account for the fact that 50 years ago there was not a whisper of social discontent among the toilers, while nowadays they are fairly seething with it. Can any one possibly be so foolish as to suppose that there is no cause for this? Fat-witted editors and economists are wont to attribute the present discontent to agitators. This is getting the cart before the horse. Every intelligent school boy is historian enough to know that agitators are the products not the causes of popular unrest. Fifty years ago the social agitator in New England had no audience; now there are not agitators enough to supply the audiences.

In view of the fact that the average operative and workingman in general works less hours, and is, on the whole, better paid, housed and clothed than fifty years ago, how shall we account for this extraordinary change in his temper?

The answer we believe to be found chiefly in the growth of social inequality and the consequent disintegration of society into classes, animated by mutual jealousy and hostility. Fifty years ago there was no such term as "the working class." Everybody worked, and everybody worked very hard. There was little social distinction between employer and employed. It used to be said of Napoleon's army that every private carried the baton of a field marshal in his knapsack, whereby it was meant that he knew the way of promotion was absolutely open to merit. In like manner fifty years ago, every clever workman felt himself a future employer. There were few wealthy families, and the wealthiest were poor compared with the poorest of the modern plutocracy, while of ostentation in living there was very little.

A profound change has taken place in these respects within a generation. It has become impossible for a man to start a business or become an employer on the easy terms it formerly was. Capital has the call everywhere, and without its backing there is little opportunity for talent to raise a man to the position of employer. With the increasing inequalities of wealth, social inequalities have come in, and the old sympathy and comradeship between master and man has given place to an opposition of interests and feelings. Young men no longer feel that the world is before them; their world they now see to be the class they were born into. In mockery of these new limitations, which now hem in their careers, they see about them a license of wealth, a pride of ostentation, a prodigality of luxury such as the rich men of their fathers' day never dreamed of.

Hard work or hard conditions in themselves do not produce social discontent, so long as they are equally shared, for there is then nobody to be discontented with. On the other hand, inequality, although it be combined with easier general conditions, becomes from its first introduction a root of bitterness.

It is useless to console people who see others better off than they are, by proving to them that they themselves are better off than their grandfathers. It is not with ancestors, but with contemporaries that people measure themselves. The only practical significance of enough is as much as those about us have. Among free men contentment can only be nourished by equality, which is the ancient and only true name for justice.

The people are discontented, because they realize that the vast and unprecedented growth of the national wealth in the last 50 years has been most unequally distributed. If it has to a certain degree benefited the masses, the great bulk of it has gone to a few. Whatever the legality of the devices by which this unequal distribution has been accomplished, the people recognize it as a substantial injustice, and it is the sense of this injustice which is at the bottom of the present discontent. That discontent will grow and spread, and never cease till the present inequalities are done away with by a better industrial system, and the new republic is founded upon the principle that a nation's wealth should be equally shared by all its members.

DOCUMENT 20.5

The Village-Town Ideal: Affirmation.*

John Fiske was a social Darwinist and a devoted follower of Spencerian evolutionism. He saw American institutions in the light of comparative history and shared a widely held theory that they were of Anglo-Saxon origins. They had been born in the German forests at a remote time, the theory ran, and had been successively replanted in primitive England and in early English settlements on the North American mainland. Favored by Providence, they would ultimately be adopted throughout the world. For Fiske, accordingly, the New England village-town had a fitting place in universal history. In his view of it, he tended, as the following excerpt shows, to screen facts and actualities through the premises of his historical philosophy. To his way of thinking, he was perceiving the true essence of the village-town: its enduring and transcending qualities, rather than qualities which were transitory and accidental. It is precisely for this reason that the excerpt below serves so well as a statement of the American village-town ideal of the late 19th century.

*Source: John Fiske, *American Political Ideas Viewed from the Standpoint of Universal History* (New York: Harper & Bros., 1885), pp. 20–26.

In the outward aspect of a village in Massachusetts or Connecticut, the feature which would be most likely first to impress itself upon the mind of a visitor from England is the manner in which the village is laid out and built. Neither in England nor anywhere else in western Europe have I ever met with a village of the New England type. In English villages one finds small houses closely crowded together, sometimes in blocks of ten or a dozen, and inhabited by people belonging to the lower orders of society; while the fine houses of gentlemen stand quite apart in the country, perhaps out of sight of one another, and surrounded by very extensive grounds. The origin of the village, in a mere aggregation of tenants of the lord of the manor, is thus vividly suggested. In France one is still more impressed, I think, with this closely packed structure of the village. In the New England village, on the other hand, the finer and the poorer houses stand side by side along the road. There are wide straight streets overarched with spreading elms and maples, and on either side stand the houses, with little green lawns in front, called in rustic parlance "door-yards." The finer houses may stand a thousand feet apart from their neighbours on either side, while between the poorer ones there may be intervals of from twenty to one hundred feet, but they are never found crowded together in blocks. Built in this capacious fashion, a village of a thousand inhabitants may have a main street more than a mile in length, with half a dozen crossing streets losing themselves gradually in long stretches of country road. The finest houses are not ducal palaces, but may be compared with the ordinary country-houses of gentlemen in England. The poorest houses are never hovels, such as one sees in the Scotch Highlands. The picturesque and cosy cottage at Shottery, where Shakespeare used to do his courting, will serve very well as a sample of the humblest sort of old-fashioned New England farm-house. But most of the dwellings in the village come between these extremes. They are plain neat wooden houses, in capaciousness more like villas than cottages. A New England village street, laid out in this way, is usually very picturesque and beautiful, and it is highly characteristic. In comparing it with things in Europe, where one rarely finds anything at all like it, one must go to something very different from a village. As you stand in the Court of Heroes at Versailles and look down the broad and noble avenue that leads to Paris, the effect of the vista is much like that of a New England village street. As American villages grow into cities, the increase in the value of land usually tends to crowd the houses together into blocks as in a European city. But in some of our western cities founded and settled by people from New England, this spacious fashion of building has been retained for streets occupied by dwelling-houses. In Cleveland—a city on the southern shore of Lake Erie, with a population about equal to that of Edinburgh—there is a street some five or six miles in length and five hundred feet in width, bordered on each side with a double row of arching trees, and with handsome stone houses, of sufficient variety and freedom in architectural design, standing at intervals of from one to two hundred feet along the entire length of the street. The effect, it is needless to add, is very noble indeed. The vistas remind one of the nave and aisles of a huge cathedral.

Now this generous way in which a New England village is built is very closely associated with the historical origin of the village and with the peculiar kind of political and social life by which it is characterized. First of all, it implies abundance of land. As a rule the head of each family owns the house in which he lives and the ground on which it is built. The relation of landlord and tenant, though not unknown, is not commonly met with. No sort of social distinction or political privilege is associated with the ownership of land; and the legal differences between real and personal property, especially as regards ease of transfer, have been reduced to the smallest minimum that practical convenience will allow. Each householder, therefore, though an absolute proprietor, cannot be called a miniature lord of the manor, because there exists no permanent dependent class such as is implied in the use of such a phrase. Each larger proprietor attends in person to the cultivation of his own land, assisted perhaps by his own sons or by neighbours working for hire in the leisure left over from the care of their own smaller estates. So in the interior of the house there is usually no domestic service that is not performed by the mother of the family and the daughters. Yet in spite of this universality of manual labour, the people are as far as possible from presenting the appearance of peasants. Poor or shabbily-dressed people are rarely seen, and there is no one in the village whom it would be proper to address in a patronizing tone, or who would not consider it a gross insult to be offered a shilling. As with poverty, so with dram-drinking and with crime; all alike are conspicuous by their absence. In a village of one thousand inhabitants there will be a poor-house where five or six decrepit old people are supported at the common charge; and there will be one tavern where it is not easy to find anything stronger to drink than light beer or cider. The danger from thieves is so slight that it is not always thought necessary to fasten the outer doors of the house at night. The universality of literary culture is as remarkable as the freedom with which all persons engage in manual labour. The village of a thousand inhabitants will be very likely to have a public circulating library, in which you may find Professor Huxley's "Lay Sermons" or Sir Henry Maine's "Ancient Law": it will surely have a high-school and half a dozen schools for small children. A person unable to read and write is as great a rarity as an albino or a person with six fingers. The farmer who threshes his own corn and cuts his

own firewood has very likely a piano in his family sitting-room, with the *Atlantic Monthly* on the table and Milton and Tennyson, Gibbon and Macaulay on his shelves, while his daughter, who has baked bread in the morning, is perhaps ready to paint on china in the afternoon. In former times theological questions largely occupied the attention of the people; and there is probably no part of the world where the Bible has been more attentively read, or where the mysteries of Christian doctrine have to so great an extent been made the subject of earnest discussion in every household. Hence we find in the New England of to-day a deep religious sense combined with singular flexibility of mind and freedom of thought.

A state of society so completely democratic as that here described has not often been found in connection with a very high and complex civilization. In contemplating these old mountain villages of New England, one descries slow modifications in the structure of society which threaten somewhat to lessen its dignity. The immense productiveness of the soil in our western states, combined with cheapness of transportation, tends to affect seriously the agricultural interests of New England as well as those of our mother-country. There is a visible tendency for farms to pass into the hands of proprietors of an inferior type to that of the former owners,—men who are content with a lower standard of comfort and culture; while the sons of the old farmers go off to the universities to prepare for a professional career, and the daughters marry merchants or lawyers in the cities. The mountain-streams of New England, too, afford so much water-power as to bring in ugly factories to disfigure the beautiful ravines, and to introduce into the community a class of people very different from the landholding descendants of the Puritans. When once a factory is established near a village, one no longer feels free to sleep with doors unbolted.

It will be long, however, I trust, before

the simple, earnest and independent type of character that has been nurtured on the Blue Hills of Massachusetts and the White Hills of New Hampshire shall cease to operate like a powerful leaven upon the whole of American society. . . .

DOCUMENT 20.6

The Village-Town Ideal: Anxiety.*

The Reverend Josiah Strong wrote *Our Country* (1885) with the purpose of enlisting contributions for the Congregational Home Missionary Society. The book's thesis was that America was to be God's instrument for redeeming the world, that the western part of the United States was the last major area of the world open for settlement, that the time for Christ's Kingdom was at hand and therefore the task of conversion was urgent, and that much money and sacrifice were needed to do God's great work. But standing in the way of achieving America's religious mission were, as Strong saw it, several grave perils, of which the most important was the city. In the excerpt that follows, Strong gives the negative side of the village-town ideal.

The city is the nerve center of our civilization. It is also the storm center. . . .

The city has become a serious menace to our civilization, because in it, excepting Mormonism, each of the dangers we have discussed is enhanced, and all are focalized. It has a peculiar attraction for the immigrant. . . .

Because our cities are so largely foreign, Romanism finds in them its chief strength.

For the same reason the saloon, together with the intemperance and the

liquor power which it represents, is multiplied in the city. . . .

It is the city where wealth is massed; and here are the tangible evidences of it piled many stories high. Here the sway of Mammon is widest, and his worship the most constant and eager. Here are luxuries gathered—everything that dazzles the eye, or tempts the appetite; here is the most extravagant expenditure. Here, also, is the *congestion* of wealth the severest. Dives and Lazarus are brought face to face; here, in sharp contrast, are the *ennui* of surfeit and the desperation of starvation. The rich are richer, and the poor are poorer, in the city than elsewhere; and, as a rule, the greater the city, the greater are the riches of the rich and the poverty of the poor. Not only does the proportion of the poor increase with the growth of the city, but their condition becomes more wretched. . . .

Socialism centers in the city, and the materials of its growth are multiplied with the growth of the city. Here is heaped the social dynamite; here roughs, gamblers, thieves, robbers, lawless and desperate men of all sorts, congregate; men who are ready on any pretext to raise riots for the purpose of destruction and plunder; here gather foreigners and wage-workers who are especially susceptible to socialist arguments; here skepticism and irreligion abound; here inequality is the greatest and most obvious, and the contrast between opulence and penury the most striking; here is suffering the sorest. . . .

If moral and religious influences are peculiarly weak at the point where our social explosives are gathered, what of city government? Are its strength and purity so exceptional as to insure the effective control of these dangerous elements? In the light of notorious facts, the question sounds satirical. It is commonly acknowledged that the government of large cities in the United States is a failure. . . .

Thus is our civilization multiplying and focalizing the elements of anarchy and destruction. Nearly forty years ago De Toc-

*Source: Josiah Strong, *Our Country* (New York: The Baker and Taylor Co., 1891), pp. 179–90.

queville wrote: "I look upon the size of certain American cities, and especially upon the nature of their population, as a real danger which threatens the security of the democratic republics of the New World." That danger grows more real and imminent every year.

DOCUMENT 20.7

The Reformational Ideal: What Would Jesus Do?*

In different degrees and from different perspectives, Henry George and the Reverend Charles M. Sheldon saw the events of their times as a drama of the corruption of American life and of the great need for its redemption. Accordingly, they not only expressed anxiety about the ways in which the reformational ideal was being imperiled and actually subverted, but they also proposed programs for reforming the nation's institutions and mores and thereby revitalizing the ideal. Both wrote best-selling volumes, which caught and spoke the troubled conscience of their generation and its insistence on seeking solace and resolution within the premises of the reformational ideal. Sheldon's novel, *In His Steps* (1898) posed the question confronting all America, the land of the Puritan ethos: What would Jesus do, if He were here among us today, in this age of great social distress and moral decay? In the excerpt below, Henry Maxwell, the hero of the novel and like its author a clergyman, gives his congregation an answer to this most besetting question.

. . . He had taken for his theme the story of the young man who came to Jesus, asking what he must do to obtain eternal life. Jesus had tested him: "Sell all that thou hast and give to the poor and thou shalt have treasure in heaven, and come,

---

*Source: Charles M. Sheldon, *In His Steps,* "*What Would Jesus Do?*" (Chicago: Advance Publishing Co., 1898), pp. 272–76.

follow me." But the young man was not willing to suffer to that extent. If following Jesus meant suffering in that way, he was not willing. He would like to follow Jesus, but not if he had to give up so much.

"Is it true," continued Henry Maxwell, and his fine, thoughtful face glowed with a passion of appeal that stirred the people as they had seldom been stirred, "is it true that the church of to-day, the church that is called after Christ's own name, would refuse to follow Jesus at the expense of suffering, of physical loss, of temporary gain? The statement was made, at a large gathering in the Settlement last week, by a leader of workingmen, that it was hopeless to look to the church for any reform or redemption of society. On what was that statement based? Plainly on the assumption that the church contained, for the most part, men and women who thought more of their own ease and luxury than of the sufferings and needs and sins of humanity. How far was that true? Are the Christians of America ready to have their discipleship tested? How about the men who possess large wealth? Are they ready to take that wealth and use it as Jesus would? How about the men and women of great talent? Are they ready to consecrate that talent to humanity as Jesus undoubtedly would do?

"Is it not true that the call has come in this age for a new exhibition of discipleship, Christian discipleship? You who live in this great, sinful city must know that, better than I do. Is it possible you can go your ways careless or thoughtless of the awful condition of men and women and children who are dying, body and soul, for Christian help? Is it not a matter of concern to you personally that the saloon kills its thousands more surely than war? Is it not a matter of personal suffering in some form for you, that thousands of able-bodied, willing men tramp the streets of this city, and all cities, crying for work, and drifting into crime and suicide because they cannot find it? Can you say that this is none of your business? Let each man look after himself? Would it not be true, think you, that if every Christian in America did as Jesus would do, society itself, the business world, yes, the very political system under which our commercial and governmental activity is carried on, would be so changed that human suffering would be reduced to a minimum?

"What would be the result if all the church members of this city tried to do as Jesus would do? It is not possible to say in detail what the effect would be. But it is easy to say and it is true that, instantly, the human problem would begin to find an adequate answer.

"What is the test of Christian discipleship? Is it not the same as in Christ's own life-time? Have our surroundings modified or changed the test? If Jesus were here to-day, would He not call some of the members of this very church to do just what He commanded the young man, and ask him to give up his wealth and literally follow Him? I believe He would do that, if He felt certain that any church member thought more of his possessions than of his Savior. The test would be the same to-day as then. I believe Jesus would demand, He does demand now, as close a following, as much suffering, as great self-denial, as when He lived in person on the earth and said, 'except a man renounceth all that he hath, he cannot be My disciple.' That is, unless he is willing to do it for My sake, he cannot be My disciple.

"What would be the result, if in this city every church member should begin to do as Jesus would do? It is not easy to go into details of the result. But we all know that certain things would be impossible that are now practiced by church members. What would Jesus do in the matter of wealth? How would He spend it? What principle would regulate His use of money? Would He be likely to live in great luxury and spend ten times as much on personal adornment and entertainment as He spent to relieve the needs of suffering humanity? How would Jesus be governed in the making of money? Would

He take rentals from saloon and other disreputable property, or even from tenement property that was so constructed that the inmates had no such thing as a home and no such possibility as privacy or cleanliness?

"What would Jesus do about the great army of unemployed and desperate who tramp the streets and curse the church, or are indifferent to it, lost in the bitter struggle for the bread that tastes bitter when it is earned, on account of the desperate conflict to get it. Would Jesus care nothing for them? Would He go His way in comparative case and comfort? Would He say it was none of His business? Would He excuse Himself from all responsibility to remove the causes of such a condition?

"What would Jesus do in the center of a civilization that hurries so fast after money that the very girls employed in great business houses are not paid enough to keep soul and body together without fearful temptations, so great that scores of them fall and are swept over the great, boiling abyss; where the demands of trade sacrifice hundreds of lads in a business that ignores all Christian duties towards them in the way of education and moral training and personal affection? Would Jesus, if He were here to-day, as a part of our age and commercial industry, feel nothing, do nothing, say nothing, in the face of these facts which every business man knows?

"What would Jesus do? Is not that what the disciple ought to do? Is he not commanded to follow in His steps? How much is the Christianity of the age suffering for Him? Is it denying itself at the cost of ease, comfort, luxury, elegance of living? What does the age need, more than personal sacrifice? Does the church do its duty in following Jesus, when it gives a little money to establish missions or relieve extreme cases of want? Is it any sacrifice for a man who is worth ten million dollars simply to give ten thousand dollars for some benevolent work? Is he not giving something that costs him practically nothing, so far as any personal pain or suffering goes? Is it true that the Christian disciples to-day in most of our churches are living soft, easy, selfish lives, very far from any sacrifice that can be called sacrifice? What would Jesus do?

"It is the personal element that Christian discipleship needs to emphasize. 'The gift, without the giver, is bare.' The Christianity that attempts to suffer by proxy is not the Christianity of Christ. Each individual Christian, business man, citizen, needs to follow in His steps along the path of personal sacrifice for Him. There is not a different path to-day from that of Jesus' own times. It is the same path. The call of this dying century and of the new one soon to be, is a call for a new discipleship, a new following of Jesus, more like the early, simple, apostolic, Christianity when the disciples left all and literally followed the Master. Nothing but a discipleship of this kind can face the destructive selfishness of the age, with any hope of overcoming it. There is a great quantity of nominal Christianity to-day. There is need of more of the real kind. We need a revival of the Christianity of Christ. We have, unconsciously, lazily, selfishly, formally, grown into a discipleship that Jesus Himself would not acknowledge. He would say to many of us, when we cry, 'Lord, Lord,' 'I never knew you.' Are we ready to take up the cross? Is it possible for this church to sing with exact truth,

> Jesus, I my cross have taken,
> All to leave and follow thee.

If we can sing that truly, then we may claim discipleship. But if our definition of being a Christian is simply to enjoy the privileges of worship, be generous at no expense to ourselves, have a good, easy time surrounded by pleasant friends and by comfortable things, live respectably, and at the same time avoid the world's great stress of sin and trouble because it is too much pain to bear it—if this is our definition of Christianity, surely we are a long way from following the steps of Him who

trod the way with groans and tears and sobs of anguish for a lost humanity, who sweat, as it were, great drops of blood, who cried out on the upreared cross, 'My God! My God! Why hast thou forsaken me.'

"Are we ready to make and live a new discipleship? Are we ready to reconsider our definition of a Christian? What is it to be a Christian? It is to imitate Jesus. It is to do as He would do. It is to walk in His steps."

DOCUMENT 20.8
The Reformational Ideal: Redemption.*

Reform was the compelling need for America, the way Henry George saw it, to redeem it from gross social inequities and moral corruption. In *Progress and Poverty* (1879), he proposed a tax on the unearned increase in land values, a device he hoped would equalize economic advantages and raise enough revenue to pay for the resolution of the major social problems.

The reform I have proposed accords with all that is politically, socially, or morally desirable. It has the qualities of a true reform, for it will make all other reforms easier. What is it but the carrying out in letter and spirit of the truth enunciated in the Declaration of Independence—the "self-evident" truth that is the heart and soul of the Declaration—*"That all men are created equal; that they are endowed by their Creator with certain unalienable rights; that among these are life, liberty, and the pursuit of happiness!"*

. . . . .

Though it may take the language of prayer, it is blasphemy that attributes to the inscrutable decrees of Providence the

---

*Source: Henry George, *Progress and Poverty* (1879; reprint ed., New York: Robert Schalkenbach Foundation, 1931), pp. 545, 549–52.

suffering and brutishness that come of poverty; that turns with folded hands to the All-Father and lays on Him the responsibility for the want and crime of our great cities. We degrade the Everlasting. We slander the Just One. A merciful man would have better ordered the world; a just man would crush with his foot such an ulcerous ant-hill! It is not the Almighty, but we who are responsible for the vice and misery that fester amid our civilization. The Creator showers upon us his gifts—more than enough for all. But like swine scrambling for food, we tread them in the mire—tread them in the mire, while we tear and rend each other!

In the very centers of our civilization to-day are want and suffering enough to make sick at heart whoever does not close his eyes and steel his nerves. Dare we turn to the Creator and ask Him to relieve it? Supposing the prayer were heard, and at the behest with which the universe sprang into being there should glow in the sun a greater power; new virtue fill the air; fresh vigor the soil; that for every blade of grass that now grows two should spring up, and the seed that now increases fifty-fold should increase a hundred-fold! Would poverty be abated or want relieved? Manifestly no! Whatever benefit would accrue would be but temporary. The new powers streaming through the material universe could be utilized only through land. And land, being private property, the classes that now monopolize the bounty of the Creator would monopolize all the new bounty. Land owners would alone be benefited. Rents would increase, but wages would still tend to the starvation point!

This is not merely a deduction of political economy; it is a fact of experience. We know it because we have seen it. Within our own times, under our very eyes, that Power which is above all, and in all, and through all; that Power of which the whole universe is but the manifestation; that Power which maketh all things, and without which is not anything made that

is made, has increased the bounty which men may enjoy, as truly as though the fertility of nature had been increased. Into the mind of one came the thought that harnessed steam for the service of mankind. To the inner ear of another was whispered the secret that compels the lightning to bear a message round the globe. In every direction have the laws of matter been revealed; in every department of industry have arisen arms of iron and fingers of steel, whose effect upon the production of wealth has been precisely the same as an increase in the fertility of nature. What has been the result? Simply that land owners get all the gain. The wonderful discoveries and inventions of our century have neither increased wages nor lightened toil. The effect has simply been to make the few richer; the many more helpless!

Can it be that the gifts of the Creator may be thus misappropriated with impunity? Is it a light thing that labor should be robbed of its earnings while greed rolls in wealth—that the many should want while the few are surfeited? Turn to history, and on every page may be read the lesson that such wrong never goes unpunished; that the Nemesis that follows injustice never falters nor sleeps! Look around to-day. Can this state of things continue? May we even say, "After us the deluge!" Nay; the pillars of the state are trembling even now, and the very foundations of society begin to quiver with pent-up forces that glow underneath. The struggle that must either revivify, or convulse in ruin, is near at hand, if it be not already begun.

The fiat has gone forth! With steam and electricity, and the new powers born of progress, forces have entered the world that will either compel us to a higher plane or overwhelm us, as nation after nation, as civilization after civilization, have been overwhelmed before. It is the delusion which precedes destruction that sees in the popular unrest with which the civilized world is feverishly pulsing only the passing effect of ephemeral causes. Between democratic ideas and the aristocratic adjustments of society there is an irreconcilable conflict. Here in the United States, as there in Europe, it may be seen arising. We cannot go on permitting men to vote and forcing them to tramp. We cannot go on educating boys and girls in our public schools and then refusing them the right to earn an honest living. We cannot go on prating of the inalienable rights of man and then denying the inalienable right to the bounty of the Creator. Even now, in old bottles the new wine begins to ferment, and elemental forces gather for the strife!

But if, while there is yet time, we turn to Justice and obey her, if we trust Liberty and follow her, the dangers that now threaten must disappear, the forces that now menace will turn to agencies of elevation. Think of the powers now wasted; of the infinite fields of knowledge yet to be explored; of the possibilities of which the wondrous inventions of this century give us but a hint. With want destroyed; with greed changed to noble passions; with the fraternity that is born of equality taking the place of the jealousy and fear that now array men against each other; with mental power loosed by conditions that give to the humblest comfort and leisure; and who shall measure the heights to which our civilization may soar? Words fail the thought! It is the Golden Age of which poets have sung and high-raised seers have told in metaphor! It is the glorious vision which has always haunted man with gleams of fitful splendor. It is what he saw whose eyes at Patmos were closed in a trance. It is the culmination of Christianity—the City of God on earth, with its walls of jasper and its gates of pearl! It is the reign of the Prince of Peace!

21 Labor's Response to Modern Industrialism

HERBERT GUTMAN
University of Rochester

The United States industrialized between 1840 and 1900. Although the process was slow and uneven, industrialism, once started, proved irrevocable and appeared irresistible. All aspects of human experience felt its consequences: where people worked, the tools they used, how they traveled, what they ate and wore, their leisure habits, their thoughts about themselves and the world in which they lived, and the pace of life itself. In many ways the industrialization of a modern nation is the most significant set of social and economic changes affecting a people—and perhaps the most difficult to analyze. Compare the problem of evaluating the impact of industrialization upon a people with, let us say, the successes of John Adams as a diplomat or Andrew Jackson's motives in attacking the second Bank of the United States, or, better still, the causes of the Mexican War. Once done, the relative difficulty of appraising the effect of industrial development and the responses to it become self-evident. The *process* of industrialization extends over a greater length of time and has many more indirect consequences than the influence of a single great leader or of particular events surrounding a momentary political and diplomatic crisis. For this reason, among others, analysis of the industrial process and the responses to it is important. Our own United States,

after all, has as its central quality the fact that it is an industrial nation.

Industrialization meant many things to 19th-century Americans: the process by which investment capital poured into the building of new railroads and factories as well as into the development of mines; the widespread application of new sources of nonanimal power to the productive process; the application of new machinery to agriculture in an effort to increase productivity; the introduction of new systems of mechanized production. And it meant more, too. Industrialization also accelerated the movement of people from farm to city. Centers of trade, manufacturing, and commerce grew rapidly, as did a laboring population dependent on others for work and income.

Part of the industrial process is revealed in the simple reporting of elementary statistical trends and the wondrous fashion in which contemporaries viewed such data. A few examples suffice. The number of Cincinnati workers engaged in manufacturing increased from 9,040 in 1840 to 58,508 in 1872. In the latter year, 350,000 wage earners lived in New York City, and more than 200,000 crowded into Philadelphia. Pittsburgh, center of the iron and steel industry, impressed one contemporary as a city "like 'hell with the lid taken off.' The entire landscape seems ablaze.... The factories are so continuous

71

on the various streets that if placed in a . . . row they would reach thirty-five miles." Steam-propelled machinery became increasingly important. In 1870, 2,346,142 horsepower was used in manufacturing; 30 years later the figure stood at 11,300,081. Coal production soared from 14,610,042 tons in 1860 to 513,525,477 tons in 1914. "One horse power," a prominent Philadelphia manufacturer declared in 1872, "equals the labor-power of ten able-bodied men. . . . This is wealth—embodied wealth in its most advanced form. . . . Human labor is economized; the ingenuity of man has devised labor-saving machinery by which vast economies are affected, and none need labor sixteen hours a day. . . ." Industrial production rose spectacularly, and four industries led the way: iron and steel and allied manufactures, food and kindred processed goods, textiles, and lumber and its finished products. In 1890, for the first time, the value of manufactured products exceeded that of agricultural goods; 10 years later, it had doubled. No less a personage than Horace Greeley paid glowing tribute to this industrial progress. Together with Albert Brisbane and others, he penned a 1,300-page paean in 1872 entitled *The Great Industries of the United States.* Characterizing leading inventors and manufacturers as men who led the people "out of the plodding ways which the feudal age . . . imposed upon the race," Greeley and his associates cheerfully concluded: "Though prompted in the main by the spirit of self-aggrandizement, these men have proved themselves the chief philanthropists of the time and have borne the standard of progress. . . ."

Yet the industrial process cannot be measured simply by statistics indicating economic growth. Industrialism also meant a new way of life for whole sectors of the population. In 1859 the nation counted 1,311,346 wage earners. By 1914, more than 7 million persons depended on wages for income. In these years, and even earlier, the skilled craftsman declined in importance, and the factory worker replaced him as the symbol of the new industrial order. The commissioners of the Massachusetts Bureau of Labor Statistics admitted the importance of economic growth in the early postbellum years; but significantly, they asked if it was "logical to reason" that the building of a railroad, itself a sign of unquestioned progress, meant that "the laborers who excavate . . . the grade . . . , dig the ore . . . , and cast the rails" automatically were "prosperous and growing rich."

A critical aspect of the industrial process is its effect on the standard of comfort. But even more is involved, for much of the history of industrialization between 1840 and 1900 is the story of the painful process by which an old way of life gave over to a new one. And in this context the central issue was the rejection or modification of traditional sets of "rules" and "commands" that no longer fit the more modern industrial context. What did it mean to work in a factory for the first time after one was used to the routine of a small shop or, better still, of agricultural life? How could an employer, himself uneasy in his new position of power, impose discipline on persons unaccustomed to the demands of factory labor? What did unemployment mean to persons entirely dependent for the first time on others for income with which to purchase necessities? Although he spoke in language peculiar to 19th-century America, Carroll D. Wright, the first Commissioner of Labor for the United States, put it well in 1878:

The divine economy takes neither the old machine nor the discarded operator of it into account, but puts in the place of one a more perfect piece of mechanism, and in the place of the other an intellect of a much higher order, and contemplates the general results to humanity, and not the loss to the individual. . . . An examination, carried in any direction, demonstrates the proposition that all progress, every step in advance, is over apparent destruction, and, like every pioneer who has startled the world by his discoveries, and by them benefited his kind, is over the graves of men.

Stripped to its essence, Wright's words capsuled a central dilemma inherent in the industrial process: The new social order, serviced by steam and coal and rails, and centering around the factory and the mine, exacted a heavy price from those who surrendered an earlier and less complex way of life. The craftsman's pride in his work lost its meaning as he was overwhelmed by specialization and the machine. The New York Wood Carvers' Union, for example, complained that "unlimited conpetition" meant lower prices and forced the manufacturer to seek cheaper productive methods. "Ingenious machinery has then to be used to such a degree that skilled workingmen ... become superfluous. All mechanics become *factory workmen* and [all] production *machine work*. There is no escape from that." Similarly, a cigar maker complained of the revolutionary effects of the cigar mold on his craft: "The mode by which most segars ... are produced to-day is so divided that skilled labor is no longer required. The inventive genius has superseeded [*sic*] skill...."

The growing importance of unskilled and semiskilled labor also altered the status of women and children. Always useful on the farm, they proved equally valuable in the factory. New England's early cotton mills illustrated this development. But it was intensified by the ethos of the entire period—by the emphasis placed on investment capital and cheap production. The Massachusetts Bureau of Labor Statistics found that factory labor proved that a woman could operate machinery and perform manual labor out of her home. Not surprisingly, one of every three factory workers in Philadelphia in 1870 was a woman. Child labor also increased in these years. Horace Greeley and his associates insisted that "the pride of the nation is in its children, and in none so much as in those who pre-eminently distinguish themselves in the arts of peace—domestic manufacturing...." A New York daily advised its readers that "a bright twelve year old girl" easily could be "taught to make a cap in four weeks." And so it went. In addition to a new status for skilled craftsmen in the bustling factories, there was a new kind of labor for women and children who worked to supplement the meager wages of unskilled fathers.

New conditions of work and life tell much about the impact of the industrial order upon the wage earner, but his response to these conditions is an equally important part of the story. At times the wage earner was passive. Was his silence the result of satisfaction? Or was protest made difficult by the very conditions of the new industrial order? At other times the wage earner protested. Bitter strikes and lockouts—most usually caused by the demand for labor organization or for better wages, hours, and working conditions—characterized innumerable industrial disputes. The violence that accompanied the great railroad strikes in 1877 and the bitterness on all sides during the Homestead strike and the Pullman boycott in the 1890s were outstanding illustrations, but there were countless unrecorded and lesser disputes between workers and employers between 1840 and 1900. What explained the bitterness of industrial conflict at that time? Were skilled workers more discontented than unskilled? Were immigrant workers more satisfied than native-born laborers? Did the violence in the United States during its prime years of industrialization, as some historians argue, far exceed that of any European nation? How does one account for such bitterness and violence?

One clue to the answer of these questions about the social behavior of wage earners rests in understanding just *who* the workers were, *what* they did *before* they entered the factory, and the *frame of mind* they carried with them into the new industrial order and used to interpret it. In general, four kinds of persons became wage earners in the United States between 1840 and 1900. Two of them already were accustomed to urban experience but knew little of factory life. One consisted of the urban skilled craftsmen, who surrendered independence and skill to the factory and the machine. Unskilled urban day laborers, so numerous in preindustrial cities, made up the other. Rural Americans, most often sons and daughters of farmers—familiar at best with the small town—were a third important element drawn to the industrial city by the dynamism of shop and factory. The fourth group—the foreign-born—came mostly from Europe and, to a much lesser extent, from the Orient. Immigrants, largely from Ireland, Germany, Great Britain, and the Scandinavian countries, totaled about one third of all the workers in the mining, mechanical, and manufacturing industries in the late 19th century. Furthermore, an increasing number of newcomers were pouring in from Southern and Eastern Europe. British immigrants excepted, few of the foreign-born brought industrial experience with them to the United States.

How did each of these groups react to the industrial order in America? Persons sensitive to the process *and* the problems of social change most often view the former in one of two ways. They compare the present with the past and judge what is becoming by what has been. Or they criticize the present by comparing it to a utopian order that lies in the future. Several problems of analysis emerge. Did those workers who questioned the direction of the industrial order use the past or the future as their point of reference? If they judged primarily by past experience, did they tend to romanticize it? If the future served as the point of reference, what ideal of social reconstruction most appealed to what group: cooperatives, socialism, abolition of the "wages system," or simple trade unions that sought through organization to improve living conditions without changing the structure of the new order?

Whatever their point of reference or particular criticism, wage earners who questioned the industrial order often shared a general revulsion against the quality of *dependence* that characterized the new way of life. Each element had its own reasons for resenting dependence. With high expectations, the immigrant came in search of opportunity, which he viewed as the fulfillment of the dream of independent ownership and self-sufficiency. The urban skilled worker, on the other hand, witnessed a genuine decline in his status and self-image. Native-born persons who entered the labor force experienced a *new* quality of dependence for the first time. What did the factory mean to the son of a farmer who moved from a western New York farm to work in a Cleveland iron mill or oil refinery? How did a person accustomed to the rigors and simplicity of a small New England or Pennsylvania town react to the regimen imposed by a Fall River textile mill or a Pittsburgh coal mine? And how did the native-born worker, a citizen *before* he became a worker and in this sense unique in the 19th-century world, react to his new dependent status?

Before the coming of industrialism, the American dream (or ideal) had abjured a dependent status. In the early years of the republic, Thomas Jefferson warned: "Dependence begets subservience and venality, suffocates the germ of virtue, and prepares fit tools for the designs of ambition." Years later, Abraham Lincoln, shortly before winning the nomination as candidate for the Presidency on the Republican ticket, asserted the ideal in positive terms. During a strike of shoe workers, Lincoln spoke in New Haven, Connecticut:

. . . What is the true condition of the laborer? I take it that it is best for all to leave each man free to acquire property as fast as he can. Some will get wealth. I don't believe in a law to prevent a man from getting rich; it would do more harm than good. So while we do not propose any war upon capital, we do wish to allow the humblest man an equal chance to get rich with everybody else. When one starts poor, as most do in the race of life, free society is such that he knows he can better his condition; he knows that there is no fixed condition of labor, for his whole life. . . . I want every man to have a chance ... in which he *can* better his condition—when he may look forward and hope to be a hired laborer this year and the next, work for himself afterward, and finally hire men to work for him! That is the true system. . . .

Here, then, was the dream—independence, self-sufficiency, and upward mobility based largely on merit and personal talent.

The industrial way of life tested this ideal in many ways. It is instructive to compare Lincoln's statement with that of Terence V. Powderly less than three decades later. In his memoir, *Thirty Years of Labor*, this head of the Knights of Labor eloquently lamented the passing of the old order. He described the new obstacles to the old ideal and revealed a characteristic response to dependent status:

> . . . With the introduction of machinery, large manufacturing establishments were erected in the cities and towns. . . . The village blacksmith shop was abandoned, the road-side shoe shop was deserted, the tailor left his bench, and all together these mechanics turned away from their country homes and wended their way to the cities wherein the large factories had been erected. . . . They no longer carried the keys of the workshop, for workshop, tools, and keys belonged not to them, but to their master. . . . Competition between man and man is healthy to both, but competition between man and the machine is injurious to the former. He who offered to sell his labor after the introduction of machinery, could not hope to compete with a fellowman in the work he proposed to do; he was forced to compete with a machine, or a whole row of machines, being managed by boys or girls who worked for inadequate wages. . . . Beneath the shadow of machinery, merit went for naught so far as man's natural ability to perform labor was concerned.

In this light, can one argue that the individualist and "entrepreneurial" tradition, which encouraged rapid capital accumulation and, at times, a ruthless insensitivity to others, also shaped the embittered response of workers to the condition of dependence?

Response to dependence took many forms. Often, it was little more than a lament. In other instances it was sheer anger and frustration. At times it revealed a deep sense of betrayal. Some workers sought only a means of escape from city and factory. Others were aggrieved that an ostensibly democratic government should support only one group, the new industrial capitalists, or merely stand by and watch the "natural laws" of social development unfold. Still others questioned the morality and ethics of the new era. And finally, some argued that dependence best could be overcome by self-organization among the wage earners. Here, too, many problems for analysis arise. In these years, unions collapsed almost as quickly as they came into being. E. L. Godkin, editor of the *Nation*, insisted in 1868 that "the trades-unions . . . have, in reality, put the laborer and the capitalist for the first time on equal terms, economically considered." Unions, Godkin explained, "have rendered, and are rendering, to the working classes, one essential service—by enabling them, for the first time in their history, to contract with masters as free agents and on equal terms." What, then, explained the rapid rise and fall of unions? Was it the rapid growth of the economy? Was it the changing composition of the labor force? Was it the attitude of employers and their power, supported by a sympathetic government? Or was it the very dream itself of independent proprietorship?

SUGGESTED READINGS

BRUCE, ROBERT V. *1877: Year of Violence*. Indianapolis: Bobbs-Merrill Co., 1959.

COMMONS, JOHN R., AND ASSOCIATES. *History of Labour in the United States*. 4 vols. New York: Macmillan Co., 1918–35.

DAVID, HENRY. *The History of the Haymarket Affair*. New York: Russell & Russell, 1958.

DESTLER, CHESTER M. *American Radicalism, 1865–1901*. New London, Conn.: Octagon Press, 1946.

DUBOFSKY, MELVYN. *We Shall Be All: A History of the IWW*. Chicago: Quadrangle Books, 1969.

ERICKSON, CHARLOTTE. *American Industry and the European Immigrant, 1860—1885*. Cambridge, Mass.: Harvard University Press, 1957.

FONER, PHILIP S. *History of the Labor Movement in the United States*. 2 vols. New York: International Publishers Co., Inc., 1947–55.

GINGER, RAY. *The Bending Cross: A Biography of Eugene Victor Debs*. New Brunswick, N.J.: Rutgers University Press, 1949.

GREENE: VICTOR R. *The Slavic Community on Strike: Immigrant Labor in Pennsylvania Anthracite*. Notre Dame, Ind.: University of Notre Dame Press, 1968.

GROB, GERALD N. *Workers and Utopia: A Study of Ideological Conflict in the American Labor Movement, 1865–1900*. Evanston, Ill.: Northwestern University Press, 1961.

GROSSMAN, JONATHAN. *William Sylvis: Pioneer of American Labor*. New York: Columbia University Press, 1945.

HANDLIN, OSCAR. *The Uprooted: The Epic Story of the Great Migrations That Made the American People*. Boston: Little, Brown & Co., 1951.

KIRKLAND, EDWARD CHASE. *Industry Comes of Age: Business, Labor, and Public Policy, 1860–1897*. New York: Holt, Rinehart & Winston, Inc., 1961.

LASLETT, JOHN P. *Labor and the Left: A Study of Socialist and Radical Influences in the American Labor Movement, 1881–1924*. New York: Basic Books, 1970.

MADISON, CHARLES. *American Labor Leaders*. New York: Harper & Bros., 1950.

MONTGOMERY, DAVID. *Beyond Equality: Labor and the Radical Republicans, 1862–1872*. New York: Alfred A. Knopf, 1967.

QUINT, HOWARD H. *The Forging of American Socialism: Origins of the Modern Movement*. Columbia: University of South Carolina Press, 1953.

TAFT, PHILIP. *The A. F. of L. in the Time of Gompers*. New York: Harper & Bros., 1957.

THERNSTROM, STEPHAN. *Poverty and Progress: Social Mobility in a Nineteenth Century City*. Cambridge, Mass.: Harvard University Press, 1964.

WARE, NORMAN J. *The Industrial Worker, 1840–1860*. Gloucester, Mass.: Peter Smith, 1958.

——. *The Labor Movement in the United States, 1860–1895*. New York: D. Appleton Co., 1929.

DOCUMENT 21.1

The Passing of the Old Order and the Recognition of Dependence

Soon after the Civil War ended, the Massachusetts Bureau of Labor Statistics compiled data and drew conclusions about the transition from a craft-oriented to a factory-dominated economy.

THE MACHINE*

Skill, once the strong defence of the artisan, is now trembling in the balance, today of value, to-morrow of none, rapidly retiring, with its apprenticed pupils before the advance of machinery. In fact, it is about conquered. Men of skill in trades which it was never supposed invention would reach, have been compelled to enlist into the service of machinery, or turned adrift to learn new trades, or gone to swell the ranks of unskilled laborers—nothing save the increased demand for articles manufactured, coming in to their rescue. . . . As the machine is the embodiment of skill, there is small need of skill on the part of the machine-tender. He is transformed from an adept to be the servant of automatic apparatus, and the subdivision of labor renders this service simple and easily acquired. But few trades remain, in all departments of which a man can become an adept, and wherein he has opportunity to exercise his constructive faculties, for he knows that the machinery he tends will adjust its work with the needed precision. He needs neither to calculate nor to make allowance; his principal function is "to feed the thing he tends," and if properly fed, the machine works up its food and digests it to the expected result, with unfailing certainty.

Charles Litchman's father manufactured shoes. For six years Litchman worked as a salesman for his father. Between 1870 and

*Source: Massachusetts Bureau of Labor Statistics, *Annual Report, 1872* (Boston, 1873), pp. 341–42.

1874, he owned his own shoe factory. He then studied law, worked "at the bench" in a shoe factory, and became Grand Servitor of the Knights of St. Crispin, a labor union of shoe workers. In November 1879 he testified before a congressional committee investigating labor conditions and the causes of industrial depression.

SPECIALIZATION*

Mr. Litchman: . . . . The first effect of the introduction of labor-saving machinery is the degradation of the labor.

The Chairman: How so?

Mr. Litchman: By the sub-division of labor a man now is no longer a tradesman. He is a part of a tradesman. In my own trade of shoe-making, twenty years ago the work was done almost entirely by hand, and the man had to learn how to make a shoe. Now with the use of machines of almost superhuman ingenuity, a man is no longer a shoemaker, but only the sixty-fourth part of a shoemaker, because there are sixty-four sub-divisions in making shoes; and a man may work forty years at our trade and at the end of forty years he will know no more about making a whole shoe than when he commenced business.

The Chairman: He would only know how to make a peg or a waxed end?

Mr. Litchman: Yes; or he would be a laster, or a beveler, or heeler, or nailer, or he would be running and using a machine, or a peg-measure, or attending to any one of the sixty-four sub-divisions into which the trade is parceled out. . . . You cannot turn back the hands upon the dial of human progress and say that all machinery must be banished. You would not take up the rails, destroy the locomotive, and break up the railroad cars, and go back to stage-coaches and horses. . . . Yet all these improvements, while in the abstract they

benefit mankind, have as their first result the degradation of labor by the sub-division of labor. Under our present wage-labor system, capital gets the whole advantage of the introduction of [the] human brain into human labor.

· · · · ·

The Chairman: How many of [the] 48,000 [Massachusetts] shoemakers can make a shoe?

Mr. Litchman: I have no means of knowing, but I would venture to assert that not one-tenth of them can make a shoe, and the shoe that they could make would be the old kind of a turned shoe. I cannot make a machine shoe. My sixty-fourth part of making shoes is standing at the bench and cutting the uppers.

The Chairman: Still you might hang out a sign, "Boots and shoes made"; but the man who only makes pegs cannot say to the world, "Here is a shoemaking shop."

Mr. Litchman: No, Sir. Of course, the man who makes pegs would not be called a shoemaker anyhow. . . .

The Chairman: Does this rule which you have applied to the manufacturing of shoes apply to all other branches of manufacturing industry?

Mr. Litchman: It does substantially. I have no hesitation in saying that. It applies to every trade, not even excepting stone cutting. . . .

DOCUMENT 21.2

The Condition of Dependence: Unemployment

Unemployment at different times resulted from technological change, seasonal patterns of work, and cyclical fluctuations.

SEASONAL WORK*

. . . Since the old system of working in little shops was abandoned for that of

---

*Source: "Testimony of Charles H. Litchman," *Causes of the General Depression in Labor and Business,* Investigation by a Select Committee of the House of Representatives, 46th Cong., 2d sess., Misc. House Doc. No. 5 (Washington, D.C.: U.S. Government Printing Office, 1879), pp. 422–33.

*Source: Massachusetts Bureau of Labor Statistics, "Testimony of Unidentified Worker," *Annual Report, 1870–1871* (Boston, 1871), pp. 242–43.

large manufactories, there has been a steady diminution in the length of the working season per year. Before the time of factories, there would be a steady run of employment for from seven to ten years, only interrupted by commercial depressions or revulsions. The working hours would be from twelve to fifteen. The season for lighting up was from September 20 to May 20. Since that time, there has never been a year of steady work. At first a month only would be lost; now it has got so that we lose over four months' time every year. The system is worse here than elsewhere because machinery has been thoroughly introduced.

In January 1874, the Federal Council of the International Workingmen's Association urged Congressman Benjamin Butler to support a bill that would "provide for all citizens who desire to settle on the public lands with transportation for themselves and families, and also lumber, seed, tools, food and all other necessaries for their establishment as farmers on the public lands for the term of one year, cost of same . . . to be a mortgage on their farm." When this petition appeared in the *New York Sun,* it caused Emanuel Richards to write to that newspaper.

CYCLICAL UNEMPLOYMENT°

Sir: The petition . . . to the Government to settle the poor on public lands . . . [is] what I have long desired and hoped for. I am a good mechanic with a family of seven children. I have no work and no hope of anything better for myself than a life of dependence, crime, or hard hand-to-mouth labor. I would like to take my children out of the city. I can till the ground. I hope you will be in this . . . the friend of the people, and help us to an independent, useful life on the great prairies of the West.

°Source: Emanuel Richards to the editor, *New York Sun,* January 15, 1874.

DOCUMENT 21.3

The Condition of Dependence: Work Contracts

Located in Johnstown, Pennsylvania, the Cambria Iron Works, according to *The New York Times,* was the "finest iron works in the country and one of the glories of Pennsylvania industry." The *Times* made its observation because the mill included 4 modern blast furnaces, 42 double-turn puddling furnaces, and more than 5,000 workers. In April, 1874, after a bitter dispute with its coal miners, the Cambria managers introduced a new contract, and the trade journal *Iron Age* admonished its readers: "If every employer in the country would adopt the same policy as that adopted by the Cambria Company and a few other large works, we would soon have an end of this whole wretched business of trade union tyranny."

RULES ADOPTED BY THE CAMBRIA IRON WORKS, APRIL 6, 1874°

. . . . .

9. Any person or persons known to belong to any secret association or open combination whose aim is to control wages or stop the works, or any part thereof, shall be promptly and finally discharged. Persons not satisfied with their work or their wages can leave honorably by giving the required notice; and persons quitting work, or inducing, or attempting to induce others to quit work other than in the manner prescribed in these rules and regulations, shall forfeit whatever may be due or owing to such person or persons absolutely.

10. Any person going to work intoxicated, or absenting himself from work, without having previously given notice and obtained leave, will be discharged or fined, at the option of the company. Any

°Source: "Rules Adopted by the Cambria Iron Works, April 6, 1874," printed in *Iron Age,* December 31, 1874.

person failing to do his work in a proper manner, or failing to do a satisfactory amount, may expect to be dismissed whenever it may suit the convenience of the company.

11. Quarreling or rioting about the works, or on the company's premises, shall be punished by a fine of not less than $5 nor more than $10, or the discharge of the offender, who may also be prosecuted for violation of the law.

12. All money collected as fines and penalties will be set apart and reserved for those workers injured by accident.

. . . . .

14. Persons detected in stealing coal will be charged the price of a load of coal for every lump stolen . . . and for a repetition of the offense will be discharged.

15. Persons living in the company's houses will be charged for all damages done to the houses beyond the ordinary wear and tear, and will be compelled to leave at once upon ceasing to be employed by the company. In renting the houses, preference will always be given to those whose business requires them to live near the works.

. . . . .

19. In hiring, promoting, and discharging workmen, superintendents and foremen must regard only the interest of the company and the merits of employees.

P. Lorillard & Company, the largest tobacco manufacturer in the country, had its works in Jersey City, New Jersey, and employed nearly 4,000 men, women, and children, including large numbers of recent immigrants, in the manufacture of smoking tobacco, chewing tobacco, and snuff. In 1880, it offered these workers a new contract.

A TOBACCO FACTORY, 1880°

I, the undersigned, in consideration of employment being furnished to me and

wages agreed to be paid me, by the firm of P. Lorillard & Co., do hereby agree and convenant with the said firm, its survivors, successors and assigns, to allow the said firm, or its proper agent or agents for the purpose appointed, to search and examine my person, clothing or other personal effects and property, at any and all times while I am upon the premises of said firm, or while leaving the said premises; and also to allow the said firm, or its proper agents, to enter and search my house or place of abode, without suit, let, hinderance, or molestation, with a view to detect and ascertain whether I have taken or secreted any of the goods, wares, tools or any other property of the said firm; and law, custom, or enactment to the contrary notwithstanding. And I do further, for the consideration above named, agree that all injury to life, limb, body, or health, by reason of my employment by said firm shall be at my own risk, and I . . . will not use or prosecute said firm for damage by reason of any such injury that may occur to me, in or upon the premises of the said firm or when about the business of the said firm. And I hereby covenant that I will faithfully observe and keep the rules of said firm, for the government of employees, which said rules are hereby made a part of this agreement; and will promptly obey the orders of my foreman, and other superiors in said employment. Witness my hand this——— day of————— 18——.

DOCUMENT 21.4

The Condition of Dependence: Health and the Factory System

Five hundred cigar workers and their supporters met in Germania Hall, New York City, in September 1874 to protest against tenement-house cigar manufacturing. This meeting started a long campaign for legislation to abolish work of this kind in the home. The following resolution was passed.

°Source: Contract enclosed in Dick ——— to the editor, n.d., *Fall River Labor Standard*, June 5, 1880.

TENEMENT-HOUSE MANUFACTURING*

... It has become the custom of many cigar manufacturers in this city to rent tenement houses, fill them with families of cigar makers, and carry on the trade of cigar making therein. These houses are used to serve as a workshop, a packing, sleeping, and dwelling room without an opportunity to purify the locality from the odor of moist tobacco. It has been proven by physicians and a committee of investigation that small pox and other contagious diseases have infected some of these tenement houses. The neighborhood and the city are threatened by disease, and are in constant danger thereof . . . [because] these poison-breeding shops are permitted to exist. The consumers of these articles, when made by workmen so affected, are likewise threatened with infection, and their health endangered in an alarming way. It is the sacred and bounden duty of the Board of Health to remove all shops of this kind because the Board has been created solely to protect the inhabitants of the city in their health. . . .

Constant contact with the cotton factory workers in Fall River led Dr. John B. Whitaker to write the following letter to the Massachusetts Bureau of Labor Statistics in 1871.

A MEDICAL REPORT†

... 1. Accidents and casualties are very numerous, partly owing to the exposed machinery and partly owing to carelessness. . . . It is really painful to go round among the operatives and find the hands and fingers mutilated, in consequence of accidents. 2. Unnatural or monotonous working positions . . . in some cases [make the worker] round-shouldered, in other cases producing curvature of the spine and bow-legs. 3. Exhaustion from overwork. In consequence of the long hours of labor, the great speed the machinery is run at, the large number of looms the weavers tend, and the general overtasking, so much exhaustion is produced, in most cases, that immediately after taking supper, the tired operatives drop to sleep in their chairs. . . . 4. Work by artificial light. It is very injurious to the eyes. The affections consist principally in conjunctiviti, opacity of cornea, granulations of the lids, &c. 5. The inhalation of foreign articles. . . . I have been called to cases where I suspected this to be the cause of trouble in the stomach. After giving an emetic, they have in some cases vomited little balls of cotton. . . . 10. Predisposition to pelvic diseases . . . among the female factory operatives produces difficulty in parturition. The necessity for instrumental delivery has very much increased within a few years, owing to the females working in the mills while they are pregnant and in consequence of deformed pelvis. . . . 11. . . . Predisposition to sexual abuse. There is no doubt that this is very much increased, the passions being excited by contact and loose conversation. . . . They are, also, as a general thing, ignorant—at least to the extent that they do not know how to control their passions nor to realize the consequences. . . . 12. Predisposition to depression of spirits. . . . Factory life predisposes very much to depression of spirits. Hence you see the careworn haggard look, the dull expression of the eye. . . . Hypochondria and hysteria are quite common amongst the females. . . . 15. Connection between continuous factory labor and premature old age. . . . Very few live to be old that work in a factory. . . . With regard to provision on the part of the operative, for sickness there is none, they having about as much as they can do to live while they are able

---

*Source: *New York Sun*, September 28, 1874.

†Source: Dr. John B. Whitaker, Fall River, 1871, to the gentlemen of the Massachusetts Bureau of Labor Statistics, printed in Massachusetts Bureau of Labor Statistics, *Annual Report, 1870–1871*, pp. 504–6.

to work. When sickness comes, they have either to assume debts they will never be able to pay, or call upon the city or State to take care of them. . . .

DOCUMENT 21.5

The Condition of Dependence: Child Labor

A Fall River textile worker criticized the use of children in factories before a special investigating committee appointed by the Massachusetts legislature in the 1860s.

A SEVEN-YEAR-OLD°

Question: How old are the children? *Answer:* Seven and eight. *Question:* Have you a child of seven working in the mills? *Answer:* Yes, I have. . . . *Question:* Does he get any schooling now? *Answer:* When he gets done in the mill, he is ready to go to bed. He has to be in the mill ten minutes before we start up, to wind spindles. Then he starts about his own work and keeps on till dinner time. Then he goes home, starts again at one and works till seven. When he's done he's tired enough to go to bed. Some days he has to clean and help scour during dinner hour. . . . Some days he has to clean spindles. Saturdays he's in all day.

The overseer who gave this testimony had 17 years' experience in the Massachusetts cotton mills.

A KINDLY OVERSEER†

. . . Six years ago I ran night work from 6:45 P.M. to 6 A.M. with 45 minutes for meals, eating in the room. The children were drowsy and sleepy. [I] have known them to fall asleep standing up at their work. I have had to sprinkle water in their faces to arouse them after having spoken to them till hoarse; this was done gently and without any intention of hurting them.

Otis G. Lynch, superintendent of the Enterprise Manufacturing Company, which employed 100 children between the ages of 10 and 15 years among its 485 workers in an Augusta, Georgia cotton mill, explained his attitude toward child labor to a U.S. Senate committee in 1883.

A SOUTHERN FACTORY°

Q. Is it a good thing according to your experience that children of from ten to fifteen years of age should work in the factories?—*A.* I think it would be better for them if they were not compelled to work at all, but,—

Q. (Interposing). You would want them to work a part of the time in order to learn a business for life, would you not?— *A.* Yes, sir. Circumstances now force them into the mill. They come in with their mothers.

. . . . .

Q. You think, I suppose, that it would be better for the children to have a chance to be outdoors?—*A.* Yes, sir.

Q. But the testimony is that many of those children seem to enjoy their work in the factory.—*A.* Oh, yes. It is not laborious work, and it is not continuous; there is more or less rest as they go along.

Q. Not much play, I suppose?— *A.* Some little; not much. Of course, we have discipline in the mill, but the labor is not continuous or excessive.

Q. Do the children remain in the mill during the whole eleven hours as the older operatives do?—*A.* Yes.

°Source: "Testimony of John Wild," *Massachusetts Report of Special Committee on the Hours of Labor and the Condition and Prospects of the Industrial Classes,* Mass. House Doc. No. 98 (Boston, n.d.), p. 6.

†Source: Massachusetts Bureau of Labor Statistics, *Annual Report, 1870–1871,* p. 126.

°Source: "Testimony of Otis G. Lynch, Augusta, Georgia," *Report of the Committee of the Senate upon the Relations between Labor and Capital,* Vol. IV (Washington, D.C.: U.S. Government Printing Office, 1885), pp. 748–58.

. . . .

Q. . . . . If you lost your present supply of white labor you think that you would be compelled to substitute foreign white labor rather than negro labor?—*A.* Yes.

Q. For some reason or other the negro is not well adapted to cotton manufacturing, I take it?—*A.* He is not adapted to the management of intricate machinery.

Q. But this intricate machinery is not so troublesome but what ten-year-old white people can take care of it and run much of it?—*A.* Oh, the colored people can be used in factories if circumstances should make it necessary.

DOCUMENT 21.6

The Condition of Dependence: Life outside the Mill or Mine*

In 1877 the Ohio commissioner of labor asked for detailed descriptions from coal and iron ore miners about the prevalence and the character of store pay, scrip money, and company stores in the coal and iron ore regions. The responses printed below are by a coal miner in Athens County and an ore digger in Lucas County.

Lucas County. Store pay is our ruin. . . . The store keeps no meat, no potatoes, no lard, and the most of the time this summer no flour, no butter, no eggs; but we can get hominy at 5 cents per pound, crackers at 10 cents per pound, and rice at 10 cents per pound. Now, it must be evident, that if I work for store-pay, and the store has no meat, I must go without it; and if they have no flour, I must buy crackers. If we were paid in cash, we could go to Toledo, and save, at least, 40 per cent. . . . How can a man be a moral, liberty-loving citizen, when he can not send his children to

school for want of clothes, or take his wife to church in decent attire?

Athens County. . . . When a man's work is done, it is money that is due him, yet he must take just what he can get, or do without. If he sues for it a stay is taken, and his family can starve. There should be no stay on the wages of labor, and the man or company should be compelled under penalty to pay wages every two weeks, in currency. . . . We cannot exchange . . . [the store money] with farmers or others. A farmer comes to my door. He has produce, just what I need. He sells for thirty cents. He also wants something out of the store, and would willingly give me the produce and take the "check" on the store, but the store will not receive the check from him, so he is obliged to sell his produce to the store, and I am forced to pay the store forty cents for the article I could have bought for thirty cents. . . .

DOCUMENT 21.7

The Reaffirmation of Individual Responsibility in an Industrial Society*

Employers vigorously defended their prerogatives and criticized efforts by trade unions and city or state governments to interfere with their freedom of action. They often drew support from eminent social theorists. Henry V. Rothschild manufactured wholesale clothing in New York City, and J. H. Walker owned a shoe factory in Worcester, Massachusetts. William Graham Sumner was professor of political and social science at Yale College. All three testified before a congressional committee in 1878.

*Source: *Investigation by a Select Committee of the House of Representatives Relative to the Causes of the General Depression in Labor and Business,* 45th Cong., 3d sess., Misc. House Doc. No. 29 (Washington, D.C.: U.S. Government Printing Office, 1879), pp. 131–36, 108–208, 310–21.

*Source: Ohio Bureau of Labor Statistics, "The Payment of Wages," *Annual Report, 1877* (Columbus, 1878), pp. 156–92.

HENRY V. ROTHSCHILD

. . . . .

Q. Your remedy is, for the moral improvement of the working classes, to keep them so busy that they cannot indulge in dissipation?—A. That is a most significant point, and it is the only form in which the workingman can be improved.... I say the legislature has no right to encroach upon me as to whether I shall employ men eight hours, or ten, or fifteen hours. It is a matter of mutual agreement, and the legislature has no right, according to the principles of the Declaration of Independence, to impose upon me what hours of labor I shall have between myself and my employes.... Political economy teaches us that the laborers and the capitalists are two different forms of society.... The laborer should do as good as he can for himself, and the capitalist should do as good as he can for himself; it is a matter between the laborer and the capitalist.

Q. You think the community have no interest in that question at all?—A. They have an interest so far as if an unprincipled employer tyrannizes in some way over the laborer; that is a different thing.

Q. How would you interfere in that case—by legislation or not?—A. If a tyranny arises, from which we are not amply protected at the present day, the legislature can always interfere, without a doubt. But this is no tyranny, if the contract arises between a laborer and the employer. The horse-car drivers of New York are employing their hands 14 and 16 hours a day. They are all willing to work; they are not bound to accept the labor; it is a matter between themselves and their employers.

Q. But do they want to work that length of time?—A. All labor is irksome.

J. H. WALKER

Q. The most important fact before this committee is that we have in this country a large amount of unemployed labor.—

A. A man might just as well hang himself because he has a boil, as to talk about changing our laws or institutions because the country has a local ache just now.

Q. What remedy are we to take for this surplus population?—A. Leave them alone; that is the remedy.

Q. You think they will take care of themselves?—A. Let them alone. "The man who will not work shall not eat."

. . . . .

Q. Are we to have these panics in the future as we have had them? Can they be avoided?—A. Nothing will prevent "panics" until human nature is radically changed. Their comparative severity will increase with advancing civilization, unless the disposition to protect themselves ... by saving a portion of their earnings is more universal among the people than it now is.... The laws and institutions of the country can no more be adjusted to them than they can be to the condition of yellow fever....

WILLIAM GRAHAM SUMNER

Q. What is the effect of machinery on those laborers whom for the time being it turns out of employment?—A. For the time being they suffer, of course, a loss of income and a loss of comfort....

Q. Is there any way to help it?—A. Not at all. There is no way on earth to help it. The only way is to meet it bravely, go ahead, make the best of circumstances; and if you cannot go on in the way you were going, try another way, and still another until you work yourself out as an individual....

Q. Do you admit that there is what you call distress among the laboring classes of this country?—A. No sir; I do not admit any such thing. I cannot get evidence of it.... I do not know of anything that the government can do that is at all specific to assist labor—to assist non-capitalists. The only things that the government can do are generally things such as are in the province of a government. The general things that a government can do to assist the non-capitalist in the accumulation of capital (for that is what he wants) are two things. The first thing is to give him the greatest possible liberty in the directing of his own energies for his own development, and the second is to give him the greatest possible security in the possession and use of the products of his own industry. I do not see any more than that that a government can do. . . . Society does not owe any man a living. In all cases that I have ever known of young men who claimed that society owed them a living, it has turned out that society paid—in the State prison. I do not see any other result. . . . The fact that a man is here is no demand upon other people that they shall keep him alive and sustain him. He has got to fight the battle with nature as every other man has; and if he fights it with the same energy and enterprise and skill and industry as any other man, I cannot imagine his failing— that is, misfortune apart. . . .

DOCUMENT 21.8

The Response to Dependence: The Railroad Strikes of 1877

The railroad strikes of 1877 affected the entire nation and for the first time made the labor question a national one. The destruction of life and property in several cities brought home to many the impact of the industrial order on the wage-earning classes. Responses varied. Henry Ward Beecher, the prominent Protestant minister, addressed his followers in Brooklyn's Plymouth Church. A. C. Buell was special correspondent in New York City for the *New Orleans Daily Democrat.*

THE REVEREND
HENRY WARD BEECHER*

. . . It is true that $1 a day is not enough to support a man and five children, if the

man insists on smoking and drinking beer. Is not a dollar a day enough to buy bread? Water costs nothing. Men cannot live by bread, it is true; but the man who cannot live on bread and water is not fit to live. When a man is educated away from the power of self-denial, he is falsely educated. A family may live on good bread and water in the morning, water and bread and midday, and good water and bread at night. Such may be called the bread of affliction, but it is fit that man should eat the bread of affliction. . . . The great laws of political economy cannot be set at defiance.

A. C. BUELL*

. . . The most striking fact developed by this movement is the terrible antipathy which has grown up among the poor and laboring classes against those who possess great wealth. . . . John Jones and William Smith, laborers, regard William H. Vanderbilt, Jay Gould, and Tom Scott, capitalists, as their natural enemies, whose welfare means their loss and whose downfall would redound to their gain. . . . Today, Tom Scott could not get through Pittsburgh, or Vanderbilt through Buffalo, alive! . . . You may call it whatsoever name you please—Communism, Agrarianism, Socialism, or anything else— . . . in the estimation of the vast majority of the American people the millionaire has come to be looked upon as a public enemy! . . . We have just now had a foretaste of real Civil War; of that conflict of classes, which is the most terrible of all species of war. . . . The inadequacy of the present governmental system to combat servile insurrections has been forced home upon the capitalistic classes as a fact that can no longer be evaded. . . . The average citizen may forget the danger as soon as it is past, but not the man of millions. He has seen the ghost of the Commune, and it will stalk his

---

*Source: *The New York Times,* July 30, 1877.

*Source: A. C. Buell, special correspondent, New York, July 30, 1877, *New Orleans Daily Democrat,* August 4, 1877.

dreams every night until he can feel with his prototype of the old world the security of mercenary bayonets enough to garrison every considerable town. . . .

DOCUMENT 21.9
Opposition to Dependence

Martin A. Foran, president of the Coopers' International Union in the early 1870s and later an Ohio congressman, disputed the popular contention that the government could not interfere in relations between employers and their workers. He spoke in Indianapolis in December 1873, a few months after the start of a severe depression.

MARTIN A. FORAN*

. . . We hear a great deal about the presumptuous absurdity of asking the government to interpose its protecting arm in behalf of the people in emergencies and crises of the nature through which we are now passing. We are told that doing so is a strange and unusual proceeding in free America, . . . that to do so would recognize a principle at variance with the spirit and genius of our institutions. . . . What, permit me to ask, is the object of government? Why do we form governments? Is it not for the purpose of having each citizen protected in all his social rights and privileges? Why give up, surrender a portion of our natural rights, those rights which God has given in *ventre sa mere*, unless it be for the purpose of having the balance of them more securely and safely protected? Certainly, the object of a true Democratic government is not to confer exclusive privileges and artificial rights upon a very small portion of the people. . . . It is the conferring of such exclusive rights, powers, and priviliges upon corporate

monopolies, national banks, especially, that has brought upon us the present panic. . . . Should we not demand, are we not justified in demanding from the sovereign power a revocation of the laws that have entailed upon us these evils? If not, then, it were better we had no government at all. . . . How shall the people be saved? Simply by repealing bad or class legislation, and by enacting wise, salutary laws, such laws, and such only, as will beneficially affect, not banks or railroads, not any special class, but such as will beneficially affect the whole people. . . .

Craft workers often argued that the principle of *scarcity* would work to their advantage and maintain or improve their status and condition. At times, such arguments meant the exclusion of ethnically different groups. The following circular was distributed by Atlanta workers in 1875. Similar documents urged the exclusion of immigrants, especially Chinese workers. The principle of scarcity was put forth in all parts of the country.

ATLANTA WORKERS*

We, the undersigned mechanics and working men, appreciating the difficulties that beset us on every hand, and which, through the cupidity of certain proprietors, contractors, and capitalists, whose greed of gain would force us into hopeless poverty, and thus virtually enslave us and our children forever, hereby, individually and collectively, pledge our sacred honor that from and after this date—

1. We will not deal in a business way, or support for public office, any man or men (whether grocer, dry goods, provision or other dealer) who oppresses us by employing negro instead of skilled white labor.

2. We will not trade with any retail dealer who purchases his supplies from a

---

*Source: Speech by Martin A. Foran printed in *Coopers' New Monthly*, Vol. I (January 1874), pp. 5–6.

*Source: Petition printed in *Iron Age*, July 22, 1875, p. 14.

man or men who employ negro instead of skilled white labor.

3. We will not rent a house or houses owned by persons who employ negro to the exclusion of skilled white labor in their construction or repairs.

In 1883, Adolph Strasser and Samuel Gompers, leaders of the cigar workers, offered broader justifications for trade unions to a committee of the United States Senate.

ADOLPH STRASSER[*]

... We have no ultimate ends. We are going on from day to day. We are fighting only for immediate objects—objects that can be realized in a few years.... We want to dress better and to live better, and become better off and better citizens generally.... No well-organized trade [union] can be riotous. New organizations having no funds to back them may become desperate and may do damage to property, but when a trade is well organized you will find that no violence will be committed under such conditions....

SAMUEL GOMPERS[†]

... If you wish to improve the condition of the people, you must improve their habits and customs. The reduction of the hours of labor reaches the very root of society. It gives the workingmen better conditions and better opportunities, and makes of him what has been too long neglected—a consumer instead of a mere producer.... A man who goes to his work before the dawn of the day requires no clean shirt to go to work in, but is content to go in an old overall or anything that will cover his members; but a man who goes to work at 8 o'clock in the morning wants a clean shirt; he is afraid his friends will see him, so he does not want to be dirty. He also requires a newspaper; while a man who goes to work early in the morning and stays at it late at night does not need a newspaper, for he has no time to read, requiring all the time he has to recuperate his strength sufficiently to get ready for his next day's work.... The general reduction of the hours per day ... would create a greater spirit in the working man; it would make him a better citizen, a better father, a better husband, a better man in general.... The trades unions are not what too many men have been led to believe they are, importations from Europe.... Modern industry evolves these organizations out of the existing conditions where there are two classes in society, one incessantly striving to obtain the labor of the other class for as little as possible ...; and the members of the other class being, as individuals, utterly helpless in a contest with their employers, naturally resort to combinations to improve their condition, and, in fact, they are forced by the conditions which surround them to organize for self-protection. Hence trade unions.... Wherever trades unions have organized and are most firmly organized, there are the rights of the people respected.... I believe that the existence of the trades-union movement, more especially where the unionists are better organized, has evoked a spirit and a demand for reform, but has held in check the more radical elements in society....

[*]Source: *Report of the Committee of the Senate upon the Relations between Labor and Capital, 1883*, Vol. 1. pp. 294–95, 373–75.

[†]Source: *Ibid.*, p. 460.

22 Populism Reexamined

THEODORE SALOUTOS
University of California, Los Angeles

Populism has meant different things to different people. To its more hostile critics, it was the sponsor of the wildest monetary schemes of the day. To the Populists themselves, Populism was a crusade in behalf of political and economic democracy that was entitled to the respect of all righteous citizens. Sympathetic scholars have viewed it as a reminder of the passing of the frontier and a warning for the federal government to adopt a more positive role in economic affairs. Still others consider it as the agrarian response to an emerging industrial order. Within recent years a handful of writers have claimed that in Populism are to be found the roots of American fascism.

Which of these analyses should one accept? Since the heyday of Populism, our experiences would indicate that it was a more involved effort, one that attempted to get to the roots of the problems of the day. It has become patently evident that the Populists were more constructive and farsighted in their approach than their harshest critics would have us believe.

Basically, Populism was a dramatic protest against those sweeping changes of the post-Civil War decades that were downgrading agriculture and upgrading the profit-making nonagricultural interests of the nation. It was middle-class in its orientation and sectional in its appeal. It sought to cushion the effects of these changes, to right the imbalance, and to restore agriculture to its position of preeminence by sponsoring a program of direct political action built chiefly upon the aims and aspirations of the grangers, Farmers Alliance men, and lesser groups. Its principles, although born and bred in rural America, were found adaptable to the needs of urban America.

The Populists were practical people who grappled with problems demanding immediate solutions instead of with justifications for some theoretical position they had assumed. They recognized that farmers were fighting with backs to the wall in an effort to preserve their way of life from forces that threatened to uproot it. From the one side, farmers were being pressed by a disappearing agricultural frontier, the unprofitableness of farming, and the breaking-up of the farm family; from the other, by a dynamic industrialism, growing cities, mammoth corporations, corrupt political machines, and swarms of immigrants. The America they knew, or believed they knew, was being ground to bits by a new, foreign, and frightening America they did not understand.

The more immediate grievances of the Populists are a matter of common knowledge. Farmers in the West complained of a long procession of low prices, heavy debts, high interest rates, farm foreclosures, and tenancy. Droughts, blizzards, grasshoppers, insects, and floods compounded their woes. Farmers in the South, too, were weighed down by these burderns, plus sharecropping, the crop-liens system, and the petty tyrannies of the country merchants.

Even the concept of "economic growth," which has become a major concern to our economists, did not escape the probing minds of the Populists. One of their more perceptive philosophers observed that the growth of agriculture lagged behind that of railroading, banking, and manufacturing. One may quibble with the accuracy of their statistics and the rate at which the various sectors of the economy grew, but certainly not with the idea of contrasting the rate of growth. The Populist Senator William A. Peffer of Kansas found that from 1850 to 1880, railroading had grown by more than 700 percent, which was far above the general average of 500; banking by more than 900 percent; and manufacturing by more than 800 percent. Agriculture's rate of growth did not exceed 200 percent. In short, the senator was showing the "railroad builder, the banker, miner, and manufacturing growing richer, . . . the farmer and his co-worker poorer as the years pass."

All this had a painful effect on the farmers, who had always believed that they were the mainstay of the American economy. For these ailing agriculturists comprised the bulk of the population, paid most of the taxes, produced the food and raw materials that sustained life, and kept going the wheels of industry, commerce, and finance. And unless these farmers, who were struggling for their economic life, were rescued, the agricultural America which nurtured them and so many of their leaders in government, business, and industry was in jeopardy.

For these reasons, rural society had to be cleansed and provision made for training of future farmers and leaders. Agriculture needed to regain its economic health. The Populists were convinced that farming was the most fundamental of all occupations—so fundamental that survival of the nation and civilization hinged upon its prosperity and prestige. As the farmers fared, so fared America.

Whether one agrees with the Populists' rationale is beside the point. They believed they were right; so did many of their disciples, who accepted the tenets of Populism in the spirit in which they accepted the teachings of the Bible. In the final analysis, what they believed was more important than the truth itself.

By the late 19th century, many if not most farmers had been cured of their pathological distrust of a strong central government. Low farm prices, high production costs, mortgage indebtedness, rising tenancy, dry summers, severe winters, and poor crops had left thousands of them in dire straits. Their inability to strike a good bargain with merchants, buyers, bankers, and large corporations caused them to look to the federal government as an ally.

The Populists, charting their course of action, surveyed the agrarian strategy of the recent past and found it wanting. Farmers and their leaders erroneously had assumed that voluntary economic action such as group buying and selling, better farming practices, diversified production, and cheaper credit facilities would bring the necessary relief and correct the imbalance. What farmers needed was vigorous, well-directed, and assertive leadership, not half measures, balance-of-power politics with apologetic overtones. These goals had to be reinforced with a vigorous program of political action by the farmers themselves.

But to influence the government and control it, the farmers had to build a People's party comprised of rank-and-file producers. They had to buttress their economic program with a political crusade aimed at the extermination of those elements that preyed on them. And the farmers were the logical ones to head this crusade, for they were the most numerous, suffered the most, and had the experience to guide them in their quest for justice.

Populist leaders were a striking and

colorful lot. The ferocious, acid-tongued Tom Watson of Georgia was one of the more eloquent. Champion of the underdog and then a friend of the Negro, Watson spoke endlessly about the money question, monopolies, and the sham of reform from within the major parties. Obstinate and strong-minded Davis H. Waite of Colorado concentrated on railroad legislation and the silver question. To his foes, he was known as "Bloody Bridles" Waite, as a result of a speech in which he said: "It is better, infinitely better, that blood should flow to the horses' bridles rather than our national liberties should be destroyed."

An interesting triumvirate came from Kansas. "Sockless Jerry" Simpson, according to one account, got his sobriquet during the congressional campaign of 1890 when he accused his opponent of wearing "silk stockings." Subsequently, someone retorted that Simpson wore no socks at all; hence the "Sockless Jerry." A dynamic speaker with a large following, Simpson's chief grievance was the railroads and their influence. Senator William A. Peffer, or "Whiskers" Peffer, was a learned and capable man who wrote and spoke on a wide variety of subjects. Although described as "a well-meaning, pin-headed anarchistic crank," Peffer was far better informed than his critics believed. The most unusual was the Irish-born and Irish-tempered Mary Elizabeth Lease. A tall, slim, attractive woman with a flair for oratory, she went up and down Kansas telling farmers to "raise less corn and more hell." The appearance of this "Patrick Henry in petticoats" on the Populist platform was evidence that the farmers were advocates of women's rights.

Populism was built on more than the shopworn argument that the producers were a sound and virtuous people. It was founded in part on a felt need for articulate spokesmen of agrarian democracy. Its leaders argued with a high degree of indignation that farmers and wage earners deserved and had to have greater representation in a government hitherto dominated by lawyers, millionaires, financiers, and their allies. The basic needs of the people must be satisfied and the integrity of the government restored.

If virtuous and industrious farmers filled the legislative chambers, they would find themselves strategically placed to challenge those self-seeking interests that obstructed the channels of economic and social justice. They might even gain control of the government and marshal its resources—that is, the resources of the people—and regulate the corporations and financial empires which had a stranglehold on the economic life of the nation. They might eliminate fraudulent business practices, assure honest elections, preserve competition, restrict immigration, block alien and corporate land controls, and perhaps revive most of the prosperity that had been choked off.

Although high in praise of the virtues and values of an agrarian order, the Populists had no intention of turning the clock backward, stifling industrialism, and checking material progress. They wanted reforms within the framework of a democratic capitalism, reforms that would give producers a fairer share for their labors and a greater voice in the government. They asked only for prosperity in place of privation, and representation in place of misrepresentation.

The Populists considered solution of the money crisis a prime requisite to recovery. With undeniable sincerity, if not always with learned accuracy, they argued that the population, industry, commerce, and transportation of the country had been increasing at a faster pace than money in circulation. This disparity in turn precipitated a fierce competitive struggle among borrowers for the limited quantities of money, forced up interest rates, and made it difficult for the small producers to borrow. Shortage of money placed the farmer in particular in a disadvantageous position, depressed his prices, and forced him to give more products for less money.

The Populist solution was for the federal government to pump more money into circulation and to assume the initiative in liberalizing the nation's credit. A judicious amount of inflation, Populists believed, was good not only for debtors but also for business elements in need of finances to expand their operations. More money in circulation promised to raise farm prices, enable the farmers to pay their debts, bring down interest rates, and make it easier to borrow. In due time, this was expected to produce a chain reaction that would have a healthy and invigorating effect on the entire economy. The farmers would be able to buy more goods and produce more employment; farm surpluses would move into the market; wheels of prosperity would hum again. In effect, this was a form of Keynesianism before John Maynard Keynes.

The Populists wanted a flexible financial system that would place money in the hands of farmers at harvesttime, when they needed it the most. Given their way, the Populists would have demolished the national banking structure and restricted the money-issuing power to the federal government, where it rightfully belonged. They would have authorized free and unlimited coinage of silver until it rose to $50 per capita, a sum considered sufficient to transact the business of the country on a cash basis.

Despite an emotional attachment to silver, Populist theoreticians actually were less concerned with the support that money had behind it than they were in having the federal government issue it. Such a responsibility could not be taken lightly, for only a government responsive to the needs of the people was truly responsible. Money, argued the Populists, obtained its value from the strength and prestige of the government that issued it, not from precious metals stored in government vaults. Paper money issued by a strong government was as sound as silver or gold money.

The Populists would pump this money into circulation through the Farmers Alliance subtreasury plan, a land-loan scheme, or any other acceptable device. The subtreasury plan was viewed as a money lending scheme by some and as a price-influencing mechanism by others. Both the subtreasury and the land-loan ideas were based on the simple fact that farmers had two kinds of property to offer as collateral: their farmlands and their nonperishable products, such as cotton, wheat, oats, barley, and tobacco.

The subtreasury plan was a forerunner of numerous credit-issuing and price-influencing devices that gained popularity after World War I. But in the 1890s, it was viewed as a harebrained scheme that could be supported only by the worst kind of money cranks. It called for creation of subtreasuries—which for all practical purposes amounted to government lending agencies and warehouses—where farmers could borrow at a nominal rate of interest up to as much as 80 percent of the market value of the stored commodity.

A singular advantage of the plan, apart from its lending geatures, was that it would enable farmers to keep their products off the market during the rush season when prices could be forced down to unreasonable levels. The government could, if it chose, sell these products at any time during the year as a means of obtaining more favorable prices. This, too, was the germ of the orderly marketing philosophy that attracted widespread support after World War I.

The land-loan idea likewise anticipated plans sponsored by various groups during the 20th century. One Populist proposal asked for the granting of loans not in excess of $3,000 or more than 80 percent of the cash value of the property offered as security. The loan was to mature within 50 years and carry no more than 2 percent interest; applications for loans were to be received until the amount of money in circulation climbed to $50 per capita.

Here, in essence, was the Populist program for adjusting the nation's money and credit to an expanding economy: Confine the money-issuing power to the federal government, and issue money generously through a combination of loans on the land and crops of farmers. Within a reasonable time the prices the farmer received would begin rising; he would then pay his debts, increase his purchases, create jobs for city people, promote commerce, force interest rates to drop, and accelerate the recovery of the general economy, which was so dependent upon a healthy agriculture.

The Populists also had some positive views on land ownership. According to their creed, man was placed on earth by the laws of God and nature, not by those of any political or economic system. Hence, man was entitled to as much land as he needed to make a living, and the government was obligated to see to it that he got it. Farmers, as producers, created all wealth; yet they had little or no voice in the distribution of the land. Far too much land had fallen into the hands of railroads, corporations, and financiers, who preyed on the producers.

This prodigality had to be supplanted by a policy of responsibility. Among other things, the federal government was obligated henceforth to reserve all lands recovered from corporations as a consequence of their failure to abide by the provisions of their grants. It was also to safeguard remnants of the public lands for homesteads by actual settlers. Ownership by corporations had to be limited to legitimate business needs. Finally, ownership by aliens had to be eliminated, for as one Farmers Alliance paper wrote: "By allowing aliens to own the lands of the country the way is open for them to own the whole country."

Adequate transportation at reasonable rates was an important part of the Populist agenda. Since state and federal regulation allegedly had failed to provide it at reasonable rates, the Populists espoused government ownership of the railroads, and even of the telephone and telegraph lines.

The Populists likewise pleaded for a more equitable system of taxation, which would shift some of the farmers' burden to the recipients of large incomes. The general property tax, source of the bulk of the local and state revenues, was virtually a real property tax, except in the farming districts, where personal property was in view of the assessors and taxed. But in the cities, much if not most of the wealth in intangibles escaped taxation, since it was concealed from tax assessors. Consequently, a disproportionate share of the load fell on the shoulders of the farmers. Enactment of an income tax would help transfer a greater part of the tax burden to those who could afford to carry it: rich urban holders of securities, wealthy businessmen, and well-to-do members of the professional classes. And still one other change had to be inaugurated: Improvements on the land had to be exempted from taxation. Levies, according to the Populists, ought to be made in terms of the assessed value of the land, without reference to improvements added by labor.

In keeping with agrarian tradition, the Populists insisted that government expenditures be cut to the bone by a policy of honesty in public office and reduction in the salaries of all state and federal officials. This policy could be counted on to bring relief to the overburdened taxpayers.

Populism further sought to broaden the base of American democracy by bringing the people closer to their government, in the hope of checking the encroachment of special interests on their economic rights. This they would help accomplish through the direct election of U.S. senators. In theory, the direct election of senators would encourage more people to take a genuine interest in the affairs of government, weaken party domination over the Senate, lessen the influence of the privileged interests, and enhance that of the people. Moreover, it would make it far more difficult to corrupt the citizenry than the existent system, which confined the power of election to a few men in the state legislature. Finally, it would eliminate the evil of a deadlock in making selections, which in the past had sometimes left states unrepresented in the Senate. Certainly, if the people had the intelligence to choose judges, state legislatures, and congressmen, they could choose senators.

Adoption of the Australian ballot was still another vehicle for bringing the government closer to the people. Such would enable the citizen to take his ballot into the polling booth, where he could make his choice and cast it without anyone knowing how he voted.

Obviously, Populism held that society suffered from too little instead of too much democracy, and that the surest way of extending its scope was by distributing political and economic power over as many people as possible. The Populists believed in the ultimate goodness of man, the very premise on which democracy is based; that honesty and decency would ultimately triumph in a society that was moneymad. And Populism sought not the eradication of the profit system, but its reform, so that its benefits could be shared by more people. It sought all this through gradual, constitutional means, and within the framework of the existing social economy. It sought to make the profit system function in a more equitable fashion, not to destroy it.

The Populists have come under attack for embracing what is referred to as the conspiratorial philosophy of history, which viewed financiers, railroad owners, middlemen, and others as partners in a babal to rob the common people, i.e., the producers, of their just rewards. The truth of the matter is that this was a widely held view over which the Populists had no monopoly. Civil service reformers, trade, unionists, preachers of the social gospel, urban humanitarians, and others bemoaned the antisocial influences that the monied interests wielded over social and political institutions. Much if not most of

the social legislation proposed by the Populists in the 1890s and by the Progressives in the following decade was geared to the undoing of these antisocial forces.

Populism hardly was encased in the class philosophy frequently ascribed to it by its critics and some of the ungrateful Progressives who borrowed copiously from its ideas. As spokesmen for agriculture, long the dominant occupation and source of wealth, the Populists were hardly more class-oriented than were the leaders of industry, finance, commerce, and labor. Unconcerned with the unschooled in the art of public relations, the Populists often used coarse and brutal language, but they spoke with sincerity. They believed that what was good for the farmers was good for the nation in the very same spirit that labor leaders claimed that what was good for the wage earner was good for the country, or as a corporation executive later more bluntly put it: "What is good for General Motors is good for America."

The ideology of Populism lived long after the movement itself had disintegrated and passed from the political scene. Many of its ideas were absorbed lock, stock, and barrel by the more adept Progressives, who benefited from the years of agitation and economic prosperity denied the Populists. "Might-have-beens" do not fall properly within the scope of the historian, but one may wonder how far Wilsonian liberalism would have progressed if during the New Freedom period the business cycle had been on the downgrade instead of the upgrade.

The Wilsonian elements, with roots in the agrarian past, ultimately strengthened the Populist mood within Progressivism. By 1912, much if not most of what the Populists espoused had gained respectability and a larger following. The income tax, for example, was placed on the statute books; it began to place some of the tax burden on those who could best afford to bear it and made available useful data to the lawmakers. The Federal Reserve Act, the most important piece of financial legislation enacted since Civil War years, was designed in part to meet the money and credit needs of the farmers. In this respect it was a disappointment, but its defects were partly overcome with the passage of the Federal Farm Loan Act and the Federal Warehouse Act. Both had familiar Populist overtones. The former offered mortgage facilities to those who otherwise might have had difficulties in obtaining them; the latter enabled farmers to store their products, obtain loans on them, and even anticipate higher prices.

Populism may be properly considered the political forebear of the Nonpartisan League, the farmer-labor party idea, and even of La Follette Progressivism. Long-standing grievances against middlemen, financiers, corporations, and special interests temporarily stirred farmers and trade unionists to adopt a common course of action.

Yet there were notable differences in general strategy and tactics, and even in the source of leadership. Populism favored formation of a new party, adoption of its own platform, and nomination of its own candidates. It drew heavily from the leadership of the Farmers Alliance. The Nonpartisan League, on the other hand, discarded the new party strategy, preferred playing balance-of-power politics from within one of the major parties, and relied for leadership in part on ex-socialists and members of the American Society of Equity. The League's strategy was one of political expediency: obtaining a favorable bargaining position within the party, or even controlling it. It also went several steps beyond the Populists in demanding that the state government of North Dakota take a more direct hand in the economic life of the farmer by building state-owned mills, elevators, banks, and industries. Despite these differences, the Populists and the Nonpartisan Leaguers were agreed on the need for farmers to take a more active role in politics.

The farmer-labor party idea was more a lineal descendant of the Populists than was the Nonpartisan League, even though it was inspired by Nonpartisan Leaguers who had become disenchanted with balance-of-power politics and belatedly felt the need for a new party. Unlike the Populist party, this new coalition appealed more to trade unionists than to farmers, giving indication that the spearhead of liberalism had become urban-industrial. But its sponsors believed that farmers and wage earners had sufficient interest in common to wage successful campaigns in behalf of public utility regulation, progressive income taxes, government assistance to farmers, and shorter hours and better wages for employees.

The La Follette Progressives, frequently treated in the Populist tradition, sought unsuccessfully to build a party on an amorphous middle-class base in which occupational lines were blurred. The principal difference between the La Follette Progressives and the farmer-laborites was that the platform of the former had less of a doctrinaire quality about it.

Echoes of the Populist philosophy were heard in other quarters as well during the 1920s and 1930s, when Old Dealers and New Dealers stressed the benefits to be had by farmers from storing their crops in warehouses, obtaining credit from the government, and marketing their products in an orderly manner. Populist philosophy affected the various commodity pools of the 1920s, the Federal Farm Board of Herbert Hoover, and the Ever-Normal Granary Plan of Henry A. Wallace. Even more graphic was the revival of the old Populist war cry for the free and unlimited coinage of silver at the ratio of 16 to 1 during the closing days of the Hoover administration and the early hours of Franklin D. Roosevelt's New Deal. Finally, the inflationary agricultural programs of the New Deal were evidence that the Populist argument had not been in vain.

Although the Populists did not win many elections, they challenged the two major parties. They agitated, argued, discussed, and demanded; for the most part, they appealed to the rank and file, though they also attracted some intellectuals. For good or for ill, they helped popularize the idea of the federal government serving as an agency of social reform and may even be considered as precursors of the "welfare state." Racism and antiforeignism hardly were the cornerstone of their thinking, as some historians seem to insist; they were incidental and probably less concentrated than in urban quarters.

Interest in Populism, as indicated, has persisted to this very day, especially among those interested in the quest for new facts, as well as among those who have been more concerned with attacking the traditional interpretation of Populism without seeking out new evidence. This latter group of revisionists has been aiming most of its fire toward what they viewed as the more antisocial aspects of Populism; and it has found more support among sociologists and social psychologists then historians. On the other hand, those who adhere to the more traditional interpretation have had their position reinforced by new scholarly findings which substantiate the thesis that Populism was an indigenous brand of reformism conditioned by the American experience.

The debates of the 1950s and 1960s over whether the Populists were reformers or something less flattering were precipitated by a peculiar twist of circumstances, rather than by an agricultural crisis comparable to that of the 1890s. Issues of particular concern to the academicians of the 1950s were projected back into the 1890s and shored-up with the argument that new scholarly techniques merited fresh and up-to-date conclusions that had escaped the earlier writers. Positions taken in the 1890s and based on values of the 1890s were appraised in terms of priorities and values of the 1950s.

The Populist argument has haunted the 1950s and 1960s despite charges that Populism is irrelevant to present day problems. The monetary views of Milton Friedman, professor of economics at the University of Chicago and one of the leading classical economists and theoreticians of the day, is a case in point. For Friedman's reasoning sounds similar to that of the Populists, in that he insists that "the key to capitalistic economic stability" is "monetary policy—the factors that govern the rate of growth or decline in the money supply." In short, Friedman is placing the Populist argument of the 1890s in an academic attire of the 1960s. The Populists maintained that the whole of industry, agriculture, and commerce could not be set in complete motion and the economic health of the nation restored unless the money supply kept pace with the growth of population and all other sectors of the economy. In the 1890s this was viewed as the harebrained notion of money cranks, but in the 1960s one of the foremost conservative economists was advocating that the money supply of the country be increased at a rate of from 3 to 5 percent annually. Friedman goes far beyond what the Populists proposed when they demanded an increase in the money supply until it reached $50 per capita.

Despite claims of irrelevance and charges of reaction, the revisionists have been unsuccessful in bringing about any major shifts in the traditional interpretation among the historians. The revisionists have stimulated much discussion and rekindled fresh interest in the subject, but as yet no scholar of the revisionist persuasion has come forward with a full-scale study buttressing this position. New scholarship, for the most part, has enhanced and solidified the position of the traditional interpretation of Populism.

SUGGESTED READINGS

BROADHEAD, MICHAEL J. *Persevering Populist: The Life of Frank Doster*. Reno: University of Nevada Press, 1969.

CLANTON, O. G. *Kansas Populism: Ideas and Men*. Lawrence, Kans., and London: University of Kansas Press, 1969.

DURDEN, ROBERT F. *The Climax of Populism*. Lexington: University of Kentucky Press, 1965.

HICKS, JOHN D. *The Populist Revolt*. Minneapolis: University of Minnesota Press, 1931.

HOFSTADTER, RICHARD C. *The Age of Reform: From Bryan to F.D.R*. New York: Alfred A. Knopf, 1955.

NOBLIN, STUART. *Leonidas LaFayette Polk*. Chapel Hill; Univesity of North Carolina Press, 1949.

NUGENT, WALTER T.K. *The Tolerant Populists*. Chicago: University of Chicago Press, 1963.

POLLACK, NORMAN. *The Populist Response to Industrial America*. Cambridge, Mass.: Harvard University Press, 1962.

————.(ed.). *The Populist Mind*. Indianapolis: Bobbs-Merrill Co., 1967.

RIDGE, MARTIN. *Ignatius Donnelly*. Chicago: University of Chicago Press, 1962.

ROCHESTER, ANNA. *The Populist Movement in the United States*. New York: International Publishers Co., Inc., 1943.

SALOUTOS, THEODORE, *Farmer Movements in the South, 1865–1933*. Berkeley and Los Angeles: University of California Press, 1960.

————. *Populism: Reaction or Reform*. New York: Holt, Rinehart, & Winston, 1968.

————. "The Professors and the Populists," *Agricultural History,* Vol. XL (October 1966), pp. 235–54.

SALOUTOS, THEODORE, and HICKS, JOHN D. *Agricultural Discontent in the Middle West, 1900–1939*. Madison: University of Wisconsin Press, 1951.

TINDALL, GEORGE B. (ed.). *A Populist Reader*. New York: Harper & Row (Torchbooks), 1966.

WOODWARD, C. VANN. *Tom Watson: Agrarian Rebel*. New York: Macmillan Co., 1938.

DOCUMENT 22.1

The Farmer: Source of American Life*

The importance of agriculture to the national well-being was a favorite Populist propaganda argument. The agrarian origins of the nation's leaders were constantly brought to public attention. The following selection by N. B. Ashby is a succinct statement of agricultural fundamentalism.

... But suppose drought or mildew should claim the whole land for a single year, and the earth would refuse her increase; or suppose the whole farming world would simultaneously go out upon a strike and refuse to market any portion of their entire products for a year—what would happen? Panic, calamity, ruin. First, the country merchant would close up store—like Othello, his occupation gone; then the country banker would close the doors of his loan-shop and retire to one of his farms secured by foreclosure, and the town would hang out the sign so frequently seen upon the wagons of returning '49ers. The freight departments of the railways would now suspend, weary and bankrupt from transporting "emptys." Next the great elevators and the stockyards would go to the wall, and the packinghouses would close. Panic would seize the whole country. The banks in the great centers would suspend, railroad stocks would collapse, the Goulds and Vanderbilts would be paupers, factories and mines would close down, trade and transportation in every line would cease, and the cities would be full of a hungry, panic-stricken, famishing mob, for whom there would be no bread, and who would re-enact the scenes in Paris in 1791. Agriculture is so inseparably connected with the whole business structure of the country as a first cause that such direful ruin would necessarily follow upon its suspension. ...

*Source: N. B. Ashby, *The Riddle of the Sphinx* (Des Moines, 1890).

Man began civilized life as a farmer, and the industrial army is ever returning to the farm for recruits. The farm constantly furnishes the brain and the brawn to the nations. The leading men in journalism, medicine, ministry, finance, law, transportation, and trade are the sons of farmers, or, a farthest remove, grandsons. A generation or two removed from the invigorating influences of the farm wears out both mental and bodily vigor. Hence, the leaders in the great moral, social, intellectual, and political movements of the race come continually from the descendants of the sturdy yeomen. And thus the farm sustains the forum and the mart in fully as substantial a way as in the furnishing of products for the shop and factory. . . .

DOCUMENT 22.2

Pastoral Vision and Plutocratic Reality*

Decrying the influence of the new plutocracy in the social and political life of the nation, the Populists singled out the United States Senate for special criticism. By the 1890s, the Senate was already gaining the reputation as a club for retired millionaires. The following selection by Populist historian N. A. Dunning is typical of such criticism.

. . . One of the relics of aristocracy that has been handed down to us is the United States Senate, a branch of our government whose uselessness is only equalled by its aristocratic notions. In connection with this old-time, blue-blooded aristocracy, and supplemental to it, has sprung into existence, in almost every part of our country, another species of aristocracy, which follows the acquirement of large fortunes. It has come to be an accepted idea, that the accumulation of money will, in some manner, divorce its possessors

*Source: N. A. Dunning, *The Farmers' Alliance History* (Washington, D.C., 1891), pp. 3–5.

from the taint of plebeian birth, obscure beginnings, or former social relations, and at once change the inner as well as the outer individual.

Aristocratic ideas, backed up by intelligence and refinement, may serve a good purpose in toning down the untamed spirit, and broadening the nature of a native American; but when this station in society is reached through the medium of a bank account, human nature revolts, and the average person becomes disgusted. This spirit of avarice, or desire to make money, has become the bane of our social relations, and threatens the perpetuity of the government itself. The desire for wealth is increased as the power and privileges which it brings become more clearly understood. When the brains of a Webster or a Calhoun must wait unnoticed in the anteroom, while the plethoric pocket-book of some conscienceless speculator, monopolist, or trickster, brings to its owner the privileges of the parlor, and the softest seat at the feast, intelligence and moral rectitude will always be at a discount, while fraud and corruption will bring a premium. In order that such conditions may exist, some portions of the people must suffer. . . .

It was to satisfy the American farmer that his calling had either become obsolete, or his environment unnatural, that agricultural organizations, for political or economic purposes, were brought into existence. Up to 1860 the economic privileges of the farmer were somewhat near a parity with other branches of productive industry. The systematic spoliation of the present was, to a large extent, practically unknown. Special laws and privileges, which operated directly against the national interests of agriculture, existed only in a mild degree. At that period immense fortunes were almost unknown, and aristocracy was confined to the better educated and more refined. Neither poverty nor crime existed in the same proportion as now, and the general trend of events was toward conservatism in all economic conditions. Moderate fortunes, moderate sized farms, and moderate business enterprises, were not only the rule of the times, but were maintained under the protecting care of society's consent. Of course there were exceptions, but not in the offensive and disturbing sense in which they now exist. All must admit that the parasitic age had not begun at this date, and that labor in production paid less tribute than at the present time. Emerson says: "The glory of the farmer is that, in the division of labors, it is his part to create. All trade rests at last on his primitive activity. He stands close to Nature; he obtains from the earth the bread and the meat. The food which was not he causes to be." It is because of the truth contained in this statement that the farmer complains. It is because he simply creates for others, with but a feeble voice, if any, in determining the measure of his remuneration, that he has at last been compelled to enter an earnest protest. Willing as he is to create, and anxious to serve all other classes with the fruits of his industry and skill, yet the farmer has learned, by sad experinece, that his toil has gone unrequited, and his anxiety has been construed into servility. The American farmer, in his present condition, is a living example of the folly and disaster which inevitably follow, where one class of citizens permits another class to formulate and administer all economic legislation. In other words, he is the victim of misplaced confidence, and has at last undertaken to regain his lost advantages and rights. . . .

DOCUMENT 22.3

The Parties Have Forgotten the People*

The Populists had little faith in the leadership of the Republican and Democratic parties. As one of their supporters saw it: "The capital of the Republican party consists in the virtues of its ancestry; and the capital of the Democratic party consists in the faults of its opponents."

The Republican party was born of the spirit of opposition to chattel slavery. It was this principle that gave it life, vitality and power. While this contest was waging it was grand in its conception of right and justice. It taught the inconsistency of slavery growing on the tree of liberty; that the two could not be blended in one harmonious setting; that the cries of the mother who was compelled to part with her child did not harmonize with the songs of heaven; that the groans of the woman compelled to become a mother without being a wife, were not consistent with the teachings of Christianity; that this was intended by the fathers of American liberty to become, indeed and in truth, a free land; that it was a Union of States having a common interest, that it was a land of free churches, free schools and free men. When the contest for these principles was over, and chattel slavery went down amid the boom of artillery, the rattle of musketry and groans of the dying, the Republican party emerged from the conflict with a prestige and glory that commanded the admiration of the world. Flushed with victory, they said in the pride of their heart—like the king of Babylon—see, we have done all this.

Then the work of despoiling began. . . . The glory of the Republican party has departed. Their bright sun has set in the hopeless misery which their financial pol-

*Source: W. A. Morgan, *History of the Wheel and Alliance* (Fort Scott, Kans., 1889), pp. 715–17.

icy has entailed upon an enterprising people. Their record on contraction of the currency, national banks, back salary steals, credit strengthening act, funding schemes and demonetization tendencies should have consigned them to political oblivion long ago, and would, but there was no power that promised any better, and the people were in the hands of corporations and combinations. . . .

. . . Since the war [the Democratic party has] aped the policy of the Republican party on every issue of vital interest to the great masses of the people. They have voted for contraction; they have favored national banks; they have aided the Republicans in their funding schemes; they have voted and worked to strike down silver; they have bowed to Baal; they have worshipped Mammon; they have built unto themselves false Gods, and set them on the hill-tops of freedom; they have courted aristocratic establishments; they have partaken of the spoils; they have received bribes; they have forsaken their principles, and their glory is deaprted from them forever. . . .

DOCUMENT 22.4
The Amount of Money Needed*

A major complaint of the Populists was the shortage of circulating money. In fact, by 1894, it became their major political issue, overshadowing all others. An eloquent speaker on the "money problem" was William A. Peffer, United States senator from Kansas. The following selection is extracted from his book, *The Farmer's Side.*

If the functions of money be public functions, the people, as a body politic, ought to provide money enough for the use of the people, and regulate its use in such a way as to make it most serviceable

---
*Source: William A. Peffer, *The Farmer's Side* (New York, 1891), pp. 227–29.

and least expensive. It is on this theory and reason that the plan herein set forth is based. It is universally agreed among workers that the amount of circulating money needed by the people is such amount as is sufficient for our business if transacted on a cash basis. That necessarily is indefinite. Whenever definiteness is attempted, the amount is put at $50 per capita. This is the amount named by the Ohio farmers at a State meeting in May, 1891. The same figures have been given frequently by other public bodies. This particular amount is agreed upon, probably, because when our great war ended and when business was prosperous, our money circulation was above that. On careful examination, however, it will be found that population alone is not a proper basis for estimating money volume. The amount of money needed in any community depends not on population, but on the amount of business done and the density of population—in other words, on the necessities of the people, not on their number. One community requires more money than another, though the number of its inhabitants may be less. If a rule must be found and applied, why should it not be the same as that adopted in the case of coffee, sugar, shoes, or axes? Let the people themselves determine the quantity they need. . . .

. . . In this case, then, suppose we adopt a rule somewhat like this: Ascertain the amount of pressing indebtedness now resting upon the people for which their homes are mortgaged as security, and which debts are due and subject to *immediate collection.* If it be ascertained that that particular class of indebtedness is $1,000,000,000, then that amount of money is needed at once to relieve the people. Besides paying the debts of this particular class of persons, the money would immediately go into circulation, and within thirty days afterward pay as many more debts, and within another thirty days as many more debts, and so on; so that by the time a year had passed the money would have paid off twelve times as much indebtedness as it did at first. Upon a plan something of that kind the people may be relieved of their debt burdens in the course of twelve or fifteen years by the practice of a very simple policy, one which has been practiced ever since money was invented. . . .

DOCUMENT 22.5
Government Control of Fiscal Affairs*

The issuance of money ought to be confined exclusively to the federal government and not to private bankers, according to the Populists. Senator William A. Peffer here uses an argument that thousands of Americans heard from the stentorian voice of William Jennings Bryan.

Is there anything unreasonable or dangerous in the request that money be issued by the government directly to the people? It must be remembered that the money of every nation is issued by the governing power. In this country Congress is authorized to "coin money and regulate the value thereof," and no other body is so empowered. Every American coin, every piece of money, whether of metal or of paper, which has been given to the people as money, was made and issued to them by authority and direction of Congress. Four hundred million dollars in treasury notes were so made and issued in 1862, and the national banking law was enacted one year later for the express purpose of giving more money to the people. At one time the aggregate amount of treasury notes (greenbacks) and national bank notes in use as money, was more than $700,000,000 dollars. Besides these, some of the bonds were used as money. The

government issuing money to the people is not a new or untried proceeding. But what the farmers object to is, that the government unnecessarily uses a very costly channel through which to effect the distribution, and the people are charged with the expense; that is to say, the money is passed to the people through banks, and they—the banks—charge anywhere from ten per cent to twenty-four per cent per annum for making the transfer; whereas, if it were issued to the people directly, without the intervention of the banks or any other private agency demanding profit on the work, the expense would not exceed one to three per cent. If the money is intended for the people (and it is), why not give it to them at once through government hands, as postage stamps, for example, are given? In the first place, money belongs to the people; the people's general agent, the government, makes the money, every dollar of it, by authority of the people and for them; why, then, should banks or any trafficking agency be permitted to trade in it before it reaches the people to whom it belongs, and for whose use it is intended? That practice is not adopted with respect to anything else which the government does for the people. Whatever else it delivers to them passes through government hands only. What reason can be assigned for delivering treasury notes to the people through banks, that would not apply with equal force to the issuing and delivering to them of patents to public lands, or postage stamps? The object in making the issuing money is, that the people shall have it to use in their business affairs. It would reach them quite as easily and early if sent out through direct channels from the treasury as it does by passing through banks, and it would not cost the people more than from one-tenth to one-eighth as much as the banks and loan agencies compel them to pay. It is believed that this exorbitant charge for the use of money, more than any other one thing, is responsible for the general depression of agriculture. . . .

*Source: N. A. Dunning, *The Farmers' Alliance History* (Washington, D. C., 1891), pp. 262–63.

DOCUMENT 22.6

The Omaha Platform*

An explicit statement of Populist aims appears in the platform of the People's Party, adopted at its National Convention on July 4, 1892. It was largely written by the colorful Ignatius Donnelly of Minnesota.

Assembled upon the 116th anniversary of the Declaration of Independence, the People's Party of America, in their first national convention, invoking upon their action the blessing of Almighty God, put forth in the name and on behalf of the people of this country, the following preamble and declaration of principles:

PREAMBLE

The conditions which surround us best justify our co-operation; we meet in the midst of a nation brought to the verge of moral, political, and material ruin. Corruption dominates the ballot-box, the Legislatures, the Congress, and touches even the ermine of the bench. The people are demoralized; most of the States have been compelled to isolate the voters at the polling places to prevent universal intimidation and bribery. The newspapers are largely subsidized or muzzled, public opinion silenced, business prostrated, homes covered with mortgages, labor impoverished, and the land concentrating in the hands of capitalists. The urban workmen are denied the right to organize for self-protection, imported pauperized labor beats down their wages, a hireling standing army, unrecognized by our laws, is established to shoot them down, and they are rapidly degenerating into European conditions. The fruits of the toil of millions are boldly stolen to build up colossal fortunes for a few, unprecedented in the history of mankind; and the possessors of these, in turn, despise the Re-

*Source: E. McPherson (ed.), *A Handbook of Politics for 1892* (Washington, 1892), pp. 269–71.

public and endanger liberty. From the same prolific womb of governmental injustice we breed the two great classes—tramps and millionaires.

The national power to create money is appropriated to enrich bond-holders; a vast public debt payable in legal-tender currency has been funded into gold-bearing bonds, thereby adding millions to the burdens of the people.

Silver, which has been accepted as coin since the dawn of history, has been demonetized to add to the purchasing power of gold by decreasing the value of all forms of property as well as human labor, and the supply of currency is purposely abridged to fatten usurers, bankrupt enterprise, and enslave industry. A vast conspiracy against mankind has been organized on two continents, and it is rapidly taking possession of the world. If not met and overthrown at once it forebodes terrible social convulsions, the destruction of civilization, or the establishment of an absolute despotism.

We have witnessed for more than a quarter of a century the struggles of the two great political parties for power and plunder, while grievous wrongs have been inflicted upon the suffering people. We charge that the controlling influences dominating both these parties have permitted the existing dreadful conditions to develop without serious effort to prevent or restrain them. Neither do they now promise us any substantial reform. They have agreed together to ignore, in the coming campaign, every issue but one. They propose to drown the outcries of a plundered people with the uproar of a sham battle over the tariff, so that capitalists, corporations, national banks, rings, trusts, watered stock, the demonetization of silver and the oppressions of the usurers may all be lost sight of. They propose to sacrifice our homes, lives, and children on the altar of mammon; to destroy the multitude in order to secure corruption funds from the millionaires.

Assembled on the anniversary of the

birthday of the nation, and filled with the spirit of the grand general and chief who established our independence, we seek to restore the government of the Republic to the hands of the "plain people," with which class it originated. We assert our purposes to be identical with the purposes of the National Constitution; to form a more perfect union and establish justice, insure domestic tranquillity, provide for the common defence, promote the general welfare, and secure the blessings of liberty for ourselves and our posterity.

We declare that this Republic can only endure as a free government while built upon the love of the people for each other and for the nation; that it cannot be pinned together by bayonets; that the Civil War is over, and that every passion and resentment which grew out of it must die with it, and that we must be in fact, as we are in name, one united brotherhood of free men.

Our country finds itself confronted by conditions for which there is no precedent in the history of the world; our annual agricultural productions amount to billions of dollars in value, which must, within a few weeks or months, be exchanged for billions of dollars' worth of commodities consumed in their production; the existing currency supply is wholly inadequate to make this exchange; the results are falling prices, the formation of combines and rings, the impoverishment of the producing class. We pledge ourselves that if given power we will labor to correct these evils by wise and reasonable legislation, in accordance with the terms of our platform.

We believe that the power of government—in other words, of the people—should be expanded (as in the case of the postal service) as rapidly and as far as the good sense of an intelligent people and the teachings of experience shall justify, to the end that oppression, injustice, and poverty shall eventually cease in the land.

While our sympathies as a party of reform are naturally upon the side of every proposition which will tend to make men intelligent, virtuous, and temperate we nevertheless regard these questions, important as they are, as secondary to the great issues now pressing for solution, and upon which not only our individual prosperity but the very existence of free institutions depend; and we ask all men to first help us to determine whether we are to have a republic to administer before we differ as to the conditions upon which it is to be administered, believing that the forces of reform this day organized will never cease to move forward until every wrong is righted and equal rights and equal privileges securely established for all the men and women of this country.

PLATFORM

We declare, therefore—

First.—That the union of the labor forces of the United States this day consummated shall be permanent and perpetual; may its spirit enter into all hearts for the salvation of the Republic and the uplifting of manking.

Second.—Wealth belongs to him who creates it, and every dollar taken from industry without an equivalent is robbery. "If any will not work, neither shall he eat." The interests of rural and civil labor are the same; their enemies are identical

Third.—We believe that the time has come when the railroad corporations will either own the people or the people must own the railroads; and should the government enter upon the work of owning and managing all railroads, we should favor an amendment to the constitution by which all persons engaged in the government service shall be placed under a civil-service regulation of the most rigid character, so as to prevent the increase of the power of the national administration by the use of such additional government employes.

Finance.—We demand a national currency, safe, sound, and flexible issued by the general government only, a full legal tender for all debts, public and private, and that without the use of banking corporations; a just, equitable, and efficient means of distribution direct to the people, at a tax not to exceed 2 per cent, per annum, to be provided as set forth in the sub-treasury plan of the Farmers' Alliance, or a better system; also by payments in discharge of its obligations for public improvements.

1. We demand free and unlimited coinage of silver and gold at the present legal ratio of 16 to 1.
2. We demand that the amount of circulating medium be speedily increased to not less than $50 per capita.
3. We demand a graduated income tax.
4. We believe that the money of the country should be kept as much as possible in the hands of the people, and hence we demand that all State and national revenues shall be limited to the necessary expenses of the government, economically and honestly administered.
5. We demand that postal savings banks be established by the government for the safe deposit of the earnings of the people and to facilitate exchange.

Transportation.—Transportation being a means of exchange and a public necessity, the government should own and operate the railroads in the interest of the people. The telegraph and telephone, like the post-office system, being a necessity for the transmission of news, should be owned and operated by the government in the interest of the people.

Land.—The land, including all the natural sources of wealth, is the heritage of the people, and should not be monopolized for speculative purposes, and alien ownership of land should be prohibited. All land now held by railroads and other corporations in excess of their actual needs, and all lands now owned by aliens should be reclaimed by the government and held for actual settlers only.

Expression of Sentiments

Your Committee on Platform and Resolutions beg leave unanimously to report the following:

Whereas, Other questions have been presented for our consideration, we hereby submit the following, not as a part of the Platform of the People's Party, but as resolutions expressive of the sentiment of this Convention.

1. Resolved, That we demand a free ballot and a fair count in all elections, and pledge ourselves to secure it to every legal voter without Federal intervention, through the adoption by the States of the unperverted Australian or secret ballot system.
2. Resolved, That the revenue derived from a graduated income tax should be applied to the reduction of the burden of taxation now levied upon the domestic industries of this country.
3. Resolved, That we pledge our support to fair and liberal pensions to ex-Union soldiers and sailors.
4. Resolved, That we condemn the fallacy of protecting American labor under the present system, which opens our ports to the pauper and criminal classes of the world and crowds out our wage-earners; and we denounce the present ineffective laws against contract labor, and demand the further restriction of undesirable emigration.
5. Resolved, That we cordially sympathize with the efforts of organized workingmen to shorten the hours of labor, and demand a rigid enforcement of the existing eight-hour law on Government work, and ask that a penalty clause be added to the said law.
6. Resolved, That we regard the maintenance of a large standing army of mercenaries, known as the Pinkerton system, as a menace to our liberties, and we demand its abolition; and we condemn the recent invasion of the Territory of Wyoming by the hired assassins of plutocracy, assisted by Federal officers.
7. Resolved, That we commend to the fa-

vorable consideration of the people and the reform press the legislative system known as the initiative and referendum.

8. Resolved, That we favor a constitutional provision limiting the office of President and Vice-President to one term, and providing for the election of Senators of the United States by a direct vote of the people.

9. Resolved, That we oppose any subsidy or national aid to any private corporation for any purpose.

10. Resolved, That this convention sympathizes with the Knights of Labor and their righteous contest with the tyrannical combine of clothing manufacturers of Rochester, and declare it to be a duty of all who hate tyranny and oppression to refuse to purchase the goods made by the said manufacturers, or to patronize any merchants who sell such goods.

DOCUMENT 22.7
The Cross of Gold*

William Jennings Bryan, contrary to legend, was never a Populist. A magnificent orator, he electrified the delegates to the Democratic National Convention of 1896 in Chicago with his famous "Cross of Gold" speech, one of the most famous public addresses in American history. The speech well summed up the frustrations and grievances of rural America. It was largely on the basis of this speech that the former Nebraska congressman was accorded the Democratic Party's nomination for the Presidency in 1896 against the strenuous opposition of conservative Democrats from the East. Bryan lost to Republican William McKinley in 1896. He was also unsuccessful in two other bids for the Presidency, as the candidate of the Democratic Party, in 1900 and 1908.

---

*Source: William Jennings Bryan, *The First Battle: A Story of the Campaign of 1896* (Chicago, 1896), pp. 199–206.

I would be presumptuous, indeed, to present myself against the distinguished gentlemen to whom you have listened if this were a mere measuring of abilities; but this is not a contest between persons. The humblest citizen in all the land, when clad in the armor of a righteous cause, is stronger than all the hosts of error. I came to speak to you in defense of a cause as holy as the cause of liberty—the cause of humanity.

When this debate is concluded, a motion will be made to lay upon the table the resolution offered in commendation of the administration, and also the resolution offered in condemnation of the administration. We object to bringing this question down to the level of persons. The individual is but an atom; he is born, he acts, he dies; but principles are eternal; and this has been a contest over a principle.

Never before in the history of this country has there been witnessed such a contest as that through which we have just passed. Never before, in the history of American politics has a great issue been fought out as this issue has been by the voters of a great party. On the fourth of March, 1895, a few Democrats, most of them members of Congress, issued an address to the Democrats of the nation, asserting that the money question was the paramount issue of the hour; declaring that a majority of the Democratic party had the right to control the action of the party on this paramount issue; and concluding with the request that the believers in the free coinage of silver in the Democratic party should organize, take charge of, and control the policy of the Democratic party. Three months later, at Memphis, an organization was perfected, and the silver Democrats went forth openly and courageously proclaiming their belief, and declaring that, if successful, they would crystallize into a platform the declaration which they had made. Then began the conflict. With a zeal approaching the zeal which inspired the Crusaders who followed Peter the Hermit, our silver Democrats went forth from victory unto victory until they are now assembled, not to discuss, not to debate, but to enter up the judgement already rendered by the plain people of this country. In this contest brother has been arrayed against brother, father against son. The warmest ties of love, acquaintance and association have been disregarded; old leaders have been cast aside when they have refused to give expression to the sentiments of those whom they would lead, and new leaders have sprung up to give direction to this cause of truth. Thus has the contest been waged, and we have assembled here under as binding and solemn instructions as were ever imposed upon representatives of the people.

We do not come as individuals. As individuals we might have been glad to compliment the gentleman from New York [Senator Hill], but we know that the people for whom we speak would never be willing to put him in a position where he could thwart the will of the Democratic party. I say it was not a question of persons; it was a question of principle, and it is not with gladness, my friends, that we find ourselves brought into conflict with those who are now arrayed on the other side.

The gentleman who preceded me [ex-Governor Russell] spoke of the State of Massachusetts; let me assure him that not one present in all this convention entertains the least hostility to the people of the State of Massachusetts, but we stand here representing the people who are the equals, before the law, of the greatest citizens in the State of Massachusetts. When you [turning to the gold delegates] come before us and tell us that we are about to disturb your business interests, we reply that you have disturbed our business interests by your course.

We say to you that you have made the definition of a business man too limited in its application. The man who is employed for wages is as much a business man as his employer, the attorney in a country town is as much a business man as the corporation counsel in a great metropolis; the merchant at the cross-roads store is as much a business man as the merchant of New York; the farmer who goes forth in the morning and toils all day—who begins in the spring and toils all summer—and who by the application of brain and muscle to the natural resources of the country creates wealth, is as much a business man as the man who goes upon the board of trade and bets upon the price of grain; the miners who go down a thousand feet into the earth, or climb two thousand feet upon the cliffs, and bring forth from their hiding places the precious metals to be poured into the channels of trade are as much business men as the few financial magnates who, in a back room, corner the money of the world. We come to speak for this broader class of business men.

Ah, my friends, we say not one word against those who live upon the Atlantic coast, but the hardy pioneers who have braved all the dangers of the wilderness, who have made the desert to blossom as the rose—the pioneers away out there [pointing to the West], who rear their children near to Nature's heart, where they can mingle their voices with the voices of the birds—out there where they have erected school houses for the education of their young, churches where they praise their Creator, and cemeteries where rest the ashes of their dead—these people, we say, are as deserving of the consideration of our party as any people in this country. It is for these that we speak. We do not come as aggressors. Our war is not a war of conquest; we are fighting in the defense of our homes, our families, and posterity. We have petitioned, and our petitions have been scorned; we have entreated, and our entreaties have been disregarded; we have begged, and they have mocked when our calamity came. We beg no longer; we petition no more. We defy them.

The gentleman from Wisconsin has said that he fears a Robespierre. My friends, in this land of the free you need not fear that a tyrant will spring up from among the people. What we need is an Andrew Jackson to stand, as Jackson stood, against the encroachments of organized wealth.

They tell us that this platform was made to catch votes. We reply to them that changing conditions make new issues; that the principles on which Democracy rests are as everlasting as the hills, but that they must be applied to new conditions as they arise. Conditions have arisen, and we are here to meet those conditions. They tell us that the income tax ought not be brought in here; that it is a new idea. They criticize us for our criticism of the Supreme Court of the United States. My friends, we have not criticized; we have simply called attention to what you already know. If you want criticisms, read the dissenting opinions of the court. There you will find criticisms. They say that we passed an unconstitutional law; we deny it. The income tax law was not unconstitutional when it was passed; it was not unconstitutional when it went before the Supreme Court for the first time; it did not become unconstitutional until one of the judges changed his mind, and we cannot be expected to know when a judge will change his mind. The income tax is just. It simply intends to put the burdens of government upon the backs of the people. I am in favor of an income tax. When I find a man who is not willing to bear his share of the burdens of the government which protects him, I find a man who is unworthy to enjoy the blessings of a government like ours.

They say that we are opposing national bank currency; it is true. If you will read what Thomas Benton said, you will find he said that, in searching history, he could find but one parallel to Andrew Jackson; that was Cicero, who destroyed the conspiracy of Cataline and saved Rome. Benton said that Cicero only did for Rome that Jackson did for us when he destroyed the bank conspiracy and saved America. We say in our platform that we believe that the right to coin and issue money is a function of government. We believe it. We believe that it is a part of sovereignty, and can no more with safety be delegated to private individuals than we could afford to delegate to private individuals the power to make penal statutes or levy taxes. Mr. Jefferson, who was once regarded as good Democratic authority, seems to have differed in opinion from the gentleman who has addrest us on the part of the minority. Those who are opposed to this proposition tell us, that the issue of paper money is a function of the bank, and that the Government ought to go out of the banking business. I stand with Jefferson rather than with them, and tell them, as he did, that the issue of money is a function of government, and that banks ought to go out of the governing business.

They complain about the plank which declares against life tenure in office. They have tried to strain it to mean that which it does not mean. What we oppose by that plank is the life tenure which is being built up in Washington, and which excludes from participation in official benefits the humbler members of society.

Let me call your attention to two or three important things. The gentleman from New York says that he will propose an amendment to the platform providing that the proposed change in our monetary system shall not affect contracts already made. Let me remind you that there is no intention of affecting those contracts which according to present laws are made payable in gold; but if he means to say that we cannot change our monetary system without protecting those who have loaned money before the change was made, I desire to ask him where, in law or in morals, he can find justification for not protecting the debtors when the act of 1873 was passed, if he now insists that we must protect the creditors.

He says he will also propose an amendment which will provide for the suspension of free coinage if we fail to maintain the parity within a year. We reply that when we advocate a policy which we believe will be successful, we are not compelled to raise a doubt as to our own sincerity by suggesting what we shall do if we fail. I ask him, if he would apply his logic to us, why he does not apply it to himself. He says he wants this country to try to secure an international agreement. Why does he not tell us what he is going to do if he fails to secure an international agreement? There is more reason for him to do that than there is for us to provide against the failure to maintain the parity. Our opponents have tried for twenty years to secure an international agreement, and those are waiting for it most patiently who do not want it at all.

And now, my friends, let me come to the paramount issue. If they ask us why it is that we say more on the money question than we say upon the tariff question, I reply that, if protection has slain its thousands, the gold standard has slain its tens of thousands. If they ask us why we do not embody in our platform all the things that we believe in, we reply that when we have restored the money of the Constitution all other necessary reforms will be possible; but that until this is done there is no other reform that can be accomplished.

Why is it that within three months such a change has come over the country? Three months ago, when it was confidently asserted that those who believe in the gold standard would frame our platform and nominate our candidates, even the advocates of the gold standard did not think that we could elect a President. And they had good reason for their doubt, because there is scarcely a State here today asking for the gold standard which is not in the absolute control of the Republican party. But note the change. Mr. McKinley was nominated at St. Louis upon a platform which declared for the maintenance of the gold standard until it can be changed into bimetalism by international agreement. Mr. McKinley was the most popular man among the Republicans, and three months ago everybody in the Republican party prophesied his election. How is it to-day? Why, the man who was once pleased to think that he looked like Napoleon—that man shudders to-day when he remembers that he was nominated on the anniversary of the battle of Waterloo. Not only that, but as he listens he can hear with ever-increasing distinctness the sounds of the waves as they beat upon the lonely shores of St. Helena.

Why this change? Ah, my friends, is not the reason for the change evident to any one who will look at the matter? No private character, however pure, no personal popularity, nowever great, can protect from the avenging wrath of an indignant people a man who will declare that he is in favor of fastening the gold standard upon this country, or who is willing to surrender the right of self-government and place the legislative control of our affairs in the hands of foreign potentates and powers.

We go forth confident that we shall win. Why? Because upon the paramount issue of this campaign there is not a spot of ground upon which the enemy will dare to challenge battle. If they tell us that the gold standard is a good thing, we shall point to their platform and tell them that their platform pledges the party to get rid of the gold standard and substitute bimetalism. If the gold standard is a good thing, why try to get rid of it? I call your attention to the fact that some of the very people who are in this convention today and who tell us that we ought to declare in favor of international bimetalism—thereby declaring that the gold standard is wrong and that the principle of bimetalism is better—these very people four months ago were open and avowed advocates of the gold standard, and were then telling us that we could not legislate two metals together, even with the aid of all the world. If the gold standard is a good thing, we ought to declare in favor of its retention and not in favor of abandoning it; and if the gold standard is a bad thing, why should we wait until other nations are willing to help us to let go? Here is the line of battle, and we care not upon which issue they force the fight; we are prepared to meet them on either issue or on both. If they tell us that the gold standard is the standard of civilization, we reply to them that this, the most enlightened of all the nations of the earth, has never declared for a gold standard and that both the great parties this year are declaring against it. If the gold standard is the standard of civilization, why, my friends, should we not have it? If they come to meet us on that issue we can present the history of our nation. More than that; we can tell them that they will search the pages of history in vain to find a single instance where the common people have ever declared themselves in favor of the gold standard. They can find where the holders of fixt investments have declared for a gold standard, but not where the masses have.

Mr. Carlisle said in 1878 that this was a struggle between "the idle holders of idle capital" and "the struggling masses, who produce the wealth and pay the taxes of the country"; and, my friends, the question we are to decide is: Upon which side will the Democratic party fight; upon the side of "the struggling masses"? That is the question which the party must answer first, and then it must be answered by each individual hereafter. The sympathies of the Democratic party, as shown by the platform, are on the side of the struggling masses who have ever been the foundation of the Democratic party. There are two ideas of government. There are those who believe that, if you will only legislate to make the well-to-do prosperous, their prosperity will leak through on those below. The Democratic idea, however, has been that if you legislate to make the masses prosperous, their prosperity will find its way up through every class which rests upon them.

You come to us and tell us that the great cities are in favor of the gold stan-

dard; we reply that the great cities rest upon our broad and fertile prairies. Burn down your cities and leave our farms, and your cities will spring up again as if by magic; but destroy our farms and the grass will grow in the streets of every city in the country.

My friends, we declare that this nation is able to legislate for its own people on every question, without waiting for the aid or consent of any other nation on earth; and upon that issue we expect to carry every State in the Union. I shall not slander the inhabitants of the fair State of Massachusetts nor the inhabitants of the State of New York by saying that, when they are confronted with the proposition, they will declare that this nation is not able to attend to its own business. It is the issue of 1776 over again. Our ancestors, when but three millions in number, had the courage to declare their political independence of every other nation; shall we, their descendants, when we have grown to seventy millions, declare that we are less independent than our forefathers? No, my friends, that will never be the verdict of our people. Therefore we care not upon what lines the battle is fought. If they say bimetalism is good, but that we cannot have it until the other nations help us, we reply that, instead of having a gold standard because England has, we will restore bimetalism, and then let England have bimetalism because the United States has it. If they dare to come out in the open field and defend the gold standard as a good thing, we will fight them to the uttermost. Having behind us the producing masses of this nation and the world, supported by the commercial interests, the laboring interests, and the toilers everywhere, we will answer their demand for a gold standard by saying to them: You shall not press down upon the brow of labor this crown of thorns, you shall not crucify mankind upon a cross of gold.

DOCUMENT 22.8

Tom Watson Speaks for the Negro*

Tom Watson, a Georgia congressman, was a new Jeffersonian at odds with his state's Democratic bourbon leadership. In his successful campaign for Congress on the Farmer's Alliance program in 1890, he denounced the "vampires" of Wall Street, proclaimed his Populist views, and was elected by the votes of both blacks and whites. Later in his career, after the turn of the century, Watson gave up his advocacy of Negro rights and became an archetypal southern demagogue.

The key to the new political movement called the People's Party has been that the Democratic farmer was as ready to leave the Democratic ranks as the Republican farmer was to leave the Republican ranks. In exact proportion as the West received the assurance that the South was ready for a new party, it has moved. In exact proportion to the proof we could bring that the West had broken Republican ties, the South has moved. *Without* a decided break in both sections, neither would move. *With* that decided break, both moved.

The very same principle governs the race question in the South. The two races can never act together permanently, harmoniously, beneficially, till each race demonstrates to the other a readiness to leave old party affiliations and to form new ones, based upon the profound conviction that, in acting together, both races are seeking new laws which will benefit both. On no other basis under heaven can the "Negro Question" be solved.

Now, suppose that the colored man were educated upon these questions just as the whites have been; suppose he were shown that his poverty and distress came

*Source: Thomas E. Watson, "The Negro Question in the South," *Arena*, Vol. VI (1892), pp. 545–50.

from the same sources as ours; suppose we should convince him that our platform principles assure him an escape from the ills he now suffers, and guarantee him the fair measure of prosperity his labor entitles him to receive,—would he not act just as the white Democrat who joined us did? Would he not abandon a party which ignores him as a farmer and laborer; which offers him no benefits of an equal and just financial system: which promises him no relief from oppressive taxation; which assures him of no legislation which will enable him to obtain a fair price for his produce?

Granting to him the same selfishness common to us all; granting him the intelligence to know what is best for him and the desire to attain it, why would he not act from that motive just as the white farmer has done?

That he would do so, is as certain as any future event can be made. Gratitude may fail; so may sympathy and friendship and generosity and patriotism; but in the long run, self-interest *always* controls. Let it once appear plainly that it is to the interest of a colored man to vote with the white man, and he will do it. Let it plainly appear that it is to the interest of the white man that the vote of the Negro should supplement his own, and the question of having that ballot freely cast and fairly counted, becomes vital to the *white man*. He will see that it is done.

Now let us illustrate: Suppose two tenants on my farm; one of them white, the other black. They cultivate their crops under precisely the same conditions. Their labors, discouragements, burdens, grievances, are the same.

The white tenant is driven by cruel necessity to examine into the causes of his continued destitution. He reaches certain conclusions which are not complimentary to either of the old parties. He leaves the Democracy in angry disgust. He joins the People's Party. Why? Simply because its platform recognizes that he is badly treated and proposes to fight his battle. Necessity drives him from the old party, and hope leads him into the new. In plain English, he joins the organization whose declaration of principles is in accord with his conception of what he needs and justly deserves.

Now go back to the colored tenant. His surroundings being the same and his interests the same, why is it impossible for him to reach the same conclusions? Why is it unnatural for him to go into the new party at the same time and with the same motives?

Cannot these two men act together in peace when the ballot of the one is a vital benefit to the other? Will not political friendship be born of the necessity and the hope which is common to both? Will not race bitterness disappear before this common suffering and this mutual desire to escape it? Will not each of these citizens feel more kindly for the other when the vote of each defends the home of both? If the white man becomes convinced that the Democratic Party has played upon his prejudices, and has used his quiescence to the benefit of interests adverse to his own, will he not despise the leaders who seek to perpetuate the system?

The People's Party will settle the race question. First, by enacting the Australian ballot system. Second, by offering to white and black a rallying point which is free from the odium of former discords and strifes. Third, by presenting a platform immensely beneficial to both races and injurious to neither. Fourth, by making it to the *interest* of both races to act together for the success of the platform. Fifth, by making it to the *interest* of the colored man to have the same patriotic zeal for the welfare of the South that the whites possess.

Now to illustrate. Take two planks of the People's Party platform: that pledging a free ballot under the Australian system and that which demands a distribution of currency to the people upon pledges of land, cotton, etc.

The guaranty as to the vote will suit the black man better than the Republican platform, because the latter contemplates Federal interference, which will lead to collisions and bloodshed. The Democratic platform contains no comfort to the Negro, because, while it denounces the Republican programme, as usual, it promises nothing which can be specified. It is a generality which does not even possess the virtue of being "glittering."

The People's Party, however, not only condemns Federal interference with elections, but also distinctly commits itself to the method by which every citizen shall have his constitutional right to the free exercise of his electoral choice. We pledge ourselves to isolate the voter from all coercive influences and give him the free and fair exercise of his franchise under state laws.

Now couple this with the financial plank which promises equality in the distribution of the national currency, at low rates of interest.

The white tenant lives adjoining the colored tenant. Their houses are almost equally destitute of comforts. Their living is confined to bare necessities. They are equally burdened with heavy taxes. They pay the same high rent for gullied and impoverished land.

They pay the same enormous prices for farm supplies. Christmas finds them both without any satisfactory return for a year's toil. Dull and heavy and unhappy, they both start the plows again when "New Year's" passes.

Now the People's Party says to these two men, "You are kept apart that you may be separately fleeced of your earnings. You are made to hate each other because upon that hatred is rested the keystone of the arch of financial despotism which enslaves you both. You are deceived and blinded that you may not see how this race antagonism perpetuates a monetary system which beggars both."

This is so obviously true it is no wonder both these unhappy laborers stop to listen. No wonder they begin to realize that no change of law can benefit the white tenant which does not benefit the black one likewise; that no system which now does injustice to one of them can fail to injure both. Their every material interest is identical. The moment this becomes a conviction, mere selfishness, the mere desire to better their conditions, escape onerous taxes, avoid usurious charges, lighten their rents, or change their precarious tenements into smiling, happy homes, will drive these two men together, just as their mutually inflamed prejudices now drive them apart.

Suppose these two men now to have become fully imbued with the idea that their material welfare depends upon the reforms we demand. Then they act together to secure them. Every white reformer finds it to the vital interst of his home, his family, his fortune, to see to it that the vote of the colored reformer is freely cast and fairly counted.

Then what? Every colored voter will be thereafter a subject of industrial education and political teaching.

Concede that in the final event, a colored man will vote where his material interests of farmers, croppers, and laborers; concede that under full and fair discussion the people can be depended upon to ascertain where their interests lie—and we reach the conclusion that the Southern race question can be solved by the People's Party on the simple proposition that each race will be led by self-interest to support that which benefits it, when so presented that neither is hindered by the bitter party antagonisms of the past.

Let the colored laborer realize that our platform gives him a better guaranty for political independence; for a fair return for his work; a better chance to buy a home and keep it; a better chance to educate his children and see them profitably employed; a better chance to have public life freed from race collisions; a better chance for every citizen to be considered as a *citizen* regardless of color in the making and enforcing of laws,—let all this be fully realized, and the race question at the South will have settled itself through the evolution of a political movement in which both whites and blacks recognize their surest way out of wretchedness into comfort and independence.

The illustration could be made quite as clearly from other planks in the People's Party platform. On questions of land, transportation and finance, especially, the welfare of the two races so clearly depends upon that which benefits either, that intelligent discussion would necessarily lead to just conclusions.

Why should the colored man always be taught that the white man of his neighborhood hates him, while a Northern man, who taxes every rag on his back, loves him? Why should not my tenant come to regard me as his friend rather than the manufacturer who plunders us both? Why should we perpetuate a policy which drives the black man into the arms of the Northern politician?

Why should we always allow Northern and Eastern Democrats to enslave us forever by threats of the Force Bill?

Let us draw the supposed teeth of this fabled dragon by founding our new policy upon justice—upon the simple but profound truth that, if the voice of passion can be hushed, the self-interest of both races will drive them to act in concert. There never was a day during the last twenty years when the South could not have flung the money power into the dust by patiently teaching the Negro that we could not be wretched under any system which would not afflict him likewise; that we could not prosper under any law which would not also bring its blessings to him.

To the emasculated individual who cries "Negro supremacy!" there is little to be said. His cowardice shows him to be a degeneration from the race which has never yet feared any other race. Existing under such conditions as they now do in this country, there is no earthly chance for Negro domination, unless we are ready to admit that the colored man is our superior in will power, courage, and intellect.

Not being prepared to make any such

admission in favor of any race the sun ever shone on, I have no words which can portray my contempt for the white men, Anglo-Saxons, who can knock their knees together, and through their chattering teeth and pale lips admit that they are afraid the Negroes will "dominate us."

The question of social equality does not enter into the calculation at all. That is a thing each citizen decides for himself. No statute ever yet drew the latch of the humblest home—or ever will. Each citizen regulates his own visting list—and always will.

The conclusion, then, seems to me to be this: the crushing burdens which now oppress both races in the South will cause each to make an effort to cast them off. They will see a similarity of cause and a similarity of remedy. They will recognize that each should help the other in the work of repealing bad laws and enacting good ones. They will become political allies, and neither can injure the other without weakening both. It will be to the interest of both that each should have justice. And on these broad lines of mutual interest, mutual forbearance, and mutual support the present will be made the stepping-stone to future peace and prosperity.

23 American Imperialism

NORMAN A. GRAEBNER
University of Virginia

Contemporaries sensed—and historians have since agreed—that 1898 was a turning point in the history of the American republic. The events of that year, culminating in Commodore George Dewey's victory at Manila, ushered the United States onto the international stage as a world power. Yet neither the concept of world power nor that of national expansion represented anything new or unique in the nation's history. Significant changes in a country's power position never occur overnight. From the moment of its birth the United States had been a world power, a nation important enough to influence the decisions of the great nations of Europe. During the 19th century, especially after the American Civil War, Europe's leaders recognized increasingly that the United States had become the equal of the traditional powers in its ability to sustain a war.

To be sure, acquisition of the Philippine Islands was a clear departure from established national precedent. If expansion had been a recurrent concern of the American people, it had been limited to regions contiguous to the United States. The only exception had been Alaska. With the annexation of the Philippines, the nation abandoned for the first time its strategy of hemispheric isolation in favor of a major strategic commitment in the western Pacific. Also, for the first time, the United States established its sovereignty over territories that were never intended for self-government under the aegis of the U.S. Constitution. Instead, the Philippine population, ethnically and culturally remote from American society, was destined from the beginning for the imposition of minority white rule.

What mattered in the events of 1898 was not that the United States had become a world power or an imperialistic nation but that, in acquiring the Philippine Islands, it had deserted those principles of statecraft which had determined important decisions throughout the previous century. The defiance of diplomatic tradition lay in the determination of American officials to anchor the nation's imperialistic behavior to abstract moral principles rather than to the political wisdom of the past. Neither war against Spain nor acquisition of the Philippines resulted from any recognizable or clearly enunciated national interest. They emanated, rather, from a sense of moral obligation. In a large measure the critical decisions of 1898 were totally incompatible with assumptions and methods upon which earlier generations of Americans had attempted to defend the national interest abroad. For this reason, they inaugurated a new age for the United States in world affairs.

American diplomacy prior to 1898 had been rooted firmly in the realistic tradition of the modern world. It had followed the precepts of President George Washington expressed in 1795: "In every act of my ad-

112

ministration I have sought the happiness of my fellow citizens. My system for the attainment of this objective has uniformly been to overlook all personal, local, and partial consideration; to contemplate the United States as one great whole, . . . and to consult only the substantial and permanent interest of our country." In 1796, in his farewell address, he warned the nation to expect no more of others, declaring that "it is a maxim, founded on the universal experience of mankind, that no nation is to be trusted further than it is bound by its interest; and no prudent statesman or politician will venture to depart from it."

Of necessity, those who believed that American policy abroad should seek fulfillment of the nation's democratic mission challenged Washington's realistic position. During the debates on the French alliance in 1793 and 1794, the Greek revolt of the early 1820s, and the European revolutions of 1848, American idealists pleaded that the United States underwrite the cause of liberty abroad. But without exception, these pleas emanated from men who had no direct responsibility for American action. Their appeals to idealism generally had less a diplomatic purpose overseas than a political purpose at home. The energy and determination with which every administration, including that of Grover Cleveland, countered all pressures to involve the nation in humanitarian movements abroad measured the true depth of the country's tradition of realism. The Spanish-American War of 1898 shattered this 19th-century tradition of diplomacy.

Historians generally agree that the United States had no legitimate cause for declaring war against Spain. The Spanish government had recognized its failure in Cuba and was doing all within its power, short of granting independence, to relieve conditions on the island. Conscious of their complete incapacity to wage a successful war, Spanish officials sought to avoid open conflict with the United States; they moved as rapidly as Spanish opinion

would permit to meet American demands. But the "yellow press" of the United States insistently clamored for war, especially after the destruction of the *Maine* in Havana harbor. The conviction of most Republican editors and politicians that Cuban liberty was popular and just mobilized both the G.O.P. majority in Congress and the McKinley administration behind the clamor for action. Warning the Republican leadership that Democratic ambition would permit no postponement of the decision to intervene in Cuba, the *Chicago Times-Herald* declared: "Let President McKinley hesitate to rise to the just expectation of the American people, and who can doubt that 'war for Cuban liberty' will be the crown of thorns that Free Silver Democrats and Populists will adopt at the elections this fall. . . . The President would be powerless to stay any legislation, however ruinous to every sober honest interest of the country." Two days after President William McKinley learned of the Spanish government's extensive concessions to his demands, he nonetheless permitted the Congress to decide the whole question, knowing full well it would vote for war.

Few Americans justified the Spanish-American War in terms of the security and well-being of the United States. Theodore Roosevelt observed in his *Autobiography:* "Our own interests [in Cuba] were great. . . . But even greater were our interests from the standpoint of humanity. Cuba was at our very doors. It was a dreadful thing for us to sit supinely and watch her death agony." Walter Hines Page termed the war "a necessary act of surgery for the health of civilization." To Senator John T. Morgan, the United States had been drawn into the war by a sense of humanity and the "duty we owe to Christian civilization." That the United States achieved its initial goal of freeing Cuba and thus fulfilled its great moral purpose at little national expense merely confirmed the growing conviction that policy anchored primarily to national interest was no longer legitimate for a nation so fortunate in its institutions and so militarily and economically powerful.

Traditional political considerations played no greater role in the decision to acquire the Philippines than in the declaration of war itself. If the solemnly declared purpose of the war did not transcend the simple liberation of Cuba, even this limited objective necessitated some degree of military victory over Spain. To destroy Spanish sea power in the Pacific and thereby protect American commerce, the administration ordered Commodore Dewey to Manila Bay. On May 1, 1898, he destroyed the Spanish squadron anchored there with loss of but one American life—through a heat stroke. No one suspected this victory would lead to the acquisition of the Philippines except, perhaps, a few administration zealots. Most Americans thought the problems of order and security in the Islands sufficient to demand the American expeditionary force which occupied Manila in August.

This sudden employment of U.S. naval power in the distant Pacific and the possibilities it held for empire building were not lost on a powerful minority of American expansionists. The dramatic events of 1898 followed a logic of their own; but they could not be divorced, at least in the expansionist mind, from the increasing American involvement in the Pacific. The foundation of this concern was commercial. On foundations generously constructed in wartime, American businessmen after 1865 quickly pushed the nation's industrial capacity beyond domestic demands. Indeed, their optimism in railroad and industrial construction led to such perennial overbuilding that it tumbled the national economy into periodic depressions, the worst two blanketing the years 1873–78 and 1893–97. Each depression stimulated further business consolidation, but it also demonstrated the need for foreign markets if the economy was ever to perform at full capacity again. Those charged with the conduct of U.S.

foreign relations accepted the challenge to encourage American commercial expansion.

In developing their overseas strategy, American leaders were careful to direct official policy toward the quest for markets and not the acquisition of islands. Secretary of State James G. Blaine emphasized this distinction between trade and annexation in a remarkable statement of August 1890:

I wish to declare the opinion that the United States has reached a point where one of its highest duties is to enlarge the area of its foreign trade. Under the beneficent policy of protection we have developed a volume of manufactures which, in many departments, overruns the demands of the home market. . . . Our great demand is expansion. I mean expansion of trade with countries where we can find profitable exchanges. We are not seeking annexation of territory.

Still, the actual penetration of the Pacific by American merchants, sea captains, and naval officers had long confronted Washington with a variety of specific policy challenges, some political as well as economic. New opportunities for easy annexations, which neither Republican nor Democratic administrations cared to ignore, produced, in the early nineties, the new philosophy of *strategic bases*. President Benjamin Harrison recorded the pressures of the Pacific on official opinion when he wrote to Blaine in October 1891: "You know I am not much of an annexationist; though I do feel that in some directions, as to naval stations and points of influence, we must look forward to a departure from the too conservative opinions which have been held heretofore." The Harrison administration concerned itself specifically with Samoa and Hawaii; it succeeded in annexing neither. This administration, however, committed the United States to the creation of a large navy to protect its expanding interests around the world.

During the depressed nineties, spokesmen of the conservative Cleveland administration perpetuated the distinction between the country's need for enlarged markets and the dangers involved in the acquisition of insular possessions. Secretary of State Walker Q. Gresham readily acknowledged in 1894 the need for expanded markets. Opposed to the annexation of Pacific islands, he suggested that the United States negotiate for coaling stations which would give it commercial advantages without involving it in dangerous military and political responsibilities. Carl Schurz, the noted Republican, accepted this formula in a significant essay which appeared in *Harper's New Monthly Magazine,* October 1893: "There is little doubt that we can secure by amicable negotiation sites for coaling stations which will serve us as well as if we possessed the countries in which they are situated. In the same manner we can obtain . . . all sorts of commercial advantages . . . without assuming any responsibilities. . . ."

Richard Olney, who succeeded Gresham in 1895, shared his predecessor's preferences for trade expansion through limited commercial arrangements. But he later concluded that the decisions of 1898 and 1899, which included the annexation of Hawaii and a settlement with Germany regarding Samoa, had been in response to changes slowly accumulating throughout the nineties. Writing in 1904, he observed that the American people had long recognized that their commercial needs required "free access to all markets; that to secure such access the nation must be formidable not merely in its wants and wishes and latent capabilities but in the means at hand wherewith to readily exert and enforce them." Such demands for markets and prestige in themselves suggested no precise actions of government which might guarantee their achievement. That the spokesmen for the nation's business wanted enlarged foreign markets was beyond question. Governmental officials recognized both the need and the desire of industry to have them. Still, it seems clear that trade expansion received little encouragement from the actual policies the government pursued and that the pressure for markets had at best a generalized, not a specific, influence on American territorial expansion into the Pacific.

Unlike Samoa and Hawaii, the Spanish Philippines had of necessity remained off limits to imperialist ambitions. Against the immediate background of the nation's varied interests in the Pacific, however, the reduction of Spanish power in the Islands confronted the United States with an unanticipated dilemma. What was to be the disposition of the Islands, now largely in American hands? Doubts and confusion within the administration were profound, for prior to Dewey's naval victory no organized sentiment for the acquisition of any portion of the Philippine archipelago existed at all. Finley Peter Dunne's Mr. Dooley remarked that the American people "did not know whether the Philippines were islands or canned goods." President McKinley himself had to resort to a globe to discover their location; he could not, he admitted, have described their position within 2,000 miles! *The New York Times* reported on May 16 that "neither in the White House nor the State Department is there any definite conviction or determination concerning the future direction of the national policy with respect to the disposal of those oversea possessions, over which the Americal flag will be flying when the war is over."

But the nation's mood, excited by persuasive arguments of a small but determined group of Republican expansionists and by dreams of empire, increasingly accepted the inevitability of acquiring the Philippines. The philosopher William James sensed the changing national spirit. In June 1898, he acknowledged a genuine sincerity in the American effort to base policy on philanthropic duty, but he also warned that

once the excitement of action gets loose, the taxes levied, the victories achieved . . . the old human instincts will get into play with all their old strength, and the ambition and sense of mastery which our nation has will set up new demands. . . . We had supposed ourselves . . . a better nation than the rest, safe at home, and without the old savage ambition, destined to exert great international influence by throwing in our "moral weight". . . . Dreams! Human Nature is everywhere the same; and at the least temptation all the old military passions rise, and sweep everything before them.

The perceptive James knew whereof he spoke, for during the summer months of 1898, imperialist sentiment rolled across the nation, capturing the support of newspaper editors and businessmen who wanted nothing less than the retention of Manila, which, according to Senator Henry Cabot Lodge, was "the thing which will give us the Eastern trade."

Slowly, a national policy emerged. At the end of July 1898, President McKinley, responding to expansionist pressure, announced that any truce with Spain must stipulate that the United States continue to occupy Manila until the conclusion of a treaty. Then, on September 16, the administration clarified its intentions more precisely in its instructions to the peace commissioners. The President wrote:

Without any original thought of complete or even partial acquisition, the presence and success of our arms at Manila imposes upon us obligations which we cannot disregard. The march of events rules and over-rules human action. . . . We cannot be unmindful that without any desire or design on our part the war has brought us new duties and responsibilities which we must meet and discharge as becomes a great nation on whose growth and career from the beginning the Ruler of Nations had plainly written the high command and pledge of civilization.

Except for a vague suggestion that American responsibility and interests might require a cession of the island of Luzon, the President assigned to the American commissioners in Paris the task of determining the actual terms of the treaty with Spain.

The commissioners, unable to agree among themselves, sought the advice of officers knowledgeable in Far Eastern affairs. William R. Day, recently Secretary of State, believed retention of Luzon, Mindoro, and Palawan sufficient for a naval base; but strategically, it appeared inescapable that the United States acquire either the entire archipelago or no portion of it. Although Senator George Gray, the lone Democratic member of the commission, opposed any acquisitions in the Philippines, the majority favored the retention of all the Islands. With this decision, McKinley eventually concurred.

That the United States perhaps acquired the Philippines reluctantly does not mean it lacked freedom of choice. But that freedom had literally become extinguished with the initial decision to conquer the Islands. Once liberated, their restoration to Spain would have defied the will of the vast majority of Filipinos. Clearly, the Islands lacked the power and resources to sustain their own independence; to cast them adrift seemed nothing less than a total negation of responsibility. The order to destroy Spanish authority in Manila was crucial. Thereafter, all avenues of escape from a self-imposed dilemma appeared closed. Like the Spanish-American War itself, the ultimate decision to annex the Islands was then rationalized in terms of humanitarianism. There was no alternative, President McKinley is said to have explained to a group of visiting clergymen, "but to take them all, and to educate the Filipinos, and uplift and Christianize them, and by God's grace do the very best we could by them, as our fellowmen, for whom Christ also died. . . ."

Opponents of expansion—and they were legion—placed powerful intellectual obstacles in the path of the imperialists. Any acquisition of territory in the Philippine archipelago, they held, would defy the spirit of both the Declaration of Independence and the Constitution. Neither of these documents, they said, provided for the government of peoples not designated for statehood. Nor was it clear how the American people could assimilate a population that was so racially and culturally different. If granted political equality, the Filipinos would merely corrupt the American democratic system. Secretary of State John Hay, who had warmly supported "the splendid little war," told McKinley in August 1898 that "the more I hear about the state of the Tagalog population and their leaders the more I am convinced of the seriousness of the task which would devolve upon us if we made ourselves permanently responsible for them."

Even more sobering was the observation that the Philippines were so distant, exposed, and defenseless that they would constitute a hostage which other world powers could employ in bargaining with the American government. Senator Alexander Clay of Georgia put his colleagues on notice of the price which might be exacted of the nation for its new involvement in the Far East:

We want no complications or war with England, France, Germany, Russia, China, Japan, or any other foreign power. We want no territory or population liable and likely to involve us in complications which may lead to war with any of these powers. The danger of frequent and almost constant wars between foreign nations in the Far East . . . should be a warning against the acquisition of this foreign territory and population. . . . The United States has heretofore been solid, compact, contiguous, and impregnable. . . . When we go out into the seas beyond the Western Hemisphere and acquire other countries, we increase our responsibilities, weaken our defenses, and enormously increase the expenses of our Army and Navy. We must not come to the conclusion because we destroyed the Spanish fleets, that we could so easily cope with the navies of the European powers.

For most Americans and even members of Congress, such warnings passed unnoticed. So remote were the burdens of empire that many assumed that the acquisition of the Philippines actually strengthened the nation.

Yet, unless the Islands themselves possessed sources of power which equaled or exceeded that required for their defense, they would become a strategic liability. As the English *Saturday Review* saw it, the new American commitment in the Far East was so extensive that the reliance of the United States on British naval power was greater than ever before. Thereafter, London officials would expect the United States to deal generously with Canada on the matter of tariffs and to support the British in the approaching conflict over China occasioned by European encroachment and rivalry. The United States, declared the *Review*, had a growing need for a stout friend, namely, Great Britain.

U.S. policy in 1898 extended the Monroe Doctrine to the western Pacific and thereby destroyed the nation's traditional isolation from the Eastern Hemisphere. Only the ridiculously easy victory over the Spanish squadron at Manila obscured the magnitude of the new obligations. The Islands were acquired so painlessly that the strategic commitment involved scarcely disturbed American isolationist habits of mind. For this challenge to the national behavior, no obvious precedent existed in the American experience. The political wisdom of the past, which had guarded carefully the concept of limited objectives and limited power, had been forgotten. After the events of 1898, it would become increasingly difficult for American officials to employ the nation's 19th-century tradition in their perennial efforts to carry out policy. Occasional warnings that the United States possessed neither the required naval forces to maintain an empire nor the intention of building them were largely ignored. The suddenness and completeness of the changes wrought by expansion measured the extent to which illusions emanating from easy success had supplanted analysis in the conduct of the nation's external affairs.

What was especially disturbing to thoughtful Americans at the turn of the century was the widespread conviction that victory would always reward the nation's effort abroad. Senator George

Turner of the state of Washington pointed disapprovingly at the "vain and boastful spirit which seems to be abroad in the land, that we of this day and age and generation are entirely sufficient unto ourselves; that there are no problems which we can not solve unaided; that there is no danger which it is not cowardly and un-American for us to fear." No longer did it appear essential that American leadership obey the principles of the past that ends be limited by means and that the long-term interests of the nation be defined in a coherent fashion. If the United States had experienced success in the past at no inordinate cost, it would continue to do so.

This baseless assumption that American will was unlimited underlay the promulgation of the open door policy toward China in the summer of 1900. The McKinley administration's intention to oppose any moves by the European powers to restrict permanently the commerce of China and to endanger that nation's territorial integrity appeared feasible enough. And the magnificent undertaking of saving China from dismemberment—through mere circulation of the famous first open door notes, to which all interested European powers gave their equivocal approval—merely intensified the illusion that great achievements abroad required little but the proper motivation. Ignoring the skepticism of other countries, the American press hailed the open door policy as one of the most brilliant diplomatic achievements in the nation's history. For the Republican leadership, facing an election year, it was highly welcome. The bold stroke in China satisfied the demand for protection of American commercial interests. Moreover, by guaranteeing Chinese rights against foreign encroachment, it supported the cause of freedom.

As had happened with regard to the Philippines in 1898, the American policy toward China overlooked the enormity of the resulting commitment. In the Boxer Rebellion crisis, China was "saved" less by American intention than by the rivalries of the European forces. Despite the momentary success of American leadership in sustaining the Manchu empire, it was soon clear to Secretary Hay, with whose name the open door was identified, that the United States was not prepared to defend Chinese political and territorial integrity with force. In the wake of the Boxer Rebellion, Hay was confronted by a series of Russian maneuvers in Manchuria which clearly defied the open door principle. The Secretary began to recognize the fallacy of building policy on high-minded declarations alone. "The talk of the papers about our 'pre-eminent moral position giving us the authority to dictate to the world,'" he observed, "is mere flapdoodle." Yet, for Hay, there was no avenue of retreat. To the popular mind, his concept of the open door appeared so laudable in objective and so sound in precept that no later administration dared retract it.

Thus, in the Fourth-of-July atmosphere of the closing years of the 19th century, the United States entered an age of overcommitment in the Far East. In the long run, the acquisition of the Philippines and the open door in China could prove disastrous. The Japanese assault on Manchuria in 1931 and the subsequent war in the Pacific demonstrated the ultimate price that must be paid for sustaining imperial designs with appeals to humanitarian sentiment rather than precise assessments of the national interest. From the beginning, both the Philippines and China rendered the nation vulnerable; both regions lay across the Pacific in a vast area where other powers deployed greater military strength than did the United States. It was only the temporary absence of any direct challenge to these distant commitments that permitted the United States to escape for a long generation the normal penalty of creating ends of policy without sufficient consideration of means.

SUGGESTED READINGS

BEISNER, ROBERT L. *Twelve Against Empire: The Anti-Imperialists, 1898–1900.* New York: McGraw-Hill Book Co., 1968.

Dennis, A.L.P. *Adventures in American Diplomacy, 1866–1906.* New York: E.P. Dutton & Co., 1928.

Dulles, Foster Rhea. *The Imperial Years.* New York: Thomas Y. Crowell Co., 1956.

Griswold, A. Whitney. *The Far Eastern Policy of the United States.* New York: Harcourt, Brace & Co., 1938.

Healy, David F. *The United States in Cuba, 1898–1902: Generals, Politicans, and the Search for Policy.* Madison: University of Wisconsin Press, 1963.

Kennan, George F. *American Diplomacy, 1900–1950.* Chicago: University of Chicago Press, 1951.

La Feber, Walter. *The New Empire: An Interpretation of American Expansion, 1860–1898.* Ithaca, N.Y.: Cornell University Press, 1963.

May, Ernest R. *Imperial Democracy.* New York: Harcourt, Brace & World, Inc., 1961.

Millis, Walter. *The Martial Spirit.* Boston: Houghton Mifflin Co., 1931.

Pratt, Julius W. *The Expansionists of 1898.* Baltimore: Johns Hopkins Press, 1936.

Varg, Paul A. *Open Door Diplomat: The Life of W. W. Rockhill.* Urbana: University of Illinois Press, 1952.

Williams, William A. *The Tragedy of American Diplomacy.* Cleveland: World Publishing Co., 1959.

Wisan, J. E. *The Cuban Crisis as Reflected in the New York Press, 1895–1898.* New York: Columbia University Press, 1934.

DOCUMENT 23.1

The Anglo-Saxon and the World's Future*

Josiah Strong, a gifted young Congregational minister, was secretary of his denomination's Home Missionary Society. A leading religious journalist, he also was a pioneer in the social gospel movement. The selection below is characteristic of his belief in the future destiny and God-given "mission" of the United States.

Every race which has deeply impressed itself on the human family has been the representative of some great idea—one or more—which has given direction to the nation's life and form to its civilization. . . . The Anglo-Saxon is the representative of two great ideas, which are closely related. One of them is that of civil liberty. . . . The noblest races have always been lovers of liberty. That love ran strong in early German blood, and has profoundly influenced the institutions of all the branches of the great German family; but it was left for the Anglo-Saxon branch fully to recognize the right of the individual to himself, and formally to declare it the foundation stone of government.

The other great idea of which the Anglo-Saxon is the exponent is that of a pure *spiritual* Christianity. . . .

It is not necessary to argue to those for whom I write that the two great needs of mankind, that all men may be lifted up into the light of the highest Christian civilization, are, first, a pure, spiritual Christianity, and, second, civil liberty. Without controversy, these are the forces which, in the past, have contributed most to the elevation of the human race, and they must continue to be, in the future, the most efficient ministers to its progress. It follows, then, that the Anglo-Saxon, as the great representative of these two ideas, the depositary of these two greatest blessings, sustains peculiar relations to the world's future, is divinely commissioned to be, in a peculiar sense, his brother's keeper. Add to this the fact of his rapidly increasing strength in modern times, and we have well nigh a demonstration of his destiny. . . .

It is not unlikely that, before the close of the next century, this race will outnumber all the other civilized races of the world. Does it not look as if God were not only preparing in our Anglo-Saxon civilization the die with which to stamp the peoples of the earth, but as if he were also massing behind that die the mighty power with which to press it? My confidence that this race is eventually to give its civilization to mankind is not based on mere numbers—China forbid! I look forward to

*Source: Josiah Strong, *Our Country* (New York: Baker and Taylor, 1885), pp. 159, 161, 165, 174–76.

what the world has never yet seen united in the same race; viz., the greatest numbers, *and* the highest civilization.

There can be no reasonable doubt that North America is to be the great home of the Anglo-Saxon, the principal seat of his power, the center of his life and influence. . . .

. . . It seems to me that God, with infinite wisdom and skill, is training the Anglo-Saxon race for an hour sure to come in the world's future. Heretofore there has always been in the history of the world a comparatively unoccupied land westward, into which the crowded countries of the East have poured their surplus populations. But the widening waves of migration, which millenniums ago rolled east and west from the valley of the Euphrates, meet to-day on our Pacific coast. There are no more new worlds. The unoccupied arable lands of the earth are limited, and will soon be taken. The time is coming when the pressure of population on the means of subsistence will be felt here as it is now felt in Europe and Asia. Then will the world enter upon a new stage of its history—*the final competition of races, for which the Anglo-Saxon is being schooled.* Long before the thousand millions are here, the mighty *centrifugal* tendency, inherent in this stock and strengthened in the United States, will assert itself. Then this race of unequaled energy, with all the majesty of numbers and the might of wealth behind it—the representative, let us hope, of the largest liberty, the purest Christianity, the highest civilization—having developed peculiarly aggressive traits calculated to impress its institutions upon mankind, will spread itself over the earth. If I read not amiss, this powerful race will move down upon Mexico, down upon Central and South America, out upon the islands of the sea, over upon Africa and beyond. And can any one doubt that the result of this competition of races will be the "survival of the fittest"? . . .

. . . "At the present day," says Mr. Darwin, "civilized nations are everywhere supplanting barbarous nations, excepting where the climate opposes a deadly barrier; and they succeed mainly, though not exclusively, through their arts, which are the products of the intellect." Thus the Finns were supplanted by the Aryan races in Europe and Asia, the Tartars by the Russians, and thus the aborigines of North America, Australia and New Zealand are now disappearing before the all-conquering Anglo-Saxons. It would seem as if these inferior tribes were only precursors of a superior race, voices in the wilderness crying: "Prepare ye the way of the Lord!" . . .

DOCUMENT 23.2

The Advantages of Naval Territorial Expansion*

Alfred Thayer Mahan was an Annapolis graduate who served in the U.S. Navy during the Civil War, was appointed to the Naval War Board in the Spanish-American War, and subsequently advanced to the rank of rear admiral. A "big-navy" man and a leading exponent of expansionism, he was admired by the entire bloc of imperialist spokesmen, Theodore Roosevelt in particular. Mahan argued that the national security demanded a growing naval force, an Isthmian canal, and Caribbean and Pacific island possessions. He presented his message within the social Darwinian framework, his central thesis being that international competition was a naked struggle for power—with control of the sea being an indispensable factor.

Indications are not wanting of an approaching change in the thoughts and pol-

*Source: Alfred Thayer Mahan, "The United States Looking Outward," in *The Interest of America in Sea Power* (New York: Harper & Bros., 1897), pp. 3–27.

icy of Americans as to their relations with the world outside their own borders. For the past quarter of a century, the predominant idea, which has asserted itself successfully at the polls and shaped the course of the government, has been to preserve the home market for the home industries. . . .

. . . Within, the home market is secured; but outside, beyond the broad seas, there are the markets of the world, that can be entered and controlled only by a vigorous contest, to which the habit of trusting to protection by statute does not conduce. . . .

. . . The interesting and significant feature of this changing attitude is the turning of the eyes outward, instead of inward only, to seek the welfare of the country. To affirm the importance of distant markets, and the relation to them of our own immense powers of production, implies logically the recognition of the link that joins the products and the markets,—that is, the carrying trade; the three together constituting that chain of maritime power to which Great Britain owes her wealth and greatness. Further, is it too much to say that, as two of these links, the shipping and the markets, are exterior to our own borders, the acknowledgment of them carries with it a view of the relations of the United States to the world radically distinct from the simple idea of self-sufficingness? We shall not follow far this line of thought before there will dawn the realization of America's unique position, facing the older worlds of the East and West, her shores washed by the oceans which touch the one or the other, but which are common to her alone.

Coincident with these signs of change in our own policy there is restlessness in the world at large which is deeply significant, if not ominous. It is beside our purpose to dwell upon the internal state of Europe, whence, if disturbances arise, the effect upon us may be but partial and indirect. But the great seaboard powers there do not stand on guard against their continental rivals only; they cherish also aspirations for commercial extension, for colonies, and for influence in distant regions, which may bring, and, even under our present contracted policy, already have brought them into collision with ourselves. The incident of the Samoa Islands, trivial apparently, was nevertheless eminently suggestive of European ambitions. America then roused from sleep as to interests closely concerning her future. At this moment internal troubles are imminent in the Sandwich Islands, where it should be our fixed determination to allow no foreign influence to equal our own. All over the world German commercial and colonial push is coming into collision with other nations. . . .

. . . In a general way, it is evident enough that this canal [through the Central American Isthmus], by modifying the direction of trade routes, will induce a great increase of commercial activity and carrying trade throughout the Caribbean Sea; and that this now comparatively deserted nook of the ocean will become, like the Red Sea, a great thoroughfare of shipping, and will attract, as never before in our day, the interest and ambition of maritime nations. Every position in that sea will have enhanced commercial and military value, and the canal itself will become a strategic centre of the most vital importance. Like the Canadian Pacific Railroad, it will be a link between the two oceans; but, unlike it, the use, unless most carefully guarded by treaties, will belong wholly to the belligerent which controls the sea by its naval power. In case of war, the United States will unquestionably command the Canadian Railroad, despite the deterrent force of operations by the hostile navy upon our seaboard; but no less unquestionably will she be impotent, as against any of the great maritime powers, to control the Central American canal. Militarily speaking, and having reference to European complications only, the piercing of the Isthmus is nothing but a disaster to the United States, in the present state of her military and naval preparation. It is especially dangerous to the Pacific coast; but the increased exposure of one part of our seaboard reacts unfavorably upon the whole military situation.

Despite a certain great original superiority conferred by our geographical nearness and immense resources,—due, in other words, to our natural advantages, and not to our intelligent preparations,—the United States is woefully unready, not only in fact but in purpose to assert in the Caribbean and Central America a weight of influence proportioned to the extent of her interests. We have not the navy, and, what is worse, we are not willing to have the navy, that will weigh seriously in any disputes with those nations whose interests will conflict there with our own. We have not, and we are not anxious to provide, the defence of the seaboard which will leave the navy free for its work at sea. We have not, but many other powers have, positions, either within or on the borders of the Caribbean which not only possess great natural advantages for the control of that sea, but have received and are receiving that artificial strength of fortification and armament which will make them practically inexpugnable. On the contrary, we have not on the Gulf of Mexico even the beginning of a navy yard which could serve as the base of our operations. . . .

. . . Though distant, our shores can be reached; being defenceless, they can detain but a short time a force sent against them. . . .

Yet, were our sea frontier as strong as it now is weak, passive self-defence, whether in trade or war, would be but a poor policy, so long as the world continues to be one of struggle and vicissitude. All around us now is strife; "the struggle of life," "the race of life," are phrases so familiar that we do not feel their significance till we stop to think about them. Everywhere nation is arrayed against nation; our own no less than others. What is our protective system but an organized warfare? . . .

DOCUMENT 23.3

Anti-Imperialism: The Argument against Expansionism*

Among the many arguments leveled at American expansion into the western Pacific at the turn of the century, one—presented by Andrew Carnegie—appeared especially significant. It challenged the popular notion that the new acquisitions would require no special military expenditures and that the new commitments would not unduly expose the United States to embarrassment or attack.

Let another phase of the question be carefully weighed. Europe is today an armed camp, not chiefly because the home territories of its various nations are threatened, but because of fear of aggressive action upon the part of other nations touching outlying "possessions." France resents British control of Egypt and is fearful of its West African possessions; Russia seeks Chinese territory, with a view to expansion in the Pacific; Germany also seeks distant possessions; Britain, who has acquired so many dependencies, is so fearful of an attack upon them that this year she is spending nearly eighty millions of dollars upon additional warships, and Russia, Germany and France follow suit. Japan is a new element of anxiety; and by the end of the year it is computed she will have 67 formidable ships of war. The naval powers of Europe, and Japan also, are apparently determined to be prepared for a terrific struggle for possessions in the Far East, close to the Philippines—and why not for these islands themselves? Into this vortex the Republic is cordially invited to enter by those powers who expect her policy to be of benefit to them, but her action is jealously watched by those who fear that her power might be used against them.

It has never been considered the part of wisdom to thrust one's hand into the

*Source: Andrew Carnegie, "Distant Possessions—The Parting of the Ways," *North American Review*, August 1898, pp. 239–48.

hornet's nest, and it does seem as if the United States must lose all claim to ordinary prudence and good sense if she enter this arena, and become involved in the intrigues and threats of war which make Europe an armed camp.

It is the parting of the ways. We have a continent to populate and develop; there are only 23 persons to the square mile in the United States. England has 370, Belgium 571, and Germany 250. A tithe of the cost of maintaining our sway over the Philippines would improve our internal waterways; deepen our harbors; build the Nicaraguan Canal; construct a waterway to the ocean from the Great Lakes; an inland canal along the Atlantic seaboard; a canal across Florida, saving 800 miles distance between New York and New Orleans; connect Lake Michigan with the Mississippi; deepen all the harbors upon the lakes; build a canal from Lake Erie to the Allegheny River; slackwater through movable dams the entire length of the Ohio River to Cairo; thoroughly improve the Lower and Upper Mississippi, and all our seaboard harbors. All these enterprises would be as nothing in cost in comparison to the sums required for the experiment of possessing the Philippine Islands, 7,000 miles from our shores. If the object be to render our Republic powerful among nations, can there be any doubt as to which policy is the better? To be more powerful at home is the surest way to be more powerful abroad. To-day the Republic stands the friend of all nations, the ally of none; she has no ambitious designs upon the territory of any power upon another continent; she crosses none of their ambitious designs, evokes no jealousy of the bitter sort, inspires no fears; she is not one of them, scrambling for "possessions"; she stands apart, pursuing her own great mission, and teaching all nations by example. Let her become a power annexing foreign territory, and all is changed in a moment.

If we are to compete with other nations for foreign possessions we must have a navy like theirs. It should be superior to any other navy, or we play a second part. It is not enough to have a navy equal to that of Russia or of France, for Russia and France may combine against us just as they may against Britain. We at once enter the field as a rival of Britain, the chief possessor of foreign possessions, and who can guarantee that we shall not even have to measure our power against her?

What it means to enter the list of military and naval powers having foreign possessions may be gathered from the following considerations. First, look at our future navy. If it is only to equal that of France it means 51 battleships; if of Russia, 40 battleships. If we cannot play the game without being at least the equal of any of our rivals, then 80 battleships is the number Britain possesses. We now have only 4, with 5 building. Cruisers, armed and unarmed, swell the number threefold, Britain having 273 ships of the line built or ordered, with 308 torpedo boats in addition; France having 134 ships of the line and 269 torpedo boats. All these nations are adding ships rapidly. Every armor and gun making plant in the world is busy night and day. Ships are indispensable, but recent experience shows that soldiers are equally so. While the immense armies of Europe need not be duplicated, yet we shall certainly be too weak unless our army is at least twenty times what it has been—say 500,000 men....

To-day two great powers in the world are compact, developing themselves in peace throughout vast coterminous territories. When war threatens they have no outlying "possessions" which can never be really "possessed," but which they are called upon to defend. They fight upon the exposed edge only of their own soil in case of attack, and are not only invulnerable, but they could not be more than inconvenienced by the world in arms against them. These powers are Russia and the United States.... Britain, France, Germany, Belgium, Spain, are all vulnerable, having departed from the sagacious policy of keeping possessions and power concentrated. Should the United States depart from this policy, she also must be so weakened in consequence as never to be able to play the commanding part in the world, disjointed, that she can play whenever she desires if she remains compact.

Whether the United States maintain its present unique position of safety or forfeit it through acquiring foreign possessions, is to be decided by its action in regard to the Philippines; for, fortunately, the independence of Cuba is assured, for this the Republic has proclaimed to the world that she has drawn the sword. But why should the less than two millions of Cuba receive national existence and the seven and a half millions of the Philippines be denied it? The United States, thus far in their history, have no page reciting self-sacrifice made for others; all their gains have been for themselves. This void is now to be grandly filled. The page which recites the resolve of the Republic to rid her neighbor Cuba from the foreign "possessor" will grow brighter with the passing centuries, which may dim many pages now deemed illustrious. Should the coming American be able to point to Cuba and the Philippines rescued from foreign domination and enjoying independence won for them by his country and given to them without money and without price, he will find no citizen of any other land able to claim for his country services so disinterested and so noble.

We repeat there is no power in the world that could do more than inconvenience the United States by attacking its fringe, which is all that the world combined could do, so long as our country is not compelled to send its forces beyond its own compact shores to defend worthless "possessions." If our country were blockaded by the united powers of the world for years, she would emerge from the embargo richer and stronger, and with her own resources more completely developed. We have little to fear from external attack. No thorough blockade of our enor-

mous seaboard is possible; but even if it were, the few indispensable articles not produced by ourselves (if there were any such) would reach us by way of Mexico or Canada at slightly increased cost. . . .

DOCUMENT 23.4

Anti-Imperialism: The Appeal to Conservative Tradition*

A major position taken by antiexpansionists challenged the new American habit of rationalizing national action with appeals to patriotism and democratic ideology. William Graham Sumner, the Yale sociologist, urged his countrymen to remember the true sources of national greatness and idealism.

. . . The war with Spain was precipitated upon us headlong, without reflection or deliberation, and without any due formulation of public opinion. Whenever a voice was raised in behalf of deliberation and the recognized maxims of statesmanship, it was howled down in a storm of vituperation and cant. Everything was done to make us throw away sobriety of thought and calmness of judgment, and to inflate all expressions with sensational epithets and turgid phrases. It cannot be denied that everything in regard to the war has been treated in an exalted strain of sentiment and rhetoric very unfavorable to the truth. At present the whole periodical press of the country seems to be occupied in tickling the national vanity to the utmost by representations about the war which are extravagant and fantastic. There will be a penalty to be paid for all this. Nervous and sensational newspapers are just as corrupting, especially to young people, as nervous and sensational novels.

*Source: William Graham Sumner, "The Conquest of the United States by Spain," *Yale Law Journal*, Vol. VIII, No. 4 (January 1899), pp. 168–93.

The habit of expecting that all mental pabulum shall be highly spiced, and the corresponding loathing for whatever is soberly truthful, undermines character as much as any other vice. Patriotism is being prostituted into a nervous intoxication which is fatal to an apprehension of truth. It builds around us a fool's paradise, and it will lead us into errors about our position and relations just like those which we have been ridiculing in the case of Spain. . . .

. . . The laws of nature and of [the] human body are just as valid for Americans as for anybody else, and if we commit acts, we shall have to take consequences, just like other people. Therefore prudence demands that we look ahead to see what we are about to do, and that we gauge the means at our disposal, if we do not want to bring calamity on ourselves and our children. We see that the peculiarities of our system of government set limitations on us. We cannot do things which a great centralized monarchy could do. The very blessings and special advantages which we enjoy, as compared with others, bring disabilities with them. That is the great fundamental cause of what I have tried to show throughout this lecture, that we cannot govern dependencies consistently with our political system, and that, if we try it, the state which our fathers founded will suffer a reaction which will transform it into another empire just after the fashion of all the old ones. That is what imperialism means. That is what it will be, and the democratic republic, which has been, will stand in history as a mere transition form like the colonial organization of earlier days.

And yet this scheme of a republic which our fathers formed was a glorious dream which demands more than a word of respect and affection before it passes away. . . .

. . . Our fathers would have an economical government, even if grand people called it a parsimonious one, and taxes should be no greater than were absolutely necessary to pay for such a government. . . .

. . . No adventurous policies of conquest or ambition, such as, in their belief, kings and nobles had forced, for their own advantage, on European states, would ever be undertaken by a free democratic republic. Therefore the citizen here would never be forced to leave his family, or to give his sons to shed blood for glory and to leave widows and orphans in misery for nothing. Justice and law were to reign in the midst of simplicity, and a government which had little to do was to offer little field for ambition. In a society where industry, frugality and prudence were honored, it was believed that the vices of wealth would never flourish.

We know that these beliefs, hopes and intentions have been only partially fulfilled. We know that, as time has gone on, and we have grown numerous and rich, some of these things have proved impossible ideals, incompatible with a large and flourishing society, but it is by virtue of this conception of a commonwealth that the United States has stood for something unique and grand in the history of mankind, and that its people have been happy. It is by virtue of these ideals that we have been "isolated," isolated in a position which the other nations of the earth have observed in silent envy, and yet there are people who are boasting of their patriotism, because they say that we have taken our place now amongst the nations of the earth by virtue of this war. My patriotism is of the kind which is outraged by the notion that the United States never was a great nation until in a petty three months campaign it knocked to pieces a poor, decrepit bankrupt old state like Spain. To hold such an opinion as that is to abandon all American standards, to put shame and scorn on all that our ancestors tried to build up here, and to go over to the standards of which Spain is a representative.

DOCUMENT 23.5

Anti-Imperialism: The Appeal to Liberal Tradition*

Senator George F. Hoar of Massachusetts, a Republican, led the anti-imperialist forces in Congress against the Philippine annexation treaty. He based his opposition to annexation on the principles of the Constitution and the Declaration of Independence. The doctrine of political liberty, he. argued, is not divisible and thus cannot be defied by the government of the United States with impunity.

. . . There are two lessons our fathers learned from the history of Greece which they hoped their children would remember—the danger of disunion and domestic strife and an indulgence in the greed and lust of empire. The Greeks stood together against the power of Persia as the American States stood together against the tyranny of England. For us the danger of disunion has happily passed by. Our Athenians and our Spartans are bound and welded together again, each lending to the other the strength of their steel and the sharpness of their tempered blade in an indissoluble Union. Our danger to-day is from the lust of empire. It is a little remarkable that the temptation that besets us now lured and brought to ruin the Athenian people in ancient times. I hope that we may be able to resist and avert that danger as we resisted and averted the peril of disunion. . . .

Mr. President, I am no strict constructionist. I am no alarmist. I believe this country to be a nation, a sovereign nation. I believe Congress to possess all the powers which are necessary to accomplish under the most generous and liberal construction the great objects which the men who framed the Constitution and the people who adopted it desired to accomplish

Source: Senator George F. Hoar's speech before the Senate, January 9, 1899, in the *Congressional Record*, pp. 494–69, 498, 503.

by its instrumentality. I was bred, I might almost say I was born, in the faith, which I inherited from the men whose blood is in my veins, of the party of Hamilton and Washington and Webster and Sumner, and not in that of Madison or Calhoun or the strict constructionists. . . .

But the question with which we now have to deal is whether Congress may conquer and may govern, without their consent and against their will, a foreign nation, a separate, distinct, and numerous people, a territory not hereafter to be populated by Americans, to be formed into American States and to take its part in fulfilling and executing the purposes for which the Constitution was framed, whether it may conquer, control, and govern this people, not for the general welfare, common defense, more perfect union, more blessed liberty of the people of the United States, but for some real or fancied benefit to be conferred against their desire upon the people so governed or in discharge of some fancied obligation to them, and not to the people of the United States.

Now, Mr. President, the question is whether the men who framed the Constitution, or the people who adopted it, meant to confer that power among the limited and restrained powers of the sovereign nation that they were creating. . . .

I declare not only that this is not among the express powers conferred upon the sovereignty they created, that it is not among the powers necessarily or reasonably or conveniently implied for the sake of carrying into effect the purposes of that instrument, but that it is a power which it can be demonstrated by the whole contemporaneous history and by our whole history since until within six months they did not mean should exist—a power that our fathers and their descendants have ever loathed and abhorred—and that they believed that no sovereign on earth could rightfully exercise it, and that no people on earth could rightfully confer it. They not only did not mean to confer it, but they would have cut off their right hands, every one of them, sooner than set them to an instrument which should confer it....

Mr. President, the persons who favor the ratification of this treaty without conditions and without amendment differ among themselves certainly in their views, purposes, and opinions, and as they are so many of them honest and well-meaning persons, we have the right to say in their actual and real opinions. In general, the state of mind and the utterance of the lips are in accord. If you ask them what they want, you are answered with a shout; "Three cheers for the Flag! Who will dare to haul it down? Hold on to everything you can get. The United States is strong enough to do what it likes. The Declaration of Independence and the counsel of Washington and the Constitution of the United States have grown rusty and musty. They are for little countries and not for great ones. There is no moral law for strong nations. America has outgrown Americanism."...

Now, Mr. President, there are Senators here yet hesitating as to what their action may be in the future, who will tell you that they loathe and hate this doctrine that we may buy nations at wholesale; that we may acquire imperial powers or imperial regions by conquest; that we may make vassal states and subject peoples without constitutional restraint, and against their will, and without any restraint but our own discretion.

Now, I appeal to those gentlemen whenever and wherever they may be called to act to answer to themselves as the one great proposition, the greatest question, not of a year or of a Congress, not of a generation, not of a century, but a question pertaining rather to the great eternity of national life, whether—even if that action be permitted or not by the letter of the Constitution—it be not repugnant to its form and spirit....

Now, I claim that under the Declaration of Independence you can not govern a foreign territory, a foreign people, another people than your own, that you can not subjugate them and govern them against their will, because you think it is for their good, when they do not; because you think you are going to give them the blessings of liberty. You have no right at the cannon's mouth to impose on an unwilling people your Declaration of Independence and your Constitution and your notions of freedom and notions of what is good....

DOCUMENT 23.6

God's Command Is on Us*

Senator Albert J. Beveridge was a Progressive Republican from Indiana. Like Josiah Strong, he was an uninhibited spokesman for Anglo-Saxon racism and proponent of "the American century"; but in the following speech, delivered during the 1900 presidential campaign, he did not omit profits from the divine mission of the United States.

...It is a noble land that God has given us; a land that can feed and clothe the world: a land whose coast lines would inclose half the countries of Europe; a land set like a sentinel between the two imperial oceans of the globe; a greater England and a nobler destiny. It is a mighty people that He has planted on this soil; a people sprung from the most masterful blood of history; a people perpetually revitalized by the virile workingfolk of all the earth; a people imperial by virtue of their power, by right of their institutions, by authority of their heaven-directed purposes, the propagandists and not the misers of liberty. It is a glorious history our God has bestowed upon His chosen people; a history whose keynote was struck by Liberty Bell; a history heroic with faith in our mission and our future; a history of statesmen, who flung the boundaries of the Republic out into unexplored lands and savage wildernesses; a history of soldiers, who carried the flag across blazing deserts and through the ranks of hostile mountains, even to the gates of sunset: a history of a multiplying people, who overran a continent in half a century; a history divinely logical, in the process of whose tremendous reasoning we find ourselves to-day.

Therefore, in this campaign the question is larger than a party question. It is an American question. It is a world question. Shall the American people continue their resistless march toward the commercial supremacy of the world? Shall free institutions broaden their blessed reign as the children of liberty wax in strength until the empire of our principles is established over the hearts of all mankind? Have we no mission to perform—no duty to discharge to our fellow-man? Has the Almighty Father endowed us with gifts beyond our deserts, and marked us as the people of His peculiar favor, merely to rot in our own selfishness, as men and nations must who take cowardice for their companion and self for their deity—as China has, as India has, as Egypt has? Shall we be as the man who had one talent and hid it, or as he who had ten talents and used them until they grew to riches? And shall we reap the reward that waits on the discharge of our high duty as the sovereign power of earth; shall we occupy new markets for what our farmers raise, new markets for what our factories make, new markets for what our merchants sell,—aye, and please God, new markets for what our ships shall carry? Shall we avail ourselves of new sources of supply of what we do not raise or make, so that what are luxuries to-day shall be necessities to-morrow? Shall we conduct the mightiest commerce of history with the best money known to man or shall we use the pauper money of Mexico, China, and the Chicago platform? Shall we be worthy of our mighty past of progress, brushing aside, as we have always done, the spider webs of technicality, and march ever onward upon the highway of development, to the doing of real deeds, the achievement of real things, and the winning of real victories?

In a sentence, shall the American people endorse at the polls the American administration of William McKinley, which, under the guidance of Divine Providence, has started the Republic on its noblest career of prosperity, duty and glory; or shall the American people rebuke that administration, reverse the wheels of history, halt the career of the flag. . . ?

. . . William McKinley is continuing the policy that Jefferson began, Monroe continued, Seward advanced, Grant promoted, Harrison championed. Hawaii is ours; Porto Rico is to be ours; at the prayer of its people Cuba will finally be ours; in the islands of the East, even to the gates of Asia, coaling stations are to be ours; at the very least the flag of a liberal government is to float over the Philippines, and it will be the stars and stripes of glory. And the burning question of this campaign is whether the American people will accept the gifts of events; whether they will rise, as lifts their soaring destiny; whether they will proceed along the lines of national development surveyed by the statesmen of our past, or whether, for the first time, the American people doubt their mission, question their fate, prove apostate to the spirit of their race, and halt the ceaseless march of free institutions?

The opposition tells us that we ought not to govern a people without their consent. I answer, the rule of liberty that all just government derives its authority from the consent of the governed, applies only to those who are capable of self-government. We govern the Indians without their consent; we govern our Territories without their consent; we govern our children without their consent. I answer, would not the natives of the Philippines prefer the just, humane, civilizing government of this Republic to the savage, bloody rule of pillage and extortion from which we have rescued them? Do not the blazing fires of joy and the ringing bells of gladness in Porto Rico prove the welcome of our flag? And regardless of this formula of words made only for enlightened, self-governing peoples, do we owe no duty to the world? Shall we turn these peoples back to the reeking hands from which we have taken them? Shall we save them from those nations, to give them to a self-rule of tragedy? It would be like giving a razor to a babe and telling it to shave itself. It would be like giving a typewriter to an Esquimau and telling him to publish one of the great dailies of the world. . . .

. . . To-day, we are making more than we can use. Therefore, we must find new markets for our produce, new occupation for our capital, new work for our labor. And so, while we did not need the territory taken during the past century at the time it was acquired, we do need what we have taken in 1898, and we need it now. Think of the thousands of Americans who will pour into Hawaii and Porto Rico when the Republic's laws cover those islands with justice and safety. Think of the tens of thousands of Americans who will invade the Philippines when a liberal government shall establish order and equity there. Think of the hundreds of thousands of Americans who will build a soap-and-water, common school civilization of energy and industry in Cuba, when a government of law replaces the double reign of anarchy and tyranny. . . .

. . . The resources of the Philippines have hardly been touched by the finger tips of modern methods. And they produce what we cannot, and they consume what we produce—the very predestination of reciprocity. And William McKinley intends that their trade shall be ours. It means an opportunity for the rich man to do something with his money, besides hoarding it or lending it. It means occupation for every workingman in the country at wages which the development of new resources, the launching of new enterprises, the monopoly of new markets always brings. . . .

. . . Why mumble the meaningless phrases of a tale that is told when the golden future is before us, the world calls us, its wealth awaits us and God's command is on us? . . .

Fellow-Americans, we are God's chosen people. Yonder at Bunker Hill and Yorktown His providence was above us. At New Orleans and on ensanguined seas His hand sustained us. Abraham Lincoln was His minister, and His was the altar of freedom the boys in blue set up on a hundred smoking battlefields. His power directed Dewey in the east, and He delivered the Spanish fleet into our hands on Liberty's natal day as He delivered the elder Armada into the hands of our English sires two centuries ago. His great purposes are revealed in the progress of the flag, which surpasses the intentions of Congresses and Cabinets, and leads us, like a holier pillar of cloud by day and pillar of fire by night, into situations unforeseen by finite wisdom and duties unexpected by the unprophetic heart of selfishness. The American people cannot use a dishonest medium of exchange; it is ours to set the world its example of right and honor. We cannot fly from our world duties; it is ours to execute the purposes of a fate that has driven us to be greater than our small intentions. We cannot retreat from any soil where Providence has unfurled our banner; it is ours to save that soil for liberty and civilization. For liberty and civilization and God's promises fulfilled, the flag must henceforth be the symbol and the sign to all mankind.

24 The Plight of the Negro after Reconstruction, 1877–1910

I. A. NEWBY
University of Hawaii

The story of Negroes in the New South is a vital segment of the history of the race in America. The issues involved in that story and the questions it raises are just as relevant now as they were in 1877 and 1910. Negroes are today the nation's most distinctive minority, distinctive not only in race but in cultural, political, and socioeconomic terms as well. Why is this so? Why have Negroes remained a distinctive minority when others have lost themselves in the majority? Can their distinctiveness be explained in historical terms? How has their experience in America affected them? Other questions are equally pertinent. What is the proper relationship between whites and Negroes? What are the surest means of achieving interracial harmony? What is the proper role of the federal government and the states, of whites and Negroes, in determining racial policy? Answers to these questions are difficult and debatable, but the story of Negroes in the New South throws light upon all of them.

In an illuminating essay, "The Search for Southern Identity," in *The Burden of Southern History*, Professor C. Vann Woodward suggests that to understand the South one must first understand "the collective [historical] experience of Southerners." The South, he suggests, is a distinctive region today because its historical experience has been unlike that of the rest of America. In contrast to other Americans, Southerners have undergone "a long and quite un-American experience with poverty"; they have endured "generations of scarcity and want"; they have suffered "large components of frustration, failure, and defeat," including "defeat in the provinces of economic, social and political life." If these are significant elements in the history of Southerners (and I think they are), they are doubly important in the history of Negroes. A "search for Negro identity," that is, an effort to understand the history of Negroes in America and to explain their distinctiveness as American citizens, must stress many of the things Woodward emphasizes in explaining the South. Whether Southerners or not, Negroes have had a long and quite un-American experience with poverty and deprivation; their experiences with frustration, failure, and defeat have been so enormous that the history of white Southerners is, by comparison, a success story. In the historical experience of Negro Americans, frustration, failure, and defeat are normal—not exceptional—occurrences. The race has endured difficulties which, in

130

poignancy as in magnitude, surpass those of all other American minorities, excepting only the Indians. Generally speaking, ethnic groups in America have suffered discrimination in proportion to the differences between themselves and the North European, Protestant, English-speaking majority. Such groups, however, have generally overcome discrimination by "Americanization"—absorbing the culture, language, and middle-class ethic of the majority. For Negroes, however, this escape was never possible. Regardless of the extent to which he absorbed the culture, character traits, and modes of conduct of the majority, a Negro could never lose himself in the majority. He remained a Negro; and in the eyes of most whites, that was the primary consideration.

Here emerges the transcendent fact: Negro Americans are today what their historical experience in this country has made them—a group apart, a distinctive minority which differs in significant respects from the majority. White Americans think of their national experience as a success story. America to them is a land of hope and opportunity, of economic abundance, social mobility, political equality. They see their society as one which cultivates such peculiarly American virtues as initiative, individualism, self-reliance, self-sacrifice. They see in America a nation whose institutions are benevolent: The law protects everyone from oppression and is not itself oppressive; the fundamental rights of citizens are spelled out in the Constitution and guaranteed to all; the right of trial by an impartial jury of one's peers is so basic as to be a commonplace; every man respects his fellowman, his person and property, his womenfolk and children, his freedom of expression and movement. This picture, of course, is overdrawn in the popular imagination; the ideals are rarely achieved in such absolute form. Nevertheless, there is a significant element of truth in this view—at least for white Americans. For them, the ideals mentioned above *are* meaningful, even though imperfectly achieved. For them, society *is* generally committed to those ideals.

For Negroes, the story is different. Picture a society in which those ideals are denied altogether or honored more in the breach than the observance, and you begin to see the difference in the historical experience of white and Negro Americans. Moreover, the difference was greater in 1877 and 1910 than it is today. In 1877, Negroes had only recently emerged from slavery; by 1910, they had been forced into a new world of rigid segregation, almost universal disfranchisement, and a deadening second-class status that destroyed the energies of all save the most persevering. The *racial* meaning of this must be understood. Slavery and segregation are the two most important facts in the history of Negro Americans. They have dominated the Negro's experience in this country just as political freedom, economic opportunity, and social mobility have dominated the white man's.

The effects of slavery persisted long after the institution itself expired. Brutal and brutalizing, slavery excluded Negroes from what white Americans had already labeled the American way of life. It did more than deprive Negroes of freedom, more than deny them civil liberty, economic opportunity, and social equality. Its most lasting effects were sociological and psychological. The slave environment tended to cultivate in Negroes certain personal and social traits, certain moral and ethical values, which together produced a way of life markedly different from that of whites. The "good" white American displayed initiative, daring, and independence; the "good" slave was imitative, humble, ingratiating, childlike—a sycophant or a clown. Nothing in his experience encouraged thrift and self-sacrifice; he had no hope for a better tomorrow. His environment encouraged him in self-indulgence, ignorance, servility, helplessness, hopelessness—all qualities which white Americans despised. There was little in his experience to inculcate respect for the law and government, for property rights, Judeo-Christian morality, the family, even his fellow Negroes. Government to him was an organized tyranny; the law a device for denying him the fruits of his own labor; society a system which permitted his "wife" to be compromised, his children sold, his honor and self-respect ruthlessly eliminated. Every "respectable" element in his society taught him that he was inferior to other men, that his was a despised, ridiculous race.

Slavery, in short, was an abject failure as a training ground for freedom, just as segregation later proved a poor school for training first-class citizens. The mass of freedmen in 1877 were still ill-prepared for the duties and responsibilities of American citizenship. This is not to argue that they should have been made second-class citizens or given an intermediate status between slavery and citizenship. If one may draw upon the experience of other ethnic groups, many of whom were originally considered unfit for citizenship by the white Anglo-Saxon Protestant American majority, citizenship is its own best training ground. One learns to be a citizen be being a citizen. In addition, it should go without saying that the conditions described did not apply equally to all Negroes. The suitability of individual Negroes for American citizenship probably varied as much as that of individual whites. What I am suggesting is that the Negro's experience in America *tended* to produce in him certain qualities which handicapped him as a free man. By 1910 the race had made major strides in overcoming the effects of slavery, but it is easy to overemphasize this progress. Slavery had done its work too well. In any case the lingering effects of slavery were a major factor in the story of Negroes in the New South.

They were not the only major factor, however. The hope instilled in Negroes by the promises of Radical Reconstruction, the bitterness stirred in southern whites

by those same promises, the disillusionment of many Northerners over the freedmen's failure to achieve white standards of accomplishment and conduct in little more than a decade of freedom, the increasing disinterest of Northerners in race relations in the South—these were also major factors. Out of them emerged the central theme of Negro history in the New South: the loss of all those guarantees of equal rights which Radical Republicans had written into the Constitution and into federal law during Reconstruction. In significant respects this was a period of retrogression for the race. The three elements responsible for racial reforms during Radical Reconstruction—the federal government, the Republican party, and northern liberals—each relaxed its vigil, lost interest in the welfare of Negroes, and thereby abandoned the race to white Southerners. The result was a tragedy from which the nation has not yet recovered. For more than two generations the majority of Americans chose to ignore a major national problem, or rather to shunt it aside, leaving it like a dark sore on the body politic to fester and grow worse. In the late 19th and early 20th centuries, Populist and Progressive reformers recognized and tried to deal with a wide spectrum of national problems; but for both, the race problem was a blind spot. Because southern whites were allowed to have their way for so long, it became an item of faith with them (and others, too) that segregation is the natural relationship between whites and Negroes, that it is the only legal, constitutional system of race relations in this country, that integration is artificial and realizable only through the use of force, and that states have primary control over racial policy.

The Compromise of 1877, which ended Radical Reconstruction, was the final episode in the sectional conflict extending back to Andrew Jackson's day, and its consummation signaled the end of that conflict. The nation had grown tired of sectional animosity and crusading idealism and was anxious to get on with the business of the Gilded Age. Negroes had been freed, their rights written into the Constitution. Wasn't that enough? Wasn't it time freedmen became "mere citizens" like everyone else? The new mood found expression in an exaggerated impulse toward national reunion. Men of every section joined together to promote spiritual reunion and heal the psychological wounds of prolonged sectional conflict.

Whatever the merits of this impulse toward reunion, and they were many, it was accomplished at the expense of Negroes. The "Negro issue" had divided the nation; dropping it would restore harmony. Not that this was calculated. Federal officials and the Republican Party continued to endorse Negro rights in rhetoric reminiscent of Reconstruction Radicalism, but they no longer matched their words with action. Indeed, they now discovered that federal "interference" in race relations was a bad thing. President Rutherford B. Hayes gave voice to this view when he declared in 1877 that he would insist upon "absolute justice and fair play to the negro." But, he added disarmingly, this could "be got best and almost surely by trusting the honorable and influential southern whites." This sentiment was the basis for federal policy throughout the era of the New South. President William Howard Taft echoed it in 1909 when he told a delegation of southern Negroes that hope for their race lay not in action by the federal government but in sympathy and help from "noble, earnest, sympathetic white men in the South."

The practical consequences of this policy may be seen in the dismemberment of the Radical Reconstruction program by the federal courts. "Practically all the relevant decisions of the United States Supreme Court during Reconstruction and to the end of the century," writes Rayford W. Logan, "nullified or curtailed those rights which the Reconstruction 'radicals' thought they had written into laws and

into the Constitution." In a series of landmark decisions, chief among them being the slaughterhouse cases (1873), *United States* v. *Cruikshank* (1876), the civil rights cases (1883), and *Plessy* v. *Ferguson* (1896), the Court destroyed the special protections which Reconstruction Radicals had devised for Negroes. In the process the federal government was stripped of power to deal effectively with race relations in the South. This was accomplished by interpreting the 13th and 14th amendments, insofar as they applied to the rights of Negroes, in the narrowest possible sense. The 14th Amendment had recognized a dual citizenship—state and national—but had not defined the rights a citizen derives from each of these citizenships. In the slaughterhouse cases the Court ruled, in effect, that those civil rights and liberties of most concern to Negroes inhere in state citizenship and are beyond the purview of federal responsibility. Negroes denied those rights must seek redress from the states, not the federal government. The Court interpreted the Due Process Clause of the 14th Amendment as adding nothing substantive to the rights of Negro citizens, but as being merely a procedural guarantee for all citizens. Equally significant, the Court ruled that the 14th Amendment prohibited discrimination by states only, and not by private individuals. Refusing Negroes access to hotels, restaurants, theaters, and railroad cars were acts of private individuals (the owner, manager, or conductor) and were not prohibited by the 14th Amendment. Negroes who objected to the resulting segregation must look for relief to state legislatures. Finally, in 1896 the Court gave its explicit sanction to racial segregation. "The object of the [14th] Amendment was undoubtedly to enforce the absolute equality of the two races before the law," the Court declared in *Plessy v. Ferguson*, but "laws permitting, and even requiring" racial segregation do no violence to that objective.

The full meaning of these decisions is

comprehensible only within a racial context. Though the Reconstruction laws and constitutional amendments were written in general language and were ostensibly applicable to all citizens, they had in fact provided Negro citizens with what amounted to *special* protection. The special protection was easily justifiable, since Negroes had a special problem, one not shared by other Americans: They were victims of racial discrimination; and without protection from it, they might never have equality before the law. It is a truism among Americans that the law must not play favorites, that no man or group of men is entitled to special consideration. It might, however, be argued that since Negroes encounter racial discrimination and whites do not, equality for Negroes can be achieved only through special protection. Statutes, constitutional interpretations, and public policies which adequately safeguard the rights of white citizens do not, sad to say, always accomplish similar results for Negroes. White Americans had no need for a law such as the Civil Rights Act of 1875, which prohibited racial discrimination in public accommodations, because they were not subject to such discrimination. Nor, for that matter, did they need the 13th, 14th, and 15th amendments. Thus, when the Supreme Court declared the Civil Rights Act unconstitutional and circumscribed the meaning of those amendments, it did not adversely affect the rights of white citizens. It merely removed the special protections which had been intended to make Negroes equal citizens. Those decisions thus assured Negro inequality—at least as long as racial discrimination existed.

The Court's rulings virtually gave southern whites a free hand in race relations. There were, of course, limitations beyond which they could not go. They could not repeal the Reconstruction amendments or overtly nullify them. But they could accomplish the same thing through indirection and subterfuge. The process began in 1890 when the constitu-

tional convention of Mississippi adopted a series of measures which disfranchised virtually all Negroes in that state. South Carolina (1895) and Louisiana (1898) soon took similar steps; and by 1910, the "Mississippi Plan" or some variation thereof was in effect in every southern state.

The specific measures varied from state to state, but everywhere the purpose was the same—to eliminate Negroes from politics by circumventing the 15th-Amendment guarantee that "the right of citizens of the United States to vote shall not be denied or abridged by the United States or by any State on account of race, color, or previous condition of servitude." The most common devices were literacy tests, property qualifications, and poll taxes. Any one of these, however, if applied with a modicum of straightforwardness, would enfranchise a considerable number of Negroes and disfranchise many whites. Some of the men responsible for disfranchising Negroes had no objection to disfranchising poor and uneducated whites as well. Others, however, who considered themselves spokesmen for poor whites, did have objections and were troubled that so many whites fell within the purview of the voter disqualification laws. Their concern was justified. At the turn of the century, in 231 counties in the South, 20 percent or more of voting-age whites were illiterate; while in many areas the new property qualification for voting, typically $300 to $500, exceeded the per capita wealth.

To overcome these factors, the disfranchisers devised a variety of loopholes through which poor, illiterate whites could escape disqualification and literate, property-owning Negroes could not. The laws themselves were written in vague and general language and gave (white) registrars wide latitude in determining who could and who could not vote. An "understanding clause" permitted an illiterate (white) to register if, in the registrar's opinion, he satisfactorily interpreted a passage in the state constitution read to him. A "good-character" clause permitted disqualification of anyone who met literacy and property qualifications but was not, in the registrar's judgment, a man of good character. A "grandfather clause," first enacted in Louisiana, made this kind of subterfuge unnecessary by simply making the right to vote hereditary for whites. This was done by exempting from voter disqualification laws anyone eligible to vote in the state on January 1, 1867 (before Radical Reconstruction and Negro voting began), or anyone whose father or grandfather was then eligible. The poll tax served a variety of uses. It was not only a tax on the right to vote, but it was administered so as to make voting difficult. The tax itself, due 6 to 18 months before election day, was usually cumulative for two or three years, and the voter was required to present his receipt of payment to registration and election officials on various occasions. Finally, if Negro voters were not discouraged or disqualified by these and other requirements and accompanying pressures, the Democratic white primary was instituted to exclude them from the only meaningful election in the one-party South. The Democratic Party declared itself to be a private club and its primary election a private function for members only. Thus the handful of Negroes who could vote did so only in general elections in which there was only one candidate—the winner of the Democratic white primary.

The impact of these measures was overwhelming. The Louisiana experience was not untypical. There, between 1897 and 1904, the total number of registered voters declined from 294,432 to 93,058. Among whites, the decline was from 164,088 to 91,716; among Negroes, from 130,344 to 1,342. More important than mere figures, however, was the effect of disfranchisement upon the Negro's status in the South. It deprived the race of the last of the guarantees inherited from Radical Reconstruction. The Radicals had intended the franchise to be the Negro's basic protection against southern whites.

It never fulfilled that purpose, at least not entirely, in part because Negroes remained economically dependent upon whites and therefore subject to economic pressure. It did, however, help to blunt anti-Negro tendencies among white politicians, a number of whom, like Wade Hampton in South Carolina and L. Q. C. Lamar in Mississippi, had in the seventies and eighties encouraged interracial cooperation in politics. Now this protection was lost and, with it, the incentive for politicians to forgo race baiting and concern themselves with the well-being of Negroes. Southern politics soon fell prey to race-baiting demagogues, and southern politicians became the most extreme advocates of white supremacy in the section. Disfranchisement thus completed a cycle. After the Compromise of 1877, Negroes could no longer look to the President and Congress for protection against southern whites. After the *Plessy* decision of 1896, they could no longer look to the federal courts—and thus to the Constitution. Now they could no longer help themselves.

Political impotence made Negroes vulnerable to attack from white-dominated governments; and between 1890 and 1910, the southern states enacted a series of laws and ordinances which did to Negroes socially and economically what disfranchisement had done politically. A new era dawned in southern race relations, an era of rigid, ubiquitous segregation which still endures in many places. That the era was new is often forgotten. But as C. Vann Woodward has convincingly demonstrated, the pervasive segregation typical of the 20th century was in significant respects an innovation of the years following 1890. It is of course easy to overstress the integration and interracial harmony of the earlier period; nevertheless, the changes wrought after 1890 were fundamental. In his recent study, *Race Relations in Virginia, 1870–1902*, Charles E. Wynes states that "the most distinguishing factor in the complexity of social relations between the races was that of inconsistency. From 1870 to 1900, there was no generally accepted code of racial mores." Moreover, he continues, "at no time was it the general demand of the white populace that the Negro be disfranchised and white supremacy be made the law of the land." Until 1900, when the Virginia legislature enacted a law requiring segregated railroad cars, "the Negro sat where he pleased and among the white passengers on perhaps a majority of the state's railroads."

None of these statements would be true for Virginia—or the rest of the South—after the first decade of the 20th century. After that time, there *was* a generally accepted code of racial mores everywhere in the section, and it was observed with remarkable consistency.

The new laws and ordinances requiring segregation are an imperfect guide to what actually happened. In many instances, passage of a law merely confirmed what was already occurring; in others, segregation became the rule without benefit of law. Nevertheless, these new statutes do reflect the changes taking place. Before 1900, only three states required segregated railroad cars, and evidence indicates that integration was a common practice in this important means of public transportation. By 1910, every southern state required segregation on railroads, and integrated travel was a thing of the past. Before 1900, only Georgia required segregated seating in streetcars; a decade later, streetcar segregation was practiced throughout the South. In short, by 1910, whites and Negroes had been systematically segregated throughout the section—in factories, hospitals, public parks, theaters, penal and eleemosynary institutions—or permitted to come together only in a master-servant relationship. A typical ordinance in Birmingham, Alabama, required racial segregation in "any room, hall, theatre, picture house, auditorium, yard, court, ball park, or other indoor or outdoor place"; and it was specified that in these areas, whites and Negroes must be "distinctly separa-

ted" by "well defined physical barriers." In one city or another across the South, everything from telephones to prostitutes was segregated, and Ray Stannard Baker reported in 1908 that separate Bibles were used to swear in white and Negro witnesses in Atlanta courts!

Again the racial significance of this must be stressed. Ostensibly, segregation laws applied equally to whites and Negroes. In reality the laws meant different things to each race. In their efforts to understand American Negro slavery, historians often note the difficulty a free man has in comprehending what it means to be a slave. The same difficulty exists for the white American who tries to understand segregation and is no doubt one reason whites have been willing to tolerate that institution. What does it mean to be a segregated man, to be told by your society in a thousand subtle and unsubtle ways that yours is a race so despised, so contaminated as it were, that other men must quarantine themselves from you? In *The Souls of Black Folk*, first published in 1903, W. E. B. Du Bois, a sensitive and incisive observer, described what life in the white man's society was like to him. (And Du Bois's experience, it must be remembered, was relatively "integrated" and comparatively free of the harsher aspects of segregation.) "It dawned upon me with a certain suddenness that I was different from [my white classmates]," he wrote of his first encounter with racial prejudice, "[that I was] shut out from their world by a vast veil. . . . The worlds I longed for, and all their dazzling opportunities, were theirs, not mine." Du Bois was better able to withstand discrimination than many of his youthful contemporaries. Of their response to life in the white man's world, he wrote:

Their youth shrunk into tasteless sycophancy, or into silent hatred of the pale world about them and mocking distrust of everything white; or wasted itself in a bitter cry, Why did God make me an outcast and a stranger in mine own house? The shades of the prison-house closed round about us all: walls strait and stubborn to the whitest, but relentlessly narrow, tall, and unscalable to sons of night who must plod darkly on in resignation, or beat unavailing palms against the stone, or steadily, half hopelessly, watch the streak of blue above.

For whites, segregation meant little more than physical separation from Negroes; for Negroes, it made *race* the supreme fact of life. At every turn it subjected the individual Negro to an invidious racial test. It meant that he could not go as far in life as his talents and ambition might otherwise carry him. Every day he encountered a racial veil which circumscribed his liberties, stifled his talents, thwarted his ambition. He could not live where he pleased, work where he pleased, play where he pleased, go to the school of his choice. Like slavery, segregation was ill suited to make "good" Americans, if the criteria of goodness be those honored by the white majority. The segregated Negro found it impossible, or virtually so, to exercise the responsibilities of citizenship or reap the rewards of the good life. He could not adequately protect himself, his family, or his property. He could not as easily as white Americans achieve a position of self-respect, independence, and virtue. The effect of segregation was to mold Negroes into second-class citizens; to keep them uneducated, ignorant, and poverty-stricken; to encourage antisocial and immoral behavior in them—and then use these shortcomings as justification for perpetuating segregation by insisting that the race is not yet "ready" for integration.

The triumph of southern segregationists did not take place in a vacuum. It was directly related to the intellectual milieu of the times. This was the era in which the American people assumed a share of "the white man's burden," excluded oriental immigrants, endorsed a variety of movements and ideologies tinged with racism or nativism. Racism—specifically, a belief in the innate inequality of races and ethnic groups—was commonly accepted

by Americans of that day, whether Northerners or Southerners, and was the basic justification offered for racial segregation. Segregation was the racists' solution to the race problem; it is justifiable, they insisted, because Negroes are innately inferior to whites. Because of this inferiority, continued the racists' argument, Negroes cannot intelligently exercise the responsibilities of citizenship; and since their inferiority is innate, it cannot be overcome by environmental reforms. In other words, the racist argument is essentially this: Negroes are second-class Americans—poor, ignorant, immoral, etc.—because they are second-rate human beings. Of course, these ideas have no validity at all, but they are widely believed at the beginning of the 20th century. One of the great cultural lags in this country today consists of the fact that segregation persists long after the ideas originally used to justify it have been exploded.

The prosegregation argument was widely accepted in this bustling era. Henry W. Grady, architect of the New South, even though he was one of his section's most imaginative and progressive leaders, insisted that whites "have clear and unmistakable control of public affairs" in the South because "they are the superior race, and will not and cannot submit to the domination of an inferior race." Theodore Roosevelt, whose racial views were more enlightened that those of many of his contemporaries, expressed similar ideas. "Now as to the negroes!" he wrote novelist Owen Wister. "I entirely agree with you that as a race and in the mass they are altogether inferior to whites."

Because of the widespread acceptance of these views, northern public opinion came to be generally sympathetic toward southern segregationists. "Northern whites are beginning to sympathize strongly with their Southern brethren in respect to the peculiar burden which the action of the National Government in liberating the Negro has imposed on them," declared

President Charles W. Eliot of Harvard in 1904. "Put the prosperous Northern whites in Southern States, in immediate contact with millions of Negroes, and they would promptly establish separate schools for the colored population, whatever the necessary cost." Men of Eliot's class were now convinced that Radical Reconstruction had been unwise. "One thing is clear, the work done by those who were in political control at the close of our Civil War was done in utter ignorance of ethnologic law and total disregard of unalterable fact," wrote the younger Charles Francis Adams in 1906. "We will in America make small progress towards a solution of our race problem until we approach it in less of a theoretic and humanitarian, and more of a scientific spirit."

The history of Negro Americans is characterized by periods of frustration and defeat alternating with moments of hope and progress. The promise of Reconstruction followed close on the heels of slavery and was itself soon succeeded by the slough of segregation and disfranchisement. In his perceptive study, *Negro Thought in America, 1880–1915*, August Meier suggests that these cycles of hope and despair have exerted a transcendent influence upon the attitude of Negroes toward racial policy. When their prospects brighten, Negroes tend to direct their energies toward equality and integration into the larger society; in darker periods they are prone to turn their interests inward, seeking escape from the white man's world and preoccupying themselves with self-help, self-improvement, and race nationalism. For the gloomy years of the New South, this pattern seems especially valid. At such a time, influential Negro leaders generally advocated self-help and self-improvement as the most likely means of promoting the welfare of their race, meliorating racial prejudice, and blunting the harshness of segregation and disfranchisement.

Part of the Negroes' difficulties in these years stemmed from the lack of broadly based and viable racial organizations. Except for religious and fraternal groups, which were escapist rather than activist in nature, there were no organizations with mass membership and broad influence among the race. There were no counterparts of the more effective civil rights groups today. Given the socioeconomic condition of the race, this was not surprising. In 1890, more than 57 percent of Negro Americans were illiterates, and no doubt most of the literates were only marginally so. In the same year, when an overwhelming majority of the nearly eight million American Negroes lived in the rural South, the Census Bureau found only 120,738 Negro farmers who owned their homes. Ten years later, more than 86 percent of Negroes still derived their livelihood from agriculture, domestic service, or related occupations. The race was thus grossly over-represented in the poorest paying jobs and, as a result, had no large middle class to supply a broadly based racial leadership. There were, however, individual Negro leaders who exercised considerable influence among their race and among whites as well, of whom first Frederick Douglass and later Booker T. Washington were preeminent. By 1900 a third leader, W. E. B. Du Bois, was emerging to challenge Washington's leadership; and from the perspective of today, he is much more significant than Washington.

Frederick Douglass, ex-slave, former abolitionist, ardent equalitarian, was the most influential Negro American from antebellum days until his death in 1895. A militant, outspoken man, Douglass insisted that Negroes should have complete equality in America and that they should be satisfied with nothing less. The only issue involved in racial policy, he reminded white Americans in 1894, is whether "American justice, American liberty, American civilization, American law, and American Christianity can be made to include and protect alike and forever all American citizens in the rights which have been guaranteed to them by the organic and fundamental laws of the land."

Even before his death, Douglass' outspoken equalitarianism was giving way to Booker T. Washington's gradualism and accommodationism. To a considerable extent, Washington became the leading spokesman of his generation not so much because he led Negroes (though subsequently he came to wield tremendous power over them) but because he voiced sentiments appealing to white men. In effect, he asked Negroes to forgo the things of which white supremacists were then depriving the race. His advice to Negroes was especially attractive to men who shared the racial views, previously quoted, of Henry W. Grady, Theodore Roosevelt, and Charles Francis Adams. However, this does not mean that Washington was an "Uncle Tom" or a "white man's Negro." He was a much more complex man than that. His discussion of ultimate goals was always ambiguous and open-ended. He never explicitly accepted segregation as the final racial policy, never endorsed the disfranchisement policies of white supremacists. It seems certain that he envisioned eventual racial equality. His approach was essentially evolutionary and gradual; and given the conditions of the time, it was in some senses realistic. Much of it, though, was unrealistic, even anachronistic. His emphasis on vocational training and agriculture, for example, came at a time when the South was industrializing and urbanizing, and would do little to help Negroes meet the challenges implicit in these changed conditions. A victim of many of the myths of agrarianism and the "southern way of life," Washington thought Negroes should stay on the farm and in the South as a permanent agricultural class. By urging his race to deemphasize politics, and by not insisting on continued federal intervention in southern race policy, he seemed to acquiesce in the loss of the chief means Negroes had of protecting themselves. He believed that through hard work, self-

sacrifice, and appeals to the white man's better nature, and not through protest, agitation, and direct action, Negroes would earn—and thus receive—full equality in the South.

The Negro's experience since the turn of the century would argue that Washington's advice was inadequate. Generally speaking, the white South has never made a substantial concession to Negro Southerners that was not forced through some form of direct action by Negroes themselves and/or through "outside" pressure from the federal government and northern reformers.

Washington's views were of course challenged by many Negroes. Throughout the period of his suzerainty, there was a growing opposition to his ideas, which came to center around W. E. B. Du Bois. Well educated (Fisk, Harvard, Berlin), a Harvard Ph.D., an accomplished author, journalist, and scholar, Du Bois was an intellectual cosmopolite to whom Washington's racial policies were not only personally repugnant and racially insulting but economically unsound and politically unwise. Increasingly critical of Washington after 1900, Du Bois advocated equality for Negroes and abolition of all invidious racial distinctions in American life. He saw the salvation of the race in its "talented tenth" of educated men. He was militant where Washington was accommodationist, demanding where Washington pleaded. Moreover, he had the ear of a small group of white liberals who shared his views, and with them in 1909 organized the National Association for the Advancement of Colored People. Through the NAACP, Du Bois was in the forefront of the movement which led Negroes away from the accommodationism of Washington and toward integration and equalitarianism. Progress, however, was agonizingly slow, and Du Bois was not a patient man. He eventually became a Marxist, a communist, but this does not detract from his earlier accomplishments. As much as any man, Du Bois is responsible for pointing Negroes in the direction of the civil rights movement, which has already accomplished more for the race than was accomplished in the previous 300 years of their American experience.

SUGGESTED READINGS

Du Bois, W. E. B. *The Souls of Black Folk.* New York: Crest Books, 1961.

Franklin, John Hope. *From Slavery to Freedom: A History of American Negroes.* New York: Alfred A. Knopf, 1961.

Gossett, Thomas F. *Race: The History of an Idea in America.* Dallas: Southern Methodist University Press, 1963.

Logan, Rayford W. *The Betrayal of the Negro: From Rutherford B. Hayes to Woodrow Wilson.* New York: Collier Books, 1965.

Meier, August. *Negro Thought in America, 1880–1915.* Ann Arbor: University of Michigan Press, 1963.

Newby, I. A. *Jim Crow's Defense: Anti-Negro Thought in America, 1900–1930.* Baton Rouge: Louisiana State University Press, 1965.

Quarles, Benjamin, and Fishel, Leslie H. Jr. *The Black American: A Documentary Collection.* Glenview, Ill.: Scott, Foresman & Co., 1970.

Washington, Booker T. *Up from Slavery: An Autobiography.* New York: A. L. Burt, 1901.

Woodward, C. Vann. *The Burden of Southern History.* Baton Rouge: Louisiana State University Press, 1960.

——. *Origins of the New South, 1877–1913.* Baton Rouge: Louisiana State University Press, 1951

——. *The Strange Career Of Jim Crow.* 2d rev. ed. New York: Oxford University Press, 1966.

Wynes, Charles E. *Race Relations in Virginia, 1870–1902.* Charlottesville: University of Virginia Press, 1961.

DOCUMENT 24.1
The Atlanta Exposition Address*

Between 1877 and 1910, Negroes faced the perennial questions of racial policy: What is the proper role (or "place") of Negroes in American life, and how might that role be most readily attained? Booker T. Washington discussed the substance of those questions on September 18, 1895, in his famous address at the opening ceremonies of the Atlanta Exposition.

A ship lost at sea for many days suddenly sighted a friendly vessel. From the mast of the unfortunate vessel was seen a signal: "Water, water; we die of thirst!" The answer from the friendly vessel at once came back: "Cast down your bucket where you are.". . . The captain of the distressed vessel, at last heeding the injuction, cast down his bucket, and it came up full of fresh, sparkling water from the mouth of the Amazon River. To those of my race who depend upon bettering their condition in a foreign land, or who underestimate the importance of cultivating friendly relations with the Southern white man who is their next-door neighbor, I would say: "Cast down your bucket where you are"—cast it down in making friends, in every manly way, of the people of all races by whom we are surrounded.

Cast it down in agriculture, in mechanics, in commerce, in domestic service, and in the professions. And in this connection it is well to bear in mind that whatever other sins the South may be called to bear, when it comes to business, pure and simple, it is in the South that the Negro is given a man's chance in the commercial world, and in nothing is this Exposition more eloquent than in emphasizing this chance. Our greatest danger is that in the great leap from slavery to freedom we may overlook the fact that the masses of us are to live by the productions of our hands,

*Source: Booker T. Washington, *Up from Slavery: An Autobiography* (New York: A. L. Burt, 1901), pp. 153–58.

and fail to keep in mind that we shall prosper in proportion as we learn to dignify and glorify common labor, and put brains and skill into the common occupations of life; shall prosper in proportion as we learn to draw the line between the superficial and the substantial, the ornamental gewgaws of life and the useful. No race can prosper till it learns that there is as much dignity in tilling a field as in writing a poem. It is at the bottom of life we must begin, and not at the top. Nor should we permit our grievances to overshadow our opportunities.

To those of the white race who look to the incoming of those of foreign birth and strange tongue and habits for the prosperity of the South, were I permitted, I would repeat what I say to my own race, "Cast down your bucket where you are." Cast it down among the eight million Negroes whose habits you know, whose fidelity and love you have tested in days when to have proved treacherous meant the ruin of your firesides. Cast down your bucket among these people who have without strikes and labor wars tilled your fields, cleared your forests, builded your railroads and cities, brought forth treasures from the bowels of the earth, and helped make possible this magnificent representation of the progress of the South. Casting down your bucket among my people, helping and encouraging them as you are doing on these grounds, and, with education of head, hand, and heart, you will find that they will buy your surplus land, make blossom the waste places in your fields, and run your factories. While doing this, you can be sure in the future, as in the past, that you and your families will be surrounded by the most patient, faithful, law-abiding, and unresentful people that the world has seen. As we have proved our loyalty to you in the past, in nursing your children, watching by the sick bed of your mothers and fathers, and often following them with tear-dimmed eyes to their graves, so in the future, in our humble way, we shall stand by you with a devotion that no foreigner can approach, ready to lay down our lives, if need be, in defense of yours, interlacing our industrial, commercial, civil, and religious life with yours in a way that shall make the interests of both races one. In all things that are purely social we can be as separate as the fingers, yet one as the hand in all things essential to mutual progress. . . .

The wisest among my race understand that the agitation of questions of social equality is the extremest folly, and that progress in the enjoyment of all the privileges that will come to us must be the result of severe and constant struggle rather than of artificial forcing. No race that has anything to contribute to the markets of the world is long, in any degree, ostracized. It is important and right that all privileges of the law be ours, but it is vastly more important that we be prepared for the exercise of those privileges. The opportunity to earn a dollar in a factory just now is worth infinitely more than the opportunity to spend a dollar in an opera house.

DOCUMENT 24.2

Of Mr. Booker T. Washington and Others*

W. E. B. Du Bois was the most important critic of Booker T. Washington's accommodationism. In the following excerpt, written in 1903, he challenges the racial policies advocated by Washington and offers alternative views.

Among his own people, . . . Mr. Washington has encountered the strongest and most lasting opposition, amounting at times to bitterness, and even to-day continuing strong and insistent even though largely silenced in outward expression by the public opinion of the nation. . . . There

*Source: W. E. B. Du Bois, *The Souls of Black Folk* (Chicago: A. C. McClurg, 1903), pp. 47–59.

is among educated and thoughtful colored men in all parts of the land a feeling of deep regret, sorrow, and apprehension at the wide currency and ascendancy which some of Mr. Washington's theories have gained. . . .

Mr. Washington represents in Negro thought the old attitude of adjustment and submission; but adjustment at such a peculiar time as to make his programme unique. This is an age of unusual economic development, and Mr. Washington's programme naturally takes an economic cast, becoming a gospel of Work and Money to such an extent as apparently almost completely to overshadow the higher aims of life. Moreover, this is an age when the more advanced races are coming in closer contact with the less developed races, and the race-feeling is therefore intensified; and Mr. Washington's programme practically accepts the alleged inferiority of the Negro races. Again, in our own land, the reaction from the sentiment of war time has given impetus to race-prejudice against Negroes, and Mr. Washington withdraws many of the high demands of Negroes as men and American citizens. In other periods of intensified prejudice all the Negro's tendency to self-assertion has been called forth; at this period a policy of submission is advocated. In the history of nearly all other races and peoples the doctrine preached at such crises has been that manly self-respect is worth more than lands and houses, and that a people who voluntarily surrender such respect, or cease striving for it, are not worth civilizing.

In answer to this, it has been claimed that the Negro can survive only through submission. Mr. Washington distinctly asks that black people give up, at least for the present, three things,—

First, political power,
Second, insistence on civil rights,
Third, higher education of Negro
    youth,—

and concentrate all their energies on industrial education, the accumulation of wealth, and the conciliation of the South. This policy has been courageously and insistently advocated for over fifteen years, and has been triumphant for perhaps ten years. As a result of this tender of the palm branch what has been the return? In these years there have occurred:

1. The disfranchisement of the Negro.
2. The legal creation of a distinct status of civil inferiority for the Negro.
3. The steady withdrawal of aid from institutions for the higher training of the Negro.

These movements are not, to be sure, direct results of Mr. Washington's teachings; but his propaganda has, without a shadow of doubt, helped their speedier accomplishment. The question then comes: Is it possible, and probable, that nine millions of men can make effective progress in economic lines if they are deprived of political rights, made a servile caste, and allowed only the most meagre chance for developing their exceptional men? If history and reason give any distinct answer to these questions, it is an emphatic *No*. . . .

. . . [Thinking classes of American Negroes] insist that the way to truth and right lies in straightforward honesty, not in indiscriminate flattery; in praising those of the South who do well and criticising uncompromisingly those who do ill; in taking advantage of the opportunities at hand and urging their fellows to do the same, but at the same time in remembering that only a firm adherence to their higher ideals and aspirations will ever keep those ideals within the realm of possibility; . . . they are absolutely certain that the way for a people to gain their reasonable rights is not by voluntarily throwing them away and insisting that they do not want them; that the way for a people to gain respect is not by continually belittling and ridiculing themselves; that, on the contrary, Negroes must insist continually, in season and out of season, that voting is necessary to modern manhood, that color discrimination is barbarism, and that black boys need education as well as white boys. . . .

. . . On the whole the distinct impression left by Mr. Washington's propaganda is, first, that the South is justified in its present attitude toward the Negro because of the Negro's degradation; secondly, that the prime cause of the Negro's failure to rise more quickly is his wrong education in the past; and, thirdly, that his future rise depends primarily on his own efforts. Each of these propositions is a dangerous half-truth. The supplementary truths must never be lost sight of: first, slavery and race-prejudice are potent if not sufficient causes of the Negro's position; second, industrial and common-school training were necessarily slow in planting because they had to await the black teachers trained by higher institutions, . . . and, third, while it is great truth to say that the Negro must strive and strive *mightily* to help himself, it is equally true that unless his striving be not simply seconded, but rather aroused and encouraged, by the initiative of the richer and wiser environing group, he cannot hope for great success.

In his failure to realize and impress this last point, Mr. Washington is especially to be criticised. His doctrine has tended to make the whites, North and South, shift the burden of the Negro problem to the Negro's shoulders and stand aside as critical and rather pessimistic spectators; when in fact the burden belongs to the nation, and the hands of none of us are clean if we bend not our energies to righting these great wrongs. . . .

DOCUMENT 24.3
A Southern Politician Defends Segregation*

In the following speech, Representative Frank Clark of Florida gives a segregationist's answer to questions concerning racial policy and the proper place of Negroes in American life. He made this speech in defense of an amendment (to a pending bill before the House of Representatives) to institute segregation on streetcars in Washington, D.C. He repeats some of the segregationist's most widely used arguments and also illustrates the intellectual level of much segregationist literature.

I am going to vote for this amendment. I am going to do it because I think it is in the interest of the black man more so than it is in the interest of the white man, and I say this because, as is well known, in every conflict between the races the black man gets the worst of it. You bring them together and you are bound to have conflicts. . . . I would not do them an injury. I would not do them a wrong. . . .

The relations of the races in the South is [sic] the one question, I believe, above all others that has been more discussed by more people who absolutely knew nothing of it than any other question that has ever challenged American thought since the formation of the Republic. The ignorance of real conditions permeating the effusions of theoretical defenders of the negro race would be ludicrous in the extreme if it were not for the fact that every speech, magazine article, or other publication of this character makes more difficult the proper and just settlement of one of the greatest problems that ever confronted any people. . . .

The average negro is perfectly happy when he finds himself eating a watermelon or going on a railroad excursion.

---

*Source: *Congressional Record*, February 22, 1908, Appendix, pp. 38–40.

The railroad companies in the South cater to this weakness of the negro for riding on trains, and scarcely a week passes in the summer time that a negro excursion is not "pulled off" in every neighborhood. They flock to these excursion trains by thousands, and of course the cars set apart for the negroes on the regular passenger trains are used for negro excursions.

Imagine a nice, new passenger coach, packed with dirty, greasy, filthy negroes, down South, in midsummer, and you can readily understand why that car does not long remain as good, as clean, and as desirable as a similar car occupied exclusively by white travelers. It is said of Sam Jones, the great Georgia revivalist, that on one occasion a certain Northern gentleman asked him if there was very much difference in the instincts of a "nigger" and a white man. Sam replied that he didn't know as to that, but of one thing he was absolutely sure, and that was that there was a vast difference in the *out stinks* of the two. . . .

Mr. Lincoln said that this nation could not exist "half slave and half free." I think it is equally true that this nation can not exist *half white* and *half black*. I am sure that no country having within its borders two distinct races, alien to each other in every essential respect, can long exist with any degree of harmony between the two upon the beautiful theory of perfect equality of all before the law.

The position which we of the South occupy on this question is not one of hostility to the negro. It is one of patriotic love for our own race. We will do the black man no harm, and we will not allow him to harm the white man. Members of Congress who are dependent upon a few negro votes in order to retain their seats in this body, a few long-haired negrophilists in various sections of the country, and a lot of short-haired white women who disgrace both their race and sex, may rant of injustice and wrong to the end of time, but they had as well realize now as at any other time that, no matter what the cost or

how great the sacrifice, we shall under any and all circumstances maintain the integrity of our race and preserve our civilization. . . .

If God Almighty had intended these two races to be equal, He would have so created them. He made the Caucasian of handsome figure, straight hair, regular features, high brow, and superior intellect. He created the negro, giving him a black skin, kinky hair, thick lips, flat nose, low brow, low order of intelligence, and repulsive features. I do not believe that these differences were the result of either accident or mistake on the part of the Creator. I believe He knew what He was doing, and I believe He did just what He wanted to do.

We believe in God, and we are willing to accept His work just as it fell from His hands. But these people who profess to believe that "a white man may be as good as a negro if the white man behaves himself" are not satisfied with God's work in this regard. They are quite sure that they can make a better job of it than did the Creator, hence we find them attempting to remove the black man from the menial sphere for which he was created, and where he may be useful, to a higher circle, for which he is entirely unfitted and where he is perfectly useless.

DOCUMENT 24.4
A Southern White Integrationist Speaks*

In the years of the New South, few southern whites spoke in favor of racial integration. One who did so was the Virginian Lewis H. Blair, whose defense of integrated public schools, though published in 1889, is still strikingly valid today.

---

*Source: Lewis H. Blair, *The Prosperity of the South Dependent upon the Elevation of the Negro* (1889), edited by C. Vann Woodward as *A Southern Prophecy* (Boston: Little, Brown & Co., 1964), pp. 137–38, 148–49.

The moral necessity is this: Separate Schools are a public proclamation to all of African or mixed blood that they are an inferior caste, fundamentally inferior and totally unfit to mingle on terms of equality with the superior caste. That this is not a temporary and ephemeral but a fundamental and caste inferiority is proven by the fact that opposition does not cease when the temporary inferiority ceases, but still operates, however cultured and refined the Negro may be. Hence it follows that separate schools brand the stigma of degradation upon one-half of the population, irrespective of character and culture, and crush their hope and self-respect, without which they can never become useful and valuable citizens. Life is hard enough and progress is slow enough with all the tonic of self-respect and with all the stimulus of hope, but deprived thereof, the boldest and the bravest among the whites cease effort and relapse into despondency, despair or recklessness; but when we make our implement of elevation, namely our public schools, simply a branding iron for stamping the letter "D", degraded, upon the foreheads of millions of black fellow-citizens, we deliberately tear up by the roots all our other efforts for their amelioration. We can improve the beauty, strength, speed and usefulness of animals by careful feeding, housing and training, but we can never make men of human beings simply by attending, however carefully, to their physical necessities—meat and drink of the best quality and in the greatest abundance leave them animals still. We can only make men of them by cultivating and stimulating their higher and nobler natures, their mental and moral parts, and this can never be done while the principle of separate schools remains in full force. . . .

Separate schools poison at its very source the stream whence spring the best and noblest fruits of education, because at the very beginning of instruction the little ones are taught two dogmas—first, that white children are and shall *forever* be fundamentally superior to black children; and, second, that black children are and *forever* shall be fundamentally inferior to white children. At the fountain of education the doctrine of caste, which elsewhere is being successfully combatted, is enshrined in fresh vigor and authority, and it seizes with its rigid, icy grasp the impressible minds of the children, and taints them; and the blind superiority thereby inculcated fosters sentiments of false pride, disregard of the rights of others, and unfeeling haughtiness to all, regardless of color, whom they deem inferiors; and the inferiority thereby taught the blacks cultivates feelings of abasement and of servile fear of all whom they consider superior—sentiments totally destructive of manliness, courage and self-respect, the noblest jewels in the character of man.

DOCUMENT 24.5

Plessy v. Ferguson: The Supreme Court Decision*

In the *Plessy* case the Supreme Court gave its answer to questions of racial policy and the Negro's proper place in American life. The result was to make segregation the law of the land.

This case turns upon the constitutionality of an act of the General Assembly of the State of Louisiana, passed in 1890, providing for separate railway carriages for the white and colored races. . . .

The constitutionality of this act is attacked upon the ground that it conflicts both with the Thirteenth Amendment of the Constitution, abolishing slavery, and the Fourteenth Amendment, which prohibits certain restrictive legislation on the part of the States.

1. That it does not conflict with the Thirteenth Amendment, which abolished slavery and involuntary servitude, except

---

*Source: *Plessy* v. *Ferguson,* 163 U.S. 537 (1896).

as a punishment for crime, is too clear for argument. . . .

A statute which implies merely a legal distinction between the white and colored races—a distinction which is founded in the color of the two races, and which must always exist so long as white men are distinguished from the other race by color—has no tendency to destroy the legal equality of the two races, or reestablish a state of involuntary servitude. . . .

The object of the [14th] amendment was undoubtedly to enforce the absolute equality of the two races before the law, but in the nature of things it could not have been intended to abolish distinctions based upon color, or to enforce social, as distinguished from political equality, or a commingling of the two races upon terms unsatisfactory to either. Laws permitting, and even requiring, their separation in places where they are liable to be brought into contact do not necessarily imply the inferiority of either race to the other, and have been generally, if not universally, recognized as within the competency of the state legislatures in the exercise of their police power. The most common instance of this is connected with the establishment of separate schools for white and colored children, which has been held to be a valid exercise of the legislative power even by courts of states where the political rights of the colored race have been longest and most earnestly enforced. . . .

So far, then, as a conflict with the Fourteenth Amendment is concerned, the case reduces itself to the question whether the statute of Louisiana is a reasonable regulation, and with respect to this there must necessarily be a large discretion on the part of the legislature. In determining the question of reasonableness it is at liberty to act with reference to the established usages, customs and traditions of the people, and with a view to the promotion of their comfort, and the preservation of the public peace and good order. Gauged by this standard, we cannot say that a law

which authorizes or even requires the separation of the two races in public conveyances is unreasonable, or more obnoxious to the Fourteenth Amendment than the acts of Congress requiring separate schools for colored children in the District of Columbia. . . .

We consider the underlying fallacy of the plaintiff's argument to consist in the assumption that the enforced separation of the two races stamps the colored race with a badge of inferiority. If this be so, it is not by reason of anything found in the act, but solely because the colored race chooses to put that construction upon it. . . . The argument also assumes that social prejudices may be overcome by legislation, and that equal rights cannot be secured to the Negro except by an enforced commingling of the two races. We cannot accept this proposition. If the two races are to meet upon terms of social equality, it must be the result of natural affinities, a mutual appreciation of each other's merits and a voluntary consent of individuals. . . . Legislation is powerless to eradicate racial instincts or to abolish distinctions based upon physical differences, and the attempt to do so can only result in accentuating the difficulties of the present situation. . . . If one race be inferior to the other socially, the Constitution of the United States cannot put them upon the same plane. . . .

DOCUMENT 24.6

Plessy v. Ferguson: Justice Harlan's Dissenting Opinion*

Justice John Marshall Harlan, a Kentuckian and former slaveholder, was the only member of the Court to dissent from the *Plessy* decision. His dissent was a stirring appeal for equality of all men before the law regardless of their race. In a series

---

*Source: *Plessy* v. *Ferguson,* 163 U.S. 537 (1896).

of decisions since 1954, the Supreme Court has fully vindicated Harlan's views.

In respect of civil rights, common to all citizens, the Constitution of the United States does not, I think, permit any public authority to know the race of those entitled to be protected in the enjoyment of such rights. Every true man has pride of race, and under appropriate circumstances when the rights of others, his equals before the law, are not to be affected, it is his privilege to express such pride and to take such action based upon it as to him seems proper. But I deny that any legislative body or judicial tribunal may have regard to the race of citizens when the civil rights of those citizens are involved. Indeed, such legislation, as that here in question, is inconsistent not only with that equality of rights which pertains to citizenship, National and State, but with the personal liberty enjoyed by every one within the United States. . . .

These notable additions to the fundamental law [i.e., the 13th, 14th, and 15th amendments] were welcomed by the friends of liberty throughout the world. They removed the race line from our governmental system. They had, as this court has said, a common purpose, namely, to secure "to a race recently emancipated, a race that through many generations have been held in slavery, all the civil rights that the superior race enjoy." They declared, in legal effect, this court has further said, "that the law in the States shall be the same for the black as for the white; that all persons, whether colored or white, shall stand equal before the laws of the States, and, in regard to the colored race, for whose protection the amendment was primarily designed, that no discrimination shall be made against them by law because of their color." We also said: "The words of the amendment, it is true, are prohibitory, but they contain a necessary implication of a positive immunity, or right, most valuable to the colored race—the right to exemption from unfriendly legislation against them distinctively as colored—exemption from legal discriminations, implying inferiority in civil society, lessening the security of their enjoyment of the rights which others enjoy, and discriminations which are steps toward reducing them to the condition of a subject race." . . .

It was said in argument that the statute of Louisiana does not discriminate against either race, but prescribes a rule applicable alike to white and colored citizens. . . . Every one knows that the statute in question had its origin in the purpose, not so much to exclude white persons from railroad cars occupied by blacks, as to exclude colored people from coaches occupied by or assigned to white persons. . . . The thing to accomplish was, under the guise of giving equal accommodation for whites and blacks, to compel the latter to keep to themselves while travelling in railroad passenger coaches. No one would be so wanting in candor as to assert the contrary. The fundamental objection, therefore, to the statute is that it interferes with the personal freedom of citizens. . . . If a white man and a black man choose to occupy the same public conveyance on a public highway, it is their right to do so, and no government, proceeding alone on grounds of race, can prevent it without infringing the personal liberty of each. . . .

The white race deems itself to be the dominant race in this country. And so it is, in prestige, in achievements, in education, in wealth and in power. . . . But in the view of the Constitution, in the eye of the law, there is in this country no superior, dominant, ruling class of citizens. There is no caste here. Our Constitution is color-blind, and neither knows nor tolerates classes among citizens. In respect of civil rights, all citizens are equal before the law. The humblest is the peer of the most powerful. The law regards man as man, and takes no account of his surroundings or of his color when his civil rights as guaranteed by the supreme law of the land are involved. . . .

The arbitrary separation of citizens, on the basis of race, while they are on a public highway, is a badge of servitude wholly inconsistent with the civil freedom and the equality before the law established by the Constitution. It cannot be justified upon any legal grounds.

If evils will result from the commingling of the two races upon public highways established for the benefit of all, they will be infinitely less than those that will surely come from state legislation regulating the enjoyment of civil rights upon the basis of race. We boast of the freedom enjoyed by our people above all other peoples. But it is difficult to reconcile that boast with a state of the law which, practically, puts the brand of servitude and degradation upon a large class of our fellow citizens, our equals before the law. The thin disguise of "equal" accommodations for passengers in railroad coaches will not mislead any one, nor atone for the wrong this day done. . . .

25 Progressivism as a Radical Movement

DAVID P. THELEN
University of Missouri at Columbia

The conservative character of the progressive movement is rapidly becoming one of the clichés of American history. Historians have reached this conclusion from two different paths. One group, carrying a briefcase full of insights from the social sciences, has suggested that reformers are generally men who advocate change to relieve some kind of personal anxiety. Since so many progressives seemed to have been members of the middle class, progressivism represented some kind of mass anxiety and guilt in that class. The second group of historians has been appalled by the failure of the generation between 1890 and 1920 to solve the problems of poverty, injustice, and big business domination. Since this period is widely called the "Progressive Era," these historians have interpreted the failures as a consequence of progressivism. To explain these failures they have assigned a number of traits to the progressives: middle class and moralistic biases; a corporatist orientation; worship at the shrine of Efficiency; lack of a Marxist critique and class consciousness; faith in professional and bureaucratic solutions to economic problems. The result of these two approaches is the prevailing view of the progressive movement as a middle-class campaign to legislate efficiency and order. Both the class and the goals justify the conservative label for the movement.

In making this judgment historians have done a very strange thing. They have attributed the results of a period to one group of actors. It is almost as though everyone who lived between 1897 and 1917 was a "progressive," and everything that happened was part of "progressivism." This curious approach has led more than one historian to throw up his hands and conclude that there was no such thing as a progressive movement. A more effective kind of analysis would acknowledge that the progressives were a minority of their times, argue that the most famous legislation of the period represented not progressive triumphs but political compromises with the enemies of progressivism and, finally, examine the inspiration, origins, beliefs, and programs of those men and women most widely hailed by their contemporaries as progressives. If we look at the major developments of the period as compromises between bitterly divided ideological and political groups, we may have to agree that progressivism was a failure, but only because the progressives failed to secure the programs they desired.

Progressivism was, from this viewpoint, an indigenous radical response to the rapid growth of cities and factories. Its radical cast developed, in large measure, from the writings of the man who inspired so many of its leaders. It has become customary today to assume that Karl Marx is

149

the father of modern American radical movements and that the radicalness of a movement should be measured by the degree to which that movement is Marxian. But for turn-of-the-century Americans the radical challenge came not from Karl Marx but from Henry George. He inspired most progressive leaders with a unique appeal. George offered an explanation and a solution to a generation of Americans that was trying to understand why the rapid spread of factories and cities—what most people called "progress" —was accompanied by the concomitantly rapid spread of poverty and the domination of big businessmen over government. The American environment, with its rich farmlands and mineral deposits, should have offered a bountiful opportunity for every American to make a decent living. The American factory, with its technological superiority, should have produced cheap enough goods for everyone to enjoy. The American heritage of relatively democratic political institutions and rule by the Jacksonian yeoman should have created a government in which the will of the majority prevailed.

What went wrong? The answer was clear: some people had acquired artificial monopolies that allowed them to deprive the majority of equal opportunity to enjoy nature's blessings. Men's laws diverted nature's rich inheritance from the needs of the majority to the pocketbooks of a mere handful. Land and tax laws created the parasitic land speculator who grabbed up lands that lay in the path of development, who waited for settlers to arrive and force up the value of lands, and who then sold the land to settlers at a fantastic profit. Land and tax laws encouraged a few wealthy men to own nature's rich mineral deposits below the land's surface without returning any of nature's wealth to the good of the community. Patent laws allowed a single company to monopolize inventions which could have been made available to all manufacturers with the result of lower costs to the consumer. Tar-iff laws permitted favored American manufacturers to escape competition from foreign manufacturers, thereby encouraging American monopolies to charge artificially high prices. Franchise laws forced city governments to award monopolistic contracts to favored capitalists to provide the rapidly growing cities with the transportation, lighting, water, and power needs of all citizens. Railroads received huge subsidies in the form of federal and state land grants. Government, in short, had become a captive of those "special interests" that used legislative privileges to monopolize nature's blessings.

If laws encouraged men to cheat nature out of her gifts to all men, they also cheated the community of the economic value created by civilization. Henry George's most famous program, the Single Tax, was an attempt to return to the community the benefits which it created. The true value of land derived not from the efforts of the individual but from those of the community. But the community never received the benefits of the rise in values. In fact, George charged, the community's tax laws hurt those very people who improved their property and benefited others who did nothing with their property but wait for the work of their neighbors to raise its value. George's Single Tax was an attempt to solve two problems: first, to return to the community in the form of taxation the value which civilization had given to the land, and second, to strike at those individuals who profited from the improvements made by others. Underlying the Single Tax were the desires for community good to take precedence over individual greed and special privilege and for government (by means of taxes) to narrow the widening gap between rich and poor.

George influenced all classes of Americans who were disturbed by the paradoxes that accompanied rapid industrialization. His books, particularly *Progress and Poverty* (1879), which the philosopher John

Dewey said in 1933 had received a wider distribution than all other books on political economy put together, and his decision to publicize the cause by seeking election to the mayoralty of New York City in 1886 and 1897, won him thousands of zealous disciples. By 1889 there were 131 Single Tax clubs scattered across the United States; George's followers published newspapers, sponsored debates, ran for office—anything to promote the cause.

Georgism, as espoused by the master and modified by his disciples, created a radical challenge in the generation between 1890 and 1920. First, it pointed out that taxation was an excellent means to redistribute wealth. Second, it noted the rapid demise of majority rule in a country where "special interests" controlled the political process because those "interests" needed the legal privileges of government in order to secure their goals. Third, Georgism profoundly challenged American social and ethical thought. It had the same kind of influence in the United States during this period that Marxism exerted over Europe. It emphasized men's ethical obligation to aid their less fortunate neighbors. Poverty need not accompany Progress. In effect, Georgism severely undercut the prevailing self-help and individualistic ethics.

While George had many supporters in organized labor during the 1880s, it was the catastrophic depression of 1893–97 that converted the challenge of Georgism into the progressive movement. The depression revealed for the average citizen a host of social and political problems that had accompanied the rapid growth of cities and factories in the previous generation. It also severely undercut popular faith that industrialism could cure its own ills. One could no longer escape the widespread suffering of the poor. In many areas unemployment rates exceeded those of the Great Depression of the 1930s. Bands of unemployed men, known as Coxey's Army, led the first March on Washington in 1894 to demand federal

relief. Angry strikers, as at Chicago in 1894, raised the threat that the poor might lead a revolution against the established order. The difficulties of the rich were just as obvious. Bank failures—583 banks failed in 1893—had helped to precipitate the depression, and thousands of other businesses were dragged into bankruptcy with them. These failures often produced courtroom trials which revealed that many businessmen had acquired their wealth not by hard work, as popular legend had maintained, but by embezzlement, graft, and special privileges. Businessmen, moreover, used their disproportionate political power to secure such privileges as tax relief, monopoly franchises, tariff benefits. Even more striking than criminality or political power was the life style of the rich. Their elaborate social life—parties, yachts, art "treasures," plays, and the things that created the ghastly stereotype of the "Gay Nineties"—was something new in America and acquired particular significance in these years of desperate suffering. Against this backdrop the social habits of the rich did indeed constitute "conspicuous consumption," as Thorstein Veblen explained in his depression-inspired book, *The Theory of the Leisure Class*. The rich and the poor, whose habits had remained tucked out of view during the widespread prosperity of the 1880's, suddenly became conspicuous indeed.

Unable to escape the discovery of the rich and the poor, Americans of all classes wanted to know how it had happened. And they wanted to know what could be done. They desperately wanted to bridge the unjust and unsafe gap between rich and poor.

Their desperation was intensified by failure of traditional ideas and political leaders to solve the problems. President Grover Cleveland was utterly unable to comprehend, let alone relieve, the situation. The only suffering he seemed to fathom was that of his Wall Street friends; he was confident, as were they, that repeal of the 1890 Sherman Silver Purchase Act would end the depression. Repeal was enacted in 1893, the depression got worse, and Cleveland seemed even more irrelevant. His policy toward labor in 1894 was to send federal troops to Chicago—over the protest of several governors—to smash a strike. Cleveland's "program" only symbolized a deeper problem: the failure of the political process to relieve the depression or solve the basic economic and social problems it revealed. For generations the tariff had been a major point of division between Republicans and Democrats, and now both parties were convinced that a lower or higher tariff would end the depression. Democrats lowered the tariff in 1894, but the depression continued. Neither the national political process nor the major party spokesmen proved responsive to the depression's dangerous mood of social unrest.

Angry and frightened Americans began casting about for new ideas and institutions to fill the void left by the irrelevance of national politics. One new forum was the discussion club, often affiliated with a church, where people from all backgrounds could share and compare economic and social programs. Another was the adult education movement, frequently connected with boards of education, farmers' institutes, churches, and universities. People hoped that lecturers might have answers to questions politicians failed to ask. In 1890, 26,632 people attended free lectures offered by the New York Board of Education; by 1898 the audiences had increased twentyfold to 509,135. Popular magazines and newspapers were other new institutions. The "yellow journals" and later the popular muckraking magazines fed the popular hunger for information, and programs geared to the new problems. By 1910 William Randolph Hearst was better known for his attacks on monopolies and campaigns for public ownership than for his foreign policy crusades. (Indeed, socialist Upton Sinclair once predicted that Hearst would be the first Socialist President.)

These new agencies—discussion groups, lecture forums, reform leagues, newspapers and magazines—provided places where troubled Americans hoped to find answers to questions that suddenly disturbed them. These agencies picked up the analyses of two groups which had long been exploring the problems most Americans discovered in the depression. One set of predepression reformers whose ideas acquired special urgency were the radical groups. Some, like the Single Tax clubs, were, of course, directly inspired by George. For others, like Edward Bellamy's Nationalist clubs or the various Populist and socialist movements, Georgism interacted with other influences to support public ownership and an ethical view of a new brotherhood. The depression's social unrest made it unwise and unsafe to ignore anyone who had an answer, and these radical groups received a much more respectful hearing than they had before the depression.

The second group of predepression reformers to find acceptance were the new social scientists who had long been critical of the conservatism and formalism of traditional social science. The American Economic Association was formed in 1885 to attack the prevailing economic individualism and to promote state intervention in the economy "as an educational and ethical agency whose positive aid is an indispensable condition to human progress." While a few of these new social scientists espoused George's specific programs, and many more had been challenged by his ideas about tax injustices, land monopoly, and government privilege, all could agree with economist Richard T. Ely that "perhaps the greatest service of all which Mr. George has rendered is to be found in the discussion of right and wrong in economic affairs and institutions which he has provoked."

Inspired by George's ethical approach to economics, the new social scientists advocated programs which became the heart of the progressive movement. They argued that men were products of their environments, not of their individual characters, and that the way to make a better man was to improve his environment. It followed that collective action (such as unions) and state action (such as social justice laws) should be used to improve living and working conditions of the poor. These new social scientists agreed with George's disciples that certain individuals and corporations received special privileges from government which promoted monopoly and perverted democracy. They believed that the political process was unresponsive to the wishes of the majority because it was controlled by privilege-seeking corporations. Consequently, new devices—direct primary, municipal home rule, initiative, referendum, recall, direct election of Senators, women's suffrage—would have to be adopted, devices which would enable the majority to destroy the ruling "establishment." In accord with George that taxation was perhaps the best way to redistribute wealth, these new social scientists proposed inheritance, income, land, franchise, and corporation taxes—to force the economically privileged to contribute to the community welfare.

These programs of the new social scientists were attractive to Americans in the depression for two major reasons. First, they were addressed specifically to the disturbing new questions that politicians had ignored. In 1895, a Wisconsin farmer, after attending a lecture, caught the popular desire for salvation by these new social scientists when he wrote the lecturer, a University of Wisconsin economist: "The science which you teach (followed from an honest desire for the best interests of the people) is the noblest of all professions and the hope of the future." The second reason for their new popularity was the involvement of the new social scientists in a major civil liberties crisis. From 1895, when the University of Chicago dismissed Edward W. Bemis, until 1900, when Stanford fired Edward A. Ross, the corporate rulers of American higher education purged more than a dozen "radical" social scientists whose ideas and reform activities they found offensive. The popular outcry was deafening. Even those people who rejected the professors' ideas believed that they should have the right of free speech. This issue of free speech, a sacred American right, produced progress in intellectual matters. A local streetcar company or an oil monopoly should not have the power to force the dismissal of a professor who had attacked them. Frequent discussions of the "academic freedom crisis" in the new agencies of mass communication exposed a great many people to the ideas of the new social scientists.

The experiences of Americans in the depression demonstrated need for programs long advocated by radicals and social scientists. Tax reform acquired special urgency as both a means to redistribute wealth and a way to attack affluent tax-dodgers. Squeezed between higher taxes to cover the rising costs of local government and their own diminishing revenues in the depression, many individuals and corporations began to hide their assets from the assessors, to lobby tax relief through local governments, and even to refuse to pay any taxes. Those citizens who did pay their full taxes mounted a crusade against tax-dodgers; it included all the tax reforms proposed by the earlier reformers. Corporate arrogance also acquired new urgency. Facing declining revenues, many corporations raised rates, lobbied special privileges through city and state governments, and refused to make necessary improvements dictated by elementary considerations of health and safety. "Corporate arrogance" was no longer the doctrinaire cry of radicals. It became an unprotected railway crossing where careless children were killed as they came home from school, or typhoid-infected water which produced epidemics of disease and death because the company refused to make the improvements necessary for healthful water, or streetcars whose lack of bumpers annually mangled and killed hundreds of Americans. For the emerging progressive movement these specific threats had three important consequences: they united all classes, for each class contained parents of careless children, drinkers of impure water, or riders of unsafe streetcars; they clearly identified the corporation as a menace; and they suggested that the menace was primarily political. The only way to stop corporate arrogance was to break the power that favored corporations had over the political process. The first step was to enact the necessary political reforms which would restore power to the people. The depression of 1893–97 thus catalyzed the challenge of Georgism into the mass-based, cross-class progressive movement.

Behind these local efforts to build a radical consciousness based on the features men and women had in common was a profound rejection of large-scale industrial capitalism which had driven deep wedges into the traditional life styles of Americans. It had destroyed the ancient dream of the united community in which men felt a sense of mutual responsibility for their neighbor's welfare. Progressivism had its roots in the late 19th century in a series of largely unorganized revolts by people who wanted to reassert the older discipline of the united community against the large-scale capitalists who had resorted to forces outside the community to achieve legitimacy, to translate their economic power into social and political power. Communities had resisted the new capitalists when they had used such external pressures as injunctions, strikebreakers (often immigrants and blacks), armed force, and bribery to rivet the new discipline onto older life styles. Interestingly enough, pre-capitalist peoples made folk heroes out of the bandits like Jesse James who had attacked the most visible symbols of the new capitalism, railroads and banks. Jesse James had received his legitimacy from the farmers and villagers of Missouri; the railroads and banks had received theirs by appeals to forces outside the new community. Progressivism was, in many ways, a more organized form of the same rebellion. Emphasizing the common qualities of men and women—as consumers, taxpayers, and citizens—progressives were trying to reassert the older discipline, to appeal to the kind of legitimacy that had supported Jesse James. As a result, the movement would be most radical at the local level.

Because the traumas of the depression were local and immediate—local factories closed, family and friends unemployed, angry strikers at nearby plants, death-dealing impure water, increased streetcar fares, higher local taxes, unscrupulous and sometimes criminal local bankers, children killed at nearby crossings, and declining income for everyone—the reaction was also local and immediate. The central fact about the progressive movement from its birth in the mid-1890s until its death in World War I was that it derived its greatest vitality from action at the *local* level. Progressives wanted to solve local and immediate problems. The more than 400 social settlement houses that grew up in poor urban neighborhoods between 1890 and World War I illustrate progressivism's grass-roots character. Instead of trying to impose programs from above, as had the charity workers of the 1880s and as would the psychiatric social workers of the 1920s, the progressive settlement leaders let their poor neighbors define the necessary programs to improve working and living environments. The settlement worker might find himself helping a labor union one day, trying to inject more practical experience into a public school the next, promoting a playground the third day, and running a day-care center the fourth. Even when social workers entered state and national politics to achieve these goals, they were basically trying to solve local neighborhood problems.

The most radical and successful political progressives operated at the local level. Progressive leaders included mayors like Hazen Pingree of Detroit (1889–96), Tom Johnson of Cleveland (1901–9), John MacVicar of Des Moines (1896–1900), Samuel M. ("Golden Rule") Jones (1897–1904) and Brand Whitlock (1905–13) of Toledo, James D. Phelan of San Francisco (1897–1901), Edward F. Dunne of Chicago (1905–7), Josiah Quincy of Boston (1896–99), and Mark Fagan of Jersey City (1901–8). The mayors were joined by such local leaders as George L. Record, Jersey City corporation counsel; Walter L. Fisher of the Chicago Municipal Voters League; Judge Ben B. Lindsey of Denver; State Senator Everett Colby of Essex County, New Jersey; and Prosecutors Francis J. Heney of San Francisco and Joseph W. Folk of St. Louis, to form the local-level radicalism of the progressive movement. Their backgrounds were remarkably diverse. Fagan and Lindsey came from poverty-stricken Catholic homes. Johnson, Jones, and Pingree were wealthy, self-made industrialists. Colby and Quincy came from Yankee aristocratic backgrounds. A child of the lawless frontier, Heney had killed a man in Arizona before prosecuting San Francisco's social and business elite.

What united these men was not their backgrounds but their analyses as well as their programs to solve the problems of rapid urban and industrial growth. Often directly inspired by Georgism, they wanted to take power from the privilege-dominated political elites and return it to the people. Reformers who wished only to replace corrupt mayors and aldermen with honest men earned the scorn of these local progressives. Their battle was with what Johnson called "Privilege," Lindsey called "The Beast," and Lincoln Steffens and Robert M. La Follette called "The System." "If you must blame" any individual, Lindsey explained, "blame those heads of the lawless public-service corporations in Colorado who corrupt judges, juries, legislators, public officials, political workers, gamblers, dive keepers, and prostitutes so that *they* and their corporations may be safe above the law and in power to loot the people." American democracy would remain a failure so long as the people lacked the weapons to recapture government. Once the people had both the political weapons and the power, they would easily enact the rest of the progressive program: public ownership of public-service corporations; abolition of what Johnson called "Privilege's most valued power—its control of taxing machinery"; protection for such consumers as pedestrians, water drinkers, and careless children; and extension of government into the social justice area.

How were progressives to destroy Privilege? Progressivism, it must be recalled, was most radical and effective at the local level; and Privilege was most apparent and blatant at this level. Americans could not escape a contest with it as they tried to solve the local and immediate problems impinging on their everyday lives—to follow Mark Fagan's lead in creating parks for Jersey City, Ben Lindsey's in helping Denver's juvenile delinquents, Tom Johnson's in taxing Cleveland's land speculators. Because these problems directly affected everyone in the city, the problem of public education, which was the key to progressivism, was most easily solved at the local level. Progressive leaders burned with a passion to share their own discoveries—about the System, the Beast, or Privilege—with their constituents; they wanted to lead a popular uprising against the establishment that they saw as preventing the solution of immediate problems. Frequently more adept at promoting popular education than at politics, they sounded the same chord: "the truth shall make us free." These local progressives stand out among major factions in American political history because of their desire to make everyone in their communities share their sense of a never-ending battle against Privilege. Hazen Pingree's mass protest meetings in Detroit, Mark Fagan's canvass of every Jersey City home, Tom Johnson's tent meetings in Cleveland suggested how heavily local progressives depended upon popular education. Ben Lindsey was proud that conservatives called him a "sensational" speaker and a "grandstander." "I appealed to [the people] directly and indirectly, from the platform, and through the newspaper whenever a reporter gave me an interview or an editor allowed me a column for an article," he wrote. Tom Johnson boasted that "the tent meeting is largely responsible for this public enlightenment of the people of Cleveland," and he regarded that enlightenment as his supreme achievement. While muckraking journalists tried to arouse the public on the national level and Theodore Roosevelt mounted the "bully pulpit" to stir his national constituents, their efforts fell notably short of the desperate tone and radical programs that dominated local-level progressivism.

As the local progressives sought to create an aroused public that would destroy the Beast, they had a number of structural advantages in their educational campaigns over those reformers who worked at the state and national levels. The structure of local government aided issue-oriented mass educators. City officials were elected separately from state and national officers and thus municipal issues were harder to obscure with party loyalties and national issues. City councils met continuously, and thus progressives could apply continual pressure. Local-level progressives received crucial support from the new newspapers that promoted the popular side of issues. Lindsey expressed a cliché among progressives when he observed that "there are no agents of reform as powerful in our American communities as the newspapers." But the most powerful advantage at the local level was the simple fact that everyone understood

local and immediate grievance. There could be no compromise with poisoned water. The greater the distance between the immediate problem and its resolution, the less public opinion could influence that resolution.

Progressivism was more effective at the local level than in almost any other area. Most people interested in social justice assumed that the cities—where progressives and the new mass communications had greatest influence—were the scenes of the real innovation. Rochester in 1897 pioneered in the war on infant mortality. Milwaukee and Chicago in 1899 led the juvenile court movement. Gary in 1907 began to create its progressive public schools. In the area of tax reform such cities as Cleveland and Fairhope, Alabama, successfully applied many basic Single Tax ideas. The most radical proposal for direct democracy—the recall of elected public officials by their constituents at any time—first appeared in Los Angeles in 1903. The most hated corporations were the utilities which intimately touched the daily lives of all the people, and progressives in hundreds of cities wrested ownership from private to public hands after bitter crusades. The public ownership movement was effective in cities everywhere: Duluth, Schenectady, Syracuse, Detroit, Bangor, Maine, Holyoke, Massachusetts, and Marshalltown, Iowa. In this period, before most cities had home rule, the campaigns of local progressives were constantly frustrated by the conservatism of state legislatures which had the power to restrain local radicalism. Voters could elect progressive and Socialist city governments, but the radical officials lacked power. George R. Lunn, Schenectady's Socialist mayor, typically complained in 1913: "Whenever we try to do anything, we run up against the charter." But the legislatures, to be sure, could not discourage voters from electing radical local officials. The election of hundreds of Socialist local officials testifies to grass-roots radicalism. In addition, many prominent progressives, like Toledo's Jones or Denver's Lindsey, were elected over the determined opposition of both major parties. At the state and national level, Socialist and independent candidates were doomed to defeat.

These local progressives created a fundamentally new and profoundly radical political style. In contrast to the ethnic-oriented politics that had dominated both reformers and bosses in American cities in the post-Civil War years, and in contrast to the producer-oriented politics of compromise among interest groups that dominated the state and national level, local progressives built a mass, issue-oriented politics that united men as taxpayers, consumers, and "citizens," in that favorite progressive word.

As an issue-oriented, mass-based, cross-class movement of popular education and insurgency against local establishments, progressivism had special problems in the connections between its leaders and supporters that produced strengths and weaknesses. It required a special role of its leaders: they had to be supermen if they were to slay the "Beast" or destroy "the System." Leaders gladly accepted this role. Encouraged by voters who were heavily ideological in outlook, and who wanted to slay the Beast, many progressives came to believe that they were truly messiahs, the only men who could save "the people." (The word "leader" as defined by many radical progressives would be translated by a later generation of Europeans as "duce" or "fuehrer.") Their constituents were particularly susceptible to messianism because they lacked the usual ethnic, occupational, and partisan allegiances which have traditionally motivated most voters and because they agreed that mass "education" was a crucial part of the movement. They could unhesitatingly support Wisconsin's progressive Senator Robert M. La Follette when he claimed that his political philosophy was simply: "The will of the people shall be the law of the land." But his critics, like those of most progressives,

charged that "the people" had simply a plebiscitarian function: they voted for him, the messiah, and he then determined the best method of salvation.

This problem of leadership helps to explain progressivism's weakness above the local level and its frequent inability to enact the radicalism implicit in the analysis. At the local level, progressives could direct public pressure against corporate arrogance and tax-dodgers. But at the state and national level progressives settled simply for their election and reelection. They never adequately figured out how to translate their effectiveness in applying public pressure to a single city council vote into an equal effectiveness in influencing the course of a state or national bill through committee hearings, both houses of the legislature, and final action by the chief executive. State and national progressives received greater freedom of action in exchange for their lesser ability to mobilize "the people."

National legislation was rarely a product of the aroused public that had such a notable influence on the local level. The Meat Inspection and Pure Food and Drug Acts of 1906 are distinctly exceptional. Most famous national laws—the acts of 1903, 1906, and 1910 regulating railroads, the 1913 act regulating banking and currency, the 1903 and 1914 regulations of business—were shaped in their details by competing interest groups. National efforts to democratize the political process—such as direct election of Senators or reform of the rules of the House of Representatives—were pale and tardy imitations of the initiative, referendum, and recall that gave such great power to voters at lower levels. Embracing the initiative with great enthusiasm, Oregon voters, greatly influenced by George's disciple William S. U'Ren, decided the fate of 37 major issues in 1912; and they hardly needed—or used—their state legislature. Such radical democracy could not exist at the national level.

The difficulty of transplanting progressivism's local-level insurgency to the national level largely explains the movement's decline and fall. The real enemy of the insurgent, in the final analysis, was not the Beast, but industrialization. Across the industrializing world, large-scale production dictated the necessity for men to organize along producer lines, as workers, manufacturers, or farmers. These new pressure groups discovered that the political system, particularly at the national level, responded well, as it had in the past, to their needs. As the railroad workers secured national laws limiting their hours of work, as small shippers secured relief from discriminatory railroad rates, as farmers received federal aid, as bankers secured a more flexible banking and currency system, they could not believe that a tight establishment—the Beast—controlled the political process. The fundamental frailty of the local-level progressives resulted from their efforts to appeal to men as consumers, taxpayers, and citizens—the common features of all men—at a time when large-scale production encouraged men to emphasize their producer roles— the features that divided them. Lacking the advantage of hindsight, which would enable them to see they were fighting the growing tendency of men to identify with their producer-oriented pressure groups, the progressives believed, in Tom Johnson's words, that "the greatest obstacle to overcome in any fight in which fundamental moral issues are involved is not opposition, but indifference." Only direct campaigns of mass education could overcome the natural inclination of men to identify with their jobs, and these were only possible at the local level. Progressivism's weakness derived from the nearly impossible task of organizing the consumer into a political spearhead. This weakness would prove fatal when World War I centralized power at the national level, emphasized production as the highest national good, and distracted attention from local and internal problems.

The progressive movement, then, raises the question of the ability of the economic and political system to respond to the aroused consumer. One interpretation of progressivism is that the consumer could produce profound changes when he could be lured from his tendency to choose his politics on the basis of his job. He could topple political establishments and enact laws without need for legislatures. But progressivism raises a second interpretation. Were the progressives correct that the economic and political systems could not easily respond to the things men have in common: as consumers of unsafe merchandise and death-dealing pollution, as consumers of a foreign policy they cannot alter, as consumers of tax structures that frustrate creative uses of governments, as consumers of social and economic priorities established by producer-oriented interest groups?

With this question the progressives were important forerunners of today's radicals. If Ben Lindsey or Tom Johnson were reborn today and were to seek a congenial political statement of the past twenty years, they might well accept the proposition of the student left of the 1960s. They would agree that "the focus of political attention is significantly distorted by the enormous lobby force . . . to the wants of private economic groupings." They would agree that politics should draw men together into a sense of community. They would believe that the "military-industrial complex" was the latest form the Beast had devised to use privilege to defeat the desires of consumers. Finally, the progressives would loudly affirm the application of the principle of participatory democracy.

SUGGESTED READINGS

BARKER, CHARLES A. *Henry George.* New York: Oxford University Press, 1955.
BEMIS, EDWARD W. (ed.) *Municipal Monopolies.* New York: Thomas Y. Crowell, 1899.
DAVIS, ALLEN F. *Spearheads for Reform: The*

Social Settlements and the Progressive Movement, 1890–1914. New York: Oxford University Press, 1967.

DEWITT, BENJAMIN PARKE. *The Progressive Movement.* New York: Macmillan, Co., 1915.

FAULKNER, HAROLD U. *The Quest for Social Justice, 1898–1914.* New York: Macmillan Co., 1931.

FILLER, LOUIS. *Crusaders for American Liberalism.* New York: Harcourt, Brace & Co., 1939.

FLOWER, BENJAMIN O. *Progressive Men, Women and Movements of the Past Twenty-five Years.* Boston: New Arena Publishing Co., 1914.

HOFFMANN, CHARLES. *The Depression of the Nineties: An Economic History.* Westport, Conn.: Greenwood Publishing Corp., 1970.

HOFSTADTER, RICHARD. *The Age of Reform: From Bryan to F.D.R.* New York: Alfred A. Knopf, 1955.

HOLLI, MELVIN G. *Reform in Detroit: Hazen S. Pingree and Urban Politics.* New York: Oxford University Press, 1969.

JOHNSON, TOM L. *My Story.* New York: B. W. Huebsch, 1913.

KOLKO, GABRIEL. *The Triumph of Conservatism: A Reinterpretation of American History, 1900–1916.* New York: Free Press of Glencoe, 1963.

LINDSEY, BEN B. and O'HIGGINS, HARVEY J. *The Beast.* Garden City, N.Y.: Doubleday, Page & Co., 1910.

MOWRY, GEORGE E. *The California Progressives.* Berkeley: University of California Press, 1951.

NOBLE, RANSOM E., JR. *New Jersey Progressivism before Wilson.* Princeton, N.J.: Princeton University Press, 1946.

STEFFENS, LINCOLN. *Autobiography.* New York: Harcourt, Brace & Co., 1931.

————. *The Shame of the Cities.* New York: McClure, Phillips & Co., 1904.

THELEN, DAVID P. *The New Citizenship: The Origins of Progressivism in Wisconsin, 1885–1900.* Columbia: University of Missouri Press, 1972.

WEINSTEIN, JAMES. *The Corporate Ideal in the Liberal State: 1900–1918.* Boston: Beacon Press, 1968.

WIEBE, ROBERT H. *The Search for Order, 1877–1920.* New York: Hill & Wang, 1967.

YOUNG, ARTHUR NICHOLS. *The Single Tax Movement in the United States.* Princeton, N.J.: Princeton University Press, 1916.

DOCUMENT 25.1

The Progressive Program*

The National Social and Political Conference that convened in Buffalo for a week in late June and early July of 1899 issued a policy statement that expresses the principles that united most progressives. The participants included political progressives like Hazen Pingree and Samuel "Golden Rule" Jones, social progressives like Florence Kelley, labor leaders like Samuel Gompers, Negro leaders like Booker T. Washington, socialists like Eugene Debs and W. D. P. Bliss, and antimonoply Populists like Henry Demarest Lloyd. More than 300 reformers, representing 22 distinct "schools" of reform thought, found in this statement a common ground.

We, the members of the National Social and Political Conference, assembled in the city of Buffalo, June 28–July 4th, 1899, address the people of the United States concerning the two great evils of militarism and plutocracy which now menace the existence of the Republic, the economic and moral well-being of every citizen, and the liberties in which these states have their birth and being. We send forth this address with the urgent purpose of co-operating with the people and with all parties and movements that represent them, in their efforts toward the redemption of our common citizenship, and in the saving and developing of the liberties and principles of self-government bequeathed to us by our fathers.

The evil of militarism is expressed in our war of conquest in the Philippine Islands; in our continued government of Cuba by armed forces and the military grants of Cuban franchises and special privileges; in the private use of the United States army for the complete and instant

*Source: *Direct Legislation Record*, July 1899, pp. 41–42.

overthrow of civil government in Idaho and the establishment in its place of military despotism; in the corporate and private use of military force to destroy and terrorize organized labor in the exercise of its sacred rights of association; in the monstrous and open public corruptions that have grown out of our Spanish and Philippine wars as their natural fruits.

A nation cannot deny the capacity and violate the right of another nation to liberty and self-government without losing faith in the capacity of its own people for self-government, and in the right of its own people to liberty. There never existed a nation that could be trusted with the liberty of another nation, or a man who could be trusted with the liberty of another. The nation that strikes at the liberties of another nation commits national suicide. No people can be free save by standing for the freedom of all peoples. The liberty of no citizen is secure so long as there remains a single oppressed or enslaved citizen in any nation. Militarism and conquest cannot co-exist with liberty and self-government. If we suffer our American government to destroy in other and struggling peoples that sacredest thing that comes from God to the common life, namely, the right of men to create their own institutions and choose and organize their own national and individual lives, then we place in the hands of our rulers the power and weapons with which to destroy our liberties, our self-governing opportunities and functions, and our rights to free lives of noble and aspiring citizenship.

We cannot too greatly emphasize the fact that the militarism that seeks conquest abroad has for its ultimate purpose the destruction of organized labor at home and the defence of government by injunctions of the federal courts, which have usurped the functions of legislation and have set aside the laws of the land. This fact is manifested not only in the increase and use of military force by private corporations against trades unions or labor organizations in settlements of questions of wages and strikes. It is manifested by the fact that we are already living under what is practically a secret military dictatorship; that we are engaged in an illegal war unauthorized by Congress, which alone has the authority of the Constitution to declare war; that constitutional government is set aside by a military usurpation which menaces the freedom of speech and of press, and which forcibly and lawlessly retains our young men in military service for which they have not volunteered, upon which service the nation did not send them. We therefore appeal to the people to join with us in the demand that our own liberties be saved and that our national dishonor be expiated in the granting of the liberties which we pledged to the Philippinos, and in the restoration of our own constitutional rights and government.

But we would urgently emphasize our belief that the militarism which menaces us as a people is but the offspring and incident of the greater menace of plutocracy, which has established monopoly government in the place of government by the people. Monopoly rule is entrenched in every branch of national, state and municipal government. By economic force based upon special privileges in law and natural resources, upon indirect taxation and consequent political corruption, monopoly is centralizing the wealth of the nation in the hands of enormous trusts, which are becoming irresponsible economic despotisms; which are using legislation, the judiciary and all the functions of government as the mere instruments of private profit; which are reducing the entire people to economic serfdom or enforced wage slavery.

Political liberty is a mockery without economic liberty. No man is in any sense free, either in politics or religion or science, so long as he is in enforced dependence upon some other man for the opportunity to earn his livelihood. No individual or political rights are secure without security and equality of economic opportunity. Equality before law and institutions must be based upon equality of opportunity and access to the resources which the common Father gave to all people in common. If the state permits a few men to own the earth, then these few own the rights, liberties and moral well-being of the people who must live upon the earth. Even the further extension of the suffrage, so as to grant political citizenship to women, which extension we urge and advocate, will avail little or nothing without economic freedom to all.

We, therefore, make urgent appeal to the people to co-operate with us in the initiation of such movements and the support of such men as shall propose:

I. Direct legislation and proportional representation by which the people shall be able to truly govern themselves, become their own legislators, judge of the constitutionality of their own law-making acts, and forever keep for the common life the self-governing power which can never be rightly delegated to representatives. Thus only, and for the first time since our fathers established the New England town meeting, will government by and for and of the people become a reality.

II. Direct taxation, in order that all values which society creates may equally benefit all men in common, and give special privileges to no man or class.

III. Public ownership of public utilities or of monopolies growing out of natural resources and the existence of society, in order that there may be equality of all men in the gifts of God to the common life; equality of economic opportunity and political power; equality in access to all the material and social resources needful for the living of free, righteous, happy and complete lives. Trust and combination are the result of economic law, and cannot be met by negative anti-trust legislation or outlawed in the courts, but only by the ownership of national and economic monopolies by the people.

IV. The sole control by the people through their government of their medium of exchange, which can never be entrusted to specially privileged financial institutions, save through the betrayal of the inherent and sovereign right of the people to create and regulate their money and its standards. The money question is not so much conflict between standards as it is a question as to whether the powerful few or the whole people shall create and control the medium of exchange. Only through making and ruling their own money can the people escape the destruction of their liberties through the rule of the nation by and for money.

In conclusion, and for the upbuilding and enduring establishment of a free, just and progressive society, based on these elemental principles of political and social democracy, we offer our services and our citizenship, and appeal to the good will inherent in the association of men for liberty and the common good.

DOCUMENT 25.2

The Influence of Henry George on Politics*

Tom L. Johnson, mayor of Cleveland from 1901 to 1909, was probably Henry George's most famous disciple. His autobiography, written to inspire others to follow George, defined the problem and revealed the great importance of mass education and the civic revival. After defining "Privilege," Johnson applied George's analysis to the biggest Privilege-based businesses, the railroads. He explained how Georgism differed from contemporary practice and the socialist alternative.

The greatest movement in the world today may be characterized as the struggle of the people against Privilege.

*Source: Tom L. Johnson, *My Story* (New York: B. W. Huebsch, 1911), pp. xxv, xxxix, 149, 151–54; 99–100; 148.

On the one side the People—slow to wake up, slow to recognize their own interests, slow to realize their power, slow to invoke it. On the other, Privilege—always awake and quick to act, owning many of the newspapers, controlling the election and appointment of judges, dictating to city councils, influencing legislatures and writing our national laws.

What is Privilege?

Privilege is the advantage conferred on one by law of denying the competition of others. It matters not whether the advantage be bestowed upon a single individual, upon a partnership, or upon an aggregation of partnerships, a trust—the essence of the evil is the same. And just to the extent that the law imposes restrictions upon some men and not on others, just to the extent that it grants special favors to some to the exclusion of others, do the people suffer from this evil.

These law-made restrictions and benefits are many, but substantially all may be grouped, in the order of their importance, in the following five classes: land monopolies, taxation monopolies, transportation monopolies, municipal monopolies and patent monopolies.

. . . .

The economic change that will correct these political abuses is one that must remove the prizes which Privilege now secures from the People. It must reserve to the public the ownership and management of public-service utilities so that they shall be regarded no longer as private loot, but as public rights to be safeguarded and protected.

That good, law-abiding corporations and good, well-meaning men cannot correct these wrongs without changing the economic conditions which produce them, has been proved times without number, and only serves to emphasize the fact that the real fight of the people is not to abolish lawbreaking, but to put an end to that lawmaking which is against the public good.

It is true that the contest looks like an unequal one; that the advantage seems to be entirely on the side of Privilege; that its position appears invulnerable.

Is there then no hope? Let us see.

The people's advance guard has been routed often, and will be time and time again. New recruits must come to the front. As the firing lines are decimated the discontented masses must rush forward to fill the gaps in the ranks. Finally, when *we are fighting all along the line*, public opinion will be strong enough to drive Privilege out of its last trench.

Agitation for the right, once set in motion, cannot be stopped. Truth can never lose its power. It presses forward gaining victories, suffering defeats, but losing nothing of momentum, augmenting its strength though seeming to expend it.

. . . .

The original idea behind the railroad was entirely different from the idea which attaches to it in common thought to-day, and to the departure from this original idea we may trace the evils now complained of. It was at first simply the idea of providing a roadway or passageway—a highway for vehicles moved by steam, just as there were then roads or highways for vehicles moved by horses. It did not provide for exclusive use, but for general use, subject to a charge or toll, just as charges were made on some horse roads. But, seeing the advantage of exclusive use, the companies building these steam highways, by means of heavy or discriminating tolls or other methods, prevented general use, stopped competition and made themselves the sole users. The rail or steam roads in the United States, instead of becoming what they were intended to be as the term applied to them, "public highways," indicates, became private highways.

. . . . .

We see the evils of this form of special privilege. Now what about the remedy? Socialism would seek the cure in government ownership. The philosophy of the natural order, which would promote competition and place as little power as possible in the hands of the government would seek the remedy in throwing the steam highway open to general use. No wonder the Socialists point to railroad centralization under present conditions as the greatest standing indictment of competition, a colossal example of its utter failure and say that competition having broken down the only alternative is government ownership and operation. The Socialist, regarding competition as the source of the evil, demands its destruction. We who hold that the evils arise from a denial of competition demand the abolition of law-made advantage, of governmental favor.

Is not the simple, easy, practicable remedy to be found in going back to the original conception underlying the railway to make a really "public" highway for private transportation companies or individuals to use? In making the highway public property, should we not destroy the essence of monopoly power in the railroad? With the States owning the roadbeds and the cities owning the terminals, and no favor shown to any transportation company, but free play being given to competition, would not the public get the maximum of service at the minimum of cost?

. . . . .

This proposal is in perfect harmony with the natural order and in absolute accord with the rule of public practice on almost every other kind of public highway that we have had or now have. The underlying principle is to make the pathway a publicly owned and controlled way, open to all on equal terms, whether absolutely free or subject to toll. And the end to strive for in the railroad problem is to open such roadways to equal use by all who desire to use them as exists on public country roads or streets, on rivers, canals, lakes and the very ocean.

. . . . .

But if I were ambitious to rule a country absolutely, I should not try to get control of its railroads even under the present system when, as we have seen, one-man power can be carried to such great lengths. I should devote myself with singleness and tenacity of purpose to becoming its landlord. The ownership of railroads gives power as, and only as, it is really ownership of land; the power of street car companies is based on the same thing, privileges in the ownership of streets which is land; the power of the Standard Oil Company rests upon the right of way for its pipe lines, and that right of way is land. A man who controlled all the land of a country would be the ruler of that country no matter who made its laws or wrote its songs.

If this is true why does it not indicate to the people their own source of power? If a tyrant can rule them by gaining control of the land of their country, why cannot they destroy tyranny by themselves resuming and retaining control of their land?

But we must have a method whereby this can be accomplished and the method, I believe, is in the single tax as Henry George's philosophy is commonly called in this country. The single tax proposes the abolition of all forms of taxation except a tax upon land values. It would eliminate taxes upon industry, personal property, buildings and all improvements. It would tax land values, including the value of all franchises and public utilities operated for private profit. It is the community which creates land values and franchise values, therefore these values belong to the community and the community should take them in taxation.

ROOTS OF PROGRESSIVISM IN LOCAL AND INTERMEDIATE PROBLEMS

In his discussion of the municipally-owned transit line that ran from Manhattan to Brooklyn, Johnson showed his confidence that radical solutions could work best for problems that affected people's daily lives.

The management was vested in the Bridge authorities appointed by the two cities. Now here was a commission appointed by two notoriously corrupt city governments yet performing its various duties with absolute fidelity to the public. Why? Because the enterprise was operating under the daily observation of the persons most interested in it. Between a privately operated enterprise and one publicly operated the people will always insist upon a higher degree of efficiency in the latter. . . . The people soon become disheartened and give up the fight in trying to get good service from a private company.

And between two public enterprises, one under the eye of the people and the other removed from their observation, the one they have closest contact with will be held to higher standards. For example, witness the placid indifference with which the ordinary citizen regards a one hundred thousand dollar robbery of customs receipts, and by contrast his virtuous wrath if by chance his postman happens to be late three days in succession. He doesn't mind being robbed indirectly and at long range, but he *will* have his mail delivered at the same time each day or know the reason why. . . .

A PLEA FOR MUNICIPAL HOME
RULE

The most pressing of all civic problems is that of municipal home rule by the people themselves, and it is more pressing in the United States than elsewhere. . . .

Municipalities must cease to be answerable to their States, except in matters of State concern, and become answerable in matter of home concern only to their own people. Every city should make its own laws, design its own organization, govern itself by the ballots of its own people, absolutely untrammeled by outside dictation

or interference, except with reference to matters of outside concern. More and more as the years go by are our cities going to reach out and demand such control of their own affairs from their States.

In that way the city will rapidly rise; she will learn more about self-government. And the voice of her people will be heard, direct, demanding of her officers the things the people want; and the officers will hear, and do—or lose their jobs.

DOCUMENT 25.3
The Many Shapes of the Beast*

Ben B. Lindsey, judge of Denver's juvenile court from 1900 to 1927, called his autobiography *The Beast*. He discovered the Beast not from ideological preconceptions but from attempts to solve the small daily problems of administering the courtroom. He soon learned that seemingly different problems all led back to the same source. In contrast to those historians who claim that reformers wanted to develop bureaucratic solutions to each separate problem in order to accomodate the different pressure groups involved in each area, Lindsey believed that all solutions would fail until the people, not the Beast, had the power to govern.

THE CHILDREN AND THE BEAST

I cannot conclude . . . without adding the final lesson . . . that leads me back again into the quarrel with the Beast. It is this: criminals are born *and* criminals are bred, but the conditions of which they are born and under which they are bred in Denver are the same conditions that de-

---

*Source: Ben B. Lindsey and Harvey J. O'Higgins, *The Beast* (Garden City, N.Y.: Doubleday, Page & Co., 1910), pp. 151–52, 220–21, 223, 315–16, 318–21.

bauch our Legislature, our judiciary, our press, our business life, and our poor. I found no "problem of the children" that was not also the problem of their parents. The young bud was blighted by the same corruption that infected the twig, killed the branch and ate out the heart of the trunk. The rule of the plutocracy in Denver was the cause of three-quarters of the crime in Denver. The dependent and delinquent children who came into my court came almost wholly from the homes of dependent and delinquent parents who were made such by the hopeless economic conditions of their lives; and those conditions were made hopeless by the remorseless tyranny of wealthy men who used their lawless power to enslave and brutalize and kill their workmen. Legislatures, corrupted by corporate wealth, refused to pass the eight-hour law that would give the child's home a parent able to fulfil his parental duties—refused to pass the employer's liability law that would save the widows from starvation and the children from the streets—refused to pass even a "three-fourths jury" law that would allow the poor victim of corporate greed to obtain a little pittance of justice in the courts. The saloons, protected by the political power of the corporations, debauched the parents and destroyed the homes of our children, and the protected gambler hunted and preyed with the protected saloon. I could not do my duty toward the children without attacking the conditions that deformed the lives of the children. And when I tried to do *this*—
... the Beast replied: "Then you shall not be allowed to save even the little children."

. . . . .

THE BEAST AND THE STATE

... I saw that the people of Colorado were not free citizens, but enfranchised serfs. They could be killed by their masters with impunity, and the jury would "hang." As a rule, they could elect no man to a political office unless he served their masters—and my own election was merely "the exception that proved the rule." If they rose, in mass, to vote for an eight-hour law, and the Legislature passed such a law, their masters, through the mouth of the Supreme Court, declared it unconstitutional. If they rose again to pass a constitutional amendment permitting such a law, their masters, through the Legislature, refused to pass it. If they rebelled against this tyranny, and went on strike for their constitutional rights, and were lawless in their opposition to lawlessness, their masters, through the Governor, called out the militia, suspended the last pretence of justice, and drove them from the state. The citizen of Colorado had no more right to "life, liberty and the pursuit of happiness" than a yellow dog on the streets of Denver, unless he wore the corporation collar and tag, came to the whistle of his master and ate scraps from his hand.

. . . . .

In the spring of 1905, ... I was prepared to stir up an insurrection among my fellow-serfs, and I believed that such an insurrection could be made successful. I had not been, for so long, an opponent of the Beast without having learned the sources of its power. I had seen that whenever it was attacked in its jungle, it took refuge up a tree. I believed that we could fell that tree, with the animal in its top— bring the brute down, stunned by its fall— and dispatch it where it lay, before it could recover. In other words, I had seen that the corporations derived their power from their control of politics, and that they controlled politics largely through the election laws. If we could reform the election laws so as to make the will of the people effective, we could overturn the throne of the plutocracy and have the king sprawling at the feet of his subjects. After that, we could make what terms with him we pleased.

. . . . .

THE CROSS-CLASS NATURE OF PROGRESSIVISM

Lindsey's campaign for reelection to the juvenile court in 1908 showed how a campaign of mass education could produce the cross-class nature of progressivism at the local level. Denied the nomination of either the Democrats or Republicans by the corporation men in both parties, Lindsey ran as an independent. Instead of discussing the juvenile court in his campaign, Lindsey ran entirely on the issue of corporation control of politics—and he won.

Corporation-dominated politicians did not deceive the labour men. I was admitted to the meetings of their unions and addressed them night after night. In company with Rev. A. H. Fish, of the Central Presbyterian Church, and Mr. L. M. French, a labour leader, I went to the factories and shops at luncheon hour, talking to the men and women workers. We made it plain that our fight was against the tyranny of the corporations. The unions passed resolutions endorsing our work, and the members of the barbers' union made every barber shop in Denver a centre of propaganda which their lathered customers could not escape. We sent out, from our headquarters, cards to the voters for them to sign, pledging their votes; and we received 23,000 of these pledges signed.

The women—not so much their suffrage leaders or their politicians, as the mothers in the homes and the working women in the factories and the shops—came out for us by the thousands. Our headquarters swarmed with newsboys and schoolchildren anxious to help; and some of those boys made the most effective campaign orators we had. It was tickling to the verge of tears to hear them, on a public platform, addressing a crowded hall with their pathetic earnestness and their childish arguments. If the "kids" were going to "stay wit'" me, they pleaded, why shouldn't "the folks"? One of these boys spoke to an audience of several thousand at a W. C. T. U. convention in the Auditorium, and raised a heart-shaking enthusiasm; and the aid and inspiration given us by these noble women was a power in the campaign. The corporation newspapers cut all mention of it from their reports of the meetings—maintaining a policy of concerted silence about my candidacy in an attempt to "bottle" us. But the Denver *Express* kept on hammering; the signed pledges kept coming in; and at last Senator Patterson's two papers swung into line and things began to move with a whoop. The Christian Citizenship Union had succeeded in reaching the "church element" in spite of the opposition of those wealthy churches whose boards were controlled by the Beast. The labouring men and their wives packed our meetings. In the foreign quarters, and particularly on the West Side among the Russian Jews, the poor mothers whose children I had befriended received us with tears running down their cheeks, so that I could hardly speak to them for the choke in my throat. The people were up—with a shout—with a shout that was at once angry and tearful with anger, for we did not yet believe we could win—and the politicians shut their ears to it, and orated about their presidential candidates. . . .

· · · · ·

. . . It was a straight campaign against corporation rule. I made no appeals to sentiment; I often left the question of our court work out of my speeches. I was determined that if I was to be beaten, I must be beaten as the opponent of the Beast; and that if I was to be saved, it must be by voters who saw who were their masters and revolted against them. All the usual tricks of the Beast were used against us. Many Democratic and Republican "workers," in going their rounds, whenever they were asked by a voter how to vote for me, replied: "Oh, that's all right. He's on our ticket. Just vote it straight." And our workers were kept busy explaining that I was on neither party ticket. In order to issue instructions to voters, we asked the clerks in the office of the County Clerk and Recorder where my name would appear on the official ballot; they replied: "In the fourth column about half way down." Accordingly, in our printed directions, we told the voters to look for my name "in the fourth column, half way down." But when the official ballot was issued, there appeared, half way down the fourth column: "For County Judge for short term, to succeed Ben. B. Lindsey," with the "Ben. B. Lindsey" in very large letters where it should not have appeared at all. Some distance below, in smaller type, my name appeared as an independent candidate for Juvenile Judge; and as a result of this trick, it was estimated, some eight thousand votes intended for me were lost. In an ordinary election, it would have been sufficient to defeat me.

But this was not an ordinary election.... Women wearing long white badges—"Vote for Judge Lindsey"—watched the approaches to the polling places all day long, without relief, and accosted every voter. A newsboy, on the previous night, had obtained a dollar from our committee for "campaign expenses," and bought a dollar's worth of coloured chalk and sent out a horde of boys to mark the sidewalks, the walls and the fences with "Vote for Judge Lindsey"—and the party henchmen with brushes and mops had not succeeded in entirely obliterating that "handwriting on the wall." ... The foreigners who could not speak English came to the polls with cards on which friends had written for them, "I want to vote for Judge Lindsey." The women, everywhere, made no secret of the fact that they intended to vote for me. We began to believe that the impossible was about to happen at last.

... The details kept coming in, from the well-to-do precincts on Capitol Hill, from the foreign quarters, from the home districts of the working men and women, and even from the wards where the "dives"

were thickest; and all but three gave me pluralities. ...

Elected? Out of 65,000 votes cast, we had polled, on the official count, 32,000, which was almost as many as my two opponents had together. Even without the 8,000 votes of which we had been cheated by the trick in the ballot—and although these votes had been counted for my opponents—I had a plurality of almost 15,000. The people had at last "seen the cat" and they had "scratched" it to the bone! I went to bed that night, no longer a slave among slaves, but a freedman in a community that had at last risen against its masters and given them a warning of the wrath to come!

DOCUMENT 25.4

The Biggest Beast: The Money Trust*

Behind the utilities of Denver and the street railroads of Cleveland that had so bitterly resisted Lindsey and Johnson there was a still more powerful beast, argued Robert M. La Follette, Wisconsin's progressive governor (1901–05) and senator (1906–25). The most radical national progressive, La Follette believed that the major investment banks controlled the entire business of the country by means of their seats on the boards of directors of hundreds of corporations. They had artificially created the panic of 1907 to recoup earlier losses, drive out competition, and silence the progressive movement. La Follette spent several weeks talking with businessmen, particularly from New York, to compile his list of the 100 men who ran the nation. This speech, which took several March days in 1908, was aimed against the Aldrich-Vreeland Currency Act, which La Follette believed gave government aid to the largest banks that already owned the country.

*Source: *Congressional Record*, 60th Cong., 1st sess., Vol. XLII, pp. 3450, 3451, 3795, 3799.

I have placed before you the record evidence that less than one hundred men own and control railroads, traction, shipping, cable, telegraph, telephone, express, mining, coal, oil, gas, electric light, copper, cotton, sugar, tobacco, agricultural implements, and the food products, as well as banking and insurance. Does anyone question the overcapitalization of these consolidated corporations which cover the business of the country? Does anyone doubt the community of interest that binds these men together? Does anyone question their vital interest in maintaining their overcapitalization and protecting their stocks and bonds? Does anyone doubt their hostility to the declared policies of President Roosevelt, and the progressive movement throughout the country, and their readiness, nay, their determination, to make an end of it at any cost? Was this not made abundantly manifest during the summer of 1907? . . .

With this enormous concentration of business it is possible to create, artificially, periods of prosperity and periods of panic. Prices can be lowered or advanced at the will of the "System." When the farmer must move his crops a scarcity of money may be created and prices lowered. When the crop passes into the control of the speculator the artificial stringency may be relieved and prices advanced, and the illegitimate profit raked off the agricultural industry may be pocketed in Wall street. . . .

Sir, can any sane man doubt the power of a little group of men in whose hands are lodged the control of the railroads and the industries, outside of agriculture, as well as the great banks, insurance, and trust companies of the principal money center of the country, to give commercial banking and general business a shock at will? Having the power, did they not have reasons (purely selfish reasons, it is true), but reasons sufficient to cause them to exercise that power in their own interest? They could even turn it to their advantage financially. From 1904 to 1906 the interests had disposed of enough stocks at artificially created prices to make it profitable to drop these same stocks and bonds still lower, taking them in finally at a profit to themselves. Owning the controlling interest of their own securities, prices are largely a matter of manipulation. They can be lowered and raised at will damaging only the outsider who is caught "long" or "short" for the time being.

Taking the general conditions of the country, it is difficult to find any sufficient reason outside of manipulation for the extraordinary panic of October, 1907. It is true that earthquake and war had destroyed some of the wealth of the world. But look for a moment at the general business condition of this country. . . .

There were no commercial reasons for a panic. There were speculative, legislative, and political reasons why a panic might serve special interests. There were business scores to settle. There was legislation to be blocked and a currency measure suited to the system to be secured. There was a third term to be disposed of and policies to be discredited.

A panic came. I believe that it needs only to be followed step by step to show that it was planned and executed, in so far as such a proceeding is subject to control, after once in motion. . . .

Sir, I have named certain individuals from time to time in the course of my argument upon the pending bill. If I am understood as making war upon these men, I disavow it here and now, I do not direct my attack against a Rockefeller, a Morgan, a Harriman. They are but types. They but embody an evil. Back of these men is the THING which we must destroy if we would preserve our free institutions. Men are as nothing; the System which we have built up by privileges, which we have allowed to take possession of Government and control legislation, is the real object of my unceasing warfare.

Mr. President, the statement that the business of the country in a national sense is controlled by less than 100 men—by less than 50 men—aye, by a mere handful of men, requires the citation of no authority further than the list of directors of transportation, industrial, and financial trusts, combinations, and corporations of the country. The official records of those institutions are in themselves the proof.

The business of the country is transacted by corporations and combinations of corporations. The control of corporations rests of necessity with a board of directors, the executive committee, and the officers of the organization. It is therefore only necessary to take the great controlling transportation and business organizations of the country, analyze the directorates, and the truth is ascertained. When the most significant names in the Standard Oil-Morgan groups are distributed with their all-powerful influence on the boards of directors controlling in a broad way transportation, industrial institutions, mining, iron and steel, coal, gas, electric light, shipping, copper, and other natural products and the industrial life resting upon them, together with the great insurance companies, and an overbalancing control of the banking institutions of the country, no amount of denunciation and personal abuse, from whatever source it may come, can by any possibility obscure the facts. So long as the official records of these controlling bodies stand as published to-day, the proof stands, and the case is made. . . .

Mr. President, I have talked in vain if I have not made plain the thought that there is just one issue before the country today. It is not currency. It is not tariff. It is not railroad regulation. These and other important questions are but phases of one great conflict.

Let no man think he is not concerned; that his State or his constituency is not interested. There is no remote corner of this country where the power of Special Interests is not encroaching on public rights.

Let no man think this is a question of party politics. It strikes down to the very foundation of our free institutions. The System knows no party. It is supplanting government.

Mr. President, I think I may say without risk of being misunderstood, at least by those of whom I speak, that I know something of the sentiment of the people of this country.

I have found no difference of opinion among them as to existing conditions and the causes underlying it all. In Wisconsin, and from New York to the Pacific States, the people I have met hold one opinion, have one conviction.

They are deeply concerned. They understand. Men back of the System seem to know not what they do.

In their strife for more money, more power—more power, more money—there is no time for thought, for reflection. They look neither forward nor backward. Government, society, and the individual are swallowed up in the struggle for greater control. The plain man living the wholesome life of peace and contentment has a better perspective, a saner judgment. He has ideals and conscience and human emotion. Home, children, neighbors, friends, church, schools, country, constitute life. He knows very definitely the conditions, affecting the rights guaranteed him by the Constitution, but he longs for expression, he longs for leadership. . . .

Blind indeed is he who does not see what the time portends. He who would remain in public service must serve the public, not the System. He must serve his country, not Special Interests.

DOCUMENT 25.5

Sin and Society*

Edward A. Ross was a sociologist whose pathbreaking studies explored changes in mechanisms of social control as increased economic complexity produced the evolution of a community into a society. Believing that academicians should not retreat into professional activities alone, Ross was a great admirer of the popular muckraking journalists. He wrote *Sin and Society* (1907), which impressed President Theodore Roosevelt, as a committed progressive who wanted the public to understand how popular moral judgments were increasingly misdirected toward unimportant sins as society became increasingly interdependent. The final product of social evolution was the soulless corporation which society lacked the moral sophistication to restrain.

To-day the sacrifice of life incidental to quick success rarely calls for the actual spilling of blood. How decent are the pale slayings of the quack, the adulterator, and the purveyor of polluted water, compared with the red slayings of the vulgar bandit or assassin! Even if there is blood-letting, the long-range, tentacular nature of modern homicide eliminates all personal collision. What an abyss between the knifeplay of brawlers and the law-defying neglect to fence dangerous machinery in a mill, or to furnish cars with safety couplers! The providing of unsuspecting passengers with "cork" life-preservers secretly loaded with bars of iron to make up for their deficiency in weight of cork, is spiritually akin to the treachery of Joab, who, taking Amasa by the beard "to kiss him," smote Amasa "in the fifth rib;" but it wears a very different aspect. The current methods of annexing the property of others are characterized

*Source: Edward Alsworth Ross, *Sin and Society: An Analysis of Latter-Day Iniquity* (Boston: Houghton, Mifflin Co., 1907), pp. 7–8, 11–16, 90–93, 109–10; 83–85.

by a pleasing indirectness and refinement. . . .

. . . . .

The covenant breaker, the suborned witness, the corrupt judge, the oppressor of the fatherless,—the old-fashioned sinner, in short,—knows his victim, must hearken, perhaps, to bitter upbraidings. But the tropical belt of sin we are sweeping into is largely impersonal. Our iniquity is wireless, and we know not whose withers are wrung by it. The hurt passes into that vague mass, the "public," and is there lost to view. . . .

Often there are no victims. If the crazy hulk sent out for "just one more trip" meets with fair weather, all is well. If no fire breaks out in the theatre, the sham "emergency exits" are blameless. The corrupt inspector who O. K.'s low-grade kerosene is chancing it, that is all. Many sins, in fact, simply augment risk. Evil does not dog their footsteps with relentless and heart-shaking certainty. When the catastrophe does come, the sinner salves his conscience by blasphemously calling it an "accident" or an "act of God."

Still more impersonal is sin when the immediate harm touches beneficent institutions rather than individuals, when, following his vein of private profit, the sinner drives a gallery under some pillar upholding our civilization. The blackguarding editor is really undermining the freedom of the press. . . . The corrupt bosses and "combines" are murdering representative government. The perpetrators of election frauds unwittingly assail the institution of the ballot. Rarely, however, are such transgressions abominated as are offenses against persons.

Because of the special qualities of the Newer Unrighteousness, because these devastating latter-day wrongs, being comely of look, do not advertise their vileness, and are without the ulcerous hag-visage of the primitive sins, it is possible for iniquity to flourish greatly, even while men are getting better. Briber and boodler and grafter are often "good men," judged by the old tests, and would have passed for virtuous in the American community of seventy years ago. . . .

One might suppose that an exasperated public would sternly castigate these modern sins. But the fact is, the very qualities that lull the conscience of the sinner blind the eyes of the onlookers. People are sentimental, and bastinado wrong-doing not according to its harmfulness, but according to the infamy that has come to attach to it. Undiscerning, they chastise with scorpions the old authentic sins, but spare the new. They do not see that boodling is treason, that blackmail is piracy, that embezzlement is theft, that speculation is gambling, that tax-dodging is larceny, that railroad discrimination is treachery, that the factory labor of children is slavery, that deleterious adulteration is murder. . . . The cloven hoof hides in patent leather. . . . The petty shoplifter is more abhorred than the stealer of a franchise, and the wife-whipper is outcast long before the man who sends his over-insured ship to founder with its crew.

· · · · ·

By *vice* we mean practices that harm one's self; by *sin* we mean conduct that harms another. They spring from different roots and call for different treatment. Sin grows largely out of the relations into which men enter, and hence social development, by constantly opening new doors to wrong-doing, calls into being new species of sin. . . . Vice, on the other hand, being personal, is less affected by social change. New forms, like the cocaine habit or bridge gambling, are *invented*, not developed by social growth.

. . . Vice encounters barriers fixed by nature; in the end its wage is death. Sin, on the other hand, flourishes if society does not make haste to check it. . . .

Sin . . . is not self-limiting. If a ring is to be put in the snout of the greedy strong, only organized society can do it. . . .

· · · · ·

. . . If the corporate owner is free from the weaknesses of the individual, it escapes also his wholesome limitations. It feels not the restraints that conscience and public sentiment lay on the business man. It fears the law no more, and public indignation far less, than does the individual. You can hiss the bad man, egg him, lampoon him, caricature him, ostracize him and his. Not so with the bad corporation. The corporation, moreover, is not in dread of hell fire. You cannot Christianize it. You may convert its stockholders, animate them with patriotism or public spirit or love of social service; but this will have little or no effect on the tenor of their corporation. In short, it is an entity that transmits the greed of investors, but not their conscience; that returns them profits, but not unpopularity.

· · · · ·

The special-interest man ignores the moral energy that inspires the uprising against latter-day sin. He scoffs at a law on the ground that it was enacted by a bare majority of "hayseed" legislators, ignorant of legal philosophy and the fitness of things. He does not care to notice that this close vote records an overwhelming public sentiment, the outcome of a long, disinterested agitation. Or he complains that the statute is "precipitate," and pleads for "conservatism."

"Conservatism!" piled on top of inertia and the strangle-hold of sinister interests, in a tumultuously changing society, where an evil condition may be rapidly worsening while we speechify and procrastinate! Here is a growing evil,—so much blood of brakemen on cars and rails. Give heed, ye legislators! No impression. The legislator removes his cigar long enough to sneer, "hot air," "mawkish sentimentality," "they take the risks." So, on with the slaughter! Let the wheels redden until the totals are formidable. "Now will you act?" No, "interference" would "undermine individual responsibility," or be "unconstitutional." So let the mangled pile up. . . . So is it with the uprooting of child labor. Once the pocket-book interest has twined itself about the evil, the wreckage of child life has to be mountainous, ghastly, and sickening, before the public can be stirred to the point of breaking the grasp of the employers on the throat of the legislature. The same obstacles delay the advent of mine inspection, tenement-house reform, the abolition of grade crossings, the enforced fencing of dangerous machinery. Thanks to the inertia of large bodies and the power of special interests, the relief inevitably comes ten to twenty years later than it should. . . .

DOCUMENT 25.6

A Progressive Attack on Government Regulation of Business*

Some recent historians have suggested that the independent regulatory commission was the progressives' favorite panacea because it allowed the new producer-oriented interest groups to reach accomodations with a minimum of friction. But most local progressives were not interested in creating a structure for the harmonious interaction of interest groups. Frank Parsons, one of the new social scientists who combined activism with research and was fired from the Kansas State Agricultural College as a result, expressed many of the progressives' reservations about regulation.

Regulation, tho of decided use, is not a solution of the problem of monopoly, because it cannot remove the root of the evil, nor the soil in which it thrives. The antagonism of interest remains as long as the private ownership remains, and the power to make the antagonism effective will also remain so long as the private ownership of the monopoly continues. Private ownership of monopoly means antagonism to

*Source: Frank Parsons, *The City for the People* (Philadelphia: C. F. Taylor, 1899), pp. 105–7.

public interest, and it also means power. If you take away the monopolist's control, you take away the heart of his ownership. The paper title is not the ownership; it is only the evidence of ownership. The substance of ownership is the power to control the property. You may *modify* this power and still leave the monopolist some ownership, but if you take the whole power you take the ownership. And if you do not take the whole power, if any loophole is left for the monopolist to use the forces of the monopoly according to his own discretion, to that extent the business will be managed in private interest (without the natural checks of competition) and the evils of monopoly will make their appearance.

As a matter of fact, regulation has met with all sorts of failures and difficulties. It works under serious disadvantages. (1) It lets one set of men do the work and employs another set to determine how it shall be done, and a third set to watch the first, and see that the regulations provided by the second set are properly obeyed. (2) It leaves the antagonism of interest rankling underneath. The monopolists and their agents resent the outside control, and scheme to evade or defy the law. The managers regard the gas plants, street railways, etc., as the property of themselves and the stockholders who elect them and pay them; they regard effective regulation as a violation of their property rights, and endeavor to nullify it; and, if compelled to serve the public instead of the stockholders, they do so in a halfhearted, rebellious way, perpetually seeking a path of escape. (3) The added impulse to fraud and evasion emphasizes the corrupting of public officers and the demoralization of business men. The most powerful and unscrupulous corporations, the very ones most in need of control, are able to avoid the law. They get their vassals appointed as commissioners, or they capture the regulators by their intelligence, wealth and courtesy, or they block them by false accounts, or tie their hands by imperfections in the law, introduced thru the force of their money and influence and the cunning of their keen attorneys. There are very few laws that the great corporations are bound to obey, and the power of the companies to defeat the will of the people is growing every day thru combination, consolidation and the increase of corporate wealth. So thoro is the control of the big monopolies over the machinery of regulation that even in the states where this method has been most fully tried the giant companies regard the system as a protection and not as a menace. (4) The courts are apt to interfere to prevent the enforcement of any regulation that cuts near the bone in the financial quarter. Over capitalization and the innocent purchaser are an infallible vaccine to keep off an epidemic of just rates, which the corporators fear worse than the plague. (5) As long as the monopolists can keep their excessive rates, they can buy the fulfillment of their wishes the rest of the way.

In short, regulation fails at the vital points. It leaves the monopolist in possession, with right of property and more or less control. He has a full purse, a cunning lawyer and a flexible conscience, bowing before the business maxim that property is to be managed in the interests of its owner, and the rest is easy. In dealing with little concerns, regulation is often successful in a high degree, tho never attaining the full perfection of a harmony of interests; but in dealing with great affairs, tho good is accomplished here and there, the general result at the vital points is failure.

26 The Failure of Political Socialism in America

HOWARD H. QUINT
University of Massachusetts

Awareness of paradox is one of the many insights we gain from history. If, for instance, we examine the 1912 platform of the Socialist Party of America, we must be struck by the fact that so many of the "radical" social and economic propositions then advocated by the Socialists are now institutionally incorporated into our national life. And what is more, they have received overwhelming general acceptance. Yet the Socialist Party, which in 1912 seemed destined to grow in national importance, has literally disappeared from our contemporary scene. How do we account for this paradox?

Turning for a moment to the countries of Western Europe, we should likewise note that much of the socialist program of the turn of the century is also an accomplished social and economic fact. In nearly all of these countries, vigorous socialist parties continue to exist and frequently hold or share political power. Why, then, should the experience of political socialism be so different in the parliamentary democracies of Western Europe and in the United States?

Several explanations with varying degrees of validity suggest themselves, but one merits particular consideration. In the United States the pervasive social and economic problems stemming from a modern industrial society have compelled the leadership of the orthodox political parties to adopt the general philosophy of state planning, once almost the exclusive property of the socialists. In this way they have been able to perpetuate the nation's capitalistic system, albeit in substantially modified form. In Western Europe the same social and economic problems have also been present and have elicited a similar response. There, however, the socialist parties, always much stronger than in the United States, became increasingly less doctrinaire and concentrated on the same kind of overall objectives as the American political parties. Thus, whereas the Democratic and Republican parties of the United States have become more "socialistic" in confronting the problems of mass security and of economic planning, the socialist parties of Western Europe have managed to survive largely by abandoning their one-time goal of revolution and settling more and more for planned welfare capitalism. In summary, then, modern industrial and technological developments—and in particular those associated with the creation and maintenance of powerful military establishments—have tended to subordinate issues of ideology. They have compelled governments, whatever their nature, to seek and adopt solutions that are exceedingly similar in character, whether they be in the form of industrial organization or in the providing of social services.

All of this is noteworthy but also in a sense academic insofar as the Socialist

174

Party of America is concerned. Despite seemingly promising beginnings, the party (notwithstanding speculations of some historians as to what it might have been or become) never really had a chance for success in the United States. Indeed, we can dispose of it quite quickly as a political organism and then return to examine the basic causes for its failure.

Even at the very height of the Socialist Party's influence during the first decade of the 20th century, it contained within itself a malignancy which contributed to its eventual destruction. A sizable portion of the SPA membership either were members of or were sympathetic to the Industrial Workers of the World, which espoused industrial unionism. On this score the Socialists, who were committed to the principle of industrial as opposed to craft unionism, had no quarrel. But the antipolitical orientation of the IWW and its advocacy of industrial sabotage antagonized the Socialist Party leadership, which in 1912 succeeded in expelling most practitioners or advocates of industrial sabotage. IWW leader "Big Bill" Haywood, who was also a member of the party's National Executive Committee, was the principal target of the purge. When he left the party, he took with him a not inconsiderable part of its membership.

Here was a sharp blow from within, but far more serious and almost fatal was a blow from without that came during the World War I years and those immediately following. During the war the Socialist Party of America was battered almost past the point of salvaging by ferocious hypernationalist persecutions. The party, which had taken an adamant antiwar stand, was deserted by a large segment of its membership which supported President Woodrow Wilson's crusade "to make the world safe for democracy." It was hobbled shamefully by a government policy of repression condoned by the President at the expense of his reputation as a liberal, a reputation which some scholars believe he had not earned or deserved. Moreover, the American people gave full endorsement to this persecution. As Alexis de Tocqueville had noted a century before, an egalitarian democracy, lacking an aristocratic tradition of tolerance of dissent, was capable of indulging in gross violations of civil rights in time of stress. Certainly this was evident in the suppression of socialists and other radicals during the war years and those immediately following. The Socialist Party never recovered from this experience and furthermore, starting in 1919 and continuing through the twenties, a large part of its membership drifted into the newly formed Communist Party. Although it limped on through the twenties and was briefly rejuvenated in the early years of the Great Depression during the following decade, it expired in the 1950s with only a few of the faithful left to mourn it.

Now that the Socialist Party seems relegated to the "ashcan of history" (to use a good Marxian phrase), a brief consideration of some Marxist tenets and their application to the American scene is in order. We know today how enormously wrong was Karl Marx's prediction that a socialist society would emanate only from an advanced form of industrial capitalism. This prediction had the sanctity of law in Marxian doctrine. Yet the truth of the matter is that wherever thoroughgoing socialist societies have come into being during the last half century, aside from those imposed by the force of Soviet political and military power, they have been in economically backward countries. And the reason for this is clear to us, if it was not to Marx: In their drive for quick industrialization the people of these countries have turned to the state because it, and it alone, possesses sufficient capital—and sometimes not too much, at that—to mobilize economic resources and to undertake ambitious production programs. The human cost of such industrialization under state auspices has come high, as witness the experience of any Communist country; but this has not lessened its appeal, particularly in those places where the great mass of poverty-stricken people has had everything to gain and very little or nothing to lose.

In the late 19th and early 20th centuries, socialists throughout the world were under the spell of Marx's seemingly inpregnable analysis. And this essentially was why they were hard pressed to explain the pronounced weakness of the socialist movement in the United States, where it should have been strong. The United States was undeniably a rising industrial colossus with a pronounced tendency toward industrial monopoly. Marx's theory of capitalistic accumulation and concentration surely applied to the American republic. Yet other components of Marx's dialectical materialism did not fit the American pattern. There had not come into being, for example, a sizable class-conscious proletariat dedicated to the overthrow of capitalism; the economic well-being of American industrial workers was not deteriorating, but improving; the middle class, contrary to Marx's prognosis, was not being ground down into the proletariat, but expanding; and the Socialist Party, which was to be the political vehicle for anticapitalist discontent, had not made a significant dent in the traditional party loyalties of American voters. Never possessing a strong network of local political organizations so necessary for success in American party politics, it made its best showing in 1912, at the very crest of the Progressive Era, when Eugene V. Debs, its perennial candidate for the Presidency, received 897,011 votes, or 5.97 percent of the total number cast. The Socialists never elected a United States senator or a state governor; the best they could claim were two lonely congressmen, Victor Berger of Wisconsin and Meyer London of New York. Both men served in the second decade of the century.

The organization of a vigorous, united socialist movement in the United States was complicated by widely differing and strongly held beliefs as to what socialism involved. But more pertinent, perhaps, than the question of ideology, though not divorced from it, was the method by which socialism was to be attained. Here the socialists ran head on into formidable socioeconomic, political, and institutional barriers imposed by a successful American capitalism and a triumphant American democracy.

The pre-World War I socialist movement, both in Europe and in the United States, was plagued by a duality of doctrine which resulted in a kind of schizophrenia and simultaneously created bitter internecine conflicts. On the one hand, the scientific socialists aimed at a revolutionary new order and were pledged to eradicate capitalism, if and when they ever came to power. But to hew close to the line of doctrinal purity, to give short shrift to contemporary issues, and to emphasize only the glory day of socialist salvation—the delivery date of which could not be guaranteed—was to limit socialism's appeal to the pragmatically minded American wage earners and middle class. On the other hand, if the socialists were to seek to mitigate conditions of the existing order and to improve the lot of those living under it, they would have to accept the major premises of a capitalistic society and ultimately be forced to play the game of social reformers. According to hard-shelled Marxists, this would have the effect of making them socialists in name only and would blur socialism's grand vistas. Socialists, then, were torn between ends and means, between millennial hopes and everyday actualities.

The Marxist overtures to American proletarians were made along orthodox lines of class solidarity and increasing misery. But this appeal lacked the magnetism that it held for European workers. As all students of the labor movement know, the United States at the turn of the century was hardly a worker's paradise. Yet the American industrial worker was well aware of and constantly reminded that the nation's capitalistic system had achieved higher real wages and living standards, and greater occupational opportunities and mobility, than were to be found elsewhere in the world. On the basis of the mass-production system, low prices, and generous credit, most Americans could enjoy consumption goods that were far beyond the reach of foreign workers.

This latter factor bears attention in the light of repeated claims by cultural nationalists that the "American dream" of a classless society, a fervently embraced idea of "uniqueness" and "givenness," and a frontier tradition of individualism were together responsible for counteracting socialism's appeal to the country's wage earners. Folk beliefs, of course, have an amazing persistency and an undeniable importance in the shaping of the national character. But what was it in the new industrial society if not the availability of consumption goods that gave to the older tradition of individualism the necessary material underpinnings? If the American worker—and here we are talking about the overwhelming majority of *white* workers—did not qualify for membership in the middle class either by job or by income status, still the fact that he could obtain or even think of acquiring most of the material comforts of life placed him psychologically in the middle class, as had been true under the older agrarian order. There is a certain irony in the fact that whereas American middle-class social reformers have invariably maintained that they have been *for* but not *of* the working class, members of the latter just as consistently have considered themselves as being *of* though not necessarily *for* the middle class.

Economically speaking, the expansion and success of the American industrial system and the emergence of the welfare state offer the best general answer to any query about the failure of socialism, as an ideology, to win more adherents in the United States. There was little cause to accept a gospel of social and economic salvation emanating from a Europe already

at the point of being surpassed by Yankee drive, technology, and ingenuity. Insofar as socialism as an organized movement was concerned, however, its essential weakness was the failure of socialists themselves to "bore from within" and to gain control of the trade union movement. Without trade union foundations, as the early-day Marxists had maintained, the socialists could have little hope of either immediate or future success in the United States.

Socialists were active in both the National Labor Union and the Knights of Labor, though by no means did they play a controlling role in either. Efforts to bore from within and capture control of the American Federation of Labor encountered formidable difficulties, since Samuel Gompers and several of its founders had been at one time confirmed Marxists. These men, while not hesitating to present as their own much of the Marxist criticism of modern capitalism, nevertheless deserted socialism's standard. The AFL leaders and the socialists differed fundamentally regarding the nature of labor organization. As has been noted, the socialists advocated inclusion of both skilled and unskilled workers into vertically structured industrial unions. Gompers and his supporters were champions of horizontal union structure. They sought the membership only of skilled workers and organized on a craft union basis. But more important was their acceptance of the permanency of industrial capitalism. They were willing to operate within its assumptions and to accept the very same stratified class society that the socialists wished to eliminate.

Socialism's high water mark within the American Federation of Labor came amidst the panic and depression of 1893 and 1894. During the latter year, one Federation affiliate followed another in voting favorably on a political program calling for the "collective ownership by the people of all the means of production and distribution." But thereafter, as the nineties wore on, socialist influence waned, and the Federation became irretrievably committed both to craft union organization and to cooperation with capital. Gompers gave the socialists no quarter. At the 1903 national convention of the AFL he achieved national acclaim when he declared in a dramatic speech:

I want to tell you, Socialists, that I have studied your philosophy; read your works upon economics, and not the meanest of them; studied your standard works, both in English and German—have not only read, but studied them. I have heard your orators and watched the work of your movement the world over. I have kept close watch upon your doctrines for thirty years; have been closely associated with many of you, and know how you think and what you propose. I know, too, what you have up your sleeve. And I want to say that I am entirely at variance with your philosophy. I declare it to you, I am not only at variance with your doctrines, but with your philosophy. Economically, you are unsound; socially, you are wrong; industrially, you are an impossibility.

And why, it may quite properly be asked, did the socialists in the AFL acquiesce to Gompers' determined leadership and to the Federation's utter rejection of industrial unionism? Perhaps the best answer is that, as trade unionists, they were more concerned with maintaining an organization dedicated to securing bread-and-butter objectives than, as socialists, in adhering unswervingly to a policy that offered the proverbial "pie in the sky."

Failure of the socialists to gain control of the trade union movement had the effect of sharpening their interest in political action. But here they encountered even greater difficulties than in the field of trade unionism. For one thing, there has been a traditional disinclination in the United States to support absolutist and abstract theories of society and government. To gain mass acceptance, socialism had to originate in and grow out of the institutional fabric of American society. Such was hardly the case. Although it had many distinct American ramifications, socialism was ideologically a foreign impor-

tation, and the great mass of Americans never ceased to regard it as such. Equally if not more important, the fact that Marxist theory condoned ultimate resort to force and violence had the effect of stigmatizing "scientific socialism." Moreover, it placed votaries of such a doctrine outside the then still honorable tradition of native American radicalism, which adhered to parliamentary and nonviolent methods. Marxist leaders, always painfully conscious of the high percentage of immigrants within their ranks, stressed the need to "Americanize" the movement, but it was not until the collapse of the People's Party after 1896 that the memberships of socialist political organizations began to be sprinkled generously with native-born Americans.

The two-party system and tradition constituted the greatest single political obstacle to the socialists as well as to other third parties. Spokesmen for the orthodox parties, when they did not ignore the socialists completely, never failed to point out the futility of throwing away one's vote on socialist candidates who were destined to certain defeat. Socialism's objectives might be alluring, but they were of little concrete value if the means of achieving them were not at hand. Under the circumstances, the socialists and their sympathizers were often unable to resist voiting for the less objectionable of the Republican or Democratic candidates. And political victories over and above the local level were important, despite the contentions of socialist leaders that elections under the existing capitalistic system were significant only as propaganda opportunities. Constant political setbacks discouraged rather than educated the socialist rank and file. In the face of such defeats, party morale was difficult to maintain, and converts were seldom made in the face of political impotence.

In those places where socialism, as a political movement, has enjoyed a modicum of success, it has been largely because of the support of middle-class adherents who were convinced that the socialists would bring about increased economic efficiency and greater social justice. During the 1890s the vogue of Edward Bellamy's *Looking Backward* caused thousands of middle-class Americans to take an interest in socialism and give it a thin veneer of respectability hitherto completely lacking. Yet, as with the working class, only a very small segment of the American middle class was attracted to socialism. A few mavericks threw in their lot with the Marxists and in some instances, notably in the Progressive Era, rose to positions of leadership. But most middle-class radicals, even those who were willing to label themselves "Fabian socialists," eschewed association with the Marxists and the political parties they dominated. First and foremost, they rejected the Marxist emphasis on the class struggle doctrine. But they were also understandably irritated by the allocation of all of humanity's virtues to the proletarians who toiled with sweat and brawn.

In any consideration of the relationship of the middle class to socialism, one must bear in mind the difficulties that confronted socialist leaders in their efforts to win over that particular hard core of the American bourgeoisie, the farmers. In the Midwest and in some parts of the South the socialists inherited some of the legacy of the agrarian discontent generated by Populism, but their appeal was fundamentally one of negative protest against the existing social and economic order rather than of positive adherence to the principles of the cooperative commonwealth. The socialists faced the same very real bugaboo that had confronted Henry George when he sought to enlist the support of farmers in his crusade against land rents. In the last analysis, socialism meant the expropriation of land, and that could not be explained away. American farmers, furthermore, were far more concerned with preserving competitive capitalism than in extirpating it. Some had been willing to go along with the mild collec-

tivist proposals of the Populists, not because they condoned state ownership per se but because it gave promise of eliminating the private monopolist. Only the most despairing saw in socialism a solution to their own personal problems.

And the socialists displayed certain attitudinal shortcomings which revealed how closely they were identified with prevailing social values of their day. The socialists, for example, made no particular appeal to minority groups in the United States except, perhaps, to some Jewish immigrants who previously had participated in the radical political movements of Eastern Europe. They refused to give special consideration or attention to Negroes and other dark-skinned ethnic Americans. Socialists told these minorities that their day of salvation would come at the same time that the working class, with whom they were automatically identified, threw off the oppressive shackles of capitalism. But even more to the point, many socialists, and particularly those among the party "intellectuals," had insulting racist viewpoints which they rarely concealed and often articulated.

Similarly, the socialists had little sympathy for American feminism. The same male chauvinism characteristic of the leadership of the orthodox political parties was also unfortunately true of most of the socialist leadership, so much so, in fact, that the party was on more than one occasion threatened by a wholesale desertion of its women members. Admittedly, the socialists were early advocates of women's suffrage, but this is not to say that taken in their collectivity they were sympathetic to women's liberation. Far from it. Women's place, for most socialist males and for most American males, was in the home.

Socialism needs a favorable disposition in the national temperament to permit it an unbiased hearing and perhaps a trial of its claims. This it has lacked in the United States, where all of the institutional cards have been thoroughly stacked on the side of the existing order. From those cradles of ideas and ideals, the public schools, the young have been early inculcated with a twin credo: the inherent superiority of American democracy and American capitalism. Nor have the nation's colleges and universities been seminaries of socialist sedition, as frightened conservatives have always complained. American professors and students have been on the whole conservative, if not completely socially and politically apathetic. Furthermore, it is a matter of public record that university administrators, spurred on by determined boards of trustees, have shown on occasion a zeal in purging their faculties of instructors who have held mildly unorthodox, let alone socialist, views.

Religious institutions, too, have been bulwarks of the status quo. Few will deny their important role in shaping the national mind; and in this regard it is perhaps well to reemphasize the traditional social conservatism of American churches of all denominations. In recent years, historians have been prone to overplay the importance of the social gospel movement in American Protestantism. One needs rather to remember that only a very meager part of the Protestant clergy was tinged with radical social Christianity. Much the same can be said of the Catholic counterpart of the social gospel. The Catholic church in America, dominated by a conservative Irish-American hierarchy, has been an important factor in immunizing Catholic workingmen against socialism. As the Reverend Bernard Vaughan, S.J., warned members of the faith in 1912: "Socialism, acting on its belief in the materialistic conception of history, expects to establish a State without reference to God. It has no special use for God. It ignores Him when it does not deny Him." Finally, Karl Marx himself had given the kiss of death to socialism in America. For try as they might, the American socialists could not live down his famous statement that religion was the "opiate of the people." To millions of Americans, socialism was identified with atheism and automatically was an anathema.

One other molder of public attitude, the press, merits a word. Even those papers which boasted of their objectivity and impartiality rarely extended press coverage to the socialists. And when by chance they did, there was usually a perceptible effort made to denigrate them. Nor were editorials on socialism the epitome of intellectual honesty, as socialist doctrines were consistently and—one cannot help but believe—purposely misrepresented. As often as not, socialism was identified with bloodshed, sexual promiscuity, and immorality.

In broad and highly general terms, then, these have been the principal reasons for the present bankruptcy of socialism in the United States. Undoubtedly, there are other reasons which may be equally significant, particularly in the context of specific situations, for, as we know, the failure of an ideological and political movement can hardly be intellectually packaged and explained in a neat and all-inclusive formula.

SUGGESTED READINGS

BEDFORD, HENRY F. *Socialism and the Workers in Massachusetts, 1886–1912.* Amherst: University of Massachusetts Press, 1966.

BELL, DANIEL. "The Background and Development of Marxian Socialism in the United States," in DONALD EGBERT and STOW PERSONS (eds.), *Socialism and American Life*, Vol. I. Princeton: Princeton University Press, 1952.

DUBOFSKY, MELVYN. *We Shall Be All: A History of the I.W.W.* Chicago: Quadrangle Books, 1969.

FINE, NATHAN. *Labor and Farmer Parties in the United States.* New York: Russell & Russell, Inc., 1961.

FRIED, ALBERT. *Socialism in America: From the Shakers to the Third International.* New York: Anchor Books, 1970.

GINGER, RAY. *The Bending Cross: A Biography of Eugene Victor Debs.* New Brunswick, N.J.: Rutgers University Press, 1949.

HERRESHOFF, DAVID. *American Disciples of Marx*. Detroit: Wayne State University Press, 1967.

HILLQUIT, MORRIS. *History of Socialism in the United States*. New York: Funk & Wagnalls Co., 1903.

————. *Loose Leaves from a Busy Life*. New York: Macmillan Co., 1934.

KARSON, MARC. *American Labor Unions and Politics, 1910–1918*. Carbondale: Southern Illinois University Press, 1958.

KIPNIS, IRA. *The American Socialist Movement, 1897–1912*. New York: Columbia University Press, 1952.

KREUTER, KENT and KREUTER, GRETCHEN. *An American Dissenter: The Life of Algie M. Simons, 1870–1950*. Lexington: University of Kentucky Press, 1969.

PETERSON, H. C., and FITE, GILBERT C. *Opponents of War, 1917–1918*. Madison: University of Wisconsin Press, 1957.

PRESTON, WILLIAM, JR. *Aliens and Dissenters: Federal Suppression of Radicals, 1903–1933*. Cambridge, Mass.: Harvard University Press, 1963.

QUINT, HOWARD H. *The Forging of American Socialism: Origins of the Modern Movement*. Columbia: University of South Carolina Press, 1953.

RENSHAW, PATRICK. *The Wobblies*. Garden City, N.Y.: Doubleday & Co., Inc., 1967.

SHANNON, DAVID A. *The Socialist Party of America*. New York: Macmillan Co., 1955.

WEINSTEIN, JAMES. *The Decline of Socialism in America, 1912–1925*. New York: Monthly Review Press, 1967.

DOCUMENT 26.1

The Socialist Platform (1912)*

Perhaps the best summary of socialist beliefs and objectives during the Progressive Era appears in the 1912 national platform of the Socialist Party of America. Not all of the planks in the platform, of course, were uniquely the political property of the socialists, since in some instances similar positions were taken by the Republican and Democratic parties as well as Theodore Roosevelt's Progressives. Yet a close reading of the Socialist platform is revealing in the light of subsequent political, social, and economic developments.

*Source: Socialist Party, *Proceedings of the National Convention of the Socialist Party, 1912* (Chicago, 1912), pp. 196–98.

WORKING PROGRAM

As measures calculated to strengthen the working class in its fight for the realization of its ultimate aim, the cooperative commonwealth, and to increase its power of resistance to capitalist oppression, we advance and pledge ourselves and our elected officers to the following program:

COLLECTIVE OWNERSHIP

a) The collective ownership and democratic management of railroads, wire and wireless telegraphs and telephones, express services, steamboat lines and all other social means of transportation and communication and of all large-scale industries.

b) The immediate acquirement by the municipalities, the states or the federal government, of all grain elevators, stock-yards, storage warehouses, and other distributing agencies, in order to reduce the present extortionate cost of living.

c) The extension of the public domain to include mines, quarries, oil wells, forests, and water power.

d) The further conservation and development of natural resources for the use and benefit of all the people:

1. By scientific forestation and timber protection.
2. By the reclamation of arid and swamp tracts.
3. By the storage of flood waters and the utilization of water power.
4. By the stoppage of the present extravagant waste of the soil and of the products of mines and oil wells.
5. By the development of highway and waterway systems.

e) The collective ownership of land wherever practicable, and in cases where such ownership is impracticable, the appropriation by taxation of the annual

rental value of all land held for speculation or exploitation.

f) The collective ownership and democratic management of the banking and
currency system.

UNEMPLOYMENT

a) The immediate government relief of
the unemployed by the extension of all
useful public works. All persons employed
on such works to be engaged directly by
the government under a workday of not
more than eight hours and at not less than
the prevailing union wages. The government also to establish employment
bureaus; to lend money to states and municipalities without interest for the purpose of carrying on public works, and to
take such other measures within its power
as will lessen the widespread misery of the
workers caused by the misrule of the capitalist class.

INDUSTRIAL DEMANDS

The conservation of human resources,
particularly of the lives and well being of
the workers and their families:

a) By shortening of the workday in
keeping with the increased productiveness
of machinery.

b) By securing to every worker a rest
period of not less than a day and a half in
each week.

c) By securing a more effective inspec-
tion of workshops, factories and mines.

d) By forbidding the employment of
children under sixteen years of age.

e) By the co-operative organization of
the industries in the federal penitentiaries
for the benefit of the convicts and their
dependents.

f) By forbidding the interstate transportation of the products of child labor, of
convict labor and of all uninspected factories and mines.

g) By abolishing the profit system in
government work and substituting either
the direct hire of labor or the awarding of
contracts to co-operative groups of
workers.

h) By establishing minimum wage
scales.

i) By abolishing official charity and
substituting a non-contributory system of
old-age pensions, a general system of insurance by the State of all its members
against unemployment and invalidism and
a system of compulsory insurance by employers of their workers, without cost to
the latter, against industrial diseases, accidents and death.

POLITICAL DEMANDS

a) The absolute freedom of press,
speech and assembly.

b) The adoption of a graduated income
tax, the increase of the rates of the present
corporation tax and the extension of inheritance taxes graduated in proportion to
the value of the estate and to nearness of
kin—the proceeds of these taxes to be
employed in the socialization of industry.

c) The abolition of the monopoly ownership of patents and the substitution of
collective ownership, with direct awards
to inventors by premiums or royalties.

d) Unrestricted and equal suffrage for
men and women.

e) The adoption of the initiative, referendum and recall and of proportional representation, nationally as well as locally.

f) The abolition of the Senate and of
the veto power of the President.

g) The election of the President and of
the Vice-President by the direct vote of
the people.

h) The abolition of the power usurped
by the Supreme Court of the United States
to pass upon the constitutionality of the
legislation enacted by Congress. National
laws to be repealed only by act of
Congress or by a referendum vote of the
whole people.

i) The abolition of the present restrictions upon the amendment of the constitution, so that instrument may be made
amendable by a majority of the voters in a
majority of the States.

j) The granting of the right of suffrage
in the District of Columbia with repre-

sentation in Congress and a democratic form of municipal government for purely local affairs.

k) The extension of democratic government to all United States territories.

l) The enactment of further measures for general education and particularly for vocational education in useful pursuits. The Bureau of Education to be made a Department.

m) The enactment of further measures for the conservation of health. The creation of an independent bureau of health, with such restrictions as will secure full liberty to all schools of practice.

n) The separation of the present Bureau of Labor from the Department of Commerce and its elevation to the rank of a department.

o) Abolition of all federal district courts and the United States circuit courts of appeals. State courts to have jurisdiction in all cases arising between citizens of the several states and foreign corporations. The election of all judges for short terms.

p) The immediate curbing of the power of the courts to issue injunctions.

q) The free administration of the law.

r) The calling of a convention for the revision of the constitution of the United States.

Such measures of relief as we may be able to force from capitalism are but a preparation of the workers to seize the whole powers of government, in order that they may thereby lay hold of the whole system of socialized industry and thus come to their rightful inheritance.

DOCUMENT 26.2

The Parable of the Water Tank*

Edward Bellamy's utopian novel *Looking Backward* (1887), the first great document of American socialism, introduced thousands of persons from all walks of life to socialist ideas and inspired formation of a network of Nationalist clubs which worked to achieve social and economic reconstruction based on cooperative rather than competitive principles. On the eve of his death in 1898, Bellamy published *Equality,* a sequel to *Looking Backward.* A more profound though less popular book, *Equality* contained "The Parable of the Water Tank," a clever simplification of socialist principles.

... "The other day, at the museum, I was delving among the relics of literature of the great Revolution, with a view to finding something that might illustrate our theme. I came across a little pamphlet of the period, yellow and almost undecipherable, which, on examination, I found to be a rather amusing skit or satirical take-off on the profit system. It struck me that probably our lesson might prepare us to appreciate it, and I made a copy. It is entitled "The Parable of the Water Tank," and runs this way:

" 'There was a certain very dry land, the people whereof were in sore need of water. And they did nothing but to seek after water from morning until night, and many perished because they could not find it.

" 'Howbeit, there were certain men in that land who were more crafty and diligent than the rest, and these had gathered stores of water where others could find none, and the name of these men was called capitalists. And it came to pass that the people of the land came unto the capitalists and prayed them that they would give them of the water they had gathered that they might drink, for their need was

*Source: Edward Bellamy, *Equality* (New York: D. Appleton & Co., 1898), pp. 195–203.

sore. But the capitalists answered them and said:

" ' "Go to, ye silly people! why should we give you of the water which we have gathered, for then we should become even as ye are, and perish with you? But behold what we will do unto you. Be ye our servants and ye shall have water."

" 'And the people said, "Only give us to drink and we will be your servants, we and our children." And it was so.

" 'Now, the capitalists were men of understanding, and wise in their generation. They ordered the people who were their servants in bands with captains and officers, and some they put at the springs to dip, and others did they make to carry the water, and others did they cause to seek for new springs. And all the water was brought together in one place, and there did the capitalists make a great tank for to hold it, and the tank was called the Market, for it was there that the people, even the servants of the capitalists, came to get water. And the capitalists said unto the people:

" ' "For every bucket of water that ye bring to us, that we may pour it into the tank, which is the Market, behold! we will give you a penny, but for every bucket that we shall draw forth to give unto you that ye may drink of it, ye and your wives and your children, ye shall give us two pennies, and the difference shall be our profit, seeing that if it were not for this profit we would not do this thing for you, but ye should all perish."

" 'And it was good in the people's eyes, for they were dull of understanding, and they diligently brought water unto the tank for many days, and for every bucket which they did bring the capitalists gave them every man a penny; but for every bucket that the capitalists drew forth from the tank to give again unto the people, behold! the people rendered to the capitalists two pennies.

" 'And after many days the water tank, which was the Market, overflowed at the top, seeing that for every bucket the peo-

ple poured in they received only so much as would buy again half of a bucket. And because of the excess that was left of every bucket, did the tank overflow, for the people were many, but the capitalists were few, and could drink no more than others. Therefore did the tank overflow.

" 'And when the capitalists saw that the water overflowed, they said to the people:

" ' "See ye not the tank, which is the Market, doth overflow? Sit ye down, therefore and be patient, for ye shall bring us no more water till the tank be empty."

" 'But when the people no more received the pennies of the capitalists for the water they brought, they could buy no more water from the capitalists, having naught wherewith to buy. And when the capitalists saw that they had no more profit because no man bought water of them, they were troubled. And they sent forth men in the highways, the byways, and the hedges, crying, "If any thirst let him come to the tank and buy water of us, for it doth overflow." For they said among themselves, "Behold, the times are dull; we must advertise."

" 'But the people answered, saying: "How can we buy unless ye hire us, for how else shall we have wherewithal to buy? Hire ye us, therefore, as before, and we will gladly buy water, for we thirst, and ye will have no need to advertise." But the capitalists said to the people: "Shall we hire you to bring water when the tank, which is the Market, doth already overflow? Buy ye, therefore, first water, and when the tank is empty, through your buying, will we hire you again." And so it was because the capitalists hired them no more to bring water that the people could not buy the water they had brought already, and because the people could not buy the water they had brought already, the capitalists no more hired them to bring water. And the saying went abroad, "It is a crisis."

" 'And the thirst of the people was great, for it was not now as it had been in the days of their fathers, when the land was open before them, for every one to seek water for himself, seeing that the capitalists had taken all the springs, and the wells, and the water wheels, and the vessels and the buckets, so that no man might come by water save from the tank, which was the Market. And the people murmured against the capitalists and said: "Behold, the tank runneth over, and we die of thirst. Give us, therefore, of the water, that we perish not."

" 'But the capitalists answered: "Not so. The water is ours. Ye shall not drink thereof unless ye buy it of us with pennies." And they confirmed it with an oath, saying, after their manner, "Business is business."

" 'But the capitalists were disquieted that the people bought no more water, whereby they had no more any profits, and they spake one to another, saying: "It seemeth that our profits have stopped our profits, and by reason of the profits we have made, we can make no more profits. How is it that our profits are become unprofitable to us, and our gains do make us poor? Let us therefore send for the soothsayers, that they may interpret this thing unto us," and they sent for them.

" 'Now, the soothsayers were men learned in dark sayings, who joined themselves to the capitalists by reason of the water of the capitalists, that they might have thereof and live, they and their children. And they spake for the capitalists unto the people, and did their embassies for them, seeing that the capitalists were not a folk quick of understanding neither ready of speech.

" 'And the capitalists demanded of the soothsayers that they should interpret this thing unto them, wherefore it was that the people bought no more water of them, although the tank was full. And certain of the soothsayers answered and said, "It is by reason of overproduction," and some said, "It is glut"; but the signification of the two words is the same. And others said, "Nay, but this thing is by reason of the spots on the sun." And yet others an-

swered, saying, "It is neither by reason of glut, nor yet of spots on the sun that this evil hath come to pass, but because of lack of confidence."

" 'And while the soothsayers contended among themselves, according to their manner, the men of profit did slumber and sleep, and when they awoke they said to the soothsayers: "It is enough. Ye have spoken comfortably unto us. Now go ye forth and speak comfortably likewise unto this people, so that they be at rest and leave us also in peace."

" 'But the soothsayers, even the men of the dismal science—for so they were named of some—were loath to go forth to the people lest they should be stoned, for the people loved them not. And they said to the capitalists:

" ' "Masters, it is a mystery of our craft that if men be full and thirst not but be at rest, then shall they find comfort in our speech even as ye. Yet if they thirst and be empty, find they no comfort therein but rather mock us, for it seemeth that unless a man be full our wisdom appeareth unto him but emptiness." But the capitalists said: "Go ye forth. Are ye not our men to do our embassies?"

" 'And the soothsayers went forth to the people and expounded to them the mystery of overproduction, and how it was that they must needs perish of thirst because there was overmuch water, and how there could not be enough because there was too much. And likewise spoke they unto the people concerning the sun spots, and also wherefore it was that these things had come upon them by reason of lack of confidence. And it was even as the soothsayers had said, for to the people their wisdom seemed emptiness. And the people reviled them, saying: "Go up, ye bald-heads! Will ye mock us? Doth plenty breed famine? Doth nothing come out of much?" And they took up stones to stone them.

" 'And when the capitalists saw that the people still murmured and would not give ear to the soothsayers, and because also they feared lest they should come upon the tank and take of the water by force, they brought forth to them certain holy men (but they were false priests), who spake unto the people that they should be quiet and trouble not the capitalists because they thirsted. And these holy men, who were false priests, testified to the people that this affliction was sent to them of God for the healing of their souls, and that if they should bear it in patience and lust not after the water, neither trouble the capitalists, it would come to pass that after they had given up the ghost they would come to a country where there should be no capitalists but an abundance of water. Howbeit, there were certain true prophets of God also, and these had compassion on the people and would not prophesy for the capitalists, but rather spake constantly against them.

" 'Now, when the capitalists saw that the people still murmured and would not be still, neither for the words of the sooth-sayers nor of the false priests, they came forth themselves unto them and put the ends of their fingers in the water that overflowed in the tank and wet the tips thereof, and they scattered the drops from the tips of their fingers abroad upon the people who thronged the tank, and the name of the drops of water was charity, and they were exceeding bitter.

" 'And when the capitalists saw yet again that neither for the words of the soothsayers, nor of the holy men who were false priests, nor yet for the drops that were called charity, would the people be still, but raged the more, and crowded upon the tank as if they would take it by force, then took they counsel together and sent men privily forth among the people. And these men sought out the mightiest among the people and all who had skill in war, and took them apart and spake craftily with them, saying:

" ' "Come, now, why cast ye not your lot in with the capitalists? If ye shall be their men and serve them against the people, that they break not in upon the tank, then

shall ye have abundance of water, that ye perish not, ye and your children."

" 'And the mighty men and they who were skilled in war hearkened unto this speech and suffered themselves to be persuaded, for their thirst constrained them, and they went within unto the capitalists and became their men, and staves and swords were put in their hands and they became a defense unto the capitalists and smote the people when they thronged upon the tank.

" 'And after many days the water was low in the tank, for the capitalists did make fountains and fish ponds of the water thereof, and did bathe therein, they and their wives and their children, and did waste the water for their pleasure.

" 'And when the capitalists saw that the tank was empty, they said, "The crisis is ended"; and they sent forth and hired the people that they should bring water to fill it again. And for the water that the people brought to the tank they received for every bucket a penny, but for the water which the capitalists drew forth from the tank to give again to the people they received two pennies, that they might have their profit. And after a time did the tank again overflow even as before.

" 'And now, when many times the people had filled the tank until it overflowed and had thirsted till the water therein had been wasted by the capitalists, it came to pass that there arose in the land certain men who were called agitators, for that they did stir up the people. And they spake to the people, saying that they should associate, and then would they have no need to be servants of the capitalists and should thirst no more for water. And in the eyes of the capitalists were the agitators pestilent fellows, and they would fain have crucified them, but durst not for fear of the people.

" 'And the words of the agitators which they spake to the people were on this wise:

" ' "Ye foolish people, how long will ye be deceived by a lie and believe to your hurt that which is not? for behold all these things that have been said unto you by the capitalists and by the soothsayers are cunningly devised fables. And likewise the holy men, who say that it is the will of God that ye should always be poor and miserable and athirst, behold! they do blaspheme God and are liars, whom he will bitterly judge though he forgive all others. How cometh it that ye may not come by the water in the tank? Is it not because ye have no money? And why have ye no money? Is it not because ye receive but one penny for every bucket that ye bring to the tank, which is the Market, but must render two pennies for every bucket ye take out, so that the capitalists may have their profit? See ye not how by this means the tank must overflow, being filled by that ye lack and made to abound out of your emptiness? See ye not also that the harder ye toil and the more diligently ye seek and bring the water, the worse and not the better it shall be for you by reason of the profit, and that forever?"

" 'After this manner spake the agitators for many days unto the people, and none heeded them, but it was so that after a time the people hearkened. And they answered and said unto the agitators:

" ' "Ye say truth. It is because of the capitalists and of their profits that we want, seeing that by reason of them and their profits we may by no means come by the fruit of our labor, so that our labor is in vain, and the more we toil to fill the tank the sooner doth it overflow, and we may receive nothing because there is too much, according to the words of the soothsayers. But behold, the capitalists are hard men and their tender mercies are cruel. Tell us if ye know any way whereby we may deliver ourselves out of our bondage unto them. But if ye know of no certain way of deliverance we beseech you to hold your peace and let us alone, that we may forget our misery."

" 'And the agitators answered and said, "We know a way."

" 'And the people said: "Deceive us not, for this thing hath been from the beginning, and none hath found a way of deliverance until now, though many have sought it carefully with tears. But if ye know a way, speak unto us quickly."

" 'Then the agitators spake unto the people of the way. And they said:

" ' "Behold, what need have ye at all of these capitalists, that ye should yield them profits upon your labor? What great thing do they wherefore ye render them this tribute? Lo! it is only because they do order you in bands and lead you out and in and set your tasks and afterward give you a little of the water yourselves have brought and not they. Now, behold the way out of this bondage! Do ye for yourselves that which is done by the capitalists—namely, the ordering of your labor, and the marshaling of your bands, and the dividing of your tasks. So shall ye have no need at all of the capitalists and no more yield to them any profit, but all the fruit of your labor shall ye share as brethren, every one having the same; and so shall the tank never overflow until every man is full, and would not wag the tongue for more, and afterward shall ye with the overflow make pleasant fountains and fish ponds to delight yourselves withal even as did the capitalists; but these shall be for the delight of all."

" 'And the people answered, "How shall we go about to do this thing, for it seemeth good to us?"

" 'And the agitators answered: "Choose ye discreet men to go in and out before you and to marshal your bands and order your labor, and these men shall be as the capitalists were; but, behold, they shall not be your masters as the capitalists are, but your brethren and officers who do your will, and they shall not take any profits, but every man his share like the others, that there may be no more masters and servants among you, but brethren only. And from time to time, as ye see fit, ye shall choose other discreet men in place of the first to order the labor."

" 'And the people hearkened, and the thing was good to them. Likewise seemed it not a hard thing. And with one voice they cried out, "So let it be as ye have said, for we will do it!"

" 'And the capitalists heard the noise of the shouting and what the people said, and the soothsayers heard it also, and likewise the false priests and the mighty men of war, who were a defense unto the capitalists; and when they heard they trembled exceedingly, so that their knees smote together and they said one to another, "It is the end of us!"

" 'Howbeit, there were certain true priests of the living God who would not prophesy for the capitalists, but had compassion on the people; and when they heard the shouting of the people and what they said, they rejoiced with exceeding great joy, and gave thanks to God because of the deliverance.

" 'And the people went and did all the things that were told them of the agitators to do. And it came to pass as the agitators had said, even according to all their words. And there was no more any thirst in that land, neither any that was ahungered, nor naked, nor cold, nor in any manner of want; and every man said unto his fellow, "My brother," and every woman said unto her companion, "My sister," and so were they with one another as brethren and sisters which do dwell together in unity. And the blessing of God rested upon that land forever.' "

DOCUMENT 26.3
The Moral Fervor of Socialism*

In attempting to explain the Progressive Era in terms of a "status revolution" or in the light of calculated and self-interested conservatism, historians today sometimes ignore the fact that much of the period's moral fervor had socialist origins. It even

*Source: *The Outlook*, Vol. XC (September 12, 1908), pp. 61–63.

may be argued that had there been no socialist agitation, there would have been, in fact, no Progressive Era. The following editorial in *The Outlook* magazine acknowledges the contribution of the socialists in establishing a climate for reform.

The Socialist programme, as interpreted by the platform of the Socialist party and by the books of its most intellectual leaders, involves the collective ownership of all producing property and the collective control of all producing industry. In this programme The Outlook does not believe. We think it would not be any remedy for present industrial ills; that it would aggravate the evils it seeks to cure.

But there is much in the Socialist spirit that is admirable. There are in it two elements that are wholly admirable.

It looks at the facts of life courageously. To thousands of men and women to-day life is a tragedy. They live in crowded sections of a city where they are denied participation in the common gifts of God—fresh air, pure water, cheering sunshine. They watch the ebbing life of their dear ones, knowing well that the deadly disease is needless; perhaps knowing that the mortality in their homes is three times what it is in the homes of the prosperous. They see their children denied the pleasures of childhood that they may help earn the daily bread of the household, or driven to seek their playgrounds in the squalid streets and their playmates among the hoodlums. They suffer sometimes the pangs of physical hunger and always the pangs of hunger of mind and soul for leisure and means to nourish the higher life. They are often unable to get work because no one will hire them, often compelled to take a wage barely sufficient to keep them in tolerable condition as working machines. The conditions of their employment are often neither comfortable nor sanitary; sometimes so far unendurable that the power to endure them is exhausted by half a score of years. When their wages are adequate and their conditions favorable, both are, or seem to be, dependent on the good will and the business capacity of an employer in the selection of whom they have no voice. They help to elect the President who administers the affairs of the Nation, but not the boss who administers the affairs of their mine or factory. In the profits of their industry they have no share; or, if some share is accorded to them, it is in the form of increased wages, not in the form of profits. And all the while they see neighbors whose problem appears to be, not how to live on their income, but how to spend it. It is not strange that, with Frederic Harrison, who is not a Socialist, they wonder, "Are rich men likely to prove of any real social use, or will it be better for society to abolish the institution?" Nor strange that they lend eager attention to reformers who propose to abolish rich men and give to the workers the ownership and the management of the mine and the factory.

Socialism has dared to see these facts and to make society see them. Socialism is making one half the world know how the other half lives. "A prudent man," says the proverb, "seeth the evil; the simple pass on and are mulcted." It was because in the century before Christ the simple would not see the evil that the Roman Republic was wrecked. It was because in the eighteenth century the simple would not see the evil that the feudal system in France was overturned by the fateful Revolution. Socialism sees, and is compelling a reluctant society to see, the evil of our present industrial system. It is true that these evils are portrayed elsewhere; by Carlyle, by Ruskin, by John Stuart Mill, by F. A. Walker. It is true that the Socialist pictures are sometimes exaggerations and often ill-proportioned. Nevertheless, for a vivid and even for a careful scientific account of the evils of the wages system the student must go to the Socialist literature. Too long the prosperous have been blind and deaf. Socialism sees and hears, and is compelling the prosperous to see and hear. For the courage and the persistence with which the Socialists reiterate their disagreeable revelation they deserve both honor and thanks.

With this spirit of courage goes a spirit of brotherhood: It is true that this is often marred by a distinctive and even a bitter class feeling, witnessed by the title of one Socialist publication, "The Class War"; indicated by the closing paragraph of the Socialist Political Platform, which demands for the workers the whole power of government and the sole control of industry.

Nevertheless, in the main a spirit of brotherhood inspires the great worldwide Socialist movement. It is not class ambition nor class jealousy that has drawn such men as Mr. [J. G. Phelps] Stokes into the Socialist movement in America, or such men as Jerome K. Jerome and R. J. Campbell and Lord Ribblesdale in England, or has won from even the conservative clergy in both continents so much sincere if not always intelligent sympathy. Even the class feeling is an advance on individual selfishness. "An injury to one is an injury to all" is as yet only a class motto, the motto of the trades union. So *Noblesse oblige* was a class motto, the motto of the feudal nobility. But either of them is better than the motto "Every man for himself and the devil take the hindmost," which is the motto of individualism.

The hopes of the Socialists are not class hopes. Illusive they may be, but they are certainly human. The Rev. Charles H. Vail, in his "Principles of Scientific Socialism," includes in his catalogue of the advantages of Socialism, increased production, orderly and equable distribution, prevention of waste, elevation of woman, better conditions for children, abolition of taxation, an end to enforced idleness, to business dishonesty, to divorce and to prostitution, the elimination of crime, the prevention of intemperance and insanity, and the cure of poverty. These hopes are very enticing. If they were only true or even plausible!

Socialism sees clearly social evils which have grown unendurable; it is animated by a spirit of brotherhood which is sometimes a class feeling, but is sometimes a feeling of humanity; and it prescribes a panacea from which it anticipates a millennium which will bring equal benefits to all. The antidote for Socialism is not in ignoring the evils which it portrays, but in seeing them more clearly and understanding more correctly the causes which have produced them. It is not in sneering at the spirit of brotherhood which the Socialists profess, but in a wider spirit of brotherhood which shall include the rich as well as the poor in its fellowship. It is not by simply pointing out the inadequacy of the proposed economic panacea, but in discerning and setting in operation those combined and co-operative forces—spiritual, intellectual, industrial, and political —which alone can regenerate society and so effectually reform its institutions. The Socialists would do well to ponder this sentence from Frederic Harrison: "We must regenerate domestic life, personal life, moral life, social life, political life, religious life, and not manufacturing and trading life alone." But that sentence the opponents of Socialism would also do well to ponder. For Socialism will win the opportunity to try its experiment, in spite of all opposition, unless its opponents have some better social order to offer to the world than a mere continuance of present conditions.

DOCUMENT 26.4

Theodore Roosevelt on Socialism*

Theodore Roosevelt lumped together socialists and "malefactors of great wealth" as being the principal enemies of American democracy. After Roosevelt left the Presidency, he became an editor of *The Outlook* magazine. Significantly, his

*Source: Theodore Roosevelt, "Socialism," *The Outlook,* Vol. XCI (March 20, 1909), pp. 619–23.

first signed article was a vituperative attack on "socialism" in general and American socialists in particular.

It is always difficult to discuss a question when it proves impossible to define the terms in which that question is to be discussed. Therefore there is not much to be gained by a discussion of Socialism *versus* Individualism in the abstract. Neither absolute Individualism nor absolute Socialism would be compatible with civilization at all; and among the arguments of the extremists of either side the only unanswerable ones are those which show the absurdity of the position of the other. . . .

With those self-styled Socialists to whom "Socialism" is merely a vaguely conceived catchword, and who use it to express their discontent with existing wrongs and their purpose to correct them, there is not much need of discussion. So far as they make any proposals which are not foolish, and which tend towards betterment, we can act with them. But the real, logical, advanced Socialists, who teach their faith as both a creed and a party platform, may deceive to their ruin decent and well-meaning but short-sighted men; and there is need of plain speaking in order accurately to show the trend of their teaching.

The immorality and absurdity of the doctrines of Socialism as propounded by these advanced advocates are quite as great as those of the advocates, if such there be, of an unlimited individualism. As an academic matter there is more need of refutation of the creed of absolute Socialism than of the creed of absolute individualism; for it happens that at the present time a greater number of visionaries, both sinister and merely dreamy, believe in the former than in the latter. One difficulty in arguing with professed Socialists of the extreme, or indeed of the opportunist, type, however, is that those of them who are sincere almost invariably suffer from great looseness of thought; for if they did not keep their faith nebulous, it would at once become abhorrent in the eyes of any upright and sensible man. The doctrinaire Socialists, the extremists, the men who represent the doctrine in its most advanced form, are, and must necessarily be, not only convinced opponents of private property, but also bitterly hostile to religion and morality; in short, they must be opposed to all those principles through which, and through which alone, even an imperfect civilization can be built up by slow advances through the ages.

Indeed, these thoroughgoing Socialists occupy, in relation to all morality, and especially to domestic morality, a position so revolting—and I choose my words carefully—that it is difficult even to discuss it in a reputable paper. In America the leaders even of this type have usually been cautious about stating frankly that they proposed to substitute free love for married and family life as we have it, although many of them do in a roundabout way uphold this position. In places on the continent of Europe, however, they are more straightforward, their attitude being that of one of the extreme French Socialist writers, M. Gabriel Deville, who announces that the Socialists intend to do away with both prostitution and marriage, which he regards as equally wicked—his method of doing away with prostitution being to make unchastity universal. Professor Carl Pearson, a leading English Socialist, states their position exactly:

The sex relation of the future will not be regarded as a union for the birth of children, but as the closest form of friendship between man and woman. It will be accompanied by no child bearing or rearing, or by this in a much more limited number than at present. With the sex relationship, so long as it does not result in children, we hold that the State in the future will in no wise interfere, but when it does result in children, then the State will have a right to interfere.

He then goes on to point out that in order to save the woman from "economic dependence" upon the father of her children, the children will be raised at the expense of the State; the usual plan being to have huge buildings like foundling asylums.

Mr. Pearson is a scientific man who, in his own realm, is as worthy of serious heed as Mr. Flinders Petrie, whom I mention later, is in his realm; and the above quotation states in naked form just what logical scientific Socialism would really come to. Aside from its thoroughly repulsive quality, it ought not to be necessary to point out that the condition of affairs aimed at would in actual practice bring about the destruction of the race within, at most, a couple of generations; and such destruction is heartily to be desired for any race of such infamous character as to tolerate such a system. Moreover, the ultra-Socialists of our own country have shown by their attitude towards one of their leaders, Mr. [George D.] Herron, that, so far as law and public sentiment will permit, they are now ready to try to realize the ideals set forth by Messrs. Deville and Pearson. As for Mr. Herron, I commend to those who desire to verify what I have said, the article in the Boston Congregationalist of June 15, 1901; and to those, by the way, who have not the time to hunt up all the original authorities, I would commend a book called "Socialism; the Nation of Fatherless Children," a book dedicated to the American Federation of Labor. The chapters on Free Love, Homeless Children, and Two Socialist Leaders are especially worth reading by any one who is for the moment confused by the statements of certain Socialist leaders to the effect that advanced Socialism does not contemplate an attack upon marriage and the family.

These same Socialist leaders, with a curious effrontery, at times deny that the exponents of "scientific Socialism" assume a position as regards industry which in condensed form may be stated as, that each man is to do what work he can, or, in other words, chooses, and in return is to take out from the common fund whatever he needs; or, what amounts to the same thing, that each man shall have equal remuneration with every other man, no matter what work is done. . . .

In other words, on the social and domestic side doctrinaire Socialism would replace the family and home life by a glorified State free-lunch counter and State foundling asylum, deliberately enthroning self-indulgence as the ideal, with, on its darker side, the absolute abandonment of all morality as between man and woman; while in place of what Socialists are pleased to call "wage slavery" there would be created a system which would necessitate either the prompt dying out of the community through sheer starvation, or an iron despotism over all workers, compared to which any slave system of the past would seem beneficent, because less utterly hopeless.

"Advanced" Socialist leaders are fond of declaiming against patriotism, of announcing their movement as international, and of claiming to treat all men alike; but on this point, as on all others, their system would not stand for one moment the test of actual experiment. If the leaders of the Socialist party in America should to-day endeavor to force their followers to admit all negroes and Chinamen to a real equality, their party would promptly disband, and, rather than submit to such putting into effect of their avowed purpose, would, as a literal fact, follow any capitalistic organization as an alternative. . . .

So much for the academic side of unadulterated, or, as its advocates style it, "advanced scientific" Socialism. Its representatives in this country who have practically striven to act up to their extreme doctrines, and have achieved leadership in any one of the branches of the Socialist party, especially the parlor Socialists and the like, be they lay or clerical, deserve scant consideration at the hands of honest and clean-living men and women. What their movement leads to may be gathered from the fact that in the last Presidential election they nominated and voted for a man who earns his livelihood as the editor of a paper which not merely practices every form of malignant and brutal slander, but condones and encourages every form of brutal wrong-doing, so long as either the slander or the violence is supposed to be at the expense of a man who owns something, wholly without regard to whether that man is himself a scoundrel, or a wise, kind, and helpful member of the community. As for the so-called Christian Socialists who associate themselves with this movement, they either are or ought to be aware of the pornographic literature, the pornographic propaganda, which make up one side of the movement; a pornographic side which is entirely proper in a movement that in this country accepts as one of its heads a man whose domestic immorality has been so open and flagrant as to merit the epithet of shameless. That criminal nonsense should be listened to eagerly by some men bowed down by the cruel condition of much of modern toil is not strange; but that men who pretend to speak with culture of mind and authority to teach, men who are or have been preachers of the Gospel or professors in universities, should affiliate themselves with the preachers of criminal nonsense is a sign of either grave mental or moral shortcoming.

I wish it to be remembered that I speak from the standpoint of, and on behalf of, the wage-worker and the tiller of the soil. These are the two men whose welfare I have ever before me, and for their sakes I would do anything, except anything that is wrong; and it is because I believe that teaching them doctrine like that which I have stigmatized represents the most cruel wrong in the long run, both to wage-worker and to earth-tiller, that I reprobate and denounce such conduct.

We need have but scant patience with those who assert that modern conditions are all that they should be, or that they cannot be improved. The wildest or most vicious of Socialistic writers could preach no more foolish doctrine than that contained in such ardent defenses of uncontrolled capitalism and individualism as

Mr. Flinders Petrie's "Janus," a book which is absurd, but which, because of this very fact, is not mischievous, for it can arouse no other emotion than the very earnest desire that this particular archæological shoemaker should stick to his early-Egyptian last. There are dreadful woes in modern life, dreadful suffering among some of those who toil, brutal wrong-doing among some of those who make colossal fortunes by exploiting the toilers. It is the duty of every honest and upright man, of every man who holds within his breast the capacity for righteous indignation, to recognize these wrongs, and to strive with all his might to bring about a better condition of things. But he will never bring about this better condition by misstating facts and advocating remedies which are not merely false, but fatal.

Take, for instance, the doctrine of the extreme Socialists, that all wealth is produced by manual workers, that the entire product of labor should be handed over every day to the laborer, that wealth is criminal in itself. Of course wealth is no more criminal than labor. Human society could not exist without both; and if all wealth were abolished this week, the majority of laborers would starve next week. As for the statement that all wealth is produced by manual workers, in order to appreciate its folly it is merely necessary for any man to look at what is happening right around him, in the next street, or the next village. Here in the city where The Outlook is edited, on Broadway between Ninth and Tenth Streets, is a huge dry goods store. The business was originally started, and the block of which I am speaking was built for the purpose, by an able New York merchant. It prospered. He and those who invested under him made a good deal of money. Their employees did well. Then he died, and certain other people took possession of it and tried to run the business. The manual labor was the same, the good-will was the same, the physical conditions were the same; but the guiding intelligence at the top had changed. The business was run at a loss. It would surely have had to shut, and all the employees, clerks, laborers, everybody turned adrift, to infinite suffering, if it had not again changed hands and another business man of capacity taken charge. The business was the same as before, the physical conditions were the same, the good-will the same, the manual labor the same, but the guiding intelligence had changed, and now everything once more prospered, and prospered as had never been the case before. With such an instance before our very eyes, with such proof of what every business proves, namely, the vast importance of the part played by the guiding intelligence in business, as in war, in invention, in art, in science, in every imaginable pursuit, it is really difficult to show patience when asked to discuss such a proposition as that all wealth is produced solely by the work of manual workers, and that the entire product should be handed over to them. Of course, if any such theory were really acted upon, there would soon be no product to be handed over to the manual laborers, and they would die of starvation. A great industry could no more be managed by a mass-meeting of manual laborers than a battle could be won in such fashion, than a painters' union could paint a Rembrandt, or a typographical union write one of Shakespeare's plays.

The fact is that this kind of Socialism represents an effort to enthrone privilege in its crudest form. Much of what we are fighting against in modern civilization is privilege. We fight against privilege when it takes the form of a franchise to a street railway company to enjoy the use of the streets of a great city without paying an adequate return; when it takes the form of a great business combination which grows rich by rebates which are denied to other shippers; when it takes the form of a stock-gambling operation which results in the watering of railway securities so that certain inside men get an enormous profit out of a swindle on the public. All these represent various forms of illegal, or, if not illegal, then anti-social, privilege. But there can be no greater abuse, no greater example of corrupt and destructive privilege, than that advocated by those who say that each man should put into a common store what he can and take out what he needs. This is merely another way of saying that the thriftless and the vicious, who could or would put in but little, should be entitled to take out the earnings of the intelligent, the foresighted, and the industrious. Such a proposition is morally base. To choose to live by theft or by charity means in each case degradation, a rapid lowering of self-respect and self-reliance. The worst wrongs that capitalism can commit upon labor would sink into insignificance when compared with the hideous wrong done by those who would degrade labor by sapping the foundations of self-respect and self-reliance. The Roman mob, living on the bread given them by the State and clamoring for excitement and amusement to be purveyed by the State, represent for all time the very nadir to which a free and self-respecting population of workers can sink if they grow habitually to rely upon others, and especially upon the State, either to furnish them charity, or to permit them to plunder, as a means of livelihood.

In short, it is simply common sense to recognize that there is the widest inequality of service, and that therefore there must be an equally wide inequality of reward, if our society is to rest upon the basis of justice and wisdom. Service is the true test by which a man's worth should be judged. We are against privilege in any form: privilege to the capitalist who exploits the poor man, and privilege to the shiftless or vicious poor man who would rob his thrifty brother of what he has earned. Certain exceedingly valuable forms of service are rendered wholly without capital. On the other hand, there are exceedingly valuable forms of service which can be rendered only by means of great accumulations of capital, and not to recog-

nize this fact would be to deprive our whole people of one of the great agencies for their betterment. The test of a man's worth to the community is the service he renders to it, and we cannot afford to make this test by material considerations alone. One of the main vices of the Socialism which was propounded by Proudhon, Lassalle, and Marx, and which is preached by their disciples and imitators, is that it is blind to everything except the merely material side of life. It is not only indifferent, but at bottom hostile, to the intellectual, the religious, the domestic and moral life; it is a form of communism with no moral foundation, but essentially based on the immediate annihilation of personal ownership of capital, and, in the near future, the annihilation of the family, and ultimately the annihilation of civilization.

DOCUMENT 26.5
An Appeal to Students*

Upton Sinclair, the socialist novelist and muckraker, was one of the founders of the Intercollegiate Socialist Society (later rechristened the League for Industrial Democracy). He appealed to college students on idealistic grounds to join the socialist movement. While the ISS was active on several campuses and could boast of a distinguished membership, it reached only a small part of the American student body.

So far as a living is concerned, the college man in our community is generally safe. If he saves himself from the grosser forms of dissipation he can always earn money in one way or another. . . . But the thing that he must ask himself is, Who it is that furnishes the wealth that constitutes the dividends upon the vested securities? It is the vast mass of the producers of the

*Source: Upton Sinclair, "The Message of Socialism to Collegians," *Independent*, Vol. LXIX (August 18, 1910), pp. 357–58.

land, the men, women and children who work upon a competitive wage and who get a bare living out of life. They furnish all the profits. These people are in the pit —they have not been given college educations. They have the sense of injustice, but they are unorganized and untaught—they do not know what to do, or how to set about it. That, at any rate, is the way the college man feels about it at first. But in time he comes to the discovery that these people whom [sic] he supposed were helpless have had the courage and persistence to go ahead at the task of organizing themselves, of founding their own publishing houses, newspapers and magazines, of developing a propaganda and a moral sentiment—undertaking this tremendous fight to deliver themselves from the chains of wage slavery and the servitude of vested interests. They are doing it, they will continue to do it—all alone if they have to—but they need the help of educated men. The college man who goes out into the world and seeks the truth—who faces the facts and keeps himself in the vital current of affairs—will come sooner or later to a knowledge of this movement and the duty which he owes to it. He will have to sacrifice his dreams of wealth; he will have to sacrifice fame; he will have to give up his idea of being recognized as an eminent citizen and a leader of public opinion. He will not be invited to address large bodies of prominent citizens, and the newspapers will not report his speeches at length. He will find the whole body of conservatism, so called, most bitterly opposed to him. He will find himself maligned. He will find that he has to face ridicule and loneliness—the path is not quite so lonely now as it was a few years ago, but it is not "the primrose path of dalliance." Whether for a lawyer, or for a doctor, or for a college professor, it is the path of struggle; but it is also the path of duty and the path which brings to a man the sense of power and righteousness which is the best thing that life has to offer to a man.

On the other hand, he may choose the easy way. He may become the legal representative of some large corporation. He may be sent to the legislature, he may become a judge, a great thinker. He will then be often called upon to speak; and the newspapers will report his speeches. But all this time the working class will continue to organize itself; this great ideal of Brotherhood will continue to arise and develop; and the man will find that all the world is sweeping by him and leaving him —with all his money, and his respectability, and his comfortable home, and his prosperous children—leaving him behind in all intellectual and spiritual ways.

If you choose the pathway of the truth you may have to wait a long time for your reward. You may have the satisfaction of knowing that your children will live to enjoy it—and if you take fairly good care of your health you may live to enjoy it yourselves. But in any case, you will have lived for the welfare of humanity, and your life will not be a failure. If you build your hopes upon humanity you are building upon the rock. The rule of the vested interest in this republic cannot last forever, and sooner or later those who toil for justice and human welfare will behold the breaking of the mighty dawn.

DOCUMENT 26.6
Subversion in Academe*

The following editorial, entitled "Socialism in the Colleges" and appearing in a 1913 issue of *Century* magazine, affords evidence that attacks on American colleges and universities for alleged dissemination of radical and "subversive" doctrines are part and parcel of an anti-intellectual tradition that is deeply embedded in the national culture.

---

*Source: "Socialism in the Colleges," *Century*, Vol. LXXXVI (July 1913), pp. 468–70.

Simon-pure Socialism is so ugly, so red in tooth and claw, that to be hated it needs but to be seen and understood. Yet there are so many dilutions of Socialism on the market, emotional adulterations and attenuations of the genuine brand, that the inexperienced seeker is pretty sure to have a mixture far below full strength palmed off on him, and after tasting he will be likely to say that the stuff is not so bad, after all. Socialism is offered in the guise of bland and salutary reforms; it takes the form of ethical standards, of social justice, of uplift, and of progress and happiness for all; now it is the shield that guards the poor and the helpless against the shafts of undeserved ill fortune, and now it stays the hand of the heartless oppressor. In its assumptions it is the Ten Commandments, it is the Sermon on the Mount, it is Christianity. Can we wonder that in these disguises it disarms suspicion and wins a tolerance that is already a halfway approval?

It is time that the men and women of this country awoke to an understanding of the true nature of Socialism, of what it is, what it aims to do, and how it seeks to achieve its ends. Socialism is revolution, it is blood, it is overthrow, spoliation, and a surrender of the priceless conquests of civilization, an extinction of the noble impulses that have raised mankind out of the condition of savagery.

It is time these things were known and understood, we say; it is time that foolish misconception gave way to clear knowledge, because Socialism is everywhere sowing its seeds, because it is spreading in the land, not insidiously, but by an open propaganda; because the principles of Socialism are taking hold upon the minds of youth through teaching permitted, or in the name of "academic freedom" actually encouraged, in our schools, colleges, universities, and even in theological seminaries. And it is only here and there that from some chair of instruction a voice is heard proclaiming the truth about Socialism, examining its foundations, subjecting its system and its principles to the test of reason and common sense, and picturing forth in the clear light of experience the consequences of substituting them for the existing social order. Having permitted this poison to be instilled into the minds of their students, it is the belief of men who have observed with growing apprehension the spread of Socialistic belief, that the country's institutions of learning will be false to their duty if they fail to supply the antidote by establishing courses of instruction in which the fallacies, the falsehoods, and the dangers of Socialism shall be combatted by competent analysis in the light of history and economic truth.

No board of trustees, no faculty, can plead an excusable ignorance as to what Socialists intend. They differ as to plan and method, but they are agreed upon this foundation article of their faith: "The Socialist program requires the public or collective ownership and operation of the principal instruments and agencies for the production and distribution of wealth—the land, mines, railroads, steamboats, telegraph and telephone lines, mills, factories, and modern machinery."

"This is the main program," says Morris Hillquit, and it "admits of no limitation, extension, or variation." The Socialist program means, then the abolition of private property in land and in investments, the abolition of rent, profits of the wage system, and of competition. Some Socialists advocate confiscation by taxing at full value—for of course Socialism aims at full control of the powers of government; some, like the Industrial Workers of the World, would have the wage-earners take forcible possession of the factories and operate them for their own account; others would make a pretense of payment, while still others preach direct seizure. All agree that the land and the instruments of production and exchange must be taken out of the hands of private owners and transferred to the State, and assent to that foundation doctrine makes every Socialist a revolutionist. Obviously, it is a revolution that could succeed only through violence and bloodshed, but the real Socialists do not shrink from that extreme. "The safety and the hope of the country," said Victor Berger, the Socialist member of the last Congress, "will finally lie in one direction only—that of violent and bloody revolution." He advises Socialists to read and think, and also "have a good rifle." But the literature of Socialism supplies proof upon proof that the capture of the Government and of property is to be effected by violence. Hence the Socialist's hatred of the Army, of the Navy, and of the National Guard; hence his detestation of all manifestations of the sentiment of patriotism. . . .

Our "altars" are the symbol of our religion. "No God, no master," is the cry of the Socialists, and it was only after a prolonged debate that a repudiation of religion was kept out of the Socialist platform of 1908. Our "fires" are our homes and hearthstones. Socialism would destroy the home. The revolting doctrine of promiscuity was applauded, and applauded by young women of the faith, at a recent meeting of Socialists. "The green graves of your sires"—those words should remind us that the earliest form of title to land was the right to inclose the graves of parents and kindred. Socialism permits no private ownership of land. "God, and your native land"—Socialism denies the Creator and puts the red flag above the Stars and Stripes. Could the grim meaning of this hideous creed be brought more directly home to the minds and hearts of American youth than by the evidence that it is a cold-blooded negation of . . . fine and lofty patriotism. . . .

Yet American youth by thousands are to-day under Socialistic teaching and conviction. In December, 1912, the Fourth Annual Convention of the Intercollegiate Socialist Society was held in New York. It was reported that there were fifty-nine "chapters" of the society in as many colleges and universities, including all the leading institutions of the country, and eleven graduate chapters. There were between 900 and 1000 members of the undergraduate chapters, and 700 graduate members. The list of "enthusiastic disciples of Karl Marx" among college faculties includes the names of many professors of national repute. Socialism is at work, too, in the schools, and it has schools of its own, and in this city its "Sunday-schools." The doctrines are put before children and youth not as doctrines of destruction and confiscation, and of revolution by violence and bloodshed, but as principles of ethics, or social justice, and the common good, all leading up to the beautiful dream of the brotherhood of man. College students are asked to consider the working of some privately managed undertaking, and then by plausible illustrations it is pointed out to them that the State could perform the service much better, and thus the ground principle of Socialism gets a lodgment in minds insufficiently informed to detect the falsity of the teaching. In the children's schools is used "The Socialist Primer," in which by text and pictures hatred of the rich and well-to-do is implanted, and the workingman is presented as the helpless victim of greed and cruel oppression. The facts of Socialism, the truth about Socialism, are open to ascertainment by every college and university trustee, by every president, by every giver of funds whose benefactions are employed in part to support the teaching of this devil's creed that is to supplant our old-time reverence for the altar, the hearth-fire, the family, the graves of kindred, and the flag. There is no vital difference between Socialists. The revolutionaries of the Haywood and Debs type and the evolutionary Socialists of the college faculties have virtually a common faith, and tend inevitably to the acceptance of one method for its attainment.

Is this teaching of revolution and confiscation to go on? A sound course of instruction devoted to the exposure of the fallacies, the falsehoods, and the destructive purposes of Socialism in every college where it has gained a foothold, would make the student immune to its poisonous delusions. Truth is the natural shield against error, yet only here and there has its protection been extended over the endangered youth of our colleges. The teaching of false history and false science would not be tolerated anywhere. Is it less important that young men should be safeguarded against false teaching in matters that go to the very groundwork of their morality and their citizenship? The trustees, presidents, and faculties of the country's seats of learning have a duty to perform that they cannot longer neglect without inviting the sternest censure of public opinion.

DOCUMENT 26.7
Socialism and Religion*

In 1913, *Everybody's* magazine invited Morris Hillquit, the nation's ablest socialist theoretician, and the Reverend John A. Ryan, then professor of moral theology and economics at St. Paul Seminary and later to become the first director of the Social Action Department of the National Catholic Welfare Conference, to debate socialism. Both accepted, and what ensued was a learned and often brilliant confrontation. Eventually, the question of socialism and religion arose. Part of the debate, later published in book form, appears below.

THE REVEREND JOHN A. RYAN

The great majority of Socialists seem to be either unfriendly to religion, or at least to have severed their connection with the church and the synagogue. While this statement is from the nature of the case incapable of mathematical demonstration, it is so well established by universal observation that no Socialist seriously attempts

---

*Source: *Socialism: Promise or Menace* (New York: Macmillan Co., 1914), pp. 192–209.

to call it in question. So far as Catholics are concerned, I am certain that only an insignificant fraction of those who become identified with the Socialist movement remain loyal sons of the Church. Except in an infinitesimal number of cases, they cannot truthfully assert that they have been "driven out of the Church by the priest." They have been driven out, or drawn out, by the irreligious teaching and influences pervading the movement. In America, as in Europe, the normal result of Catholic affiliation with Socialism is that noted by the editor of *Justice*: "Roman Catholics, I gladly recognize, have become very good Socialists, but only on condition of becoming very bad Catholics."

It is occasionally asserted by Socialists that the irreligious utterances of the movement should not be charged against the Socialist organization, any more than similar expressions from prominent Democrats and Republicans should be set down to the discredit of their respective political parties.

But the cases are not parallel. In the first place, there is a very great difference of proportion. Only a small minority of the distinguished members of the old parties are avowed atheists or agnostics, while practically *all* the leaders of Socialism must be so classified. . . .

In the second place, the Socialist leaders deliberately connect their irreligion with their Socialism, and propagate it in books and periodicals which are primarily intended for the advocacy of Socialism. Their agnosticism and their Socialism go hand in hand.

We are sometimes told that Socialism in the United States shows very little of that antagonism to religion which prevails on the Continent. This is a mistake. Both the leaders and the literature of the American movement are in harmony with the International Socialist position on this subject. Whatever minor differences exist are of method, not of substance or spirit. The opposition of American members of the party to religion is apparently less outspoken, less crude, and less direct than that of their European comrades; but it is not less positive, insidious, and menacing. . . .

The materialistic view of the universe and of life . . . has been made quite explicit by the leaders and scholars of the Socialist movement. They have applied it specifically to the phenomenon of religion. They have expressly declared that religion is a product of economic conditions, that it changes with the changes in these conditions, and that the present forms of religion will disappear with the disappearance of the existing economic system. . . .

If there be any intelligent student of Socialism who honestly thinks that it is merely an economic theory, or who hopes that the Socialist State is likely to be instituted and maintained in conformity with the traditional principles of religion and morals, he will be constrained to accept the following suggestions as entirely reasonable from the viewpoint of the Christian and the Theist:—

Let Socialists eliminate from their postulates, principles, and propaganda every element which is contrary to the traditional teaching on morals and religion. This will mean repudiation of the theory of economic determinism in so far as the theory implies materialism in philosophy, relativity in ethics, and in religion agnosticism.

It will mean that they will no longer defend confiscation and "love unions," nor make the working-class and the Socialist State the supreme standard of morality, nor teach that the principles of morality are essentially variable.

It will mean the cessation of their antagonism toward religion, and of their attempts to explain the origin and development of religion on social and economic grounds.

It will mean that capitalists whose property is to be taken by the Socialist State are to receive full compensation, and that no industry which is not a natural monopoly is to be operated by the State until experience has proved that the latter is more efficient than private enterprise.

How can Socialists accomplish this task of elimination, expurgation, and purification? By a method that is elementary in its simplicity. Let the Socialist party in national convention formally repudiate all the printed works which contain teaching contrary to the doctrines and proposals advocated in the last four paragraphs; or let it appoint a committee charged with the duty of relentlessly expurgating from the approved books and pamphlets everything but the *economic* arguments and proposals of Socialism. Let the convention solemnly condemn beforehand all periodicals, writers and speakers who refuse to conform to the new policy; and let it commit the party to a programme of "socialization" by a gradual process, through the method of competition in all competitive industries, and with full compensation to all capitalists whose property is taken over by the Socialist State.

Only through formal action of this kind can the Socialist movement purge itself of responsibility for anti-religious and immoral teaching, or become a purely economic organization and agency. When this has been done, and the new policy in good faith enforced, religious opposition to Socialism will probably cease. Until it has been done, no such result can be expected by any intelligent man who is honest in his thinking.

MORRIS HILLQUIT

At the outset it cannot be too strongly emphasized that the organized Socialist movement as such is not hostile to religion. Nor is it friendly to it. It is entirely neutral in all matters of religious belief. . . .

Still I am inclined to believe that the majority of Socialists find it difficult, if not impossible, to reconcile their general philosophic views with the doctrines and practices of dogmatic religious creeds. In that sense my opponent is perhaps justified in asserting that the Socialist party contains a larger proportion of "agnostics" than either the Republican or the Democratic party.

But Dr. Ryan is entirely in the wrong when he points to the Marxian philosophy, and particularly to the theory of economic determinism, as the specific source of the non-orthodox religious views of the average Socialist. Orthodox and dogmatic religious beliefs and formalistic religious practices are as inconsistent with any other scientific system of social or philosophic thought as they are with Marxism, and the "irreligion" of the Socialists is neither greater nor less than the "irreligion" of the average enlightened person who has been trained in the methods of contemporaneous thought and who accepts the conclusions of modern science. The only reason why the type of the "agnostic" occurs more frequently in the Socialist movement than in the ranks of the old political parties is that the average Socialist is better instructed and more independent in his thinking than the average Republican or Democratic voter.

Dr. Ryan assures us that to-day "genuine science no longer puts itself in opposition to religion"; but unfortunately he fails to specify the sciences which he considers "genuine," or to define the term *religion* in this bold sentence. If he has in mind the more modern and rather vague idealistic conceptions of religion, then I repeat that Socialism also does not "put itself in opposition" to it; but if he refers to the more orthodox and cruder forms of religious belief, I know of no pact of reconciliation between them and modern sciences.

"Genuine" modern science shows no inclination to compromise with traditional dogmatic theology, and the conflict between the two world views is sharpest where the latter exerts its strongest sway. Thus Italy, Spain, and France, the strongholds of Catholicism, are also the seats of the most aggressive and militant atheism. The Socialist movement in those countries

likewise presents a much larger proportion of agnostics than it does in the United States and in other countries of modernized liberal creeds. In this it merely reflects the general state of the enlightened public mind in precisely the same way as any other advanced section of the population—no more and no less.

The attitude of the average individual Socialist toward Religion and Christianity may thus be said to be identical with the attitude of the average non-Socialist of similar state of general enlightenment. What are his relations to the Church as an organization distinct from the general institutions of Religion or Christianity?

As a rule, these relations must be admitted to be rather strained, and I believe Dr. Ryan's observation that the majority of Socialists "seem to have severed their connection with the Church" contains a large element of truth. Not alone the Socialist movement, but organized labour all over the world seems to develop an ever growing sentiment of distrust and suspicion toward the Church. And the responsibility for that attitude rests entirely with the Church, and particularly with its social and economic attitude and activities.

For the Church has undergone very radical changes within the nineteen centuries since its original foundation. Born as a revolt of the lowly and disinherited against the oppression of the rich and powerful of the world, it had for several centuries remained the true and class-conscious organization of the proletariat for their mutual economic protection and social salvation. The primitive Christian community at Jerusalem was, in the testimony of St. Luke, a purely communistic institution, in which all members "who were possessed of lands or houses sold them, and brought the price of the things that were sold, and laid them down at the apostles' feet; and the distribution was made to every man according as he had need."

Throughout the first centuries of our era the fathers of the Church, following the example of their Master, condemned the wealthy as "robbers of the poor" and championed the right of all human beings to the earth and the fruits thereof. It was owing to this proletarian and revolutionary character of the primitive Christian Church that it grew and expanded into a world power; and when it had attained that power, it fell. The Christian Church never had a concrete social and economic programme. Its teachings were purely abstract, purely ethical. Its sole social significance lay in its negative expression of revolt; and when the shrewd ruling classes of the Roman Empire, under Constantine, turned persecution into favour, and elevated Christianity to the dignity of a State and court religion, they drew the fangs from the dangerous movement. The meaningless form was preserved, but the living substance was destroyed. . . .

In modern times the Church has been shorn of much of its temporal power, but it has remained the steadfast ally and the loyal apologist of the classes in power, and the determined foe of the common people. Every form of political tyranny and social and economic oppression has invariably had its spiritual support and pastoral blessing. Every effort of the downtrodden to lift their heads has infallibly met with its stern rebuke. Serfdom and slavery were sanctioned by the Church as God-ordained institutions. The brutal and rapacious feudal lord was acclaimed by it as the "soldier of Christ," and the autocratic tyrant as the "anointed of God." The struggles of the nations for political liberty in the eighteenth century and the American antislavery movement in the earlier half of the nineteenth century were combated by the Church as wicked, and so, on the whole, are the modern struggles of the workers for economic justice.

The Church can be relied on to take the employer's side in every important labour struggle. It counsels "Christian" resignation and preaches to the exploited workers the paralyzing and immoral gospel of ser-

vile submission. It hates and execrates all revolts against the ruling classes, and that is the true reason for its embittered war against Socialism, the most radical and potent expression of the modern working-class revolt.

It is not true that the strenuous anti-Socialist agitation of the Catholic Church was inspired by the alleged "immorality" or "irreligion" of the movement. The Catholic Church remains indifferent and inactive in the face of the most shocking spread of prostitution, white slavery, and all forms of moral degeneracy, as well as to the rankest manifestations of atheism, so long as they do not endanger the material power of the dominant classes. The Catholic Church cares little for morality *per se*. Its active and aggressive attacks are always directed against liberating movements, and the charges of immorality and irreligion are its invariable weapons of warfare in such cases.

Of course, this rule, as all rules, does not operate without exceptions. All modern movements for human uplift have had the active and enthusiastic support of some, often many, high-minded ministers of the Church. But they have been the exception; and, particularly in the case of Catholic priests, the exceptional and anomalous position of clerical champions of popular liberty has often been accentuated by severe discipline from the Mother Church.

And still I should advise my good Catholic comrades in the Socialist and labour movement not to take the attacks of their Church too much to heart. For just as the Church has ever opposed every progressive and revolutionary movement, just so has it uniformly reconciled itself with those movements in the hours of their triumph and victory. The Catholic Church seems quite loyal in its support of republicanism, personal liberty, and even religious freedom in all countries where these privileges have been won, although it had bitterly opposed all these institutions before their establishment, and still opposes them in countries of monarchical form of government and backward social organizations. It is therefore quite within the realm of the possible that when the Socialist movement shall have attained its object, and the Socialist commonwealth shall be an accomplished fact, the Catholic Church will confer on it its belated blessings, and proclaim it the only God-ordained social order. . . .

27 War, Revolution, and Wilsonian Diplomacy

N. GORDON LEVIN, JR.
Amherst College

Broadly speaking, two approaches toward the great war in Europe interacted within the Wilson administration from the outbreak of the conflict in August 1914 to the moment of America's entry in April 1917. One approach emphasized neutrality, uniqueness and isolation from the horrors of war, and the evils of Old World diplomacy. This neutral orientation was characterized by attempts to use American influence on behalf of a compromise peace and the creation of a new liberal world order based on international law. The other approach eschewed neutrality, and directly supported the Allied side. It firmly opposed German submarine warfare and called for mediation between the warring parties in a manner acceptable to Great Britain. Yet like its neutral opposite, the pro-Allied orientation included a vision of a new international liberal order to emerge from the wreckage of war, one, incidentally, which made no accommodation to the Russian Bolsheviks who would transform world politics through revolutionary socialism.

Some basic questions are posed by a consideration of Woodrow Wilson's foreign policy. Was the President predominantly a realist or an idealist in his conduct of diplomacy? Or did he fuse realism and idealism in a missionary vision of a liberal world order which also served the political and economic interests of the American nation-state? More specifically, did America enter World War I for reasons of idealism or of power politics? How did President Wilson justify fighting a war to end war in the company of Allies with more traditionally imperialistic war aims? Why did he oppose the more revolutionary visions and programs of Lenin's Bolshevik Revolution in Russia, and why did the President eventually come to sanction a limited American military intervention in Siberia? In connection with the problems of imperialism and revolution, can we see Wilson's policies at the Paris Peace Conference as an effort to support his vision of liberal world order against challenges from both the left and the right? Was the League of Nations which emerged from the deliberations at Paris predominantly an expression of liberal idealism or of power politics? Finally, how can we explain Wilson's difficulties in bringing the American people into the League of Nations?

The enormity of the European conflict reinforced traditional isolationist attitudes in the United States. Editors and Congressmen emphasized America's geographic and moral isolation from Old World power politics. American neutrality was taken to be the diplomatic expression of the difference between a liberal and peaceful United States and a Europe cursed by reaction and war.

America, it followed, should keep its distance from a conflict in which it had no conceivable moral or strategic interest.

Within the Wilson administration, this neutralist perspective on the war was embodied most fully in the views of Secretary of State William Jennings Bryan. The Commoner cherished a sense of America's unique moral virtue and, while he was not averse to offering the nation's liberal exceptionalism as a model for the Old World to follow, he opposed any suggestion of involvement with the war beyond the most neutral of mediation efforts. Bryan's desire to keep the United States at peace and free from European power politics led to his resignation in the spring of 1915 as an act of protest against President Wilson's hard line on the issue of the sinking of the *Lusitania* in particular and the German submarine question in general.

President Wilson was not immune to this neutralist and isolationist persuasion in the 1914–17 period. Time and again his speeches conveyed a sense that the war was essentially a European phenomenon which did not concern the United States. Relatedly, the President projected a neutralist vision of the United States as best serving the cause of world peace by her own peaceful example and by the use of her moral and economic power. The United States would assist the warring nations in achieving a peace without victory for either side as the foundation for a new American-inspired system of international law and open trade supported by an association of nations. In short, part of President Wilson's response to the war in Europe involved a fusion of neutralism with a messianic search for a liberal order for the postwar world. Yet, this vision of global reform could also come to be linked with a more pro-Allied approach to the war.

In Wilson's case such a transition meant moving from a neutralist, liberal America confronting a war-ridden and reactionary Europe to a pro-Allied, liberal America joining with progressive and democratic European Allies to confront a uniquely reactionary and militaristic Imperial Germany. On the ideological level, a redefinition of the war as a conflict between German autocracy and Allied democracy was furthered by a growing Anglo-American diplomatic and cultural rapprochement. Strong Anglophile sentiments were found especially among cosmopolitan Anglo-Saxon Protestant elites. Led by Theodore Roosevelt and Massachusetts Senator Henry Cabot Lodge, pro-Allied Republicans maintained political pressure on the Wilson administration after 1914, although to some extent this pressure was balanced by the anti-Allied or neutralist views of Irish and German Americans and radical agrarian neutralists. However, whatever the strength of his neutralist predilections, President Wilson partly shared general American suspicion of Germany and support for England and France. Two of his closest advisers, Colonel Edward M. House and Secretary of State Robert Lansing strongly favored the Allied cause and perceived German autocracy as a moral and strategic threat to the United States and its hopes for a future liberal world order. Still, tradition and ideology might not have been enough to push Wilson toward the pro-Allied persuasion had important diplomatic factors not added their weight to the balance.

America's war trade with the Allies grew to immense proportions between 1914 and 1917, as the British control of the sea complemented the availability of food, arms, and credits in the United States. The desire of the Wilson administration to bring about a return to economic prosperity in America led it to make decisions favorable to the Allies regardless of their implications for America's neutral status. Economic motives fused with broader political and cultural factors to bring the administration to acquiesce de facto to British methods of enforcing their maritime system during the early years of the war. But on the contrary, the President took an unyielding stance toward German submarine warfare. The submarine was seen as a direct challenge to America's neutral trading rights as well as human rights generally.

Thus, while maritime conflicts with the British were filed away for future settlement, the United States moved from crisis to crisis with the Germans over the submarine issue until early 1917, when those elements that favored unlimited submarine warfare regardless of American reaction won out in Germany. Wilson had tended to ignore the extent to which the United States provoked Germany by giving de facto support to the Allied cause. And he had made a clear moral distinction between British and German naval war methods. Consequently, the President's ethical rejection of the submarine went a long way toward bringing him to perceive of Imperial Germany as uniquely reactionary and militaristic and the war as a contest between the forces of European autocracy and democracy.

The efforts of Wilson and Colonel House to mediate the European war in the 1915–16 period also evolved in an implicitly pro-Allied context. By the second year of the war the Kaiser's armies had advanced well into Allied territory on both the eastern and western fronts and Germany possessed a clear advantage on the war map. Under such circumstances Wilson's efforts to achieve a mediated peace without victory based on the status quo antebellum involved the implicit notion of uncompensated German troop withdrawals on both fronts and the end of German annexationist hopes. Moreover, Colonel House's attempts at mediation in the winter of 1915–16 involved a commitment of American support for ambiguous British war aims of an annexationist nature.

The pro-Allied nature of much Wilsonian diplomacy did not go unchallenged in the United States. Conservative anti-German Republicans were balanced by southern and midwestern agrarian progressives who demanded that America avoid participation in what they saw as an imperialist war on both sides. William Jennings Bryan, Senator Robert La Follette, Senator George Norris, and others believed the United States was being dragged into war on behalf of war traders and Anglophile banking elites. They sought to limit the right of travel on armed Allied merchantmen and to balance diplomatic assaults on the German submarine policy with stronger protests against British naval practices. This agrarian radical position later expressed itself in postwar opposition to Wilson's League of Nations.

Wilson rejected criticism of his submarine diplomacy, defended the need for military preparedness, and argued that acquiescence on the submarine question would cost the United States heavily in moral prestige as well as strike a blow at neutral commercial rights and international law. The President was prepared, however, to attempt a more neutral stance on the mediation issue in a last desperate effort to achieve peace before the United States was finally forced to go to war over the submarine. By late 1916 he had checked the pro-Allied direction of House's attempts at mediation, campaigned successfully for reelection as a peace-oriented progressive, and launched a public effort to mediate the conflict on the basis of a peace without victory. The culmination of this last Wilsonian peace endeavor, which was taken against the opposition of House and Lansing, was the famous "Peter without Victory" address of January 22, 1917. Here Wilson adopted a neutralist perspective on the war and offered U.S. participation in a League of Nations to stabilize a new liberal world order erected on the foundation of a true compromise peace.

Wilson's last attempt at a really neutral settlement was rejected by both sides, which continued to prefer victory to peace. The German government not only declined mediation on Wilson's terms but also decided to launch unlimited submarine warfare. Soon afterward German diplomatic intrigues with Mexico against the United States came to light in the Zimmerman telegram. In early 1917, then, these German policies, combined with the pro-Allied urgings of House and Lansing and the triumph in March of liberal and pro-Allied Russian revolutionaries, led a tortured Wilson finally to abandon his neutralism. By April the President had made his decision for war. His message to Congress blamed Imperial Germany specifically and not Europe in general for the war. Wilson retained his vision of an American-inspired postwar liberal world order, but that vision was no longer attainable through a peace without victory but rather through the triumph of the Allied "democracies" whose ranks suddenly included Russia. For no longer did a tsarist autocracy serve as a political embarrassment in the struggle against reactionary German imperialism.

During the spring and summer of 1917 the United States developed its economic and military capacities and, at the same time, the President's ideological commitment to the defeat of German imperialism deepened. In August, the administration rejected a Vatican appeal for a compromise peace, with Wilson arguing that a secure peace could be established only with a Germany democratized from within and controlled militarily from without. Yet, while maintaining a firm stance against Germany in the early months of America's participation in the war, the President also had to consider the possible threat of Allied imperialism to his projected liberal world order. He discovered that Allied postwar plans were embodied in a series of secret treaties. These treaties envisioned the dismemberment of the Austro-Hungarian Empire, the partition of the Ottoman Empire, and the economic and political isolation of a territorially diminished Germany. Such plans, if realized, could undermine Wilsonian hopes of a war to end war. Wilson was in a dilemma, for how could the United States

oppose these secret treaties openly without fatally upsetting Allied unity against a powerful foe whose own war aims were no less imperialistic? The President's natural inclination was to play down the war aims issue, carry through to victory, and rely upon the moral and economic power of the United States to moderate Allied imperialism and reform world politics at the resultant peace conference. But by late 1917 and early 1918, political and diplomatic realities impinged and prevented him from postponing the question of war aims until victory.

One major problem was the decline in morale in the Allied countries due to military reversals and the protracted nature of the brutal conflict. Liberal and radical forces in all these nations, but most especially in Russia, were more and more critical of Entente war aims and called for a compromise peace without annexations or indemnities. As 1917 drew to a close, Wilsonians increasingly saw the necessity for a declaration on Allied war aims in order to raise Allied morale, particularly among the disaffected. Such a statement of war aims, with its projection of a new liberal world order, would hopefully firm up the Allied liberals and radicals behind the war and also appeal over the heads of Germany's leaders to peace-oriented moderates and socialists in Germany itself.

One should read the President's Fourteen Points speech of January 8, 1918, in this general context. Indeed, the Fourteen Points were a skillful political platform. Liberals and socialists in Allied countries could support those points that projected a new postwar liberal world order characterized by open diplomacy, freedom of the seas, respect for international law, and global cooperation in a League of Nations. On the other hand, conservatives could draw solace from those of the Fourteen Points that kept the door open to political and territorial changes at the expense of Germany, Turkey, and Austria-Hungary. In spite of or perhaps because of their very ambiguity, the Fourteen Points helped to maintain Allied support for the conflict throughout the final difficult year of 1918. In Germany, however, even the moderates rejected them as a prescription for German defeat. Eventually in late 1918 German liberals and socialists would turn to them out of fear of military collapse. And finally, regardless of their success in England, France, and Italy, the Wilsonian war aims appeal met a setback in Russia where the Bolshevik Revolution of November, 1917, destroyed the power of Russian liberal-nationalism and took Russia out of both the war and the Entente alliance.

Throughout the summer and early autumn of 1917, the Wilson administration, along with its European Allies, sought to buttress the prowar Russian provisional government against its radical opponents. After the Bolshevik triumph, many in Washington continued to hope that a declaration of liberalized Allied war aims might move the Bolsheviks away from their revolutionary absolutism toward approving a liberal war for liberal peace. For this reason, the Fourteen Points address was most specifically aimed at the Bolshevik leaders then engaged in separate peace talks with Germany at Brest-Litovsk.

The Fourteen Points did not move Lenin. Having failed to end the war through a universal revolutionary peace, he preferred to gain a breathing space for internal Bolshevik consolidation by means of a separate peace with Germany. Lenin hoped that Germany's imperialistic gains made at Russian expense at Brest-Litovsk would ultimately be wiped out by revolutionary socialist triumphs throughout Europe. Furthermore, not only did Lenin upset Wilson's diplomatic hopes by signing a separate peace, but the Bolshevik dispersal of the Constituent Assembly early in 1918 dashed any lingering hopes for a return to liberal nationalist control in Russian politics. These developments in Russia reinforced the increased influence of anti-Bolshevik elements within the Wilson administration. The President moved steadily during 1918 to accept Secretary of State Lansing's view that any appeasement of Russian Bolshevism or Allied radicalism would hurt the war effort and redound to the interests of German imperialism. By the late winter and early spring of 1918, then, the Wilson administration was defending the position of liberal war against the interrelated challenges of revolutionary socialism on the left and German power on the right. In Europe this policy was expressed by an expanding American combat role on the western front; in Russia it led eventually to intervention in Siberia.

Initially, Wilson resisted Allied promptings for a Japanese or Japanese-American intervention in Siberia. He believed that grandiose Allied plans for a new eastern front were impractical and feared that Allied support for Russian reactionaries, coupled with the use of Japanese troops, could well alienate liberal and anti-German Russians from the Entente cause. But by the spring of 1918, as Allied pressure continued, Wilson's opposition to intervention began to erode. Diplomatic reports, moreover, suggested that a joint American-Japanese force would be well received in the Russian east. Failure to intervene might drive many anti-Bolshevik Russians irrevocably into the arms of Germany for refuge from revolutionary socialism. Increasingly, Washington came to view economic or military-political action in Siberia as a way to support the forces of Russian liberal nationalism. An opportunity presented itself in the summer of 1918 when a division of Czech troops, in alliance with anti-Bolshevik Russian elements, became involved in a conflict with the Bolsheviks along the entire Trans-Siberian Railroad. Wilson's administration, in cooperation with Japan, used this occasion for limited military and economic intervention in Siberia. Moreover, the President hoped such cooperation would serve to prevent unilateral Japanese designs in Russian Asia.

During the autumn of 1918 Germany collapsed militarily and politically and, as the Paris Peace Conference approached, President Wilson set his sights on combining peacemaking with the construction of a postwar liberal international order. Wilson envisaged the moral, political and economic preeminence of the United States. But Allied conservatives, politically ascendant in Britain, France, and Italy posed a threat to his postwar design in that they intended to use the peace conference to reaffirm the terms of the secret treaties. On the left, the President was challenged in the defeated countries by revolutionary socialist elements which sought to activate the potential for revolution latent in sociopolitical dislocation and national humiliation. Consequently, when the Paris Peace Conference opened in early 1919, Wilson faced a Europe where liberals and moderate socialists were on the defensive, whereas radicals and rightists alike were projecting postwar programs hostile to Wilson's new world order.

During the peace conference American policy aimed at containing Bolshevism without simultaneously encouraging either Allied militarism or political reaction. In Eastern Europe Wilson and his advisors favored creation of liberal-nationalist successor states to the Dual Monarchy. They were concerned in that area, with the mutually reinforcing challenges posed by French-supported militarism among the victors and by revolutionary socialism among the defeated. The American answer stressed free trade, food relief, and diplomatic pressures designed to maintain peace in the region and to oust the Hungarian Bolshevik regime of Béla Kun in the summer of 1919.

With regard to Russia, the Wilson administration pursued a limited anti-Bolshevik policy during 1919. At Paris, the President opposed plans for massive Allied intervention in Russia and sought unsuccessfully to negotiate the Bolsheviks out of power by means of an all-Russian peace conference. Wilson naively intended any conference with the Bolsheviks to involve their acceptance of the status of one of several political parties in a democratic and pluralistic Russia. Despite the hopes of Lenin and the urgings of such liberals as William C. Bullitt, Wilson never planned to recognize a Bolshevik regime.

In addition, Wilson continued to support the joint American-Japanese military intervention in Siberia designed to maintain the Trans-Siberian Railroad supply line for Admiral Kolchak's White Russian forces in the Russian east. The President hoped that Kolchak might organize a new government and bring Russia back to the community of democratic states. As matters turned out, Kolchak's forces were eventually destroyed by the Red Army, and the Siberian intervention ended with few concrete results.

When the Paris Peace Conference opened, there was great concern that Germany might go Bolshevik. There was likewise worry among American delegates lest Allied extremism exacerbate the danger of revolution in Germany. The German settlement had to be moderate enough to buttress those German social democrats and liberals who sought Wilson's support against extreme Allied demands in return for combatting German Bolshevism. Toward this end, the Americans tried to get food relief into Germany, to lessen the severity of the Allied blockade, and to arrange a more rational reparations settlement.

Yet this American reintegrationist tendency toward Germany was counterbalanced by the President's desire to punish and control the defeated Germans. In other words, Wilson was more moderate toward Germany than Clemenceau and Lloyd George, but his greater moderation was a matter of degree. It was never enough to please those German political elements that had hoped for his support. Indeed, on the issues surrounding the Polish and Czechoslovakian borders with Germany, the President took an even more anti-German position than Lloyd George. While fearing a successful Communist revolution in Germany, the President was also concerned lest conservatives there would retain excessive influence after the Kaiser's fall. Wilson, then, was not entirely averse to controlling Germany from the outside, since he did not completely trust the Germans within.

Wilson's uneasiness united with his fear of revolution in Germany to inhibit him from openly confronting Allied extremism. Anxious to retain Allied unity, the President sought to obtain concessions from the French on the Rhineland and other issues in return for American security guarantees. In this manner, the League of Nations that emerged from Paris was as much a power-political alliance of the victors as it was the nucleus for a new liberal world order. In other words, the League of Nations contained within itself the basic Wilsonian contradiction at Paris between a reintegrationist and a punitive policy toward Germany.

In a broader sense still, the League's colonial mandate system involved an uneasy compromise between a pragmatic Wilsonian acquiescence in the division of the colonial spoils and an idealistic American attempt to reform the political and economic relations between advanced and backward nations. The President's grudging acceptance of Japanese control of the Chinese province of Shantung, after the Japanese threatened to boycott the League of Nations, reflected this broader Wilsonian tendency to compromise temporarily with Allied imperialism in the hope of eventually moderating and reforming it through the League of Nations.

After his return to the United States in mid-1919, the President had to defend the League concept against opposition from both left and right. On one level, Wilson presented the League as the potential institutional basis for a transformation of world politics. Nations would be pledged to the mutual defense of each other's independence and territorial integrity, even in cases when their own particular interests were not immediately involved in a case of aggression. Yet always fused inextricably with Wilson's missionary idealism was a realistic sense of America's national interests.

The President wished to impress the American people regarding the connection between a League-supported liberal world order and the concrete interests of an expansive American capitalism anxious to move goods and credits into a stable international market. Also, he argued that the Covenant and Article X would provide the necessary deterrent to any possible German efforts to undo the Versailles Treaty. He was especially anxious to protect the new states of Eastern Europe from German pressure. Finally, Wilson and League defenders in the Senate spoke of the containment of Bolshevism in the context of the expected achievement of international stability.

Above all, the President as realist stressed the necessity for an American commitment through the League to a permanent role in the maintenance of international peace. Germany was to be controlled, liberalized, and eventually reintegrated into the western political economy. The Allies and the new states were to join in maintaining world order. Bolshevism was to be spatially contained in European Russia, while liberal reformism elsewhere would, in time, moderate Lenin's regime and draw men everywhere away from revolutionary socialism. Problems left in the treaty, such as Shantung and reparations, were to be remedied over time through the League and its related committees. And all this was to be possible because the United States would fulfill its missionary liberal destiny by remaining committed to securing world peace and stability.

In the Senate, Wilson's vision was criticized by such progressive isolationists as Senators Borah, Johnson, Norris, and La Follette. These men repeatedly attacked the League as a defensive alliance of the major Allied powers designed to preserve by force the imperialistic settlements of the Paris Peace Conference. Thus, while the President was often accused by Senate conservatives of an excess of idealism, he was constantly criticized by the Senate's progressive isolationists as a fellow traveler of Allied imperialism. The progressive isolationists called for America's extrication from a hopelessly flawed world.

In the final analysis, however, the attack by Senate conservatives led by Senator Henry Cabot Lodge, who had an intense personal animosity for Wilson, was even more crucial than the criticism by Senate progressives in the defeat of the Versailles Treaty. Lodge was no isolationist, and ironically he shared with Wilson a number of specific goals in postwar international affairs. Both Lodge and Wilson were concerned with containing Germany within the borders of the treaty framework. And Lodge favored the Anglo-American Treaty of Guarantee for France against future German aggression which the President had negotiated at Paris. Like Wilson but unlike the progressive isolationists, Lodge hoped to see the expansion of Bolshevism actively checked in postwar Europe. Given such common goals, how can we understand the great distance between Wilson and Lodge over the League?

Beyond personal factors, the key point would appear to be that Lodge had a greater faith than Wilson in the self-equilibrating potential of a world run along traditional lines by the victorious Allied powers. Wilson feared a world collapse into the chaos of war and revolution if the United States were not involved in future major world political issues. On the other hand, Lodge was confident that Germany could be controlled and Bolshevism successfully contained if Wilson would stop meddling and simply permit the world to be governed on the basis of a spheres-of-influence consortium by the Entente victors. Lodge disapproved of Wilson's efforts to moderate Allied imperialism at

Paris in return for American security guarantees through the League. Moreover, in exchange for a largely free hand in Eurasia, Lodge expected that the European Allies and Japan would continue to respect the Monroe Doctrine as an instrument of American security. In short, Lodge looked forward to the United States resuming its growing but still limited role in world politics as one among several peaceful and satisfied imperial powers.

Wilson clearly contemplated a far larger role for the United States in world politics than did Lodge who, along with Theodore Roosevelt, Elihu Root and former Secretary of State Philander C. Knox, had possessed rather a monopoly on the "large policy" prior to 1917. The President was advocating a real and steady American involvement in world affairs: in mandates, reparations, and territorial guarantees. But, paradoxically, at the very moment that Wilson sought permanently to involve the United States as never before beyond the Western Hemisphere, he argued that the nation was entering world politics not simply to participate but also to transform it through the League.

During the entire League debate the left isolationists were largely beyond Wilson's reach. Wilson could have brought the United States into the League, however, by uniting his supporters with Lodge's followers to accept the League with reservations. In one way or another the President was urged to compromise by Lansing, Taft, Hoover, House and many others who had come to share much if not all of his vision of America's postwar world role. Reflecting upon the course of world events after 1920, it might have been far better had the President been willing to compromise on the issue of reservations. In his stubbornness over detail Wilson played into the hands of inveterate foes of the League and denied America the possibility of a partial realization of his grander vision.

In conclusion, what can we say about

the Wilsonian heritage in American diplomacy? Did Wilsonian values live on in later periods of American history, in the efforts of Henry Stimson, Cordell Hull, Franklin Roosevelt, Harry Truman and others, to fashion a liberal world order around the principle of collective security? Did Wilsonian anti-Bolshevism preview America's cold war stance? Or, can we say that the superpower rivalry between Russia and the United States which has characterized the cold war world reality since 1945 involves a much stronger power-political and strategic component than Wilson's more ideological rivalry with a weak Soviet Union in the period of World War I?

SUGGESTED READINGS

Buehrig, Edward H. *Woodrow Wilson and the Balance of Power*. Bloomington: Indiana University Press, 1955.

Diamond, William. *The Economic Thought of Woodrow Wilson*. Baltimore: The Johns Hopkins University Press, 1943.

Farnsworth, Beatrice. *William C. Bullitt and the Soviet Union*. Bloomington: Indiana University Press, 1967.

Fifield, Russell H. *Woodrow Wilson and the Far East, The Diplomacy of the Shantung Question*. New York: Thomas Y. Crowell Co., 1952.

Lasch, Christopher. *The American Liberals and the Russian Revolution*. New York: Columbia University Press, 1962.

Levin, N. Gordon, Jr. *Woodrow Wilson and World Politics*. New York: Oxford University Press, 1968.

Link, Arthur S. *Wilson the Diplomatist*. Baltimore: The Johns Hopkins University Press, 1957.

Martin, Laurence W. *Peace without Victory, Woodrow Wilson and the British Liberals*. New Haven, Conn.: Yale University Press, 1958.

May, Ernest R. *The World War and American Isolation*. Cambridge, Mass.: Harvard University Press, 1959.

Mayer, Arno J. *The Political Origins of the New Diplomacy, 1917–1918*. New Haven, Conn.: Yale University Press, 1959.

——. *Politics and Diplomacy of Peacemaking, Containment, and Counterrevolution at Versailles, 1918–1919*. New York: Alfred A. Knopf, Inc., 1968.

Smith, Daniel M. *The Great Departure, The United States and World War One, 1914–1920*. New York: John Wiley & Sons, 1965.

Thompson, John M. *Russia, Bolshevism, and the Versailles Peace*. Princeton, N.J.: Princeton University Press, 1966.

Tillman, Seth P. *Anglo-American Relations at the Paris Peace Conference of 1919*. Princeton: Princeton University Press, 1961.

DOCUMENT 27.1

Secretary of State Lansing and Germany: 1915*

As the following selection makes clear, Robert Lansing had come to view Imperial Germany as a moral and strategic threat to the United States early in the war. President Wilson did not come entirely to share this perspective until early 1917.

Consideration and Outline of Policies

July 11, 1915

I have come to the conclusion that the German Government is utterly hostile to all nations with democratic institutions because those who compose it see in democracy a menace to absolutism and the defeat of the German ambition for world domination. Everywhere German agents are plotting and intriguing to accomplish the supreme purpose of their government.

Only recently has the conviction come to me that democracy throughout the world is threatened. Suspicions of the vaguest sort only a few months ago have been more and more confirmed. From many sources evidence has been coming until it would be folly to close one's eyes to it.

German agents have undoubtedly been at work in Mexico arousing anti-American

*Source: Robert Lansing, *The War Memoirs of Robert Lansing*, (Indianapolis: Bobbs-Merrill Co., 1935), pp. 19–21. Copyright, 1935, reprinted by permission of the publishers, The Bobbs-Merrill Company, Inc.

feeling and holding out false hopes of support. The proof is not conclusive but is sufficient to compel belief. Germans also appear to be operating in Haiti and San Domingo and are probably doing so in other Latin American Republics.

I think that this is being done so that this nation will have troubles in America and be unable to take part in the European War if a repetition of such outrages as the *Lusitania* sinking should require us to act. It may even go further and have in mind the possibility of a future war with this Republic in case the Allies should be defeated.

In these circumstances the policies we adopt are vital to the future of the United States and, I firmly believe, to the welfare of mankind, for I see in the perpetuation of democracy the only hope of universal peace and progress for the world. Today German absolutism is the great menace to democracy.

I think that we should, therefore, adopt the following for the present and pursue these policies until conditions materially change:

1. The settlement, for the time being at least, of the present submarine controversy because the American people are still much divided on the merits of the war. As it progresses, I believe that the real objects of the German Government will be disclosed and there will be united opposition. Meanwhile we should get ready to meet the worst.

2. A rigorous and continuing prosecution of all plots in this country and a vigilant watch on Germans and their activities here.

3. Secret investigations of German activities in Latin America, particularly Mexico, and the adoption of means to frustrate them.

4. The cultivation of a Pan-American doctrine with the object of alienating the American republics from European influence, especially the German influence.

5. The maintenance of friendly relations with Mexico. To do this it will be necessary to recognize Carranza's faction, which seems to be the stronger. Union with the other American republics will have a good effect upon them.

6. The purchase of the Danish West Indies as soon and as secretly as possible because Germany may conquer Denmark and come in that way into legal title. If Denmark believes that Germany covets the islands she will sell to us and prevent their possession being a menace to Danish independence. The Danish Government must be told this.

7. The prevention by all means in our power of German influence becoming dominant in any nation bordering the Caribbean or near the Panama Canal. In this connection we should settle in some way with Colombia, for the Germans are particularly active there.

8. The actual participation of this country in the war in case it becomes evident that Germany will be the victor. A triumph for German imperialism *must not be*. We ought to look forward to this possibility and make ready to meet it.

There is a future possibility, which does not change the foregoing policies but which emphasizes the last one. It is that the war may end in a draw or with the German Empire dominant over its enemies.

The argument could then be made by the German Government that, in spite of the fact that the world was arrayed against it, it succeeded in preventing the defeat of the Empire, and that having thus proved its superior efficiency it should be continued and supported as the agency best fitted to restore the German nation to a state of prosperity.

I believe that this argument would be potent with the German people, who are in the habit of unquestioning obedience to their rulers in thought as well as action. Of course, the terrible cost of war, when the time to consider that arrives, will weaken the argument, for the people will ask what is the recompense for the great sacrifices they have made, the great suffering which they have endured, and the government will have nothing to show. The nation may then rise and demand a change to a political system in which their voice will be supreme. But, if the argument should prevail and the present military oligarchy be perpetuated, then what?

My judgment is that the German Government, cherishing the same ambition of world power which now possesses it, would with its usual vigor and thoroughness prepare to renew its attack on democracy. I think, however, that it would not pursue the course taken in this war, which has failed, because it would realize that the democratic nations would be more watchful and less trustful and better prepared to resist. It would probably endeavor to sow dissensions among the nations with liberal institutions and seek an alliance with other governments based to a more or less degree on the principle of absolutism.

The remedy seems to me to be plain. It is that Germany must not be permitted to win this war or to break even, though to prevent it this country is forced to take an active part. This ultimate necessity must be constantly in our minds in all our controversies with the belligerents. American public opinion must be prepared for the time, which may come, when we will have to cast aside our neutrality and become one of the champions of democracy.

We must in fact risk everything rather than leave the way open for a new combination of powers, stronger and more dangerous to liberty than the Central Allies are today.

DOCUMENT 27.2

President Wilson Searches for Peace without Victory*

On January 22, 1917, the President climaxed his last great personal peace effort with the "Peace without Victory" address before the Senate. Wilson combined a neutralist stance on the issues dividing the European powers with the projection of an American-inspired liberal world order.

... Is the present war a struggle for a just and secure peace, or only for a new balance of power? If it be only a struggle for a new balance of power, who will guarantee, who can guarantee the stable equilibrium of the new arrangement? Only a tranquil Europe can be a stable Europe. There must be, not a balance of power, but a community of power; not organized rivalries, but an organized common peace.

Fortunately we have received very explicit assurances on this point. The statesmen of both of the groups of nations now arrayed against one another have said, in terms that could not be misinterpreted, that it was no part of the purpose they had in mind to crush their antagonists. But the implications of these assurances may not be equally clear to all—may not be the same on both sides of the water. I think it will be serviceable if I attempt to set forth what we understand them to be.

They imply, first of all, that it must be a peace without victory. It is not pleasant to say this. I beg that I may be permitted to put my own interpretation upon it and that it may be understood that no other interpretation was in my thought. I am seeking only to face realities and to face them without soft concealments. Victory would mean peace forced upon the loser,

*Source: Ray Stannard Baker and William E. Dodd (eds.), *The Public Papers of Woodrow Wilson*, Vol. IV, *The New Democracy* (New York: Harper & Bros., 1927). pp. 410–14. Copyright 1926, 1954 by Edith Boling Wilson.

a victor's terms imposed upon the vanquished. It would be accepted in humiliation, under duress, at an intolerable sacrifice, and would leave a sting, a resentment, a bitter memory upon which terms of peace would rest, not permanently, but only as upon quicksand. Only a peace between equals can last. Only a peace the very principle of which is equality and a common participation in a common benefit. The right state of mind, the right feeling between nations, is as necessary for a lasting peace as is the just settlement of vexed questions of territory or of racial and national allegiance.

The equality of nations upon which peace must be founded if it is to last must be an equality of rights; the guarantees exchanged must neither recognize nor imply a difference between big nations and small, between those that are powerful and those that are weak. Right must be based upon the common strength, not upon the individual strength, of the nations upon whose concert peace will depend. Equality of territory or of resources there of course cannot be; nor any other sort of equality not gained in the ordinary peaceful and legitimate development of the peoples themselves. But no one asks or expects anything more than an equality of rights. Mankind is looking now for freedom of life, not for equipoises of power.

And there is a deeper thing involved than even equality of right among organized nations. No peace can last, or ought to last, which does not recognize and accept the principle that governments derive all their just powers from the consent of the governed, and that no right anywhere exists to hand peoples about from sovereignty to sovereignty as if they were property. I take it for granted, for instance, if I may venture upon a single example, that statesmen everywhere are agreed that there should be a united, independent, and autonomous Poland, and that henceforth inviolable security of life, of worship, and of industrial and social development should be guaranteed to all peoples who have lived hitherto under the power of governments devoted to a faith and purpose hostile to their own.

I speak of this, not because of any desire to exalt an abstract political principle which has always been held very dear by those who have sought to build up liberty in America, but for the same reason that I have spoken of the other conditions of peace which seem to me clearly indispensable—because I wish frankly to uncover realities. Any peace which does not recognize and accept this principle will inevitably be upset. It will not rest upon the affections or the convictions of mankind. The ferment of spirit of whole populations will fight subtly and constantly against it, and all the world will sympathize. The world can be at peace only if its life is stable, and there can be no stability where the will is in rebellion, where there is not tranquillity of spirit and a sense of justice, of freedom, and of right.

So far as practicable, moreover, every great people now struggling towards a full development of its resources and of its powers should be assured a direct outlet to the great highways of the sea. Where this cannot be done by the cession of territory, it can no doubt be done by the neutralization of direct rights of way under the general guarantee which will assure the peace itself. With a right comity of arrangement no nation need be shut away from free access to the open paths of the world's commerce.

And the paths of the sea must alike in law and in fact be free. The freedom of the seas is the *sine qua non* of peace, equality, and co-operation. No doubt a somewhat radical reconsideration of many of the rules of international practice hitherto thought to be established may be necessary in order to make the seas indeed free and common in practically all circumstances for the use of mankind, but the motive for such changes is convincing and compelling. There can be no trust or intimacy between the peoples of the world without them. The free, constant, un-threatened intercourse of nations is an essential part of the process of peace and of development. It need not be difficult either to define or to secure the freedom of the seas if the governments of the world sincerely desire to come to an agreement concerning it.

It is a problem closely connected with the limitation of naval armaments and the co-operation of the navies of the world in keeping the seas at once free and safe. And the question of limiting naval armaments opens the wider and perhaps more difficult question of the limitation of armies and of all programs of military preparation. Difficult and delicate as these questions are, they must be faced with the utmost candor and decided in a spirit of real accommodation if peace is to come with healing in its wings, and come to stay. Peace cannot be had without concession and sacrifice. There can be no sense of safety and equality among the nations if great preponderating armaments are henceforth to continue here and there to be built up and maintained. The statesmen of the world must plan for peace and nations must adjust and accommodate their policy to it as they have planned for war and made ready for pitiless contest and rivalry. The question of armaments, whether on land or sea, is the most immediately and intensely practical question connected with the future fortunes of nations and of mankind.

I have spoken upon these great matters without reserve and with the utmost explicitness because it has seemed to me to be necessary if the world's yearning desire for peace was anywhere to find free voice and utterance. Perhaps I am the only person in high authority amongst all the peoples of the world who is at liberty to speak and hold nothing back. I am speaking as an individual, and yet I am speaking also, of course, as the responsible head of a great government, and I feel confident that I have said what the people of the United States would wish me to say.

May I not add that I hope and believe that I am in effect speaking for liberals and friends of humanity in every nation and of every program of liberty? I would fain believe that I am speaking of the silent mass of mankind everywhere who have as yet had no place or opportunity to speak their real hearts out concerning the death and ruin they see to have come already upon the persons and the homes they hold dear.

And in holding out the expectation that the people and Government of the United States will join the other civilized nations of the world in guaranteeing the permanence of peace upon such terms as I have named I speak with the greater boldness and confidence because it is clear to every man who can think that there is in this promise no breach in either our traditions or our policy as a nation, but a fulfilment, rather, of all that we have professed or striven for.

I am proposing, as it were, that the nations should with one accord adopt the doctrine of President Monroe as the doctrine of the world: that no nation should seek to extend its polity over any other nation or people, but that every people should be left free to determine its own polity, its own way of development, unhindered, unthreatened, unafraid, the little along with the great and powerful.

I am proposing that all nations henceforth avoid entangling alliances which would draw them into competitions of power; catch them in a net of intrigue and selfish rivalry, and disturb their own affairs with influences intruded from without. There is no entangling alliance in a concert of power. When all unite to act in the same sense and with the same purpose all act in the common interest and are free to live their own lives under a common protection.

I am proposing government by the consent of the governed; that freedom of the seas which in international conference after conference representatives of the United States have urged with the eloquence of those who are the convinced disciples of liberty; and that moderation of armaments which makes of armies and navies a power for order merely, not an instrument of aggression or of selfish violence.

These are American principles, American policies. We could stand for no others. And they are also the principles and policies of forward looking men and women everywhere, of every modern nation, of every enlightened community. They are the principles of mankind and must prevail.

DOCUMENT 27.3

President Wilson Seeks Peace through Liberal War*

Wilson's War Message of April 2, 1917 —delivered at a Joint Session of Congress —revealed that he had come to accept the Lansing view of the war as a struggle between Allied democracy and German autocracy. It is clear that the Russian Revolution played a role in the President's ideological transition. Yet, a vision of an eventual postwar liberal world order links this address with the earlier one of January 22.

While we do these things, these deeply momentous things, let us be very clear, and make very clear to all the world what our motives and our objects are. My own thought has not been driven from its habitual and normal course by the unhappy events of the last two months, and I do not believe that the thought of the Nation has been altered or clouded by them. I have exactly the same things in mind now that I had in mind when I addressed the Senate

*Source: Ray Stannard Baker and William E. Dodd (eds.), *The Public Papers of Woodrow Wilson*, Vol. V. *War and Peace* (New York: Harper & Bros., 1927), pp. 11–16. Copyright 1926, 1954 by Edith Boling Wilson.

on the twenty-second of January last, the same that I had in mind when I addressed the Congress on the third of February and on the twenty-sixth of February. Our object now, as then, is to vindicate the principles of peace and justice in the life of the world as against selfish and autocratic power and to set up amongst the really free and self-governed peoples of the world such a concert of purpose and of action as will henceforth insure the observance of those principles. Neutrality is no longer feasible or desirable where the peace of the world is involved and the freedom of its peoples, and the menace to that peace and freedom lies in the existence of autocratic governments backed by organized force which is controlled wholly by their will, not by the will of their people. We have seen the last of neutrality in such circumstances. We are at the beginning of an age in which it will be insisted that the same standards of conduct and of responsibility for wrong done shall be observed among nations and their governments that are observed among the individual citizens of civilized states.

We have no quarrel with the German people. We have no feeling towards them but one of sympathy and friendship. It was not upon their impulse that their government acted in entering this war. It was not with their previous knowledge or approval. It was a war determined upon as wars used to be determined upon in the old, unhappy days when peoples were nowhere consulted by their rulers and wars were provoked and waged in the interest of dynasties or of little groups of ambitious men who were accustomed to use their fellow men as pawns and tools. Self-governed nations do not fill their neighbor states with spies or set the course of intrigue to bring about some critical posture of affairs which will give them an opportunity to strike and make conquest. Such designs can be successfully worked out only under cover and where no one has the right to ask questions. Cunningly contrived plans of deception or aggression, carried, it may be, from generation to generation, can be worked out and kept from the light only within the privacy of courts or behind the carefully guarded confidences of a narrow and privileged class. They are happily impossible where public opinion commands and insists upon full information concerning all the nation's affairs.

A steadfast concert for peace can never be maintained except by a partnership of democratic nations. No autocratic government could be trusted to keep faith within it or observe its covenants. It must be a league of honor, a partnership of opinion. Intrigue would eat its vitals away; the plottings of inner circles who could plan what they would and render account to no one would be a corruption seated at its very heart. Only free peoples can hold their purpose and their honor steady to a common end and prefer the interests of mankind to any narrow interest of their own.

Does not every American feel that assurance has been added to our hope for the future peace of the world by the wonderful and heartening things that have been happening within the last few weeks in Russia? Russia was known by those who knew it best to have been always in fact democratic at heart, in all the vital habits of her thought, in all the intimate relationships of her people that spoke their natural instinct, their habitual attitude towards life. The autocracy that crowned the summit of her political structure, long as it had stood and terrible as was the reality of its power, was not in fact Russian in origin, character, or purpose; and now it has been shaken off and the great, generous Russian people have been added in all their naïve majesty and might to the forces that are fighting for freedom in the world, for justice, and for peace. Here is a fit partner for a League of Honor.

One of the things that has served to convince us that the Prussian autocracy was not and could never be our friend is that from the very outset of the present war it has filled our unsuspecting communities and even our offices of government with spies and set criminal intrigues everywhere afoot against our national unity of counsel, our peace within and without, our industries and our commerce. Indeed, it is now evident that its spies were here even before the war began; and it is unhappily not a matter of conjecture but a fact proved in our courts of justice that the intrigues which have more than once come perilously near to disturbing the peace and dislocating the industries of the country have been carried on at the instigation, with the support, and even under the personal direction of official agents of the Imperial Government accredited to the Government of the United States. Even in checking these things and trying to extirpate them we have sought to put the most generous interpretation possible upon them because we knew that their source lay not in any hostile feeling or purpose of the German people towards us (who were no doubt as ignorant of them as we ourselves were), but only in the selfish designs of a Government that did what it pleased and told its people nothing. But they have played their part in serving to convince us at last that that Government entertains no real friendship for us and means to act against our peace and security at its convenience. That it means to stir up enemies against us at our very doors the intercepted note to the German Minister at Mexico City is eloquent evidence.

We are accepting this challenge of hostile purpose because we know that in such a Government, following such methods, we can never have a friend; and that in the presence of its organized power, always lying in wait to accomplish we know not what purpose, there can be no assured security for the democratic Governments of the world. We are now about to accept gage of battle with this natural foe to liberty and shall, if necessary, spend the whole force of the Nation to check and nullify its pretensions and its power. We are glad, now that we see the facts with no veil of false pretense about them, to fight thus for the ultimate peace of the world and for the liberation of its peoples, the German peoples included: for the rights of nations great and small and the privilege of men everywhere to choose their way of life and of obedience. The world must be made safe for democracy. Its peace must be planted upon the tested foundations of political liberty. We have no selfish ends to serve. We desire no conquest, no dominion. We seek no indemnities for ourselves, no material compensation for the sacrifices we shall freely make. We are but one of the champions of the rights of mankind. We shall be satisfied when those rights have been made as secure as the faith and the freedom of nations can make them.

Just because we fight without rancor and without selfish object, seeking nothing for ourselves but what we shall wish to share with all free peoples, we shall, I feel confident, conduct our operations as belligerents without passion and ourselves observe with proud punctilio the principles of right and of fair play we profess to be fighting for.

I have said nothing of the Governments allied with the Imperial Government of Germany because they have not made war upon us or challenged us to defend our right and our honor. The Austro-Hungarian Government has, indeed, avowed its unqualified indorsement and acceptance of the reckless and lawless submarine warfare adopted now without disguise by the Imperial German Government, and it has therefore not been possible for this Government to receive Count Tarnowski, the Ambassador recently accredited to this Government by the Imperial and Royal Government of Austria-Hungary; but that Government has not actually engaged in warfare against citizens of the United States on the seas, and I take the liberty, for the present at least, of postponing a discussion of our relations with the authorities at Vienna. We enter this war only where we are clearly forced into it because there are no other means of defending our rights.

It will be all the easier for us to conduct ourselves as belligerents in a high spirit of right and fairness because we act without animus, not in enmity towards a people or with the desire to bring any injury or disadvantage upon them, but only in armed opposition to an irresponsible government which has thrown aside all considerations of humanity and of right and is running amuck. We are, let me say again, the sincere friends of the German people, and shall desire nothing so much as the early reëstablishment of intimate relations of mutual advantage between us,— however hard it may be for them, for the time being, to believe that this is spoken from our hearts. We have borne with their present Government through all these bitter months because of that friendship,— exercising a patience and forbearance which would otherwise have been impossible. We shall, happily, still have an opportunity to prove that friendship in our daily attitude and actions towards the millions of men and women of German birth and native sympathy who live amongst us and share our life, and we shall be proud to prove it towards all who are in fact loyal to their neighbors and to the Government in the hour of test. They are, most of them, as true and loyal Americans as if they had never known any other fealty or allegiance. They will be prompt to stand with us in rebuking and restraining the few who may be of a different mind and purpose. If there should be disloyalty, it will be dealt with with a firm hand of stern repression; but, if it lifts its head at all, it will lift it only here and there and without countenance except from a lawless and malignant few.

It is a distressing and oppressive duty, Gentlemen of the Congress, which I have performed in thus addressing you. There are, it may be, many months of fiery trial and sacrifice ahead of us. It is a fearful thing to lead this great peaceful people into war, into the most terrible and disastrous of all wars, civilization itself seeming to be in the balance. But the right is more precious than peace, and we shall fight for the things which we have always carried nearest our hearts,—for democracy, for the right of those who submit to authority to have a voice in their own Governments, for the rights and liberties of small nations, for a universal dominion of right by such a concert of free peoples as shall bring peace and safety to all nations and make the world itself at last free. To such a task we can dedicate our lives and our fortunes, everything that we are and everything that we have, with the pride of those who know that the day has come when America is privileged to spend her blood and her might for the principles that gave her birth and happiness and the peace which she has treasured. God helping her, she can do no other.

DOCUMENT 27.4

President Wilson on Russia and War Aims*

The famous Fourteen Points address represented an effort by Wilson to appeal to liberals and radicals in Russia and the other Allied countries with a war aims program which would legitimate a continuation of the war against Imperial Germany. The message was successful in Western Europe, but in Russia it was rejected by the Bolsheviks, who went on to sign a separate peace with Germany at Brest-Litovsk shortly after.

Once more, as repeatedly before, the spokesmen of the Central Empires have

*Source: Ray Stannard Baker and William E. Dodd (eds.), *The Public Papers of Woodrow Wilson*, Vol. V. *War and Peace* (New York: Harper & Bros., 1927), pp. 155–62. Copyright 1926, 1954 by Edith Boling Wilson.

indicated their desire to discuss the objects of the war and the possible bases of a general peace. Parleys have been in progress at Brest-Litovsk between representatives of the Central Powers to which the attention of all the belligerents has been invited for the purpose of ascertaining whether it may be possible to extend these parleys into a general conference with regard to terms of peace and settlement. The Russian representatives presented not only a perfectly definite statement of the principles upon which they would be willing to conclude peace but also an equally definite program of the concrete application of those principles. The representatives of the Central Powers, on their part, presented an outline of settlement which, if much less definite, seemed susceptible of liberal interpretation until their specific program of practical terms was added. . . .

. . . Whatever the results of the parleys at Brest-Litovsk, whatever the confusions of counsel and of purpose in the utterances of the spokesmen of the Central Empires, they have again attempted to acquaint the world with their objects in the war and have again challenged their adversaries to say what their objects are and what sort of settlement they would deem just and satisfactory. There is no good reason why that challenge should not be responded to, and responded to with the utmost candor. We did not wait for it. Not once, but again and again, we have laid our whole thought and purpose before the world, not in general terms only, but each time with sufficient definition to make it clear what sort of definitive terms of settlement must necessarily spring out of them. . . .

There is, moreover, a voice calling for these definitions of principle and of purpose which is, it seems to me, more thrilling and more compelling than any of the many moving voices with which the troubled air of the world is filled. It is the voice of the Russian people. They are prostrate and all but helpless, it would seem, before the grim power of Germany, which has hitherto known no relenting and no pity. Their power, apparently, is shattered. And yet their soul is not subservient. They will not yield either in principle or in action. Their conception of what is right, of what it is humane and honorable for them to accept, has been stated with a frankness, a largeness of view, a generosity of spirit, and a universal human sympathy which must challenge the admiration of every friend of mankind; and they have refused to compound their ideals or desert others that they themselves may be safe. They call to us to say what it is that we desire, in what, if in anything, our purpose and our spirit differ from theirs; and I believe that the people of the United States would wish me to respond, with utter simplicity and frankness. Whether their present leaders believe it or not, it is our heartfelt desire and hope that some way may be opened whereby we may be privileged to assist the people of Russia to attain their utmost hope of liberty and ordered peace.

It will be our wish and purpose that the processes of peace, when they are begun, shall be absolutely open and that they shall involve and permit henceforth no secret understandings of any kind. The day of conquest and aggrandizement is gone by; so is also the day of secret covenants entered into in the interest of particular governments and likely at some unlooked-for moment to upset the peace of the world. It is this happy fact, now clear to the view of every public man whose thoughts do not still linger in an age that is dead and gone, which makes it possible for every nation whose purposes are consistent with justice and the peace of the world to avow now or at any other time the objects it has in view.

We entered this war because violations of right had occurred which touched us to the quick and made the life of our own people impossible unless they were corrected and the world secured once for all against their recurrence. What we de-

mand in this war, therefore, is nothing peculiar to ourselves. It is that the world be made fit and safe to live in; and particularly that it be made safe for every peace-loving nation which, like our own, wishes to live its own life, determine its own institutions, be assured of justice and fair dealing by the other peoples of the world as against force and selfish aggression. All the peoples of the world are in effect partners in this interest, and for our own part we see very clearly that unless justice be done to others it will not be done to us. The program of the world's peace, therefore, is our program; and that program, the only possible program, as we see it, is this:

I. Open covenants of peace, openly arrived at, after which there shall be no private international understandings of any kind but diplomacy shall proceed always frankly and in the public view.

II. Absolute freedom of navigation upon the seas, outside territorial waters, alike in peace and in war, except as the seas may be closed in whole or in part by international action for the enforcement of international covenants.

III. The removal, so far as possible, of all economic barriers and the establishment of an equality of trade conditions among all the nations consenting to the peace and associating themselves for its maintenance.

IV. Adequate guarantees given and taken that national armaments will be reduced to the lowest point consistent with domestic safety.

V. A free, open-minded, and absolutely impartial adjustment of all colonial claims, based upon a strict observance of the principle that in determining all such questions of sovereignty the interests of the populations concerned must have equal weight with the equitable claims of the government whose title is to be determined.

VI. The evacuation of all Russian territory and such a settlement of all questions affecting Russia as will secure the best and freest coöperation of the other nations of the world in obtaining for her an unhampered and unembarrassed opportunity for the independent determination of her own political development and national policy and assure her of a sincere welcome into the society of free nations under institutions of her own choosing; and, more than a welcome, assistance also of every kind that she may need and may herself desire. The treatment accorded Russia by her sister nations in the months to come will be the acid test of their good will, of their comprehension of her needs as distinguished from their own interests, and of their intelligent and unselfish sympathy.

VII. Belgium, the whole world will agree, must be evacuated and restored, without any attempt to limit the sovereignty which she enjoys in common with all other free nations. No other single act will serve as this will serve to restore confidence among the nations in the laws which they have themselves set and determined for the government of their relations with one another. Without this healing act the whole structure and validity of international law is forever impaired.

VIII. All French territory should be freed and the invaded portions restored, and the wrong done to France by Prussia in 1871 in the matter of Alsace-Lorraine, which has unsettled the peace of the world for nearly fifty years, should be righted, in order that peace may once more be made secure in the interest of all.

IX. A readjustment of the frontiers of Italy should be effected along clearly recognizable lines of nationality.

X. The peoples of Austria-Hungary, whose place among the nations we wish to see safeguarded and assured, should be accorded the freest opportunity of autonomous development.

XI. Rumania, Serbia, and Montenegro should be evacuated; occupied territories restored; Serbia accorded free and secure access to the sea; and the relations of the several Balkan states to one another deter- mined by friendly counsel along historically established lines of allegiance and nationality; and international guarantees of the political and economic independence and territorial integrity of the several Balkan states should be entered into.

XII. The Turkish portions of the present Ottoman Empire should be assured a secure sovereignty, but the other nationalities which are now under Turkish rule would be assured an undoubted security of life and an absolutely unmolested opportunity of autonomous development, and the Dardanelles should be permanently opened as a free passage to the ships and commerce of all nations under international guarantees.

XIII. An independent Polish state should be erected which should include the territories inhabited by indisputably Polish populations, which should be assured a free and secure access to the sea, and whose political and economic independence and territorial integrity should be guaranteed by international covenant.

XIV. A general association of nations must be formed under specific covenants for the purpose of affording mutual guarantees of political independence and territorial integrity to great and small states alike.

In regard to these essential rectifications of wrong and assertions of right we feel ourselves to be intimate partners of all the governments and peoples associated together against the Imperialists. We cannot be separated in interest or divided in purpose. We stand together until the end.

For such arrangements and covenants we are willing to fight and to continue to fight until they are achieved; but only because we wish the right to prevail and desire a just and stable peace such as can be secured only by removing the chief provocations to war, which this program does remove. We have no jealousy of German greatness, and there is nothing in this program that impairs it. We grudge her no achievement or distinction of learning or of pacific enterprise such as have made her record very bright and very enviable. We do not wish to injure her or to block in any way her legitimate influence or power. We do not wish to fight her either with arms or with hostile arrangements of trade if she is willing to associate herself with us and the other peace-loving nations of the world in covenants of justice and law and fair dealing. We wish her only to accept a place of equality among the peoples of the world,—the new world in which we now live,—instead of a place of mastery.

Neither do we presume to suggest to her any alteration or modification of her institutions. But it is necessary, we must frankly say, and necessary as a preliminary to any intelligent dealings with her on our part, that we should know whom her spokesmen speak for when they speak to us, whether for the Reichstag majority or for the military party and the men whose creed is imperial domination.

We have spoken now, surely, in terms too concrete to admit of any further doubt or question. An evident principle runs through the whole program I have outlined. It is the principle of justice to all peoples and nationalities, and their right to live on equal terms of liberty and safety with one another, whether they be strong or weak. Unless this principle be made its foundation no part of the structure of international justice can stand. The people of the United States could act upon no other principle; and to the vindication of this principle they are ready to devote their lives, their honor, and everything that they possess. The moral climax of this the culminating and final war for human liberty has come, and they are ready to put their own strength, their own highest purpose, their own integrity and devotion to the test.

DOCUMENT 27.5

Robert Lansing on the Bolshevik Revolution*

The following selection reveals the depth of Lansing's anti-Bolshevik commitment. After the separate peace of Brest-Litovsk and the Bolshevik dispersal of the Russian Constituent Assembly in early 1918, views such as these came to dominate the Wilson administration and pave the way for the eventual intervention in Siberia.

There are a number of people who are telling us about Russia and advising us as to what the outcome will be and what we ought to do. I have seen several and a number have written me their views. The conclusions and opinions are almost as many as the advisers, and their advice as to our policy is about as harmonious. I have yet to find one, who, pinned down to the application of his theory, is able to furnish a plan that is practical except one who frankly asserts that the best thing to do is to let things alone as far as it is possible to do so.

With this latter policy I am in entire accord. The Russian situation is to me an unanswered and unanswerable riddle. None of our observers, and some are well trained, has been able to find a way out or to advise a course of action leading to satisfactory results.

When the Root Mission returned, they were all, with the exception of Charles R. Crane, who knew Russia better than the others, most optimistic as to the power of the Kerensky Government to restore order and to keep the Russian armies in the field. But not long after their return Kerensky was overthrown and the Bolsheviks seized the government at Pet-

*Source: Robert Lansing, *The War Memoirs of Robert Lansing*, (Indianapolis: Bobbs-Merrill Co., 1935), pp. 339–42. Copyright 1935, reprinted by permission of the publishers, The Bobbs-Merrill Company, Inc.

rograd. Thus their recommendations predicated on the success of the Provisional Government could not be adopted, or, if they had been, would have been useless. Yet the Root Mission was composed of very able men who were doubtless as capable of judging the situation and giving advice as any this government could have sent out.

I confess that I do not feel warranted in hazarding even a guess as to what the outcome will be. This makes the adopting of an active policy most difficult.

Historically the Russian situation is unprecedented. It is wholly novel. It seems to me that the controlling forces are idealism and ignorance supported by weapons. The especial characteristics of the idealists who are masters in Petrograd are lack of any sentiment of nationality and a determination, frankly avowed, to overthrow all existing governments and establish on the ruins a despotism of the proletariat in every country. The Bolsheviki are anarchists rather than Socialists, though they would undoubtedly repudiate such a charge.

I cannot see how this element which is hostile to the very idea of nationality can claim that they are the government of a nation or expect to be recognized as such. They are avowedly opposed to every government on earth; they openly propose to excite revolutions in all countries against existing governments; they are as hostile to democracy as they are to autocracy. If we should recognize them in Russia, we would encourage them and their followers in other lands. That would be a serious error. Both France and Great Britain seem to be tempted. If they decide to deal with them I believe it will be a mistake.

The correct policy for a government which believes in political institutions as they now exist and based on nationality and private property is to leave these dangerous idealists alone and have no direct dealings with them. To recognize them would give them an exalted idea of their own power, make them more insolent and

impossible, and win their contempt, not their friendship.

It is true that the Teutonic Powers are recognizing them. They may profit temporarily by this policy, but it is my belief that they may suffer in the end. Of course these governments are tempted by the possibility of obtaining supplies to arrange peace with these people, or rather by disorganizing the Russian armies and causing confusion in the Russian provinces ... [making] peace unavoidable. The result would be that Germany and Austria could remove their military forces for use elsewhere and Russia's resources would be at their mercy. They will probably succeed in these objects, but they may have to pay a heavy price in the end. The truth lies in the future.

It was my belief that the Bolsheviki, pursuing their doctrine of breaking down political power, would go to pieces. Thus far my belief has not been justified. Their cry of "Peace and Land" is popular with the ignorant Russians who have suffered grievously in the past. And yet I cannot see how unorganized and undirected physical power such as now dominates affairs in Petrograd can continue. It has in itself every element of destruction. Up to the present, however, the logic of events has failed.

Of one thing I am convinced, and that is that it would be unwise to give recognition to Lenin, Trotsky and their crew of radicals. We ought to sit tight and wait and see how the Germans come out. If they do not burn their fingers I will admit I am mistaken. Of course Russia as a nation will never come under the Petrograd Bolsheviki. They are far more likely to break up into separate units claiming independence. We are apt to see several distinct states each managing its own affairs. The danger is that Germany may conquer or make peace with these piecemeal. When that time comes we will have new conditions to face. I cannot see how recognition of the Bolsheviks would prevent this, as it would not be the slightest inducement for them to continue the war. If they should continue it, it will only be because their power is menaced.

As to Lenin and Trotsky I am in doubt. They may be acting entirely in Germany's interest, but I cannot make that belief harmonize with some things which they have done. In fact they may be honest in purpose and utterly dishonest in methods. For national and personal honor, for truth and for the individual rights of life, liberty and property they seem to have no regard. How can anyone deal with such people? They are wanting in international virtue. International obligation and comity mean nothing to them. The one thing they are striving to bring about is the "Social Revolution," which will sweep away national boundaries, racial distinctions and modern political, religious and social institutions, and make the ignorant and incapable mass of humanity dominant in the earth. They indeed plan to destroy civilization by mob violence.

As far as one can judge from the ever-changing and confused conditions, the Bolshevik program is to make way with the military and political authority in Russia and to incite similar destruction in other countries. This will undoubtedly first result in the division of Russia into separate states, some favorable and some hostile to the Bolshevik idea. A general disorganization of trade, industry and transportation will follow with discontent and disorder everywhere. People will become hungry and demand food. They will become desperate and rob and kill, aided by the criminal element. With weakened military and political power the Bolsheviki will be unable to suppress these outrages.

It seems to me that Russia is about to be the stage on which will be acted one of the most terrible tragedies of all history. Civil war seems certain. The cities will be the prey of mobs, thieves and murderers. Factions will struggle for mastery. Russia will fairly swim in blood, a prey to lawlessness and violence. And then to add to these horrors will come the ruthless Germans to take from this struggling mass of humanity their lands and property and to force them to obey.

I believe that the Russian "Terror" will far surpass in brutality and destruction of life and property the Terror of the French Revolution. The latter at least possessed the semblance of government and made pretense of legality. Russia possesses neither. There is no authority, no law. It is a seething caldron of anarchy and violence. I can conceive of no more frightful calamity for a people than that which seems about to fall upon Russia.

The only possible remedy would be for a strong commanding personality to arise who would be able to gather a disciplined military force sufficiently strong to restore order and maintain a government. As yet no leader has shown enough strength to organize the Cossacks into an effective army. They may succeed, but no one knows how much the Cossacks returning from the front are inoculated with Bolshevism. Many are very hopeful, but I cannot say that I am overconfident. However, they are at present the only hope that has appeared. I am opposed to giving these leaders any open support, as their enterprise seems to me too uncertain and the whole situation too chaotic to put faith in any one group or faction.

"Do nothing" should be our policy until the black period of terrorism comes to an end and the rising tide of blood has run its course. It cannot last forever, but Russia will sink lower before better days come.

DOCUMENT 27.6

Motives for the Siberian Intervention*

The following dispatch from the American Consul (Poole) at Moscow in the summer of 1918 reveals the anti-German and anti-Bolshevik motives behind the Siberian intervention.

To the Secretary of State

683. The situation has come to the most critical pass which has yet been experienced. The Department no doubt has full reports from the Embassy concerning developments at Archangel. Chicherin assured me on the 28th that the note to the British representative, . . . unlike the previous protests concerning Murman, is really meant, and that the Soviet government is dispatching troops to Murman and to Archangel. Respecting the expedition to Murman, he said that there will be an inevitable conflict with any foreign troops encountered and that it is not to be foreseen where such conflict may end. Admitting by inference that the local Murman soviets deplore the withdrawal of the Allied forces, he said that they will nevertheless have to bend to the will of the central authorities. Concerning the dispatch of troops to Archangel, he remarked that, with so much talk of intervention, the Soviets must be prepared to resist a landing.

As the Red Army is of slight military value, and has already more than it can do on the Czech front, this belligerent attitude of the Soviets derives its chief importance from the menace of direct German cooperation. The British have learned from a source they consider sure that reported, 27th, Chicherin instructed Soviet representatives at Berlin to request formally of the supreme German command military assistance against the Allies and

the British. Observers fail so far to confirm persistent rumors of the passage east or north Ukraine of actual German units, and the situation in the Ukraine as well as events on the western front suggest their general improbability. However, the Department is aware of German war prisoners in Russia and of the presence of number of important German forces in Finland. An observer just returned from Kem reports continuance of military activities in Karelia threatening the Murman railway at various points, and reports come from good sources of preparations for a movement northward toward Pechenga Bay or Murmansk.

The development of the political situation during the week lends color to the view that the Germans have decided to support the Bolsheviki for the moment, and that the Bolsheviki, in despair of dealing with the situation themselves, have accepted. The general bearing of the Bolshevik leaders has become most assured during the week and they are most active and outspoken respecting Allied intervention. Some of the most indiscreet among them have stated openly that the general mobilization, which is now being attempted with only moderate success, is directed against the Allies. Their subservience to German domination has become most manifest. . . . On the other hand the anti-Bolshevik parties are experiencing a resurge of pro-Ally sentiment, resulting from conviction of a German-Bolshevik understanding and the success of the Allied arms in the west.

The moment is peculiarly ripe for Allied intervention, of the unavoidable necessity for which sooner or later I trust the Department is also convinced. Coming at this time, it promises to result in a declaration of war against the Allies by the Bolsheviki and an alliance with Germany. This will have two important effects: (1) A reciprocal alliance with imperial Germany will come as a final revelation of the sordid and insincere selfishness which characterizes the greater part of the Bol-

*Source: *Foreign Relations, 1918, Russia,* Vol. II (Washington, D.C.: U.S. Government Printing Office, 1932), pp. 236–38.

shevik leaders; it will place the onus of action on them and throw definitely into the Allied camp the parties of opposition. (2) It will draw Germany into central Russia, increasing her military effort in the east and widening the surface of the Russian [theater of war].

While . . . the Russian press exaggerates the unrest in the Ukraine, it claims it is still certain that the Ukraine situation seriously hampers German freedom of action in the west. Chicherin argues that if the Allies intervene they will encounter the same difficulties in the portions of Russia occupied by them. There is a fundamental difference. Germany has nothing to give and ruthlessly strips occupied territory of food and manufactures. I take it for granted that the Allies will not overlook the political aspects of intervention which in some ways overtop the purely military in importance and that within the regions defended the good will of the population will be secured not only by tactful administration but direct economic assistance. In this way the influence of intervention will spread far beyond the field of military operations, based on the formula that, while Germany takes, the Allies give, food.

It [is] generally understood that the feeding of even small portions of northern Russia is an enormous undertaking, but its assumption can not be avoided by non-intervention, as the famine of the coming winter will imperatively command the attention of civilized nations by its humanitarian, if not military and political aspects. Obviously we cannot and should not undertake to send our own food, except possibly a few initial shiploads to appease the population in the territory immediately to be defended. Northern Russia can be adequately fed only from the granary of western Siberia. To effect this the new front must include Semipalatinsk . . . , and Ekaterinburg, as well as the points now held by the Czechs.

On this account and in view of favorable military situation created by the un-successful Soviet attack on the Czechs and because the Czechs, if not promptly supported, will inevitably be crushed by direct or indirect German military pressure, the moment is also ripe for intervention in Siberia. While action in northern Russia might be limited to an armed demonstration designed only to draw Germany into central Russia, intervention in Siberia must be especially [effected by] sufficient military force to create a secure secondary base for operations in northern Russia and to maintain communication with Archangel via Vyatka and Kotlas, if not Verkhneuralsk. If intervention can also in time project itself down the Volga with your [sic] supporting expeditions towards Ekaterinoslav on the one hand and towards the Caucasus on the other, so much the better, but that is for the future.

Like intervention in northern Russia, that in Siberia will fail if undertaken as a purely military enterprise. There is need for as good political and economic administrative genius as can be found. . . . The Siberians are disgusted with Bolshevism and consider Allied intervention the only means of escaping German domination, but they distrust the Japanese. Against this we have their faith in America and we must develop this asset by every conceivable means.

Regarding intervention in general the people of the Allied countries must not permit themselves illusions. The bulk of the Russians are generally ignorant and moved only by immediate and material considerations. The educated political leaders are party men lacking in the western conception of patriotism. No class has developed self-reliance and all dislike hard work. They look to others for guidance and support and delude them [selves] with the thought that foreign intervention will forthwith bring order and comfort without special privation or effort on their part. It is certain therefore that even with the good will of the Russian people we can count upon very little serious practical help from them. We must also foresee that, following a possibly enthusiastic initial reception, there will be a reaction of disillusion and discontent.

DOCUMENT 27.7

The Problem of Bolshevism at the Paris Conference*

At Paris the Wilson administration sought to check Bolshevism and reintegrate Germany with a program of timely food relief. The following cablegram was sent in January 1919 to the chairman of the Appropriations Committee, House of Representatives.

I cannot too earnestly or solemnly urge upon the Congress the appropriation for which Mr. Hoover has asked for the administration of food relief. Food relief is now the key to the whole European situation and to the solutions of peace. Bolshevism is steadily advancing westward, is poisoning Germany. It cannot be stopped by force, but it can be stopped by food; and all the leaders with whom I am in conference agree that concerted action in this matter is of immediate and vital importance. The money will not be spent for food for Germany itself, because Germany can buy its food; but it will be spent for financing the movement of food to our real friends in Poland and to the people of the liberated units of the Austo-Hungarian Empire and to our associates in the Balkans. I beg that you will present this matter with all possible urgency and force to the Congress. I do not see how we can find definite powers with whom to conclude peace unless this means of stemming the tide of anarchism be employed.

WOODROW WILSON

*Source: Ray Stannard Baker and William E. Dodd (eds.), *The Public Papers of Woodrow Wilson*, Vol. V. *War and Peace* (New York: Harper & Bros., 1927), p. 389. Copyright 1926, 1954 by Edith Boling Wilson.

DOCUMENT 27.8

Wilson and the Blockade of Bolshevik Russia: 1919*

The following statement of President Wilson makes clear that his opposition to the Bolshevik regime in Russia continued throughout the Paris Peace Conference. The President participated throughout 1919, albeit often ambivalently, in a variety of diplomatic, political, and military measures designed to contain and remove Lenin's government.

Reply of President Wilson to Inquiry of July 27, From the British, French, Italian and Japanese Representatives in the Council of Five, on the Question of a Proposed Blockade of Soviet Russia.

The President is not unmindful of the serious situation which exists in relation to neutral trade in the Baltic with the Russian ports controlled by the Bolsheviks. He has given careful consideration to the arguments advanced in the message transmitted at the request of Monsieur Clemenceau, and is not unmindful of their force in support of the proposed interruption of commerce with the ports mentioned. However, while he fully understands the reasons for employing war measures to prevent the importation of munitions and food supplies into the portion of Russia now in the hands of the Bolsheviks, he labours under the difficulty of being without constitutional right to prosecute an act of war such as a blockade affecting neutrals unless there has been a declaration of war by the Congress of the United States against the nation so blockaded.

The landing of troops at Archangel and Murmansk was done to protect the property and supplies of the American and Allied Governments until they could be removed. The sending of troops to Siberia was to keep open the railway for the pro-

*Source: *Foreign Relations, The Paris Peace Conference, 1919,* Vol. VII (Washington, D.C.: U.S. Government Printing Office, 1946), pp. 644–45.

tection of Americans engaged in its operation and to make safe from possible German and Austrian attack the retiring Czecho-Slovaks. The furnishing of supplies to the Russians in Siberia, while indicating a sympathy with the efforts to restore order and safety of life and property, cannot be construed as a belligerent act.

The President is convinced that if proper representations are made to the neutral countries during the war they can be induced to prohibit traffic in arms and munitions with the portions of Russia controlled by the Bolsheviks. The avowed hostility of the Bolsheviks to all Governments and the announced programme of international revolution make them as great a menace to the national safety of neutral countries as to Allied countries. For any Government to permit them to increase their power through commercial intercourse with its nationals would be to encourage a movement which is frankly directed against all Governments and would certainly invite the condemnation of all peoples desirous of restoring peace and social order.

The President cannot believe that any Government whose people might be in a position to carry on commerce with the Russian ports referred to would be so indifferent to the opinion of the civilised world as to permit it. The President therefore suggests that the so-called neutral Governments be approached by the Allied and Associated Governments in joint note setting forth the facts of the case and the menace to such countries and to the world of any increase of the Bolshevik power, and requesting the neutral Governments to take immediate steps to prevent trade and commerce with Bolshevik Russia and to give assurance that the policy will be rigorously enforced in conjunction with other Governments which are equally menaced.

DOCUMENT 27.9
President Wilson Defends the Treaty and the League*

In his speeches in defense of the League of Nations the President argued that the League would preserve the peace settlement of Versailles, help to contain the threat of revolution, and fulfill America's destiny of inspiring a liberal world order.

At Columbus, Ohio, September 4, 1919

MR. CHAIRMAN, GOVERNOR CAMPBELL,
MY FELLOW CITIZENS:

It is with very profound pleasure that I find myself face to face with you. I have for a long time chafed at the confinement of Washington. I have for a long time wished to fulfill the purpose with which my heart was full when I returned to our beloved country, namely, to go out and report to my fellow countrymen concerning those affairs of the world which now need to be settled. The only people I owe any report to are you and the other citizens of the United States.

And it has become increasingly necessary, apparently, that I should report to you. After all the various angles at which you have heard the treaty held up, perhaps you would like to know what is in the treaty. I find it very difficult in reading some of the speeches that I have read to form any conception of that great document. It is a document unique in the history of the world for many reasons, and I think I cannot do you a better service, or the peace of the world a better service, than by pointing out to you just what this treaty contains and what it seeks to do.

In the first place, my fellow countrymen, it seeks to punish one of the great-

*Source: Ray Stannard Baker and William E. Dodd (eds.), *The Public Papers of Woodrow Wilson*, Vol. VI. *War and Peace* (New York: Harper & Bros., 1927), pp. 590–98. Copyright 1926, 1954 by Edith Boling Wilson.

est wrongs ever done in history, the wrong which Germany sought to do to the world and to civilization; and there ought to be no weak purpose with regard to the application of the punishment. She attempted an intolerable thing, and she must be made to pay for the attempt. The terms of the treaty are severe, but they are not unjust. I can testify that the men associated with me at the Peace Conference in Paris had it in their hearts to do justice and not wrong. But they knew, perhaps, with a more vivid sense of what had happened than we could possibly know on this side of the water, the many solemn covenants which Germany had disregarded, the long preparation she had made to overwhelm her neighbors, and the utter disregard which she had shown for human rights, for the rights of women, of children, of those who were helpless. They had seen their lands devastated by an enemy that devoted himself not only to the effort at victory, but to the effort at terror—seeking to terrify the people whom he fought. And I wish to testify that they exercised restraint in the terms of this treaty. They did not wish to overwhelm any great nation. They acknowledged that Germany was a great nation, and they had no purpose of overwhelming the German people, but they did think that it ought to be burned into the consciousness of men forever that no people ought to permit its government to do what the German Government did.

In the last analysis, my fellow countrymen, as we in America would be the first to claim, a people are responsible for the acts of their Government. If their Government purposes things that are wrong, they ought to take measures to see to it that that purpose is not executed. Germany was self-governed; her rulers had not concealed the purposes that they had in mind, but they had deceived their people as to the character of the methods they were going to use, and I believe from what I can learn that there is an awakened consciousness in Germany itself of the deep iniquity of the thing that was attempted.

When the Austrian delegates came before the Peace Conference, they in so many words spoke of the origination of the war as a crime and admitted in our presence that it was a thing intolerable to contemplate. They knew in their hearts that it had done them the deepest conceivable wrong, that it had put their people and the people of Germany at the judgment seat of mankind, and throughout this treaty every term that was applied to Germany was meant, not to humiliate Germany, but to rectify the wrong that she had done.

Look even into the severe terms of reparation—for there was no indemnity. No indemnity of any sort was claimed, merely reparation, merely paying for the destruction done, merely making good the losses so far as such losses could be made good which she had unjustly inflicted, not upon the governments, for the reparation is not to go to the governments, but upon the people whose rights she had trodden upon with absolute absence of everything that even resembled pity. There was no indemnity in this treaty, but there is reparation, and even in the terms of reparation a method is devised by which the reparation shall be adjusted to Germany's ability to pay it.

I am astonished at some of the statements I hear made about this treaty. The truth is that they are made by persons who have not read the treaty or who, if they have read it, have not comprehended its meaning. There is a method of adjustment in that treaty by which the reparation shall not be pressed beyond the point which Germany can pay, but which will be pressed to the utmost point that Germany can pay—which is just, which is righteous. It would have been intolerable if there had been anything else. For, my fellow citizens, this treaty is not meant merely to end this single war. It is meant as a notice to every government which in the future will attempt this thing that mankind will unite to inflict the same punishment. There is no national triumph sought to be recorded in this treaty. There is no glory sought for any particular nation. The thought of the statesmen collected around that table was of their people, of the sufferings that they had gone through, of the losses they had incurred—that great throbbing heart which was so depressed, so forlorn, so sad in every memory that it had had of the five tragical years that have gone. Let us never forget those years, my fellow countrymen. Let us never forget the purpose—the high purpose, the disinterested purpose—with which America lent its strength for its own glory but for the defense of mankind.

As I said, this treaty was not intended merely to end this war. It was intended to prevent any similar war. I wonder if some of the opponents of the League of Nations have forgotten the promises we made our people before we went to that peace table. We had taken by processes of law the flower of our youth from every household, and we told those mothers and fathers and sisters and wives and sweethearts that we were taking those men to fight a war which would end business of that sort; and if we do not end it, if we do not do the best that human concert of action can do to end it, we are of all men the most unfaithful, the most unfaithful to the loving hearts who suffered in this war, the most unfaithful to those households bowed in grief and yet lifted with the feeling that the lad laid down his life for a great thing and, among other things, in order that other lads might never have to do the same thing. That is what the League of Nations is for, to end this war justly, and then not merely to serve notice on governments which would contemplate the same things that Germany contemplated that they will do it at their peril, but also concerning the combination of power which will prove to them that they will do it at their peril. It is idle to say the world *will* combine against you, because it may not, but it is persuasive to say the world *is* combined against you, and will remain combined against the things that Germany attempted. The League of Nations is the only thing that can prevent the recurrence of this dreadful catastrophe and redeem our promises.

The character of the League is based upon the experience of this very war. I did not meet a single public man who did not admit these things, that Germany would not have gone into this war if she had thought Great Britain was going into it, and that she most certainly would never have gone into this war if she dreamed America was going into it. And they all admitted that a notice beforehand that the greatest powers of the world would combine to prevent this sort of thing would prevent it absolutely. When gentlemen tell you, therefore, that the League of Nations is intended for some other purpose than this, merely reply this to them: If we do not do this thing, we have neglected the central covenant that we made to our people, and there will then be no statesmen of any country who can thereafter promise his people alleviation from the perils of war. The passions of this world are not dead. The rivalries of this world have not cooled. They have been rendered hotter than ever. The harness that is to unite nations is more necessary now than it ever was before, and unless there is this assurance of combined action before wrong is attempted, wrong will be attempted just so soon as the most ambitious nations can recover from the financial stress of this war.

Now, look what else is in the treaty. This treaty is unique in the history of mankind, because the center of it is the redemption of weak nations. There never was a congress of nations before that considered the rights of those who could not enforce their rights. There never was a congress of nations before that did not seek to effect some balance of power brought about by means of serving the strength and interest of the strongest powers concerned; whereas this treaty builds up nations that never could have won their freedom in any other way; builds them up by gift, by largess, not by obligations; builds them up because of the conviction of the men who wrote the treaty that the rights of people transcend the rights of governments, because of the conviction of the men who wrote that treaty that the fertile source of war is wrong. The Austro-Hungarian Empire, for example, was held together by military force and consisted of peoples who did not want to live together, who did not have the spirit of nationality as towards each other, who were constantly chafing at the bands that held them. Hungary, though a willing partner of Austria, was willing to be a partner because she could share Austria's strength to accomplish her own ambitions, and her own ambitions were to hold under her the Jugo-Slavic peoples that lay to the south of her; Bohemia, an unhappy partner, a partner by duress, beating in all her veins the strongest national impulse that was to be found anywhere in Europe; and north of that, pitiful Poland, a great nation divided up among the great powers of Europe, torn asunder, kinship disregarded, natural ties treated with contempt, and an obligatory division among sovereigns imposed upon her—a part of her given to Russia, a part of her given to Austria, a part of her given to Germany—great bodies of Polish people never permitted to have the normal intercourse with their kinsmen for fear that that fine instinct of the heart should assert itself which binds families together. Poland could never have won her independence. Bohemia never could have broken away from the Austro-Hungarian combination. The Slavic peoples to the south, running down into the great Balkan peninsula, had again and again tried to assert their nationality and independence, and had as often been crushed, not by the immediate power they were fighting, but by the combined power of Europe. The old alliances, the old balances of power, were meant to see to it that no little nation asserted its right to the disturbance of the peace of Europe, and every time an assertion of rights was attempted they were suppressed by combined influence and force.

This treaty tears away all that: says these people have a right to live their own lives under the governments which they themselves choose to set up. That is the American principle, and I was glad to fight for it. When strategic claims were urged, it was matter of common counsel that such considerations were not in our thought. We were not now arranging for future wars. We were giving people what belonged to them. My fellow citizens, I do not think there is any man alive who has a more tender sympathy for the great people of Italy than I have, and a very stern duty was presented to us when we had to consider some of the claims of Italy on the Adriatic, because strategically, from the point of view of future wars, Italy needed a military foothold on the other side of the Adriatic, but her people did not live there except in little spots. It was a Slavic people, and I had to say to my Italian friends, "Everywhere else in this treaty we have given territory to the people who lived on it, and I do not think that it is for the advantage of Italy, and I am sure it is not for the advantage of the world, to give Italy territory where other people live." I felt the force of the argument for what they wanted, and it was the old argument that had always prevailed, namely, that they needed it from a military point of view, and I have no doubt that if there is no league of nations, they will need it from a military point of view; but if there is a league of nations, they will not need it from a military point of view.

If there is no league of nations, the military point of view will prevail in every instance, and peace will be brought into contempt, but if there is a league of nations, Italy need not fear the fact that the shores on the other side of the Adriatic tower above the lower and sandy shores on her side the sea, because there will be no threatening guns there, and the nations of the world will have concerted, not merely to see that the Slavic peoples have their rights, but that the Italian people have their rights as well. I had rather have everybody on my side than be armed to the teeth. Every settlement that is right, every settlement that is based on the principles I have alluded to, is a safe settlement, because the sympathy of mankind will be behind it.

Some gentlemen have feared with regard to the League of Nations that we will be obliged to do things we do not want to do. If the treaty was wrong, that might be so, but if the treaty is right, we will wish to preserve right. I think I know the heart of this great people whom I, for the time being have the high honor to represent better than some other men that I hear talk. I have been bred, and am proud to have been bred, in the old revolutionary school which set this Government up, when it was set up as the friend of mankind, and I know if they do not that America has never lost that vision or that purpose. But I have not the slightest fear that arms will be necessary if the purpose is there. If I know that my adversary is armed and I am not, I do not press the controversy, and if any nation entertains selfish purposes set against the principles established in this treaty and is told by the rest of the world that it must withdraw its claims, it will not press them.

The heart of this treaty then, my fellow citizens, is not even that it punishes Germany. That is a temporary thing. It is that it rectifies the age-long wrongs which characterized the history of Europe. There were some of us who wished that the scope of the treaty would reach some other age-long wrongs. It was a big job, and I do not say that we wished that it were bigger, but there were other wrongs elsewhere than in Europe and of the same kind which no doubt ought to be righted, and some day will be righted, but which we could not draw into the treaty because

we could deal only with the countries whom the war had engulfed and affected. But so far as the scope of our authority went, we rectified the wrongs which have been the fertile source of war in Europe.

Have you ever reflected, my fellow countrymen, on the real source of revolution? Men do not start revolutions in a sudden passion. Do you remember what Thomas Carlyle said about the French Revolution? He was speaking of the so-called Hundred Days Terror which reigned not only in Paris, but throughout France, in the days of the French Revolution, and he reminded his readers that back of that hundred days lay several hundred years of agony and of wrong. The French people had been deeply and consistently wronged by their Government, robbed, their human rights disregarded, and the slow agony of those hundreds of years had after awhile gathered into a hot anger that could not be suppressed. Revolutions do not spring up overnight. Revolutions come from the long suppression of the human spirit. Revolutions come because men know that they have rights and that they are disregarded; and when we think of the future of the world in connection with this treaty we must remember that one of the chief efforts of those who made this treaty was to remove that anger from the heart of great peoples, great peoples who had always been suppressed, who had always been used, and who had always been the tools in the hands of governments, generally alien governments, not their own. The makers of the treaty knew that if these wrongs were not removed, there could be no peace in the world, because, after all, my fellow citizens, war comes from the seed of wrong and not from the seed of right. This treaty is an attempt to right the history of Europe, and, in my humble judgment, it is a measurable success. . . .

28 Rural-Urban Conflict in the 1920s

DAVID N. CHALMERS
University of Florida

The decade of the 1920s has held considerable nostalgic appeal for later generations of Americans. Aided primarily by the motion pictures and the phonograph, seconded by misty memory, we have pictured the period as one of frenetic hedonism, based on booze, blues, and jazz; Sigmund Freud and Henry Ford; raccoon coats, rumrunners, and Runyonesque gangsters. It was an era in which "the younger generation" made its bow as America's institutionalized No. 1 problem and most emulated symbol in a society which small-town fundamentalism was never able to repress. This was the world of William Faulkner, Scott Fitzgerald, Ernest Hemingway, Ezra Pound, Hart Crane, and T. S. Eliot; of Al Capone, Babe Ruth, Theda Bara, and Rudy Vallee; of Warren Harding playing poker with the boys in the "little green house on K Street" and of Calvin Coolidge asleep in the White House. Many of the people who lived through the succeeding decades of depression, world war, and cold war looked back at the twenties with considerable, though not always accurate, longing. Only in the midsixties, when the twist, LSD, and the miniskirt had replaced the Charleston, booze, and the flapper, would the exaggerated glow of the not-so-golden twenties begin to fade.

By the 1920s the United States was well on its way to becoming an urban society, and the value of industrial production had exceeded that of the farms for at least three decades. In 1900 the total national population reached 76 million, of which some 60 percent were rural. By 1920, out of 106 million people, the nonurban portion had fallen to 48 percent, a growing part of which lived in rural hamlets and villages. This movement was to continue during the twenties at an increasing rate, and for the first time the actual number of people on the farms declined.

Of course, percentage points only supply information and symbolize movement; they do not in themselves create discontent. Why had it taken until the 1920s for a reaction to rural decline to take place? After the hard times and turbulent agrarian protest of the 1870s, eighties, and nineties, the 20th century had brought two decades of prosperity for the farmer, climaxing in the boom times of World War I. The Progressive Era was a period of great optimism, based upon a belief in human rationality and progress. Traditional standards of truth, justice, patriotism, and morality seemed unchallenged. It was a period which the historian Henry F. May (*The End of American Innocence*) has described as "the time when people wanted to make a number of sharp changes because they were so confident in the basic rightness of things as they were." America might be changing and the proportion of the rural population decreasing, but it was not initially apparent that the traditional, comforting American values were also on the decline. When these supports were clearly disappearing by the 1920s, the crisis of rural America took on psychological as well as economic dimensions.

With high wartime demand and prices, the farmer had expanded his production and his indebtedness. But the government withdrew its support from wheat and pork by the end of 1919. The following year, with a falling market—though not necessarily lower freight rates, interest, and taxes—agriculture went into a depression which continued until war broke out again in Europe at the end of the thirties.

Agriculture was not so sick, however, that it could not fight back. Its struggle was in part a rational attempt to increase farm income, which became focused on the McNary-Haugen bill to require the government to prop up domestic prices by dumping agricultural surpluses abroad. This ran into conflict with the prevailing business orientation of the Republican Party, which was willing to offer tax and tariff relief to industry and believed that the only solution for agriculture would be for farmers to reduce production and for economic law to reduce the number of farmers. A farm bloc in Congress, led by Republican progressives, got some tariff protection and farm credit, but Presidents Calvin Coolidge and Herbert Hoover vetoed the McNary-Haugen bill.

The farmer was not inclined, however, to blame all of his problems on mortgage costs and commodity prices. While some farm leaders, such as the Iowa spokesman *Wallace's Farmer*, shifted their concern from the primacy of agrarianism to the necessity for parity, there were others who had a profound feeling that society itself was being destroyed. Foreclosures and tenancy were increasing, as was the drift of the rural population, particularly the young, to the cities, drawn by the superior opportunities for money, mobility, and pleasure.

The values of the old-stock, traditional American society seemed to be increasingly overshadowed by the machine-centered, materialistic ones created by the racial and religious pluralism of the cities. The farmer's response to this changing society often took the form of an attack upon it rather than an attempt to find a place for agriculture within it. In a world in which President Coolidge could comment that the farmers never made any money anyway and in which the Democratic Party had not yet assumed its role as a broad group-interest broker, "rum, race, and religion" were often more politically potent than economics. The Presidential candidacy of Robert M. La Follette in 1924 did well in the western farm, mountain, and coastal states, but it represented a protest, hardly a program or a party. In the rural South, post-Populist frustration had long been focused upon the polyglot eastern cities.

But American society was too complex to be summed up only in terms of a simple rural-urban dichotomy. By 1920, approximately two out of every five persons classified as rural lived not on farms but in small hamlets and towns. These villages acted as the commercial intermediates between the farms and the cities, transmitting and producing goods, supplying services, and handling the farmer's transactions. Although a good share of their population was made up of retired, tax-wary farmers, the conflict between farm and hamlet had reached back into the previous century. The division was most pronounced in the Middle West, but there was a widespread tendency for townspeople to look down on the farmer. He in turn sensed slight where he did not see it and considered the villager to be concerned primarily with the middleman's profit at his expense. The story is told of one small town which was forced to restore the old water trough and hitching post when the farmers took the removal as a personal insult and began motoring to neighboring villages to do their marketing. Arguments about bank interest rates, mortgages, and retail prices and credit were joined by disagreement over Sunday movies, sermons, and whether young John Thomas Scopes should have been allowed to teach Dayton, Tennessee, high school students that man "descended from a lower order of animals."

The small towns also had their economic problems. They too had over-expanded during the war, and now they suffered contraction and often banking failure. The great building boom of the twenties passed them by. Business property was deteriorating, and civic and social organizations were becoming less active. More and more, the rural community was being overshadowed by the city, which, while contributing the automobile service trade, drew the flivverized farmers and took over the role of supplier of nationally manufactured goods, replacing the blacksmith, butcher, and miller.

The townspeople saw the city as an anonymous, impersonal, dog-eat-dog society, ruled by corrupt politicians, immigrant bosses, labor leaders, and monopolists, all of whom lived off the hardworking countryfolk. The big cities embodied the opulent and immoral life of the very rich, and the secularism and agnostic atheism of the city churches and universities. The eastern metropolises were wet, Roman Catholic, immigrant, perhaps Bolshevik, probably un-American, and certainly not safe, either in their streets or in their influences. They were, in short, responsible for the problems which faced country life.

Many major cities such as Cincinnati, Birmingham, Columbus, Indianapolis, Kansas City, Dallas, and Denver, and most of the smaller ones, were not greatly touched by the waves of immigrants from Southern and Eastern Europe who flooded into the country after the 1880s.

Like Muncie, Indiana, which the sociologists Robert S. Lynd and Helen M. Lynd profiled in *Middletown: A Study in American Culture* (1929), such cities had been populated by old-stock Americans from the nearby farm lands. They had come to the city at a time when new industrial processes were successfully undercutting the formerly well-paid, prestigious craftworkers and shifting unchallenged civic leadership to the business community. The Rotary and Kiwanis culture was rapidly becoming both lord and symbol of the small cities. So too was the pursuit of status in the form of conspicuous consumption which Sinclair Lewis presented so forcefully that the titles of his books *Main Street* and *Babbit* became an unflattering part of the American language. Common values joined Lewis's prototypic town of Gopher Prairie and Muncie's bustling, boosting, 35,000 population; and perhaps most acutely in Muncie, the former deep sense of community was being lost in the newly dominant worlds of business and consumption. When a movement came along that could bring men together to seek aggressively the older community, it might well have great power. Such a force was the Ku Klux Klan during its brief life in the early and middle twenties.

The Ku Klux Klan, which had become a folk legend in the South as the savior of a downtrodden people during Reconstruction, was revived as a fraternal organization in 1915 by an ex-Methodist minister, "Colonel" William J. Simmons. Like many such orders, it was restricted to white, native-born Protestants, and Simmons expected it to have a mild success in southeastern United States. Its purposes were in-group gregariousness and money-making. It was not originally intended to be particularly anti-Negro or anti-anybody else. However, in the hands of skilled fraternal salesmen, operating in times still touched by wartime conformity, animosities, and restlessness, the Klan spread like a prairie fire up the Mississippi Valley, jumped the mountains to the West Coast, fanned out in the American hinterland, and pushed powerfully toward the North and East. The Klan was the great lodge of the American twenties, a parasite feeding upon the gregarious, xenophobic, small-town, old-stock American subculture.

While its main appeal was togetherness and excitement, its cause and its cohesiveness derived from nativism. The hundreds of thousands who flocked to the Klan had found their society changing and disturbing, and they sought a personified explanation. Who was at fault? Presidents Warren G. Harding and Calvin Coolidge were hardly active forces for change, nor was the Supreme Court, while Congress was safely Protestant and Masonic. It never occurred to the Klansmen to blame it all on structural steel, the dynamo, and the internal-combustion engine; the Klan's answer was conspiracy. It appealed to the uneasy feeling that the American way of life was under attack. The aggressor was identified as the unassimilable alien outsider, primarily the Southern and Eastern European immigrant, particularly the Roman Catholic, and then the Jew and the Negro. The highly fragmented American Protestant majority had a persecution complex out of which grew the Ku Klux Klan. The Klansman saw himself as a sentry on guard against alien subversion and the erosion of the old morality in the guise of the roadhouse and urban sin.

The Klan was more than just a small-town organization; the cities, great and small, were being populated by the same native American stock as was to be found in the Ku Klux Klan, and these internal migrants brought their heartland values and their defensiveness with them.

The Klan marched, elected, and terrorized—literally—from Portland, Maine, to Portland, Oregon. It helped to elect at least 16 senators and 11 governors, a number of them members of the hooded order, and reached its peak strength of about two million members in 1924. It was powerful in states such as Ohio, Indiana, Texas, Colorado, and Kansas, as well as Georgia and Alabama, and in cities such as Los Angeles, Indianapolis, Milwaukee, Detroit, Dallas, Denver, and Philadelphia. It was as prone to violence in California's San Joaquin Valley as in the North Carolina piedmont, although never to the extent of its night riding in Texas and Oklahoma.

Although the Klan sought to enforce its version of moral behavior, fought for prohibition and immigration restriction, and strove to keep "the church in the wildwood" and "the little red schoolhouse" American, it had no constructive program. The Klan's underlying meaning lay not in its moral stance or its vigilantism, but in its attempt to explain and resist the changes that had taken place in the national society. Masking defensiveness in an aggressive form, the Klan became, during its period of power, as much a parody of the values it sought to support as any caustic epitaph ever written by H. L. Mencken.

Perhaps if the Klan had grown more slowly and had achieved better leadership, it might have endured as a fraternal order. However, continuous inner conflict over spoils and power, as well as the Klan's general violence and disruptiveness, lost it membership and community support; after 1925, it rapidly declined.

The high level of bitterness that marked the social conflicts of the 1920s was indicated by the degree which intellectuals proclaimed their loss of faith and interest in popular government and traditional values, and by the degree to which Yankee-Protestant rural and village America felt itself isolated, under attack, and—somehow—losing. This schism within the culture represented a national loss of security and direction in the face of great social change.

Many of the value drives of American life in the 20th century seemed to converge on prohibition. Fundamentalist attack on "evil," southern uneasiness over the Negro, midwestern nativist distrust of the immigrant, the organizational fervor of the Women's Christian Temperance Union, and the political single-mindedness of the Anti-Saloon League combined with the opposition of middle-class social workers and progressives to the corrupting influence of the saloon and the liquor interests. The evangelical need to make men good and the progressive belief that law could be used to change the outer environment and thus reshape the inner one joined to drive alcohol from national life.

By the beginning of World War I, local option or outright prohibition had swept the states. The national movement acted with the wartime need for foodstuffs and willingness to accept sacrifices to produce the Lever Act, halting the production of liquor during the emergency. The 18th Amendment to the Constitution sought to make prohibition permanent. But what was begun as a noble experiment to redeem mankind soon became a defensive cause and symbol of the old village morality—bolstered by the Methodist, Episcopal, and Baptist churches—against urban, immigrant citadels controlled by rum and Rome. As Andrew Sinclair pointed out in *Prohibition: The Era of Excess* (1962), prohibition left no room for temperance and appealed to the psychology of excess in both its supporters and its opponents. From the beach counties of New Jersey and the rural southern tier of New York State to the delta country of Illinois and the plains of Oklahoma, Klansmen rallied to the defense of a dry America. In 1924, for the first time, the Prohibition Party added planks on the Americanization of aliens and on the Bible to its platform. By the midtwenties, prohibition had moved from the camp of optimistic, idealistic reform to that of defensive fundamentalism.

Although Klansmen often marched down church aisles while the choirs sang "Onward, Christian Soldiers," and listened with bowed heads while ministers intoned Romans 12:1 or sermonized about the evils of drink, the defense of Protestant fundamentals against the corrosive doctrines of modernism and Darwinism was the great issue that raged around many pulpits and schools. It was somewhat difficult to fuel general protest against modernism alone, for it did emphasize the transcendence of the ethical and moral nature of Jesus' ministry. Evolutionary doctrines, however, conflicted with the biblical story of creation and the uniqueness of man as the center of God's concern. Further, it offered both ape and Darwin as suitably graphic antagonists. The loss of confidence and sense of security that increasingly afflicted rural and small-town America made many of its churches a defensive battlement for religion and morality. Leading *his* people for the last time against a corrupting urban East which had always rejected him, William Jennings Bryan devoted himself to defending the "Blood of the Lamb" against that of "the beast."

Although, in one form or another, Oklahoma, Florida, North Carolina, Texas, Louisiana, Missouri, and Arkansas also restricted the teaching of evolution, Tennessee's law of 1925 gained national attention. The state legislature, over the supine silence of the University of Tennessee, made it illegal to teach "any theory that denies the story of the divine creation of man as taught in the Bible, and to teach instead that man descended from a lower order of animals." Having discussed the situation over ice-cream sodas at the local drugstore in the small town of Dayton, a young high school teacher named John Thomas Scopes taught his class that "the earth was once a hot molten mass" which had cooled sufficiently for a "little germ of one-cell organism" to form, and that the organism "kept on evolving and from this was man."

The American Civil Liberties Union sent counsel, including the nation's most famous defense lawyer, Clarence Darrow, to defend Scopes, and William Jennings Bryan came up from Florida to help the prosecution. When the judge refused to let the defense use expert testimony to support the evolutionary hypothesis, Bryan permitted himself to be called to the stand to be cross-examined on the Bible. The high drama of a battle over the book of Genesis was exciting but inconclusive— and Bryan's death a few days after the trial deprived fundamentalism of its national champion. As with the declining membership of the Klan and the effect of prohibition, fundamentalism remained more a memorial pillar than a victorious arch to the one-time moral hegemony of old-stock, Yankee-Protestant America.

The frustration of rural and small-town America and the emergence of an urban society did not mean sudden political revolution or the emergence of a cosmopolitan cultural synthesis. The inflow of city dwellers, both from immigrant ships and from the farm, created conglomerates rather than a new politically conscious community. However, a crucial long-run political shift was under way. On the national scene it was appropriate that in Al Smith, New York City should produce the first truly big-city candidate for President. Smith was wet, Roman Catholic, only one generation away from his mother's Irish soil, and had come up through the Tammany machine from the Lower East Side's Fulton Fish Market. In defeating him in 1928, Iowa-born Herbert Hoover broke the hitherto solid South and carried all but 6 of the 48 states. Nevertheless, by the late 1920s the sons and daughters of the new immigration from southern and eastern Europe were reaching voting age. Across the nation, major cities which had earlier cast their vote for Harding and Coolidge were moving into the Democratic column, while Klansmen, fundamentalists, and prohibitionists helped to contribute to Republican successes in the North and Midwest.

For the business community, whether in Muncie or New York City, the clash and confusion of values did not dilute a high sense of optimism. Herbert Hoover, America's outstanding Secretary of Commerce, was pushing trade associations and writing that "American individualism" depended upon cooperation and upon the reduction of the great wastes of "over-reckless competition." The businessman's self-image was not one of conservatism, but of innovation, with technology and business leadership producing never-ending prosperity. On the whole, the social scientists, led by Charles A. Beard and Mary Beard, the economist Wesley C. Mitchell, the psychologist James M. Watson, and the educator John Dewey, agreed on the potential of enlightened social intelligence. In their intensive study of Muncie, the Lynds maintained that tensions and other social problems developed because habit and institutions lagged unreasonably behind technology.

It was not the social scientists but the expressive intellectuals who sensed society's deeper fault lines in the 1920s. If rural, small-town America felt something slipping away, the artists, writers, and critics maintained that developments had not gone far enough. Intellectuals of the Progressive Era had believed in progress and morality, both natural and environmental, and had looked to and worked for the improvement of society. They had found in the people, as a mass, and in government, instruments which they trusted. The trauma of war, the peace that was not a peace, the prejudice of the masses, the misuse of government, and the materialism of America's business civilization led to a sense of alienation that Freud's teachings fostered and to which the cities gave refuge.

Intellectuals blamed their loss on the traditional establishment culture of America, which they denounced as stifling, repressive, and firmly intrenched in the puritanism of the American village. Ludwig Lewisohn spoke for many of the alienated when he asked: "What will you say to a man who believes in hell, or that the Pope in Rome wants to run the country or that the Jews caused the war? How would you argue with a Methodist minister from an Arkansas village, with a Kleagle of the Klan, with a 'this-is-a-white-man's-country' politician from central Georgia?" Seeking freedom in escape and exile, the intellectuals fled to Greenwich Village, or to the Left Bank, or into a world of art which was dedicated not to society but to private experience.

The old American belief in progress, the people, and the neighborliness of the small town once had been the strength and the refuge of American society; now the urbanites rejected it. Led by Sherwood Anderson in *Winesburg, Ohio* (1919), Sinclair Lewis in *Main Street* (1920) and *Babbit* (1922), and H. L. Mencken in the *Smart Set* and the *American Mercury*, they flayed the idea that "the people" could save themselves or were worth saving. The most powerful army of creative artistic talent assembled since the days of Henry Thoreau and Herman Melville, chief among them being Ezra Pound and T. S. Eliot, Ernest Hemingway and William Faulkner, Scott Fitzgerald and Eugene O'Neill, E. E. Cummings and Hart Crane, found that their private paths led toward no American dream. Their alienation marked the passing of the old America. As Thomas Wolfe would show in his later description of the 20's, *You Can't Go Home Again* (1940), they had sensed that the dynamic forces and the home of America was no longer in the countryside.

SUGGESTED READINGS

CHALMERS, DAVID M. *Hooded Americanism: The First Century of the Klu Klux Klan.* New York: Doubleday & Co., 1965.

FITE, GILBERT C. *George N. Peek and the Fight for Farm Parity.* Norman: University of Oklahoma Press, 1954.

FURNISS, NORMAN F. *The Fundamentalist Controversy, 1918–1931.* New Haven: Yale University Press, 1954.

HICKS, JOHN D. *Republican Ascendancy, 1921–1933.* New York: Harper & Bros., 1960.

JACKSON, KENNETH T. *The Klu Klux Klan in the City, 1915–1930.* New York: Oxford University Press, 1967.

LEUCHTENBURG, WILLIAM E. *The Perils of Prosperity, 1914–1932.* Chicago: University of Chicago Press, 1958.

LEVINE, LAWRENCE W. *Defender of the Faith, William Jennings Bryan: The Last Decade, 1915–1925.* New York: Oxford University Press, 1965.

LYND, ROBERT S., and LYND, HELEN M. *Middletown: A Study in American Culture.* New York: Harcourt, Brace & Co., 1929.

MAY, HENRY F. *The End of American Innocence.* New York: Alfred A. Knopf, 1959.

NASH, RODERICK, *The Nervous Generation: American Thought, 1917–1930.* Chicago: Rand McNally & Co., 1970.

PLESUR, MILTON (ed.), *The 1920's: Problems and Paradoxes.* Boston: Allyn & Bacon, Inc., 1969.

PRESIDENT'S RESEARCH COMMITTEE ON SOCIAL TRENDS. *Recent Social Trends in the United States.* New York: McGraw-Hill Co., 1933.

SALOUTOS, THEODORE, and HICKS, JOHN D. *Agricultural Discontent in the Middle West, 1900–1939.* Madison: University of Wisconsin Press, 1951.

SINCLAIR, ANDREW. *Prohibition: The Era of Excess.* Boston: Little, Brown & Co., 1962.

STEIN, MAURICE R. *The Eclipse of Community.* Princeton: Princeton University Press, 1960.

VEBLEN, THORSTEIN. *Absentee Ownership and Business Enterprise in Recent Times.* New York: B. W. Huebsch, Inc., 1923.

DOCUMENT 28.1
Immigration Restriction*

With the passage of the National Origins Act of 1924, the United States made the restriction of immigration its national policy. People from most of Asia were excluded, and a quota system was set up which heavily favored Northwestern

---

*Source: *Congressional Record*, April 16–28, 1924, pp. 6461–62, 6464–65, 6468, 6537, 6545.

Europe. A yearly limit of 164,000 persons of origin outside the Western Hemisphere was set. In the Senate debate over the act, a sense of belligerent insecurity underlay many of the arguments.

Mr. SHIELDS. [Tenn.] Mr. President, the future immigration policy of the United States is challenging the most serious attention of the American people. They demand that this policy be changed from one of practically the open door to all peoples of the world to one of rigid restriction if not absolute prohibition of immigration. . . . The immigrants we are receiving to-day are of different character from those that came in the early history of our country, and the great numbers in which they are arriving is a cause of serious alarm and menaces the purity of the blood, the homogeneity, and the supremacy of the American people and the integrity and perpetuity of our representative form of government. . . .

The great majority of the present-day immigrants do not, like the old ones, distribute themselves over the States, mingle with and become absorbed in the great body of American people, and build homes, cultivate lands, or, in other words, become permanent and loyal American citizens. They do not have the social characteristics of the original stock. They are not assimilable and do not seem to desire to be assimilated. They bring with them lower standards of living and labor conditions and strange customs and ideals of social justice and government. Civil and religious liberty do not attract them, but they come here to enjoy our prosperity and possess the country our forefathers redeemed from the wilderness and improved as none other in the world.

They largely congregate in cities and form communities of their several foreign nationalities; they speak their own languages and train their children to do so. . . . [M]ore than half of them remain unnaturalized and owe allegiance to foreign governments. . . There are whole wards in New York and Chicago where the English language is seldom heard and no newspapers printed in it read. . . .

Mr. President, these undesirable immigrants are seriously endangering the peace and tranquillity of our people and the supremacy of our laws and Government. . . . There are many who are intolerant of all restraint and all law and would introduce into this country the wildest doctrines of Bolshevism. We get the majority of the communists, the I.W.W.'s, the dynamiters, and the assassins of public officers from the ranks of the present-day immigrant. . . .

Mr. GEORGE. [Georgia] . . . So, Mr. President, there were two evils. One was presented in the sheer number of immigrants coming, and the other in the character and in the class of immigrants coming. About 1880, and certainly as late as 1890, as I have just said, the immigrant coming to this country established his own quarter; he established his own section; he established his own institutions; he established his own printing presses. In fact, he solidified himself, and out of his solidity grew a form, consciously or unconsciously, of aggression; and this was precisely the cause of the restless and unhappy mood and attitude of the old or native stock. . . .

Mr. KING. [Utah] Does not the Senator think . . . that the fact that the immigrant . . . rather isolated himself from the mass of the American people, resulted largely because of the exclusive manifestations of the native populations? . . . We assumed . . . a superiority over them; and the tendency of our manifestations was to make them herd together, to become gregarious, because they felt that we were drawing a line of cleavage between the American citizen, the native born, and the immigrant. Does not the Senator think that much of the situation is due to the failure of the people of the United States to adopt a proper attitude toward the immigrant, to provide means of Americanization, and to prove legitimate and proper means more quickly to assimilate the immigrant into the social organism? . . .

Mr. REED. [Mo.] . . . There has not been a race of men who have ever established themselves upon this earth but have assumed that they were God's chosen children. They have set up barriers against the stranger. In the savage days they imprisoned him or slaughtered him if he entered within their domains; and just in proportion as they adhered to that narrow policy they have circumscribed their own well-being and limited their own development; and just in proportion as nations have recognized the fact that they are only one of the great family of nations, just in proportion as they have generously opened their doors to the peoples of other countries, have nations grown into magnitude and power. . . .

Mr. SHEPPARD. [Texas] . . . As long as a stream of migrating peoples rushes over the gangways of the ships that bear them from other lands to this they produce a swirling, turbulent, disordered mass that is never permitted to reach an angle of racial, political, intellectual, or spiritual repose. While fertile lands in public or in private possession remained available on fairly easy terms and while the cities were still small the new accessions were distributed with a minimum of disturbance and maladjustment. With the disappearance, however, of the public-land frontier, the rise in price and the almost complete occupation of the habitable, cultivable, and readily obtainable areas until they are beyond the reach of the masses, who have only their labor to exchange, the extensive concentration of people in the factory districts and the cities, a condition has developed whereby the American standard of living . . . is being seriously imperiled, and whereby the discord and the turmoil of former years are rendered tenfold more dangerous and intense. . . .

Mr. HEFLIN. [Alabama] . . . Mr. President, down at Fort Mims, in my State . . . there was a fort in which the white people of that section dwelt. . . . [T]here was a

big gate in the wall around the fort, and when they closed that mighty gate to this walled-in place they were safe from the Indians. But they grew careless and indifferent, as some Americans have done on this question. One day . . . one of the girls living in the houses within this inclosure, looked down and saw the big gate open, and she said, "Who left that gate open?" They said, "That don't make any difference. There isn't an Indian in 50 miles of here." . . . Just then a little white boy . . . ran through the open gate and said, "I saw a man down by the river side with red paint on his face and feathers in his hair." They screamed with one voice, "Indians! Close the gates!" They started with a rush to the gate, but the Red Eagle, with his Creek warriors, had already entered. It was too late! Too late! . . . With the exception of two or three prisoners, they massacred the whole white population at Fort Mims.

I am appealing to the Senate of the Unites States to close the gates, close them now while we can. If we do not close them now, the time will come when we will be unable to close them at all. And in that sad day we will cry in vain, "Close the gates."

DOCUMENT 28.2

How the Ku Klux Klan Saw Things*

In 1922 a *coup d'etat* in the Imperial Palace of the Ku Klux Klan, on Peachtree Street, in Atlanta, Georgia, replaced "Colonel" William J. Simmons with a Dallas, Texas, dentist named Hiram Wesley Evans. Although they had differed over the best way to develop the full financial possibilities of the Klan and over who was to enjoy

---

*Source: Hiram Wesley Evans, "The Klan's Fight for Americanism," *North American Review*, March 1926, pp. 38–39.

the profits and the power, there was basic agreement about the menace that threatened America.

The Klan, therefore, has now come to speak for the great mass of Americans of the old pioneer stock. We believe that it does fairly and faithfully represent them, and our proof lies in their support. To understand the Klan, then, it is necessary to understand the character and present mind of the mass of old-stock Americans. The mass, it must be remembered, as distinguished from the intellectually mongrelized "Liberals."

These are, in the first place, a blend of various peoples of the so-called Nordic race, the race which, with all its faults, has given the world almost the whole of modern civilization. The Klan does not try to represent any people but these. . . .

In spite of it, however, these Nordic Americans for the last generation have found themselves increasingly uncomfortable, and finally deeply distressed. There appeared first confusion in thought and opinion, a groping and hesitancy about national affairs and the private life alike, in sharp contrast to the clear, straightforward purposes of our earlier years. There was futility in religion, too, which was in many ways even more distressing. Presently we began to find that we were dealing with strange ideas; policies that always sounded well, but somehow always made us still more uncomfortable.

Finally came the moral breakdown that has been going on for two decades. One by one all our traditional moral standards went by the boards, or were so disregarded that they ceased to be binding. The sacredness of our Sabbath, of our homes, of chastity, and finally even of our right to teach our own children in our own schools fundamental facts and truths were torn away from us. Those who maintained the old standards did so only in the face of constant ridicule.

Along with this went economic distress.

The assurance for the future of our children dwindled. We found our great cities and the control of much of our industry and commerce taken over by strangers, who stacked the cards of success and prosperity against us. Shortly they came to dominate our government. The *bloc* system by which this was done is now familiar to all. Every kind of inhabitant except the Americans gathered in groups which operated as units in politics, under orders of corrupt, self-seeking and un-American leaders, who both by purchase and threat enforced their demands on politicians. Thus it came about that the interests of Americans were always the last to be considered by either national or city governments, and that the native Americans were constantly discriminated against, in business, in legislation and in administrative government.

So the Nordic American today is a stranger in large parts of the land his fathers gave him. . . .

DOCUMENT 28.3
H. L. Mencken on Prohibition*

The most caustic critic of rural and small-town America was the outspoken Baltimore newspaperman, H. L. Mencken. His basic Nietzschean distrust of the people, or the "yokels," as he liked to call them, made his journal, the *American Mercury*, required reading for the "in" set during the 1920s.

. . . [T]he issue of Prohibition emerges as the only one that the voters of the Republic are really interested in, and under it lies the issue of city or country hegemony. The yokels, it seems to me, are in for a drubbing, if not in November, then in some November not far ahead. The

*Source: H.L. Mencken, *A Carnival of Buncombe*, ed. Malcolm Moos (Baltimore: Johns Hopkins Press, 1956), pp. 160–61, 163.

trouble with them is that they have lost all their old-time leaders to the towns, and are now led by a rabble of frauds and fanatics. The typical American statesman of the better sort, in the early days of the Republic, was a country gentleman. But now he is a city man—born on a farm, perhaps, but raised on hard paving-stones, and with urban prejudices in his blood.

The yokels hang on because old apportionments give them unfair advantages. The vote of a malarious peasant on the lower Eastern Shore counts as much as the votes of twelve Baltimoreans. But that can't last. It is not only unjust and undemocratic; it is absurd. For the lowest city proletarian, even though he may be farm-bred, is at least superior to the yokel. He has had enterprise enough to escape from the cow and the plow, and he has enjoyed contact with relatively enlightened men. He knows a great deal more than the rustic, and his tastes are more civilized. In the long run he is bound to revolt against being governed from the dung-hill.

His refusal to accept Prohibition is the first sign of that revolt. Prohibition is essentially a yokel idea. It mirrors alike the farmer's fear of himself and his envy of city men. Unable to drink at all without making a hog of himself, he naturally hates those who can. When a city man goes on a grand drunk the police take charge of him humanely and he is restrained from doing any great damage. The worst that happens to him is that his wife beats him and he loses his job. But when a farmer succumbs to the jug his unmilked cows burst, his hogs and chickens starve, his pastor denounces him as an atheist (or even an Episcopalian), and he is ruined. Thus he favors Prohibition, especially if he is given to heavy drinking —first because he hopes it will protect him against himself, and secondly because it harasses his superior and enemy, the city man.

There are, of course, Prohibitionists in the cities also, but they are not numerous, and most of them will be found, on inspec-tion, to be defectively assimilated yokels. The more intelligent countrymen, escaping to the cities, become urbanized very rapidly, and some of them take on a high polish. But there are others so dumb that it is impossible to civilize them, and they continue to be yokels. Baltimore houses a great many such poor nitwits. They support the Hell-fire ecclesiastics who survive among us, and are run amuck by Klan whisperings in every campaign. The time will come when the emancipated cities will send such morons back to the country.

. . . Once the cities have liberated themselves from yokel rule, civilization will be free to develop in the United States. Today it is woefully hobbled by the ideas of peasants. We have many huge and grandiose villages, but, with the possible exception of New York and San Francisco, we have no cities. When an American, acquiring money, feels a yearning for civilized living, he has to go abroad. That is surely not a sound state of affairs. No one wants to civilize the peasant against his will, but it is plainly against reason to let him go on riding his betters.

DOCUMENT 28.4

William Jennings Bryan Defends the Faith*

Throughout his political life, William Jennings Bryan combined a struggle for political success with belief in a Christian moral order. In his earlier career he fought against the attempts of corporate wealth to undo that order, and in the 1920s he came to believe that science and a secular urban society were undercutting its religious foundations. In his last years he led the fundamentalist battle to protect biblical

*Source: William Jennings Bryan, *The Menace of Darwinism* (New York: Fleming H. Revell Co., 1922), pp. 15–17, 22–23, 49–51.

truths from being undermined in the schools by the doctrines and followers of Darwinism.

When the mainspring is broken a watch ceases to be useful as a timekeeper. A handsome case may make it still an ornament and the parts may have a market value, but it cannot serve the purpose of a watch. There is that in each human life that corresponds to the mainspring of a watch—that which is absolutely necessary if the life is to be what it should be, a real life and not a mere existence. That necessary thing is a *belief in God.* . . .

. . . If there is at work in the world today anything that tends to break this mainspring, it is the duty of the moral, as well as the Christian, world to combat this influence in every possible way.

I believe there is such a menace to fundamental morality. The hypothesis to which the name of Darwin has been given —the hypothesis that links man to the lower forms of life and makes him a lineal descendant of the brute—is obscuring God and weakening all the virtues that rest upon the religious tie between God and man. . . .

Science has rendered invaluable service to society; her achievements are innumerable—and the hypotheses of scientists should be considered with an open mind. Their theories should be carefully examined and their arguments fairly weighted, but the scientist cannot compel acceptance of any argument he advances, except as, judged upon its merits, it is convincing. Man is infinitely more than science; science, as well as the Sabbath, was made for man. It must be remembered, also that all sciences are of equal importance. Tolstoy insists that the science of "How to Live" is more important than any other science, and is this not true? It is better to trust in the Rock of Ages, than to know the age of the rocks; it is better for none to know that he is close to the Heavenly Father, than to know how far the stars in the heavens are apart. And is it not just as im-

portant that the scientists who deal with matter should respect the scientists who deal with spiritual things, as that the latter should respect the former? If it be true, as Paul declares, that "the things that are seen are temporal" while "the things that are unseen are eternal," why should those who deal with temporal things think themselves superior to those who deal with the things that are eternal? Why should the Bible, which the centuries have not been able to shake, be discarded for scientific works that have to be revised and corrected every few years? The preference should be given to the Bible.

The two lines of work are parallel. There should be no conflict between the discoverers of *real* truths, because real truths do not conflict. Every truth harmonizes with every other truth, but why should an hypothesis, suggested by a scientist, be accepted as true until its truth is established? Science should be the last to make such a demand because science to be truly science is classified knowledge; it is the explanation of facts. Tested by this definition, Darwinism is not science at all; it is guesses strung together. There is more science in the twenty-fourth verse of the first chapter of Genesis (And God said, let the earth bring forth the living creature after his kind, cattle and creeping things, and beast of the earth after his kind; and it was so.) than in all that Darwin wrote. . . .

. . . At the University of Wisconsin (so a Methodist preacher told me) a teacher told his class that the Bible was a collection of myths. When I brought the matter to the attention of the President of the University, he criticized me but avoided all reference to the Professor. At Ann Arbor a professor argued with students against religion and asserted that no thinking man could believe in God or the Bible. At Columbia (I learned this from a Baptist preacher) a professor began his course in geology by telling his class to throw away all that they had learned in the Sunday school. There is a professor in Yale of whom it is said that no one leaves his class a believer in God. (This came from a young man who told me that his brother was being led away from the Christian faith by this professor.) A father (a Congressman) tells me that a daughter on her return from Wellesley told him that nobody believed in the Bible stories now. . . .

I submit three propositions for the consideration of the Christians of the nation:

First, preachers who break the bread of life to lay members should believe that man has in him the breath of the Almighty, as the Bible declares—not the blood of the brute, as the evolutionists affirm. He should also believe in the virgin birth of the Saviour.

Second, none but Christians in good standing and with spiritual conception of life should be allowed to teach in Christian schools. Church schools are worse than useless if they bring students under the influence of those who do not believe in the religion upon which the Church and church schools are built. Atheism and agnosticism are more dangerous when hidden under the cloak of religion than when they are exposed to view.

Third, the tax-payers should prevent the teaching in the public schools of atheism, agnosticism, Darwinism, or any other hypothesis that links man in blood relationship with the brutes. Christians build their own colleges in which to teach Christianity; let atheists and agnostics build their own schools in which to teach their doctrines—whether they call it atheism, agnosticism, or a scientific interpretation of the Bible.

If it is contended that an instructor has a right to teach anything he likes, I reply that the tax-payers must decide what shall be taught. The hand that writes the pay check rules the school. . . . [A] person can expose himself to the smallpox if he desires to do so, but he has no right to communicate it to others. So a man can believe anything he pleases but he has no right to teach it against the protest of his employers. . . .

DOCUMENT 28.5
Cultural Lag*

Middletown: A Study in American Culture was a complete inventory and analysis of the American small city, here represented by Muncie, Indiana. Still regarded as a major milestone in American sociology, it presented the clash between the old and new in a changing society.

. . . It is apparent that Middletown is carrying on certain . . . habitual pursuits in almost precisely the same manner as a generation ago, while in the performance of others its present methods bear little resemblance to the earlier ones. . . . Getting a living seemingly exhibits the most pervasive change, particularly in its technological and mechanical aspects; leisure time, again most markedly in material developments such as the automobile and motion picture, is almost as mobile; training the young in schools, community activities, and making a home would come third, fourth, and fifth in varying order, depending upon which traits are scrutinized; while, finally on the whole exhibiting least change, come the formal religious activities.

Thus Middletown, due allowance always being made for wide variations in practice within the city, may be observed to employ in the main the psychology of the last century in training its children in the home and the psychology of the current century in persuading its citizens to buy articles from its stores; it may be observed in its courts of law to be commencing to regard individuals as not entirely responsible for their acts, while in its institutional machinery for selling homes, failure to pay, whether due to unemployment, sickness, or other factors, is regarded as a deliberate violation of an agreement voiding all right to consideration; a man may get his living by operating a twentieth-century machine and at the same time hunt for a job under a *laissez-faire* individualism which dates back more than a century; a mother may accept community responsibility for the education of her children but not for the care of their health; she may be living in one era in the way she cleans her house or does her washing and in another in the care of her children or in her marital relations.

. . . Whether one is temperamentally well disposed towards social change or resistant to it, however, the fact remains that Middletown's life exhibits at almost every point either some change or some stress arising from failure to change. . . .

. . . New tools and inventions have been the most prolific breeders of change. They have entered Middletown's industrial life more rapidly than new business and management devices. Bathrooms and electricity have pervaded the homes of the city more rapidly than innovations in the personal adjustments between husband and wife or between parents and children. The automobile has changed the leisure-time life more drastically than have the literature courses taught the young, and tool-using vocational courses have appeared more rapidly in the school curriculum than changes in the arts courses. The development of the linotype and radio are changing the technique of winning political elections more than developments in the art of speech-making or in Middletown's methods of voting. The Y.M.C.A., built about a gymnasium, exhibits more change in Middletown's religious institutions than do the weekly sermons of its ministers or the deliberations of the Ministerial Association. By and large, a new tool or material device, the specific efficacy of which can be tested decisively and impersonally, is fairly certain to be fitted somehow into Middletown's accepted scheme of things, while opposed non-material factors, such as tradition and

sentiment, slowly open up to make room for it. . . .

. . . As Middletown has become reluctantly conscious from time to time of discrepancies in its institutional system it has frequently tended to avoid "doing something about" these "social problems" of "bad times," "the younger generation," "corrupt politics," "housing," "street traffic," and so on, by blaming the difficulty on the "nature of things" or upon the willfulness of individuals. When the "problem" has become so urgent that the community has felt compelled to seek and apply a "remedy," this remedy has tended to be a logical extension of old categories to the new situation, or an emotional defense of the earlier situation with a renewed insistence upon traditional verbal or other symbols, or a stricter enforcement or further elaboration of existing institutional devices: thus difficulties in the business world are met by a greater elaboration of financial devices and by an attempt to apply the familiar individual ethics to corporate activities, increase in crime by an elaboration of the police and court systems or the doubling of penalties, political corruption by harking back to the Constitution in all the schools, by nationwide oratorical contests, by getting more people out to vote, indifference to the church by the forming of more church organizations. . . .

DOCUMENT 28.6

The Small Town as "Dullness Made God"*

Sinclair Lewis' novel about the unsuccessful efforts of a vivacious young wife, named Carol Kennicott, to bring vitality and culture to the mythical midwestern town of Gopher Prairie was taken up in the 1920s as the classic description of

*Source: Sinclair Lewis, *Main Street* (New York: Harcourt, Brace & Co., 1920), pp. 264–65. Copyright 1920 by Harcourt Brace Jovanovich, Inc.; copyright 1948, by Sinclair Lewis. Reprinted by permission of the publisher.

the philistine monotony of small-town America.

In reading popular stories and seeing plays, asserted Carol, she had found only two traditions of the American small town. The first tradition, repeated in scores of magazines every month, is that the American village remains the one sure abode of friendship, honesty, and clean sweet marriageable girls. Therefore all men who succeed in painting in Paris or in finance in New York at last become weary of smart women, return to their native towns, assert that cities are vicious, marry their childhood sweethearts and, presumably, joyously abide in those towns until death.

The other tradition is that the significant features of all villages are whiskers, iron dogs upon lawns, gold bricks, checkers, jars of gilded cattails, and shrewd comic old men who are known as "hicks" and who ejaculate "Waal I swan." This altogether admirable tradition rules the vaudeville stage, facetious illustrators, and syndicated newspaper humor, but out of actual life it passed forty years ago. Carol's small town thinks not in hoss-swapping but in cheap motor cars, telephones, ready-made clothes, silos, alfalfa, kodaks, phonographs, leather-upholstered Morris chairs, bridge-prizes, oil-stocks, motion-pictures, land-deals, unread sets of Mark Twain, and a chaste version of national politics.

With such a small-town life a Kennicott or a Champ Perry is content, but there are also hundreds of thousands, particularly women and young men, who are not at all content. The more intelligent young people (and the fortunate widows!) flee to the cities with agility and, despite the fictional tradition, resolutely stay there, seldom returning even for holidays. The most protesting patriots of the towns leave them in old age, if they can afford it, and go to live in California or in the cities.

The reason, Carol insisted, is not a whiskered rusticity. It is nothing so amusing!

It is an unimaginatively standardized background, a sluggishness of speech and manners, a rigid ruling of the spirit by the desire to appear respectable. It is contentment ... the contentment of the quiet dead, who are scornful of the living for their restless walking. It is negation canonized as the one positive virtue. It is the prohibition of happiness. It is slavery self-sought and self-defended. It is dullness made God.

A savorless people, gulping tasteless food, and sitting afterward, coatless and thoughtless, in rocking-chairs prickly with inane decorations, listening to mechanical music, saying mechanical things about the excellence of Ford automobiles, and viewing themselves as the greatest race in the world.

29 The New Deal

DEAN ALBERTSON
University of Massachusetts

"The story of the New Deal," according to historian Paul K. Conkin, "is a sad story, the ever recurring story of what might have been." In a similar vein Rexford Guy Tugwell, one of the New Deal's major architects, has written recently: "At some moments I thought Roosevelt saw how radical a reconstruction was called for; at others I guessed he would temporize.... I was right in this last. The New Deal was mild medicine.... [Roosevelt] could have emerged from the orthodox progressive chrysalis and led us into a new world. He chose rather rickety repairs for an old one."

Was the crisis of 1933 of such awesome proportion that the President of the United States could have done anything he wanted to do? How well did business leaders, government administrators, and the people, understand the changing nature of American capitalism during the era of the New Deal? In judging the New Deal, should we accept Roosevelt's statement that it ended prior to 1941, or should we regard the entire 12 years of Roosevelt's Presidency as relevant to the assessment? Finally, to what extent do the social and economic problems of the 1970s have their roots in the accomplishments or failures of Roosevelt's New Deal administrations?

For many Americans of today's New Left, the New Deal was a total failure in that it preserved the market economy and paved the way for the coming of an alleged Pentagon "state-managed" economy.

For a larger number of Americans styled as liberals, New Deal reforms fortunately shored up an ailing capitalism and rescued democratic structures which were seriously threatened by fascism or communism or both.

For a minority of conservative older Americans, the New Deal's movement toward today's welfare capitalism and a semimanaged economy were nothing less than "creeping socialism." Accordingly, Roosevelt was a "traitor to his class."

For black Americans, who under New Deal relief programs were treated not unlike other poor people, the Roosevelt regime was an improvement over past administrations; yet, in retrospect, New Deal politics and policies had little effect in mitigating, let alone eliminating, racism in the United States.

President Herbert Hoover in his inaugural address on March 4, 1929, could observe with equanimity that "Through liberation from widespread poverty we have reached a higher degree of individua' freedom than ever before.... In no nation are the fruits of accomplishment more secure." Less than eight months later, the great speculative bull market broke, and the U. S. economy spiraled down into the reaches of depression more pervasive and terrifying than had ever been known.

Hoover understood capitalism in all it

248

parts. As Secretary of Commerce under Warren Harding and Calvin Coolidge, he had helped build the system. And the system which he envisaged was a capitalism emergent from the rapacious days of laissez-faire, and governed—on behalf of business, labor, and "the people"—by a national administration which served as an impartial umpire. The whole conception depended upon all three groups coming together in a sense of a voluntarily self-governing "American community."

And what were the corporate interests building in the twenties? Even then the dim outlines of a conceptualized "monster machine" had appeared. Henry Ford's cars were rolling off the assembly line at a rate of well over two million a year, and as President Coolidge presciently noted, "The business of America was business." But people in Muncie, Indiana, were working harder than ever for diminishing satisfactions: male factory workers (in 1924) had a 1 in 424 chance of promotion; females earned a third less than males for comparable work; and only 15 percent of Muncie's families earned enough to pay an income tax. If Muncie's experience was typical, millions of Americans, ironically, were excluded from the benefits of the nation's vaunted consumption-oriented economy.

And there were other indications that American capitalism was less than healthy. Despite a rising national income (from $60.7 billion in 1922 to $87.2 billion in 1929), 26 million of the total 27.5 million American families earned less than $2,500 per year, which in 1929 was deemed necessary for a decent standard of living. As technological efficiency increased, production and profits rose. Between 1922 and 1929 managerial profit and dividends increased a hundredfold. During the same period, as American Federation of Labor leadership sought to convince management of its true conservatism and devotion to capitalism, Federation membership dropped from 5.1 million to 3.4 million. Thus was management able to keep down the wages of people who were magically expected to consume the goods which were produced in profusion. It was perfectly clear that technology had brought capitalism to its post-scarcity phase in America in the twenties and yet, in order to preserve capitalism itself, scarcity continued to be artificially maintained. It was no longer a matter of having to work in order to consume—it had become a matter of having to work for wages in order to buy goods at a price which yielded profits. Few Americans perceived an alternative.

Out of the glut of profits arose the speculative mania of the twenties. It began in real estate, spearheaded by ever-increasing lines of automobiles bound nightly for the suburbs over newly constructed macadam roads. Then it shifted to the stock market. During 1927 and into 1928 the market advanced—Radio Corporation of America from 85 to 420, Montgomery Ward from 117 to 440, DuPont from 310 to 525. By the beginning of 1929 a rising tide of prosperity, a New Era, bloomed for the thin stratum of upper middle-class families earning more than $2,500 per year. As the number of investment trusts increased, so did the activity of commercial banks in granting broker's loans. Buying stock on margin came to be a common gambit in fortune winning. One paid a small percentage of the stock price in cash, financing the remainder with a broker's loan at 12 percent interest. From 1927 to 1929, broker's loans rose from $3.4 billion to $8.5 billion, or roughly 8 percent of the gross national product value. Brokers' loans seemed at the time so comparatively risk-free that some corporations began to invest their surplus funds in them.

Meanwhile, the perils of a runaway market were known to Herbert Hoover. His choice, on assuming office, was to ease the market down in March 1929—or to let it plunge to its end. He could have publicly warned against further speculation. He could have asked for legislation curbing brokers' loans and margin buying. He could have suggested that the Federal Reserve System raise the rediscount rate. He did none of these things. And on "Black Thursday," October 24, 1929, nearly 13 million stock shares were traded at prices ruinous to their former owners. Five days later, over 16 million shares crossed the counter, and within a few weeks the devastation would be computed at a 40 percent decline in stock values. That elusive quality called "business confidence," so crucial to the proper functioning of a capitalistic economy, had been lost. Businesses cut inventories. Industry shelved expansion plans. American investment abroad was curtailed.

For the remaining three years of his administration, Herbert Hoover pleaded in vain for the shock of depression to fall on profits, not on wages. He begged his ideal "community" to look after its own—to solve nationwide depression locally and to disdain an enslaving federal bureaucracy. And he undertook, more than any other President before him, to use federal money and power to combat economic adversity. Indeed, the encouragement given to trade associations prefigured Roosevelt's National Recovery Act, and Hoover's Agricultural Marketing Act and the Reconstruction Finance Corporation Act were harbingers of major New Deal legislation. Such measures suggest a continuity between the Hoover and Roosevelt administrations. But Hoover's efforts more often than not consisted of government loans to big businesses and banks, leaving the President prey to Democratic Party propaganda that he was a heartless, unfeeling leader. As if to confirm his aloofness from the suffering in July 1932, he loosed the army on several thousand veterans who had come to Washington demanding payment of a World War I bonus.

In the end, all was bootless. American capitalism sank to its knees under the crushing weight of nearly 15 million unemployed.

Franklin Delano Roosevelt stood before thousands of applauding delegates to the Democratic National Convention in Chicago on July 2, 1932, to accept the Presidential nomination which he and his "brains trust" associates had with consummate political skill managed to wrest from the other contenders. When the cheers and the last booming organ notes of "Happy Days Are Here Again" had stilled, the candidate seemed to serve notice of a break with the past. "Throughout the nation," he told them, "men and women, forgotten in the political philosophy of the government of the last years look to us here for guidance and for more equitable opportunity to share in the distribution of national wealth. . . . " And then: "I pledge you, I pledge myself, to a new deal for the American people. Let us all here assembled constitute ourselves prophets of a new order of competence and of courage. This is more than a political campaign; it is a call to arms. . . ."

Roosevelt then made an analysis of past American history, one which was to be the hallmark of New Deal rhetoric for a generation. The partnership of laissez-faire government and buccaneering capitalism may have been contributive to American industrial growth at a time when the nation was filling in its frontiers and creating the mightiest productive machinery on earth. But times had changed. The free land of the frontier was gone. The United States had entered World War I as a debtor nation and emerged as the largest international creditor. Infant industries had matured into complex, engulfing giants, unrestrained either by government or by moral self-regulation. Ownership of land, businesses, and factories (and the concomitant fruits of ownership—economic security, success, prestige and the like) once were available on a small scale for many amidst national abundance. But by the 1930s, ownership was possible on a modest scale for only a few lucky winners. National and international cartels had replaced the family-owned factory. A managerial elite, hired by corporations on annual salaries to manage their affairs, had superseded the plant owner who had known his foreman and most of his workers by their first names.

With such changes as these could democracy and individualism endure by 19th century definitions? These values were thought to be the cornerstones of American greatness. But the old democracy and the old individualism were based on the competitive economics envisioned in Adam Smith's metaphysical "invisible hand" system, which saw society automatically propelling itself toward abundance by simply competing in accordance with the laws of the marketplace—laws which were far beyond the manipulation of mortal men. Clearly, an Industrial Revolution and a managerial revolution had occurred since Adam Smith revealed these "immutable" laws. Most Americans, to be sure, had been encouraged from grade school onward to glorify the virtue and necessity of competition. Could they continue to do so? Could capitalistic competition retain the guiding principle of business and industry when one tenth of 1 percent of American corporations earned nearly half of the net income and owned over half of the assets of all corporations in the United States?

Thus came the New Deal in a period of profound, apathetic despair. But it was not the season for revolution: out of nearly 40 million votes cast in 1932, the socialists and communists combined polled less than a million, and this in face of the fact that one quarter of the entire working force was jobless, their savings often wiped out. State funds for the relief of hunger and destitution were exhausted. Foreclosure and bankruptcy stalked the homes, farms, factories, and businesses of the nation. Iowa corn was being burned for fuel while poverty-stricken urbanites shivered in breadlines. Some people with an eye on the European scene, were talking about a "dictator"—by which they meant a Leader. "All we have to fear is

fear itself," Roosevelt optimistically told them in his inaugural. "Something far more positive than acquiescence vests the President with the authority of a dictator," said newspaperwoman Anne O'Hare McCormick. "There is a country-wide dumping of responsibility on the Federal Government. If Mr. Roosevelt goes on collecting mandates, one after another, until their sum is startling, it is because all the other powers . . . virtually abdicate in his favor. America today literally asks for orders." Yes, the President probably could have done anything he wanted to do!

But Roosevelt came to the Presidency with no clear idea of what should be done. He hated the dole and believed in the morality of a balanced budget. With these dull tools, the tasks ahead were formidable. Clearly, business must be reinvigorated. The jobless must be sustained, then reemployed. The farmer must be raised from the threat of peasantry. Along with the measures for *recovery*, however, the institutions of the economy must be *reformed* so that the tragedy of depression might not again shake the foundations of democracy.

American democracy was said to follow the paths of free enterprise and individual initiative. Roosevelt saw it this way and never wavered. Despite occasional references to socialism by Tugwell and a few other advisors and cries of "Bolshevism" from the hysterical right, a Marxian analysis let alone a solution, of the American situation was never contemplated. That being so, how, then, could a free government wage war on national adversity without wrenching the entire political and economic machinery into such a high degree of centralization as to destroy both freedom and individualism? And what reforms could be carried out which hopefully would prevent depression from recurring and yet not alter the American system as to make it unpalatable to the majority vote required in an essentially conservative nation? In short, what could possibly be new about a New Deal that was locked into the capitalistic mode of production?

During the early years of the New Deal the question emphatically was not whether political democracy still prevailed in the nation. As recently as November 1932, after all, American democracy was sufficiently viable to throw Hoover and the Republicans out of office; presumably it might be used at a later date to visit similar retribution upon the Democrats. Rather the issue concerned the relevance of political democracy to economic democracy. *If*, as New Dealers suggested, a worker was no longer free to choose his job and be reasonably sure of steady employment, *if* a farmer could be told on market day that his crop would bring less than the cost of growing it, *if* the small businessman had as his only alternatives ruinous competition or the sale of his plant to a chain operation, *if* the ordinary citizen had so little control over his destiny that one third of a nation would be "ill-housed, ill-clad, ill-nourished," then of what practical value was the ballot? It was not government, said the New Dealers, which had taken economic liberty. It was the concentrated wealth and power of business and finance, and a fossilized belief in the inexorability of economic law.

To contemporaries the New Deal was incredibly confusing because of its many inconsistencies and the complexity of its proposals. The personality of President Roosevelt himself did little to alleviate the confusion. "There never was a prominent leader, who was more determined about his objectives, and never one who was more flexible about his means," said Tugwell of F.D.R. This very flexibility, this willingness on the part of Roosevelt and the rest of the New Dealers to "tinker with the works," contributed heavily to the unpatterned quality of the New Deal era.

Nonetheless, in retrospect, the goals of the Roosevelt "revolution" emerge with singular clarity—to preserve the dignity of the individual and his right to private property within the context of a capital-istic democratic society. Or, as Secretary of Agriculture Henry A. Wallace would round out the rhetoric, "the New Deal places human rights above property rights and aims to modify special privilege for the few to the extent that such modification will aid in providing economic security for the many." If in tone it made itself appear as a break with past traditions, in content it was a direct line continuum with the progressivism of Theodore Roosevelt and Woodrow Wilson.

The immediate response of the New Deal to the problems it faced was a masterful discernment of the traditional American "middle" way. The new government set about following the only mandate given it by the citizenry—to do *something*! Closed banks were examined, nearly all found to be solvent, and reopened. The gold content of the dollar was reduced and the nation moved to a semi-managed currency. White city boys who volunteered were packed off to the mountains in the dull green uniforms of the Civilian Conservation Corps to hew undergrowth and plant trees. Mild beer and light wines were provided for a thirsty nation while the 21st Amendment to the Constitution made its way among the states. Salaries of government workers were slashed 15 percent across the board. Permissible stock margins were reduced. It was indeed a kaleidoscopic program. The principal themes of New Deal policy lay buried deep within the legislation.

The first major tenet of the early New Deal evoked anguished cries from the conservative right since it embodied *planning*. Rooseveltian planning was basically experimentation rather than the comprehensive planning of a socialist regime. For the prudent householder or the shrewd businessman *not* to plan ahead was considered the height of folly. But, according to the philosophy of conservative businessmen, planning by a government was the first step toward absolute regimentation. "If city planning has been worth while," asked Secretary of the Interior Harold L. Ickes, "why not plan nationally? Why not, for instance, plan so that the ample resources which we have, may be made to go around?" Gloomily replied the deposed Hoover: "This direction must ultimately be reposed in government bureaus and they are comprised of human beings with dictatorial powers over us all." New Deal planning generally meant the formulation of interrelated national programs for rural and urban land use, for human and resource conservation, and for the overcoming of the depression. Contrary to Hoover's dire predictions, local individuals were usually consulted when it came to the implementation of national plans. In nearly all instances they approved the government's proposals, and they were asked to staff and assist in the administration of the resultant bureaucracy, as in the case of the world-renowned Tennessee Valley Authority (TVA).

A second precept of Roosevelt's administrations, deficit financing, caused even greater consternation. Congress gave the President authority to increase the national debt—to use the people's tax money for their benefit at a time when they desperately needed it. Roosevelt had promised to wage war on the depression, and, thus armed, the New Deal called forth what William James termed the "moral equivalents of war." It spent sums which were then thought to be enormous on work relief and public works. To Relief Administrator Harry Hopkins, cynics attributed the apocryphal quotation: "We will tax and tax, spend and spend, elect and elect." But from John Maynard Keynes, the brilliant British economist, came more cheering words: "You, Mr. President, having cast off such fetters [as regarding war to be the sole legitimate excuse for deficit financing], are free to engage in the interests of peace and prosperity the technique which has hitherto only been allowed to serve the purposes of war and destruction." New Deal budgets for

the relief of human suffering between 1933 and 1940 totaled a little over $20 billion. In 1940, the public debt stood at nearly $43 billion. But, it is instructive to note, at the end of World War II, in 1945, the public debt had reached well over $258 billion. American priorities were roughly six times as destructive as constructive.

A third aspect of the early New Deal to provoke cynicism was its idealistic faith in cooperation. If rational, comprehensive planning, use of deficit financing, and invocation of "moral equivalents" could enlist a people to cooperate with its government to fight hunger and poverty, government might utilize the same instruments to achieve an "economic constitutional order." Initially, the Roosevelt administration decided not to attempt ineffectual trustbusting against the concentrated power of finance and industry. Neither would it attack the "economic royalists" head on by socializing major units of industry. The New Deal would *cooperate* with big business to bring about recovery from depression. The National Recovery Administration (NRA) defined the terms of that cooperation. Under NRA auspices, each segment of industry would draw up "codes of fair competition" which would set aside the old Sherman Act injunctions against restraint of trade. Competition of the Adam Smith sort was not obliterated. "It means only," said NRA Administrator Hugh S. Johnson, "that competition must keep its blows above the belt, and that there can be no competition at the expense of decent living." To the relief of profit-minded management, it also meant no real interference with the capitalistic market economy.

Having asserted that government was to be the servant of its constituents, the New Deal was next faced with the promised redistribution of opportunity and wealth. Roosevelt approached this problem with a somewhat different conception of competition, one which existed among such groups as farmers, workers, and small businessmen. He professed to see his constituency as investors or voters or consumers. Such competiton might produce the best chance for economic democracy. Wittingly or not, the New Deal program created, in the words of Reinhold Niebuhr, "the equilibrium of power which is the basis of justice in any society." Competition among large corporations had been rationalized in the earlier Progressive Era, while competition between labor and capital had been an uneven conflict between the financially impotent and the financially powerful, with the influence of government usually thrown toward the latter. Henceforth, it was hoped that the farmers and the unions, as claimants for shares of the national wealth, might address either government or business on more equal terms.

If an equilibrium of power—involving farmers, workers, and businessmen—could endow society with a climate of economic justice, there still remained the average man's desire for economic security. Under terms of pre-World War I progressivism, such security could be had by climbing the ladder of advancement from hired hand to tenant farmer to landholder, or from worker to foreman to partner. The goal in either case was ownership. By the 1930s, it was apparent that the ladder to ownership had lost some of its rungs. Tenancy was increasing. Mobility upward from wages to salary was decreasing. Ownership of the nation's land, productive plants, and service enterprises had become concentrated in fewer and fewer hands. Recognizing that only an infinitesimal number of tenants or workers would ever achieve ownership, New Deal policies had the effect of bestowing upon the average American at least the *fruits of ownership*—security. Slum-clearance projects, low-interest home purchase loans, bank deposit insurance, and, above all, unemployment and old-age insurance provided an enlarged opportunity for the majority to enjoy some of the material well-being of the opulent and to be freed from

a measure of dependence upon the turn of economic fate. President Roosevelt, regarding the Social Security Act as the domestic capstone of his administration, took greater satisfaction from it than anything else he did. For this was the beginning of what since has come to be described as the "cradle-to-grave" security of the welfare state.

By the middle of Roosevelt's second term, times had changed, and so had the New Deal. From Europe came the threatening portents of World War II. America's unemployed had been largely absorbed by government work relief agencies. The NRA, poorly conceived, badly managed, and business dominated, had been swept from the scene in one of many laissez-faire decisions by the Supreme Court. Cooperation had failed. As conservatives in both parties gained strength, their demands for the end of a nationally planned economy grew more insistent. Early New Dealers of the planning-cooperation persuasion were dispatched on foreign missions—far from Washington. As their replacements entered the halls of government, the broad view of an interrelated economy, managed with high moral purpose in presumed accordance with the terms of human existence, gave way before "realistic" legalism and attempts to recover and regulate the classical competitive market. In 1933 the Secretary of Agriculture had seen in the first Agricultural Adjustment Act the cooperative, democratically planned use of land, blazing new trails toward a controlled economy, common sense, and social decency. In 1938 the Solicitor of the Department of Agriculture saw in the second Agricultural Adjustment Act an opportunity to move the basic farm legislation from its precarious footing under the Welfare Clause of the Constitution to a more solid foundation under the Commerce Clause. Paraphrasing Reinhold Niebuhr again, the early New Dealers had believed in man's capacity for justice, which made democracy possible; their successors in 1938 believed in man's inclination to injustice, which made democracy necessary.

Never was the New Deal alone able to defeat depression for those who endured its horror from 1929 to 1940. Never did Roosevelt gain suzerainty over the captains of finance and industry. The President, ever keen to achieve a balanced budget, put an end to deficit financing until a severe business recession in 1938 brought the government hastily back to "prime the pump." War appropriations, dwarfing the small sums allocated for the relief of human misery, soon restored economic good health to the nation.

Should the New Deal have carried America into "democratic socialism?" Could it have done so? Some early New Dealers, such as Tugwell, would have replied affirmatively to both questions. Tugwell saw the nation as being at that critical point in its development when it must recognize fundamental changes in the relationship of citizen to government, of government to economy. America, he said, must update its policies to bring them into the 20th century or, as he presciently phrased it, the American government would be either "ignored or contemptuously brushed aside by those in the community who have important affairs afoot which they desire shall not be interferred with." Tugwell had in mind what he conceived to be a rising tide of socialism. But Tugwell's hopes were groundless. The average citizen, however much he may have suffered during the depression, was not inclined to consider fundamental political or economic changes. Moreover he remained oblivious to the needs of black and poor Americans. John Dewey, indeed, had reason to be dismayed that so little had actually been done to change the root causes of human suffering. While applauding the progressive melioration that accompanied New Deal politics, he nonetheless lamented (in 1939) that his fellow countrymen still lived under scarcity capitalism and that the relationship between workers and the mode of production remained untouched. Dewey's observations were accurate. The New Deal was no radical revision of old values. Progressive to the core, it set out to save capitalism; and it did that.

SUGGESTED READINGS

ARNOLD, THURMAN W. *The Folklore of Capitalism*. New Haven: Yale University Press, 1937.

BURNS, JAMES MACGREGOR. *Roosevelt: The Lion and the Fox*. New York: Harcourt, Brace & Co., 1956.

———. *Roosevelt: The Soldier of Freedom*. New York: Harcourt, Brace Jovanovich, 1970.

CHAMBERS, CLARKE A. *The New Deal at Home and Abroad*. New York: Free Press, 1965.

CONKIN, PAUL K. *The New Deal*. New York: Thomas Y. Crowell Co. 1967.

FRANK FREIDEL. *The New Deal*. Englewood Cliffs, N.J.: Prentiss-Hall, 1964.

———. *Franklin D. Roosevelt*. 3 vols. Boston: Little, Brown & Co., 1952–56.

HAMBY, ALONZO L. *The New Deal*. New York: Weybright & Talley, 1969.

LEUCHTENBURG, WILLIAM E. *Franklin D. Roosevelt and the New Deal, 1932–1940*. New York: Harper & Row, 1963.

LILIENTHAL, DAVID E. *TVA: Democracy on the March*. New York: Harper & Bros., 1944.

SCHLESINGER, ARTHUR M., JR. *The Coming of the New Deal*. Boston: Houghton Mifflin Co., 1959.

———. *The Politics of Upheaval*. Boston: Houghton Mifflin Co., 1960.

SHERWOOD, ROBERT E. *Roosevelt and Hopkins*, New York: Harper & Bros., 1948.

TUGWELL, REXFORD G. *The Democratic Roosevelt*. Garden City, N.Y.: Doubleday & Co., 1957.

ZINN, HOWARD. *New Deal Thought*. Indianapolis: The Bobbs-Merrill Co., 1966.

DOCUMENT 29.1
Local Solutions for Local Problems*

Until 1932 the Hoover administration's efforts to relieve depression suffering were largely of a public relations nature. One such attempt was the President's Organization on Unemployment Relief (P.O.U.R.), headed by Walter S. Gifford, which in the fall of 1931 sought to persuade Americans to give more generously to their local community chest organizations. Gifford's and Hoover's limited view of P.O.U.R.'s mission may be seen in the following advertisement, which pictured an unemployed worker cheerfully tightening his belt and declaring: "I'll see it through if *you* will!"

"I'll see it through if y<u>ou</u> will!"

"THEY tell me there's five or six million of us—out of jobs.

"I know that's not your fault, any more than it is mine.

"But that doesn't change the fact that some of us right now are in a pretty tough spot—with families to worry about—and a workless winter ahead.

"Understand, we're not begging. We'd rather have a job than anything else you can give us.

"We're not scared, either. If you think the good old U. S. A. is in a bad way more than temporarily, just try to figure out some other place you'd rather be.

"But, until times do loosen up, we've got to have a little help.

"So I'm asking *you* to give us a lift, just as I would give one to you if I stood in your shoes and you in mine.

"Now don't send me any money—that isn't the idea. Don't even send any to the Committee which signs this appeal.

"The best way to help us is to give as generously as you can to your *local* welfare and charity organizations, your community chest or your emergency relief committee—if you have one.

"That's my story, the rest is up to you.
"I'll see it through—if *you* will!"

—*Unemployed, 1931*

THE PRESIDENT'S ORGANIZATION ON UNEMPLOYMENT RELIEF

Walter S. Gifford Director
WALTER S. GIFFORD

COMMITTEE ON MOBILIZATION OF RELIEF RESOURCES

Owen D. Young Chairman
OWEN D. YOUNG

The President's Organization on Unemployment Relief is non-political and non-sectarian. Its purpose is to aid local welfare and relief agencies everywhere to provide for local needs. All facilities for the nation-wide program, including this advertisement, have been furnished to the Committee without cost.

DOCUMENT 29.2

Belt Tightening at the Local Level*

It is difficult to generalize about the impact of the depression, of course, for this varied considerably among individuals and communities. By 1932, however, there was little doubt that millions of Americans were in real distress and that the system of local unemployment relief had broken down in many parts of the country. One such area was Fayette County, Pennsylvania, a coal-mining community whose plight was described to a congressional committee by an unemployed miner, Joseph Rade.

Mr. RADE. I represent the committee of unemployed of the township of Washington, Fayette County, Pa.

In Washington Township there are more than 1,350 families on the county unemployed fund, and the heads of those families have been unemployed anywhere from eight months to more than a year. The principal industry with us is coal mining. There are some farmers, but they have not done anything to any extent. They have not produced much; and the coal miners are the principal sufferers, because they do not make much, and what they have made in the past has gone very largely to the stores, which are owned by the mining people. It has all been taken by the stores.

I, myself, have been unemployed during the last eight months. I am a coal miner and have been such for the last 16 years. I have been born and raised in Fayette County, of which Washington Township is a part. I was born and raised there; I was educated in the coal mines, you might say, and I never saw such hard times as we have there now. About three

---

*Source: U.S. Congress, House Subcommittee of the Committee on Labor, *Unemployment in the United States*, Hearings, 72d Cong., 1st sess. (Washington, D.C.: U.S. Government Printing Office, 1932), pp. 46–47.

or four months ago conditions got so bad that people were approaching actual starvation, so we appealed to the miners' relief committee, who have been helping miners, and what little they gave us, such as flour, which was baked in an open oven into bread, and beans and barley, and what other little stuff we could get we had to solicit. All of this was made into a soup and we had about 70 people on our relief list who depended upon the soup kitchen for their existence.

This miners' relief has reached the end of its resources. In other words, the funds are about completely exhausted. In our community we have 50 or 60 families, it being a mining town, and those families are facing utter despair. There is no prospect whatsoever of getting anything for them. Our farmers have nothing. Our small merchants have gone bankrupt in trying to carry us. The banks have gone under, and there are only a few general stores.

I have heard the miners say, including myself, if it comes to the point where we must do it, we are going together and take over those general stores and take things we need to eat. We can not let our families starve. Our county is practically broke. It has nothing to give us by way of relief. They have been giving some families as low as $8 whether the family consists of two or, say, nine. Miners, as a general thing, as you know, have very large families, averaging five or six children to the family, and it takes a lot to keep them. And, what is worse, the children are the principal sufferers. I have known several cases where children collapsed in school, and that is the only time they would get relief from the county—when the child would collapse in school from hunger.

I have a school child myself, but it is not able to attend because I have not been able to give it proper food. That child was sick—at least I thought it was sick—but I found that it was simply starving. Again, my wife is on the verge of nervous prostration. I can not hardly speak from my emotions, but I am telling you the truth and nothing but the truth.

In our community we have a soup kitchen, as I have said, and this soup kitchen was maintained primarily by the donation from the miners' relief of which the previous speaker is the distributor of this relief from our soup kitchens.

I want to tell you gentlemen what we serve at the soup kitchen—bread and black coffee, and just enough sugar to make it palatable, and dry bread. That is served to the children who go to school. At dinner time they get the same thing, bread and black coffee. At night time the principal things they eat are soup and bread. The soup contains rice, barley, and a little potatoes when we can get them.

Mr. JACOBSEN. Besides the miners' relief, does not the county itself do something?

Mr. COLE. The county has not given us a cent. The county is, as I have said, broke.

DOCUMENT 29.3

We Shall Not Rest until That Minimum Is Achieved*

Columbia University Professor of Economics Rexford G. Tugwell was 41 years old when he became a member of Roosevelt's preelection "brain trust." Soon after the inauguration of the New Deal, he rose from Assistant Secretary of Agriculture to Undersecretary, to become one of the President's principal advisers. An outspoken protagonist of government planning and disciplined industry, he became a favored target of conservative opposition. Leaving Washington in 1937, Tugwell

---

*Source: Rexford G. Tugwell, *The Battle for Democracy* (New York: Columbia University Press, 1935), pp. 1–16, 78–96, and 256–67.

became successively Governor of Puerto Rico and distinguished professor at the University of Chicago. The selections from speeches which he made during 1933 and 1934, given below, illustrate the directions his followers hoped the President would take during the early New Deal period.

There is no prearranged field of government which is set apart from the circumstances of those who are governed. Relations here are always interdependent. As the circumstances of the people change, functions of government change. . . . It is a truism, too, to say that what is done by each of its divisions is affected by the whole orientation of the state. Like most truisms, this one contains a kernel of vital truth; it means, as respects ourselves, that executive, legislative, and judicial functions are not unalterably fixed, but are subject to revision. Government, or any part of it, is not in itself something; it is for something. It must do what we expect of it or it must be changed so that it will. . . .

Past circumstances produced needs (or supposed needs) which yielded theories in support of them. Toughest of those theories—so tough that, in the thinking of most men, it became an unalterable fact— was that which made competition a vital necessity, an end in itself, to be preserved at all costs. Competition was assumed to be an inherent part of democracy. Indeed competition and democracy came to be thought of as two aspects of one and the same value: a noncompetitive world was an undemocratic world.

Some two decades ago, it began to be apparent—or should have been—that competition and democracy were not Siamese twins, that they were separable, that in fact the separation had to be carried out if democracy were not to be stifled by competition. . . .

Competition, to depart from which was made unlawful, became a matter of legal compulsion. It meant compelled business confusion. Cooperative impulses, demanded by the current economic trend, were thwarted and repulsed. They expressed themselves only indirectly and unhealthily. What was sound and economically necessary was branded as wrong legally. . . .

. . . In this era of our economic existence, I believe it is manifest that a public interest well within the functions of government and well within the authority of government under our Constitution, commands the protection, the maintenance, the conservation, of our industrial faculties against the destructive forces of the unrestrained competition. And certainly the Constitution was never designed to impose upon one era the obsolete economic dogma which may have been glorified under it in an earlier one. For today and for tomorrow our problem is that of our national economic maintenance for the public welfare by governmental intervention—any theory of government, law or economics to the contrary notwithstanding. Hence the National Recovery Act and the Agricultural Adjustment Act of this administration. . . .

. . . Has the theory of a republican form of government explicit in the Constitution been violated by the new Democratic President and Congress? Has the philosophy of "checks and balances" within the Federal Government been infringed? These questions naturally arise; they command respect, for they concern our faith in the organization and functioning of our national Government. But must faiths, political more than economic, be preserved at any cost—that is, in disregard of the obviously necessary requirements of the public welfare? May our faiths in "checks and balances" yield to necessity, or even to expediency? If these faiths, and this necessity for more expeditious government action, are to clash, must we sacrifice efficiency or shall we establish a new faith? . . .

. . . To check and balance government to a point just short of inaction was the desideratum. The prevailing constitutional theory, and therefore the constitu-

tional law, of course corresponded to this prevailing economic outlook.

At the center of this constitutional law was the conception of government as policeman. Government was to stop flagrant abuses, but not, in any circumstances, to do more. It was to be negative and arresting, not positive and stimulating. Its role was minor and peripheral. It was important in this one sense: It was to prevent interferences with the competitive system. Behind that system (so it was said and thoroughly believed) was an invisible hand which beneficently guided warring business men to the promotion of the general welfare.

The jig is up. The cat is out of the bag. There is no invisible hand. There never was. If the depression has not taught us that, we are incapable of education. Time was when the anarchy of the competitive struggle was not too costly. Today it is tragically wasteful. It leads to disaster. We must now supply a real and visible guiding hand to do the task which that mythical, nonexistent, invisible agency was supposed to perform, but never did.

Men are, by impulse, predominantly cooperative. They have their competitive impulses, to be sure; but these are normally subordinate. Laissez-faire exalted the competitive and maimed the cooperative impulses. It deluded men with the false notion that the sum of many petty struggles was aggregate cooperation. Men were taught to believe that they were, paradoxically, advancing cooperation when they were defying it. That was a viciously false paradox. Of that, today, most of us are convinced and, as a consequence, the cooperative impulse is asserting itself openly and forcibly, no longer content to achieve its ends obliquely and by stealth. We are openly and notoriously on the way to mutual endeavors.

And here is the importance of the rediscovery of the Constitution. We are turning our back on the policeman doctrine of government and recapturing the vision of a government equipped to fight and overcome the forces of economic disintegration. A strong government with an executive amply empowered by legislative delegation is the one way out of our dilemma, and on to the realization of our vast social and economic possibilities.

THE ECONOMICS OF
THE RECOVERY PROGRAM

The general objective is clear and easily stated—to restore a workable exchangeability among the separate parts of our economic machine and to set it to functioning again; and beyond this to perfect arrangements which may prevent its future disorganization. This means that we must insure adequate income to the farmers, adequate wages to the workers, an adequate return to useful capital, and an adequate remuneration to management. What we want, really, is to provide the opportunity for every individual and every group to work and to be able to consume the product of others' work. This involves a creation of buying power which is coordinate with the creation of goods. We shall not rest nor be diverted to lesser things until that minimum is achieved. . . .

It is quite impossible to predict the shape of our newly invented economic institutions may take in the future. That seems to me, in any case, unimportant. What is important is that we have undertaken a venture which is theoretically new in the sense that it calls for control rather than drift. In the years to come much ingenuity will be needed in the effort to isolate and strengthen the nerve centers of industrial civilization. We have yet to discover in determinate fashion what efforts are naturally those of common service, and so require a high degree of socialization, and what ones can safely be left to relatively free individual or group contrivance. We are turning away from the entrusting of crucial decisions, and the operation of institutions whose social consequences are their most characteristic feature, to individuals who are motivated by private interests.

· · · · ·

The twentieth century found the American people psychologically and financially unprepared to utilize the wealth which the technological revolution of the last thirty years had made possible. . . .

As it became apparent that a more abundant life was within the reach of all our people, if we could only display the social inventiveness necessary to deal with this new abundance in such form as to convert anxious unemployment into secure leisure, we were shaken by a profound moral crisis. On the one side stood the sincere group of wishful beneficiaries of the Old Order, who . . . sat "waiting for the twentieth century to blow over." On the other side stood the mass of our people, who were increasingly bewildered by the failure of the old principles of our society to assure the distribution of those goods which were there for all to see and which were rotting away for want of buyers. The result of this crisis and conflict was the New Deal.

A new deal was absolutely inevitable. People will submit to grave privations and will even starve peaceably, if they realize that actual dearth exists, but no man and no race will starve in the presence of abundance. . . .

The objective of this administration is accordingly a simple one: it is to give our citizens the opportunity for a richer life. But simple and easily stated as this objective is, the methods it imposes are difficult and complex. . . .

In order to understand, it seems to me necessary to keep far up in the foreground always the idea that the possibilities of the future are always greater than were those of any time in the past. . . . That is why, in my opinion, it is a fundamental error to assume that we have now reached the end of the "swing to the left" and that we ought to forego any further important policy changes. The real economic revolution is just beginning and social policy will have to move rapidly to keep pace with it.

I have very little patience, therefore, with those who say we have come to the end of a period of progress, that we must now retrench and economize, hoarding our gains against a poverty-stricken future. . . . We do not seem to realize that it is our own abundance which compels us to make radical changes, first in our ideas and then in the institutions based on our ideas. . . . All the prejudices and shibboleths which survive in people's heads seem to crystallize in government—perhaps because, very rightly, we think of it as somehow sacred. But it will not stay sacred long if it is set apart from change in a changing world. It will simply become atrophied and obsolete and will either be ignored or contemptuously brushed aside by those in the community who have important affairs afoot which they desire shall not be interfered with.

Something like this has been happening to our Government. I think it is fair to say that until last March it was fast becoming ineffectual in its relationships with industry. It insisted on an interpretation of industrial life which belonged to an era which had disappeared. It broke up trusts as a sufficient answer to the pressing problem of control; and when it discovered that the more they were broken up, the more they remained as they had been, it fell into a kind of trance. It was unwilling to give up competitive theory; it could therefore think of nothing to do except to restore competition; and when competition refused to be restored, industry continued to exist in a kind of purgatory—half the heaven of freedom and half the hell of ineffectual public disapproval.

The various recovery acts proceeded from a theory which . . . recognized the changes which had occurred in industrial society and it sought to secure the benefits of industry as it actually existed for the public good. It said, "Industry has developed out of the face-to-face stage; huge factories exist; central-office organizations control many even of these organizations, great as they are in themselves; financial controls are superimposed on this; scientific management has come to stay—therefore, the Government must legalize all these heretofore horrid developments so that it may shape them into social instruments. . . .

. . . Up to now much of the energy of business men has been dissipated in the overpraised conflicts of competition. Each was trying to beat the other fellow—to reach success by standing on the exhausted bodies of fallen competitors. And the success for which all this striving took place was usually defined as the right to exploit consumers by selling them goods of doubtful quality at prices which lowered the general standard of living. . . .

. . . We are fast approaching the time, therefore, when each industry will be able to devote its best energy to the fundamental purpose of industry—which is to produce goods rather than competition. . . .

This reconciliation of differences, however quickly it may come, or whatever contractual relationships it may establish among industries, is not, however, sufficient. For there always remains the essentially defenseless ultimate consumer. The Government may turn out to be his only refuge; and if this is so, the Government will have to assume more and more responsibility for pushing his case.

There are two broad ways in which industrial policy may be shaped from this point on to secure this objective. Industry may be required to define the quality of the goods it offers and to sell them at prices which are suitably low, so that when the transactions of a year, for instance, are totaled up it will be found that our energies and our producing plant have been used to the utmost and that the goods and services they yield have gone to consumers without increase of debt; or industry may be allowed to proceed with the policy of establishing high prices and maintaining them by limitation, and of selling goods whose qualities are mysterious to most consumers; and much of the resulting profits may be taken in taxes and returned to consumers as free goods by the Government—in the form of facilities for health and recreation, insurance against old age, sickness and unemployment, or in other ways. We shall have to accept one or the other of these policies because unless we do we shall sacrifice most of those objectives which we associate with what has been called the New Deal. The choice which lies before us is, therefore, a choice between a socially wise economic policy and the application of socialistic taxation. I prefer the former method.

One, certainly, of the distinguishing characteristics of the present is the power of our industrial machine to produce goods. This power has astonished and frightened us. We have not known what to do about it. It required that we should either chain it up and prevent its free functioning or that we should reorganize our machinery of distribution so that consumers could take possession of the vast flow of goods. . . .

It is my belief that we shall prove unwilling to accept limitation in this sense as a permanent policy. This does not mean that we may not plan; it does not mean that we may not choose to use our resources in one way rather than another, limiting in some instances and expanding in others, so that all may run smoothly together as a considered and coordinated whole. . . .

I think it is perfectly obvious that we can have nothing new in the Government which does not correspond to a new need on the part of our people and of their economic institutions. The New Deal is a very definite attempt to evolve a new governmental-economic relationship in response to the needs and opportunities created by the past methods of operating our economy. To inhibit further growth of these new methods is, therefore, impos-

sible and to attempt to deny their application is the ultimate folly of fossilized ways of thought. Using the traditional methods of a free people, we are going forward toward a realm of cooperative plenty the like of which the world has never seen. It will be no antiseptic utopia and no socialistic paradise, but a changing system in which free American human beings can live their changing lives. . . .

I have also stressed their experimental nature. That seems to me their most important characteristic, and that is something which is American if anything is. . . . There is no reason to think that year by year we shall not learn to better ourselves with the full use of energies and instruments which we have at our disposal. If this be Socialism, make the most of it!

DOCUMENT 29.4
Competition Must Keep Its Blows above the Belt*

According to the Bloomingdale's Department Store advertisement reproduced here, two seemingly identical men's shirts are offered to the buying public at a 36-cent price differential. The unknown author of the copy makes it clear that the purchaser of the 89-cent shirt is betraying his fellow workers, the NRA, and the nation. Pressure to *cooperate*, to "do his part," extended in the early New Deal period clear down to the unfortunate man with the frayed cuffs.

See Figure 1, p. 265.

---

*Source: *New York Daily News*, October 14, 1933.

Figure 1 (Document 29.4)

WHICH ONE WOULD YOU PREFER TO WEAR?

COLLAR ATTACHED SHIRT
Pre-shrunk fast color broadcloth of long
staple cotton yarn. Six-button front. **89c**

COLLAR ATTACHED SHIRT
Pre-shrunk fast color broadcloth of long
staple cotton yarn. Six-button front. **1.25**

This shirt, and tens of thousands like it, were made and sold just a few months ago when the country was not as sound as it is today.

The man that grew the cotton for it lost money. His cotton pickers were not paid with cash...they received canned goods and groceries so that they could eat and have strength to work. The workers in the mill where the cotton was spun into yarn and in the mill where the yarn was woven into fabric received starvation wages...$4 and $5 a week. The girls that fashioned it into a shirt tried to keep the wolf from the door with $5 a week, and in many instances, even less. Their employer lost money. Cut-throat competition, together with curtailed buying power, forced the retailer to sell it at a price which would attract you to buy it, but which netted him a loss.

At 89 cents it was a bargain. A bargain built on misery ...distress...losses...and suffering, all along the line. A bargain that threatened the very structure of this country.

Here is another shirt...manufactured under the Code of the N R A. Looks just like the other one, but it's different.

True, the cotton is the same, the machine-made material is the same, BUT . . . . . the workers now receive at least $13 a week. The workmanship, however, *is different.* Girls that are now receiving a living wage do better work than they did with hungry stomachs and with fear in their hearts.

Yes, it's a different shirt. They will all tell you that ... from the cotton picker to the one who sells it to you. Thanks to N R A it is *different* . . . . and not a single child labored in its making.

At $1.25, it is a *real* bargain, a *sound* bargain, *sound* for your welfare and *sound* for the welfare of our country. Which one do you prefer to wear?

* * *

Similar Encouraging Facts Could Be Published
Regarding Scores of Other Industries

Written and published in the interest of NRA and all it stands for by

Bloomingdale's
NEW YORK

Bloomingdale's will send reproduction proofs of art work and copy
to any firm or organization wishing to reprint or publish this advertisement over its own signature. To know the NRA is to like it.

DOCUMENT 29.5

Agriculture Cannot Survive in a Capitalistic Society as a Philanthropic Enterprise

Henry A. Wallace was Roosevelt's first Secretary of Agriculture, second Vice President, and fourth Secretary of Commerce. In the selections presented here from his books, *New Frontiers* and *Democracy Reborn*, he speaks out sharply on behalf of economic democracy for the farmer. In line with early New Deal thinking, Wallace calls for planning, cooperation, and obedience to the higher moral goals of democracy; contrary to the President's early policy of economic nationalism, Wallace already held definite views on the interrelatedness of the world's peoples and institutions. Seemingly beguiled here by a vision of the neighborly sharing of untrammeled production, the tough-minded Secretary pursued farm parity by administering the Agricultural Adjustment acts as instruments of scarcity capitalism.

AN AGRARIAN DRIVE TO CHANGE THE RULES°

The experimental method of democracy may be slow, but it has the advantage of being sure. When you change people's minds you change the course of a nation.

Though abundance is at hand, we still live by old standards of denial. The situation is confusing. There are those who say that there cannot be a surplus so long as there is a single hungry Chinaman. Fundamentally and eventually this may be true; but these standpat sentimentalists who weep that farmers should practice controlled production do not suggest that clothing factories go on producing *ad infinitum*, regardless of effective demand for their merchandise, until every naked Chinaman is clad. Nor do they feel that plow factories should abandon production control until every hungry Chinaman has a plow. We must play with the cards that are dealt. Agriculture cannot survive in a capitalistic society as a philanthropic enterprise. If the cry of those who bid our farmers think of all those hungry Chinamen, and plant more land, were heeded, it would mean that long before the last hungry Chinaman was taken care of, hundreds of thousands of American farm families would be destroyed.

The feeling that man should live by providing goods for his neighbors, not by withholding goods, goes very deep; and I believe that it is spreading. But the condition of greater balance and justice we now seek, in a capitalistic structure hastily mended, can certainly not be obtained by arranging that everybody work under the profit system except the farmer. The farmer's instinct has always been to be decent and unbusinesslike, to provide to the uttermost, never to deny. This instinct, obeyed by millions of scattered individuals in a society seeking profits and setting prices on a scarcity basis, took our farmers up the long hill to the poorhouse; and killed them as customers. Their death as consumers closed thousands of factories and helped to throw millions out of work. Now we are trying to give our farmers their rightful place in a more decent and balanced system, a system that will work democratically and make for neighborliness and a shared abundance. The people who raise the cry about the last hungry Chinaman are not really criticizing the farmers or the AAA, but the profit system, as we have inherited it from our past.

THE PURPOSES OF THE AAA°

To organize agriculture, co-operatively, democratically, so that the surplus lands on which men and women now are toiling,

°Source: Henry A. Wallace, *New Frontiers* (New York: Reynal and Hitchcock, 1934), pp. 138–39. Reprinted by permission of Harcourt Brace Jovanovich, Inc.

°Source: Henry A. Wallace, *Democracy Reborn*, ed. Russell Lord (New York: Reynal and Hitchcock, 1944), pp. 45–46. Reprinted by permission of Harcourt Brace Jovanovich, Inc.

wasting their time, wearing out their lives to no good end, shall be taken out of production—that is a tremendous task. The adjustment we seek calls first of all for a mental adjustment, a willing reversal, of driving, pioneer opportunism and ungoverned *laissez faire*. The ungoverned push of rugged individualism perhaps had an economic justification in the days when we had all the West to surge upon and conquer; but this country has filled up now, and grown up. There are no more Indians to fight. No more land worth taking may be had for the grabbing. We must experience a change of mind and heart.

The frontiers that challenge us now are of the mind and spirit. We must blaze new trails in scientific accomplishment, in the peaceful arts and industries. Above all, we must blaze new trails in the direction of a controlled economy, common sense, and social decency. . . .

. . . This Act offers you promise of a balanced abundance, a shared prosperity, and a richer life. It will work, if you will make it yours, and make it work. I hope that you will come to see in this Act, as I do now, a Declaration of Interdependence, a recognition of our essential unity and of our absolute reliance upon one another.

DOCUMENT 29.6
A Great Plan Is Democracy's Answer*

Born in 1899, David E. Lilienthal became director of the Tennessee Valley Authority in 1933, chairman of its board of directors in 1941. The following selections from his book *TVA: Democracy on the March* make a strong case for public power, which has

*Source: David E. Lilienthal, *TVA: Democracy on the March* (New York: Harper & Bros., 1944), pp. 46, 75–76, 105–6, 125, 127, 192–3, 195, 218, abridgment. Copyright, 1944 by David E. Lilienthal. Reprinted by permission of the publishers.

been part of the Democratic Party creed since the age of Franklin D. Roosevelt. In describing government planning in the field of resource development, Lilienthal reveals his fundamental faith in democracy and his deeply felt sense of morality. The implication is clear: A democracy can plan without becoming dictatorial, and it can carry out its plans without enslaving its citizens.

A new chapter in American public policy was written when Congress in May of 1933 passed the law creating the TVA. For the first time since the trees fell before the settlers' ax, America set out to command nature not by defying her, as in that wasteful past, but by understanding and acting upon her first law—the oneness of men and natural resources, the unity that binds together land, streams, forests, minerals, farming, industry, mankind. . . .

People are the most important fact in resource development. Not only is the welfare and happiness of individuals its true purpose, but they are the means by which that development is accomplished; their genius, their energies and spirit are the instruments; it is not only "for the people" but "by the people." . . .

This hankering to be an *individual* is probably greater today than ever before. Huge factories, assembly lines, mysterious mechanisms, standardization—these underline the smallness of the individual, because they are so fatally impersonal. If the intensive development of resources, the central fact in the immediate future of the world, could be made personal to the life of most men; if they could see themselves, because it was true, as actual participants in that development in their own communities, on their own land, at their own jobs and businesses—there would be an opportunity for this kind of individual satisfaction, and there would be something to tie to. . . .

It is the unique strength of democratic methods that they provide a way of stimulating and releasing the individual resourcefulness and inventiveness, the pride of workmanship, the creative genius of human beings whatever their station or function. A world of science and great machines is still a world of men; our modern task is more difficult, but the opportunity for democratic methods is greater even than in the days of the ax and the hand loom. . . .

With the eyes of industry now upon this valley (as they are indeed upon many valleys the world over) planning a considerable industrial expansion here after the war, there is an opportunity to plan and to build so that our resources will endure, our natural beauty be spared despoliation. Here there is a chance to see to it that human well-being in city and town will not, through lack of ingenuity and foresight, be needlessly sacrificed. Shall we succeed? Is the only choice one between pastoral poverty and industrial slums? Can private industry utilize these resources, at a profit, and yet sustain their vigor and longevity? Can business and the common weal both be served? To be able to make an affirmative reply is a matter of the greatest moment.

In the Tennessee Valley the answers will turn to some extent upon how successful the TVA is in its efforts to weld a union of the public interest and the private interests of businessmen. We appear to be uncovering and developing in this valley principles and practices for effecting a jointure of public interests with private, by methods that are voluntary and noncoercive. Our actual experience is unpretentious as measured by the scope of the problem, but it is definitely encouraging and of not a little significance for industry and the people of the country generally. . . .

What the TVA, in specific ways, has sought to do can be simply stated: to accept an obligation to harmonize the private interest in earning a return from resources, with the dominant public interest in their unified and efficient development. The method—and this is the distinc-

tive part of the experiment—is to bring to bear at the grass roots the skills of public experts and administrators not for negative regulation but *to make affirmative action in the public interest both feasible and appealing to private industry*. By public interest I mean the interest of people—people as human beings—not "the people" in their institutional roles as wage earners or investors or voters or consumers. "Underneath all, individuals," men and women and children. . . .

The unified development of resources requires the broadest coalition of effort. This is a job not only for all the people, but for all of the people's institutions. The purpose is national, but the task is one that calls for a partnership of *every* agency of government, state and local as well as federal, that can further the common purpose. Therefore the grass-roots policy of drawing in private organizations and individuals—such as those of farmers, workers, and businessmen . . . —has in like manner been applied by TVA, a *federal* organization, so that the governmental agencies of *local* communities and of the *states* of the Tennessee Valley have become TVA's active and responsible partners.

Decentralizing the administration of government functions that are clearly national has been carried so far in this valley . . . that, whenever there is a state or local institution which can perform part of the task that has been assigned by law to the TVA, we have sought to have that non-federal agency do it. This way of getting results is an exacting test of managerial skill in defining functions clearly and in securing a union of effort. Legalistic arguments about "states' rights" or "federal supremacy" have faded into irrelevance. . . .

In calling upon a state or local agency to share responsibility instead of setting up a TVA organization to do a specific job alone, and in negotiating the contracts upon which such joint efforts rest, we have deliberately tried to "start something" that local forces might later carry on, on their own. We have tried to place each new activity into the stream of the region's life, in the hands of local agencies to be continued when the initial federal support is withdrawn. . . .

The TVA *is* a planning agency, the first of its kind in the United States. The great change going on in this valley is an authentic example of modern democratic planning; this was the expressed intent of Congress, by whose authority we act. . . .

. . . "Unified development" as I have described the idea in action is, in substance, the valley's synonym for "planning. . . ."

Planning by businessmen, often under some other name, is recognized as necessary to the conduct of private enterprise. It has the virtue of a single and direct objective, one that can be currently measured, that is, the making of a profit. . . .

This is admittedly a grave defect of planning by the businessman. For his legitimate object, namely a profitable business, is not necessarily consistent with the object of society, that is, a prosperous and happy people. . . .

The idea of unified resource development is based upon the premise that by democratic planning the individual's interest, the interest of private undertakings, can increasingly be made one with the interest of all of us, i.e., the community interest. . . .

A great Plan, a moral and indeed a religious purpose, deep and fundamental, is democracy's answer both to our own home-grown would-be dictators and foreign antidemocracy alike. In the unified development of resources there is such a Great Plan: the Unity of Nature and Mankind. Under such a Plan in our valley we move forward. True, it is but a step at a time. But we assume responsibility not simply for the little advance we make each day, but for that vast and all-pervasive end and purpose of all our labors, the material well-being of all men and the opportunity for them to build for themselves spiritual strength.

Here is the life principle of democratic planning—an awakening in the whole people of a sense of this common moral purpose. Not one goal, but a direction. Not one plan, once and for all, but *the conscious selection by the people of successive plans. . . .*

We have a choice. There is the important fact. Men are not powerless; they have it in their hands to use the machine to augment the dignity of human existence. True, they may have so long denied themselves the use of that power to decide, which is theirs, may so long have meekly accepted the dictation of bosses of one stripe or another or the ministrations of benevolent nursemaids, that the muscles of democratic choice have atrophied. But that strength is always latent; history has shown how quickly it revives. How we shall *use* physical betterment—that decision is ours to make. We are not carried irresistibly by forces beyond our control, whether they are given some mystic terms or described as the "laws of economics." We are not inert objects on a wave of the future. . . .

DOCUMENT 29.7

Collectivism in Industry Compels Collectivism in Government*

In his hard-hitting acceptance speech before the Democratic National Convention of 1936, Franklin D. Roosevelt began his attack on the "economic royalists"— the "privileged princes of these new economic dynasties, thirsting for power, [reaching] out for control over Government itself." By 1938 the President had gleaned some startling statistics from the income tax rolls. In 1929, for instance, three tenths of 1 percent of the American

*Source: Samuel I. Rosenman (ed.), *The Public Papers and Addresses of Franklin D. Roosevelt*, 1938 vol., *The Continuing Struggle for Liberalism* (New York: Macmillan Co., 1941), pp. 305–20.

people received 78 percent of the stock dividends reported by individuals. In 1935–36, 47 percent of American families were living on less than $1,000 per year, while 1½ percent of American families were living on incomes totaling the combined income of the 47 percent. On April 29, 1938, Roosevelt sent his message to Congress on the concentration of economic power, proposing a program to "preserve private enterprise for profit." It is apparent from this message, selections from which are given below, that the earlier New Deal policy of cooperation with business had ended and that competition was to be restored to a government-regulated market. At the same time, it must also be realized that there had been no change whatever in the President's goals of individualism, private property, and democracy. The result of his message was the creation of the Temporary National Economic Committee, with Senator Joseph C. O'Mahoney as chairman. After three years of hearings, Senator O'Mahoney presented the committee's recommendations: that national corporations be chartered, that competition be maintained through effective enforcement of the antitrust laws, and that new business and small enterprise be given tax advantages. By the time the committee reported its findings, the United States was at war, and the whole matter was left to the searching scrutiny of future economists.

Unhappy events abroad have retaught us two simple truths about the liberty of a democratic people.

The first truth is that the liberty of a democracy is not safe if the people tolerate the growth of private power to a point where it becomes stronger than their democratic state itself. That, in its essence, is Fascism—ownership of Government by an individual, by a group, or by any other controlling private power.

The second truth is that the liberty of a democracy is not safe if its business system does not provide employment and produce and distribute goods in such a way as to sustain an acceptable standard of living.

Both lessons hit home.

Among us today a concentration of private power without equal in history is growing.

This concentration is seriously impairing the economic effectiveness of private enterprise as a way of providing employment for labor and capital and as a way of assuring a more equitable distribution of income and earnings among the people of the nation as a whole. . . .

We believe in a way of living in which political democracy and free private enterprise for profit should serve and protect each other—to ensure a maximum of human liberty not for a few but for all. . . .

That heavy hand of integrated financial and management control lies upon large and strategic areas of American industry. The small business man is unfortunately being driven into a less and less independent position in American life. You and I must admit that.

Private enterprise is ceasing to be free enterprise and is becoming a cluster of private collectivisms: masking itself as a system of free enterprise after the American model, it is in fact becoming a concealed cartel system after the European model. . . .

If you believe with me in private initiative, you must acknowledge the right of well-managed small business to expect to make reasonable profits. You must admit that the destruction of this opportunity follows concentration of control of any given industry into a small number of dominating corporations.

One of the primary causes of our present difficulties lies in the disappearance of price competition in many industrial fields, particularly in basic manufacture where concentrated economic power is most evident—and where rigid prices and fluctuating payrolls are general.

Managed industrial prices mean fewer jobs. It is no accident that in industries, like cement and steel, where prices have remained firm in the face of a falling demand, payrolls have shrunk as much as 40 and 50 per cent in recent months. Nor is it mere chance that in most competitive industries where prices adjust themselves quickly to falling demand, payrolls and employment have been far better maintained. . . .

If private enterprise left to its own devices becomes half-regimented and half-competitive, half-slave and half-free, as it is today, it obviously cannot adjust itself to meet the needs and the demands of the country.

Most complaints for violations of the antitrust laws are made by business men against other business men. Even the most monopolistic business man disapproves of all monopolies but his own. We may smile at this as being just an example of human nature, but we cannot laugh away the fact that the combined effect of the monopolistic controls which each business group imposes for its own benefit, inevitably destroys the buying power of a nation as a whole.

Competition, of course, like all other good things, can be carried to excess. Competition should not extend to fields where it has demonstrably bad social and economic consequences. The exploitation of child labor, the chiseling of workers' wages, the stretching of workers' hours, are not necessary, fair or proper methods of competition. I have consistently urged a federal wages and hours bill to take the minimum decencies of life for the working man and woman out of the field of competition. . . .

But generally over the field of industry and finance we must revive and strengthen competition if we wish to preserve and make workable our traditional system of free private enterprise.

The justification of private profit is private risk. We cannot safely make America safe for the business man who does not want to take the burdens and risks of being a business man. . . .

A discerning magazine of business has editorially pointed out that big business collectivism in industry compels an ultimate collectivism in government.

The power of a few to manage the economic life of the nation must be diffused among the many or be transferred to the public and its democratically responsible government. If prices are to be managed and administered, if the nation's business is to be allotted by plan and not by competition, that power should not be vested in any private group or cartel, however benevolent its professions profess to be.

Those people, in and out of the halls of government, who encourage the growing restriction of competition either by active efforts or by passive resistance to sincere attempts to change the trend, are shouldering a terrific responsibility. Consciously, or unconsciously, they are working for centralized business and financial control. Consciously or unconsciously, they are therefore either working for control of the government itself by business and finance or the other alternative—a growing concentration of public power in the government to cope with such concentration of private power.

The enforcement of free competition is the least regulation business can expect.

The traditional approach to the problems I have discussed has been through the anti-trust laws. That approach we do not propose to abandon. On the contrary, although we must recognize the inadequacies of the existing laws, we seek to enforce them so that the public shall not be deprived of such protection as they afford. To enforce them properly requires thorough investigation not only to discover such violations as may exist but to avoid hit-and-miss prosecutions harmful to business and government alike. . . .

But the existing anti-trust laws are inadequate—most importantly because of new financial economic conditions with which they are powerless to cope. . . .

We have witnessed the merging-out of effective competition in many fields of enterprise. We have learned that the so-called competitive system works differently in an industry where there are many independent units, from the way it works in an industry where a few large producers dominate the market.

We have also learned that a realistic system of business regulation has to reach more than consciously immoral acts. The community is interested in economic results. It must be protected from economic as well as moral wrongs. We must find practical controls over blind economic forces as over blindly selfish men.

Government can deal and should deal with blindly selfish men. But that is a comparatively small part—the easier part—of our problem. The larger, more important and more difficult part of our problem is to deal with men who are not selfish and who are good citizens, but who cannot see the social and economic consequences of their actions in a modern economically interdependent community. They fail to grasp the significance of some of our most vital social and economic problems because they see them only in the light of their own personal experience and not in perspective with the experience of other men and other industries. They, therefore, fail to see these problems for the nation as a whole.

To meet the situation I have described, there should be a thorough study of the concentration of economic power in American industry and the effect of that concentration upon the decline of competition. . . .

It is not intended as the beginning of any ill-considered "trust-busting" activity which lacks proper consideration for economic results. . . .

It is a program whose basic purpose is to stop the progress of collectivism in business and turn business back to the democratic competitive order.

It is a program whose basic thesis is not that the system of free private enterprise for profit has failed in this generation, but that it has not yet been tried. . . .

DOCUMENT 29.8
Old Problems Unsolved*

Locked into the dogma of "declining competition," "trustbusting," and "free private enterprise for profit," Roosevelt and most New Deal thinkers were unable to contemplate the basic human relationship between workers and work. Writing in 1939, philosopher John Dewey reviewed the New Deal and concluded that as a force for fundamental change, it was little more than a slogan.

After the world depression of 1929, the earlier idea of reconstruction revived, not under that name but, in this country, under the slogan of the New Deal. It has become increasingly evident that the conditions which caused the World War remain in full force, intensified indeed by the growth of exacerbated Nationalism—which is the direction in which "internal social reorganization" has in fact mainly moved. Failure of the world communities to "meet and forestall" needed change with "sympathy and intelligence" has left us with the old problems unsolved and new ones added. . . .

How much progress has been made in the intervening years? How does the situation now stand? We have a recognition which did not exist before of social responsibility for the care of the unemployed whose resources are exhausted in consequence of unemployment. But at best, the method we employ is palliative: it comes after the event. The positive problem of instituting a social-economic

*Source: John Dewey, "The Economic Basis of the New Society," in *Intelligence in the Modern World* (New York: Random House, 1939), pp. 416–33. Reprinted with the permission of Joseph Ratner.

order in which all those capable of productive work will do the work for which they are fitted remains practically untouched. . . .

In saying these things, I am expressing no sympathy for those who complain about the growing amount of money spent upon taking care of those thrown out of productive work and the consequent increase in taxation. Much less am I expressing sympathy with the reckless charges brought against the unemployed of loving idleness and wishing to live at the expense of society. Such complaints and charges are the product of refusal to look at the causes which produce the situation and of desire to find an alibi for their refusal to do anything to remove the causes—causes which are inherent in the existing social-economic regime. The problem of establishing social conditions which will make it possible for all who are capable to do socially productive work is not an easy one. I am not engaging in criticism because it has not been solved. I am pointing out that the problem is not even being thought much about, not to speak of being systematically faced. The reason for the great refusal is clear. To face it would involve the problem of remaking a profit system into a system conducted not just, as is sometimes said, in the interest of consumption, important as that is, but also in the interest of positive and enduring opportunity for productive and creative activity and all that signifies for the development of the potentialities of human nature.

What gain has been made in the matter of establishing conditions that give the mass of workers not only what is called "security" but also constructive interest in the work they do? What gain has been made in giving individuals, the great mass of individuals, an opportunity to find themselves and then to educate themselves for what they can best do in work which is socially useful and such as to give free play in development of themselves? The managers of industries here and there have learned that it pays to have condi-

tions such that those who are employed know enough about what they are doing so as to take an interest in it. Educators here and there are awake to the need of discovering vocational and occupational abilities and to the need of readjusting the school system to build upon what is discovered. But the basic trouble is not the scantiness of efforts in these directions, serious as is their paucity. It is again that the whole existing industrial system tends to nullify in large measure the effects of these efforts even when they are made. The problem of the adjustment of individual capacities and their development to actual occupations is not a one-sided or unilateral one. It is bilateral and reciprocal. It is a matter of the state of existing occupations, of the whole set-up of productive work, of the sturcture of the industrial system. Even if there were a much more widespread and searching concern with the capacities of individuals and much more preparation of them along the lines of their inherent fitness and needs than now exists, what assurance is there in the existing system that there will be opportunity to use their gifts and the education they have obtained? As far as the mass is concerned, we are now putting the social cart before the social horse.

If we take the question of production, what do we find? I pass by the basic fact that real production is completed only through distribution and consumption, so that mere improvement in the mechanical means of mass production may, and does, intensify the problem instead of solving it. I pass it over here because recurring crises and depressions, with the paradox of want amid plenty, has forced the fact upon the attention of every thoughtful person. The outcome is sufficient proof that the problem of production cannot be solved in isolation from distribution and consumption. I want here to call attention rather to the fact that the present method of dealing with the problem is *restriction* of productive capacity. For scarcity of materials and surplus of those who want to work is the ideal situation for profit on the part of those situated to take advantage of it. *Restriction of production* at the very time when *expansion* of production is most needed has long been the rule of *industrialists. . . .*

The ultimate problem of production is the production of human beings. To this end, the production of goods is intermediate and auxiliary. It is by this standard that the present system stands condemned. "Security" is a means, and although an indispensable social means, it is not the end. Machinery and technological improvement are means, but again are not the end. Discovery of individual needs and capacities is a means to the end, but only a means. The means have to be implemented by a social-economic system that establishes and uses the means for the production of free human beings associating with one another on terms of equality. Then and then only will these means be an integral part of the end, not frustrated and self-defeating, bringing new evils and generating new problems.

The problem today remains one of using available intelligence, of employing the immense resources science has put at our disposal: a pooled and coördinated social intelligence, not the mere scattered individualized intelligences of persons here and there, however high their I.Q.'s may be. Mere individual intellectual capacities are as ineffective as are mere personal good intentions. The existence of social objective intelligence brings us back to the point where we started. Social control effected through organized application of social intelligence is the sole form of social control that can and will get rid of existing evils without landing us finally in some form of coercive control from above and outside.

A great tragedy of the present situation may turn out to be that those most conscious of present evils and of the need of thorough-going change in the social-economic system will trust to some short-cut way out, like the method of civil war

and violence. Instead of relying upon the constant application of all socially available resources of knowledge and continuous inquiry they may rely upon the frozen intelligence of some past thinker, sect and party cult: frozen because arrested into a dogma.

That "intelligence," when frozen in dogmatic social philosophies, themselves the fruit of arrested philosophies of history, generates a vicious circle of blind oscillation is tragically exemplified in the present state of the world. What *claims* to be social planning is now found in Communist and Fascist countries. The *social* consequence is complete suppression of freedom of inquiry, communication and voluntary association, by means of a combination of personal violence, culminating in extirpation, and systematic partisan propaganda. The results are such that in the minds of many persons the very idea of social planning and of violation of the integrity of the individual are becoming intimately bound together. But an immense difference divides the *planned* society from a *continuously planning* society. The former requires fixed blueprints imposed from above and therefore involving reliance upon physical and psychological force to secure conformity to them. The latter means the release of intelligence through the widest form of coöperative give-and-take. The attempt to *plan* social organization and association without the freest possible play of intelligence contradicts the very idea in *social* plann*ing*. For the latter is an operative method of activity, not a predetermined set of final "truths."

When social "planning" is predicated on a set of "*final*" truths, the social end is fixed once for all, and the "end" is then used to justify whatever means are deemed necessary to attain it. "Planning" then takes place only with respect to means of the latter sort, not with respect to ends, so that planning with respect to even means is constrained and coercive. The social result is that the means used have quite other consequences than the end originally set up in idea and afterwards progressively reduced to mere words. As the events of the past twenty years have shown, the seizure of political power by force signifies the continued maintenance of power by force with its continued suppression of the most precious freedoms of the individual spirit. Maintenance of power in order to use force becomes the actual end. Means used determine the end actually reached. The end justifies the means only when the means used are such as actually bring about the desired and desirable end.

Only when reflection upon means and choice of ends are free can there be actual social planning. Every arrest of intelligence (and every form of social dogma is an arrest) obstructs and finally suppresses free consideration and choice of means. The method of social intelligence is primarily concerned with free determination of means to be employed. Until that method of social action is adopted we shall remain in a period of drift and unrest whose final outcome is likely to be force and counterforce, with temporary victory to the side possessed of the most machine guns.

30 President Roosevelt and American Foreign Policy

ROBERT H. FERRELL
Indiana University

Historical reputations have a way of going up and down, depending upon the judgment of individual generations, and it is fair to say that at the present time the reputation of President Franklin D. Roosevelt in the handling of American foreign relations may well be going down. The concern of Americans in the 1970s is, of course, foreign affairs, and within that large category of public policy lie many problems, not least the problem of presidential leadership. The leadership of the Democratic Roosevelt in international affairs now appears to have been seriously, perhaps gravely, flawed.

For Americans who have lived through the 1960s and can now see the difficulties in foreign policy produced by decisions of that crisis-ridden decade, there is an almost overwhelming desire for presidential responsibility in foreign relations—one needs merely to mention the name of Vietnam to explain the reason for this desire. The administration of President Lyndon B. Johnson was less than candid with the American people over its trials and tribulations in Vietnam, with the result that by the end of the decade Americans had a first-class Asian war on their hands, a war which, as events turned out, they could not win. Honesty in foreign affairs, a willingness to consult the individuals—the people—who would have to bear the burden, became more than a theoreti-

cal proposition. If Americans of the next decade, the 1970s, would find a single principle of foreign relations more attractive than any other, it is the need for candid leadership by the President of the United States. All this is to say nothing about the feeling of many Americans in the early 1970s that President Richard M. Nixon was being no more responsible about problems and difficulties of the war in Vietnam than his predecessor, Johnson, had been.

If one considers, then, this desire of people a quarter century and more after the death of President Franklin D. Roosevelt, he can understand how the reputation of the President of 1933–45 is no longer as appealing as it once was. Consider the three full terms of President Roosevelt, together with the slightly more than three months he served of his fourth term. A lack of candid presidential leadership marked at least an important part of this period, and it is a deeply troubling heritage for Americans of the 1970s.

In the first full Roosevelt term the principal problem of the American nation was domestic affairs, getting out of the Great Depression, and the foreign relations of that era have often seemed shadowy and insubstantial compared to the grand procession of domestic enactments and programs sponsored by the New Deal. There can be no question about it—the country was in deep economic trouble in March 1933. And there can be no question but what the appearance of a new President, Franklin D. Roosevelt, the first Democratic incumbent of the nation's highest office since Woodrow Wilson departed the White House in 1921, was a tonic to people of the time. The Hundred Days of economic and social reform, and subsequent measures by the Roosevelt administration, may well have saved capitalism in America, as Raymond Moley later was to write. Yet of revolution there probably was not much chance; there was talk of revolution, but in retrospect it does not appear to have been serious. The major task, and the major accomplishment, of the Roosevelt administration in 1933, and in subsequent years down to, say, the recession of 1937, was to lift the nation out of an economic morass.

In this first four-year period of the Roosevelt administistation the mistakes of foreign policy were errors of omission rather than of commission, and they were not intentional. They resulted from lack of wisdom. Few Americans, not least the President of the United States, understood that the most serious problem of the era was not within the United States but abroad—was not the domestic economy but foreign policy. It was the movement of international disorder, first appearing in the Japanese conquest of Manchuria in 1931–33, then in the attack by Italian troops upon Ethiopia in 1935, and then in the occupation of the Rhineland by German troops the following year, contrary to the Treaty of Versailles. The signal event of the era, an event that passed with little more than superficial comment by the people and government of the United States, was the accession to power of Adolf Hitler, who became chancellor of Germany in January 1933, a few weeks before Roosevelt became President of the United States.

The President, like his countrymen, was not alert to the danger. The three volumes of personal Roosevelt letters for 1933–37 published recently by the Harvard University Press in cooperation with the Roosevelt Library at Hyde Park show presidential unawareness. The best one can say for the dismal period 1933–37, when dictatorships in Germany, Japan, and Italy were beginning to consider a second World War, is that insofar as the United States was concerned, there was a policy as close to true isolation as any American government had practiced in the 20th century, and perhaps even in the isolationist 19th century. President Roosevelt, in his first term, was simply inadequate as a leader in foreign affairs, whatever the successes of his domestic policy.

These Roosevelt letters are fascinating reading, for one is struck with the trivial nature of the correspondence—the schoolboyish commentaries about the politics of foreign nations, the exchange of sophomoric hunches with American ambassadors abroad, the amusement at the customs of foreigners, the concern for personalities of foreign statesmen which seemed to be almost the observations of a social climber looking over the qualities of the competition.

Presidential leadership in foreign affairs during the first term, one should add, was not through the Department of State, for the President distrusted or at least found himself bored with the old Wilsonian Secretary of State Cordell Hull, whom he had taken into the Cabinet as a gesture to the southern conservatives of his party. The President preferred to work through the ambassadors and sought to maintain a spirit of camaraderie with them, encouraging personal letters to the White House which would bypass Department of State policy desks, not to mention the desk of Secretary Hull. And in this regard the present-day reader of the Roosevelt correspondence is struck with the "old boy network" quality of the exchanges and the impressionistic nature of the information. Ambassador Breckinridge ("Breck") Long in Rome informed the President of how straight the young fascists stood in their black-shirted uniforms, how impressive they were. The President learned from Ambassador William C. ("Bill") Bullitt in Moscow of how the ambassador was equipping some regiments of the Moscow garrison with baseball bats and gloves, to give them a feeling for American culture. Bullitt had gone to the Soviet Union under the impression that friendship and enthusiasm would improve Soviet-American relations, which had been in a deep-freeze since the Revolution of 1917. Perhaps, too, trade could be increased and an entente achieved against Japanese aggression in the Far East. By 1936, when Bullitt left the Soviet Union (he was transferred to an even more crucial embassy, that of Paris), he discovered that a personal approach gained nothing with the Russians and maybe less than nothing, because he may have brought the government of the United States into disrepute among the insular and insulated rulers of the Soviet Union, Stalin not least. In the increasingly dangerous 1930s Roosevelt allowed such representation of American interests, although one must hasten to add that the nation's diplomats were probably no worse than in former times. The President corresponded lightly with his second-raters and chose to ignore the clear warnings of trouble advanced by the only historically minded ambassador in Europe, William E. Dodd, a professor of American history at the University of Chicago whom Roosevelt impulsively had accredited to the Nazi government in Berlin.

If the first Roosevelt term passed in epistolary exchanges, with little policy or presidential concern, the second term found the President forced to take a close interest in foreign relations. By the time his second term came to an end in January 1941, Roosevelt had proposed what was to become the Lend-Lease Act of March of that year, the single most important action in foreign affairs taken by the U.S. government prior to entrance into World War II.

It was the second term, and the opening months of the third in the spring and summer of 1941, in which President Roosevelt's leadership in foreign affairs appeared at its worst, at least in the perspective of the 1970s that demands openness in presidential conduct of foreign affairs. In 1937–41 the problem was the obviously worsening international scene—the Japanese invasion of China beginning in 1937, the occupation of Austria in March, 1938, the Munich crisis over Czechoslovakia in September–October, 1938, the crisis over Danzig which became ever more serious in the summer of 1939 and eventuated in the German attack on Poland on September 1 of that year, and the declaration of war on Germany by Britain and France a few days later. In the United States the first question was what the administration, which had managed to lead the nation to better economic arrangements although not out of the Depression (this did not happen until the nation went to war in December 1941), would do. The President at the outset was highly uncertain. Then, when at long last he realized the threat to American interests both in Europe and in Asia, he chose a course which was something less than candid, an oblique approach to aiding Britain against Germany and Japan.

At the beginning of his second term in 1937, Roosevelt had his hands full with the recession of that year, and he confused his domestic friends and enlivened his domestic foes by seeking to "pack" the Supreme Court. The next year he made another maladroit political move by trying to "purge" (his enemies used the word attributed to Stalin's contemporary wholesale trials and executions of opponents in Russia) Congress of conservatives who had voted against New Deal measures. The President, however, was now looking carefully to the increasing triumphs of aggression in Europe and Asia (among other adverse changes in the international climate, the Spanish Civil War had commenced in 1936 and was proceeding toward the defeat of the democratically elected if inept Loyalist government in 1939). He was concerned that the United States enter the balance of power in Europe and Asia in favor of democracy. In a famous speech in Chicago in October 1937, the year before the Munich crisis, Roosevelt spoke of "quarantining" aggressors:

The peace-loving nations must make a concerted effort in opposition to those violations of treaties and those ignorings of humane instincts which today are creating a state of international anarchy and instability from which there is no escape through mere isolation or neutrality. . . . When an epidemic of physical disease starts to spread, the community approves and joins in a quarantine of the patients in order to protect the health of the community against the spread of the disease. . . . War is a contagion, whether it be declared or undeclared.

Faced with uncertainty in the Department of State, and believing that he had raised more domestic opposition than was wise, the President backed down from this declaration almost immediately. Always sensitive to public opinion, he decided that he had failed to win approval, and wrote off the Chicago speech as a trial balloon that had come down. "It's a terrible thing," he told one of his associates, "to look over your shoulder when you are trying to lead—and to find no one there."

It would be possible to list the increasingly anti-Axis speeches of President Roosevelt in 1938, 1939, and 1940 and show how at least with words Roosevelt was castigating the aggressive rulers of Europe and Asia, how he was trying to marshal the power of the United States to the support of democratic nations such as Britain and France. But words were about as far as he went. There was little rearmament, except passage of the Vinson Act in 1937, which promised to build the American navy up to the limit set by the Washington Naval Conference of 1921–22 and the London Naval Conferences of 1930 and 1935–36.

Perhaps words were all the President had to work with in the later 1930s, and yet one is not altogether certain. It may be that to be critical of presidential speech-making before and after the beginning of World War II in Europe is to ask of the President an impossible thing—to use the phrase of Woodrow Wilson just prior to U.S. entry into World War I. The President faced an isolationist American public. So sensitive were the Americans to the possibility of entrance into the war that they might well have voted Roosevelt out of office in the election of 1940 if the President had passed from words against the aggressors to proposals for rearmament. It is always easy for students or professors in a later time to point out weaknesses of political leadership, to note the artifices of leadership. It is also easy to sacrifice leaders and statesmen on the altar of truth when it is their careers, and not our own, which will go down. There is probably a theoretical quality in all college and university studies, and it is likewise easy to send goats into the wilderness. Still, in the light of present-day concerns about presidential leadership, one has the feeling that the President of 1937—41 moved too slowly, and eventually (as we will see) too obliquely, with his countrymen.

The statement-making of the later 1930s turned into outright misrepresentation in 1940–41. There was the notable competitive dissimulation during the presidential election of 1940. After the defeat of France in June 1940, Roosevelt had arranged for the British to receive American munitions, and in September he signed an executive agreement exchanging 50 World War I destroyers for the lease of airfields and naval stations in British territories in the New World. Taking the issue to the electorate, Roosevelt's opponents claimed he was pushing the country into war. Republican presidential candidate Wendell Willkie said that "if you elect me president I will never send an American boy to fight in any European war." The President then outdid his opponent. In Boston on October 30, 1940, Roosevelt went all the way; he told his audience that day that "while I am talking to you, fathers and mothers, I give you one more assurance. I have said this before, but I shall say it again, and again and again. Your boys are not going to be sent into any foreign wars." Three days later in Buffalo he declared: "Your President says this country is not going to war." Willkie afterward explained his own promise as "a piece of campaign oratory." Roosevelt at the time had pointed out to intimates that he, the President, had spoken only of "foreign wars" and not wars of national defense, an exhibition of verbal trickery.

This kind of trimming of public statements to fit the hallucinations of the American people, whatever the realities of international affairs, of presidential actions, and of the national interest, appeared almost as a motif in President Roosevelt's behavior, once the third inaugural had taken place in January 1941. Confident that his reelection had given him a mandate to extend aid to the government of Great Britain in the war against Hitler, the President pushed through Congress the Lend-Lease Act of March 11, 1941, a record-breaking appropriation of $7,000,000,000. It empowered the President to sell, transfer, lease, or lend munitions, weapons, airplanes, ships, food, and industrial materials to "the government of any country whose defense the President deems vital to the defense of the United States." This grant of authority, denounced by isolationists as a blank check, was the most sweeping ever given a chief executive. It was virtually a declaration of war on the European Axis powers. The President unfortunately announced the act as a measure of national self-defense and chose not to announce it as virtual involvement in World War II.

In the summer months of 1941, Roosevelt's action in foreign affairs diverged the farthest from the truth of all the years of his Presidency, from March 1933 until his death on April 12, 1945. Even before lend-lease passed Congress the President was attempting to obscure the principal problem raised by the measure, which was to get lend-lease material to Britain after it had been manufactured and put aboard ship: If German submarines sank ships en route, there was not much point in the Lend-Lease Act. The President knew the British navy was not strong enough to ensure the safety of lend-lease material, and in the spring and summer of 1941 he engaged in a playful use of words in which he virtually ordered the American navy to convoy lend-lease ships as far as Greenland and Iceland. He described U.S. Navy convoys in the Atlantic as "patrols." When during a press conference a reporter asked the difference between a patrol and a convoy, the President said it was the same difference as between a cow and a horse ("If one looks at a cow and calls it a horse that is all right with the President, but that does not make a cow a horse").

Probably the most singular of presidential deceptions before Pearl Harbor was Roosevelt's radio talk on September 11, 1941, after an action between the United States destroyer *Greer* and a German submarine. The *Greer* had trailed the submarine for three hours and 28 minutes and broadcast its position to a nearby British plane, which dropped four depth charges. Whereupon the Nazi vessel attacked the *Greer*, which answered with depth charges. According to the President's radio explanation the *Greer*

was carrying American mail to Iceland. . . . She was then and there attacked by a submarine. . . . I tell you the blunt fact that the German submarine fired first upon this American destroyer without warning, and with deliberate design to sink her. . . . We have sought no shooting war with Hitler. We do not seek it now. But neither do we want peace so much that we are willing to pay for it by permitting him to attack our naval . . . ships while they are on legitimate business. . . when you see a rattlesnake poised to strike you do not wait until he has struck before you crush him. These Nazi submarines and raiders are the rattlesnakes of the Atlantic.

The President then announced to his radio audience that he had ordered the navy to begin convoys and to "shoot on sight."

In an article published after World War II, historian Thomas A. Bailey contended that the President had had to "fool" the American people into war. The mood of the nation, Bailey claimed, was so euphoric in the summer and autumn of 1941 that it was necessary to deceive the people for their own good. This is an arresting thesis, and Bailey is a very able historian, but its point did not read well at the time, whatever the possible truth about the old argument of the means justifying the end. One does not like to feel that the future of a great democratic country should rest upon the deception of its citizenry.

One should hasten to add that the contention sometimes heard about President Roosevelt, during and after the war, that in the summer and autumn of 1941 he was engaged in an even larger piece of foolery, fooling the American people into war by exposing the American Fleet at Pearl Harbor and thereby getting the country into World War II by the "back door" after the German government had refused to oblige by opening the Atlantic front door (that is, had failed to declare war on the United States despite hostilities in the Atlantic). This contention has no truth, or at least no proof of so diabolical a plot has ever appeared. The government of the United States is too large and unwieldy a mechanism to allow the carrying out of such a plan, a scheme sounding as if it came out of Renaissance Italy in the days of Niccolo Machiavelli.

During the years of American involvement in World War II, from December 1941 to September 1945, the Roosevelt leadership was responsible for foreign policy for all except the last five months, and it is fair to say that this leadership was forthright and open, even if it did tend to gloss the difficulties of getting along with the Russians. It is difficult to fault Roosevelt's war leadership, other than to cite failures which perhaps could have appeared only in retrospect. Some of the President's contemporary and later critics were to remark that Roosevelt was a marvelous leader if he could move in a straight line. During the war there was not much need for decorating the problems of the time, and the President found the war years much more to his liking than the uneasy years 1933–41.

There remains, however, the concern of present-day Americans for the Roosevelt record of leadership in foreign affairs—if not much concern for the years of involvement, then for the years that preceded Pearl Harbor. There remains a feeling that in the early and mid-1930s the President did not face up to the realities of world affairs, and, especially, that when at last he confronted them, he did so largely in private and refused for reasons of political survival to share his perceptions with the people of his country. With a considerable lack of candor he moved the nation into an involvement with Nazi Germany. As we now can see, it was a war the nation needed to enter, a war against the most amoral ruler the world has known since the statistically clouded times of Genghis Khan. Roosevelt's left-handed leadership in foreign affairs is nonetheless an uneasy heritage for Americans of the 1970s.

SUGGESTED READINGS

ADLER, SELIG. *Isolationist Impulse.* New York: Abelard-Schuman, 1957.

BEARD, CHARLES A. *President Roosevelt and the Coming of the War: A Study in Appearances and Realities.* New Haven, Conn.: Yale University Press, 1948.

BURNS, JAMES MACGREGOR. *Roosevelt: The Lion and the Fox.* New York: Harcourt, Brace & Co., 1956.

———. *Roosevelt: The Soldier of Freedom, 1940–45.* New York: Harcourt, Brace & Co., 1970.

COLE, WAYNE. *America First: The Battle Against Intervention, 1940–41.* Madison: University of Wisconsin Press, 1953.

JONAS, MANFRED. *Isolationism in America.* Ithaca, N.Y.: Cornell University Press, 1966.

LANGER, WILLIAM L., and GLEASON, S. EVERETT. *The Challenge of Isolation, 1937–40.* New York: Harper & Bros., 1952.

———. *The Undeclared War, September 1940–December 1941.* New York: Harper & Bros., 1953.

OFFNER, ARNOLD A. *American Appeasement.* Cambridge, Mass.: Harvard University Press, 1969.

THEOBALD, ROBERT A. *The Final Secret of Pearl Harbor: The Washington Contribution to the Japanese Attack.* New York: Devin-Adair Co., 1954.

DOCUMENT 30.1

Advice from Ambassador Bullitt*

Ambassador William C. Bullitt, who represented American interests in Moscow until 1936, liked to write chatty letters to President Roosevelt showing how personal diplomacy "paid off" in the Russian capital. As was to become apparent many years later, after World War II, when one of Stalin's successors, Nikita Khrushchev, informed the 20th Party Congress in 1956 of some details of Stalin's rule, there was only one man in charge of the Soviet government in the 1930s and 1940s. Hence the personal evaluations of Ambassador Bullitt, not to mention the ambassador's friendships with ordinary Russians, were rather wide of the mark.

Moscow, August 5, 1934

MY DEAR MR. PRESIDENT:

I hope you had as good a time in Hawaii as we expected to have. I regretted not seeing you every day of your trip.

———
*Source: Edgar B. Nixon, (ed.), *Franklin D. Roosevelt and Foreign Affairs,* Vol. II (3 vols.: Cambridge, Mass.: The Balknap Press of Harvard University Press, 1969). pp. 171–72.

Jean Monnet,[1] one of my closest French friends, who has just spent six months advising the Chinese Government on financial reorganization, passed through Moscow a few days ago and gave me a creatively intimate picture of China and Japan. He is definitely of the opinion that the Japanese can be handled in such a way as to settle Eastern questions by peaceful means and I should like to spend a couple of weeks in China and Japan trying to verify his observations.

When our Hawaiian meeting was "spurlos versenkt," you suggested that you would want me to come back this autumn. If you still want to see me you might order me to report in Washington for a conference about December 1 and to come by way of the East. I could leave Vladivostok about October 15 and be in Washington by December 1st with the latest Far Eastern and Russian information. Do let me know soon how you feel about such a trip as I shall not make any plans to leave here until I know your personal wishes.

I have not been able to get anywhere with Litvinov and, while maintaining very cordial personal relations with him, have tried to build a backfire in the Kremlin by way of Voroshilov[2] and Karakhan.[3]

As a means to develop close relations with Voroshilov I imported a lot of polo equipment and have taught the Red Army Cavalry to play the game. We play every other day on a broad plain. The game at the outset had a number of unusual features not provided at Meadowbrook. All the ponies were sixteen-hand stallions who savaged each other and the riders whenever they came to close quarters, and on the first day a Mongolian soldier with an undeveloped genius for the game carried the ball in a bee-line three miles cross country before he could be stopped! The

———
[1] French diplomat; for a time first Deputy Secretary General of the League of Nations.
[2] Kliment E. Voroshilov, People's Commissar for Defense.
[3] Lev M. Karakhan, Vice-Commissar of Foreign Affairs.

polo has brought not only myself but our military men into the closest relations with the Red Army leaders and has been most useful.

As you know, I have also started baseball here and that has helped to bring us into intimate relations with the Moscow Soviet.

We have had dozens of indications lately that Stalin, Voroshilov and Molotov are most anxious to develop really friendly relations with us and I think the most important thing I can do at the moment is to get my feeble Russian into shape to have conversations with them about various matters without the aid of an interpreter. I got word from the Kremlin the other day that all the leaders of the Government, including Stalin, would be glad to see a great deal more of me than they have been seeing and in the end I think we shall be able to beat down Litvinov's resistance. I do not expect any immediate results, however, as Litvinov is about to leave Moscow for a two months' holiday and Stalin is leaving for a cure in the Caucasus. . . .

I am really too eager to see you all. The summer here has been delightful with plenty of polo, baseball, tennis and swimming in the late afternoons but the sun is already beginning to leave us and Washington is beginning to look more alluring than ever.

My very best wishes to Mrs. Roosevelt and Miss LeHand, and the hope that I may see you all soon.[4]

Yours permanently,

WILLIAM C. BULLITT

---

[4]Answered Aug. 29, 1934 (*Personal Letters, 1928–1945*, I, 416–17). Roosevelt said that he had not seen Ambassador Troyanovsky since Bullitt had returned to his post, "but everybody likes him at the State Department and I am very certain terms could be arranged if he had a more free hand."

DOCUMENT 30.2
Advice from Ambassador Dodd*

William E. Dodd was a distinguished historian of the American South and had taught many years at the University of Chicago. He was a Jeffersonian Republican in the antique sense of that designation, and his choice by President Roosevelt for the American embassy in Berlin seemed strange at the time and seems strange even in retrospect. Dodd's historical judgment proved a great help, however, even for Europe—for which area of the world, he was hardly expert. His dispatches from Berlin; his diary, which was published in later years; and his personal letters to the President all showed his perception. The dates of June 30 and July 25, 1934, referred to in the present letter, concern the so-called Blood Purge of many of Hitler's opponents and the attempted Nazi takeover of Austria by an internal coup. In the course of the latter affair Austrian Chancellor Engelbert Dollfuss was murdered.

BERLIN, August 15, 1934

DEAR MR. PRESIDENT:

According to your suggestion of May 3rd when you gave me a few minutes of your time, I am summarizing the situation in Europe, with especial reference to Germany:

1. On October 17, I had a long interview with the Chancellor in the presence of the Foreign Minister. When I reminded them of your attitude about crossing borders in a military way, Hitler asserted most positively that he would not allow a German advance across the border even if border enemies had made trouble. I named the French, Austrian and Polish fronts, and he said war might be started by violent S.A. men contrary to his command. That would be the only way.

---

*Source: Edgar B. Nixon (ed.), *Franklin D. Roosevelt and Foreign Affairs*, Vol. II (3 vols.; Cambridge, Mass.: The Belknap Press of Harvard University Press, 1969). pp. 180–81.

Now what has happened since? More men are trained, uniformed and armed (perhaps not heavy guns) than in 1914, at least a million and a half; and the funeral all the Ambassadors and Ministers attended at Tannenberg August 7 was one grand military display, contrary to von Hindenburg's known request. Every diplomat with whom I spoke regarded the whole thing as a challenge under cover. And we have plenty of evidence that up to 10 o'clock July 25 the Vienna *Putsch* against Austria was boasted of here and being put over the radio as a great German performance. Only when defeat became known was the tone changed and the radio speaker removed from his post, Habicht of Munich. So, I am sure war was just around the corner, 30,000 Austro-German Nazis waiting near Munich for the signal to march upon Vienna. These men had been maintained for a year on the Austrian border at the expense of the German people. So, it seems to me that war and not peace is the objective, and the Hitler enthusiasts think they can beat Italy and France in a month—nor is high-power aircraft wanting, the Wrights having sold them machines last April.

2. Last March, in another interview, the Chancellor almost swore to me, without witnesses, that he would never again allow German propaganda in the United States. On March 12 or 13, he issued an order that no man must be arrested and held in restraint more than 24 hours without a warrant. This was supposed to be in response to my representations about the harm done in the United States by violent treatment of the Jews here. I explained to you how, on the assumption that these promises would be kept, I managed to prevent a Hitler mock-trial in Chicago and otherwise persuaded American Jews to restrain themselves. But on the 12th of May I read excerpt on the boat from a speech of Goebbels which declared that "Jews were the syphilis of all European peoples." Of course this aroused all the animosities of the preceding winter, and I was put in the position of having been humbugged, as indeed I was. All the personal protests which I made late in May were without effect, except that the Foreign Office people expressed great sorrow.

I have reviewed these points because I think we can not depend on the promises of the highest authority when we have such facts before us. I am sorry to have to say this of a man who proclaims himself the savior of his country and assumes on occasion the powers of President, the legislature and the supreme court. But you know all this side of the matter: June 30 and July 25!

3. One other point: Germany is ceasing as fast as possible the purchase of all raw stuffs from the United States, in some cases in direct violation of treaty obligations. She is mixing wood fibre in her cotton and woolen cloth, and is setting up plants for this purpose at great expense. Schacht acknowledged this today in conversation. He said: "We can not sell you anything but hairpins and knitting needles. How can we pay you anything?" He does not believe in the system, but he says it can not be stopped. . . .

WILLIAM E. DODD

DOCUMENT 30.3

Roosevelt Replies to Ambassador Dodd*

President Roosevelt's friends and enemies have all remarked his passion for politics, and it is of interest that in response to the forebodings of Ambassador Dodd's letter of August 15, 1934, the President after a few comments turned to his primary concern, the congressional elections of November 1934.

*Source: Edgar B. Nixon (ed.), *Franklin D. Roosevelt and Foreign Affairs*, Vol. II (3 Vols. Cambridge, Mass.: The Belknap Press of Harvard University Press, 1969). pp. 186–87.

[WASHINGTON] August 25, 1934

MY DEAR DODD:

I am glad indeed to have your letter even though your situation cannot exactly be called a rosy one. It confirms my fear that the drift in Germany, and perhaps in other countries in Europe, is definitely downward and that something must break within the next six months or a year.

Harry Hopkins is back today and he is equally pessimistic. So was George Harrison of the Federal Reserve Bank.

I am on the whole fairly well satisfied with our own progress. We are under bitter political attack and will be until after election. You will have read of the formation of the American Liberty League by [Jouett] Shouse, Al Smith, James W. Wadsworth, Irenee Du Pont and John W. Davis. It has already been nicknamed the "suicide club."

I hope to see Perkins when I go to Hyde Park. I too am downhearted about Europe but I watch for any ray of hope or opening to give me an opportunity to lend a helping hand. There is nothing in sight at present.

Take care of yourself and keep on letting me have an occasional line.

As ever yours,

DOCUMENT 30.4

Quarantining the Aggressors*

The address at Chicago, October 5, 1937, has long been considered one of the President's first major efforts to awake the country to the danger to world peace presented by the aggressors in Europe and the Far East. Response to the measured condemnations of this speech was so adverse that the President quickly backed down.

---

*Source: *Peace and War: United States Foreign Policy, 1931–41* (Washington, D.C.: U.S. Government Printing Office, 1943), pp. 383–87.

PRESIDENT ROOSEVELT'S
QUARANTINE SPEECH

... The political situation in the world, which of late has been growing progressively worse, is such as to cause grave concern and anxiety to all the peoples and nations who wish to live in peace and amity with their neighbors.

Some 15 years ago the hopes of mankind for a continuing era of international peace were raised to great heights when more than 60 nations solemnly pledged themselves not to resort to arms in furtherance of their national aims and policies. The high aspirations expressed in the Briand-Kellogg Peace Pact and the hopes for peace thus raised have of late given away to a haunting fear of calamity. The present reign of terror and international lawlessness began a few years ago.

It began through unjustified interference in the internal affairs of other nations or the invasion of alien territory in violation of treaties and has now reached a stage where the very foundations of civilization are seriously threatened. The landmarks and traditions which have marked the progress of civilization toward a condition of law, order, and justice are being wiped away.

Without a declaration of war and without warning or justification of any kind, civilians, including women and children, are being ruthlessly murdered with bombs from the air. In times of so-called peace ships are being attacked and sunk by submarines without cause or notice. Nations are fomenting and taking sides in civil warfare in nations that have never done them any harm. Nations claiming freedom for themselves deny it to others.

Innocent peoples and nations are being cruelly sacrificed to a greed for power and supremacy which is devoid of all sense of justice and humane consideration.

To paraphrase a recent author, "perhaps we foresee a time when men, exultant in the technique of homicide, will rage so hotly over the world that every precious thing will be in danger, every book and picture and harmony, every treasure garnered through two millenniums, the small, the delicate, the defenseless—all will be lost or wrecked or utterly destroyed."

If those things come to pass in other parts of the world let no one imagine that America will escape, that it may expect mercy, that this Western Hemisphere will not be attacked, and that it will continue tranquilly and peacefully to carry on the ethics and the arts of civilization.

If those days come "there will be no safety by arms, no help from authority, no answer in science. The storm will rage till every flower of culture is trampled and all human beings are leveled in a vast chaos."

If those days are not to come to pass—if we are to have a world in which we can breathe freely and live in amity without fear—the peace-loving nations must make a concerted effort to uphold laws and principles on which alone peace can rest secure.

The peace-loving nations must make a concerted effort in opposition to those violations of treaties and those ignorings of humane instincts which today are creating a state of international anarchy and instability from which there is no escape through mere isolation or neutrality.

Those who cherish their freedom and recognize and respect the equal right of their neighbors to be free and live in peace, must work together for the triumph of law and moral principles in order that peace, justice, and confidence may prevail in the world. There must be a return to a belief in the pledged word, in the value of a signed treaty. There must be recognition of the fact that national morality is as vital as private morality. . . .

There is a solidarity and interdependence about the modern world, both technically and morally, which makes it impossible for any nation completely to isolate itself from economic and political upheavals in the rest of the world, especially when such upheavals appear to be spreading and not declining. There can be no stability or peace either within nations or between nations except under laws and moral standards adhered to by all. International anarchy destroys every foundation for peace. It jeopardizes either the immediate or the future security of every nation, large or small. It is, therefore, a matter of vital interest and concern to the people of the United States that the sanctity of international treaties and the maintenance of international morality be restored.

The overwhelming majority of the peoples and nations of the world today want to live in peace. They seek the removal of barriers against trade. They want to exert themselves in industry, in agriculture, and in business, that they may increase their wealth through the production of wealth-producing goods rather than striving to produce military planes and bombs and machine guns and cannon for the destruction of human lives and useful property.

In those nations of the world which seem to be piling armament on armament for purposes of aggression, and those other nations which fear acts of aggression against them and their security, a very high proportion of their national income is being spent directly for armaments. It runs from 30 to as high as 50 percent. . . .

The situation is definitely of universal concern. The questions involved relate not merely to violations of specific provisions of particular treaties; they are questions of war and of peace, of international law, and especially of principles of humanity. It is true that they involve definite violations of agreements, and especially of the Covenant of the League of Nations, the Briand-Kellogg Pact, and the Nine Power Treaty. But they also involve problems of world economy, world security, and world humanity.

It is true that the moral consciousness of the world must recognize the importance of removing injustices and well-founded grievances; but at the same time it must be aroused to the cardinal necessity of honoring sanctity of treaties, of respecting the rights and liberties of others, and of putting an end to acts of international aggression.

It seems to be unfortunately true that the epidemic of world lawlessness is spreading.

When an epidemic of physical disease starts to spread, the community approves and joins in a quarantine of the patients in order to protect the health of the community against the spread of the disease.

It is my determination to pursue a policy of peace and to adopt every practicable measure to avoid involvement in war. It ought to be inconceivable that in this modern era, and in the face of experience, any nation could be so foolish and ruthless as to run the risk of plunging the whole world into war by invading and violating in contravention of solemn treaties the territory of other nations that have done them no real harm and which are too weak to protect themselves adequately. Yet the peace of the world and the welfare and security of every nation is today being threatened by that very thing.

No nation which refuses to exercise forbearance and to respect the freedom and rights of others can long remain strong and retain the confidence and respect of other nations. No nation ever loses its dignity or good standing by conciliating its differences and by exercising great patience with and consideration for the rights of other nations.

War is a contagion, whether it be declared or undeclared. It can engulf states and peoples remote from the original scene of hostilities. We are determined to keep out of war, yet we cannot insure ourselves against the disastrous effects of war and the dangers of involvement. We are adopting such measures as will minimize our risk of involvement, but we cannot have complete protection in a world of disorder in which confidence and security have broken down.

If civilization is to survive the principles of the Prince of Peace must be restored. Shattered trust between nations must be revived.

Most important of all, the will for peace on the part of peace-loving nations must express itself to the end that nations that may be tempted to violate their agreements and the rights of others will desist from such a cause. There must be positive endeavors to preserve peace.

America hates war. America hopes for peace. Therefore, America actively engages in the search for peace.

DOCUMENT 30.5

We Must Be the Great Arsenal of Democracy*

Roosevelt's most effective means of rallying the American people behind his policies and programs was the radio fireside chat. The President, a masterful speaker, clearly enjoyed addressing the nation over the airwaves; he accompanied his words with gestures which in the days before television unfortunately could not be seen by the audience. The principal ideas expressed in this fireside chat on national security, December 29, 1940, were to be repeated in a presidential address to Congress delivered eight days later.

My friends:

This is not a fireside chat on war. It is a talk on national security; because the nub of the whole purpose of your President is to keep you now, and your children later, and your grandchildren much later, out of a last-ditch war for the preservation of American independence and all the things that American independence means to you and to me and to ours.

*Source: Samuel I. Rosenman (ed.), *The Public Papers and Addresses of Franklin D. Roosevelt: War—and Aid to Democracies* (New York: Macmillan Co., 1941), pp. 633–44.

Tonight, in the presence of a world crisis, my mind goes back eight years to a night in the midst of a domestic crisis. It was a time when the wheels of American industry were grinding to a full stop, when the whole banking system of our country had ceased to function.

I well remember that while I sat in my study in the White House, preparing to talk with the people of the United States, I had before my eyes the picture of all those Americans with whom I was talking. I saw the workmen in the mills, the mines, the factories; the girl behind the counter; the small shopkeeper; the farmer doing his spring plowing; the widows and the old men wondering about their life's savings.

I tried to convey to the great mass of American people what the banking crisis meant to them in their daily lives.

Tonight, I want to do the same thing, with the same people, in this new crisis which faces America.

We met the issue of 1933 with courage and realism.

We face this new crisis—this new threat to the security of our nation—with the same courage and realism.

Never before since Jamestown and Plymouth Rock has our American civilization been in such danger as now.

For, on September 27, 1940, by an agreement signed in Berlin, three powerful nations, two in Europe and one in Asia, joined themselves together in the threat that if the United States of America interfered with or blocked the expansion program of these three nations—a program aimed at world control—they would unite in ultimate action against the United States.

The Nazi masters of Germany have made it clear that they intend not only to dominate all life and thought in their own country, but also to enslave the whole of Europe, and then to use the resources of Europe to dominate the rest of the world.

It was only three weeks ago their leader stated this: "There are two words that stand opposed to each other." And then in defiant reply to his opponents, he said this: "Others are correct when they say: With this world we cannot ever reconcile ourselves. . . . I can beat any other power in the world." So said the leader of the Nazis.

In other words, the Axis not merely admits but *proclaims* that there can be no ultimate peace between their philosophy of government and our philosophy of government.

In view of the nature of this undeniable threat, it can be asserted, properly and categorically, that the United States has no right or reason to encourage talk of peace, until the day shall come when there is a clear intention on the part of the aggressor nations to abandon all thought of dominating or conquering the world.

At this moment, the forces of the states that are leagued against all peoples who live in freedom, are being held away from our shores. The Germans and the Italians are being blocked on the other side of the Atlantic by the British, and by the Greeks, and by thousands of soldiers and sailors who were able to escape from subjugated countries. In Asia, the Japanese are being engaged by the Chinese nation in another great defense.

In the Pacific Ocean is our fleet.

Some of our people like to believe that wars in Europe and Asia are of no concern to us. But it is a matter of most vital concern to us that European and Asiatic warmakers should not gain control of the oceans which lead to this hemisphere.

One hundred and seventeen years ago the Monroe Doctrine was conceived by our Government as a measure of defense in the face of a threat against this hemisphere by an alliance in Continental Europe. Thereafter, we stood on guard in the Atlantic, with the British as neighbors. There was no treaty. There was no "unwritten agreement."

And yet, there was the feeling, proven correct by history, that we as neighbors could settle any disputes in peaceful fashion. The fact is that during the whole of this time the Western Hemisphere has remained free from aggression from Europe or from Asia.

Does anyone seriously believe that we need to fear attack anywhere in the Americas while a free Britain remains our most powerful naval neighbor in the Atlantic? Does anyone seriously believe, on the other hand, that we could rest easy if the Axis powers were our neighbors there?

If Great Britain goes down, the Axis powers will control the continents of Europe, Asia, Africa, Australasia, and the high seas—and they will be in a position to bring enormous military and naval resources against this hemisphere. It is no exaggeration to say that all of us, in all the Americas, would be living at the point of a gun—a gun loaded with explosive bullets, economic as well as military.

We should enter upon a new and terrible era in which the whole world, our hemisphere included, would be run by threats of brute force. To survive in such a world, we would have to convert ourselves permanently into a militaristic power on the basis of war economy.

Some of us like to believe that even if Great Britain falls, we are still safe, because of the broad expanse of the Atlantic and of the Pacific.

But the width of those oceans is not what it was in the days of clipper ships. At one point between Africa and Brazil the distance is less than from Washington to Denver, Colorado—five hours for the latest type of bomber. And at the North end of the Pacific Ocean America and Asia almost touch each other.

Even today we have planes that could fly from the British Isles to New England and back again without refueling. And remember that the range of the modern bomber is ever being increased.

During the past week many people in all parts of the nation have told me what they wanted me to say tonight. Almost all of them expressed a courageous desire to hear the plain truth about the gravity of the situation. One telegram, however, expressed the attitude of the small minority who want to see no evil and hear no evil, even though they know in their hearts that evil exists. That telegram begged me not to tell again of the ease with which our American cities could be bombed by any hostile power which had gained bases in this Western Hemisphere. The gist of that telegram was: "Please, Mr. President, don't frighten us by telling us the facts."

Frankly and definitely there is danger ahead—danger against which we must prepare. But we well know that we cannot escape danger, or the fear of danger, by crawling into bed and pulling the covers over our heads.

Some nations of Europe were bound by solemn non-intervention pacts with Germany. Other nations were assured by Germany that they need *never* fear invasion. Non-intervention pact or not, the fact remains that they *were* attacked, overrun and thrown into the modern form of slavery at an hour's notice, or even without any notice at all. As an exiled leader of one of these nations said to me the other day—"The notice was a minus quantity. It was given to my Government two hours after German troops had poured into my country in a hundred places."

The fate of these nations tells us what it means to live at the point of a Nazi gun.

The Nazis have justified such actions by various pious frauds. One of these frauds is the claim that they are occupying a nation for the purpose of "restoring order." Another is that they are occupying or controlling a nation on the excuse that they are "protecting it" against the aggression of somebody else.

For example, Germany has said that she was occupying Belgium to save the Belgians from the British. Would she then hesitate to say to any South American country, "We are occupying you to protect you from aggression by the United States"?

Belgium today is being used as an invasion base against Britain, now fighting for its life. Any South American country, in Nazi hands, would always constitute a jumping-off place for German attack on any one of the other Republics of this hemisphere.

Analyze for yourselves the future of two other places even nearer to Germany if the Nazis won. Could Ireland hold out? Would Irish freedom be permitted as an amazing pet exception in an unfree world? Or the Islands of the Azores which still fly the flag of Portugal after five centuries? You and I think of Hawaii as an outpost of defense in the Pacific. And yet, the Azores are closer to our shores in the Atlantic than Hawaii is on the other side.

There are those who say that the Axis powers would never have any desire to attack the Western Hemisphere. That is the same dangerous form of wishful thinking which has destroyed the powers of resistance of so many conquered peoples. The plain facts are that the Nazis have proclaimed, time and again, that all other races are their inferiors and therefore subject to their orders. And most important of all, the vast resources and wealth of this American Hemisphere constitute the most tempting loot in all the round world.

Let us no longer blind ourselves to the undeniable fact that the evil forces which have crushed and undermined and corrupted so many others are already within our own gates. Your Government knows much about them and every day is ferreting them out.

Their secret emissaries are active in our own and in neighboring countries. They seek to stir up suspicion and dissension to cause internal strife. They try to turn capital against labor, and vice versa. They try to reawaken long slumbering racial and religious enmities which should have no place in this country. They are active in every group that promotes intolerance. They exploit for their own ends our natural abhorrence of war. These trouble-breeders have but one purpose. It is to divide our people into hostile groups and to destroy our unity and shatter our will to defend ourselves.

There are also American citizens, many of them in high places, who, unwittingly in most cases, are aiding and abetting the work of these agents. I do not charge these American citizens with being foreign agents. But I do charge them with doing exactly the kind of work that the dictators want done in the United States.

These people not only believe that we can save our own skins by shutting our eyes to the fate of other nations. Some of them go much further than that. They say that we can and should become the friends and even the partners of the Axis powers. Some of them even suggest that we should imitate the methods of the dictatorships. Americans never can and never will do that.

The experience of the past two years has proven beyond doubt that no nation can appease the Nazis. No man can tame a tiger into a kitten by stroking it. There can be no appeasement with ruthlessness. There can be no reasoning with an incendiary bomb. We know now that a nation can have peace with the Nazis only at the price of total surrender.

Even the people of Italy have been forced to become accomplices of the Nazis; but at this moment they do not know how soon they will be embraced to death by their allies.

The American appeasers ignore the warning to be found in the fate of Austria, Czechoslovakia, Poland, Norway, Belgium, the Netherlands, Denmark, and France. They tell you that the Axis powers are going to win anyway; that all this bloodshed in the world could be saved; that the United States might just as well throw its influence into the scale of a dictated peace, and get the best out of it that we can.

They call it a "negotiated peace." Nonsense! Is it a negotiated peace if a gang of outlaws surrounds your community and on threat of extermination makes you pay tribute to save your own skins?

Such a dictated peace would be no peace at all. It would be only another armistice, leading to the most gigantic armament race and the most devastating trade wars in all history. And in these contests the Americas would offer the only real resistance to the Axis powers.

With all their vaunted efficiency, with all their parade of pious purpose in this war, there are still in their background the concentration camp and the servants of God in chains.

The history of recent years proves that shootings and chains and concentration camps are not simply the transient tools but the very altars of modern dictatorships. They may talk of a "new order" in the world, but what they have in mind is only a revival of the oldest and the worst tyranny. In that there is no liberty, no religion, no hope.

The proposed "new order" is the very opposite of a United States of Europe or a United States of Asia. It is not a Government based upon the consent of the governed. It is not a union of ordinary, self-respecting men and women to protect themselves and their freedom and their dignity from oppression. It is an unholy alliance of power and pelf to dominate and enslave the human race.

The British people and their allies today are conducting an active war against this unholy alliance. Our own future security is greatly dependent on the outcome of that fight. Our ability to "keep out of war" is going to be affected by that outcome.

Thinking in terms of today and tomorrow, I make the direct statement to the American people that there is far less chance of the United States getting into war, if we do all we can now to support the nations defending themselves against attack by the Axis than if we acquiesce in their defeat, submit tamely to an Axis victory, and wait our turn to be the object of attack in another war later on.

If we are to be completely honest with ourselves, we must admit that there is risk in any course we may take. But I deeply believe that the great majority of our people agree that the course that I advocate involves the least risk now and the greatest hope for world peace in the future.

The people of Europe who are defending themselves do not ask us to do their fighting. They ask us for the implements of war, the planes, the tanks, the guns, the freighters which will enable them to fight for their liberty and for our security. Emphatically we must get these weapons to them in sufficient volume and quickly enough, so that we and our children will be saved the agony and suffering of war which others have had to endure.

Let not the defeatists tell us that it is too late. It will never be earlier. Tomorrow will be later than today.

Certain facts are self-evident.

In a military sense Great Britain and the British Empire are today the spearhead of resistance to world conquest. They are putting up a fight which will live forever in the story of human gallantry.

There is no demand for sending an American Expeditionary Force outside our own borders. There is no intention by any member of your Government to send such a force. You can, therefore, nail any talk about sending armies to Europe as deliberate untruth.

Our national policy is not directed toward war. Its sole purpose is to keep war away from our country and our people.

Democracy's fight against world conquest is being greatly aided, and must be more greatly aided, by the rearmament of the United States and by sending every ounce and every ton of munitions and supplies that we can possibly spare to help the defenders who are in the front lines. It is not more unneutral for us to do that than it is for Sweden, Russia and other nations near Germany, to send steel and ore and oil and other war materials into Germany every day in the week.

We are planning our own defense with the utmost urgency; and in its vast scale we must integrate the war needs of Britain and the other free nations which are resisting aggression.

This is not a matter of sentiment or of controversial personal opinion. It is a matter of realistic, practical military policy, based on the advice of our military experts who are in close touch with existing warfare. These military and naval experts and the members of the Congress and the Administration have a single-minded purpose—the defense of the United States.

This nation is making a great effort to produce everything that is necessary in this emergency—and with all possible speed. This great effort requires great sacrifice.

I would ask no one to defend a democracy which in turn would not defend everyone in the nation against want and privation. The strength of this nation shall not be diluted by the failure of the Government to protect the economic well-being of its citizens.

If our capacity to produce is limited by machines, it must ever be remembered that these machines are operated by the skill and the stamina of the workers. As the Goverment is determined to protect the rights of the workers, so the nation has a right to expect that the men who man the machines will discharge their full responsibilities to the urgent needs of defense.

The worker possesses the same human dignity and is entitled to the same security of position as the engineer or the manager or the owner. For the workers provide the human power that turns out the destroyers, the airplanes and the tanks.

The nation expects our defense industries to continue operation without interruption by strikes or lock-outs. It expects and insists that management and workers will reconcile their differences by voluntary or legal means, to continue to produce the supplies that are so sorely needed.

And on the economic side of our great defense program, we are, as you know, bending every effort to maintain stability of prices and with that the stability of the cost of living.

Nine days ago I announced the setting up of a more effective organization to direct our gigantic efforts to increase the production of munitions. The appropriation of vast sums of money and a well coordinated executive direction of our defense efforts are not in themselves enough. Guns, planes, ships and many other things have to be built in the factories and arsenals of America. They have to be produced by workers and managers and engineers with the aid of machines which in turn have to be built by hundreds of thousands of workers throughout the land.

In this great work there has been splendid cooperation between the Government and industry and labor; and I am very thankful.

American industrial genius, unmatched throughout the world in the solution of production problems, has been called upon to bring its resources and its talents into action. Manufacturers of watches, farm implements, linotypes, cash registers, automobiles, sewing machines, lawn mowers and locomotives are now making fuses, bomb packing crates, telescope mounts, shells, pistols and tanks.

But all our present efforts are not enough. We must have more ships, more guns, more plans—more of everything. This can only be accomplished if we discard the notion of "business as usual." This job cannot be done merely by superimposing on the existing productive facilities the added requirements of the nation for defense.

Our defense efforts must not be blocked by those who fear the future consequences of surplus plant capacity. The possible consequences of failure of our defense efforts now are much more to be feared.

After the present needs of our defenses are past, a proper handling of the country's peace-time needs will require all the new productive capacity—if not more.

No pessimistic policy about the future of America shall delay the immediate expansion of those industries essential to defense. We need them.

I want to make it clear that it is the purpose of the nation to build now with all possible speed every machine, every arsenal, every factory that we need to manufacture our defense material. We have the men—the skill—the wealth—and above all, the will.

I am confident that if and when production of consumer or luxury goods in certain industries requires the use of machines and raw materials that are essential for defense purposes, then such production must yield, and will gladly yield, to our primary and compelling purpose.

I appeal to the owners of plants—to the managers—to the workers—to our own Government employees—to put every ounce of effort into producing these munitions swiftly and without stint. With this appeal I give you the pledge that all of us who are officers of your Government will devote ourselves to the same wholehearted extent to the great task that lies ahead.

As planes and ships and guns and shells are produced, your Government, with its defense experts, can then determine how best to use them to defend this hemisphere. The decision as to how much shall be sent abroad and how much shall remain at home must be made on the basis of our over-all military necessities.

We must be the great arsenal of democracy. For us this is an emergency as serious as war itself. We must apply ourselves to our task with the same resolution, the same sense of urgency, the same spirit of patriotism and sacrifice as we would show were we at war.

We have furnished the British great material support and we will furnish far more in the future.

There will be no "bottlenecks" in our determination to aid Great Britain. No dictator, no combination of dictators, will weaken that determination, by threats of how they will construe that determination.

The British have received invaluable military support from the heroic Greek army, and from the forces of all the governments in exile. Their strength is growing. It is the strength of men and women who value their freedom more highly than they value their lives.

I believe that the Axis powers are not going to win this war. I base that belief on the latest and best information.

We have no excuse for defeatism. We have every good reason for hope—hope for peace, hope for the defense of our civilization and for the building of a better civilization in the future.

I have the profound conviction that the American people are now determined to put forth a mightier effort than they have ever yet made to increase our production of all the implements of defense, to meet the threat to our democratic faith.

As President of the United States I call for that national effort. I call for it in the name of this nation which we love and honor and which we are privileged and proud to serve. I call upon our people with absolute confidence that our common cause will greatly succeed.

DOCUMENT 30.6
The Attorney General Gives an Opinion*

American Presidents often have depended upon experts from the various executive departments of the federal government to produce legal justification for acts of dubious constitutionality. For example, in 1917—prior to the nation's entry into World War I—Woodrow Wilson circumvented a Senate filibuster to prevent the arming of merchant vessels by obtaining an opinion from Secretary of State Robert Lansing which held that such action could be taken under terms of an unrepealed statute of 1797. Attorney General Robert H. Jackson's opinion of August 27, 1940, justifying lend-lease, displays more than a little ingenuity.

*Source: *Department of State Bulletin*, Vol. III, No. 63 (September 7, 1940), pp. 201–7.

My Dear Mr. President:

In accordance with your request I have considered your constitutional and statutory authority to proceed by Executive Agreement with the British Government immediately to acquire for the United States certain off-shore naval and air bases in the Atlantic Ocean without awaiting the inevitable delays which would accompany the conclusion of a formal treaty. . . .

The questions of constitutional and statutory authority, with which alone I am concerned, seem to be these.

First. May such an acquisition be concluded by the President under an Executive Agreement or must it be negotiated as a Treaty subject to ratification by the Senate?

Second. Does authority exist in the President to alienate the title to such ships . . . , and if so, on what conditions?

Third. Do the statutes of the United States limit the right to deliver . . . the over-age destroyers by reason of the belligerent status of Great Britain? . . .

Happily, there has been little occasion in our history for the interpretation of the powers of the President as Commander-in-Chief of the Army and Navy. I do not find it necessary to rest upon that power alone to sustain the present proposal. But it will hardly be open to controversy that the vesting of such a function in the President also places upon him a responsibility to use all constitutional authority which he may possess to provide adequate bases and stations for the utilization of the naval and air weapons of the United States at their highest efficiency in our defense. It seems equally beyond doubt that present world conditions forbid him to risk any delay that is constitutionally avoidable.

The second power to be considered is that control of foreign relations which the Constitution vests in the President as a part of the Executive function. . . . The President's power over foreign relations . . . is not unlimited. Some negotiations involve commitments as to the future which would carry an obligation to exercise powers vested in the Congress. Such Presidential arrangements are customarily submitted for ratification by a two-thirds vote of the Senate before the future legislative power of the country is committed. However, the acquisitions which you are proposing to accept are without express or implied promises on the part of the United States to be performed in the future. The consideration . . . is completed upon transfer of the specified items. The Executive Agreement obtains an opportunity to establish naval and air bases for the protection of our coastline but it imposes no obligation upon the Congress to appropriate money to improve the opportunity. It is not necessary for the Senate to ratify an opportunity that entails no obligation.

There are precedents which might be cited, but not all strictly pertinent. The proposition falls far short in magnitude of the acquisition by President Jefferson of the Louisiana Territory from a belligerent during a European war, the Congress later appropriating the consideration and the Senate later ratifying a treaty embodying the agreement.

I am also reminded that in 1850, Secretary of State Daniel Webster acquired Horse Shoe Reef, at the entrance of Buffalo Harbor, upon condition that the United States would engage to erect a lighthouse and maintain a light but would erect no fortification thereon. This was done without awaiting legislative authority. Subsequently the Congress made appropriations for the lighthouse, which was erected in 1856. . . .

It is not believed, however, that it is necessary here to rely exclusively upon your constitutional power. . . . I think there is also ample statutory authority to support the acquisition of these bases, and the precedents perhaps most nearly in point are the numerous acquisitions of rights in foreign countries for sites of diplomatic and consular establishments—perhaps also the trade agreements recently negotiated under statutory authority and the acquisition in 1903 of coaling and naval stations and rights in Cuba. . . .

The transaction now proposed represents only an exchange with no statutory requirement for the embodiment thereof in any treaty and involving no promises or undertakings by the United States that might raise the question of the propriety of incorporation in a treaty. I therefore advise that acquisition by Executive Agreement of the rights proposed to be conveyed to the United States by Great Britain will not require ratification by the Senate.

The right of the President to dispose of vessels of the Navy . . . finds clear recognition in at least two enactments of the Congress and a decision of the Supreme Court—and any who assert that the authority does not exist must assume the burden of establishing that both the Congress and the Supreme Court meant something less than the clear import of seemingly plain language [acts of March 3, 1883 and June 28, 1940; *Levinson* v. *United States*, 258 U.S. 198, 201] . . . .

Whether the statutes of the United States prevent the dispatch to Great Britain, a belligerent power, of the . . . over-age destroyers depends upon the interpretation to be placed on section 3 of title V of the act of June 15, 1917. . . . This section reads:

During a war in which the United States is a neutral nation, it shall be unlawful to send out of the jurisdiction of the United States any vessel, built, armed, or equipped as a vessel of war, or converted from a private vessel into a vessel of war, with any intent or under any agreement or contract, written or oral, that such vessel shall be delivered to a belligerent nation, or to an agent, officer, or citizen of such nation, or with reasonable cause to believe that the said vessel shall or will be employed in the service of any such belligerent nation after its departure from the jurisdiction of the United States.

This section . . . is inapplicable to vessels, like the over-age destroyers, which were not built, armed, equipped as, or converted into, vessels of war with the intent that they should enter the service of a belligerent. . . .

In this connection it has been noted that during the war between Russia and Japan in 1904 and 1905, the German Government permitted the sale to Russia of torpedo boats and also of ocean liners belonging to its auxiliary navy. . . .

Accordingly, you are respectfully advised:

a) That the proposed arrangement may be concluded as an Executive Agreement, effective without awaiting ratification.

b) That there is presidential power to transfer title and possession of the proposed considerations. . . .

c) That . . . there is no legal obstacle to . . . delivery.

Respectfully submitted,
ROBERT H. JACKSON
Attorney General

DOCUMENT 30.7
Roosevelt Speaks in Boston*

President Roosevelt's speech of October 30 came shortly after Wendell L. Willkie, his Republican opponent in the 1940 election campaign, told a GOP rally in Baltimore: "If you elect him [Roosevelt] you may expect war in April, 1941." Roosevelt and his jittery advisers believed they had to reassure the mothers and fathers of America that their sons were not ticketed for slaughter on the battlefield. They were particularly anxious because of the location. Boston was marked by the Anglophobia of its citizens of Irish descent, and Massachusetts Democratic Senator David I. Walsh was a pronounced isolationist. Consequently, in his address the President catered to national fears and to local prejudices; he had sufficient political courage, however, to emphasize the necessity of extending further American aid to the British.

---

*Source: *The New York Times*, October 31, 1940. Copyright by *The New York Times*; reprinted by permission.

Mr. Mayor, my friends of
New England:

I've had a glorious day here in New England. And I don't need to tell you that I've been glad to come back to my old stamping ground in Boston. There's only one thing about this trip that I regret. I have to return to Washington tonight, without getting a chance to go into my two favorite States, Maine and Vermont.

This is the third inning. In New York City, two nights ago, I showed ... how Republican leaders, with their votes and in their speeches, have been playing and still are playing politics with national defense.

Even during the past three years, when the dangers to all forms of democracy throughout the world have been obvious, the Republican team in the Congress has been acting only as a party team.

Time after time, Republican leadership refused to see that what this country needs is an all-American team. . . .

Our objective is to keep any potential attacker as far from our continental shores as we possibly can.

And you, here in New England, know well and visualize it, that within the past two months your government has acquired new naval and air bases in British territory in the Atlantic Ocean, extending all the way from Newfoundland on the north to that part of South America where the Atlantic Ocean begins to narrow, with Africa not far away. . . .

And while I am talking to you, fathers and mothers, I give you one more assurance.

I have said this before, but I shall say it again, and again and again. Your boys are not going to be sent into any foreign wars.

They are going into training to form a force so strong that, by its very existence, it will keep the threat of war far away from our shores. Yes, the purpose of our defense is defense. . . .

I have discussed the falsifications which Republican campaign orators have been making about the economic condition of the nation, the condition of labor and the condition of business.

They are even more ridiculous when they shed those old crocodile tears over the plight of the American farmer.

Now, if there is any one that a Republican candidate loves more than the laboring man in October and up to election day, it's the farmer.

And the very first one that he forgets after election day is the farmer. . . .

No, the American farmers will not be deceived by pictures of Old Guard candidates, patting cows and pitching hay in front of moving-picture cameras. . . .

Now, among the Republican leaders, among the Republican leaders who have voted against . . . practically every . . . farm bill for the United States is the present chairman of the Republican National Committee, that "peerless leader," that "farmers' friend"—Congressman Joe Martin of Massachusetts. . . .

I will have to let you in on a secret. It will come as a great surprise to you, and it's this:

I'm enjoying this campaign and I am really having a fine time. . . .

DOCUMENT 30.8
This Was Piracy*

President Roosevelt's fireside chat of September 11, 1941, was an explanation and defense of his administration's policy of naval and air patrols in the Atlantic. The occasion for it was the sinking of an American destroyer by a German submarine a week earlier.

My Fellow-Americans:

The Navy Department of the United States has reported to me that on the morning of Sept. 4 the United States de-

*Source: The New York Times, September 12, 1941. Copyright by The New York Times; reprinted by permission.

stroyer Greer, proceeding in full daylight toward Iceland, had reached a point southeast of Greenland. She was carrying American mail to Iceland. She was flying the American flag. Her identity as an American ship was unmistakable.

She was then and there attacked by a submarine. Germany admits that it was a German submarine. The submarine deliberately fired a torpedo at the Greer, followed later by another torpedo attack. In spite of what Hitler's propaganda bureau has invented, and in spite of what any American obstructionist organization may prefer to believe, I tell you the blunt fact that the German submarine fired first upon this American destroyer without warning, and with deliberate design to sink her.

Our destroyer, at the time, was in waters which the Government of the United States had declared to be waters of self-defense, surrounding outposts of American protection in the Atlantic. . . .

This was piracy, piracy legally and morally. It was not the first nor the last act of piracy which the Nazi government has committed against the American flag in this war, for attack has followed attack. . . .

In the face of all this we Americans are keeping our feet on the ground. Our type of democratic civilization has outgrown the thought of feeling compelled to fight some other nation by reason of any single piratical attack on one of our ships. We are not becoming hysterical or losing our sense of proportion. Therefore, what I am thinking and saying tonight does not relate to any isolated episode. . . .

To be ultimately successful in world mastery, Hitler knows that he must get control of the seas. He must first destroy the bridge of ships which we are building across the Atlantic and over which we shall continue to roll the implements of war to help destroy him, to destroy all his works in the end. He must wipe out our patrol on sea and in the air if he is to do it. He must silence the British Navy. . . .

This attack on the Greer was no local-ized military operation in the North Atlantic. This was no mere episode in a struggle between two nations. This was one determined step toward creating a permanent world system based on force, terror and on murder. . . .

Normal practices of diplomacy—note writing—are of no possible use in dealing with international outlaws who sink our ships and kill our citizens. . . .

We have sought no shooting war with Hitler. We do not seek it now. But neither do we want peace so much that we are willing to pay for it by permitting him to attack our naval and merchant ships while they are on legitimate business.

I assume that the German leaders are not deeply concerned tonight, or any other time, by what the real Americans or the American Government says or publishes about them. We cannot bring about the downfall of nazism by the use of long-range invective.

But when you see a rattlesnake poised to strike, you do not wait until he has struck before you crush him.

These Nazi submarines and raiders are the rattlesnakes of the Atlantic. They are a menace to the free pathways of the high seas. They are a challenge to our own sovereignty. They hammer at out most precious rights when they attack ships of the American flag—symbols of our independence, our freedom, our very life. . . .

Do not let us be hair-splitters. Let us not ask ourselves whether the Americans should begin to defend themselves after the first attack, or the fifth attack, or the tenth attack, or the twentieth attack.

The time for active defense is now.

Do not let us split hairs. Let us not say, "We will only defend ourselves if the torpedo succeeds in getting home, or if the crew and the passengers are drowned." . . .

Upon our naval and air patrol—now operating a large number over a vast expanse of the Atlantic Ocean—falls the duty of maintaining the American policy of freedom of the seas—now. That means, very simply, very clearly, that our patrolling vessels and planes will protect all merchant ships—not only American ships but ships of any flag—engaged in commerce in our defensive waters. They will protect them from submarines; they will protect them from surface raiders.

This situation is not new. The second President of the United States, John Adams, ordered the United States Navy to clean out European privateers and European ships of war which were infesting the Caribbean and South American waters, destroying American commerce.

The third President of the United States, Thomas Jefferson, ordered the United States Navy to end the attacks being made upon American and other ships by the corsairs of the nations of North Africa.

My obligation as President is historic; it is clear; yes, it is inescapable.

It is no act of war on our part when we decide to protect the seas that are vital to American defense. The aggression is not ours. Ours is solely defense.

But let this warning be clear. From now on, if German or Italian vessels of war enter the waters the protection of which is necessary for American defense, they do so at their own peril. . . .

I have no illusions about the gravity of this step. I have not taken it hurriedly or lightly. It is the result of months and months of constant thought and anxiety and prayer. . . .

The American people have faced other grave crises in their history. . . . And with that inner strength that comes to a free people conscious of their duty, conscious of the righteousness of what they do, they will—with divine help and guidance—stand their ground against this latest assault upon their democracy, their sovereignty and their freedom.

31 Postwar America: The Homefront

JOHN EDWARD WILTZ
Indiana University

For all of the grim headlines of the years 1941–45 proclaiming the disasters on Bataan, the slaughter on the beaches of Tarawa, and the bloodletting in the Ardennes, World War II had not been a particularly agonizing experience for Americans. Less than a half million Americans had died as a result of enemy action (roughly one thirtieth the toll suffered by the Soviet Union), no bombs had fallen on American cities, and no invading armies had scarred the American countryside. On the contrary, the war had yielded large benefits to the United States. In addition to forging unity among the national population and giving Americans fresh confidence in their technical and organizational skills and their courage, the war had cast the Great Depression of the 1930s into the dustbin of unpleasant memories, brought unprecedented prosperity to the country, and enabled most workers and farmers to accumulate savings on a scale which only a decade before would have seemed an impossible dream.

Looking to the future, Americans and their leaders, when the war ended, inclined toward optimism. Was it justified?

According to one view in the 1970s, the immediate postwar years, insofar as life inside America was concerned, were not marked by important achievement. On the contrary, they were a sort of dark period in the domestic history of the republic.

The years which unfolded after Japan's surrender, so the argument goes, were a time of economic turmoil when Americans, while trying "to get back to normal," were plagued by a succession of work stoppages and rising prices. Politically, "statehouse rings" were despoiling state treasuries and the infamous "Missouri gang", which had accompanied Harry Truman into the White House, was peddling its influence in the national capital. In the Congress a "conservative coalition" of northern Republicans and southern Democrats on Capitol Hill were unceremoniously shooting down President Truman's "Fair Deal" proposals, through which the President hoped to revive the progressive movement in America and inaugurate a sweeping program of social reform.

More disheartening, the postwar era was a time when countless millions of white Americans, in the North as well as the South, shared the sentiments of Senator Richard B. Russell of Georgia, who declared in 1946 that "we will resist to the bitter end, whatever the consequences, any measure or any movement which would have a tendency to bring about social equality and intermingling and amalgamation of the races." The "conservative coalition" unceremoniously had scuttled President Truman's requests for civil rights legislation. In the South whites had prevented movie houses from showing such films as *Pinky* and *Intruder in the Dust,* which dealt sympathetically with the plight of black Americans. Throughout the nation the great preponderance of Negroes found it almost impossible to break out of the chains of discrimination and segregation, to achieve dignity, equal opportunity, equal justice and, in the South at least, that most basic right of a citizen in a democracy, the right to vote.

It has been fashionable to compare the years after World War II in America with those after the Civil War and the World War I. Countless students in college history courses have written examination essays pointing out the similarities between the political conservatism of Americans in the years after 1865, 1918, and 1945; the corruption in the administrations of Presidents Grant, Harding, and Truman; and the racism of the Ku Klux Klans of the 1870s and the 1920s as well as of such white supremacists as Senator Russell in the later 1940s. Still, the years after World War II were not entirely devoid of domestic achievement in America and, lest one have a distorted view, he should take cognizance of some of the era's accomplishments as well as its shortcomings. Of those domestic achievements the one that commands first attention was the successful reconversion of the national economy to a peacetime basis.

Some Americans after World War II, still clinging to the conventional wisdom that economic bust must follow upon economic boom, calculated that another great crisis was bound to follow the prosperity of 1941-45. The prophets of gloom in America were not alone in predicting economic calamity; Marxist-Leninist theorists held similar views. The Kremlin apparently was counting on a collapse of the citadel of world capitalism, the United States, to open the way for the grand triumph of communism in the postwar era. How did events unfold?

America's reconversion presented fewer and less troublesome problems than any-body had dared to anticipate. The civil economy absorbed some 10,000,000 service men and women with hardly a ripple of distress. To be sure, there were strikes, shortages, price increases, and a black market. Still, reconversion came off with amazing dispatch and must rank as one of the premier economic triumphs in the national history. There was no depression, nor, as many Americans had feared, was there runaway inflation. On the contrary, the country's war-born prosperity, fed by savings accumulated during the war and an insatiable demand for consumer goods —and also by a continuing high level of federal spending—continued to expand. There was no serious unemployment, and in the five years after the war national output increased from $213,000,000,000 annually to $284,000,000,000. National income soared from $181,000,000,000 to $214,000,000,000. Even the farmer, for several generations "the sick man" of the American economy, shared handsomely in the postwar prosperity, and tenancy, a central index of the state of agriculture in America, reached its lowest point in the 20th century.

Notwithstanding the mood of conservatism in the country and the strength of the conservative coalition on Capitol Hill, the time after Japan's surrender was not barren of significant legislation. One of the most important of the new laws was the Employment Act of 1946 which was intended to reassure working people against the fear of a new depression in the postwar era. Substantively, it gave legal sanction to the New Deal principle that maintenance of a high level of prosperity was a responsibility of the national government. The Employment Act—or Full Employment Act, as it sometimes was called— resulted from President Truman's famous message to Congress in September 1945 in which he spelled out his program of innovation and reform known as the "Fair Deal." When the President asked for full employment legislation, many conservatives were aghast. They argued that private enterprise alone should assume responsibility for the country's economic welfare. But the legislation embodying the president's proposal passed Congress in early 1946. To guarantee maximum employment and, more than that, to keep the entire economy prosperous, the legislation established the Council of Economic Advisers, which was to maintain a continual watch on the economy, advise the President, and assist in preparing an annual economic report to Congress. In event the economy showed signs of weakness, the act obliged the President to fashion policies and recommend legislation that would maintain full employment and restore the economy to prosperity. The Employment Act, while not wholly effective, was nonetheless noteworthy in that it required the federal government to look after the national economic welfare and to take positive action to maintain a healthy economy. In a word, government inaction, particularly in time of depression—and also in time of runaway inflation—became illegal.

Apart from reconversion of the economy, the most important achievements inside America in the postwar period came in the area of equal rights. Employment and professional opportunities for blacks, for example, slowly enlarged, and discrimination in wages and seniority rights declined. Scattered cities and towns approved ordinances opening hotels and parks and swimming pools to citizens of minority groups. Blacks gained entry to graduate and professional schools in several state universities of the South, here and there religious congregations integrated memberships, and Archbishop Joseph E. Ritter ordered desegregation of the large Catholic school system of St. Louis. In 1947 a federal judge ordered the Democratic Party of South Carolina to permit blacks to vote in its primary elections. Most dramatic, perhaps, was desegregation of major league baseball, when, in 1947, Jackie Robinson became the first baseman of the Brooklyn Dodgers.

And so, if the walls of prejudice, discrimination, and segregation did not come tumbling down in the years after the war, black Americans—because of their own long campaign for civil rights as well as the awakening of many whites to the evils of racism—made a beginning in their quest for equality.

While the most portentous foreign policy development of the two decades following the defeat of the Nazis and the Japanese was the cold war, it was also in this same period that fundamental American liberties of freedom of expression, association, and political activity were under attack on the domestic front. Indeed, internal and external events were causally linked as part of the same seamless web. In this regard there is a certain irony in the unfolding events, considering that Americans had recently fought a global war for the alleged purpose of striking down the enemies of freedom. But in retrospect, what happened was not so surprising, particularly given the superheated patriotism nourished by the war; in no small part it prepared the way for postwar illiberalism and infringements on freedom.

"Red baiting," of course, was not a new phenomenon in America. Back in the last decades of the 19th century "regular" Americans had become exercised over the views and activities of anarchists and other assorted radicals; and, on occasion, they responded in ways which did not exactly square with heralded American ideals. In the first years of the 20th century and during World War I, socialists and "Wobblies" (members of the radical labor organization the Industrial Workers of the World), were targets of harassment and intimidation; then, after the war, in 1919–20, the country experienced the "Red Scare," which was spurred largely by fear that alien radicals were conspiring a takeover in America similar to that engineered by the Bolsheviks in Russia. Through the 1920s and into the 1930s members of Congress occasionally sought to win attention by lashing out at the communists and other radicals who allegedly were "boring from within" to bring about collapse of America's democratic–free enterprise society. Then, in 1938, the House of Representatives created the House Un-American Activities Committee, and before long the newspaper-reading public was absorbing with credulity solemn charges that the Boy Scouts and Campfire Girls had become targets of communist subversives and that child actress Shirley Temple had been connected with communist causes. In 1940, Congress passed the Smith Act, making it unlawful for any person to advocate or teach the violent overthrow of any government in the United States, local, state, or national, or to organize or become a member of any group dedicated to teaching such a doctrine.

The nation's Red baiters more or less went into eclipse after America's entry in World War II and the forging of the Grand Alliance between the United States and the world leader of communism, the Soviet Union. But even before the end of the war fears of communist subversion in America were rekindled when federal officials swooped down on the offices of *Amerasia*, a communist-sponsored monthly magazine which sought to influence American policy in the Far East, and found piles of classified diplomatic and military documents. A few months later the war ended, and almost at once it was evident that optimism about the postwar era was tempered by concern over communist subversion in the United States, more so when Americans pondered Soviet behavior in Eastern Europe and read that communist parties in Western Europe and elsewhere were beginning to stir. When a Soviet espionage ring in Canada was exposed in 1946, fear of subversion in the United States heightened.

By 1947, when all Americans were aware that their republic and its allies were locked in a cold war with the Soviet Union, the outcome was increasing popular determination to guard against the rav-

ages of internal subversion. Among those who set about to check the nation's communists was President Truman, who, by instituting a comprehensive loyalty investigation of all federal employees, added to the anticommunist hysteria. Although he urged investigators to move with fair regard for justice, most civil libertarians complained that the investigation (which lasted from 1947 until 1951 and resulted in dismissal of 212 employees whose loyalty seemed doubtful) operated with a heavy hand and showed scant concern for the rights of those under scrutiny. Meanwhile the FBI was gathering evidence that leaders of the American Communist Party had violated the Smith Act by plotting violent overthrow of the national government. At length, in 1949, the government brought 11 leaders of the CPUSA to trial, and all were found guilty, fined $10,000 each, and sentenced to prison terms ranging from three to five years. Their convictions were upheld by the Supreme Court in 1951, on the ground that constitutional guarantees of freedom of speech and political activity afforded no protection to conspirators seeking violent destruction of the American constitutional system: Some Americans felt that freedom of expression and political activity had suffered a grievous blow. Could a nation, in effect, preserve democracy by whittling away its very props?

Notwithstanding the administration's drive against domestic communists, millions of Americans, their suspicions heightened by the frenetic investigations of the House Un-American Activities Committee (HUAC), continued to fear that the country—and particularly the government in Washington—was honeycombed with communist traitors. Such fear dramatically increased when the HUAC charged that Alger Hiss, a one-time official in the State Department, had been a Soviet spy. Hiss vehemently denied the charge. Those who deplored what they believed were HUAC's "witch hunting" tactics shared Truman's view, given as the presidential election campaign of 1948 was getting underway, that the investigation of Hiss by the Republican-controlled committee was "a red herring" intended to embarrass the Democrats. Then, largely as a consequence of the enterprise of Representative Richard M. Nixon of California, a committee member, the HUAC produced evidence that Hiss, back in the 1930s, had indeed passed copies of classified documents to a Soviet spy ring, whereupon Hiss was indicted for perjury. A trial in 1949 ended in a hung jury, but a second trial, completed in early 1950, resulted in conviction and a prison term for Hiss. How did Americans view the Hiss affair? Millions of them agreed with Congressman Nixon that no greater treason had marked the pages of American history than that of Alger Hiss.

If Americans felt numbed and sickened that a handsome, charming, and intelligent man such as Hiss would betray the trust of his countrymen, in 1949 and 1950 they endured still other shocks which reinforced a growing mood of fright and suspicion. First, in March 1949, came the arrest of Judith Coplon, a young Justice Department political analyst charged with having given Soviet agents important information on the FBI's counterespionage system. Then, in September 1949, came news that the Soviets had exploded an atomic bomb and broken the atomic monopoly which had provided the ultimate guarantee of America's security. This development was at least a half dozen years earlier than American scientists had thought possible. Next, in December 1949, came news that Chiang Kai-shek had given up the struggle against China's communists, fled to the island of Formosa, and conceded, for the time being at least, control of nearly one fourth of the world's population to the regime of Mao Tse-tung. The outcome of Chiang's fall was an acceleration of charges echoing across the United States for a year or more that communist successes in China were the consequence of concessions American leaders had made to the Soviets in Manchuria during the World War II, notably at the Yalta Conference in 1945. Also the Truman administration was faulted for allegedly having failed to support Chiang, although, in truth, it had made available to his venally corrupt Kuomintang regime huge quantities of surplus American war equipment and had arranged for more than $2,000,000,000 in military and economic assistance in the period 1945–49. Finally, in February 1950, came exposure of a Soviet spy ring which had penetrated America's atomic installation at Los Alamos in New Mexico.

And so it was that the right psychic moment had arrived for appearance of a demagogue who pretended to explain to a frightened, confused, and angry citizenry what had gone wrong—why it was that the communists had been able to spy on the FBI, take over the world's most populous country, and steal secrets of the atomic bomb. That demagogue was Joseph R. McCarthy, the junior senator from Wisconsin. His explanation was marvelously uncomplicated; dupes and communist sympathizers and even "card-carrying" Communists in the national government, particularly in the State Department, had fashioned policies which had enabled the communists to achieve their recent triumphs, gain the initiative in the cold war, and threaten the very survival of the United States.

The outcome was mind boggling. In an astonishingly short time McCarthy, one of the most sinister demagogues ever to move across the American landscape, turned the national mood from one of fear and depression and frustration into one of hysteria. The outcome was a wave of harassment and intimidation of individuals who were suspected of being instruments, either consciously or unconsciously, of "the communist conspiracy." The nation was shaken to its foundations, and the word "McCarthyism" was introduced into the vocabulary of Americans.

By his vicious and irresponsible attacks McCarthy wrecked the careers of Philip C. Jessup and John Stewart Service, both distinguished diplomatists. He helped induce the resignation from President Truman's Cabinet of Secretary of Defense George C. Marshall, the chief architect of America's military victories in World War II. He raised doubts about the loyalty of Secretary of State Dean G. Acheson, Ambassador Charles E. Bohlen, and the Democratic Party's candidate for President in 1952, Adlai E. Stevenson. (In one speech he referred to Stevenson as "Alger—I mean Adlai.") He branded Professor Owen Lattimore of Johns Hopkins University, a leading scholar of East Asian affairs who had intimated that America might do well to try to do business with Mao Tse-Tung, as the No. 1 communist traitor in the United States. He sent aides on a mission to rid America's overseas libraries of "subversive" literature and heaped abuse on army leaders who, he charged, had permitted traitors to infiltrate the military establishment. He apparently convinced such Republican chieftains as Senator Robert A. Taft of Ohio who announced that "the pro-Communists policies of the State Department fully justified Joe McCarthy in his demand for an investigation." (One wonders which "pro-Communist policies" Taft was referring to. The American intervention in Greece and Turkey? The Berlin airlift? The Marshall Plan? The formulation of NATO?) At the Republican National Convention of 1952 delegates cheered wildly and held up placards reading "Acheson, Hiss, Lattimore" following McCarthy's introduction as "Wisconsin's fighting Marine." (In truth McCarthy had not been a combat officer while in the Marines in the World War II and, although in postwar political campaigns he sometimes affected a limp and complained to audiences about the discomfort caused by shrapnel in his leg, he had never been wounded.)

Manifestations of the scourge of McCarthyism seemed omnipresent in America in the early 1950s. Over the veto of President Truman, Congress in 1950 passed the McCarran Internal Security Act requiring communist and communist-front organizations to register with the federal government. The act authorized the government, in time of national emergencies, to round up suspected subversives and to place them in detention centers. There were also less serious but more zany happenings. Because Henry Wadsworth Longfellow's Indian hero Hiawatha had tried to promote peace between Indian tribes—and because communists were notorious for organizing "peace offensives"—a Hollywood studio canceled plans for a film based on the Hiawatha story. An outcry occurred in Wheeling, West Virginia, when local McCarthyites discovered that inside the wrappers of candy bonbons being sold in the city were little pieces of paper offering miniature geography lessons. One piece of paper carried a likeness of the Soviet flag and read: "U.S.S.R. Population 211,000,000. Capital Moscow. Largest country in the world." Lamented the city manager of Wheeling: "This is a terrible thing to expose our children to." School textbooks, particularly those in history, political science, and economics, came under close scrutiny, and those which did not take a sufficiently hard line against communism and other forms of "leftist radicalism"—and that sometimes meant a hard line against the New Deal of the 1930s and the United Nations—were banned from classrooms. In some areas bitter debate raged over the question of whether the theory and practice of communism was a fit subject for consideration in high school social studies courses. Several state legislatures passed laws requiring state employees, especially teachers in public schools and professors of state colleges and universities, to take oaths that they were not communists and not affiliated with any "communist front" organizations. And, of course, one risked the charge that he was a traitor if, while sipping beer at a corner saloon or lecturing to undergraduate students in a college classroom, he surmised that communism might have some good points. If one was in the foreign service he was apt to be very careful about suggesting that American interests in the world might be better served if the government would consider a softer policy vis-à-vis the Soviet Union or China.

Then, in 1953–54, McCarthy made the fatal error of tangling with the administration of President Eisenhower, a national symbol of integrity and "the American way." Next came a series of televised hearings—the celebrated "Army-McCarthy hearings"—which brought the image of the demagogue from Wisconsin into millions of living rooms and gave a close-up view of his crude, bully-boy tactics. Gradually and painfully, the country began to sober up.

Still, the fling with McCarthy had been quite a binge.

What, in conclusion, can one say about the way in which Americans met their problems at home in the time after World War II?

As in every other period of their history, the record of the people of the United States in the half dozen or so years after the war presented a mixture of successes and failures. On the credit side, the country successfully engineered the transition of the national economy from war to peace and, more than that, maintained an impressive rate of economic growth throughout the entire period. Not that the country was free of economic difficulties in the postwar era. Far from it. People grumbled and many one-time Democratic voters expressed discontent over such difficulties by voting Republican in the election of 1946. Likewise the benefits of the postwar prosperity were not always evenly distributed, and large sectors of poverty, both urban and rural, continued to exist amidst rampaging affluence. Be that as it may, the years after the war, on balance, were a time of economic triumph for the people of the United States. And when one recalls the famous observation of Franklin D. Roosevelt's "minister of

relief," Harry Hopkins, that people have to eat every day he must ask himself: What could have been more important to Americans in the time after the war, particularly when they pondered the Great Depression of the previous decade, than continuing prosperity?

Then, unlike after World War I, Americans in the time after defeat of the Axis were not taken up in a political reaction. The postwar era in America, it was true, was politically conservative. But those ultrarightists in the republic who dreamed of turning the clock of history back to the 1920s and repealing the social advances of the New Deal of the 1930s scored only one success of any consequence, enactment of the Taft-Hartley labor relations act in 1947. Otherwise their record was blank. And, on the contrary, liberals or progressives in America could claim some modest successes in the time after the war. They secured passage of the Employment Act, which formally committed the government to maintenance of prosperity, and the Atomic Energy Act, which assured civil control of the atomic energy program. More important, many Americans who hitherto had taken the nation's racial caste system for granted began to realize that discrimination on account of race was a horrendous evil which had to be abolished in democratic America. This new sensitivity, combined with an increasing determination on the part of black Americans to achieve the promise of American democracy, gave new strength to the equal rights crusade, resulted in a measure of racial progress in the postwar years, and prepared the way for great triumphs in race relations in America in the decades to come.

But there is the other side of the coin. There were the failures and shortcomings of postwar America; the continuing high level of racism in the country was the most obvious and the most painful. One might have hoped, in light of the numerous declarations of commitment to democratic ideals during the war and, as the war in

Europe was ending, the sickening revelation—at Auschwitz, Belsen, and Buchenwald—of the potential consequences of racism, that America's, whites (after raising their voices in a collective utterance of *mea culpa*) might have put aside racist attitudes and welcomed their black countrymen to full membership in the democratic community. Instead tens of millions reasserted their racism with a vengeance and often had the audacity to cloak their vicious ideology behind the banner of liberty and equal opportunity, namely, the Stars and Stripes. Then there was the American contribution to the hardening of cold war attitudes. America's leaders, after onset of the cold war, seemed to give up the search for ways to bring about a reconciliation with their recent wartime allies. Likewise, after the cold war started, Americans allowed themselves to fall into a self-righteous posture about "international communism" which clouded their judgment and brought them into dubious alliance with assorted rightist dictatorships around the entire world. Finally, there was the tendency to infringe the rights of freedom of expression and political activity, the awful climax coming with the nightmare of McCarthyism.

Whatever the credits and debits of America's performance in meeting the challenges of the postwar era, and however one chooses to strike a balance between those credits and debits, nobody can deny that the time after the World War II was, as Eric Goldman later called it, a crucial period in American history—and one pregnant with meaning for Americans in the 1970s.

SUGGESTED READINGS

ANDERSON, JACK, and MAY, R. W. *McCarthy*. Boston: Beacon Press, 1952.

BARTH, ALAN. *The Loyalty of Free Men*. New York: Viking Press, 1951.

BERNSTEIN, BARTON J., and MATUSOW, ALLEN J. (eds.). *The Truman Administration: A Documentary History*. New York: Harper & Row, 1966.

BIDDLE, FRANCIS. *The Fear of Freedom*. Garden City, N.Y.: Doubleday & Co., 1951.

BONTECOU, ELEANOR. *The Federal Loyalty and Security Program*. Ithaca, N.Y.: Cornell University Press, 1953.

BROWN, RALPH. *Loyalty and Security*. New Haven, Conn.: Yale University Press, 1958.

BUCKLEY, WILLIAM, JR., and BOZELL, L. BRENT. *McCarthy and His Enemies*. Chicago: Henry Regnery Co., 1954.

CARR, ROBERT. *The House Committee on Un-American Activities, 1945–1950*. Ithaca, N.Y.: Cornell University Press, 1952.

CHAMBERS, WHITTAKER. *Witness*. New York: Random House, 1952.

CHASE, HAROLD. *Security and Liberty: The Problem of Native Communists, 1947–1955*. Garden City, N.Y.: Doubleday, 1955.

COOKE, ALISTAIR. *A Generation on Trial: U.S.A. vs. Alger Hiss*. London: Rupert Hart-Davis, 1950.

CUSHMAN, ROBERT. *Civil Liberties in the United States*. Ithaca, N.Y.: Cornell University Press, 1956.

DANIELS, JONATHAN. *The Man of Independence*. Philadelphia: J. P. Lippincott, 1948.

DAVIS, ELMER. *But We Were Born Free*. Garden City, N.Y.: Doubleday & Co., 1954.

EISENHOWER, DWIGHT D. *Mandate for Change, 1953–1956: The White House Years*. Garden City, N.Y.: Doubleday & Co., 1963.

EMERSON, THOMAS, and HABER, DAVID. *Political and Civil Rights in the United States*. Boston: Little, Brown & Co., 1952.

ERNST, MORRIS, and LOTH, DAVID. *Report on the American Communist*. N.Y.: Capricorn Books, 1952.

GARDNER, LLOYD C. *Architects of Illusion: Men and Ideas in American Foreign Policy, 1941–1949*. Chicago: Quadrangle Press, 1970.

GOLDMAN, ERIC F. *The Crucial Decade In and After: America, 1945–1955*. New York: Vintage Books, 1960.

GRIFFIN, ROBERT. *The Politics of Fear: Joseph R. McCarthy and the Senate*. Lexington: University of Kentucky Press, 1970.

HARPER, ALAN D. *The Politics of Loyalty: The White House and the Communist Issue, 1946–1952*. Westport, Conn.: Greenwood Publishing Co., 1969.

Hiss, Alger. *In the Court of Public Opinion.* New York: Alfred A. Knopf, 1957.

Hughes, Emmet John. *The Ordeal of Power: A Political Memoir of the Eisenhower Years.* New York: Atheneum Publishers, 1963.

Jowitt, William Allen. *The Strange Case of Alger Hiss.* London: Hodder and Stoughton, 1953.

Larson, Arthur. *Eisenhower: The President Nobody Knew.* New York: Charles Scribner's Sons, 1968.

Lasswell, Harold. *National Security and Individual Freedom.* New York: McGraw-Hill Book Co., 1950.

Lattimore, Owen. *Ordeal by Slander.* Boston: Little, Brown & Co., 1950.

McWilliams, Carey. *Brothers under the Skin.* Boston: Little, Brown & Co., 1951.

——— ,*Witch Hunt: The Revival of Heresy.* Boston: Little, Brown & Co., 1950.

Nixon, Richard M. *Six Crises.* Garden City, N.Y.: Doubleday & Co., 1962.

Phillips, Cabell. *The Truman Presidency.* New York: Macmillan Co., 1966.

Pritchett, C. H. *Civil Liberties and the Vinson Court.* Chicago: University of Chicago Press, 1954.

Rovere, Richard H. *Senator Joe McCarthy.* New York: Harcourt, Brace, 1959.

Shannon, David. *The Decline of American Communism: A History of the Communist Party of the United States since 1945.* New York: Harcourt, Brace, 1959.

Stouffer, Samuel. *Communism, Conformity, and Civil Liberties.* Garden City, N.Y.: Doubleday & Co., 1955.

Truman, Harry S. *Memoirs by Harry S Truman,* Vol. I, *Year of Decisions,* Vol. II, *Years of Trial and Hope.* Garden City, N.Y.: Doubleday & Co., 1955–56.

Wilcox, Clair (ed.). *Civil Liberties Under Attack.* Philadelphia: University of Pennsylvania Press, 1951.

DOCUMENT 31.1

Toward a Better World*

When World War II came to a close, Americans felt a burning pride as a result of their contribution to the victory over the Axis tyrants and believed that the end of the global conflict marked the dawning of a great new day of prosperity, freedom, and happiness for mankind. Those sentiments were captured in a radio address by a congressman from Massachusetts, Thomas J. Lane, to his constituents on September 2, 1945—the day the Japanese formally surrendered.

A short time after the sneak attack on Pearl Harbor, when most of our battle-wagons were sunk or crippled, a certain admiral named Yamamoto said: "I am looking forward to dictating peace to the United States in the White House at Washington."

Peace has been dictated—in the White House at Washington—with a slight correction. The peace has been won and its terms were unconditional surrender. It was expressed by President Truman, who spoke for you and me for the will of the American Nation.

A few years before, the late Herr Hitler said that the two ways of life—the democratic one and his own—could not exist together. One of the two must disappear.

In a way he could not foresee, he was right. One of the two had to prevail, but it was not fascism and its enslavement, but democracy and its liberation that has won. The entire world has been saved from the foul doctrine that force shall govern mankind.

In Lawrence, Boston, San Francisco, Washington, in every village and home, we rejoice. But there is more to it than this. In all nations of the world there is happiness today, yes, even in the hearts of a few intelligent Japanese. For we are not

---

*Source: *Congressional Record,* 79th Cong., 1st sess., Vol. 19, Part 12, Appendix, pp. A3747–8.

going backward into the darkness of tyranny but forward into the light of a new and challenging day. Everywhere, mankind looks upward with new hope in the vision of a better world. . . .

As we look back over the hard road we have traveled, we are amazed by the things we have done. This young Nation, under the spur of necessity has become the strongest power in the long history of man. The reason lies not in the power itself but the faith that built it. Today as never before, we believe in those values which underscore our way of life. Once we wise-cracked about them as we would about some legend which had lost its meaning in the present. "Democracy," "rights of man," "human dignity," "equality of race, creed, color, and opportunity," these were phrases dimly remembered from our schooldays. Under the impact of war these half-forgotten values took on new life and meaning. We were suddenly aware that they were good, that they were at work in America, and that they were menaced from without. As freemen, we stood ready to die, if need be, to save them for ourselves and our posterity. We knew that democracy when fully awake was capable of solving the many crises which challenge the progress of man. . . .

DOCUMENT 31.2
The Government Loyalty Program*

Harry Truman was on record as antagonistic to communism and to the Soviet Union before the postwar events which precipitated the cold war, even before the actual disruption of the wartime alliance. His actions after the cessation of hostilities

*Source: Leonard A. Nikolorić, "The Government loyalty Program" Reprinted from *The American Scholar*, Vol. 19 No. 3 (Summer 1950), pp. 285–98. Copyright © by the United Chapters of Phi Beta Kappa. By permission of the publisher.

contributed to the belligerent and uncompromising approach to communism at home and abroad out of which McCarthyism ineluctably evolved. Not only did the President fail to resist the mounting anticommunism (his veto of the McCarran Act of 1950 notwithstanding), he also handicapped himself by this failure. For he boxed himself in, and his response to McCarthyism was predictable and in the nature of things; he established a federal loyalty and security program (when still accused of being "soft on communism," he would defensively react by tightening this program). Consequently, he was on the way to becoming one of the victims of the anti-communist campaign to which he contributed. Executive Order 9835, proclaimed on March 22, 1947, established a comprehensive loyalty program for all federal employees—from diplomats to gardeners—and was undertaken to head off similar legislation by the Republicans (the Mundt-Nixon bill). One view of how the program operated is described below by Leonard A. Nikoloric, a Washington lawyer whose firm frequently defended government employees before loyalty boards and in the courts.

Established by the President's Executive Order 9835 in March, 1947, the government's loyalty program moves into its fourth year. The program presents a complex problem: whether, in the name of "loyalty" and "national security," our society is justified in abusing most of the basic tenets of Anglo-American jurisprudence and legal philosophy traditional since the seventeenth century.

The purpose of the program is not to discharge employees expressly because of what they have done in the past. President Truman has stated that it is aimed at "potentially disloyal" persons who, because of attitudes and ideas they entertain today or subscribed to yesterday, might in the future undertake action contrary to the best interests of the United States. The basic concept of the program—to ferret out the "potentially disloyal"—violates a most important principle of Anglo-American law: that one cannot be punished for merely considering the commission of a crime, or for thinking in such a way that a body determines that one might undertake action contrary to the law.

The program also violates judicial safeguards against punishment which are traditional in free societies. The rights to have a reasonable notice of charges, to cross-examine and confront one's accusers, to judicial review before punishment is meted out, to be judged by an impartial tribunal—these are, among others, eliminated from the program.

The loyalty program also distorts the concept of equal justice under the law. It assumes that a democratic government may exact from its employees special standards of conduct wholly offensive to constitutional guarantees of freedom and justice as applied to ordinary citizens. We deny two and a half million government employees political and intellectual freedoms in order to protect ourselves from the potentially subversive.

These innovations are spreading not only to some three and a half million state and local employees (the County of Los Angeles, among other local governments, has instituted a loyalty check), but elsewhere. The AFL and the CIO have undertaken to purge the Communists. The Army, the Navy and the Air Force pass on the loyalty of the employees of private contractors who bid successfully on government jobs having to do with classified material. Congressmen have urged that all employees working for industries connected with the national security be subjected to a similar screening. Presumably this concerns the various utilities—in steel, automobile, transportation and others. Teachers and scientists have been discharged for entertaining unpopular ideas. Even veterans' organizations have pledged themselves to loyalty programs. The most liberal of these, the American Veterans Committee, has adopted resolutions directing its officers to purge the Communists.

Since we are rapidly accepting the proposition that American institutions have a right to examine their membership on the basis of their "loyalty," it is appropriate to determine what the government's loyalty program is and how it operates, its ideology, and the concrete effects of its operation. . . .

The discovery of the potentially disloyal is no easy task. Executive Order 9835 directs the Boards to take action if

. . . on the basis of all the evidence, reasonable grounds exist for belief that the person involved is disloyal.

It is, therefore, the duty of the Boards to determine the existence of a nebulous state of mind which might lead an employee to commit in the future a disloyal act, either willfully or through an indiscretion. The most important elements of consideration are of necessity the employee's political beliefs, the organizations to which he has belonged, and the associations he has had.

Experience proves that it is not necessary for the employee to have been a member of either a Communist or Fascist organization. He will be found wanting if he has been "sympathetic" to communism or fascism, friendly to persons or organizations that are sympathetic, associated with such persons or organizations, or even "unduly talkative" in the presence of persons who are associated with sympathetic persons. The Boards do not find it necessary to prove any of these matters. They are required only to find "a reasonable doubt."

In order to assist the Boards, the Attorney General, in December, 1947, and by various supplements, designated some 150 organizations—membership in or sympathy for which is held to be indicative of disloyalty. These lists were promulgated without hearings. No explanation for the inclusion of any organization was given. . . . The generalities employed in loyalty charges are demonstrated by a typical example:

You are charged with having associated with Communists or with persons or organizations in sympathy with communism.

Although the order provides that the employee is entitled to a charge stating the offense with some particularity, this is limited by the discretion of the agency in the interest of security considerations. Practice has shown that it has been almost impossible for an employee or his lawyer to secure a full or complete statement of the offenses.

Defending against such charges is difficult. The burden is placed on the employee to recall all the persons with whom, and organizations with which, he has ever been in contact, and to explain them. He must also prove affirmatively that he adheres to certain nebulous standards that might be construed by the Board as indicative of so loyal a state of mind that the employee will never commit a disloyal act. . . .

The case of B is also typical. B was charged with "associating with persons in sympathy with communism." B's lawyer asked the department Board for a list of the persons. The department gave the names of three persons—of whom B knew only one, and him slightly. Counsel made an additional request and received six more names, of which B did know two. At the hearing B was met with four more names and was unprepared to make an adequate defense.

Even when names and organizations are specified, the employee is not told what is wrong with the alleged associate. Again defense is difficult. The process which ties in the accused with the associate is also used to tar the associate. For example, C was charged with associating with ten persons. C was closely associated with only one of them. Not only was C faced with the job of clearing himself, but in order to "purify" his association, found it necesary also to present long testimony in his associate's behalf.

In this connection, even the Boards themselves are not told by the FBI the source of derogatory information. It is, therefore, impossible even for them to weigh the evidence. This is revealed by the hearing of D before a Board at the Brooklyn Navy Yard. The FBI had designated its informants to the Board by symbols, "T-1, T-2, etc."

The following colloquy took place:

Board Member: Did you ever act as an organizer for the Communist Party or attempt to recruit others?
D: No.
B M: [It] has been corroborated, checked and verified—
Attorney for D: By whom?
B M: I can't tell you. . . . We don't even know who the accuser is.

Nor are the accusations made under oath. The following took place during an appeal hearing before the Review Board. In reply to counsel's questions, asking whether the statements of the accusers were sworn, and also the identity of the accusers, the Chairman replied:

I don't think so. . . . I haven't the slightest knowledge as to who they were. . . .

The employee is not tried by an impartial judge. The Board accusing him conducts the inquiry, questions the employee, and renders judgment.

There is no confrontation of the persons who have given derogatory reports to the FBI. Nor has the employee any right to cross-examine the informer. These rights are denied under the theory that they might dry up sources of information. The Chairman of the Review Board, Mr. Seth Richardson, has stated:

We have concluded that the objection to no confrontation and no cross-examination, which are important, is not essentially controlling.

Examples of double jeopardy occur when a provisional employee (over whom the Civil Service Commission has concurrent jurisdiction with the employing agency) is charged with disloyalty. For example, E was charged and cleared by a Civil Service Commission Board. Thereafter, the Army, by whom E was employed, instituted new proceedings on the same charges.

The proper presentation of an appeal is complicated by the order's requirement that Boards "shall state merely the action taken." It is impossible to tell what evidence the Board relied on, what findings of fact it made (other than the result), or even if all of its evidence was revealed to the employee. For that reason, there is no way to specify in what respects the lower Board was in error.

None of these things could happen in any other court or board proceeding directed against an individual in the United States. Axis Sally and Judith Coplon, who were charged with overt acts of treason and espionage, have received more procedural protection than is accorded the potentially disloyal. A common pickpocket may insist on every traditional and fundamental safeguard. A government employee may not. No one would dream of indicting Axis Sally for merely contemplating broadcasting Nazi propaganda; we would not consider putting a petty thief in jail for thinking about picking his neighbor's pocket. Yet we discharge and publicly smear government employees who have done nothing wrongful, who may not consider committing an act of disloyalty. We fire them because, on the basis of standards of the status quo, the Board suspects that they might do so in the future.

Those who would defend the program argue that the government is not required to secure to its employees procedural safeguards when it fires them. It is said that no citizen has an inherent right to government employment. Thus the government may fire arbitrarily—because it does not like the color of the employee's hair, because he is inefficient, or because the government fears that the employee may become a security risk. The procedural safeguards that are provided—charges and a hearing—are a matter of the sovereign's largess. They do not accrue to the employee as a matter of constitutional right. Therefore, the employee may not ask for other safeguards as a matter of constitutional right.

The opponents have a convincing case. Many judges, notably Mr. Justice Black, have argued that once having been hired, a government employee does secure a vested interest in his job which shall not be taken from him without cause. Cause may not be a matter of speculation; it must be a reality—such as inefficiency or overt acts of disloyalty.

Furthermore, a dismissal for disloyalty entails a permanent brand amounting to treason. Experience has shown that an employee who has been discharged under the loyalty program is unable to get another job; his career is ruined; he loses the respect of the community. Dismissal on loyalty or security grounds transcends the arbitrary right to fire. It amounts to punishment by government, which is protected by the Constitution. If this be the case, an employee who is fired on these grounds does have the constitutional right to traditional due process and safeguards.

Regardless of the coldly legal interpretation of the situation, it is obvious that a loyalty proceeding is a serious matter. On moral grounds, the government should not ruin an employee's career on a conjectural determination that he may in the future become disloyal. It must be remembered that the loyalty program was not designed or intended to punish people who have committed overt acts of disloyalty or treason. Not an employee fired has been charged with the commission of a wrongful act. During a recent public discussion with me, Mr. Seth Richardson, Chairman of the Loyalty Review Board, stated that the loyalty program has not discovered a single instance of espionage or any other overt action contrary to the best interests of the United States.

There are innumerable statutes calculated to deal with persons who are or have been acting contrary to our best interests. They include sanctions against espionage, sabotage, treason or advocacy of the overthrow of the government by force. More important to the inquiry here, any government agency may fire an employee for cause. "Cause" includes everything from simple inefficiency to disagreement with the agency's policy. Every applicant for government employment must sign, under oath, a statement that he does not subscribe to subversive doctrines and does not belong to any organization that does. Failure to make full disclosure is punishable as a criminal offense.

If we are to commit ourselves to a program that is (at least in moral, and probably in constitutional terms) repugnant to traditional jurisprudence, it is only fair to evaluate the reasons for calling such a program into being, the resulting ideology, and the results in practical terms.

The program was instituted for two major reasons. The first was political. In March, 1947, when the order was signed, the future of the Democratic Party was not bright. One of the principal issues on which the Republicans had won the off-year election of 1946 was that the Administration had been lax in permitting spies and subversives to infiltrate into government. It became politically expedient for the Democrats to take positive steps to appear diligent in the matter of Communists.

The second reason is the more important. It is our fear of Russia and the ideology of communism. The War left Russia the only power capable of arguing with our new role in world leadership. We are afraid of Russia's military power and fearful of the consequences to society as a whole in the event of a test of strength employing frightening new weapons. We therefore justify stringent methods to root out of government actual or potential Communist agents and spies.

Perhaps even more important (we have before been faced with threatening world powers) is our fear of the Communist ideology. The Communists have promised the world that capitalism will collapse of its own weight and inefficiencies. England, France and other traditionally capitalist countries are making concessions to various government controls. We are doing the same thing. Even in great prosperity, our governmental and pirvate economic bureaucracies, unwieldy and frozen, are unable to feed, clothe and house our people with relative adequacy. The prediction of the Communists makes us uneasy. This is particularly true because we have come to think of Communists as supermen—more clever and efficient than we. In spite of the fact that communism has never been more unpopular in America, we have never been more apprehensive of the scrubby little group of fanatics who straggle up Eighth Avenue in New York on May Day.

These fears are not clearly defined. We are suspicious of change. Confusion is added from the semantic designation of both communism and so-called liberalism as "left-wing." To many the two are synonymous. Hence, to find a potentially disloyal American, find a man who expresses dissatisfaction with the established order of things—a man who believes in racial equality, socialized medicine, labor unions, equalization of economic opportunity, or increased government activity in economic affairs—particularly if the believer is not of Anglo-American stock. These things are "left-wing"; so is communism. A *fortiori*, a man who believes in them may become in the future a Communist agent.

DOCUMENT 31.3
The Tests of Loyalty*

McCarthyism opened up a Pandora's box of problems for Americans, including that of political loyalty and its tests. A recurrent problem in Anglo-American history, it often took the form of loyalty oaths demanded by the state (for example, in Elizabethan England or during the American Revolution). Almost all Americans in the 1950s demanded absolute and unassailable proof, as if it could be had, of patriotic faith, and they constantly wondered whether communists had infiltrated Hollywood, labor, industry, schools and colleges, or the highest state and federal offices. They almost never asked the fundamental question: How is "loyalty" defined in a democratic state? And the related questions: What are legally and morally acceptable standards of "disloyalty"? How real are the existing dangers? Are they such as to demand such tests? Carey McWilliams, a distinguished editor, presents one view of the issue.

THE MODERN
AMERICAN WITCH HUNT

The issuance by President Truman of Executive Order No. 9835 on March 22, 1947, setting up a federal loyalty program, marks the beginning of an American obsession with loyalty that, in broad outline, parallels a similar Russian obsession dating from the "all-out campaign" against the Leningrad Literary Group in August 1946. Since then states, counties, and cities have imitated the federal program; many industries and plants now require affidavits of loyalty from their employees; scores of trade unions have adopted a similar requirement, along with schools and colleges; and, in California, an association of amateur archers now demands an affidavit of loyalty from its members! Not

*Source: Carey McWilliams, *Witch Hunt: The Revival of Heresy* (Boston: Little, Brown & Co., 1950), pp. 27–45, 47–48, 246–50.

since the time of the Alien and Sedition Acts has the federal government been so intensely and morbidly preoccupied with the loyalty of the American people.

As citizens, we are asked to believe that this preoccupation with *our* loyalty finds immediate justification in a series of "revelations" about spy rings and espionage activities and, generally, in a tense international situation. However, when our officials comment upon the parallel preoccupation of the Soviet government, the mote suddenly obscures the beam. For example, Lieutenant General Walter Bedell Smith, by way of answering the question: "Why were the Soviet authorities so apprehensive about the loyalty of the masses, particularly after the conclusion of a successful war?" points unerringly to the impact of the war upon internal tensions in the Soviet Union. Superficially the American obsession with loyalty appears to stem from the facts and implications of "the cold war"; but in this respect we could be the victims of a serious delusion.

One way to clarify the meaning of the loyalty program is to identify some of the instruments being used to determine who is loyal and who is disloyal. Properly identified, these instruments provide the key to an understanding of the curious psychological warfare which the government has been waging against the people for the last three years. Surely the use of the political court-martial to coerce conformity and the revival in the United States, in the middle of the twentieth century, of the discredited and abhorrent "test oath" should remind us that a concern with loyalty has often served as cover for an attack on civil liberties.

．　．　．　．　．

HERESY HUNTING IS NOT SCAPEGOATING

Just as heresy is to be distinguished from dissent, so heresy hunting is not synonymous with scapegoating. Scapegoating is universal and perennial; it is based on the simplest form of delusion. Witch hunting is a form of social madness based on delusions which are paranoid.

Scapegoating is largely an individual phenomenon; witch hunting is a product of collective madness. The key to the distinction is to be found in the fact that scapegoating may be stimulated by mild frustration but witch hunting stems only from major social dislocations. Witch hunting, as Marion L. Starkey has pointed out, always comes "in the wake of stress and social disorganization"; after wars, disasters, plagues, famines, and revolutions. Scapegoating appears in all seasons; but witch hunting only reappears in time of storm. The nature of witch hunts as such, the manner in which they unfold, and the dynamics which they set in motion, form an important chapter in the sociology of heresy.

The psychology of the witch trial is the psychology of the un-American investigation. Witches will lie; so will Communists. Witches get innocent people to do their bidding; so do Communists. One can be a witch without knowing it just as one can be a Communist without knowing it. Witches were convicted on "spectral" evidence and today a "spectral" use is made of the doctrine of guilt by association. Abigail Williams, whose fantasies damned the innocent in Salem in 1691, can be identified today as a fairly obvious psychological type; but even the wise, intelligent, and honest Samuel Sewall was taken in, at the time, by the antics of Abigail. And so today, equally wise and honest men seem quite incapable of detecting the element of fantasy and delusion which appears in the neurotically embroidered tales of Abigail's modern counterparts, whose passion for truth and patriotism is reborn simultaneously with the disappearance of their fifth-column lovers. . . .

Before social disorganization can produce a witch hunt, however, a well-organized system of police terror must be in existence. It is this factor which calls forth the mania of denunciation which is so characteristic of witch hunts. The motives for denunciation are usually mixed— fanaticism, the conforming tendency, covetousness, fear—but it is police terror which directly inspires the mania. The susceptibility of the Germans to the form of witch hunt launched by the Nazis is to be explained by the fact that a long acquaintance with the methods of a political police, and a long political police tradition, had bred in many Germans a passion for conformity. In all terroristic regimes, as Bramstedt points out, ". . . the accused is everybody outside the limited circle of privileged organizations and the ruling clique"; therefore, those outside this limited circle must *constantly prove*, by words and deed, and principally by denunciations, that they are loyal. The mania of denunciation springs not from the fear of heretics but from a well-founded and quite realistic fear of the machinery which has been set up to catch heretics.

Although this heresy-catching machinery provides an ingenious form of social control, it has distinct limitations. For one thing, the price to be paid for the suppression of heresies in terms of what it will purchase is clearly prohibitive. If we were to enact every measure proposed by the anti-Communists for the suppression of Communism we would find that we had destroyed the fabric of civil rights and that the number of Communists would probably be the same or greater today! The self-defeating character of the anti-Communist strategy is reflected in the headline of a story by W. H. Lawrence in the *New York Times* of January 2, 1950: "Brazil Reds Busy, Though Outlawed." Outlawed three years previously, the Communists of Brazil, Mr. Lawrence discovered, were more numerous and more active than ever. Thus those who favor measures to suppress heresy must be made to carry a dual burden of proof. They must be made to prove: (1) that the dangers are "clear and present"; and (2) that repressive measures will actually guard against these dangers. It is on the second point that their case invariably breaks down

Not only are heresy hunts expensive in terms of what they will actually accomplish, but they involve a peculiar law of diminishing returns. At first, only the vulnerable, the easily "fingered" victims are selected. For example, the first witches arrested in Salem were an illiterate slave, an old crone, and a lascivious grandmother. Carting these victims off to the gallows aroused little opposition; indeed it fanned the flames of intolerance. But heresy hunts must be kept going; new victims must be found. The second batch of victims will be less vulnerable than the first but their immolation will not arouse much protest either because these victims are usually unpopular, poor, and lacking in social prestige. By this time, however, the informers, inquisitors, and psychopathic witnesses have become drunk with the new-found power of denunciation. They begin to enjoy the notoriety that goes with being an expert on witchcraft and a professional "denouncer"; they thrill to the feeling of being able to destroy another person by merely voicing a phrase, or pointing a finger, or whispering an accusation.

As the accusers become bolder, the range of accusation broadens and "heresy" ceases to have any definable meaning. Individuals are now haled before the tribunal who have real roots in the community, who are generally liked and respected. Doubts then begin to arise, for the first time, that the informers are truthful, doubts which never arose when the victims were marginal types. But by this time the machinery of persecution cannot be stopped, much less reversed. To admit error would be to cast doubt on the prior convictions and to undermine the concept of heresy. The informers, during this second act, usually become frightened of the consequences of their perjuries, and the more frightened they become, the bolder their accusations, the wilder their denunciations. Informers then begin to inform on informers in an effort to prevent any possible betrayal of their fraudulent

charges and counterfeit "revelations." By this time, too, the power of denunciation has become truly frightening. A destructive self-hatred then exists in the society, like the fumes of an explosive gas, that anyone can ignite by merely striking a match. Sooner or later, however, the list of "expendable" victims must be exhausted, and at this point society recoils from the excesses of witch hunting, in weariness and horror. "Sound" elements, silent all this while, then step forward to exert a moderating influence, and gradually, slowly, like a patient recovering from a long fever, with its attendant hallucinations, society begins to recover its sanity and health.

But sanity does not always return; sometimes the society destroys itself, for the cost of eradicating heresy is in direct proportion to the success of the operation. Who would care to estimate the price paid for the Salem persecutions? Nor should it be forgotten that Spain was the one nation in which the Inquisition was really successful and the price, there, was intellectual ruin and political and moral decay. Once society starts burning heretics, figuratively or literally, the flames are likely to engulf the whole structure of society. Thus the basic reason why heresy persecutions are futile is the risk that they might succeed and the price of success is utter ruin.

DOCUMENT 31.4

Communists under the Legal Gun*

The Truman administration's drive against internal communism opened in 1948, with the indictment of 11 high-ranking Communist Party functionaries for conspiracy to teach and advocate the violent overthrow of the government in viola-

---

*Source: *Dennis et al.* v. *United States*, 341 U.S. 497 (1951).

tion of the 1940 Smith Act. Convicted in the lower courts, the defendants carried their case to the Supreme Court. The high tribunal, in the course of finding that such a conspiracy did indeed exist, modified the Holmesian criterion of "clear and present danger." Once again, the underlying issues involved the meaning of "loyalty" in a democratic society. Were belief, inquiry, advocacy, planning, persuasion, criticism now unprotected by the First Amendment? Did anything but "actions" now constitute a legitimate test of loyalty and legality? Can any democratic government afford to label its citizens "loyal" and "disloyal"? Does it not do so at its peril? Below are excerpts of the majority and dissenting views of the Justices. In a painfully obvious way, they tell us something about the Court's sensitivity to public opinion and the temper of the times.

VINSON, C.J. Petitioners were indicted in July, 1948, for violation of the conspiracy provisions of the Smith Act . . . during the period of April, 1945, to July, 1948. The pre-trial motion to quash the indictment on the grounds, *inter alia*, that the statute was unconstitutional was denied, . . . and the case was set for trial on January 17, 1949. A verdict of guilty as to all the petitioners was returned by the jury on October 14, 1949. The Court of Appeals affirmed the convictions. . . . We granted certiorari, . . . limited to the following two questions: (1) whether either sec. 2 or sec. 3 of the Smith Act, inherently or as construed and applied in the instant case, violates the First Amendment and other provisions of the Bill of Rights; (2) whether either sec. 2 or sec. 3 of the Act, inherently or as construed and applied in the instant case, violates the First and Fifth Amendments because of indefiniteness. . . .

The indictment charged the petitioners with willfully and knowingly conspiring (1) to organize as the Communist Party of the United States of America a society, group and assembly of persons who teach and advocate the overthrow and destruction of the Government of the United States by force and violence, and (2) knowingly and willfully to advocate and teach the duty and necessity of overthrowing and destroying the Government of the United States by force and violence. The indictment further alleged that sec. 2 of the Smith Act proscribes these acts and that any conspiracy to take such action is a violation of sec. 3 of the Act.

The trial of the case extended over nine months, six of which were devoted to the taking of evidence, resulting in a record of 16,000 pages. Our limited grant of the writ of certiorari has removed from our consideration any question as to the sufficiency of the evidence to support the jury's determination that petitioners are guilty of the offense charged. Whether on this record petitioners did in fact advocate the overthrow of the Government by force and violence is not before us, and we must base any discussion of this point upon the conclusions stated in the opinion of the Court of Appeals, which treated the issue in great detail. That court held that the record in this case amply supports the necessary finding of the jury that petitioners, the leaders of the Communist Party in this country, were unwilling to work within our framework of democracy, but intended to initiate a violent revolution whenever the propitious occasion appeared. Petitioners dispute the meaning to be drawn from the evidence, contending that the Marxist-Leninist doctrine they advocated taught that force and violence to achieve a Communist form of government in an existing democratic state would be necessary only because the ruling classes of that state would never permit the transformation to be accomplished peacefully, but would use force and violence to defeat any peaceful political and economic gain the Communists could achieve. But the Court of Appeals held that the record supports the following broad conclusions: By virtue of their control over the political apparatus of the Communist Political Association, petitioners were able to transform that organization into the Communist Party; that the policies of the Association were changed from peaceful cooperation with the United States and its economic and political structure to a policy which had existed before the United States and the Soviet Union were fighting a common enemy, namely, a policy which worked for the overthrow of the Government by force and violence; that the Communist Party is a highly disciplined organization, adept at infiltration into strategic positions, use of aliases, and double-meaning language; that the Party is rigidly controlled; that Communists, unlike other political parties, tolerate no dissension from the policy laid down by the guiding forces, but that the approved program is slavishly followed by the members of the Party; that the literature of the Party and the statements and activities of its leaders, petitioners here, advocate, and the general goal of the Party was, during the period in question, to achieve a successful overthrow of the existing order by force and violence. . . .

The obvious purpose of the statute is to protect existing Government, not from change by peaceable, lawful and constitutional means, but from change by violence, revolution and terrorism. That it is within the *power* of the Congress to protect the Government of the United States from armed rebellion is a proposition which requires little discussion. Whatever theoretical merit there may be to the argument that there is a "right" to rebellion against dictatorial governments is without force where the existing structure of the government provides for peaceful and orderly change. We reject any principle of governmental helplessness in the face of preparation for revolution, which principle, carried to its logical conclusion, must lead to anarchy. No one could conceive that it is not within the power of Congress to prohibit acts intended to overthrow the Government by force and violence. The question with which we are concerned here is not whether Congress has such *power*, but whether the *means* which it has employed conflict with the First and Fifth Amendments to the Constitution. . . .

In this case we are squarely presented with the application of the "clear and present danger" test, and must decide what that phrase imports. We first note that many of the cases in which this Court has reversed convictions by use of this or similar tests have been based on the fact that the interest which the State was attempting to protect was itself too insubstantial to warrant restriction of speech. . . . Overthrow of the Government by force and violence is certainly a substantial enough interest for the Government to limit speech. Indeed, this is the ultimate value of any society, for if a society cannot protect its very structure, from armed internal attack, it must follow that no subordinate value can be protected. If, then, this interest may be protected, the literal problem which is presented is what has been meant by the use of the phrase "clear and present danger" of the utterances bringing about the evil within the power of Congress to punish.

Obviously, the words cannot mean that before the Government may act, it must wait until the *putsch* is about to be executed, the plans have been laid and the signal is awaited. If Government is aware that a group aiming at its overthrow is attempting to indoctrinate its members and to commit them to a course whereby they will strike when the leaders feel the circumstances permit, action by the Government is required. The argument that there is no need for Government to concern itself, for Government is strong, it possesses ample powers to put down a rebellion, it may defeat the revolution with ease, needs no answer. For that is not the question. Certainly an attempt to overthrow the Government by force, even though doomed from the outset because of inadequate numbers or power of the revolutionists, is a sufficient evil for Congress to prevent. The damage which such attempts create both physically and politically to a nation makes it impossible to measure the validity in terms of the probability of success, or the immediacy of a successful attempt. . . .

Chief Judge Learned Hand, writing for the majority [of the Court of Appeals, interpreted "clear and present danger"] as follows: "In each case [courts] must ask whether the gravity of the 'evil,' discounted by its improbability, justifies such invasion of free speech as is necessary to avoid the danger." . . . We adopt this statement of the rule. As articulated by Chief Judge Hand, it is as succinct and inclusive as any other we might devise at this time. It takes into consideration those factors which we deem relevant, and relates their significances. More we cannot expect from words.

Likewise, we are in accord with the court below, which affirmed the trial court's finding that the requisite danger existed. The mere fact that from the period 1945 to 1948 petitioners' activities did not result in an attempt to overthrow the Government by force and violence is of course no answer to the fact that there was a group that was ready to make the attempt. The formation by petitioners of such a highly organized conspiracy, with rigidly disciplined members subject to call when the leaders, these petitioners, felt that the time had come for action, coupled with the inflammable nature of world conditions, similar uprisings in other countries, and the touch-and-go nature of our relations with countries with whom petitioners were in the very least ideologically attuned, convince us that their convictions were justified on this score. And this analysis disposes of the contention that a conspiracy to advocate, as distinguished from the advocacy itself, cannot be constitutionally restrained, because it comprises only the preparation. It is the existence of the conspiracy which creates the danger. . . . If the ingredients of the reaction are present, we cannot bind the Government to wait until the catalyst is added. . . .

There remains to be discussed the question of vagueness—whether the statute as we have interpreted it is too vague, not sufficiently advising those who would speak of the limitations upon their activity. It is urged that such vagueness contravenes the First and Fifth Amendments. This argument is particularly nonpersuasive when presented by petitioners, who, the jury found, intended to overthrow the Government as speedily as circumstances would permit. . . . A claim of guilelessness ill becomes those with evil intent. . . .

We agree that the standard as defined is not a neat, mathematical formulary. Like all verbalizations it is subject to criticism on the score of indefiniteness. But petitioners themselves contend that the verbalization "clear and present danger" is the proper standard. We see no difference from the standpoint of vagueness, whether the standard of "clear and present danger" is one contained *in haec verba* within the statute, or whether it is the judicial measure of constitutional applicability. We have shown the indeterminate standard the phrase necessarily connotes. We do not think we have rendered that standard any more indefinite by our attempt to sum up the factors which are included within its scope. We think it well serves to indicate to those who would advocate constitutionally prohibited conduct that there is a line beyond which they may not go—a line which they, in full knowledge of what they intend and the circumstances in which their activity takes place, will well appreciate and understand. . . . Where there is doubt as to the intent of the defendants, the nature of their activities, or their power to bring about the evil, this Court will review the convictions with the scrupulous care demanded by our Constitution. But we are not convinced that because there may be borderline cases at some time in the future, these convictions should be reversed because of the argument that these petitioners could not know that their activities were constitutionally proscribed by the statute. . . .

We hold that secs. 2(a) (1), 2(a) (3) and 3 of the Smith Act do not inherently, or as construed or applied in the instant case, violate the First Amendment and other provisions of the Bill of Rights, or the First and Fifth Amendments because of indefiniteness. Petitioners intended to overthrow the Government of the United States as speedily as the circumstances would permit. Their conspiracy to organize the Communist Party and to teach and advocate the overthrow of the Government of the United States by force and violence created a "clear and present danger" of an attempt to overthrow the Government by force and violence. They were properly and constitutionally convicted for violation of the Smith Act. The judgments of conviction are

Affirmed.

BLACK J., DISSENTING. At the outset I want to emphasize what the crime involved in this case is, and what it is not. These petitioners were not charged with an attempt to overthrow the Government. They were not charged with overt acts of any kind designed to overthrow the Government. They were not even charged with saying anything or with writing anything designed to overthrow the Government. The charge was that they agreed to assemble and to talk and to publish certain ideas at a later date: The indictment is that they conspired to organize the Communist Party and to use speech or newspapers and other publications in the future to teach and advocate the forcible overthrow of the Government. No matter how it is worded, this is a virulent form of prior censorship of speech and press, which I believe the First Amendment forbids. I would hold sec. 3 of the Smith Act authorizing this prior restraint unconstitutional on its face and as applied.

But let us assume, contrary to all constitutional ideas of fair criminal procedure, that petitioners although not indicted for the crime of actual advocacy may be punished for it. Even on this radical assumption, the other opinions in that case show that the only way to affirm these convictions is to repudiate directly or indirectly the established "clear and present danger" rule. This the Court does in a way which greatly restricts the protections afforded by the First Amendment . . . .

Public opinion being what it now is, few will protest the conviction of these Communist petitioners. There is hope, however, that in calmer times, when present pressures, passions and fears subside, this or some later Court will restore the First Amendment liberties to the high preferred place where they belong in a free society.

DOCUMENT 31.5

The Hiss Case*

The Alger Hiss perjury trial and the revelation that a Soviet spy ring had secured American atomic secrets brought a wave of suspicion that communists had infiltrated the U.S. government and were "boring from within" to destroy the American system. Remarks by administration leaders—such as Secretary Acheson's statement that he would not turn his back on Alger Hiss and President Truman's reference to spy hunts as "red herrings"—provided potent ammunition to critics of recent American policies. Senator Edward Martin, Republican of Pennsylvania, speaking to his constituents on February 13, 1950, is typical of these critics.

There is no doubt that the disclosures of the Alger Hiss trial have been tremendously important. Now no one can fail to be convinced—despite official denials—that Communists had worked their way into high places in our Government and

*Source: *Congressional Record*, February 17, 1950, pp. A1175–76.

were coloring our foreign and domestic policies.

I don't know whether these men have all been rooted out yet. I do know that much of their influence remains.

I do know that some of the policies which the Administration has been following at home and abroad are policies which Communists, or fellow travelers, or their innocent dupes, would set in motion and support.

Think that over. I'll come back to it later. . . .

I want to talk briefly about Dean Acheson, the Secretary of State. In the press and in my mail there have been many demands for his impeachment.

First of all, I am sure he is not a Communist. But I do believe he made a bad and indecent blunder when, after the conviction of Alger Hiss, Mr. Acheson said in effect that this traitor was his friend, and that even if the Supreme Court should uphold the conviction, he, Acheson, would not desert his friend.

Had Dean Acheson first resigned as Secretary of State, and then made that statement, it might have been a courageous and noble thing. He, as a private individual, would be standing by a friend. But Dean Acheson did not resign. He is not merely a private citizen.

Dean Acheson stands at the head of the department which makes, directs, and carries out the foreign policy for this Nation of 150,000,000 men, women, and children. Dean Acheson speaks not only for that department, but to the rest of the world he is the official spokesman for the United States.

Alger Hiss was formerly a high official of the State Department. Alger Hiss betrayed his country by stealing secrets of the State Department and transmitting them to a foreign dictatorship whose sole aim is to enslave the world by climbing over a prostrate America.

Thus we have the head of our State Department endorsing and supporting a man in his own department who resorted to perjury and hide his part in a disloyal conspiracy.

And, as I said earlier, Dean Acheson's policies regarding China and other places strongly indicate that he is the victim of policies laid down by Communists and Communist sympathizers, like Alger Hiss. . . .

Then Mr. Truman went on to make another charge. He declared that these investigations into a spy system working right here in Washington, in Government agencies, was—and I quote—"a red herring."

Surely you all remember that. It was the considered judgment of an administration which asks you to trust it to make foreign and domestic policy in your best interests.

There was still another Presidential statement in June 1948, when Mr. Truman was pooh-poohing what he called a red herring. He said—and I quote:

"I went to Potsdam in 1945 . . . with the kindliest feelings toward Russia and we made certain agreements, specific agreements. I got very well acquainted with Joe Stalin and I like old Joe. He's a decent fellow." End of quote.

Do you folks all remember that?

My fellow Pennsylvanians, I have a confession to make.

I like old Harry. I believe that deep down he's a decent fellow.

But let me add this. I'd like old Harry a lot better if he would just confess error once in a while.

I'd like him a lot better if he'd admit to the country that he was wrong about the red herring and wrong about Joe Stalin.

I'd like him a lot better if he'd clamp down on his high officials so they would not go around extending the hand of friendship to traitors to our country.

I'd like him a lot better if he'd admit that a terrible blunder was made at Yalta —that a sick Franklin Roosevelt, influenced by Communist Alger Hiss, sold out anti-Communist China to Joe Stalin and the Soviet Union.

I'd like him a lot better if he would admit that he, Harry Truman, blundered terribly when, fooled by his pro-Communist advisers, he made a deal which gave us a zone of Berlin but without a highway leading to it, so that we had to use the airlift, and are having more trouble even now.

I'd like old Harry better if he'd admit error in the Chinese policy which caused us to sell out the Nationalists to the Communists.

But I guess he won't.

The disclosures of the Hiss case and the more recent revelation that atomic secrets have been betrayed to Soviet Russia make it imperative for every American to be on his guard. . . .

DOCUMENT 31.6
McCarthy on the Loose*

The suggestion of Louis Budenz and others that failure of Chiang Kai-shek and the anticommunists in China was largely a consequence of U.S. policies which were in effect procommunist found a mark with many Americans, among them Senator Joseph R. McCarthy of Wisconsin. Virtually unknown outside his home state in early 1950, McCarthy began his meteorlike rise to prominence and power as the country's No. 1 communist hunter via a speech given at Wheeling, West Virginia, in February 1950 in connection with the Republican Party's traditional "Lincoln Day" observances.

Ladies and gentlemen, tonight as we celebrate the one hundred and forty-first birthday of one of the greatest men in American history, I would like to be able to talk about what a glorious day today is in the history of the world. As we cele-

*Source: *Congressional Record*, 81st Cong., 2nd sess., Vol. 96, Part 2 (February 20, 1950), pp. 1954–57.

brate the birth of this man who with his whole heart and soul hated war, I would like to be able to speak of peace in our time, of war being outlawed, and of worldwide disarmament. These would be truly appropriate things to be able to mention as we celebrate the birthday of Abraham Lincoln.

Five years after a world war has been won, men's hearts should anticipate a long peace, and men's minds should be free from the heavy weight that comes with war. But this is not such a period—for this is not a period of peace. This is a time of the "cold war." This is a time when all the world is split into two vast, increasingly hostile armed camps—a time of a great armaments race.

Today we can almost physically hear the mutterings and rumblings of an invigorated god of war. You can see it, feel it, and hear it all the way from the hills of Indochina, from the shores of Formosa, right over into the very heart of Europe itself. . . .

Today we are engaged in a final, all-out battle between communistic atheism and Christianity. The modern champions of communism have selected this as the time. And, ladies and gentlemen, the chips are down—they are truly down. . . .

Six years ago, at the time of the first conference to map out the peace—Dumbarton Oaks—there was within the Soviet orbit 180,000,000 people. Lined up on the antitotalitarian side there were in the world at that time roughly 1,625,000,000 people. Today, only 6 years later, there are 800,000,000 people under the absolute domination of Soviet Russia—an increase of over 400 percent. On our side, the figure has shrunk to around 500,000,000. In other words, in less than 6 years the odds have changed from 9 to 1 in our favor to 8 to 5 against us. This indicates the swiftness of the tempo of Communist victories and American defeats in the cold war. As one of our outstanding historical figures once said, "When a great democracy is destroyed, it will not be because of enemies from without, but rather because of enemies from within."

The truth of this statement is becoming terrifyingly clear as we see this country each day losing on every front. . . .

The reason why we find ourselves in a position of impotency is not because our only powerful potential enemy has sent men to invade our shores, but rather because of the traitorous actions of those who have been treated so well by this Nation. It has not been the less fortunate or members of minority groups who have been selling this Nation out, but rather those who have had all the benefits that the wealthiest nation on earth has had to offer—the finest homes, the finest college education, and the finest jobs in Government we can give.

This is glaringly true in the State Department. There the bright young men who are born with silver spoons in their mouths are the ones who have been worst. . . .

When Chiang Kai-shek was fighting our war, the State Department had in China a young man named John S. Service. His task, obviously, was not to work for the communization of China. Strangely, however, he sent official reports back to the State Department urging that we torpedo our ally Chiang Kai-shek and stating, in effect, that communism was the best hope of China.

Later, this man—John Service—was picked up by the Federal Bureau of Investigation for turning over to the Communists secret State Department information. Strangely, however, he was never prosecuted. However, Joseph Grew, the Under Secretary of State, who insisted on his prosecution, was forced to resign. Two days after Grew's successor, Dean Acheson, took over as Under Secretary of State, this man—John Service—who had been picked up by the FBI and who had previously urged that communism was the best hope of China, was not only reinstated in the State Department but promoted. And finally, under Acheson, placed in charge of all placements and promotions.

Today, ladies and gentlemen, this man Service is on his way to represent the State Department and Acheson in Calcutta—by far and away the most important listening post in the Far East. . . .

Then there was a Mrs. Mary Jane Kenny, from the Board of Economic Warfare in the State Department, who was named in an FBI report and in a House committee report as a courier for the Communist Party while working for the Government. And where do you think Mrs. Kenny is—she is now an editor in the United Nations Document Bureau. . . .

This, ladies and gentlemen, gives you somewhat of a picture of the type of individuals who have been helping to shape our foreign policy. In my opinion the State Department, which is one of the most important government departments, is thoroughly infested with Communists.

I have in my hand 57 cases of individuals who would appear to be either card carrying members or certainly loyal to the Communist Party, but who nevertheless are still helping to shape our foreign policy.

One thing to remember in discussing the Communists in our Government is that we are not dealing with spies who get 30 pieces of silver to steal the blueprints of a new weapon. We are dealing with a far more sinister type of activity because it permits the enemy to guide and shape our policy. . . .

As you hear this story of high treason, I know that you are saying to yourself, "Well, why doesn't the Congress do something about it?" Actually, ladies and gentlemen, one of the important reasons for the graft, the corruption, the dishonesty, the disloyalty, the treason in high Government positions—one of the most important reasons why this continues is a lack of moral uprising on the part of the 140,000,000 American people. In the light of history, however, this is not hard to explain.

It is the result of an emotional hangover and a temporary moral lapse which follows every war. It is the apathy to evil which people who have been subjected to the tremendous evils of war feel. As the people of the world see mass murder, the destruction of defenseless and innocent people, and all of the crime and lack of morals which go with war, they become numb and apathetic. It has always been thus after war.

However, the morals of our people have not been destroyed. They still exist. This cloak of numbness and apathy has only needed a spark to rekindle them. Happily, this spark has finally been supplied.

As you know, very recently the Secretary of State proclaimed his loyalty to a man [Alger Hiss] guilty of what has always been considered as the most abominable of all crimes—of being a traitor to the people who gave him a position of great trust. The Secretary of State in attempting to justify his continued devotion to the man who sold out the Christian world to the atheistic world, referred to Christ's Sermon on the Mount as a justification and reason therefor, and the reaction of the American people to this would have made the heart of Abraham Lincoln happy.

When this pompous diplomat in striped pants, with a phony British accent, proclaimed to the American people that Christ on the Mount endorsed communism, high treason, and betrayal of a sacred trust, the blasphemy was so great that it awakened the dormant indignation of the American people.

He has lighted the spark which is resulting in a moral uprising and will end only when the whole sorry mess of twisted, warped thinkers are swept from the national scene so that we may have a new birth of national honesty and decency in Government.

DOCUMENT 31.7
The Republican Declaration of Conscience*

Not all members of McCarthy's party approved the senator's reckless and vicious tactics but, on the contrary, felt disgusted by them. Among those Republicans who spoke out against McCarthy was Senator Margaret Chase Smith of Maine. In June 1950 six other Republican senators joined Mrs. Smith in signing a "Declaration of Conscience" which was a clear repudiation of McCarthyism.

THE GROWING CONFUSION—NEED FOR PATRIOTIC THINKING

Mrs. [Margaret Chase] Smith of Maine. Mr. President, I would like to speak briefly and simply about a serious national condition. It is a national feeling of fear and frustration that could result in national suicide and the end of everything that we Americans hold dear....

I speak as briefly as possible because too much harm has already been done with irresponsible words of bitterness and selfish political opportunism. I speak as simply as possible because the issue is too great to be obscured by eloquence. I speak simply and briefly in the hope that my words will be taken to heart.

Mr. President, I speak as a Republican. I speak as a woman. I speak as a United States Senator. I speak as an American.

The United States Senate has long enjoyed world-wide respect as the greatest deliberative body in the world. But recently that deliberative character has too often been debased to the level of a forum of hate and character assassination sheltered by the shield of congressional immunity.

It is ironical that we Senators can in debate in the Senate, directly or indirectly, by any form of words, impute to

*Source: Congressional Record, 81st Cong., 2nd sess., Vol. 96, Part 6 (June 1, 1950), pp. 7894–95.

any American who is not a Senator any conduct or motive unworthy or unbecoming an American—and without that non-Senator American having any legal redress against us—yet if we say the same thing in the Senate about our colleagues we can be stopped on the grounds of being out of order.

It is strange that we can verbally attack anyone else without restraint and with full protection, and yet we hold ourselves above the same type of criticism here on the Senate floor. Surely the United States Senate is big enough to take self-criticism and self-appraisal. Surely we should be able to take the same kind of character attacks that we "dish out" to outsiders.

I think that it is high time for the United States Senate and its Members to do some real soul searching and to weigh our consciences as to the manner in which we are performing our duty to the people of America and the manner in which we are using or abusing our individual powers and privileges.

I think it is high time that we remembered that we have sworn to uphold and defend the Constitution. I think it is high time that we remembered that the Constitution, as amended, speaks not only of the freedom of speech but also of trial by jury instead of trial by accusation.

Whether it be a criminal prosecution in court or a character prosecution in the Senate, there is little practical distinction when the life of a person has been ruined.

Those of us who shout the loudest about Americanism in making character assassinations are all too frequently those who, by our own words and acts, ignore some of the basic principles of Americanism—

The right to criticize.

The right to hold unpopular beliefs.

The right to protest.

The right of independent thought.

The exercise of these rights should not cost one single American citizen his reputation or his right to a livelihood nor should he be in danger of losing his reputation or livelihood merely because he happens to know some one who holds unpopular beliefs. Who of us does not? Otherwise none of us could call our souls our own. Otherwise thought control would have set in.

The American people are sick and tired of being afraid to speak their minds lest they be politically smeared as Communists or Fascists by their opponents. Freedom of speech is not what it used to be in America. It has been so abused by some that it is not exercised by others. . . .

Surely these are sufficient reasons to make it clear to the American people that it is time for a change and that a Republican victory is necessary to the security of the country. Surely it is clear that this Nation will continue to suffer so long as it is governed by the present ineffective Democratic administration.

Yet to displace it with a Republican regime embracing a philosophy that lacks political integrity or intellectual honesty would prove equally disastrous to the Nation. The Nation sorely needs a Republican victory. But I do not want to see the Republican Party ride to political victory on the Four Horsemen of Calumny—fear, ignorance, bigotry, and smear. . . .

As a woman, I wonder how the mothers, wives, sisters, and daughters feel about the way in which members of their families have been politically mangled in Senate debate—and I use the word "debate" advisedly.

As a United States Senator, I am not proud of the way in which the Senate has been made a publicity platform for irresponsible sensationalism. I am not proud of the reckless abandon in which unproved charges have been hurled from this side of the aisle. I am not proud of the obviously staged, undignified countercharges which have been attempted in retaliation from the other side of the aisle.

I do not like the way the Senate has been made a rendezvous for vilification, for selfish political gain at the sacrifice of individual reputations and national unity.

I am not proud of the way we smear outsiders from the floor of the Senate and hide behind the cloak of congressional immunity and still place ourselves beyond criticism on the floor, of the Senate. . . .

It is with these thoughts that I have drafted what I call a Declaration of Conscience. I am gratified that the Senator from New Hampshire [Mr. Tobey], the Senator from Vermont [Mr. Aiken], the Senator from Oregon [Mr. Morse], the Senator from New York [Mr. Ives], the Senator from Minnesota [Mr. Thye], and the Senator from New Jersey [Mr. Hendrickson] have concurred in that declaration and have authorized me to announce their concurrence.

The declaration reads as follows:

Statement of Seven Republican Senators

1. We are Republicans. But we are Americans first. It is as Americans that we express our concern with the growing confusion that threatens the security and stability of our country. Democrats and Republicans alike have contributed to that confusion.

2. The Democratic administration has initially created the confusion by its lack of effective leadership, by its contradictory grave warnings and optimistic assurances, by its complacency to the threat of communism here at home, by its oversensitiveness to rightful criticism, by its petty bitterness against its critics.

3. Certain elements of the Republican Party have materially added to this confusion in the hopes of riding the Republican Party to victory through the selfish political exploitation of fear, bigotry, ignorance, and intolerance. There are enough mistakes of the Democrats for Republicans to criticize constructively without resorting to political smears.

4. To this extent, Democrats and Republicans alike have unwittingly, but undeniably, played directly into the Communist design of "confuse, divide, and conquer."

5. It is high time that we stopped thinking politically as Republicans and Democrats about elections and started thinking patriotically as Americans about national security based on individual freedom. It is high time that we all stopped being tools and victims of totalitarian techniques—techniques that, if continued here unchecked, will surely end what we have come to cherish as the American way of life.

MARGARET CHASE SMITH,
Maine

CHARLES W. TOBEY,
New Hampshire

GEORGE D. AIKEN,
Vermont

WAYNE L. MORSE,
Oregon

IRVING M. IVES,
New York

EDWARD J. THYE,
Minnesota

ROBERT C. HENDRICKSON,
New Jersey

32 The United States and the Cold War

RICHARD J. BARNET
Institute for Policy Studies

The Cold War is the story of two great powers, each with a set of expectations as to how the other should behave, which neither was willing to fulfill. For anyone concerned with historical understanding rather than propagandistic rhetoric the question "Who started the cold war?" has little meaning. A better way to put it is: How did the Cold War happen? What has kept it going? It is impossible to understand the dynamics of this conflict without keeping in mind the stage on which the opening act was played, the smouldering world of 1945.

The United States emerged from World War II the most powerful nation in the history of the world. By almost any historical definition the United States was supreme. She alone possessed the secret of the atomic bomb, short-lived as that monopoly was to be. U.S. military forces, located on every inhabited continent, took permanent control of much of Japan's Pacific empire in the form of "strategic trusts." The war, which had brought all other participants close to economic ruin, victor and vanquished alike, had restored the American economy and left the United States in a position to manage the reconstruction of the world economy. The dollar was now the global currency. The United States was the No. 1 banker, creditor, and consumer of resources. The leader of what soon came to be known as the "Free World," with 6 percent of the population of the earth, swiftly proceeded to burn, melt, or eat each year more than 50 percent of the earth's consumable resources to feed its expanding industrial base and affluent consumer economy.

The picture of the Soviet Union in 1945 could not provide more of a contrast. With more than 20 million of her people dead, her relatively primitive industrial facilities largely in ruins, and her territory wasted by four years of "scorched earth" war, the Soviet Union, having purchased survival at a terrible price, was still weak and vulnerable. True, she was unquestionably the No. 2 power on the planet, in part because of her impressive military victories over Hitler, but principally because "victory" had spelled the end of the British and French empires that had long dominated European politics, along, of course, with the Italian, German, and Japanese empires. Soviet troops were in the middle of Europe, but the new Soviet empire was shaky indeed.

The United States entered the postwar era with a well-developed imperial creed. The United States, declared President Harry Truman in April 1945, should "take the lead in running the world in the way that the world ought to be run." From now on the 20th century was, in Henry Luce's words, to be "The American Century." "It now becomes our time," Luce wrote in a widely circulated editorial in 1941, "to be the powerhouse from which the ideals spread throughout the world." Walter Lippmann warned in 1943 that America stood now at the center of Western civilization. She must assume the role of guarantor of the "Atlantic community" or face the prospect that Europe would fall under the pressure of an expanding Soviet Union and the "emerging peoples of Asia." Henry Wallace predicted that "the English-speaking peoples of the world will have to take the lead in underwriting world prosperity for a generation to come." Frank Knox, the Secretary of the Navy, declared that the United States and Britain, having crushed the Axis, should "police the seven seas." In the 1943 hearings on Lend-Lease, Republican Congressmen Karl Mundt and Charles Eaton found themselves in agreement with the old New Dealer Adolph Berle, that the United States must now seek world power "as a trustee for civilization." The basic tenet of the new imperial creed was anti-imperialism. The United States sought power not to perpetuate the "selfish" policies of the old colonial powers but to "organize the peace" and to "impose international law."

How was the Soviet Union to fit into the American Century? American attitudes toward the Soviet Union had evolved since the days of the 1917 Revolution when Woodrow Wilson sent an American expeditionary force to Russia to help, in Winston Churchill's famous phrase, strangle Bolshevism in its cradle. When the military intervention failed the United States tried the same tactic of nonrecognition it would use 30 years later with respect to Communist China. It was not until 1933 that the Roosevelt administration finally entered into diplomatic relations with the Soviet Union. But suspicion and hostility toward the self-proclaimed revolutionary state remained. Even the wartime alliance, during which the Soviet Union held down the major force of the German armies for four years, did not dissipate the deep fear and antagonism toward Communist Russia felt in many quarters in the United States. All during the war much of the Catholic press maintained strong attacks on the godless Soviet state. Poles, Czechs, and other ethnic minorities kept alive the ancient fears and hatreds of Great Russia they had brought with them from Eastern Europe. American intellectuals, some of them former communists, knew and cared about Stalin's conniving and murderous domestic policies; they saw him as the embodiment of evil and hence a world menace. The professional military like Admiral William Leahy, Franklin Roosevelt's and Truman's personal Chief of Staff, and the professional foreign service officers like Robert Murphy and, above all, the conservative bankers, lawyers, and businessmen—Forrestal, Clayton, McCloy, Lovett, Harriman, Acheson—who had been called in to manage the war, were always nervous about the Soviet Union, which they saw not as just another state but as the embodiment of Bolshevism. The very existence of a powerful socialist state, legitimated by its struggles against Hitler, professing an alternative model for achieving consumer affluence and social justice, posed a threat to an American Century of global free enterprise. Then, too, the peculiar Soviet diplomatic style, with its capricious treatment of Western diplomats and its hostile rhetoric, aroused suspicion among those who had worked most closely with the Soviet Union. (In studying the cold war, one should not underestimate the importance of personal encounters. General Lucius Clay, the U.S. commander in Berlin, once sent Washington into a war panic by sending a telegram suggesting that, while he couldn't say anything more definite, he just didn't like the way his Soviet opposite number was acting.) Yet the men who managed American foreign policy at the end of the war prided themselves above all in being "realists." They knew that they would have to deal with a Soviet Union which was the No. 2 power in the world.

At the end of World War II the United

States was uncertain as to how much power would have to be shared with the Soviet Union in the American Century. The Truman administration was prepared to recognize the Kremlin as the legitimate ruler of the prewar Soviet empire, but it was extremely reluctant to acquiesce in any further territorial expansion as a consequence of the Soviet victory. U.S.–Soviet relations, which had always been prickly even at the height of the wartime alliance, quickly became embittered over the issue of the control of Poland. At Yalta, Franklin D. Roosevelt had accepted a vague agreement about a "democratic" Poland which, as the hard-liner Admiral Leahy observed, was "so elastic that the Russians can stretch it all the way from Yalta to Washington without ever technically breaking it." Despite its cosmetic language, it is hard to read the Yalta agreements in their proper context of big power trading as anything other than a consignment of Poland to the Soviet sphere of influence. The Republicans would soon charge Roosevelt with "treason" for the "betrayal" of Poland, and the 1946 congressional elections showed conspicuous gains for Republican candidates in districts with large Polish and Eastern European populations. But in 1945, with the Red Army at the gates of Warsaw, the Americans had little bargaining power. "In this atmosphere of disturbance and collapse, atrocities and disarrangement," Assistant Secretary of War John J. McCloy reported to President Truman in April 1945, "we are going to have to work out a practical relationship with the Russians."

For the State Department in the spring of 1945 a "practical relationship" could be based on Soviet political domination of Poland, providing it did not result in "any interference with American property or trade in these sovereign countries." The old prewar *cordon sanitaire*, a string of western-oriented, anti-Soviet regimes, was gone, but the United States still hoped to maintain "its own trading interests and

position" in Eastern Europe. The United States, then, did not intend to accord the Soviet Union the same exclusive hegemony in Eastern Europe that she had demanded for herself in Latin America ever since the Monroe Doctrine. The managers of the Truman administration saw nothing anomalous about insisting on the very rights for the No. 1 nation they would deny to the No. 2 nation. "I think that it's not asking too much," Secretary of War Stimson remarked in May 1945 in defense of this double standard, "to have our little region over here which has never bothered anybody."

The United States believed that the Soviet Union ought to behave in accordance with the new balance of power in the world and expected that the military superiority that the atomic bomb had brought it, together with America's economic might, would insure a properly "cooperative" Soviet policy. The United States would make the major decisions regarding the reconstruction of Japan and Germany, the role and character of the new world organization, the United Nations, and the management of the world economy. But Stalin lost no time in signalling his unwillingness to play the role assigned to him in the American Century.

Stalin emerged from World War II resolved to preserve the Soviet state in what he believed to be an even more hostile environment than the prewar world. Suspicious by nature, conscious that Hitler was only the latest of a wave of foreign invaders that had ravaged the Russian earth throughout her history, aware that a fundamentally anti-Soviet capitalist state had become the giant among nations, the Soviet dictator was obsessed with the question of national security. Hitler, the only man he had ever trusted, had betrayed him and almost cost him his empire. The generation of warfare Stalin had carried on against his own people in the form of purges, trials, deportations, and executions had left Soviet society weakened and the loyalty of her citizens in doubt. Much of the industrial plant for which Stalin had sacrificed a generation of peasants now lay in ruins.

At the same time the international prestige of the Soviet Union had never stood higher. A Soviet army was at the Elbe. Communist parties of Western Europe, which had played a heroic role in the resistance to the Nazis, emerged as the leading political forces in France and Italy. Unlike the Greek and Yugoslav parties, they were under the tight control of Moscow. The old vacillating regimes of prewar Europe, with their tired aristocrats, temporizing politicians, scheming clerics, and fascist collaborators, were discredited. Was it not possible that communism, personified by the heroic partisans of the antifascist struggle, was the true wave of the future?

Stalin's innate caution and his negative view of indigenous revolutionary movements kept him from exploiting these considerable political advantages. His eye was fixed on the borders of the Soviet Union. In Eastern Europe he moved with hesitation, despite his overwhelming military power over the area. Finland was allowed to maintain an independent, moderate noncommunist government at the price of declaring a "friendly" foreign policy toward the Soviet Union. In Austria a noncommunist government was set up under Red Army occupation. The Soviets held free elections in their zone in Austria in 1945 and suffered a resounding defeat. In Poland, Stalin moved ruthlessly to purge politicians of an independent bent, including many communists, but, as former State Department planner Louis Halle has observed, he was genuinely reluctant to make Poland a satellite. A noncommunist Poland with a "friendly" foreign policy could have served as a buffer. A communist Poland was a provocation to the West. Elsewhere in Eastern Europe Stalin exhibited the same pattern. In Romania Foreign Minister Andre Vishinsky suddenly descended in the midst of mounting chaos and demanded the premiership for Petru Groza, a conservative who was willing to work closely with communists. (Vishinsky's nominee for Vice Premier and Minister of Foreign Affairs, as a member of a previous government, had sent the Romanian Communist leader, Anna Pauker, to prison for 10 years.) As late as November 8, 1946, the communist daily *Scinteia* was wishing King Michael "a long life, good health, and a reign rich in democratic achievements." It was not until several months later that Romania became a People's Republic. Hungary's communists did not obtain control until August 1947. In the same year a communist dictatorship was finally imposed on Poland.

Just as the Truman administration expected a properly respectful Soviet Union not to stray far from its prewar borders and to acquiesce in the extension of American authority throughout the world, so Stalin expected that the Soviet Union, as a consequence of its great victory over Nazism, would be accorded a junior partnership in a global duopoly with the United States. Stalin, as State Department analysts at the time correctly saw it, wanted to carve up the world, but compared with the United States his appetites were modest. It was not that he was altruistic, self-effacing, or anti-imperialist. It was simply that his power was limited and that, perhaps as a result of his disastrous overconfidence in his dealings with Hitler, he consistently underestimated the power he had.

Stalin, according to Winston Churchill's account, "strictly and faithfully" kept to the agreement he made with the British not to aid the Greek communists in their 1944 bid to take over the government. (Four years later when the United States under the Truman Doctrine had replaced Britain as the mainstay of the beleagured Greek government, Stalin is said to have exclaimed to the Yugoslavs, "The uprising in Greece must be stopped, and as quickly as possible.") In accepting Churchill's mathematical descriptions of the Soviet

and Western spheres of influence in Eastern Europe ("90 percent" Soviet influence
in Romania, "80 percent" in Bulgaria,
"50—50" in Yugoslavia) Stalin may well
have assumed that these agreements,
though the Roosevelt administration remained officially aloof from them, constituted a model for future relations, at once
correct and cynical, among the strange
allies of the victorious coalition.

There is much evidence for Marshall
Tito's observation that Stalin moved to
tighten his control over Eastern Europe
in response to a series of American military and political moves including
the dispatch in early 1946 of a permanent
U.S. flotilla to the Mediterranean. The
United States could not have adopted a
policy more calculated to induce Stalin to
lay a heavy hand on Eastern Europe,
including the takeover of Czechoslovakia
in 1948. But that is not the whole story.
Elsewhere at the periphery of his empire,
Stalin sought to achieve some strategic improvements, to reclaim some former Russian territory as a tangible recompense for
the sacrifices of the war, to get some new
territorial concessions cheaply, all in the
quest for a margin of security behind
which he could reconstruct his shattered
country. At the Teheran Conference in
1943 Churchill had looked with favor on
the Soviets acquiring controlled access
from the Black Sea to the Mediterranean
through the Dardanelles, a traditional
Russian objective. After the dispute over
Poland had erupted, the British Prime
Minister was less ready to make such a
concession. Stalin began to put pressure
on the Turkish government, demanding
the return of the provinces of Khars and
Ardahan, which had belonged to Imperial
Russia between 1878 and 1918, and insisting upon Soviet naval bases on the
Dardanelles and a revision of the Mon-
treux Convention, which regulated the use
of the Straits. The Soviets engaged in
propaganda with Turkish minorities and
ostentatiously deployed their military
forces in Transcaucasia, near the Turkish

border. The Turks sent repeated alarmist
messages to Washington. In August 1946,
Truman dispatched a stern note to Stalin
and reinforced the U.S. Mediterranean
fleet, remarking to his Cabinet that "we
might just as well find out now as in five or
ten years whether the Russians are bent
on world conquest." Stalin quickly gave
up his plans for the Dardanelles.

Crude and unjustified as it was, there
was nothing in Stalin's move toward
Turkey to suggest world conquest. This
diplomatic thrust was an attempt by Stalin
to take advantage of something he thought
entitled to by virtue of his geographic
position and his military power, and in
this respect it was like his move toward
Iran later the same year. Stalin directed
the communist-controlled Tudeh Party to
agitate for an autonomous provincial government in the Iranian province of Azer-
baijan in an attempt to gain valuable oil
concessions in the region. The United
States dispatched another note which a
State Department official at the time
called "virtually an ultimatum," and Stalin
backed down once more. The strong
American reaction meant that there was to
be no junior partnership for the U.S.S.R.
The world had not only been divided, but
divided into two very unequal "camps."

Wherever Stalin made his cautious
moves to consolidate his hold over Eastern Europe or the abortive moves at the
periphery of his empire, the Red Army
was either on the scene or had been
recently withdrawn. Beyond the reach of
the Red Army Stalin followed his prewar
policy of discouraging communist revolutionary movements that could not be
tightly controlled from Moscow or that
could embarrass the Soviet Union in its
diplomatic relations with other states.
Stalin, who had advised Mao Tse-tung to
accept Chiang's leadership in the 1920s
and ordered the Spanish communists in
the 1930s to abandon their revolutionary
goals, continued in the postwar period to
pursue a frankly counterrevolutionary policy. The Soviet dictator believed, correctly

as it turned out, that independent communist revolutions did nothing to enhance the security of the Soviet state. Indeed they posed a threat to Soviet interests. (Thus it is no accident, as the Soviets themselves like to say, that two of the three communist governments established by local revolutionaries independent of the Red Army—China and Albania—became enemies of the Soviet state, and a third, Yugoslavia, once also an enemy, is now at best a wary neighbor.)

Stalin, who had been right in minimizing the possibilities of revolution in the interwar period, now underestimated the revolutionary implications of the upheavals of World War II. He discouraged the French resistance and told the communists who played a dominant role in it to line up behind General de Gaulle. Communist ministers in the early French cabinets were instructed to play a correct and cooperative role. He directed the Italian communists, who were in a very strong position, to come to terms with the government of Marshal Badoglio. Tito, he demanded, must agree to the restoration of the Yugoslav monarchy. "The bourgeoisie is very strong," Stalin warned, "not only in Serbia but in China, Poland, Romania, France, Italy—everywhere." He was well aware that, at the moment of victory, the U.S. Army in Europe had orders to disarm the partisans in Italy and France and to take control of the factories and city governments that the communists had seized.

The crucial questions for understanding this period have to do with the American response. Did the Truman administration understand what Stalin was up to? If Truman made the correct analysis, why did he adopt the policies he did? Assuming he made the wrong analysis, on the other hand, what was it about the triumphant, frightened America of 1946 that led it to see Stalin as the new Hitler?

Unfortunately, historical truth does not sort itself out quite so neatly. The fact is that the men of the Truman administration made a remarkably accurate estimate of Stalin's psychology and immediate intentions—and at the same time flew in the face of both in constructing American policies. An understanding of why that happened takes us beyond the history of international relations into the internal workings of the American government and American society.

Charles Bohlen, Dean Acheson, and other participants in the formation of U.S. Cold War policy now admit that they may have oversold the Soviet menace in 1946 and 1947. Following Senator Arthur Vandenberg's admonition of the time that they must "scare hell out of the American people," the managers of the Truman administration tried to enlist public support for a policy too subtle to be easily sold. There was, after four years of war, little sentiment in the United States for the jingoism of the American Century. The American people, suspicious of the "power politics" of Europe and eager to "bring the boys home," were not much attracted to the idea of taking over the "burdens" and "responsibilities" of the British and French empires. This was of course precisely the national security policy advanced by State Department and Pentagon planners beginning in 1943. For the planners themselves, the imperial model of national security needed no rationalization. The United States was merely stepping into an old role now left vacant by the upheavals of war. But for the public it did need rationalization. For a country that had had its first "red scare" in 1919, "Soviet Imperialism" was a perfect threat on which to build the new American empire.

That the men of the Truman administration had a less hysterical private view of Soviet intentions than their public statements indicated is suggested by the historical record and from such recent admissions as Dean Acheson's that they "may have exaggerated" the Soviet military threat. The Joint Chiefs of Staff testified repeatedly in Congress that there was no evidence that the Soviets intended to invade Western Europe, although the buildup of NATO was rooted in the opposite assumption. (Indeed, the Soviets, far more concerned about an invasion to the east, tore up the only rail tracks across Poland that fitted the odd Russian gauge.) State Department analysts such as Eldridge Durbrow were writing in 1944 that the Soviet Union would face economic collapse at the end of the war and would be in no shape to pose a military challenge to the United States.

More significant are the key documents that defined the official attitude toward Stalin's Russia and outlined the policy of containment. The most influential of these were the long dispatches which George Kennan, a senior foreign service officer stationed at the Moscow embassy, wrote to Washington in early 1946. These dispatches, which offered learned and elegant support for his own strong feelings of anticommunism, were promoted throughout the national security bureaucracy by James Forrestal, Secretary of the Navy, like a best-seller. They eventually found their way into a report which Clark Clifford, President Truman's Counsel, prepared for him and which was to become the key statement in setting the tone and direction of cold war policy. The Clifford memorandum, drawing on Kennan's analysis, correctly emphasized Stalin's security fears: the Soviets feared "encirclement" by the capitalist states and believed that they would eventually initiate a war against the Soviet Union. Thus the Soviet Union must be prepared "for any eventuality" and must strengthen its military forces. Clifford argued that it was a "direct threat to American security" for the Soviets to prepare for a war with the leading capitalist nations which, according to the Soviets' own ideology, the capitalist nations would initiate. There was only one way to deal with such a threat:

The language of military power is the only language which disciples of power politics understand. The United States must use that language in order that Soviet leaders will realize that our government is determined to uphold the interest of its citizens and the rights of small nations. Compromise and concessions are considered, by the Soviets, to be evidence of weakness and they are encouraged by our "retreats" to make new and greater demands.

This was, of course, the policy of containment which with small modifications has been carried on to this day. The Soviet Union has been ringed with military bases, constantly challenged to keep up in an arms race in which the United States has had, until recently, overwhelmingly superior military power. The Clifford memorandum makes curious —and tragic—reading a generation later. Why Stalin, described as a paranoid leader who believes that dangerous enemies are about to encircle him, should "mellow," to use Kennan's term, by having his paranoid fantasies realized is never made clear. Of course the policy of "containment" had precisely the opposite effect. Stalin rearmed, launched a crash program to produce the atomic bomb, tightened his hold on Eastern Europe and half of Germany, blockaded Berlin in 1948, and, in the name of national security, resumed his permanent war against the Russian people.

Were the men of the Truman administration genuinely afraid of the Soviets, or was the "Soviet threat" just a pretext for the military policies necessary to establish the American Century? The answer, it seems to me, is that the Truman administration was dominated by a fear which, though often publicly exaggerated, was, nonetheless, as genuine as it was irrational.

Men like Averell Harriman, who dealt with the Soviets on a day-to-day basis as ambassador to Moscow, voiced the deepest alarm in the highest circles of government. "We might well have to face an ideological warfare just as vigorous and dangerous as fascism or Nazism," Harriman told Forrestal in the spring of 1945 while the war was still on. It was not Soviet military power but communist ideology that was perceived as the great threat. In April 1945, Harriman warned that "half and maybe all of Europe might be communistic by the end of next winter." "No permanently safe international relations can be established," Secretary of War Stimson warned, "between two such fundamentally different national systems. With the best of efforts we cannot understand each other." As the war ended Harriman told the American commander in Berlin that "Hitler's greatest crime" was "opening the gates of East Europe to Asia." It was the difference in "ideology" that posed the great threat to American interests, and there would be no security until the Soviet Union reformed itself of its dangerous beliefs and stopped exporting them to the wretched, vulnerable masses of the earth.

Washington's view of Soviet ideology was heavily colored by its own ideology. The State Department's view of Stalinism bore little resemblance to what Stalin was preaching or practising. In France communist ministers joined the government and pursued a united-front strategy under which they were the strongest force in the country favoring a strong France with a formidable army and retention of the empire in Algeria as well as in Indo-China. It was hardly the policy of international conspirators ready to serve their country up to the Russians. In Italy, too, the communists sought to become a respectable, legitimate national party. (Only after the Cold War had split Europe did the French and Italian communist parties briefly attempt mass antigovernment strikes, a strategy which failed spectacularly.)

But the State Department, poring over the turgid literature of the communist ideologues, professed to see a blueprint for world conquest. Jacques Duclos, leading French communist, wrote an article in April 1945 in *Cahiers du Communisme* which the State Department took to be Moscow's "instructions" to the world communist movement for protracted conflict with the West. All the article said was that the communist parties should not dissolve, as the American communist party had done during the World War II, and that they should pursue a struggle for "national unity" while fighting the "trusts." Like Stalin's "election speech" a few months later, this document was taken by highly placed Americans to be the "declaration of World War III."

Stalin, in Truman's eyes, had become the Hitler of today: "Unless Russia is faced with an iron fist and strong language, another war is in the making." The fear of the Soviet Union that pervaded the Truman administration was real enough, although it was based on virtually no objective evidence that the Soviet Union was going to commit "aggression" outside of the area of Eastern Europe which it had staked out as its minimum reward of victory. Years later defenders of the Truman administration's Cold War policy point to allegedly threatening documents and speeches of the Soviets rather than actions to justify the early American Cold War policy. (It was not until five years later, in 1950, with the North Korean invasion of South Korea that Stalin could be plausibly painted as a Hitler-like aggressor. That move, so uncharacteristic of the cautious Stalin, has been explained in Khrushchev's memoirs as a case of Stalin's entrapment by his obstreperous North Korean puppets. Whatever the case, Korea, which was correctly analyzed in the State Department as a local action, was publicly presented as evidence of a worldwide communist military threat and was made the pretext for German rearmament, the strengthening of NATO, and the enormous rise in the U.S. military budget that has continued to this day.)

The fear of Stalinism grew out of the unwillingness of the United States to share power with a suspicious, treacherous Soviet dictator and the awareness that the Soviet Union had the military and economic potential to compel her to share that power eventually. The American Century meant American supremacy. The United States had inherited the mantle of Britain as the peacemaker of the planet and, as the Truman Doctrine made clear, its writ ran throughout the globe. It was not America's destiny to share her new power with the old discredited empires like England and France, much less with a bloody dictatorship that espoused an alien, godless ideology. This then was the American dilemma: how to be supreme in the face of another power willing to acknowledge superiority but not supremacy. Some Americans thought the answer lay in preventive war. In 1950 the Secretary of the Navy Francis Matthews publicly suggested dropping some atom bombs on the Soviet Union. Though he was publicly reprimanded, many military men have publicly and privately endorsed the policy which Barry Goldwater once described as "lobbing one into the Kremlin's men's room." Lyndon Johnson and Melvin Laird, the present Secretary of Defense, are two of a long line of American statesmen who have suggested the nuclear annihilation of the Soviet Union in a surprise attack in the event of unspecified "Soviet aggression" not necessarily involving a nuclear attack on the United States.

But that policy was not adopted. Instead, the United States asserted its supremacy by the policy of the double standard. Thus the United States established missiles within a few miles of the Soviet border in Turkey but was prepared to fight a nuclear war to compel the Soviets to remove their missiles from Cuba. American aircraft flew over the air space of the Soviet Union at a time when a Soviet attempt to duplicate that feat in American air space would have meant a major confrontation. The United States still asserts the right to maintain a permanent fleet in the Mediterranean, but a small Soviet fleet is a "threat." The United States began building military alliances in the Middle East in 1950, but Soviet penetra-

tion into the area in recent years is a menace to world peace. It has been easy to justify the double standard by using ideology. When the United States took over Britain's oil concessions in Iran, Roosevelt was thrilled at the chance to use Iran as an example of "what we could do by an unselfish American policy." What is imperialism when done by other countries is development when done by the United States. By the same token the U.S.S.R. now insists that its ships in the Mediterranean are a "peace" fleet while U.S. ships are a "war" fleet.

In recent years, as the Soviet Union has become more powerful, its leaders have relied less on bluster and invective. To use the State Department term, the "atmospherics" of U.S.–Soviet relations have improved. It is not because the Soviets have "mellowed," but because the Soviet Union is now powerful enough to compel the United States to accept something like the duopoly Stalin hoped for at the end of the war. Since the midfifties the Soviet Union has had the military capability to destroy American society no matter how many missiles or antimissiles the United States chooses to build. Thus, despite the militant rhetoric of John Foster Dulles, Secretary of State under President Eisenhower, both sides accepted the existence of a standoff which has led slowly to a bizarre partnership of political convenience, accompanied by an intensified arms race. The Soviet Union now has the power to counter America's intervention in Indo-China which it lacked in Greece, Lebanon, Iran, Dominican Republic, and many other places where the United States used its military power to shore up subservient governments or to undermine governments deemed hostile to American interests. After a generation of Cold War the Soviets are, indeed, "becoming more like us," as many commentators have observed, but this is hardly an encouraging development from the viewpoint of U.S. security. With far greater power at their disposal than Stalin ever had, with

America's nuclear monopoly broken and her vaunted "superiority" rendered meaningless, Stalin's successors are far more adventurous in their foreign policy, notably in Cuba and the Middle East, than the old dictator ever dared to be. The Soviet Union is undoubtedly, despite continuing restrictions on human liberty, a pleasanter place in which to live than in Stalin's day, and with the split in the communist world it is harder to believe in the ideological terrors of a monolithic "world communism." But the Soviet Union is a far more formidable rival of the United States than it ever was in the Stalin era. There is little in the history of the last quarter century to suggest that "containment" has kept the peace or brought added security to the American people.

SUGGESTED READINGS

ACHESON, DEAN. *Present at the Creation: My Years in the State Department.* New York: W. W. Norton & Co., 1969.

ALPEROVITZ, GAR. *Cold War Essays.* New York: Anchor Books, 1970.

BARNET, RICHARD. *Intervention and Revolution: America's Confrontation with Insurgent Movements around the World.* New York: New American Library, 1968.

BUNDY, McGEORGE, and STIMSON, HENRY L. *On Active Service in Peace and War.* New York: Harper, 1948.

BYRNES, JAMES F. *Speaking Frankly.* New York: Harper, 1947.

FORRESTAL, JAMES J. *The Forrestal Diaries,* ed. WALTER MILLIS. New York: Viking, 1951.

HALLE, LOUIS J. *The Cold War as History.* New York: Harper & Row, 1967.

KENNAN, GEORGE F. *Memoirs, 1925–1950.* Boston: Little, Brown & Co., 1967.

KOLKO, GABRIEL. *The Politics of War: The World and United States Foreign Policy, 1943–1945.* New York: Random House, 1969.

LAFEBER, WALTER. *America, Russia, and the Cold War, 1945–66.* New York: John Wiley & Sons, 1967.

LUKACS, JOHN A. *A New History of the Cold War.* 3rd ed., expanded. New York: Anchor Books, 1966.

WILLIAMS, WILLIAM APPLEMAN. *The Tragedy of American Diplomacy.* New York: Dell Publishing Co., 1968.

DOCUMENT 32.1

The Soviet Union and American Power*

In September of 1946, the Truman administration developed an analysis of the Soviet Union and a comprehensive view of the use of power in the American Century. These views were distilled in a memo by Clark Clifford, then Counsel to President Truman.

It is perhaps the greatest paradox of the present day that the leaders of a nation, now stronger than it has ever been before, should embark on so agressive a course because their nation is "weak." And yet Stalin and his cohorts proclaim that "monopoly capitalism" threatens the world with war and that Russia must strengthen her defenses against the danger of foreign attacks. The U.S.S.R., according to Kremlin propaganda, is imperilled so long as it remains within a "capitalistic encirclement." This idea is absurd when adopted by so vast a country with such great natural wealth, a population of almost 200 million and no powerful or aggressive neighbors. But the process of injecting this propaganda into the minds of the Soviet people goes on with increasing intensity.

The concept of danger from the outside is deeply rooted in the Russian people's haunting sense of insecurity inherited from their past. It is maintained by their present leaders as a justification for the oppressive nature of the Soviet police state. The thesis, that the capitalist world is conspiring to attack the Soviet Union, is

*Source: Clark Clifford, in Arthur Krock, *Sixty Years on the Firing Line,* (New York: Funk & Wagnalls, 1968), Appendix.

not based on any objective analysis of the situation beyond Russia's borders. It has little to do, indeed, with conditions outside the Soviet Union, and it has arisen mainly from basic inner-Russian necessities which existed before the second World War and which exist today. . . .

The Soviet Government, in developing the theme of "encirclement," maintains continuous propaganda for domestic consumption regarding the dangerously aggressive intentions of American "atom diplomacy" and British imperialism, designed to arouse in the Soviet people fear and suspicion of all capitalistic nations.

Despite the fact that the Soviet Government believes in the inevitability of a conflict with the capitalist world and prepares for that conflict by building up its own strength and undermining that of other nations, its leaders want to postpone the conflict for many years. The western powers are still too strong, the U.S.S.R. is still too weak. Soviet officials must therefore not provoke, by their policies of expansion and aggression, too strong a reaction by other powers.

The Kremlin acknowledges no limit to the eventual power of the Soviet Union, but it is practical enough to be concerned with the actual position of the U.S.S.R. today. In any matter deemed essential to the security of the Soviet Union, Soviet leaders will prove adamant in their claims and demands. In other matters they will prove grasping and opportunistic, but flexible in proportion to the degree and nature of the resistance encountered.

Recognition of the need to postpone the "inevitable" conflict is in no sense a betrayal of the Communist faith. Marx and Lenin encouraged compromise and collaboration with non-communists for the accomplishment of ultimate communistic purposes. The U.S.S.R. has followed such a course in the past. In 1939 the Kremlin signed a non-aggression pact with Germany and in 1941 a neutrality pact with Japan. Soviet leaders will continue to collaborate whenever it seems expedient, for

time is needed to build up Soviet strength and weaken the opposition. Time is on the side of the Soviet Union, since population growth and economic development will, in the Soviet view, bring an increase in its relative strength. . . .

A direct threat to American security is implicit in Soviet foreign policy which is designed to prepare the Soviet Union for war with the leading capitalistic nations of the world. Soviet leaders recognize that the United States will be the Soviet Union's most powerful enemy if such a war as that predicted by Communist theory ever comes about and therefore the United States is the chief target of Soviet foreign and military policy.

A recent Soviet shift of emphasis from Great Britain to the United States as the principal "enemy" has been made known to the world by harsh and strident propaganda attacks upon the United States and upon American activities and interests around the globe. The United States, as seen by radio Moscow and the Soviet press, is the principal architect of the "capitalistic encirclement" which now "menaces the liberty and welfare of the great Soviet masses." These verbal assaults on the United States are designed to justify to the Russian people the expense and hardships of maintaining a powerful military establishment and to insure the support of the Russian people for the agressive actions of the Soviet Government.

The most obvious Soviet threat to American security is the growing ability of the U.S.S.R. to wage an offensive war against the United States. This has not hitherto been possible, in the absence of Soviet long-range strategic air power and an almost total lack of sea power. Now, however, the U.S.S.R. is rapidly developing elements of her military strength which she hitherto lacked and which will give the Soviet Union great offensive capabilities. Stalin has declared his intention of sparing no effort to build up the military strength of the Soviet Union. Development of atomic weapons, guided missiles, materials for biological warfare, a strategic air force, submarines of great cruising range, naval mines and mine craft, to name the most important, are extending the effective range of Soviet military power well into areas which the United States regards as vital to its security. . . .

Although the Soviet Union at the present moment is precluded from military aggression beyond the land mass of Eurasia, the acquisition of a strategic air force, naval forces and atomic bombs in quantity would give the U.S.S.R. the capability of striking anywhere on the globe. Ability to wage aggressive warfare in any area of the world is the ultimate goal of Soviet military policy.

. . . . .

The primary objective of United States policy toward the Soviet Union is to convince Soviet leaders that it is in their interest to participate in a system of world cooperation, that there are no fundamental causes for war between our two nations, and that the security and prosperity of the Soviet Union, and that of the rest of the world as well, is being jeopardized by the aggressive militaristic imperialism such as that in which the Soviet Union is now engaged.

However, these same leaders with whom we hope to achieve an understanding on the principles of international peace appear to believe that a war with the United States and the other leading capitalistic nations is inevitable. They are increasing their military power and the sphere of Soviet influence in preparation for the "inevitable" conflict, and they are trying to weaken and subvert their potential opponents by every means at their disposal. So long as these men adhere to these beliefs, it is highly dangerous to conclude that hope of international peace lies only in "accord," "mutual understanding," or "solidarity" with the Soviet Union.

Adoption of such a policy would impel the United States to make sacrifices for the sake of Soviet–U.S. relations, which would only have the effect of raising Soviet hopes and increasing Soviet demands, and to ignore alternative lines of policy, which might be much more compatible with our own national and international interests.

The Soviet Government will never be easy to "get along with." The American people must accustom themselves to this thought, not as a cause for despair, but as a fact to be faced objectively and courageously. If we find it impossible to enlist Soviet cooperation in the solution of world problems, we should be prepared to join with the British and other Western countries in an attempt to build up a world of our own which will pursue its own objectives and will recognize the Soviet orbit as a distinct entity with which conflict is not predestined but with which we cannot pursue common aims.

As long as the Soviet Government maintains its present foreign policy, based upon the theory of an ultimate struggle between communism and capitalism, the United States must assume that the U.S.S.R. might fight at any time for the two-fold purpose of expanding the territory under communist control and weakening its potential capitalist opponents. The Soviet Union was able to flow into the political vacuum of the Balkans, Eastern Europe, the Near East, Manchuria and Korea because no other nation was both willing and able to prevent it. Soviet leaders were encouraged by easy success and they are now preparing to take over new areas in the same way. The Soviet Union, as Stalin euphemistically phrased it, is preparing "for any eventuality."

Unless the United States is willing to sacrifice its future security for the sake of "accord" with the U.S.S.R. now, this government must, as a first step toward world stabilization, seek to prevent additional Soviet aggression. The greater the area controlled by the Soviet Union, the greater the military requirements of this country will be. Our present military plans are based on the assumption that, for the next few years at least, Western Europe, the Middle East, China and Japan will remain outside the Soviet sphere. If the Soviet Union acquires control of one or more of these areas, the military forces required to hold in check those of the U.S.S.R. and prevent still further acquisitions will be substantially enlarged. That will also be true if any of the naval and air bases in the Atlantic and Pacific, upon which our present plans rest, are given up. This government should be prepared, while scrupulously avoiding any act which would be an excuse for the Soviets to begin a war, to resist vigorously and successfully any efforts of the U.S.S.R. to expand into areas vital to American security.

The language of military power is the only language which disciples of power politics understand. The United States must use that language in order that Soviet leaders will realize that our government is determined to uphold the interests of its citizens and the rights of small nations. Compromise and concessions are considered, by the Soviets, to be evidences of weakness and they are encouraged by our "retreats" to make new and greater demands. . . .

Whether it would actually be in this country's interest to employ atomic and biological weapons against the Soviet Union in the event of hostilities is a question which would require careful consideration in the light of the circumstances prevailing at the time. The decision would probably be influenced by a number of factors, such as the Soviet Union's capacity to employ similar weapons, which can not now be estimated. But the important point is that the United States must be prepared to wage atomic and biological warfare if necessary. The mere fact of preparedness may be the only powerful deterrent to Soviet aggressive action and in this sense the only sure guaranty of peace. . . .

In conclusion, as long as the Soviet Government adheres to its present policy, the United States should maintain military forces powerful enough to restrain the Soviet Union and to confine Soviet influence to its present area. All nations not now within the Soviet sphere should be given generous economic assistance and political support in their opposition to Soviet penetration. Economic aid may also be given to the Soviet Government and private trade with the U.S.S.R. permitted provided the results are beneficial to our interests and do not simply strengthen the Soviet program. We should contine to work for the cultural and intellectual understanding between the United States and the Soviet Union but that does not mean that, under the guise of an exchange program, communist subversion and infiltration in the United States will be tolerated. In order to carry out an effective policy toward the Soviet Union, the United States Government should coordinate its own activities, inform and instruct the American people about the Soviet Union, and enlist their support based upon knowledge and confidence. These actions by the United States are necessary before we shall ever be able to achieve understanding and accord with the Soviet Government on any terms other than its own.

Even though Soviet leaders profess to believe that the conflict between Capitalism and Communism is irreconcilable and must eventually be resolved by the triumph of the latter, it is our hope that they will change their minds and work out with us a fair and equitable settlement when they realize that we are too strong to be beaten and too determined to be frightened.

DOCUMENT 32.2
The Truman Doctrine*

Perhaps the most crucial foreign policy statement of the postwar era was the following message of President Truman to Congress. In the speech many of the basic premises which have remained at the heart of U.S. policy for a generation are spelled out.

MR. PRESIDENT, MR. SPEAKER, MEMBERS OF THE CONGRESS OF THE UNITED STATES:

The gravity of the situation which confronts the world today necessitates my appearance before a joint session of the Congress.

The foreign policy and the national security of this country are involved.

One aspect of the present situation, which I wish to present to you at this time for your consideration and decision, concerns Greece and Turkey.

The United States has received from the Greek Government an urgent appeal for financial and economic assistance. Preliminary reports from the American Economic Mission now in Greece and reports from the American Ambassador in Greece corroborate the statement of the Greek Government that assistance is imperative if Greece is to survive as a free nation.

I do not believe that the American people and the Congress wish to turn a deaf ear to the appeal of the Greek Government.

Greece is not a rich country. Lack of sufficient natural resources has always forced the Greek people to work hard to make both ends meet. Since 1940 this industrious and peace-loving country has suffered invasion, four years of cruel enemy occupation, and bitter internal strife.

When forces of liberation entered

*Source: Message of the President to Congress, March 12, 1947, in *Public Papers of the Presidents . . . Harry S. Truman . . . 1947*. (Washington, D.C.: Government Printing Office, 1963), pp. 176–80.

Greece they found that the retreating Germans had destroyed virtually all the railways, roads, port facilities, communications, and merchant marine. More than a thousand villages had been burned. Eighty-five percent of the children were tubercular. Livestock, poultry, and draft animals had almost disappeared. Inflation had wiped out practically all savings.

As a result of these tragic conditions, a militant minority, exploiting human want and misery, was able to create political chaos which, until now, has made economic recovery impossible.

Greece is today without funds to finance the importation of those goods which are essential to bare subsistence. Under these circumstances the people of Greece cannot make progress in solving their problems of reconstruction. Greece is in desperate need of financial and economic assistance to enable it to resume purchases of food, clothing, fuel, and seeds. These are indispensable for the subsistence of its people and are obtainable only from abroad. Greece must have help to import the goods necessary to restore internal order and security so essential for economic and political recovery.

The Greek Government has also asked for the assistance of experienced American administrators, economists, and technicians to insure that the financial and other aid given to Greece shall be used effectively in creating a stable and self-sustaining economy and in improving its public administration.

The very existence of the Greek state is today threatened by the terrorist activities of several thousand armed men, led by Communists, who defy the Government's authority at a number of points, particularly along the northern boundaries. A commission appointed by the United Nations Security Council is at present investigating disturbed conditions in northern Greece and alleged border violations along the frontier between Greece on the one hand and Albania, Bulgaria, and Yugoslavia on the other.

Meanwhile, the Greek Government is unable to cope with the situation. The Greek Army is small and poorly equipped. It needs supplies and equipment if it is to restore authority to the Government throughout Greek territory.

Greece must have assistance if it is to become a self-supporting and self-respecting democracy.

The United States must supply that assistance. We have already extended to Greece certain types of relief and economic aid, but these are inadequate.

There is no other country to which democratic Greece can turn.

No other nation is willing and able to provide the necessary support for a democratic Greek Government.

The British Government, which has been helping Greece, can give no further financial or economic aid after March 31. Great Britain finds itself under the necessity of reducing or liquidating its commitments in several parts of the world, including Greece.

We have considered how the United Nations might assist in this crisis. But the situation is an urgent one requiring immediate action, and the United Nations and its related organizations are not in a position to extend help of the kind that is required.

It is important to note that the Greek Government has asked for our aid in utilizing effectively the financial and other assistance we may give to Greece, and in improving its public administration. It is of the utmost importance that we supervise the use of any funds made available to Greece, in such a manner that each dollar spent will count toward making Greece self-supporting, and will help to build an economy in which a healthy democracy can flourish.

No government is perfect. One of the chief virtues of a democracy, however, is that its defects are always visible and under democratic processes can be pointed out and corrected. The Government of Greece is not perfect. Neverthe-

less it represents 85 percent of the members of the Greek Parliament who were chosen in an election last year. Foreign observers, including 692 Americans, considered this election to be a fair expression of the views of the Greek people.

The Greek Government has been operating in an atmosphere of chaos and extremism. It has made mistakes. The extension of aid by this country does not mean that the United States condones everything that the Greek Government has done or will do. We have condemned in the past, and we condemn now, extremist measures of the right or the left. We have in the past advised tolerance, and we advise tolerance now.

Greece's neighbor, Turkey, also deserves our attention.

The future of Turkey as an independent and economically sound state is clearly no less important to the freedom-loving peoples of the world than the future of Greece. The circumstances in which Turkey finds itself today are considerably different from those of Greece. Turkey has been spared the disasters that have beset Greece. And during the war the United States and Great Britain furnished Turkey with material aid.

Nevertheless, Turkey now needs our support.

Since the war Turkey has sought additional financial assistance from Great Britain and the United States for the purpose of effecting that modernization necessary for the maintenance of its national integrity.

That integrity is essential to the preservation of order in the Middle East.

The British Government has informed us that, owing to its own difficulties, it can no longer extend financial or economic aid to Turkey.

As in the case of Greece, if Turkey is to have the assistance it needs, the United States must supply it. We are the only country able to provide that help.

I am fully aware of the broad implica

tions involved if the United States extends assistance to Greece and Turkey, and I shall discuss these implications with you at this time.

One of the primary objectives of the foreign policy of the United States is the creation of conditions in which we and other nations will be able to work out a way of life free from coercion. This was a fundamental issue in the war with Germany and Japan. Our victory was won over countries which sought to impose their will, and their way of life, upon other nations.

To insure the peaceful development of nations, free from coercion, the United States has taken a leading part in establishing the United Nations. The United Nations is designed to make possible lasting freedom and independence for all its members. We shall not realize our objectives, however, unless we are willing to help free peoples to maintain their free institutions and their national integrity against aggressive movements that seek to impose upon them totalitarian regimes. This is no more than a frank recognition that totalitarian regimes imposed upon free peoples, by direct or indirect aggression, undermine the foundations of international peace and hence the security of the United States.

The peoples of a number of countries of the world have recently had totalitarian regimes forced upon them against their will. The Government of the United States has made frequent protests against coercion and intimidation, in violation of the Yalta agreement, in Poland, Rumania, and Bulgaria. I must also state that in a number of other countries there have been similar developments.

At the present moment in world history nearly every nation must choose between alternative ways of life. The choice is too often not a free one.

One way of life is based upon the will of the majority, and is distinguished by free institutions, representative government, free elections, guaranties, of individual liberty, freedom of speech and religion, and freedom from political oppression.

The second way of life is based upon the will of a minority forcibly imposed upon the majority. It relies upon terror and oppression, a controlled press and radio, fixed elections, and the suppression of personal freedoms.

I believe that it must be the policy of the United States to support free peoples who are resisting attempted subjugation by armed minorities or by outside pressures.

I believe that we must assist free peoples to work out their own destinies in their own way.

I believe that our help should be primarily through economic and financial aid which is essential to economic stability and orderly political processes.

The world is not static, and the *status quo* is not sacred. But we cannot allow changes in the *status quo* in violation of the Charter of the United Nations by such methods as coercion, or by such subterfuges as political infiltration. In helping free and independent nations to maintain their freedom, the United States will be giving effect to the principles of the Charter of the United Nations.

It is necessary only to glance at a map to realize that the survival and integrity of the Greek nation are of grave importance in a much wider situation. If Greece should fall under the control of an armed minority, the effect upon its neighbor, Turkey, would be immediate and serious. Confusion and disorder might well spread throughout the entire Middle East.

Moreover, the disappearance of Greece as an independent state would have a profound effect upon those countries in Europe whose peoples are struggling against great difficulties to maintain their freedoms and their independence while they repair the damages of war.

It would be an unspeakable tragedy if these countries, which have struggled so long against overwhelming odds, should lose that victory for which they sacrificed so much. Collapse of free institutions and loss of independence would be disastrous not only for them but for the world. Discouragement and possibly failure would quickly be the lot of neighboring peoples striving to maintain their freedom and independence.

Should we fail to aid Greece and Turkey in this fateful hour, the effect will be far-reaching to the West as well as to the East.

We must take immediate and resolute action.

I therefore ask the Congress to provide authority for assistance to Greece and Turkey in the amount of $400,000,000 for the period ending June 30, 1948. In requesting these funds, I have taken into consideration the maximum amount of relief assistance which would be furnished to Greece out of the $350,000,000 which I recently requested that the Congress authorize for the prevention of starvation and suffering in countries devastated by the war.

In addition to funds, I ask the Congress to authorize the detail of American civilian and military personnel to Greece and Turkey, at the request of those countries, to assist in the tasks of reconstruction, and for the purpose of supervising the use of such financial and material assistance as may be furnished. I recommend that authority also be provided for the instruction and training of selected Greek and Turkish personnel.

Finally, I ask that the Congress provide authority which will permit the speediest and most effective use, in terms of needed commodities, supplies, and equipment, of such funds as may be authorized.

If further funds, or further authority, should be needed for purposes indicated in this message, I shall not hesitate to bring the situation before the Congress. On this subject the Executive and legislative branches of the Government must work together.

This is a serious course upon which we embark.

I would not recommend it except that the alternative is much more serious.

The United States contributed $341,000,000,000 toward winning World War II. This is an investment in world freedom and world peace.

The assistance that I am recommending for Greece and Turkey amounts to little more than one-tenth of one percent of this investment. It is only common sense that we should safeguard this investment and make sure that it was not in vain.

The seeds of totalitarian regimes are nurtured by misery and want. They spread and grow in the evil soil of poverty and strife. They reach their full growth when the hope of a people for a better life has died.

We must keep that hope alive.

The free peoples of the world look to us for support in maintaining their freedoms.

If we falter in our leadership, we may endanger the peace of the world—and we shall surely endanger the welfare of our own Nation.

Great responsibilities have been placed upon us by the swift movement of events.

I am confident that the Congress will face these responsibilities squarely.

DOCUMENT 32.3

Soviet Policy in Eastern Europe*

The Soviet Union reacted to the diplomacy of the Truman administration by tightening its grip on Eastern Europe. In a speech on the 30th anniversary of the Revolution of November 7, 1917, V. M. Molotov, Foreign Minister of the U.S.S.R., explained Soviet policy.

---

*Source: *The New York Times*, November 7 1947, p. 3.

The Soviet Union has invariably carried out, and is carrying out, the policy of peace and international collaboration. Such are the relations of the Soviet Union with all the countries which evince a desire to collaborate.

The policy outlined by Comrade Stalin is opposed at present by another policy, based on quite different principles. Here we can talk first and foremost of the foreign policy of the United States, as well as that of Great Britain. Possibly there exists in the United States a program of economic development of the country for some period ahead. However, the press has not yet announced anything about this, although press conferences take place there quite frequently. On the other hand, much noise is being spread about various American projects, connected now with the Truman Doctrine, now with the Marshall plan.

Reading of all these American plans for aid to Europe, aid to China, and so on, one might think that the domestic problems of the United States have long ago been solved, and that now it is only a question of America's putting the affairs of other states in order, dictating its policy to them and even the composition of their governments.

In reality, matters are not like that. If the ruling circles of the U.S.A. had no cause for anxiety concerning domestic affairs especially in connection with an approaching economic crisis, there would not be such a superfluity of economic projects of U.S.A. expansion, which in their turn are based on the aggressive military-political plans of American imperialism.

Now they no longer hide the fact that the United States of America, not infrequently together with Great Britain, is acquiring ever new naval and air bases in all parts of the globe, and even adapts whole states for such like aims, especially if closely situated to the Soviet Union.

Who does not complain about the pressure of American imperialism in that respect? Even if the governments of certain big states of Europe, Asia and America preserve a kind of solid silence in regard to this matter, it is clear that certain small states are faced by an absolutely intolerable position. Denmark, for instance, cannot achieve the restoration of her national sovereignty over Greenland, which the Americans do not want to leave after the end of the war. Egypt legitimately demands the withdrawal of British troops from her territory. Britain refuses to do that, and America supports the British imperialists in these matters also.

It is, however, clear that the creation of military bases in various parts of the world is not designed for defense purposes, but as a preparation for aggression. It is also clear that if, up to now, the combined British-American General Staff, created during the second World War, has been maintained, this is not being done for peace-loving purposes, but for the purpose of intimidating with the possibility of new aggression.

It would be a good thing for all this to be known to the American people, for under the so-called Western freedom of the press, when almost all newspapers and radio stations are in the hands of small cliques, the aggressive cliques of the capitalists and their servitors, it is difficult for the people to know the real truth.

It is interesting that in expansionist circles of the U.S.A. a new, peculiar sort of illusion is widespread—while having no faith in their internal strength—faith is placed in the secret of the atom bomb, although this secret has long ceased to exist.

Evidently the imperialists need this faith in the atom bomb which, as is known, is not a means of defense but a weapon of aggression. . . .

It is well known that the industry of the United States of America in the period between the two world wars has grown, although its development proceeded extremely unevenly and twice fell considerably below the level of 1913. For all that, during the second World War American industry grew rapidly, became inflated and began to yield enormous profits to the capitalists and state revenues, which American state monopoly capitalism is putting into circulation and applying to exert pressure everywhere in Europe and China, in Greece and Turkey, in South America and in the Middle East.

Certainly there are not a few who like to make use of a war situation. . . .

Today the ruling circles of the U.S.A. and Great Britain head one international grouping, which has as its aim the consolidation of capitalism and the achievement of the dominations of these countries over other peoples. These countries are headed by imperialist and anti-democratic forces in international affairs, with the active participation of certain Socialist leaders in several European states. . . .

As a result of post-war Anglo-American policy the British and American zones of occupation of Germany were united into a jointly administered bizonal territory—which has been given the name of "Bizonia" in the press—so that an Anglo-American policy could be unilaterally carried out there independently of the Control Council, in which representatives of all four occupying powers participate.

Our representatives in Germany are today virtually concerned only with the Soviet zone. A situation has arisen which cannot but produce alarm among the German people also, since, as the result of the Anglo-American policy, there exists the joint zone and other zones, but there is no Germany, no single German state.

The Soviet Union considers it necessary that the decisions of the Yalta and Potsdam conferences on the German question, decisions which provided for the restoration of Germany as a single, democratic state, should be put into effect. Moreoover, in the Soviet Union it is entirely understood that the joint zone is not Germany and that the German people has a right to the existence of its own state which, it goes without saying, must be a democratic state and must not create the threat of new aggression for other peace-loving states.

At the present time there exists the Anglo-American plan—by giving some aims to calm the population of the Anglo-American zone of Germany—for basing themselves here on the former capitalists who were recently the Hitlerite support, and for utilizing with their aid the joint zone with its Ruhr industrial basin as a threat against those countries which do not display slavish submissiveness with regard to the Anglo-American plans for domination in Europe.

But these adventurists' plans, based on Germany, will lead to nothing good and it goes without saying, will be rejected by democratic Europe.

From the example of the German question, one can see how widely present day Anglo-American principles diverge from the principles of the Soviet state, how Anglo-American principles are steeped in open imperialism, while the Soviet stands firmly on democratic positions.

The Soviet Union, in common with other democratic states, stands for peace and international collaboration on democratic principles. Under present conditions, this demands the uniting of all forces of the anti-imperialist and democratic camp in Europe and beyond the boundaries of Europe, so that an insurmountable barrier shall be created against imperialism, which is becoming more active, and against its new policy of aggression.

The rallying of democratic forces and courageous struggle against imperialism in its new plans for war adventures will unite the peoples into a powerful army, the equal of which cannot be possessed by imperialism, which denies the democratic rights of the people, infringing on the sovereignty of the nations and basing its plans on threats and adventures.

Uneasiness and alarm are growing in the imperialist ranks, since everybody sees that the ground is shaking under the feet of imperialism, while the forces of democracy and socialism are daily growing and consolidating.

What can the policy of imperialism offer people? Nothing but strengthening of oppression, the rebirth of the vestiges of hated fascism and imperialistic adventures.

It is necessary to open the peoples' eyes and to unite all the democratic and anti-imperialistic forces in order to foil any plans for the economic enslavement of nations and any new adventures on the part of the imperialists.

The historic experience of the Soviet Union has confirmed the justice of the great Lenin's words on the invincibility of the people which took power into their hands. Lenin said: "One can never conquer a people where the majority of workers and peasants have realized, sensed and seen that they are upholding their own sovereign power, the power of the working people, the victory of whose cause, if upheld, will secure for them and their children the possibility of enjoying all the benefits of culture, all the achievements of human labor."

The task of our time is to unite all the anti-imperialistic and democratic forces of the nations into one mighty camp, welded together by the unity of their vital interests against the imperialist and anti-democratic camp and its policy of enslavement of the peoples and new adventures.

A sober attitude to the matter shows simultaneously that in our time new imperialistic adventures constitute a dangerous game with destinies of capitalism.

DOCUMENT 32.4
Henry Wallace Opposes American Policy*

Although the Cold War policy of the Truman administration won a broad consensus of support, there were a number of dissenters, including columnist Walter Lippmann and leading Republican Senator Robert A. Taft. The most prominent contemporary critic of cold war policy was Henry A. Wallace, who in 1948 ran for the Presidency on a third-party ticket largely because of the issues raised in the article which follows.

How do American actions since V-J Day appear to other nations? I mean by actions the concrete things like $13 billion for the War and Navy Departments, the Bikini tests of the atomic bomb and continued production of bombs, the plan to arm Latin America with our weapons, production of B-29's and planned production of B-36's, and the effort to secure air bases spread over half the globe from which the other half of the globe can be bombed. I cannot but feel that these actions must make it look to the rest of the world as if we were only paying lip-service to peace at the conference table. These facts rather make it appear either (1) that we are preparing ourselves to win the war which we regard as inevitable or (2) that we are trying to build up a predominance of force to intimidate the rest of mankind. How would it look to us if Russia had the atomic bomb and we did not, if Russia had 10,000-mile bombers and air bases within a thousand miles of our coast lines and we did not?

Some of the military men and self-styled "realists" are saying: "What's wrong with trying to build up a predominance of force? The only way to preserve peace is for this country to be so well armed that

*Source: Henry A. Wallace, "The Path to Peace with Russia," *The New Republic*, Vol. 115 (September 30, 1946), pp. 401–6. Reprinted by permission of *The New Republic*.

no one will dare attack us. We know that America will never start a war."

The flaw in this policy is simply that it will not work. In a world of atomic bombs and other revolutionary new weapons, such as radioactive poison gases and biological warfare, a peace maintained by a predominance of force is no longer possible.

Why is this so? The reasons are clear:

First. Atomic warfare is cheap and easy compared with old-fashioned war. Within a very few years several countries can have atomic bombs and other atomic weapons. Compared with the cost of large armies and the manufacture of old-fashioned weapons, atomic bombs cost very little and require only a relatively small part of a nation's production plant and labor force.

Second. So far as winning a war is concerned, having more bombs—even many more bombs—than the other fellow is no longer a decisive advantage. If another nation had enough bombs to eliminate all of our principal cities and our heavy industry, it wouldn't help us very much if we had ten times as many bombs as we needed to do the same to them.

Third. The most important, the very fact that several nations have atomic bombs will inevitably result in a neurotic, fear-ridden, itching-trigger psychology in all the peoples of the world, and because of our wealth and vulnerability we would be among the most seriously affected. Atomic war will not require vast and time-consuming preparations, the mobilization of large armies, the conversion of a large proportion of a country's industrial plants to the manufacture of weapons. In a world armed with atomic weapons, some incident will lead to the use of those weapons.

There is a school of military thinking which recognizes these facts, recognizes that when several nations have atomic bombs, a war which will destroy modern civilization will result and that no nation or combination of nations can win such a war. This school of thought therefore advocates a "preventive war," an attack on Russia now, before Russia has atomic bombs. This scheme is not only immoral but stupid. If we should attempt to destroy all the principal Russian cities and her heavy industry, we might well succeed. But the immediate counter-measure which such an attack would call forth is the prompt occupation of all continental Europe by the Red Army. Would we be prepared to destroy the cities of all Europe in trying to finish what we had started? This idea is so contrary to all the basic instincts and principles of the American people that any such action would be possible only under a dictatorship at home.

Thus the "predominance of force" idea and the notion of a "defensive attack" are both unworkable. The only solution is the one which you have so wisely advanced and which forms the basis of the Moscow statement on atomic energy. That solution consists of mutual trust and confidence among nations, atomic disarmament and an effective system of enforcing that disarmament. . . .

I should list the factors which make for Russian distrust of the United States and of the Western world as follows: The first is Russian history, which we must take into account because it is the setting in which Russians see all actions and policies of the rest of the world. Russian history for over a thousand years has been a succession of attempts, often unsuccessful, to resist invasion and conquest—by the Mongols, the Turks, the Swedes, the Germans and the Poles. The scant thirty years of the existence of the Soviet government has in Russian eyes been a continuation of their historical struggle for national existence. The first four years of the new regime, from 1917 through 1921, were spent in resisting attempts at destruction by the Japanese, British and French, with some American assistance and by the several White Russian armies encouraged and financed by the Western powers. Then, in 1941, the Soviet state was almost conquered by the Germans after a period during which the Western European powers had apparently acquiesced in the rearming of Germany in the belief that the Nazis would seek to expand eastward rather than westward. The Russians, therefore, obviously see themselves as fighting for their existence in a hostile world.

Second, it follows that to the Russians all of the defense and security measures of the Western powers seem to have an aggressive intent. Our actions to expand our military security system—such steps as extending the Monroe Doctrine to include the arming of the Western Hemisphere nations, our present monopoly of the atomic bomb, our interest in outlying bases and our general support of the British Empire—appear to them as going far beyond the requirements of defense. I think we might feel the same if the United States were the only capitalistic country in the world and the principal socialistic countries were creating a level of armed strength far exceeding anything in their previous history. From the Russian point of view, also, the granting of a loan to Britain and the lack of tangible results on their request to borrow for rehabilitation purposes may be regarded as another evidence of strengthening of an anti-Soviet bloc.

Finally, our resistance to her attempts to obtain warm-water ports and her own security system in the form of "friendly" neighboring states seems, from the Russian point of view, to clinch the case. After twenty-five years of isolation and after having achieved the status of a major power, Russia believes that she is entitled to recognition of her new status. Our interest in establishing democracy in Eastern Europe, where democracy by and large has never existed, seems to her an attempt to reëstablish the encirclement of unfriendly neighbors which was created after the last war and which might serve as a springboard of still another effort to destroy her.

If this analysis is correct, and there is ample evidence to support it, the action to improve the situation is clearly indicated. The fundamental objective of such action should be to allay any reasonable Russian grounds for fear, suspicions and distrust. We must recognize that the world has changed and that today there can be no "one world" unless the United States and Russia can find some way of living together. For example, most of us are firmly convinced of the soundness of our position when we suggest the internationalization and defortification of the Danube or of the Dardanelles, but we would be horrified and angered by any Russian counterproposal that would involve also the internationalizing and disarming of Suez or Panama. We must recognize that to the Russians these seem to be identical situations.

We should ascertain from a fresh point of view what Russia believes to be essential to her own security as a prerequisite to the writing of the peace and to coöperation in the construction of a world order. We should be prepared to judge her requirements against the background of what we ourselves and the British have insisted upon as essential to our respective security. We should be prepared, even at the expense of risking epithets of appeasement, to agree to reasonable Russian guarantees of security. . . .

American products, especially machines of all kinds, are well established in the Soviet Union. For example, American equipment, practices and methods are standard in coal mining, iron and steel, oil and non-ferrous metals.

Nor would this trade be one-sided. Although the Soviet Union has been an excellent credit risk in the past, eventually the goods and services exported from this country must be paid for by the Russians by exports to us and to other countries. Russian products which are either definitely needed or which are non-competitive in this country are various non-ferrous metal ores, furs, linen products, lumber products, vegetable drugs, paper and pulp and native handicrafts. . . .

Many of the problems relating to the countries bordering on Russia could more readily be solved once an atmosphere of mutual trust and confidence is established and some form of economic arrangements is worked out with Russia. These problems also might be helped by discussions of an economic nature. Russian economic penetration of the Danube area, for example, might be countered by concrete proposals for economic collaboration in the development of the resources of this area, rather than by insisting that the Russians should cease their unilateral penetration and offering no solution to the present economic chaos there.

This proposal admittedly calls for a shift in some of our thinking about international matters. It is imperative that we make this shift. We have little time to lose. Our post-war actions have not yet been adjusted to the lessons to be gained from experience of Allied coöperation during the war and the facts of the atomic age.

It is certainly desirable that, as far as possible, we achieve unity on the home front with respect to our international relations; but unity on the basis of building up conflict abroad would prove to be not only unsound but disastrous. I think there is some reason to fear that in our earnest efforts to achieve bipartisan unity in this country we may have given way too much to isolationism masquerading as tough realism in international affairs.

DOCUMENT 32.5

A Warning from the Chamber of Commerce*

The government was not alone in devoting energies to public education on foreign policy issues. In a pamphlet, entitled *Communist Infiltration in the United States,* the Chamber of Commerce of the United States raised the issue of the connection between domestic subversion and foreign policy.

COMMUNISM AN ORGANIZED MOVEMENT

Communism is an organized and even fanatical world movement. Its ideology holds that the opposition between it and private capitalism is complete and unalterable. As a result, it holds that capitalism must die in the throes of bloody revolution. Such a movement cannot be appeased by improvements in the standard of living of the people in capitalist nations. It is dangerous to make any contrary assumption. Marx said that capitalism is essentially exploitive, that it must oppress the workers, and hence that it must be overthrown by force. Communists believe this with blind fanaticism and privately preach violent revolution. The successful working of free enterprise may make it difficult for Communism to gain recruits, but it will not dampen the faith of the confirmed Communist. Nor would it prevent the triumph of Communism here through conquest by a foreign power, aided by our domestic Fifth Column, namely, the infiltration of Communists and their sympathizers in government, the armed forces, labor, and other important spheres of American life.

This dogma of essential conflict must be understood in order properly to evaluate Soviet policy. Thus, when Stalin, in Feb-

*Source: Report of the Committee on Socialism and Communism, Copyright, Chamber of Commerce of the United States, *Communist Infiltration in the United States* (Washington, D.C. 1946), pp. 7–11; 16–24.

ruary, 1946, announced a vast military program to counter foreign "encirclement," and in September, 1946, derided the idea of encirclement as a myth, the average reader was confused. Actually, the first proclamation was in harmony with the basic principles of Communism. The subsequent retraction was but another temporary tactical retreat, similar to many others which Stalin describes in his own writings. Significantly, there was no let-up in military preparations or stay in aggressive Soviet actions to prove the sincerity of Stalin's "peace message."

THE COMINTERN

As the instrument of the crusade to crush private capitalism, the Communist International has been organized. The aims of this world movement, called the Comintern, are to organize and stimulate Communist movements in all the nations of the world. Its openly professed objectives are to foster revolution in all capitalist lands. While technically distinct from the Soviet Government, it is in fact an agency of that State. Its headquarters are in Moscow and its leaders are the most powerful men in the Communist hierarchy.

The Comintern was ostensibly dissolved in 1943 as a gesture of cooperation between the Soviet Union and its allies. A detailed study of the *Report of the Royal Commission*, issued in June, 1946, in connection with the Canadian espionage trials casts grave doubt upon the reality of the dissolution. On the contrary, there is documented and irrefutable evidence that the Comintern organized major espionage rings among its allies throughout the war.

Furthermore, the scope of coordinated propaganda activities of the Comintern since war's end is almost unbelievable both in extent and intensity. Such widely diverse regions as the Arab world, the colonial countries of Asia and the newly independent Philippines, and practically all Latin American countries are being thoroughly cultivated. Comintern agents were the guiding forces behind the 1946 elections in Chile, where Communists showed astonishing strength. In the small island of Cuba, they have a powerful radio station and a subsidized news service, both used to spread propaganda through other Latin American countries. Their staff in Mexico is large and skillfully organized.

Little information has been released in regard to Comintern activities in the United States. Nevertheless, the Canadian Report shows that the several groups there worked closely with similar and more extensive rings in the United States. It also reveals that the Tass News Agency in New York sends lengthy reports to the Soviet Union, of which only an infinitesimal fraction is used for the Soviet press. Purchasing commissions and other economic groups transmit most minute details of commercial and industrial activity, sending abroad tons of blueprints and elaborate reports. In the fields of military and diplomatic secrets, according to the Canadian Commission, the Comintern seeks and usually obtains detailed and circumstantial accounts.

The Canadian Report indicates that the present headquarters of the Comintern are still in Moscow. Nevertheless, there are indications that some of its functions have been transferred to Paris. At least, this latter city is the headquarters for the various international Communist groups of labor, youth, and women. Other groups still to be formed, such as a world federation of scientists, will undoubtedly center there. This transfer permits such groups to pose as democratic organizations. Furthermore, Pairs is a better communication center for the purpose of reaching Western Europe and the Americas.

The spirit of this movement was expressed by Comrade Yudin, one of the chief molders of the USSR policy, as quoted by Victor Kravchenko in *I Chose Freedom:* "there are two worlds ... The two worlds of capitalism and Communism cannot forever exist side by side. As long as we exist in a capitalist encirclement, we are in danger." Stalin reiterated this same view in his February, 1946, address.

Soviet Expansionism

In addition to the ideology of Communism, many persons see in the Comintern a tool of a new form of old-fashioned power politics. Indeed, the Trotsky branch of Communism maintains that the Stalinists have deserted Marx and are merely seeking personal power on a world scale. Whatever be the merits of this theory, it is a fact that the Soviet Union has expanded its territories tremendously as a result of the war. It currently controls Eastern and much of Central Europe, the Balkans (except Greece), Manchuria, Northern Korea and North China. It is pressing towards Turkey and the Near East, in order to control the Mediterranean and the Persian Gulf.

The Soviet Union has openly announced plans for the greatest army, navy, air force, and military scientific arm in the world. It is questionable whether its own industrial potential could maintain such a force, although the new five-year plans are directed towards such a goal. But Soviet technology has been strengthened through the use of German and Czech workers and technology. Currently, the Soviet Union is putting pressure upon Sweden to orient its economy towards the East. Many analysts feel that the Molotov plan for a unified Germany would bring all German technology within the Soviet sphere. If the skill of the West can be wedded to the unlimited human and natural resources of the East, within twenty years the Soviet Union might be more powerful militarily than any combination of nations arrayed against her.

Against this background of Soviet hostility towards the capitalist world, gigantic military preparations, and an unabashed expansionist policy, the role of the Comintern seems ominous. It is revealed as a Fifth Column preparing the way for internal Communist revolution, when feasible, or for conquest from without by imperial Communism. It is at once an agency for espionage and revolutionary agitation. Such were the clear findings of the Canadian Commissioners, who reported that domestic Communists admitted a loyalty to the Soviet Union higher than that to their own country.

. . . . .

What Communism Means to America

The system just described in general terms is by no means remote from American life. On the contrary, it affects us in many important ways. Among these the first in order of importance may well be the domain of international affairs. One has but to accept the surface, not the worst, interpretation of recent Soviet moves, and one is left with profound feelings of disquiet.

The Soviet Union has proclaimed its intention to become the greatest military power on earth. It has already stretched beyond its borders to absorb nearly half of Europe and some of the richest parts of Asia. Parties under its control are active in the other half of Europe, with reasonable chances of extending Soviet influence to the Atlantic. Finally, the Comintern is meddling in most of the rest of the world, with special attention to Latin America, the orient, colonial countries, and the Arab world. Its theme is one of unremitting hostility towards the English-speaking world.

When this activity is compared with that of the Axis during the late Thirties, the points of similarity are greater than the points of difference. Those who then perceived the drift before others and cried out, as did Winston Churchill, were called warmongers. The same treatment is given today to those who observe the well-publicized facts summarized above. Yet we would be remiss in duty towards our country if we ignored them. We know that the Soviet people themselves want peace and good will towards other nations. But in the too familiar pattern, their leaders feed them warlike propaganda instead of peace, and military preparations instead of a higher standard of living. Observers of these facts tend to discount Stalin's peace line of September, 1946, as being a mere tactical move. The axiom that actions speak louder than words must be invoked once against world Communism.

WHAT COMMUNISM MEANS TO WORLD TRADE

If the recital of facts as given above savors too much of prediction, attention might be called to the immediate repercussions of Communism in the international sphere. Some American firms have suffered directly through the confiscation of their property abroad. We have virtually lost all oil wells and refineries in the Balkans, as well as giant industrial plants in Germany and Hungary. While present and future losses of this type may not be a major item to the Nation as a whole, they are a serious loss to the investors involved. They are a blow to future international investment, so badly needed to restore world production and American foreign trade. Thus, would American investors be wise to develop regions of Latin America or China, if it were probable that Communist regimes would arise to seize possession of this wealth?

Present Communist policies are badly disruptive of world trade. They have cut off the Danube, one of the great waterways of commerce. They are paralyzing economic life in Hungary, Austria, Korea, and Italy. Their reparations demands upon Italy are such as to make this nation an economic satellite. Strong pressure is being put upon Sweden and Denmark with the same aim. In many regions they are engaged in pre-emptive buying of scarce raw materials, disrupting prices and production in other lands. Thus, they seek hides from Uruguay and linseed oil from Argentina. Some of these products are not needed for their own economy. The time will come when the destructive character of these activites to multilateral trade will work to our disadvantage.

COMMUNISTS AND THE LABOR MOVEMENT

Communists have striven successfully to infiltrate the American labor movement. Organized labor, when captured, is to them a source of funds, a propaganda outlet, a means for stirring discontent, and, if necessary, a weapon of sabotage. Controlled unions contribute heavily to the various Party fronts and causes. They in turn serve as fronts for diverse propaganda schemes. They can picket consulates and government offices with practiced skill. When conditions warrant, strikes can be provoked so as to create the atmosphere of unrest in which Communism thrives. And, finally, if Comintern policy so dictates, they can actually sabotage essential production. Thus, the 1945 shipping strike "to bring back the soldiers" (American, not Russian) was an example of political sabotage.

In general, American Communists have been more successful in seizing power in the Congress of Industrial Organizations than in the American Federation of Labor. In the latter organization, they have some strength in New York and Los Angeles, and scattered control elsewhere. They have achieved real footholds in the painters union, in the hotel and restaurant unions, and in the film and stage unions. They are seeking, with some success, to infiltrate some of the independent railroad unions and the International Association of Machinists. But their stronghold is the Congress of Industrial Organizations.

History explains this success. When John L. Lewis sought to organize mass production industry, he suffered from an acute shortage of trained organizers. He used experienced Communist help, planning to discard it when the task was done. Nevertheless, he was outmaneuvered. Communists installed themselves and their sympathizers in key positions in many of the new unions. The newly organized workers, with no experience in unionism, were no match for these skilled tacticians. The result was that in union after union, Communists controlled the top levels, although the membership was overwhelmingly American in its sympathies. In spite of this fact, the C.I.O. has been slow to learn. When its Southern organizing drive bogged down in 1946, it quietly accepted support from the Communist organizers. Earlier statements that no leftist aid would be used were conveniently ignored.

Present Trend in the Labor Movement

The situation today is fluid, since Communist control is being occasionally challenged with success. On the other hand, Communists in turn make new gains periodically. At the time of this writing, two excellent surveys have been made of radicalism in labor. The correctness of these studies is attested privately by non-Communist labor leaders.

In general, the studies found that Communists had control of about one-third of the voting strength of the C. I. O. Executive Board. Their die-hard opponents controlled about one-fifth. Among the remainder, there were enough fellow-travelers to bring Communist strength to a majority in complex and obscure issues, such as foreign policy. On domestic issues the lines have been sharply drawn, with non-Communists having the balance of power.

How Communists Control Labor

While communists initially seized power through organizing unions, they maintain or lose control largely in terms of their strength in the locals of these unions. To understand their control over labor, it is vitally necessary to realize how they gain control over the various locals. If they must start from scratch in a given sit-uation, they usually send a few key organizers to work in a plant to join a union. These men show skill in speaking and fighting for workers' "rights," and soon obtain a minor office. At the same time, they cultivate ambitious opportunists and disgruntled minorities.

When they are ready to seize control, they usually make impossible demands upon the existing union officers and circulate slanderous rumors about them. Then they form an election slate consisting of opportunists with some following, representatives of racial and national minorities, and pleasant but weak characters who will be dependent upon them for advice. In large plants, where personal knowledge of the union officers is slight, the rumor campaigns and the aggressive program put out by the Communists are usually sufficient to install their slate in office in whole or in part.

Once Communists have gained power in a local, they often try to expel or discredit any potential opposition. They prolong meetings so that the membership will not attend. This permits their minority to vote funds, pass resolutions, and adopt action programs. By such tactics they often perpetuate power indefinitely. If in the beginning the Communists control the international union, they can often assume and maintain power from the very beginning of a new local.

Such tactics explain the comparative helplessness of non-Communists such as Philip Murray and James Carey. Carey was deposed from his own giant union, the United Electrical, Radio, and Machine Workers, when he opposed the Communist clique which dominated it. The issues at the time were the Hitler-Stalin pact, our foreign policy, and national defense. Murray does not dare to discharge the two powerful Communist officials who exercise such major influence in the national C. I. O. He submits to a large proportion of Communists among the legislative representatives of the C. I. O. unions. H tamely accepts resolution after resolution which show remarkable similarity to the Communist Party Line.

Communist Labor and the Businessman

Until recently the average American tended to dismiss such maneuverings as something foreign to his life. But the tremendous power of labor today permits no such complacency. Many an industrialist and businessman, and millions of union workers, have learned from experience that these moves do affect their lives vitally. When a businessman or industrialist finds that nothing he does can please his union, he tends at first to form a sour view of organized labor. But, as he becomes more sophisticated, he realizes that his difficulties may not arise from his own workers, who usually understand his problems, but from the outside forces controlling his local union. Their demands are insatiable, because they thrive on trouble. His workers are no more happy than he in such a situation but they are not trained to cope with it. They may at times even be constrained to support extreme and impossible demands.

Even where workers or their employers are not directly involved they are often affected in an oblique manner. The national policies of organized labor, if influenced by the Communists, can sometimes involve unions led by non-Communists. This is particularly the case where the objective *seems* reasonable to labor. An instance of this would be the Political Action Committee of the C. I. O. The general principle that labor has an interest in politics is almost as old as unionism itself. The more direct and aggressive methods of the C. I. O. are new and in contrast to the established approach of the A. F. of L. Even here, however, many workers who are by no means radical would accept the new approach.

The result is that practically all C. I. O. unions readily support P. A. C. Its philosophy and its program sound reasonable to them. What they do not realize is the nature of the forces which infiltrated this program. While Hillman was not a Communist, nor is Philip Murray, two of their top advisers are Communists, taking direct and frequent orders on P. A. C. policies from the very top levels of the Communist Party. At the other end of the scale, in many cities and regions, the local committees are Communist-controlled. They have the organization for ringing doorbells and getting out the vote. The easy thing is to use them, and many labor leaders take the easy way. As a result, at the time of writing such important Councils as those in New York and Detroit are Communist-controlled.

The direct national effect of Communist infiltration in P. A. C. may not have been serious. A few candidates deserving of labor's favor may have suffered because their foreign policy was opposed to the Communist line. A half dozen Communists may have gotten into our national legislature. The net effect of these moves would not be tragic. The real danger lies in the threat of the future. The feared power of P. A. C. forces politicians to select candidates in accord with the views of those who control the vote. In the day by day running of government, administrators hesitate to clash with the left wing, lest their Party suffer reprisals at the polls. It was the follow-up of the November 1944 elections in the form of pressure, demands, and suggestions which made left-wing control of P. A. C. a real force in shaping national policy.

Nor should the ambition of the local leader be overlooked. When a Communist minority can give the aggressive support needed to win an election, some politicians are willing to give their verbal aid in some specific policy, in order to obtain their help. Thus, a governor may attack our so-called "tough" policy towards Russia, knowing that he has no direct responsibility to make good on his promises.

This has happened, not only in large metropolitan centers, but also in some less settled Southern and Western states. It was the cumulative effect of all these moves which led to increased Communist influence in both domestic and foreign polices of the United States.

COMMUNISM AND GOVERNMENT

Both truth and much nonsense have been written about Communist penetration into government. There were those who visualized all New Dealers as starry-eyed radicals. Some labeled any program which changed the established order of things as Communist. This loose use of terms has caused considerable mischief. The result has been that at times the Communists could take credit for widely popular reform measures. Indiscriminate denunciation threatened to make Communism quite respectable. This was unfortunate, since it covered up a real and dangerous penetration of government.

Communist penetration of government since 1933 stems primarily from one phenomenon: the broadmindedness of the average liberal both in government and on the outside. The period characterized as the New Deal was humanitarian and reformist in its aims. As a result, there flocked to Washington large numbers of self-styled liberals, bent on reforming the Nation's economic system and curing social ills as seen by them. Bold experimentation became the order of the day. Our capitalist system was alleged to be so feeble that only daring and even recklessness could save the day.

In such an atmosphere, practically any philosophy was tolerated, provided only that it promised some modification of capitalist free enterprise. No political system was too extreme for the liberal to treat with sympathy, save only Fascism, which Communist propaganda had cleverly distorted into a "tool of reactionary big business." It was only natural that under these conditions, a considerable portion of Communists attained civil service status. Some

reached positions of authority. Once they had power, they behaved in a most illiberal manner. They were careful to appoint only like-minded individuals to officers under their control, and they schemed relentlessly to drive their opponents from government service. They achieved a considerable measure of success.

DOCUMENT 32.6
The Cuban Missile Crisis*

The high water mark of the U.S.–Soviet confrontation was the Cuban Missile Crisis of October 1962. In this television speech to the American people, President Kennedy gives his reasons for the quarantine of Cuba and the threat of military action.

GOOD EVENING, MY FELLOW CITIZENS:

This Government, as promised, has maintained the closest surveillance of the Soviet military build-up on the Island of Cuba. Within the past week, unmistakable evidence had estalished the fact that a series of offensive missile sites is now in preparation on that imprisoned island. The purpose of these bases can be none other than to provide a nuclear strike capability against the Western Hemisphere.

Upon receiving the first preliminary hard information of this nature last Tuesday morning at 9 A.M., I directed that our surveillance be stepped up. And having now confirmed and completed our evaluation of the evidence and our decision on a course of action, this Government feels obliged to report this new crisis to you in fullest detail.

The characteristics of these new missile sites indicate two distinct types of installations. Several of them include medium-range ballistic missiles, capable of carrying a nuclear warhead for a distance of more than 1,000 nautical miles. Each of these missiles, in short, is capable of

*President Kennedy's radio-television address October 22, 1962. *Bulletin*, The Department of State, Vol. 47 (November 12, 1962) pp. 715–20.

striking Washington, D.C., the Panama Canal, Cape Canaveral, Mexico City, or any other city in the southeastern part of the United States, in Central America or in the Caribbean area.

Additional sites not yet completed appear to be designed for intermediate range ballistic missiles—capable of travelling more than twice as far—and thus capable of striking most of the major cities in the Western Hemisphere, ranging as far north as Hudson's Bay, Canada, and as far south as Lima, Peru. In addition, jet bombers, capable of carrying nuclear weapons, are now being uncrated and assembled in Cuba, while the necessary air bases are being prepared.

This urgent transformation of Cuba into an important strategic base—by the presence of these large, long-range and clearly offensive weapons of sudden mass destruction—constitutes an explicit threat to the peace and security of all the Americas, in flagrant and deliberate defiance of the Rio Pact of 1947, the traditions of this Nation and Hemisphere, the Joint Resolution of the 87th Congress, the Charter of the United Nations, and my own public warnings to the Soviets on September 4 and 13. This action also contradicts the repeated assurances of Soviet spokesmen, both publicly and privately delivered, that the arms build-up in Cuba would retain its original defensive character, and that the Soviet Union had no need or desire to station strategic missiles on the territory of any other nation.

The size of this undertaking makes clear that it had been planned for some months. Yet only last month, after I had made clear the distinction between any introduction of ground-to-ground missiles and the existence of defensive anti-aircraft missiles, the Soviet Government publicly stated on September 11 that, and I quote, "the armaments and military equipment sent to Cuba are designed exclusively for defensive purposes," and there is, and I quote the Soviet Government, "no need for the Soviet Union to shift

weapons . . . for a retaliatory blow to any other country, for instance Cuba," and that, and I quote the Soviet Government, "the Soviet Union has so powerful rockets to carry these nuclear warheads that there is no need to search for sites for them beyond the boundaries of the Soviet Union," That statement was false.

Only last Thursday, as evidence of this rapid offensive build-up was already in my hand, Soviet Foreign Minister Gromyko told me in my office that he was instructed to make it clear once again, as he said his Government had already done, that Soviet assistance to Cuba, and I quote "pursued solely the purpose of contributing to the defence capabilities of Cuba," that, and I quote him, "training by Soviet specialists of Cuban nationals in handling defensive armaments was by no means offensive," and that "If it were otherwise," Mr. Gromyko went on, "the Soviet Government would never become involved in rendering such assistance." That statement also was false.

Neither the United States of America nor the world community of nations can tolerate deliberate deception and offensive threats on the part of any nation, large or small. We no longer live in a world where only the actual firing of weapons represents a sufficient challenge to a nation's security to constitute maximum peril. Nuclear weapons are so destructive, and ballistic missiles are so swift, that any substantially increased possibility of their use or any sudden change in their deployment may well be regarded as a definte threat to peace.

For many years, both the Soviet Union and the United States—recognizing this fact—have deployed strategic nuclear weapons with great care, never upsetting the precarious status quo which ensured that these weapons would not be used in the absence of some vital challenge. Our own strategic missiles have never been transferred to the territory of any other nation under a cloak of secrecy and deception. And our history—unlike that of the

Soviets since we ended World War II—demonstrates that we have no desire to dominate or conquer any other nation or impose our system upon its people. Nevertheless, American citizens have become adjusted to living daily on the bulls eye of Soviet missiles located inside the U.S.S.R. or in submarines. In that sense, missiles in Cuba add to an already clear and present danger—although, it should be noted, the nations of Latin America have never previously been subjected to a potential nuclear threat.

But this secret, swift, extraordinary build-up of Communist missiles—in an area well-known to have a special and historical relationship to the United States and the nations of the Western Hemisphere, in violation of Soviet assurances, and in defiance of American and hemispheric policy—this sudden, clandestine decision to station strategic weapons for the first time outside of Soviet soil—is a deliberately provocative and unjustified change in the status quo which cannot be accepted by this country and if our courage and our commitments are ever to be trusted again by either friend or foe.

The 1930's taught us a clear lesson: aggressive conduct, if allowed to go unchecked and unchallenged, ultimately leads to war. This Nation is opposed to war. We are also true to our word. Our unswerving objective, therefore, must be to prevent the use of these missiles against this or any other country, and to secure their withdrawal or elimination from the Western Hemisphere.

Our policy has been one of patience and restraint, as befits a peaceful and powerful nation, which leads a world-wide alliance. We have been determined not to be diverted from our central concerns by mere irritants and fanatics. But now further action is required—and it is under way—and these actions may only be the beginning. We will not prematurely or unnecessarily risk the course of world-wide nuclear war in which even the fruits of victory would be ashes in our mouth—but

neither will we shrink from that risk at any time it must be faced.

Acting, therefore, in the defense of our own security and of the entire Western Hemisphere, and under the authority entrusted to me by the Constitution as endorsed by the Resolution of the Congress, I have directed that the following initial steps be taken immediately:

First: To halt this offensive build-up, a strict quarantine on all offensive military equipment under shipment to Cuba is being initiated. All ships of any kind bound for Cuba, from whatever nation or port, will, if found to contain cargoes of offensive weapons, be turned back. This quarantine will be extended, if needed, to other types of cargo and carriers. We are not at this time, however, denying the necessities of life as the Soviets attempted to do in their Berlin Blockade of 1948.

Second: I have directed the continued and increased close surveillance of Cuba and its military build-up. The Foreign Ministers of the OAS, in their communique of October 6, rejected secrecy on such matters in this hemisphere. Should these offensive military preparations continue, thus increasing the threat to the hemisphere, further action will be justified. I have directed the Armed Forces to prepare for any eventualities—and I trust that, in the interest of both the Cuban people and the Soviet technicians at the sites, the hazards to all concerned of continuing this threat will be recognized.

Third: It shall be the policy of this nation to regard any nuclear missile launched from Cuba against any nation in the Western Hemisphere as an attack by the Soviet Union on the United States, requiring a full retaliatory response upon the Soviet Union.

Fourth: As a necessary military precaution, I have reinforced our Base at Guantanamo, evacuated to-day the dependents of our personnel there and ordered additional military units on a stand-by on an emergency basis.

Fifth: We are calling tonight for an immediate meeting of the Organization of Consultation under the Organization of American States, to consider this threat to hemispheric security and to invoke Articles 6 and 8 of the Rio Treaty in support of all necessary action. The United Nations charter allows for regional security arrangements—and the nations of this hemisphere decided long ago against the military presence of outside powers. Our other allies around the world have also been alerted.

Sixth: Under the Charter of the United Nations, we are asking tonight that an emergency meeting of the Security Council be convoked without delay to take action against this latest Soviet threat to world peace. Our Resolution will call for the prompt dismantling and withdrawal of all offensive weapons in Cuba, under the supervision of U.N. observers, before the quarantine can be lifted.

Seventh and Finally: I call upon Chairman Khrushchev to halt and eliminate this clandestine, reckless and provocative threat to world peace and to stable relations between our two Nations. I call upon him further to abandon this course of world domination, and to join in an historic effort to end the perilous arms race and to transform the history of man. He has an opportunity now to move the world back from the abyss of destruction—by returning to his Government's own words that it had no need to station missiles outside its own territory, and withdrawing these weapons from Cuba—by refraining from any action which will widen or deepen the present crisis—and then by participating in a search for peaceful and permanent solutions.

This Nation is prepared to present its case against this Soviet threat to peace, and our own proposals for a peaceful world, at any time and in any forum—in the OAS, in the United Nations, or in any other meeting that could be useful—without limiting our freedom of action. We have in the past made strenuous efforts to limit the spread of nuclear weap-

ons. We have proposed the elimination of all arms and military bases in a fair and effective disarmament treaty. We are prepared to discuss new proposals for the removal of tensions on both sides—including the possibilities of a genuinely independent Cuba, free to determine its own destiny. We have no wish to war with the Soviet Union—for we are a peaceful people who desire to live in peace with all other peoples.

But it is difficult to settle or even discuss these problems in an atmosphere of intimidation. That is why this latest Soviet threat—or any other threat which is made either independently or in response to our actions this week—must and will be met with determination. Any hostile move anywhere in the world against the safety and freedom of peoples to whom we are committed—including in particular the brave people of West Berlin—will be met by whatever action is needed.

Finally, I want to say a few words to the captive people of Cuba, to whom this speech is being directly carried by special radio facilities. I speak to you as a friend, as one who knows of your deep attachment to your Fatherland, as one who shares your aspirations for liberty and justice for all. And I have watched, and the American people have watched, with deep sorrow how your nationalist revolution was betrayed—and how your Fatherland fell under foreign domination. Now your leaders are no longer Cuban leaders inspired by Cuban ideals. They are puppets and agents of an international conspiracy which has turned Cuba against your friends and neighbors in the Americas—and turned it into the first Latin American Country to become a target for nuclear war—the first Latin American Country to have these weapons on its soil.

These new weapons are not in your interest. They contribute nothing to your peace and well-being. They can only undermine it. But this country has no wish to cause you to suffer or to impose any system upon you. We know that your lives and land are being used as pawns by those who deny you freedom.

Many times in the past, the Cuban people have risen to throw out tyrants who destroyed their liberty. And I have no doubt that most Cubans today look forward to the time when they will be truly free—free from foreign domination, free to choose their own leaders, free to select their own system, free to own their own land, free to speak and write and worship without fear or degradation. And then shall Cuba be welcomed back to the society of free nations and to the associations of this hemisphere.

My fellow citizens: Let no one doubt that this is a difficult and dangerous effort on which we have set out. No one can foresee precisely what course it will take or what costs or casualties will be incurred. Many months of sacrifice and self-discipline lie ahead—months in which both our patience, and our will, will be tested—months in which many threats and denunciations will keep us aware of our dangers. But the greatest danger of all would be to do nothing.

The path we have chosen for the present is full of hazards, as all paths are—but it is the one most consistent with our character and courage as a Nation and our commitments around the world. The cost of freedom is always high—but Americans have always paid it. And one path we shall never choose, and that is the path of surrender or submission.

Our goal is not the victory of might but the vindication of right—not peace at the expense of freedom, but both peace and freedom, here in this hemisphere, and, we hope, around the world. God willing, that goal will be achieved.

Thank you and good night.

33 The Military-Industrial Complex, 1952-72

PETER d'A. JONES
University of Illinois at Chicago Circle

On January 20, 1961, the oldest President in U.S. history handed over the White House to his successor, the youngest. Just three days before, in an unusual farewell address, President Dwight D. Eisenhower had warned the incoming Kennedy administration and the country in general of two "threats" which faced Americans. The first was institutional: the growth of what Eisenhower called the "military-industrial complex." The second was complementary: the danger of public policy falling "captive" to the dictates of an emerging "scientific-technological elite."

What were Americans to make of this sudden pronouncement? There was more to President Eisenhower's anxiety about the military-industrial complex than a sudden fear at the end of an eight-year term of office that all had not gone well. Even as a general, Eisenhower had expressed suspicion of the power of the military in the civilian sphere and, as the coordinator of victory in Europe against the Nazis, as leader of NATO, and as stant military advisor to his own ment, he knew more about the military-economic relatio men. Though unexpected cans, Eisenhower's fa no recent lesson to He had battled appropriation

For Ike the warning was "the most challenging message I could leave with the people of this country."

The retiring President had beaten Adlai Stevenson in the election of 1952. Genuinely hesitant at first to enter politics at all, by the time of his electoral victory General Eisenhower had certain very clear and firm intentions in mind. The uppermost was what he called, repeatedly, "fiscal responsibility": He would cut and balance the budget and put an end to deficit spending as soon as possible. In addition, Eisenhower felt that there really was a "mess" in Washington; that the last years of Harry S Truman's administration were characterized by sl government, irresponsibility, al, despite his political places. The ould at least, he thought, inexperie mess. Sadly and ironically, clean litical career opened up with his of charges against his running ichard M. Nixon, in 19 and his st friend and right and man, rman Adams, was forced ut of politics n 1958 after a scandal As for Eisen- hower's first aim, fiscal sponsibility, the federal budget continu to grow over the years and was made ree out of Ike's very narrowly) in o and 1960. The eight budgets: 195 largest in 13 years. deficit of 1959 w Washington no Neither the m

357

unbalanced budget were as tractable as the general and his aides had thought before taking over the administration.

The truth is that if the federal establishment was large in 1952, it was larger still in 1961 (and larger still again in 1964). If the government was "meddling" in the economy in 1952, it was still further involved eight years later, in spite of the President's attempts to increase the scope of the private sector in such areas as public utilities and atomic power. Not even an avowedly conservative two-term Republican administration could check the incursion of the federal government in any serious or lasting way. In fact, the economy of the 1960s needed a new name. "Capitalism," at least without some heavily qualifying adjective, was clearly a misnomer. Certain structural economic and social changes had taken place and were ongoing. The rhetoric of the politicians, whether conservatives or neo-Keynesian reformers, had not caught up with changed realities.

President Eisenhower's own phrase, "the military-industrial complex," was close to the mark in identifying some of the recent changes in American capitalism, especially since he added the even deeper insight—the associated danger of the "scientific technological elite." The farewell speech was written by Ike's adviser, the political scientist Dr. Malcolm Moos (president of the University of Minnesota after 1967), who was inspired by the flood of armaments that inspired by crossed his desk. Ike agreed that crossed his desk. Ike applicity that Moos's adverse reaction to such with Dr. But at the heart of the preside licity. was the massive growth of federal publicity. was the massive growth of federal Navy since the New Deal and World War creasingly tied after the Korean con. the fact that an ever-larger sector of national economy was engaged in work federal defense contracts. Such contract were in turn contracts. Such contract itary's own estident only upon the mil- very imperfect of its needs, as filtered tion and Congreugh the administra- the 1950s and 1960s,

at least down to about 1968, Congress was reluctant to cut, or even to scrutinize, military appropriations. The ever-present cold war, local hot wars, the competition of Soviet Russia, and the national phobia about communism and security encouraged politicians to give the military a free hand with national income while they themselves played the attractive role of super-patriots before the electorate.

An early critic to bring the problem to public attention was the late C. Wright Mills, a brilliant sociologist at Columbia University (of which Eisenhower was president from 1948 to 1953). Lesser critics and journalists followed Mills's analysis, enlarging his paragraphs into their chapters; some added to and deepened his thesis. In *The Power Elite* (1956), Mills popularized the notion that there existed an American "power structure." Mills portrayed the personnel in the higher echelons of several walks of life in the United States—millionaires, military chiefs, politicians, executives, "celebrities"—and the mass society which created them and made their prestige and power possible. He found extensive overlap of personnel among elites. Two of his chapters, "The Warlords" and "The Military Ascendancy," set the tone for future criticism and debate about the military-industrial complex. Two years later, in *The Causes of World War III* (1958), Mills spoke of America's "permanent war economy," and claimed that many people in the power elite understood clearly that national prosperity was tied to the war economy. Thus, "peace scares" caused panics on Wall Street, and federal spokesmen justified bigger and better bombs as a cure for unemployment. Mills regarded the connection between prosperity and war contracts as the chief reason the elite was to accept what he called "the mili-metaphysic." This would hence be a cause of World War III. President of course, was unlikely to went this far. But he did concern that civilian control of the military was now at stake in American society.

In 1961 this concern was reiterated in a much stronger fashion in an influential special issue of the *Nation* written by the journalist Fred J. Cook, entitled *Juggernaut: The Warfare State*. Cook took a conspiratorial view of events, and talked of a "master design" to merge the military with big business and impose government "from the top." Cook and other writers made Americans aware of the process by which, over the 1950s, the defense budget had risen to about half of all federal expenditures and to about 10 percent of the gross national product, and had left taxpayers with a military bill of about $50 billion a year.

This military-industrial complex grew even more rapidly in power and influence during the next decade under Presidents John F. Kennedy and Lyndon B. Johnson, particularly once Ike's relatively restraining hand was gone and war had broken out in Vietnam. At its center lay the massive Department of Defense (DOD). By 1968 the office of Secretary of Defense had largely overshadowed others under the White House—including the State Department that John Foster Dulles had built up in the 1950s. After commandeering 8 to 10 percent of the nation's total output for 20 years or so, the DOD came to regard such a slice of the national income as its own by right.

the national soil. It became America's largest buyer, spender, employer of labor and contractor. It wielded enormous monopoly-buying power which could force suppliers to do the bidding of the customer—over large areas of the economy. The DOD could outbid any rival, public or private, that tried to compete with it for skilled labor, scientific and technical manpower, raw materials, and production facilities. After all, it had a certain income each year, guaranteed by Congress and the public.

By the 1960s the DOD was controlling an internal empire of about 20,000 prime contracting corporations and perhaps 100,000 subcontracting firms, with all their managers, accountants, office staff, scientists and technicians, production workers, and stockholders. Small wonder that the official AFL–CIO union leadership consistently supported defense spending and escalations of the Vietnam War at each annual convention; that cities, states, and regions became dependent on federal war contracts and constantly pushed their Congressmen to do something for them; that four key committees chaired by conservative Southerners, the House and Senate Armed Services and Appropriations Committees could make political decisions that affect by their whole regions the entire economy of some regions of the United States; that some Americans, like C. Wright Mills and President Eisenhower, began to fear what might happen "if peace broke out."

By 1967 the US Labor Department estimated that almost eight million workers owed their living to of the government's decision-making power over aspects of defense policy are trends that should worry us," he said. Who in fact had the greatest influence on defense and military policy? The importance of the *economic* aspects of defense decisions was openly admitted in official documents, perhaps most openly when Humphrey himself was Vice-President. The President's *Economic Report* of 1967 for example, made clear that "the expansion of defense spending contributed to a significant change in the climate of public opinion. The Vietnam buildup assured American businessmen that no economic reverse would occur in the near future." And not only the business community was softened in its attitude toward the administration and the war, for ". . . Defense investment and social security liberalisation in combination speeded the growth of disposable income. Consumer spending responded strongly . . ." Clearly, by the late 1960s it was difficult to discover who in the United States was *not* affected by the military-industrial complex: its influence had proliferated throughout the economy, to universities, to labor unions, to American consumers in general, and ___ abroad to "satellite" military-indus- ___ maintained by friendly ___ American help. Mili- ___ created a ___ rs in ___

said Bosch, was a helpless mass society trying to live by an obsolete individualistic value structure. More specifically, the complex grew out of World War II. There was interpenetration of business corporations, the military, and the government earlier in American history—for instance, during World War I—but no permanent "complex" survived that war. Indeed, the American 1920s and 1930s saw a classic revulsion against war and armaments and sensationalist attacks on war contract profiteers and munitions salesmen as "merchants of death." Politicians like Senator Gerald P. Nye of North Dakota built careers on such issues. World War II was the real turning point. First, President Roosevelt dealt directly with the Joint Chiefs of Staff in running the war, going over the heads of his Cabinet secretaries. Major war decisions were made essentially by Roosevelt himself, aided by the Joint Chiefs and Harry Hopkins. The Secretaries of War and the Navy often did not hear about such decisions until after they were made. Military chiefs attended diplomatic conferences, helped Roosevelt negotiate with the Allies, and cloaked everything with heavy security. Meanwhile Congress, spurred by the attack on Pearl Harbor, gave Roosevelt and the military a free hand financially. The President inflated his military budgets against all possible contingencies as early as he could. The Manhattan Project, which built the ___ sed against Japan, despite ___ plexity as an opera- ___ Harry S.

control of the military was now at stake in American society.

In 1961 this concern was reiterated in a much stronger fashion in an influential special issue of the *Nation* written by the journalist Fred J. Cook, entitled *Juggernaut: The Warfare State*. Cook took a conspiratorial view of events, and talked of a "master design" to merge the military with big business and impose government "from the top." Cook and other writers made Americans aware of the process by which, over the 1950s, the defense budget had risen to about half of all federal expenditures and to about 10 percent of the gross national product, and had left taxpayers with a military bill of about $50 billion a year.

This military-industrial complex grew even more rapidly in power and influence during the next decade under Presidents John F. Kennedy and Lyndon B. Johnson, particularly once Ike's relatively restraining hand was gone and war had broken out in Vietnam. At its center lay the massive Department of Defense (DOD). By 1968 the office of Secretary of Defense had largely overshadowed others under the White House—including the State Department that John Foster Dulles had built up in the 1950s. After commandeering 8 to 10 percent of the nation's total output for 20 years or so, the DOD came to regard such a slice of the national income as its own by right. Ironically, a fashionable economic theory of the 1960s that claimed that a nation could achieve an industrial revolution by creatively reinvesting 10 percent of its gross national product each year was developed by White House adviser Walt W. Rostow, possibly the most famous "hawk" in Washington. If true, Rostow's theory is a good measure of what the United States lost over the years through defense spending.

As early as 1952, DOD had investments estimated at four times the book value of all manufacturing corporations in the United States—about $200 billion. It came to own about 30 million or more acres of the national soil. It became America's largest buyer, spender, employer of labor and contractor. It wielded enormous monopoly-buying power which could force suppliers to do the bidding of the customer—over large areas of the economy. The DOD could outbid any rival, public or private, that tried to compete with it for skilled labor, scientific and technical manpower, raw materials, and production facilities. After all, it had a certain income each year, guaranteed by Congress and the public.

By the 1960s the DOD was controlling an internal empire of about 20,000 prime contracting corporations and perhaps 100,000 subcontracting firms, with all their managers, accountants, office staff, scientists and technicians, production workers, and stockholders. Small wonder that the official AFL–CIO union leadership consistently supported defense spending and escalations of the Vietnam War at each annual convention; that cities, states, and regions became dependent on federal war contracts and constantly pushed their Congressmen to do something for them; that four key committees chaired by conservative Southerners, the House and Senate Armed Services and Appropriations Committees could vitally affect by their political decisions the entire economy of whole regions of the United States; that some Americans, like C. Wright Mills and President Eisenhower, began to fear what might happen "if peace broke out."

By 1967 the U.S. Labor Department estimated that almost eight million workers owed their livings directly to war contracts—over 10 percent of the entire labor force. Multiplied by a modest family factor of three, this made about 23 million Americans dependent on the military-industrial complex; but these were only those *directly* affected. Hubert H. Humphrey, while still a senator in 1964, began to ask questions about the power not only of the DOD, but also of the large firms taking the contracts. "The continued concentration of economic power and loss of the government's decision-making power over aspects of defense policy are trends that should worry us," he said. Who in fact had the greatest influence on defense and military policy? The importance of the *economic* aspects of defense decisions was openly admitted in official documents, perhaps most openly when Humphrey himself was Vice-President. The President's *Economic Report* of 1967 for example, made clear that "the expansion of defense spending contributed to a significant change in the climate of public opinion. The Vietnam buildup assured American businessmen that no economic reverse would occur in the near future." And not only the business community was softened in its attitude toward the administration and the war, for ". . . Defense investment and social security liberalisation in combination speeded the growth of disposable income. Consumer spending responded strongly . . ." Clearly, by the late 1960s it was difficult to discover who in the United States was *not* affected by the military-industrial complex: its influence had proliferated throughout the economy, to universities, to labor unions, to American consumers in general, and even abroad to "satellite" military-industrial complexes maintained by friendly foreign powers with American help. Military spending abroad, in fact, created a chronic oversupply of U.S. dollars in Europe, threatened American balance of payments very seriously, and brought ignominious pressure on the dollar, as happened in 1971.

It is easy to be moralistic or "conspiratorial" in describing the rise of the military-industrial complex. Under what historical conditions did the complex arise? Why did the American people allow it to grow and support it? Juan Bosch, ex-President of the Dominican Republic, regards "Pentagonism," as he calls it, as a new substitute for old-fashioned imperialism; it grew up, he claims, because the United States had no restraining institutions to stop it growing. The United States,

said Bosch, was a helpless mass society trying to live by an obsolete individualistic value structure. More specifically, the complex grew out of World War II. There was interpenetration of business corporations, the military, and the government earlier in American history—for instance, during World War I—but no permanent "complex" survived that war. Indeed, the American 1920s and 1930s saw a classic revulsion against war and armaments and sensationalist attacks on war contract profiteers and munitions salesmen as "merchants of death." Politicians like Senator Gerald P. Nye of North Dakota built careers on such issues. World War II was the real turning point. First, President Roosevelt dealt directly with the Joint Chiefs of Staff in running the war, going over the heads of his Cabinet secretaries. Major war decisions were made essentially by Roosevelt himself, aided by the Joint Chiefs and Harry Hopkins. The Secretaries of War and the Navy often did not hear about such decisions until after they were made. Military chiefs attended diplomatic conferences, helped Roosevelt negotiate with the Allies, and cloaked everything with heavy security. Meanwhile Congress, spurred by the attack on Pearl Harbor, gave Roosevelt and the military a free hand financially. The President inflated his military budgets against all possible contingencies as early as he could. The Manhattan Project, which built the atomic bomb used against Japan, despite its great size and complexity as an operation, went on entirely unknown to Harry S. Truman—either as chairman of the committee to investigate war production, or, later, as Vice-President of the United States. He had been President some days before he finally learned the details of the bomb.

This project alone (and there were others) brought the universities, the government, the military, and private industry together in a "complex" which would not conveniently evaporate once the war was over. Demands of the Allies for unconditional surrender of both Germany and Japan, their insistence on total military victory, and their occupation of the enemy territories for some years after the war all gave great prestige, power, and experience to military leaders and kept the complex going. A man like General Douglas MacArthur was supreme in his theater of war and remained supreme in Japan afterwards.

Harry Truman did nothing to reverse Roosevelt's policy of heavy dependence on military chiefs in diplomatic policy making. They accompanied him to Potsdam, and as his cold war policy of containment of communism developed, Truman reorganized the defense structure of the nation. He was the essential creator of the system under which Americans lived for 20 years thereafter. In 1947 his National Security Act and other measures established the National Security Council, the National Security Resources Board, the Central Intelligence Agency, and the unified Department of Defence. It was now hard to draw the lines among diplomacy, military policy, academic life, business, and government. The "external" constraints or "threats" were, of course, the apparent menace of Soviet Russia in Europe and the spread of communism in Asia. Here, 1949 was the crucial year, with the revelation of a Soviet atomic bomb and the victory of the Red forces in China. A security mania built up rapidly in the nation, with purges of government officials; oaths of loyalty imposed on schoolteachers, trade unionists and, others; and official investigations launched by Truman himself. While the president tried to pursue a policy of Fair Deal reforms at home coupled with strong anticommunism abroad, lobbying groups were emerging to support a growing military-industrial complex, groups that only needed the Korean War to push the complex toward self-sustaining growth.

As early as 1944 the business executive Charles E. Wilson advocated a "permanent war economy" (the source of C. Wright Mill's phrase). This was to be directed by the President as Commander-in-Chief and was to be "insured and supported" by Congress. Industry must cooperate with the postwar military and "must not be hampered by political witchhunts, or thrown to the fanatical isolationist fringe tagged with the 'merchants of death' label." Critics may have made too much of this speech, Wilson's main concern being that the United States avoid any repetition of its traditional unpreparedness before a major war. But his rhetoric was strong, and it echoed throughout the 1950s; he asked every major war contractor to appoint a senior executive with experience in the defense establishment and the reserve rank of Colonel or above. One of the most sinister and collusive aspects of the complex of the later 1950s and 1960s was indeed the open hiring of military retirees by defense coroporations. The step from military procurement officer to adviser of a firm, or even chairman of the board, was easy and logical, in view of the early age set for military retirement.

Senator William Proxmire's hearings of 1969 revealed that the top 100 contractors employed over 2,000 officers of the rank of colonel or above (navy captain)— including ex-admirals and generals. The biggest defense company, Lockheed, used 210 ex-officers. (In 1971 Lockheed, in dire financial difficulties, had to be bailed out by the federal government with public funds.) Another company, Litton, which already employed a general and an ex-Assistant Defense Secretary, more than doubled its defense business just before hiring yet another Assistant Secretary in 1969. As General MacArthur foresaw in December 1954: ". . . the Armed Forces of a nation and its industrial power have become one and inseparable. The integration of the leadership of one into the leadership of the other is not only logical but inescapable." Writers have tried to pinpoint the emergence of the military-industrial complex with one single incident—such as

Eisenhower's own memorandum of 1946 urging continued collaboration among the military, scholars, and business; or "NSC 68," a defense paper submitted to the White House in 1950, urging a defense build-up *before* the Korean war broke out —but it is clear that the industry-military relationship is one of natural symbiosis arising out of a historical matrix of events and conditions.

Each vested interest soon developed lobbying groups. The National Security Industrial Association, created by Navy Secretary James Forrestal, in 1944 grouped together defense companies that hoped to keep in close touch with the armed servies after the war. Other lobbies included the American Ordnance Association, the Aerospace Industries Association, and the three armed service groups—the Navy League, the Air Force Association, and the Association of the U.S. Army. Veterans groups, parts of the mass media, chambers of commerce, house publications of contracting corporations, all helped. The Pentagon itself, with its over 6,000 public relations experts, spent vast sums of public money on hard-sell campaigns for particular viewpoints or weapons systems and to influence public policy. Total publicity spending of the military, according to the Proxmire investigation, came to over $47 million a year in the late sixties—including "public information services" of the branches, films, television shows, pamphlets, tours, speeches, seminars, and "legislative liaison" with Congressmen.

Should the military in a democratic society be in a position to use public money to influence policy? When General A. D. Starbird, project manager of the Sentinel-Safeguard ABM system, began to launch a massive propaganda campaign for the system and his 17-page directive was published by a sharp journalist, the American public began to wonder what was going on. But the Senate committee that checked on the "Starbird Memorandum" in 1969 was far more interested in uncovering evidence of waste, cost overruns, inefficiency, and high profits in defense contracting than in the overall question: Who was in charge of national priorities? President Eisenhower's warning of 1961 was still largely unheeded.

The politicians of the years 1952 to 1972 saw most things in terms of "national defense" and the "threat" of communism. In 1958 the ludicrous condition had been reached whereby a major and badly needed educational reform, itself stimulated mainly by the success of the Russian *Sputnik*, had to be given the title the National *Defense* Education Act. Eisenhower fought the military on defense spending. In 1953 he cut its budget in the face of heavy lobbying and propaganda and the public resignation of several generals in protest against their Commander-in-Chief. Despite log rolling and vote switching in Congress, Ike stood firm on his demand: "security *with solvency*." Again in 1958 he struggled with Congress over necessary defense reorganization and warned it to beware of "overindulging sentimental attachment to outmoded military machines and concepts." Many congressmen held reserve officerships and served in the National Guard, a venerable political symbol. By 1959 Eisenhower was convinced that what he called "obviously political and financial considerations" were pushing the United States towards militarism. "Everybody with any sense knows that we are finally going to a garrison state," he said angrily in March. The President came to fear that too many generals had "all sorts of ideas," and his final press conference condemned the publicity of arms manufacturers. Such propaganda, said Ike, produced "almost an insidious penetration of our own minds that the only thing this country is engaged in is weaponry and missiles."

Among the pressures Eisenhower had to resist were two "hawkish" reports. One, the Henry A. Kissinger Report (written for the Rockefeller brothers), suggested a steady increase of $3 billion a year in defense spending to a ceiling of $70 billion by 1967 (which was in fact the exact figure of that year); it also considered the tactical use of nuclear weapons. The second, the H. S. Gaither Report from the RAND Corporation, demanded an enormous fall-out shelter program to cost $22 billion in 1957. Ike resisted both, just as he had rejected the notion that the United States give the French nuclear warheads for use against the Vietnamese at Dien Bien Phu in 1954. Employment of nuclear weapons would have been a "logical" extension of the "massive retalitation" doctrine of his Secretary of State, John Foster Dulles.

Eisenhower's restraint was made possible partly by a reduction of general-purpose forces and partly by greater dependence for defense (at least against any supposed attack from Russia) on nuclear "deterrence" and the use of strategic nuclear weapons. The 1950s saw the budding of a strange blossom on the tree of scholarship: defense studies, "thinking about the unthinkable"—usually in rich "think tanks," private research organizations heavily subsidized by the Department of Defense. The best known of the war gamesmen, Herman Kahn, had pretensions to being scientific. He helped to popularize a new vocabulary of "deterrence"—not of "defense," since that was acknowledged to be impossible in the nuclear age. Minimum deterrence, counterforce strategy, preemptive strike, escalation, credible first-strike capability—such pseudo-scientific phrases encouraged Americans to believe they could hold "value-free" debates on the atomic holocaust. Although Kahn's methodology has since been exposed, he and others gave the benediction of "science" to the workings of the military-industrial complex.

Ike's Defense Secretary, Charles Wilson, put it more earthily: "More bang for the buck!" is what he called the policy of concentrating on production of strategic weapons. John F. Kennedy disliked Eisenhower's policy and tried to bring in more "options." During the 1960 presidential campaign he accused Ike of causing a "missile gap" (later disavowed); Kennedy sought a policy of "flexible response." This cost money. He immediately increased defense spending in 1961—both on general purpose and on strategic forces. As late as 1962 Ike was still complaining about defense costs, but meanwhile the "McNamara revolution" was taking place in the Defense Department.

The warning of Eisenhower did not fall entirely into a void in 1961, even though his successor began a large program of defense spending. For Kennedy had appointed as Defense Secretary a management genius, a man of fortitude and toughness, Robert McNamara, who was determined to reestablish civilian control over defense planning and spending. He proposed to do this by applying the latest industrial management techniques to his department—the PPB system (Planning, Programming and Budgeting) to allow rational forward planning and use of systems analysis and operations research; and cost-benefit tools. McNamara's whole aim was to make the choices as well as the relative costs of the choices clear to those who had to make the decisions on defense policy. No doubt his own advice to the President often went beyond this modest aim. Critics might complain that the Secretary gave more heed to the cost than to the effectiveness of certain proposals, but few would deny that McNamara had irrevocably changed the way of doing things at the Defense Department.

McNamara resigned in 1968 to take a post more congenial to him as head of the World Bank. His later years in the DOD were dogged by the escalating, never-ending Vietnam War. Overall defense spending rose. The military-industrial complex thrived. It seemed as if all that McNamara's genius and dedication had achieved was to make the complex more *efficient*. Power had certainly been concentrated in the hands of the Secretary of Defense—a matter heavily criticized later by President Richard Nixon's Blue-Ribbon

Defense Panel of 1970. Did greater efficiency produce greater civilian control over the military? Hardly. For many Americans the complex seemed even bigger and more out of control than ever. McNamara won most of his own battles with the military and the corporate contractors—over the TFX plane, the F–111, and over the M–16 rifle—though whether his winning views were in the end the correct ones has remained in doubt. He lost a struggle to cut National Guard and army reserve strength and to merge the two. He did manage, if not to cut, at least to maintain defense spending at an even level down to 1965—before large Vietnam expenditures changed the picture. The United States received more in both conventional and nuclear capability for its defense outlays of 1965 than for roughly similar size outlays in 1960. Yet, most of McNamara's savings were in general-purpose forces—controversial base closings, for example. According to Senator Paul H. Douglas of Illinois, the Vietnam War prevented McNamara from ever getting around to real defense savings on strategic weapons, where cost-benefit analysis would have been easier than on general-purpose forces. He never managed to control the huge prime contracts and cost overruns on advanced weapons systems.

Finally McNamara became associated in the public mind with the ABM system, which could lead only to ever-growing expenditures and the magnification of the military-industrial complex for years ahead. For some time he stubbornly opposed deploying the anti-ballistic missile system: he found it too expensive, unreliable, and inferior in deterrence effect to strong offensive forces. However, electoral politics building up toward the presidential year of 1968 probably brought him around to favor the so-called "thin" ABM system as protection against the Chinese rather than against the Russian "threat." He was attacked bitterly by military spokesmen who wanted a "thick" ABM system and still feared sudden attack from

Soviet Russia as well as China. Other sectors regarded his move over to the ABM as a clear victory for the military-industrial complex. Under the new Republican administration after the election of 1968, many of the civilian controllers and "whiz kids" that McNamara had brought into the Defense Department were released, and the Joint Chiefs appeared in the ascendant once more as advisers on policy matters.

Behind the huge defense buildup of the Kennedy and Johnson years lay a deeply held popular belief that America was so rich it could afford both "guns and butter." The nation could *afford* to spend 10 percent of GNP on defense. As the chairman of the House Armed Services Committee said in 1967 about the "thin" and "thick" ABM systems: "We are an affluent nation. . . . We are now right at $750 billion GNP; and responsible people tell us it is headed for a trillion. So we can afford it. Why not have the two of them, and keep the Soviets off balance. . . ?" Kennedy, Johnson, and their aides all believed in this idea. But by about 1968 a newer realization was creeping in. First, the Vietnam War was costing far more than anyone ever intended—more than Korea; it was already America's second costliest war and would not seem to end. Second, the decline and depletion of the nonmilitary sector, pointed out years before by writers like John Kenneth Galbraith, was now even more evident, with rotting cities, decayed public transportation, private and public education on the edge of bankruptcy, racial conflicts and crime mounting, and millions of Americans officially admitted as being poverty-stricken.

So around 1968 the press and the American public rediscovered the military-industrial complex, and floods of articles and books appeared to denounce it in great detail. For the first time since the Korean War the military sector was really under fire at home; Congress began investigating cost overruns and paying more attention to its public duties in scanning appropriations. A new Presidency and a new Secretary of Defense also attracted attention to the complex. As Vietnam War news got worse and antiwar opposition at home became more strident, even members of armed services committees began to ask whether it was worth it. For a variety of reasons, American public opinion had previously allowed the military-industrial complex to blossom; it seemed public opinion was now changing after a quarter of a century. Where John F. Kennedy had built up defenses against the communist menace, Robert F. Kennedy opposed the war in Vietnam, decried the ABM and military spending, and demanded a switch of priorities to urban problems. Would Richard Nixon follow the example of President Eisenhower? Would he make genuine attempts to cut defense costs and get out of Vietnam the way Ike got out of Korea? Moves were made in this direction, though only very tentatively, by the new administration.

The 1972 Budget proposed cutting defense costs to about one third of federal spending, though this was still an enormous sum of $77 billion. The question of when the Vietnam War could end was still open, as was that of what would happen to the "Vietnam dividend"—the money saved, if any. Some contended that rising costs of ongoing programs, both civilian and military, would absorb any saving. Clearly, the military-industrial complex was not about to vanish overnight. Its vested interests in the ABM system spread throughout the nation: 15,000 or 20,000 companies would profit from it, and millions of workers would find jobs in it in countless congressional districts and most of the 50 states. Meanwhile, the small defense savings that had been attempted had produced the specter of joblessness and regional dislocation. Jobs were scarce in 1971–72 in places like the state of Washington and Southern California, areas of high-technology defense industries that were tied to military-industrial contracting. Could the complex really be

genuinely reduced in such a time of general economic lethargy and persistent unemployment—recession with inflation? Already ex-defense technicians were feeling the bite of unemployment after the years of boom. In Seattle, a great aerospace city, a huge placard asked bitterly in 1971: WILL THE LAST PERSON TO LEAVE SEATTLE PLEASE TURN OUT THE LIGHTS?

While the nation still had to prove to itself and to the world that peace pays better than war and that its economic prosperity was not entirely dependent on defense contracts, the military-industrial complex itself was not likely to give up on further expansion. Such would not be in the nature of large management enterprises.

But the complex, after all, was poorly named. It was tripartite: a military-industrial-*governmental* complex. Presumably the federal part still held the upper hand. If peace broke out, or rather, if disarmament were to be phased in by stages, the need for federal action to maintain growth and stability would be even greater, not less. The government's role in the complex, though not named in Eisenhower's phrase, was the one part which was sure to survive, come what may.

The federal government had not suddenly emerged on the economic scene, of course. Contrary to accepted business beliefs, the country's economy was not built on simple private enterprise, laissez-faire principles; in American history the government had always intervened to stimulate economic growth—at the local, state, and federal levels. Even long before the Civil War the American economy could more truthfully be described as a *mixed* system of public enterprise (e.g., the Erie Canal), public aid to private enterprise (e.g., some of the canals and railroads, and various other "internal improvements"), and private initiative. Federal intervention for *welfare* as well as for economic growth became noticeable with the New Deal; World War II and the subsequent cold war produced a massive growth of federal intervention on both fronts. Before the 1920s, most economic crises seemed to be *production* problems; afterwards, the massive and tragic "demand failure" of the thirties made it clear that a structural economic change of some sort had taken place. In the mature consumer economy of later years the major problem was not production but distribution—the maintaining of effective demand. Hence the flood of welfare measures of the New Deal and since—measures which have manifest and latent functions: *manifest*—to help the underprivileged and needy, the unemployed and minorities; *latent*—to redistribute income, spread the wealth through income taxation, social security payments, and so on, in order to stimulate demand. The income tax and federal welfare payments also have the second latent function of injecting an element of stability into the economy; they are called "built-in stabilizers" (as opposed to "discretionary stabilizers" such as fiscal policy) because they come into action automatically to help maintain demand in periods of depression.

While the growth of the federal government can be explained in such neutral (if not deterministic) economic terms, so can that of the large corporations. Essentially economic and technological reasons can be found for the emergence of corporate power in American society. The centralized, corporate state (called by the economist J.K. Galbraith "the new industrial state" in a book of that title in 1967) can be shown to have evolved as a stage in the history of the American economy—a stage, indeed, through which most societies might eventually pass after they have industrialized. In Galbraith's analysis the corporate "technostructures" need and demand the help and protection of the state. The central "complex," therefore, is not in essence "military-industrial" but more accurately corporate-governmental.

SUGGESTED READINGS

ALBERTSON, DEAN (ed.). *Eisenhower as President*. New York: Hill & Wang, 1963.

BARNET, RICHARD J. *The Economy of Death*. New York: Atheneum, 1969.

BOSCH, JUAN. Pentagonism: *A Substitute for Imperialism*. New York: Evergreen Books, 1968.

COOK, FRED J. *Juggernaut: The Warfare State*. New York: Macmillan Co., 1962.

EISENHOWER, DWIGHT D. *The White House Years*, Vols. I and II. Garden City, N.Y.: Doubleday & Co., 1963, 1965.

ENKE, STEPHEN (ed.). *Defense Management*. Englewood Cliffs, N.J.: Prentice-Hall, 1967.

GALBRAITH, JOHN KENNETH. *The New Industrial State*. Boston: Houghton Mifflin Co., 1967.

GREEN, PHILIP. *Deadly Logic: The Theory of Nuclear Deterrence*. New York: Schocken Books, 1968.

HUGHES, EMMET J. *The Ordeal of Power*. New York: Atheneum Publishers, 1963.

JONES, PETER d' A. *The Consumer Society: A History of American Capitalism*. Baltimore and London: Penguin Books, 1965.

LAPP, RALPH. *The Weapons Culture*. Baltimore: Penguin Books, Inc., 1969.

MELMAN, SEYMOUR. *Pentagon Capitalism*. New York: McGraw-Hill Book Co., 1970.

MILLS, C. WRIGHT. *The Power Elite*. New York: Oxford University Press, 1956.

PROXMIRE, WILLIAM. *Report from the Wasteland*. New York: Frederick A. Praeger, 1970.

REAGAN, M. D. *The Managed Economy*. New York: Oxford University Press, 1963.

Report from Iron Mountain: On the Possibility and Desirabilty of Peace. New York: Delta Books, 1967.

STONE, I. F. *The Haunted Fifties*. New York: Vintage Books, Inc., 1963.

U.S. BUREAU OF THE BUDGET, *Budget of the United States Government, Fiscal Year 1972*. Washington, D.C.: U.S. Government Printing Office, 1971.

DOCUMENT 33.1

President Eisenhower's Warning*

The anxiety over the military-industrial complex was not created by President Eisenhower's farewell address to the nation, but his revelations certainly surprised and shocked many Americans and gave greater credence to the fears of earlier critics. The address was delivered on January 18, 1961.

My fellow Americans, 3 days from now, after half a century in the service of our country, I shall lay down the responsibilities of office as, in traditional and solemn ceremony, the authority of the Presidency is vested in my successor.

This evening I come to you with a message of leavetaking and farewell, and to share a few final thoughts with you, my countrymen.

Like every other citizen, I wish the new President, and all who will labor with him, Godspeed. I pray that the coming years will be blessed with peace and prosperity for all.

Our people expect their President and the Congress to find essential agreement on issues of great moment, the wise resolution of which will better shape the future of the Nation.

My own relations with the Congress, which began on a remote and tenuous basis when, long ago, a Member of the Senate appointed me to West Point, have since ranged to the intimate during the war and immediate postwar period, and, finally, to the mutually interdependent during these past 8 years.

HIS RELATIONSHIP GOOD

In this final relationship, the Congress and the administration have, on most vital issues, cooperated well, to serve the national good rather than mere partisanship,

and so have assured that the business of the Nation should go forward. So, my official relationship with the Congress ends in a feeling, on my part, of gratitude that we have been able to do so much together.

We now stand 10 years past the midpoint of a century that has witnessed four major wars among great nations. Three of these involved our own country. Despite these holocausts America is today the strongest, the most influential and most productive nation in the world. Understandably proud of this preeminence, we yet realize that America's leadership and prestige depend, not merely upon our unmatched material progress, riches, and military strength, but on how we use our power in the interests of world peace and human betterment.

Throughout America's adventure in free government our basic purposes have been to keep the peace; to foster progress in human achievement, and to enhance liberty, dignity, and integrity among people and among nations. To strive for less would be unworthy of a free and religious people. Any future traceable to arrogance, or our lack of comprehensive or readiness to sacrifice would inflict upon us grievous hurt both at home and abroad.

Progress toward these noble goals is persistently threatened by the conflict now engulfing the world. It commands our whole attention, absorbs our very beings. We face a hostile ideology—global in scope, atheistic in character, ruthless in purpose, and insidious in method. Unhappily, the danger it poses promises to be of indefinite duration. To meet it successfully, there is called for, not so much the emotional and transitory sacrifices of crisis, but rather those which enable us to carry forward steadily, surely, and without complaint the burdens of a prolonged and complex struggle—with liberty the stake. Only thus shall we remain, despite every provocation, on our charted course toward permanent peace and human betterment.

---

*Source: *Congressional Record*, February 16, 1961, pp. 2210–11.

Crises there will continue to be. In meeting them, whether foreign or domestic, great or small, there is a recurring temptation to feel costly action could become the miraculous solution to all current difficulties. A huge increase in newer elements of our defense; development of unrealistic programs to cure every ill in agriculture; a dramatic expansion in basic and applied research—these many other possibilities, each possibly promising in itself, may be suggested as the only way to the road we wish to travel.

Balance Held Essential

But each proposal must be weighed in the light of a broader consideration: The need to maintain balance in and among national programs—balance between the private and the public economy, balance between cost and hoped-for advantage—balance between the clearly necessary and the comfortably desirable; balance between our essential requirements as a nation and the duties imposed by the Nation upon the individual; balance between actions of the moment and the national welfare of the future. Good judgement seeks balance and progress; lack of it eventually finds imbalance and frustration.

The record of many decades stands as proof that our people and their Government have, in the main, understood these truths and have responded to them well, in the face of stress and threat. But threats, new in kind or degree, constantly arise. I mention two only.

A vital element in keeping the peace is our military establishment. Our arms must be mighty, ready for instant action, so that no potential aggressor may be tempted to risk his own destruction.

Our military organization today bears little relation to that known by any of my predecessors in peacetime, or indeed by the fighting men of World War II or Korea.

Until the latest of our world conflicts, the United States had no armaments industry. American makers of plowshares could, with time and as required, make swords as well. But now we can no longer risk emergency improvisation of national defense; we have been compelled to create a permanent armaments industry of vast proportions.

Added to this, 3½ million men and women are directly engaged in the defense establishment. We annually spend on military security more than the net income of all U.S. corporations.

New to America

This conjunction of an immense military establishment and a large arms industry is new in the American experience. The total influence—economic, political, even spiritual—is felt in every city, every statehouse, every office of the Federal Government.

We recognize the imperative need for this development. Yet we must not fail to comprehend its grave implications. Our toil, resources, and livelihood are all involved; so is the very structure of our society.

In the councils of government, we must guard against the acquisition of unwarranted influence, whether sought or unsought, by the military-industrial complex. The potential for the disastrous rise of misplaced power exists and will persist.

We must never let the weight of this combination endanger our liberties or democratic processes. We should take nothing for granted. Only an alert and knowledgeable citizenry can compel the proper meshing of the huge industrial and military machinery of defense without peaceful methods and goals, so that security and liberty may prosper together.

Akin to, and largely responsible for the sweeping changes in our industrial-military posture, has been the technological revolution during recent decades.

In this revolution, research has become central; it also becomes more formalized complex, and costly. A steadily increasing share is conducted for, by, or at the direction of, the Federal Government.

Today, the solitary inventor, tinkering in his shop, has been overshadowed by task forces of scientists in laboratories and testing fields. In the same fashion, the free university, historically the fountainhead of free ideas and scientific discovery, has experienced a revolution in the conduct of research.

Partly because of the huge costs involved, a Government contract becomes virtually a substitute for intellectual curiosity. For every old blackboard there are now hundreds of new electronic computers.

The prospect of domination of the Nation's scholars by Federal employment, project allocations, and the power of money is ever present—and is gravely to be regarded.

Yet, in holding scientific research and discovery in respect, as we should, we must also be alert to the equal and opposite danger that public policy could itself become the captive of a scientific-technological elite.

It is the task of statesmanship to mold, to balance, and to integrate these and other forces, new, and old, within the principles of our democratic system—ever aiming toward the supreme goals of our free society.

Another factor in maintaining balance involves the element of time. As we peer into society's future, we—you and I, and our Government—must avoid the impulse to live only for today, plundering, for our own ease and convenience, the previous resources of tomorrow.

We cannot mortgage the material assets of our grandchildren without risking the loss also of their political and spiritual heritage. We want democracy to survive for all generations to come, not to become the insolvent phantom of tomorrow.

Down the long lane of the history yet to be written America knows that this world of ours, ever growing smaller, must avoid becoming a community of dreadful fear and hate, and be, instead, a proud consideration [sic] of mutual trust and respect.

Such a confederation must be one of equals. The weakest must come to the conference table with the same confidence as do we, protected as we are by our moral, economic, and military strength. That table, though scarred by many past frustrations, cannot be abandoned for the certain agony of the battlefield.

The Need for Disarmament

Disarmament with mutual honor and confidence, is a continuing imperative. Together we must learn how to compose differences, not with arms, but with intellect and decent purpose. Because this need is so sharp and apparent I confess that I lay down my official responsibilities in this field with a definite sense of disappointment.

As one who has witnessed the horror and lingering sadness of war—as one who knows that another war could utterly destroy this civilization which has been so slowly and painfully built over thousands of years—I wish I could say tonight that a lasting peace is in sight.

Happily, I can say that war has been avoided. Steady progress toward our ultimate goal has been made. But, so much remains to be done. As a private citizen, I shall never cease to do what little I can to help the world advance along that road.

So—in this my last good night to you as your President—I thank you for the many opportunities you have given me for public service in war and peace. I trust that in that service you find some things worthy; as for the rest of it, I know you will find ways to improve performance in the future.

You and I—my fellow citizens—need to be strong in our faith that all nations, under God, will reach the goal of peace with justice. May we be ever unswerving in devotion to principle, confident but humble with power, diligent in pursuit of the Nation's great goals.

Prayer for Peace

To all the peoples of the world, I once

more give expression to America's prayerful and continuing aspiration:

We pray that peoples of all faiths, all races, all nations, may have their great human needs satisfied; that those now denied opportunity shall come to enjoy it to the full; that all who yearn for freedom may experience its spiritual blessings; that those who have freedom will understand, also, its heavy responsibilities; that all who are insensitive to the needs of others will learn charity; that the scourges of poverty, disease, and ignorance will be made to disappear from the earth, and that, in the goodness of time, all peoples will come to live together in a peace guaranteed by the binding force of mutual respect and love.

DOCUMENT 33.2

Military Procurement Policies: A Community of Interests*

Senator William Proxmire of Wisconsin has long been a major legislative investigator of the military-industrial complex. His Senate subcommittee has been looking into "pyramiding profits and costs in the missile procurement program" and other aspects of Pentagon purchasing since 1964. In the selection below, Senator Proxmire suggests the close correspondence of business and military interests.

... Recently I asked the Department of Defense for a list of certain high ranking retired military officers employed by the 100 companies who had the largest volume of military prime contracts. I did this in connection with the hearings of the Subcommittee on Economy in Government of the Joint Economic Committee.

In fiscal year 1968 these 100 companies held 67.4 percent of the $38.8 billion of prime military contracts, or $26.2 billion.

The Defense Department has now supplied to me the list of high ranking military officers who work for these 100 companies. They include the subsidiaries. In

*Source: *Congressional Record,* March 24, 1969, pp. S3072–S3078.

one case, that of the 35th ranking contractor, four firms were involved in a joint venture.

I asked only for the names of those retired military officers of the rank of Army, Air Force, Marine Corps colonel or Navy captain and above. Excluded are all officers below those ranks. I asked for only retired regular officers and not reserve officers, although in a very few cases the reserve officers may be included.

TOP 100 COMPANIES EMPLOY OVER 2,000 RETIRED OFFICERS

The facts are that as of February, 1969, some 2,072 retired military officers of the rank of colonel or Navy captain and above were employed by the 100 contractors who reported. This is an average of almost 22 per firm. I shall ask to have printed in the *Record* as exhibit A of my statement a list of the 100 companies, ranked according to the dollar volume of their prime military contracts, and the number of high ranking retired officers they employ.

TEN COMPANIES EMPLOY OVER 1,000

The 10 companies with the largest

TABLE 1. Ten military prime contractors employing largest number of high ranking retired military officers, and value of their fiscal year 1968 contracts

Company and rank by number of high-ranking retired officers employed	Number employed Feb. 1 1969	Net dollar value of defense contracts, fiscal year 1968 (in millions)
1. Lockheed Aircraft Corp	210	$1,870
2. Boeing Co.	169	762
3. McDonnell Douglas Corp	141	1,101
4. General Dynamics	113	2,239
5. North American Rockwell Corp	104	669
6. General Electric Co	89	1,489
7. Ling-Temco-Vought, Inc	69	758
8. Westinghouse Electric Corp	59	251
9. TRW, Inc	56	127
10. Hughes Aircraft Co	55	286
Total	1,065	$9,552

number on their payrolls employed 1,065 retired officers. This is an average of 106 per firm. These 10 companies employed over half the total number of high ranking former officers employed by all the top 100 defense contractors. These companies, listed according to the number of retired officers employed by them, are given in Table 1.

KEY ABM CONTRACTORS
EMPLOY 22 PERCENT OF TOTAL

Among the major defense contractors involved in producing the key components of the anti-ballistic-missile system—ABM—nine of them employ 465 retired officers. This is an average of 51 each.

In 1968 they held contracts valued at $5.78 billion and, of course, will receive many billions more if the ABM system is deployed. These companies and the number of retired officers they employ are given in Table 2.

TABLE 2. Major prime contractors involved in ABM system and number of high ranking retired military officers employed by them

1. McConnell Douglas	141
2. General Electric	89
3. Hughes Aircraft	55
4. Martin Marietta	40
5. Raytheon	37
6. Sperry Rand	36
7. RCA	35
8. AVCO	23
9. A. T. &. T.	9
Total	465

COMPARISON OF 1969 WITH 1959

Almost 10 years ago in connection with hearings before the Senate Finance Committee on the extension of the Renegotiation Act, former Senator Paul H. Douglas asked for and received a similar list from the Pentagon. We can, therefore, make comparisons over a decade as to what has happened with respect to the employment of high ranking retired military officers by the top 100 defense contractors.

In 1959, the total number employed was only 721—88 of 100 companies re-

porting—or an average of slightly more than eight per company.

In 1969 the 100 largest defense contractors—95 of the 100 companies reporting—employed 2,072 former high military officers, or an average of almost 22 per company.

In 1959 the 10 companies with the highest number of former officers employed 372 of them.

In 1969 the top 10 had 1,065, or about three times as many.

Some 43 companies which reported were on both the 1959 and 1969 list of the top 100 largest contractors. There were several more who were on the list in both years but failed to report in one or the other year. But we can compare the 43 companies. These 43 companies employed 588 high ranking former officers in 1959. In 1969 these same companies employed 1,642 retired high ranking retired officers.

In each case where a comparison can be made, namely, in the total number of former high ranking officers employed by the top 100 contractors, the top 10 contractors employing the largest number, and the number employed by firms reporting in both 1959 and 1969, the number employed has tripled. It has increased threefold.

Roughly three times the number of retired high ranking military officers are employed by the top 100 companies in 1969 as compared with 1959.

SIGNIFICANCE

What is the significance of this situation? What does it mean and what are some of its implications?

First of all, it bears out the statement I made on March 10 when I spoke on the "blank check" for the military, that the warning by former President Eisenhower against the danger of "unwarranted influence, whether sought or unsought, by the military-industrial complex," is not just some future danger.

That danger is here. Whether sought or unsought there is today unwarranted influence by the military-industrial complex which results in excessive costs, burgeoning military budgets, and scandalous performances. The danger has long since materialized. The 2,072 retired high-ranking officers employed by the top 100 military contractors is one major facet of this influence.

No Conspiracy or Wrongdoing

Second, I do not claim nor even suggest that any conspiracy exists between the military and the 100 largest defense contractors. I do not believe in the conspiracy theory of history. I charge no general wrongdoing on the part of either group.

In the past many of the officers have performed valiant and even heroic service on behalf of the United States. The country is indeed grateful to them for their past service and for their patriotic endeavors.

We should eschew even the slightest suggestion of any conspiracy between the Pentagon, on the one hand, and the companies who hire former employees, on the other. There is not a scintilla of evidence that it exists.

Community of Interest

But what can be said, and should properly be said, is that there is a continuing community of interest between the military, on the one hand, and these industries on the other.

What we have here is almost a classic example of how the military-industrial complex works.

It is not a question of wrongdoing. It is a question of what can be called the "old boy network" or the "old school tie."

This is a most dangerous and shocking situation. It indicates the increasing influence of the big contractors with the military and the military with the big contractors. It shows an intensification of the problem and the growing community of interest which exists between the two. It makes it imperative that new weapon systems receive the most critical review and that defense contracts be examined in microscopic detail.

I am alarmed about this trend not because I question the integrity or the good will of the retired officers who have found employment with military contractors but because I believe that the trend itself represents a distinct threat to the public interest.

Dangers when coupled with Negotiated Contracts

Third, this matter is particularly dangerous in a situation where only 11.5 percent of military contracts are awarded on a formally advertised competitive bid basis. It lends itself to major abuse when almost 90 percent of all military contracts are negotiated, and where a very high proportion of them are negotiated with only one, or one or two, contractors.

Former high-ranking military officers have an entree to the Pentagon that others do not have. I am not charging that is necessarily wrong. I am saying that it is true.

Former high-ranking officers have personal friendships with those still at the Pentagon which most people do not have. Again, I charge no specific wrongdoing. But it is a fact.

In some cases former officers may even negotiate contracts with their former fellow officers. Or they may be involved in developing plans and specifications, making proposals, drawing up blueprints, or taking part in the planning process or proposing prospective weapon systems. And they may be doing this in cooperation with their former fellow officers with whom they served with and by whom, in some cases, even promoted.

With such a high proportion of negotiated contracts there is a great danger of abuse.

In addition, there is the subtle or unconscious temptation to the officer still on active duty. After all, he can see that over 2,000 of his fellow officers work for the big companies. How hard a bargain does he drive with them when he is 1 or 2 years away from retirement?

This danger does not come from corruption. Except in rare circumstances this is no more prevalent among military officers than among those with comparable civilian responsibilities.

MUTUAL INTERESTS—UNCRITICAL VIEWS

The danger to the public interest is that these firms and the former officers they employ have a community of interest with the military itself. They hold a narrow view of public priorities based on self-interest. They have a largely uncritical view of military spending.

As a group they have what has been termed "tunnelvision." But in this case their narrow training can be fortified by self-interest. In too many cases they may see only military answers to exceedingly complex diplomatic and political problems. A military response, or the ability to make one, may seem to them to be the most appropriate answer to every international threat.

SUMMARY

When the bulk of the budget goes for military purposes; when 100 companies get 67 percent of the defense contract dollars; when cost overruns are routine and prime military weapon system contracts normally exceed their estimates by 100 to 200 percent; when these contracts are let by negotiation and not by competitive bidding; and when the top contractors have over 2,000 retired highranking military officers on their payrolls; there are very real questions as to how critically these matters are reviewed and how well the public interest is served.

That ... is the point. That is why I think it important that there be public disclosure of these facts so that the American public can know more about the community of interests involved in our huge defense contract spending. . . .

DOCUMENT 33.3
Origins of the Military-Industrial Complex*

The military-industrial complex arose out of a tangled matrix of historical forces and circumstances during World War II; it was kept alive by the Cold War and thrived mightily after the Korean conflict. Among early suggestions that the postwar world would have to see a continued close cooperation among research scientists, the military, and industry was a Memorandum sent out by General Dwight D. Eisenhower in 1946 as Chief of Staff.

Memorandum for Directors and Chiefs of War Department General and Special Staff Divisions and Bureaus and the Commanding Generals of the Major Commands:
Subject: *Scientific and Technological Resources as Military Assets.*

The recent conflict has demonstrated more convincingly than ever before the strength our nation can best derive from the integration of all of our national resources in time of war. It is of the utmost importance that the lessons of this experience be not forgotten in the peacetime planning and training of the Army. The future security of the nation demands that all those civilian resources which by conversion or redirection constitute our main support in time of emergency be associated closely with the activities of the Army in time of peace.

The lessons of the last war are clear. The military effort required for victory threw upon the Army an unprecedented range of responsibilities, many of which were effectively discharged only through the invaluable assistance supplied by our cumulative resources in the natural and social sciences and the talents and experience furnished by management and labor.

---

*Source: The original memorandum signed by Eisenhower may be seen in the Henry L. Stimson Papers. By permission of Yale University Library.

The armed forces could not have won the war alone. Scientists and business men contributed techniques and weapons which enabled us to outwit and overwhelm the enemy. Their understanding of the Army's needs made possible the highest degree of cooperation. This pattern of integration must be translated into a peacetime counterpart which will not merely familiarize the Army with the progress made in science and industry, but draw into our planning for national security all the civilian resources which can contribute to the defense of the country.

Success in this enterprise depends to a large degree on the cooperation which the nation as a whole is willing to contribute. However, the Army as one of the main agencies responsible for the defense of the nation has the duty to take the initiative in promoting closer relation between civilian and military interests. It must establish definite policies and administrative leadership which will make possible even greater contributions from science, technology, and management than during the last war.

In order to ensure the full use of our national resources in case of emergency, the following general policies will be put into effect:

(1) *The Army must have civilian assistance in military planning as well as for the production of weapons.* Effective long-range military planning can be done only in the light of predicted developments in science and technology. As further scientific achievements accelerate the tempo and expand the area of our operations, this interrelationship will become of even greater importance. In the past we have often deprived ourselves of vital help by limiting our use of scientific and technological resources to contracts for equipment. More often than not we can find much of the talent we need for comprehensive planning in industry or universities. Proper employment of this talent requires that the civilian agency shall have the benefit of our estimates of future military problems and shall work closely with Plans and the Research and Development authorities. A most effective procedure is the letting of contracts for aid in planning. The use of such a procedure will greatly enhance the validity of our planning as well as ensure sounder strategic equipment programs.

(2) *Scientists and industrialists must be given the greatest possible freedom to carry out their research.* The fullest utilization by the Army of the civilian resources of the nation cannot be procured merely by prescribing the military characteristics and requirements of certain types of equipment. Scientists and industrialists are more likely to make new and unsuspected contributions to the development of the Army if detailed directions are held to a minimum. The solicitation of assistance under these conditions would not only make available to the army talents and experience otherwise beyond our reach, but also establish mutual confidence between ourselves and civilians. It would familiarize them with our fundamental problems and strengthen greatly the foundation upon which our national security depends.

(3) *The possibility of utilizing some of our industrial and technological resources as organic parts of our military structure in time of emergency should be carefully examined.* The degree of cooperation with science and industry achieved during the recent war should by no means be considered the ultimate. There appears little reason for duplicating within the Army an outside organization which by its experience is better qualified than we are to carry out some of our tasks. The advantages to our nation in economy and to the Army in efficiency are compelling reason for this procedure.

(4) *Within the Army we must separate responsibility for research and development from the functions of procurement, purchase, storage and distribution.* Our experience during the war and the experience of industry in time of peace indicate

the need for such a policy. The inevitable gap between the scientist or technologist and the user can be bridged, as during the last war, by field experimentation with equipment still in the developmental stage. For example, restricted-visibility operations with the aid of radar, such as blind bombing and control of tactical air, were made possible largely by bringing together technologists who knew the potentialities of the equipment and field commanders familiar with combat conditions and needs. Future cooperation of this type requires that research and development groups have authority to procure experimental items for similar tests.

(5) *Officers of all arms and services must become fully aware of the advantages which the Army can derive from the close integration of civilian talent with military plans and developments.* This end cannot be achieved merely by sending officers to universities for professional training. It is true that the Army's need for officers well trained in the natural and social sciences requires a thorough program of advanced study for selected military personnel, but in addition we must supply inducements which will encourage these men in the continued practical application of scientific and technological thought to military problems. A premium must be placed on professional attainments in the natural and social sciences as well as other branches of military science. Officers in each arm and service must familiarize themselves as much as possible with progress and plans made in other branches. Only then can the Army obtain the administrative and operative talents essential to its task and mutual understanding by the arms and services of their respective problems.

In general, the more we can achieve the objectives indicated above with respect to the cultivation, support and direct use of outside resources, the more energy will we have left to devote to strictly military problems for which there are no outside facilities or which for special security

reasons can only be handled by the military. In fact, it is our responsibility deliberately to examine all outside resources as to adequacy, diversity, and geographical distribution and to ensure their full utilization as factors of security. It is our job to take the initiative to promote the development of new resources, if our national security indicates the need. It is our duty to support broad research programs in educational institutions, in industry, and in whatever field might be of importance to the Army. Close integration of military and civilian resources will not only directly benefit the Army, but indirectly contribute to the nation's security, as civilians are prepared for their role in an emergency by the experience gained in time of peace. The association of military and civilians in educational institutions and industry will level barriers, engender mutual understanding, and lead to the cultivation of friendships invaluable for future cooperation. The realization of our objectives places upon us, the military, the challenge to make our professional officers the equals in knowledge and training of civilians in similar fields and make our professional environment as inviting as those outside.

In the interest of cultivating to the utmost the integration of civilian and military resources and of securing the most effective unified direction of our research and development activities, this responsibility is being consolidated in a separate section on the highest War Department level. The Director of this section will be directly supported by one or more civilians, thus ensuring full confidence of both the military and the civilian in this undertaking. By the rotation of civilian specialists in this capacity we should have the benefit of broad guidance and should be able to furnish science and industry with a firsthand understanding of our problems and objectives. By developing the general policies outlined above under the leadership of the Director of Research and Development the Army will demonstrate the value it places upon science and technology and further the integration of civilian and military resources.

GENERAL EISENHOWER
April 27, 1946

DOCUMENT 33.4

War Games: The Rowen Report*

Part of the military-industrial complex was the war games industry: groups of defense theorists, sometimes with backgrounds in physics and mathematics—rarely humanists—who advised the policy makers. A report to the Joint Economic Committee of Congress by Henry Rowen (later president of RAND) on the national security needs of the 1960s helped set the tone for that whole decade. Oberve that he suggests that the United States might *initiate* use of tactical nuclear weapons.

A significant proportion of U.S. economic resources are devoted to national security. At the present time, we allocate to this crucial national objective over one-half of all Federal expenditures and just under 10 percent of our gross national product. In return for these expenditures we do not receive security in any absolute sense, for that goal is clearly unattainable in the nuclear age. On the contrary, our defense objectives are multiple, they interact and partially conflict, they exist in an environment of great strategic, technological, and political uncertainty. The object of this paper is to describe these objectives, the relations among them, the alternative policies we might choose in their support, the risks and sacrifices they might entail, and the range of possible defense

---

*Source: Joint Economic Committee, *Study of Employment, Growth and Price Levels*, Study Paper No. 18: "National Security and the American Economy in the 1960's" (Washington, D.C.: U.S. Government Printing Office, 1960).

expenditures we might experience in the 1960's.

By now it is well understood that the role of the economy in war has been drastically changed by the advent of nuclear weapons. No longer can the United States base its military strength almost entirely on mobilization potential for war. Mobilization after nuclear attack can be ruled out; the task of survival would be dominant. However, there are many respects in which our economic strength for war remains of central importance, and our ability to increase our military force in response to aggression abroad or the threat of all-out war remains a vital source of strength. Our large economy makes it possible for us to support our Military Establishment with a much smaller proportion of our total output than in the Soviet Union whose considerably smaller economy supports a military establishment comparable to ours. This enables us to greatly expand our defense effort if we choose.

During the decade of the 1960's, however, the Soviet and Chinese economies will be growing rapidly; and so will their capacity for supporting arms and for waging war. The gross national product of the Soviet Union, now one-quarter to one-half as large as ours, will be one-third to two-thirds the size of ours by 1970. This growth will permit a large increase in defense spending while also permitting a large increase in consumption standards. This is not to say that such increases are inevitable; there are clearly opposed influences in the Soviet Union. But its capacity for supporting arms will increase and we cannot be confident that a great increase in Soviet armaments will not occur in the future.

The probable economic growth of China is in some respects more ominous both because of China's overt expanionist tendencies and because of the relative weakness of its neighbors. Although the future growth and political development of Communist China is highly uncertain by 1970 Chinese heavy industry, and consequently its ability to support armed forces, may bulk very large indeed in comparison to China's non-Communist neighbors. In brief, if the Communist bloc remains aggressive, we, our allies, and the free world will have to face the prospect of increased spending on arms.

However, even large increases in defense spending would not have drastic consequences for our way of life. We could manage moderate increases in defense without any reduction of our present levels of consumption and investment. Even large increases might be possible without any reduction in the private sector of the economy. This, in fact, was done during the Korean war. The direct effects on the economy were reduced unemployment, and leisure, and some price and wage inflation. Inflation could be avoided by offsetting moderate tax increases to limit demand in the private sector of the economy.

The major defense objectives the United States has adopted in the postwar period can be summarized as follows: Deterring nuclear assault on the United States, limiting damage to this country if war comes, while seeking a favorable war outcome; deterring aggression against our major allies and aiding in their defense; and, finally, helping to defend other allies and the free world.

The principal objective of U.S. military policy has come to be the deterrence of nuclear attack on the United States. We must attain it. But attaining it means having the ability to receive a well-designed and well-executed surprise nuclear attack and to strike back effectively. The advantage a nuclear-armed aggressor possesses in a surprise attack is formidable, and we must not depreciate the great effect of the many obstacles to retaliation the aggressor can create. This task of deterring attack will remain difficult not only because of the rapid growth of Soviet nuclear strength but also because of revolutionary changes in military technology

that are taking place, some of which may introduce greater uncertainty into the military balance. We will have to work hard and work continually throughout the decade of the 1960's to try to preserve a strong retaliatory power. And, should we succeed, we will not have complete assurance that war will not come, for the power to retaliate is not identical with the power to deter. General war might still come, perhaps by miscalculation, perhaps without either side really preferring war to peace.

If general war were to come, our military forces would be primarily concerned with limiting damage to the United States and its allies and with obtaining the best civil and military outcome that could be obtained. We should not expect the best outcome to be very good, however. Each delivered enemy bomb could do great damage, especially given our low level of civil defense preparation, and a large attack might destroy most of our population and economy. However, there are important possibilities for limiting damage through a combination of active and passive defense, through the use of offensive force, and, especially, through preparations which would enable us to fight a general nuclear war in a controlled manner. With an expanded program aimed at limiting nuclear damage, and with luck, much of our population and economy might survive a general war. . . . On general war, it is convenience to distinguish five distinct positions:

The World Annihilation View. Not everyone holds that it is rational to deter war through the threat of nuclear retaliation. Many distinguished people regard a general thermonuclear war as risking all mankind. They hold that nuclear war cannot be a rational instrument of policy. This view focuses attention on the worldwide effects of radiation that would follow a general nuclear war. It appears that such a war would lead to a shortening of life, an increased incidence of genetic defects and of leukemia and bone cancer throughout the world. Serious as these effects are, these worldwide radiation effects would probably come to less than that from natural background radiation. Moreover, there is little evidence that the nuclear powers are planning to procure weapon systems that will lead to greater worldwide fallout damage in the future. The opposite may be true. Without depreciating the awful consequences of a large nuclear war, especially for the participants, it would be dangerous to assume that an aggressor would be deterred from launching a war by worldwide radiation effects. However, there are uncertainties: the fallout problem is not entirely understood, more serious effects may yet be discovered, and new and more devastating weapons may be developed and procured in the course of the 1960's. In any case, there would be worldwide damage from a general nuclear war, and governments have an urgent obligation to take this damage into account in their preparations just as they have an obligation to weigh the prospective damage to their own population, that of their immediate neighbors, their allies, and their enemies.

The Mutual Suicide View. Much more serious would be the effect of a general nuclear war on the participants. Possible attacks, equivalent to several thousand megatons of TNT delivered on the United States, could kill over half of our population. Moreover, our entire population is at risk. This fact, along with the expectations that Soviet civil society is similarly exposed, leads to the view that a general war would inevitably mean the destruction of both sides.

Belief that nuclear war inevitably would result in mutual suicide results in an almost exclusive focus on deterrence-only policies; that is, policies intended to prevent war, not to mitigate its consequences if it were to come nonetheless. This view, often implicit, is made explicit in the doctrine of finite or minimum deterrence. ("Minimum" deterrence, in another sense, that of preventing war at minimum cost, enjoys practically universal accep-

tance.) The minimum deterrence doctrine holds that we should unilaterally reduce our general war capability by cutting down the active defenses of our cities, by not spending money on civil defense, and by limiting our offensive forces to a level adequate to destroy in retaliation some, perhaps only a few, enemy cities. It assumes that deterrence is *easy* and that working toward deterrence is *enough*.

The minimum deterrence doctrine recognizes two important truths: First, that it is not necessary to promise total destruction to a nation to deter it. Second, that the strategic nuclear balance is unstable and that we should try to stabilize it. However, this doctrine has important limitations. Contrary to the view that deterrence is easy, the difficulties of assuring retaliation *are* great. The effective weight of attack delivered in retaliation might be very much less than the level that would be lethal to a nation. It might, in some circumstances, permit the aggressor to recover rapidly. Most importantly, this view assumes that both sides would inevitably direct a great weight of attack against opposing civil targets. It is by no means certain that this would happen in a general war; both sides might have a great incentive to avoid cities. A nuclear war might be blind destruction, but on the other hand it might not. At best, it would offer a risky prospect. Nevertheless, although well-chosen defense policies can reduce the likelihood of war, it seems doubtful they can reduce its likelihood to zero. These considerations argue for something more than complete dependence on nuclear deterrence.

Deterrence Plus Insurance. This view gives great emphasis to the difficulty of having an assured retaliatory capability. also holds that different possible outcome of a general war can be distinguished an that the outcome would depend on the preparations of the contenders, their war objectives, and circumstances at the war inception. This view does not place primary reliance for the defense of any ve large part of the world on the threat of general nuclear war. For that objective, it emphasizes capabilities for direct defense abroad. It includes insurance as well as deterrence capabilities—insurance in the form of strong active and passive defenses in the United States and strategic forces designed to attack the enemy's military forces. And it includes insurance in the form of an ability to fight a nuclear war in a controlled manner. Finally, it is concerned about the stability of the balance of terror, the danger of a crisis exploding into a general war.

Extended Deterrence. Much of the burden of the defense of Europe in the 1950's has rested on the threat of a U.S. attack against the Soviet Union even in the face of nonnuclear aggression. The extended deterrence doctrine recognizes that the threat of U.S. initiation of general nuclear war has been and is an important bulwark of our defense abroad and seeks to make it more credible. (It should be distinguished from the declaratory policy of making threats of general war in circumstances in which very great devastation to the United States would seem to be a *certain* result.) This increased credibility would come from an expansion of offense forces, our air defenses, and our civil defenses. However, although much could be done to strengthen our ability to wage general war, the net effectiveness of such a program in the 1960's must inevitably be uncertain. And a greatly expanded program to increase our general war capabilities might increase the chances of general war, because it would make us look more threatening. It might increase *his* likelihood of hitting us first. This is not to say that a program aimed at sustaining the force of our general war threat as a deterrence to aggression abroad would be infeasible or without effect; it is to say that such a program would be difficult, costly, uncertain, and risky.

Massive Retaliation. This doctrine applies the threat of general nuclear war, or the threat of actions which make a big war

substantially more likely, to the defense of much of the free world. However, if our threat of general war retains some validity in the defense of so vital an area as Europe, it loses much for other parts of the world. And the expected shifts in the military power balance in the 1960's will diminish the validity of this doctrine throughout. In sum, it appears that a greater concentration on direct defense of all overseas areas will be needed.

The principal views to be found for the direct defense of overseas areas are as follows:

Dependence on Tactical Nuclear Forces. A policy of defending overseas areas by using small nuclear weapons on the battlefield would interpose a level of defense between the use of nonnuclear weapons and all-out nuclear war. They would give us graduated deterrence. However, the Russians have these weapons, too; a tactical nuclear war would be two-sided. One consequence is that such an exchange might result in great civilian damage in the area fought over. Another is that although any war between the United States and the Communist bloc carries the grave risk of exploding into all-out war, a nuclear war would seem substantially more likely to do so than a nonnuclear one. Even so, we cannot dispense with a tactical nuclear capability; in some circumstances we might elect to initiate this type of war. On the other hand, perhaps we are preparing our overseas forces too exclusively for this type of combat, and neglecting preparations for nonnuclear conflict.

Establishment of Independent Nuclear Forces. A second alternative for the more direct defense of oversea areas, one already chosen by Britain and France, is to build up independent nuclear forces. Or a European force might be created. However, if either a European or separate national force is to have a stable retaliatory capability in the face of a nuclear assault, it must be designed to survive an enemy first strike. This task is difficult even in the

United States. If not attained abroad, or worse, if not even attempted, additional nuclear forces could be seriously destabilizing to world peace. And for the United States to aid in the establishment of independent nuclear forces runs counter to our policy of discouraging the spread of nuclear weapons around the world. This policy has been based on the belief that the long-term security of the United States and the entire world would be prejudiced by the wider diffusion of bombs—especially if they were to get into the hands of irresponsible powers. Nevertheless, the process of diffusion is underway. Though difficult or impossible to stop it, it may be possible to slow it down. In the end, we might find ourselves forced to help build up the nuclear capabilities of some of our allies if feasible alternatives have been foreclosed. We should be ready for this contingency. . . .

DOCUMENT 33.5

Guns and Butter: The U.S. Reply to the United Nations*

Behind much of the American public's acceptance of the existence of the military-industrial complex lay the notion that the United States was so rich it could afford a policy of both "guns and butter"— high defense spending and continued economic growth. This idea was badly shaken by the coming of recession with inflation in the later 1960s. But in December 1961 "guns and butter" dominated American thought, as was revealed in this confident reply to the UN Secretary-General on the possible impact of disarmament for the U.S. economy.

The motivating force behind the efforts of the United States to achieve general

---

*Source: U.S. Arms Control and Disarmament Agency: *The Economic and Social Consequences of Disarmament* (Washington, D.C., June 1964).

and complete disarmament under effective international control is to save present and future generations from the scourge of war and to attain for them a more certain and beneficent security.

This basic and vital objective completely overshadows any economic calculations of gain or loss connected with disarmament. Actually, the United States can maintain as high or as low a level of defense expenditures as is deemed necessary for its security. At the same time it is clear that a basic change in our methods of achieving security will have distinct effects on our economy. Any examination of the question of disarmament therefore requires study of its economic impact in order to enlarge our understanding of the policies, programs, and actions required to derive the maximum economic and social benefit from it for ourselves and the rest of mankind.

It must be stressed that the allocation of resources to purely military purposes is not an economically creative process, except in an incidental way. It yields relatively few goods or services which contribute to the enrichment of individual lives or to the growth of the national economy. It prevents or retards the satisfaction of many civilian needs. By the same token, if the world should be fortunate enough to be able to rid itself of the burden of national defense efforts, resources would then be released everywhere which could be devoted to the production of those goods and services which advance man's material, cultural, and spiritual state. This is the basic economic interest of the United States in disarmament, and it is an entirely positive one.

This study of the extent to which the defense effort affects the American economy, and of the economic problems and opportunities which would be encountered under a program of general and complete disarmament, is in no sense definitive. This is because there are important gaps in our basic knowledge of detailed facts and because there is as yet no indication as to the timing, phasing, and duration of the disarmament program which may eventually emerge from international negotiations.

Despite these limitations, it is possible to arrive at several significant conclusions.

(1) The current national defense effort of the United States takes about one-tenth of our gross national product and employs somewhat less than that portion of our employed labor force. This allocation of human and material resources must be seen against the background of the vast and costly changes which have been taking place in the technology of arms, and of the tremendous enlargement, geographically and otherwise, in the security requirements of the United States as the leading power in the free world. As a component of total economic demand, defense expenditures are not of such magnitude that the economy is vitally dependent on them. In fact, the American economy proved itself after World War II to be very resilient to a considerably greater and more rapid reduction in defense expenditure than would be involved under any disarmament program starting at the present level of armaments.

(2) The currently recognized needs of Americans individually and collectively are so extensive that, if translated into economic demand, they would more than offset the loss of demand resulting from an agreed disarmament program. The factors required to effect this translation of civilian needs into economic demand are well understood. Moreover, there are increasingly refined tools available with which to observe, analyze, and influence the development of the economy. Advance planning and sensible policies at all levels of government will be essential to the maintenance of overall economic activity in the face of the progressive elimination of defense demand.

(3) Unquestionably, any program of disarmament will in the short and intermediate run give rise to problems of ad-

justment in all factors of production. However, these adjustment problems—of varying intensity depending on the timing, phasing, and duration of any agreed disarmament program—are not novel to the American economy; quite apart from previous successful adjustments to major changes in defense expenditures, the economy is constantly undergoing adjustment in a wide range of industries as a result of changes in technology and economic demand. Concerted effort on the part of government at all levels and of business and labor, to bring to bear numerous available instruments and, if necessary, to create additional ones, can reduce to a minimum any hardship and waste in the adjustment process under a program for general and complete disarmament.

(4) The United States has long recognized that general and complete disarmament would present opportunities for enlarged assistance to less developed countries and has sponsored United Nations resolutions in this sense. However, the United States has not waited for disarmament; it has extended foreign economic aid over the past 20 years on a scale unequaled by any other country. The United Nations, recognizing that added impetus needs to be given in the current decade to economic cooperation for development in underdeveloped countries, has designated the 1960's as the International Decade of Development. The United States, as one of the sponsors of this resolution, will do its part. When and as disarmament is achieved, the American people can be expected to face imaginatively the added challenges and opportunities which this development would hold for the welfare of mankind.

(5) In the area of international economic relations the elimination, as a result of disarmament, of U.S. Government defense-related expenditures abroad, and of defense-related imports of raw materials and other commodities, would have a corrective effect on the U.S. balance-of-

payments deficit. There would probably be a noticeably adverse effect in only a few countries; these effects could be overcome with increased external economic assistance and growth and diversification in the respective economies. The elimination of military-oriented production and trade controls under disarmament would permit more international trade to flow on the basis of comparative advantage.

DOCUMENT 33.6:

The Language of Threat*

The idea that the United States was somehow beleagured, threatened from without and within by communist conspiracies, produced the "Fortress America" psychology of the 1950s. Like the guns and butter argument, it helped underpin the hold of the military-industrial complex on the economy and society. Yet, despite the changes in national style from the late 1960s on, we can see in Defense Secretary Melvin Laird's report for fiscal year 1971 continued reliance on the language of "threat." Notice also, toward the end of this reading, that Secretary Laird criticizes McNamara's overcentralisation of the Defense Department.

A.   THE THREAT TO NATIONAL SECURITY

The first requirement we faced upon assuming office was to reappraise the spectrum of threats that exist in the world today. These threats dictate to a large degree how we should implement our basic policies in conjunction with our allies. As I noted earlier, changes in the strategic threat that might result from suc-

---

*Source: Department of Defense, *Statement of Secretary to House Subcommittee on Defense Appropriations, Fiscal Year 1971* (Washington, D.C.: U.S. Government Printing Office, 1970).

cessful arms limitation talks could have a major impact on the direction we take in our future strategic programs. Similarly the emergence of additional nuclear-capable nations such as Communist China influences our force planning.

Because the new strategy we are pursuing stresses a critical review of our obligations and of the contributions of our allies to regional defense, it will have a major impact on our general purpose forces as well as our strategic forces. In designing our forces to reflect the new strategy, we must therefore assess the full range of threats which we and our allies face, including limited war as well as strategic nuclear threats.

Permit me to highlight the four major aspects of the military threat which we have had to consider and which we must constantly review.

1.   THE STRATEGIC NUCLEAR THREAT

The Soviet strategic nuclear threat is impressive and it is growing. We now estimate the number of SS–9 Intercontinental Ballistic Missiles (ICBMs) deployed or under construction to be over 275, rather than 230 as I reported publicly less than a year ago. The number of SS–11 ICBMs has also increased significantly. The Soviets continue to test improvements in offensive weapons, including SS–9 multiple re-entry vehicles and modified SS–11 payloads. Production of nuclearpowered ballistic missile submarines has continued above previously projected rates at two Soviet shipyards.

Communist China has continued to test nuclear weapons in the megaton range and could test its first ICBM within the next year. However, the earliest estimated date that they could have an operational ICBM capability now appears to be 1973 or about one year later than last year's projection. It appears more likely that such a capability will be achieved by the mid-1970s. A force of 10 to 25 ICBM might be operational some two to three years later.

2. THE GENERAL PURPOSE FORCES THREAT

The general purpose forces threat also remains strong. In the most critical theater, that facing the NATO Central Region, the Warsaw Pact could, in a relatively short time, assemble a force of about 1.3 million men and associated combat equipment. In Asia, Communist China and North Korea continue to maintain substantial armed forces.

The major Soviet naval threat continues to be from the torpedo and cruise-missile firing submarine force. By mid-1971, the Soviets should have about 300 submarines, including 65 with nuclear power. These forces could pose a considerable threat to our deployed naval forces and to the merchant shipping essential to the support of our European and Asian allies. Additionally, Soviet Naval Air Force bombers equipped with cruise missiles could pose a threat to our naval forces operating within range of the Soviet Union.

It is clear that the Soviet Union is embarked on an amibitious program to achieve a global military capability.

Besides the strength of the forces deployed by potential enemies, we must recognize that general purpose force requirements are affected to a large degree by geography. Our forces must be structured to account for this important factor as well.

3. THE TECHNOLOGICAL THREAT

In the long term, one of the most serious threats confronting the United States is the large and growing military research and development effort of the Soviet Union.

The implications of this Soviet effort for our future security cannot be clearly foreseen at this time. Because the Soviet Union is a closed society, they can conduct their military research and development programs behind a thick veil of secrecy, making it very difficult for us to assess their progress in a timely manner.

However, we have seen evidence of this technology in the new systems they are deploying, including the FOXBAT interceptor aircraft, nuclear-powered ballistic missile and attack submarines, and other impressive weapons.

We cannot base our own research and development effort solely on an estimate of the Soviet technological threat. We simply do not have enough knowledge to assess the threat properly. The only prudent course is to advance our knowledge at a reasonable pace in every area of significance to our future military strength.

4. THE INSURGENCY THREAT

One of the most effective techniques used by Communist nations has been insurgency supported by external assistance. As the President noted in proclaiming the Nixon Doctrine on November 3rd, we intend to assist our friends and allies in coping with such threats, largely through military and economic assistance when requested and as appropriate, while looking to the nation directly threatened to assume the primary responsibility for providing the manpower for its defense. . . .

B. THE CHALLENGE AT HOME

In addition to the military threats posed from outside our borders, we faced significant challenges within our borders.

At home, there was a growing mood of self-doubt. Our youth and other segments of our population were becoming increasingly frustrated over the war in Vietnam which was pushing defense expenditures higher and higher, while our casualties were second only to those we suffered in World War II. Despite the rising costs in human and material resources, hope for success seemed dim. As we assumed office in January 1969, no clear end was in sight, either in Southeast Asia or at the conference table in Paris.

Partly as a result of the Vietnam war, high prices and growing taxes were threatening the living standards of the pensioned and the salaried. There was a clear need and a growing demand to put our Government's fiscal affairs back in order. The Federal Budget needed to be balanced to start bringing serious inflation under control. Most importantly, our national priorities had to be reordered.

Moreover, our society was troubled by divisions which too often alienated the races and divided the generations.

As we assumed office in this environment, the Department of Defense was also confronted with frustration and disillusionment. Blame for mediocre results of some past policies and programs fell largely on the shoulders of the military. Our Code of Conduct for servicemen imprisoned by hostile forces was questioned as a result of the experiences of the PUEBLO crew. The administration of post exchanges and military prisons and the use of non-appropriated funds for such activities as Non-commissioned Officers' clubs were problem areas that came to light early in the year. These were followed by other and more serious charges of misconduct in alleged violation of the Uniform Code of Military Justice.

As a result of repeated modernization deferrals, the Navy fleet was threatened with approaching obsolescence. The controversial TFX, or F–111, and the Main Battle Tank seemed to be plagued by one structural or technical defect after another. Other programs that troubled us included the Cheyenne Helicopter, the C–5A, and the Mark 48 torpedo. I found and reported to Congress in my first ap-

pearance last year that current funding deficiencies on major weapons systems amounted to about $2 billion, and subsequently reported that cost growth, for various reasons, amounted to more than $16 billion. This situation forced us to cancel some programs, to order cutbacks in other production schedules, and to rely further on aging weapons and equipment.

In addition, there were administrative problems within the Department of Defense.

I inherited a system designed for highly centralized decisionmaking. Overcentralization of decisionmaking in so large an organization as the Department of Defense leads to a kind of paralysis. Many decisions are not made at all, or, if they are made, lack full coordination and commitment by those who must implement the decisions. The traffic from lower to higher echelons may be inhibited; relevant and essential inputs for the decisionmaker can be lost. In addition, there seemed to be insufficient participation by other agencies with important responsibilities for national security.

I was also disturbed that although longrange plans existed, they did not always reflect realistic planning within foreseeable resources.

All of these challenges and problems convinced us that an overriding and immediate need was for the new Administration to devise far better methods to deal with national security matters than existed in January 1969. . . .

34 Segregation and Discrimination in the 20th Century

LOUIS RUCHAMES
University of Massachusetts—Boston

Earliest examples of legislative enactments of Negro segregation are to be found in colonial Maryland, Virginia, and Massachusetts. The first two, in 1664, and the latter, in 1705, prohibited marriage between Negroes and whites. In all three states, slavery was then lawful. Thus, segregation in America was first born within societies legally committed to slavery; its primary purpose was to help maintain slavery; and it was dedicated to the proposition that the slave, identified by his black skin, was too inferior and degraded to enter into the relationship of marriage with a white person.

While segregation grew out of slavery, its greatest development came after abolition of the "peculiar institution." The reason is quite clear. While the laws of slavery were adequate to prevent slaves as a class from rising out of bondage, the existence of the free Negro represented both an anomaly and a threat to the entire system. Segregation served to remind the free Negro that though his status resulted from an accident of fate, nevertheless, by reason of his race, he partook of the inferiority of all Negroes. And he was not to enter white society except as an inferior.

When slavery disappeared in the North after the colonial period, racial attitudes toward the Negro which had prevailed under it did not disappear but, in fact, were strengthened by the continued existence of slavery in the South. For some northern states, then, the result was an increase in segregation. In Massachusetts, for instance, "Jim Crow" railroads and an antimiscegenation law existed as late as the 1840s, and Negro children were segregated in Boston's public schools until 1855.

Similarly, the greatest development of segregation in the South occurred in the years after the end of slavery and some time after the close of the Reconstruction period in 1877. Not only did segregation grow out of attitudes concerning Negro inferiority prevailing under slavery but, indeed, it served as a substitute for slavery. Segregation helped to keep the Negro "in his place" and guaranteed that he would remain a docile "hewer of wood and drawer of water," subservient and obedient to the white man's will. Consequently, beginning with the end of Reconstruction and continuing until the early thirties of this century, there evolved, at first slowly and hesitantly but then more quickly, a dense network of racial segregation covering almost every area of society in the South.

A popular misconception is that the history of racial discrimination in America

385

has been one of gradual improvement and progress. As Professor Newby makes clear (Problem 24 above) nothing could be further from the truth. In 1900, Negro discrimination and segregation were far worse than they had been 25 years earlier; 25 years later, in many respects, the situation had further deteriorated. Charles W. Chestnutt, a Negro novelist, remarked at the turn of the century that "the rights of the Negro are at a lower ebb than at any time during the thirty-five years of their freedom, and the race-prejudice more intense and uncompromising." Professor C. Vann Woodward, in a recent study of segregation, has written: "Wide agreement prevailed in the early years of the century that there was less sympathy, tolerance, and understanding between the races than there had been during the Reconstruction period, and some put the case even more strongly."

For the Negro the pre-World War I years of the 20th century were marked by mob violence and lynchings, disfranchisement, relegation to menial and low-paid jobs, and increasing segregation in all walks of life by state and municipal laws as well as informal custom. These trends continued well after the war. As late as 1944, Gunnar Myrdal, the Swedish economist and sociologist, could say that "segregation is now becoming so complete that the white Southerner practically never sees a Negro except as his servant and in other standardized and formalized caste situations."

Despite Myrdal's doleful observation regarding segregation in 1944, conditions were already maturing which would lead to an improvement in the Negro's status throughout the nation and to a weakening of the entire structure of racial discrimination. These conditions included (1) the movement of Negroes from South to North, during World War I and ensuing years, and a subsequent increase in their political influence in several northern states; (2) mounting Negro group consciousness and militancy, marked by the decline of Booker T. Washington's philosophy of accommodation and the growth of the National Association for the Advancement of Colored People, created during the first decade of the century, with its aggressive, mass-action strategy for securing Negro rights; (3) the liberal tide which flowed across the country during the 1930s and was symbolized in Franklin D. Roosevelt's New Deal, with its greater concern for the oppressed and poverty-stricken; (4) the assistance given by New Deal agencies to the Negroes, thereby stimulating among them a new sense of their own worth and dignity; (5) the augmented interest of major religious organizations in the expansion of opportunities for all minority groups, including Negroes; (6) the insistence by the newly formed CIO, created during the 1930s, upon equality of treatment for white and Negro workers and, concomitantly, the admission of numerous Negroes into the organization; and (7) the emergence, during the 1920s and 1930s, of new and influential organizations, such as the American Civil Liberties Union and the Southern Conference for Human Welfare, which were deeply concerned for the rights of minority groups.

In June 1941, several months before the United States entered the war and in the midst of a mounting defense effort, these conditions converged to bring about one of the major advances in the history of Negro and other minority groups. It was an advance which in turn helped pave the way, 13 years later, for the epochal Supreme Court decision barring segregation in public education. This was the issuance by President Franklin D. Roosevelt of Executive Order 8802, which prohibited discrimination in government employment and defense industries on the basis of race, creed, color, or national origin. A Fair Employment Practice Committee was created to enforce the order. The President's action came in response to a prolonged campaign by Negro and other or ganizations culminating in a threatened march on Washington by more than 100,000 Negroes.

Executive Order 8802 had a twofold significance. It challenged the widely held belief of historians, social scientists, and political leaders that racial discrimination and segregation could not be eliminated through legal action. Such had been the position taken by the Supreme Court in *Plessy* v. *Ferguson*, when it ruled that "legislation is powerless to eradicate social instincts or to abolish distinctions based upon physical differences, and the attempt to do so can only result in accentuating the difficulties of the present situation." And it opened the way to new economic opportunities for Negroes and other minority groups in many of the most important sectors of the economy. Negro leaders hailed the order as "the most significant move on the part of the Government since the Emancipation Proclamation."

The Fair Employment Practice Committee existed for about five years. It practically ceased functioning during the early months of 1943 but was revived by a new executive order on May 27, 1943. It continued in effect until June 28, 1946. During its lifetime the FEPC was subjected to unremitting attack by southern members of Congress and had to endure a hostile congressional investigation. The commission suffered from insufficient funds; indifference, if not hostility, from other government agencies; and limited powers. Despite these handicaps, it achieved notable results.

The committee held public hearings, investigated complaints, brought the glare of publicity and the power of the presidential office to bear upon recalcitrant employers and labor unions, issued educational materials, and succeeded in opening many opportunities in industry and government to Negroes and others where previously none had existed. Whereas, in March 1942, Negroes were only 2.5 percent of all workers employed in war production, by November 1944,

they made up approximately 8 percent of the war workers for whom statistics were available. A very significant increase also took place in the employment of Negroes in government. While these developments in both industry and government were due partly to the wartime labor shortage, much of it undoubtedly came from FEPC efforts. Available statistics indicate that plants involved in public hearings or otherwise investigated by committee members showed a greater increase in Negro employment than did defense industries in general. Numerous employers who at one time had discriminated against Negroes or other minority groups hired a few Negroes as a result of FEPC persuasion; subsequently, they employed other workers without any discrimination. Diminishing, too, were those forms of segregation which had resulted from the hiring of Negroes for only certain types of work. Where Negroes and whites began to work side by side and to learn more about one another, prejudice often seemed to lessen. And finally, political leaders and the well-informed public generally began to realize that law, even in the form of an executive order which did not confer all the powers of a congressional statute, could be effective in eliminating discrimination.

These lessons, learned on a national level, stimulated passage of FEPC laws in states and cities throughout the North. On March 12, 1945, New York enacted the first state Fair Employment Practice law. By July 1960, 17 states and over 40 municipalities had passed similar laws. These frequently were expanded to include prohibitions against educational, housing, and other forms of discrimination. The antidiscrimination laws had a significant impact upon segregation and racial bias in the North, leading especially to more job and educational opportunities for Negroes.

As the climate of opinion in America during the late 1930s and 1940s veered toward a more sympathetic view of Negro needs and rights, so too did the Supreme Court, which both symbolized the change and contributed toward it. In far-reaching decisions, the Court pronounced against the South's white primaries, judicial enforcement of racial restrictive covenants, segregation in interstate travel, and unequal provisions for Negro and white students in segregated schools. But its greatest contribution to equal rights was made on May 17, 1954, and again on May 31, 1955 when, in the "school segregation cases," it ruled that "in the field of public education the doctrine of 'separate but equal' has no place." "Separate educational facilities are inherently unequal," the Court affirmed; and Negro pupils, by being segregated, are "deprived of the equal protection of the laws guaranteed by the Fourteenth Amendment." In ruling against school segregation in these decisions the Court implicitly challenged the entire system of legalized segregation as it existed in 21 states and in the District of Columbia.

How effective have the decisions been? During the first 12 or 13 years after the decisions, progress was extremely slow. According to Elliot L. Richardson, Nixon's Secretary of Health, Education, and Welfare, as late as the fall of 1967 "4.3 percent of the South's [1] black children were in school systems that had desegregated under current law." Even in the fall of 1968, the percentage was only 6.1 percent.

These results were in part due to the fierce resistance with which southern political leaders and large sections of the southern population met the decision. Moreover, President Eisenhower, by failing to give positive and wholehearted support to the decision, contributed to the snaillike pace of early school desegregation. Slow progress was also partially inherent in the nature of the judicial process, in which each Supreme Court

ruling pertains to the case at hand, while its application to other school systems requires additional lawsuits which may be carried to the Supreme Court. Each evasion of the law, if it is to be overcome, can be corrected only through court action, which may also be litigated up to the Supreme Court. Thus the possibilities for delaying action are almost infinite. Finally, a recent historian of the Supreme Court and the Negro has argued that the Court's "great mistake" was in its decision of May 31, 1955, that schools were to be desegregated, not immediately, but "with all deliberate speed." This proviso afforded a rationale for delay and suggested "that a *personal* and *present* constitutional right," the right to attend unsegregated schools, "could be deferred and extended gradually to those who were entitled to exercise it" immediately. The result of this ruling was that the Court "only succeeded in opening a Pandora's box of troubles."

More recently, a real breakthrough seems to have occurred in school integration. According to Secretary Richardson, the percentage of southern black children in desegregated school systems increased markedly to 27.2 percent in 1969, and in 1970 it leaped forward to 90.5 percent. He noted, too, that "Of the approximately 2,700 school districts in the 11 Southern states more than 97 percent—or all but 76 districts—have desegregated pursuant to voluntary plans and court orders."

An important factor in recent progress has been the threat by the U.S. Office of Education to withhold federal aid from those public schools that refuse to comply with the provision against segregation in education of the Civil Rights Acts of 1964. Perhaps even more important was the refusal by federal courts to permit any further delay in the implementation of integration in the fall of 1970. In this respect, the Supreme Court's *Alexander* decision, in October 1969, which set aside its earlier "deliberate speed" formula and called for desegregation forthwith, has been of vital importance.

---

[1] The states included were Alabama, Arkansas, Florida, Georgia, Louisiana, Mississippi, North Carolina, South Carolina, Tennessee, Texas, and Virginia.

What of the future? Seen nationally, segregation is today constantly narrowing and decreasing. At one time, it was supported by the national government and the Supreme Court, and its area extended throughout the United States. Today, segregation is being challenged everywhere, and its area of dominance is gradually being compressed further and further into the deep South. It should be remembered, too, that as a result of President Harry S Truman's Executive Order 9981, issued in July 1948, the army, the navy, and the air force are now completely integrated. Even the South itself has been the scene of changes which sooner or later are bound to be felt. Despite terror and intimidation, many more Negroes are voting today than ever before. They have been elected to public office; they serve on school boards; they sit on juries in increasing numbers; they participate in professional athletics; and they have entered southern colleges and universities in growing numbers, even in the deep South. Many southern cities have desegregated their parks, museums, and public libraries.

Indeed, a survey conducted by *The New York Times* on the condition of southern Negroes in August 1970 concluded that there had been notable advances in the elimination of segregation and in the achievement of equal rights. It noted that "the changes . . . are visible everywhere in the South nowadays; not only in statistics and official reports but in people's eyes and voices and manner of walking as well. . . . Discrimination still exists . . . but . . . the 'Old South' is just not the same, and the contrast is often dramatic." Moreover, the number of Negro and other minority families earning $8,000 or more doubled between 1960 and 1968, although the South lagged behind the rest of the country. Outside the South, the gap between the earnings of young husband-wife Negro families and those of whites seems to be closing. Negro families headed by a male between the ages of 25 to 34 have 87 percent of the income of

whites. The number of black technical and professional employees doubled between 1960 and 1968; this increase was more than twice that for whites. In 1968, too, the percentage of 18- and 19-year-old Negroes in school was only 6 percent lower than that of whites. Negro college enrollment rose 85 percent between 1964 and 1968, when there were 434,000 Negro college students.

Conceivably, the most significant development is the attitude of the Negro people themselves. It takes two races to make segregation work. The powerful resistance of Negroes to every manifestation of segregation, and their refusal to accept anything less than equal treatment and equal rights, are guarantees that the problem will never be solved except on the basis of complete integration. The constructive results of department store "sit-ins" in various southern cities, the sustained efforts of "freedom riders," the continuous testing of segregation ordinances, and the voter registration drives in the South have provided evidence of the new Negro spirit.

So fundamental has been the change in Negro attitudes and actions that it may be justly regarded as a revolution, as Louis E. Lomax has called it in his very perceptive book, *The Negro Revolt* (1962). The onset of this change may be traced to December 1955, when Mrs. Rosa Parks, a Negro woman of Montgomery, Alabama, refused to surrender her seat in a municipal bus to a white passenger and was subsequently arrested. Her arrest evoked the bus boycott by Montgomery Negroes which lasted for months, showed masterful organization and determination, and ended in a complete victory with the issuance of a U.S. Supreme Court decision, in October 1956, declaring segregating seating on municipal buses illegal.

The Montgomery boycott catapulted into national prominence the Rev. Martin Luther King, Jr., who perhaps better than any other Negro leader articulated the feelings and hopes of his people. The boycott also inspired Negroes throughout the country to emulate the Montgomery protest. Typifying the new Negro spirit were two forms of action which ensued: the sit-ins and the freedom rides.

The sit-ins began in February 1960, when four freshmen from an all-Negro college in Greensboro, North Carolina, entered a Woolworth store, sat down at a white lunch counter, and refused to move until served. The tactic spread to numerous other cities and states across the nation. Associated with it was the technique of nonviolent, direct mass action perfected by the Congress of Racial Equality, or CORE, and taught by its representatives to sit-in participants across the country. Over 800 sit-ins occurred, involving "more people than any other civil rights movement in history"—about 70 thousand Negroes and whites in over a hundred cities, with more than four thousand arrested, most of them Negro students. In many cities, such as Nashville, sit-ins were accompanied by economic boycotts by the entire Negro community, and the combined pressure, frequently proving decisive, brought success to the advocates of integration.

Freedom rides were initiated by James Farmer, a former Methodist clergyman and program director for the NAACP, who had resigned from the latter organization to become national director of CORE in February 1961. In March 1961, CORE announced its intention to test segregation in interstate travel terminals by undertaking freedom rides, and on May 4 the first freedom riders headed south from the national capital. Soon other groups—the Nashville Student Movement, the Student Non-Violent Coordinating Committee, and Martin Luther King's Southern Christian Leadership Conference—sent riders southward. About a thousand persons, both Negro and white, were involved. Facilities were tested in several cities, among them Nashville, New Orleans, Montgomery, Birmingham, Augusta, Athens and Jackson. In several municipalities the riders met with violence and bloodshed, but they subsequently achieved their objective when, at the request of President John F. Kennedy, the Interstate Commerce Commission banned segregation in interstate terminals. Its order became effective on November 1, 1961.

Sit-ins and freedom rides confirmed the importance of nonviolent mass action, accompanied where feasible by an economic boycott, as the vital catalytic agents for achieving results in the drive against discrimination and segregation. This became evident in the Birmingham racial crisis of April and May, 1963, in which thousands of Negroes—men, women, and children—demonstrated for more than a month. Beaten, shot at, attacked by dogs, sprayed by hoses, and imprisoned, they nevertheless refused to submit. Finally, through mass action and economic boycott, they forced the Birmingham white community —or at least some of its more important business and civil leaders—to accede to several of their demands and to begin the process of desegregation.

In any evaluation of the Negro revolt, one point bears stressing: Had similar demonstrations occurred at the turn of the century in cities and towns of the deep South, they probably would have been confronted with violence and bloodshed on a scale unimaginable today. In 1963 beatings and bombings were relatively infrequent, and even the dogs were used with some restraint. The difference lies not only in a changed climate of opinion but in the even more important fact that today the judicial and executive branches of the federal government are pledged to support the basic Negro objectives— elimination of segregation and discrimination as well as the attainment of full equality of opportunity. Freedom rides and attempts at school desegregation were first made feasible by Supreme Court rulings on interstate travel and education. The successful entrance of James Meredith, a Negro veteran, into the University of Mississippi in September 1962 and of two Negroes into the University of Alabama in June 1963, despite opposition from the governors of both states, was due ultimately to the support given to Court decisions by the late President Kennedy, however vacillating his efforts may have seemed during the early stages of the Meredith case.

President Lyndon B. Johnson also gave strong backing to the civil rights movement. Most noteworthy was the passage of the Civil Rights Act of July 1964 and the Voting Rights Act of August 1965. The former provided for the elimination of discrimination in public accommodations, education, voter registration, and employment. The latter nullified southern literacy tests, which had been used primarily against Negroes, and provided federal examiners to register Negroes in Alabama, Georgia, Louisiana, Mississippi, South Carolina, Virginia, and various counties of North Carolina.

In recent years, questions involving tactics became increasingly important to Negro organizations. These were not only tactical questions but involved fundamental differences of opinion concerning the nature of American society. CORE and the Southern Christian Leadership Conference advocated and practiced nonviolent mass action. So, too, did the Student Non-Violent Coordinating Committee, which participated in sit-ins, voter registration programs, and freedom rides. The National Association for the Advancement of Colored People, the largest and most influential Negro organization on the American scene, favored mass action in theory, but in recent years it has concentrated primarily on legal action through test cases in the courts. Confronted by the sit-ins, freedom rides, and other forms of mass action, the NAACP has lent its approval and sponsorship to such efforts.

A few leaders of the Negro community have rejected the principle of nonviolence in the face of white violence. Robert F. Williams, a former president of the local NAACP branch in Monroe, North Carolina, who lived in China, after fleeing to Cuba (to avoid prosecution), has advocated meeting violence with violence. Birmingham Negroes, after suffering police brutality without retaliation for more than a month, finally turned on the police in an outburst of violence. Similar instances have occurred elsewhere. The Black Muslims, who represent a small minority voice in the Negro community, neither advocate nor abjure violence. Yet they frequently express hatred of the white man, advocate the complete separation of Negroes and whites, demand the establishment of a separate Negro state, and emphasize the innate supremacy of the black man. Ability of Negroes to gain their objectives through methods advocated by the established organizations has undoubtedly limited Black Muslim growth. Further gains toward integration and acceptance of the Negro as a full-fledged, equal member of American society would make the Muslim program of separation even less tenable.

More recently, the slogan of "Black Power" has been raised, thereby emphasizing Negro leadership in the movement for Negro rights, a greater effort to mobilize Negro economic and political power, and an insistence upon forceful resistance to white violence against Negroes. The slogan has been attacked by the major Negro organizations—the NAACP, the National Urban League, and the Southern Christian Leadership Conference—as an incitement to violence and a repudiation of Negro-white cooperation in the civil rights movement.

"Black Power" is but one manifestation of a resurgence of "black nationalism" during the 1960s. As Theodore Draper has suggested in his *The Rediscovery of Black Nationalism*, "this resurgence has manifested itself in Black Studies or Afro-American programs and departments in our universities; in the Black Panther, Republic of New Africa, and other militant movements; and in the vogue for Afro styles in dress and hairdos."

One of the most eloquent spokesmen for black nationalism was the late Malcolm X, characterized as "perhaps the most remarkable figure as yet produced by the resurgence of black nationalism." His autobiography is referred to as belonging "with the great human documents of our time." Murdered in February 1965, he had been a Black Muslim follower of Elijah Muhammad for 12 years, until about the end of 1963, and an independent leader during the last year of his life. As a nationalist he called for "complete separation" and the emigration of America's blacks back to Africa or the creation of a black state on separate territory in the Western Hemisphere, "where the two races can live apart from each other." Several months later, his emphasis was less on physical emigration to Africa than on identification by American blacks with Africa "culturally, philosophically and psychologically" as a means of strengthening and enriching the nationalist identity of America's blacks. About a month before his death, Malcolm X abandoned his emphasis on territorial nationalism. In a television interview he announced that he no longer believed in a black state and affirmed that "I believe in a state in which people can live like human beings on the basis of equality."

The most important development in Black Nationalism during the late 1960s was the emergence of the Black Panther Party, formed on October 1966 by two black militants, Huey P. Newton and Bobby Seale, in Oakland, California, with Seale as Chairman and Newton as Minister of Defense. They were joined in 1967 by Eldridge Cleaver. The "Black Panther" was the emblem of Alabama's Lowndes County Freedom Party, formed in 1965. According to Philip Foner, the name and symbol were chosen "because the panther is reputed never to make an unprovoked attack but to defend itself ferociously whenever it is attacked." Newton and Seale were, at first, deeply influenced by the writings of Macolm X, Frantz Fanon, and later Marx, Engels, Lenin, Mao Tse-Tung, Ho Chi Minh and Ché Guevara. Their earliest activities consisted of sending armed patrol cars through Oakland's slums to prevent and combat police brutality. The movement spread and became national in membership and influence. Within three years the Panthers had set up about 30 chapters, with their membership reaching perhaps five thousand at its peak. Their primary purpose is the "national liberation" of this "black colony" in the "white mother country." "Revolutionary nationalists" in America, they also "identify with the revolutionary Black people of Africa and people of color throughout the world." Moreover, they call for a socialist as well as a nationalist revolution, and for cooperation with white revolutionary groups to achieve both socialism and black liberation. In their emphasis upon black-white cooperation, then, they differ from the separatism of earlier black nationalist movements. Despite their growth through much of 1969, their numbers and efforts appear to have declined drastically during 1970 and 1971. A *New York Times* survey, printed on March 1, 1971, reports that "a check of the Party's chapters across the country suggests that the operation is now only a skeleton of what it was just a year ago." Riven by serious ideological differences, the Party has suffered from violent encounters with the police and from the arrests and convictions of many of its leaders.

As one looks upon the current racial scene, there are several reasons for disquiet, despite gains that have been made over the past quarter century. A report of the U.S. Commission on Civil Rights of October 1970, entitled *The Federal Civil Rights Enforcement Effort*, told of a "major breakdown" in the enforcement of existing federal laws and executive order against racial discrimination. The committee's chairman, Rev. Theodore M. Hesburgh, acknowledged passage of an impressive volume of recent laws in education, employment, housing, voting, administration of justice and use of public accommodations. But he also noted "a gap between what the guarantees have promised and what has actually been delivered." Especially in such areas as employment, housing and education, "discrimination persists and the goal of equal opportunity is far from achievement." Equally disturbing has been the seemingly lackadaisical attitude of the Nixon administration toward problems of racial discrimination and segregation. Indeed, Bishop Stephen G. Spottswood of the National Association for the Advancement of Colored People observed in June 1970 that "for the first time since Woodrow Wilson, we have a National Administration that can be rightly characterized as anti-Negro." As evidence he cited the administration's refusal to act against companies violating defense contract antidiscrimination provisions, the attempt to secure court delays in the enforcement of school desegregation, the nominations of Clement Haynsworth and G. Harrold Carswell to the Supreme Court, the Moynihan Memorandum calling for "benign neglect" of racial discrimination, and administration support for tax exemption for white private schools designed to circumvent desegregation in the public schools.

Moreover, the rate of unemployment among Negroes is twice that among whites. Residential segregation throughout the country is advancing, notably in the suburbs. Despite gains in educational integration in the South, there has also been widespread evasion. A report issued in March 1971 by the Southern Regional Council, entitled *The South and Her Children: School Desegregation 1970–1971*, noted that Elliot Richardson's figures on the progress of desegregation in the South, previously cited in this essay, had obscured the fact that the pattern of segregation within so-called desegregated districts was widespread. It also noted that the Nixon administration, by empha-

sizing desegregation within districts, had avoided an examination of segregation within schools and thus "appeared to be playing a deceptive game of numbers." While observing that "it would be fair to say that, for the first time, school desegregation in one degree or another is the rule rather than the exception for the children of the South," the report noted that "this is a far cry, however, from the final dismantling of the dual system." Black children in "integrated" schools sometimes attend separate all-black classes in separate wings of a building. Attendance at private segregated schools in the fall of 1970 in the 11-state South was between 450,000 and 500,000, more than 10 times greater than before the Civil Rights Act of 1964, and up from the 400,000 of the previous spring.

In another area, the war in Vietnam has placed a disproportionate burden upon Negro young men, who constitute a larger percentage of soldiers and casualties than their percentage of the total population. Similarly, budgetary cuts in welfare and poverty programs within the United States, due to the increased needs of war, have constituted a greater loss to the Negro than to other groups in the population.

Despite current difficulties, further progress is certainly possible. But it will not come automatically. It will result from continued struggle on the part of the Negro people, supported by whites who are willing to join them. Much will depend upon the efforts of the President and other federal officials to enforce the Civil Rights Act and upon Court decisions. (Extremely heartening is the unanimous decision of the Supreme Court on April 20, 1971, on desegregation of the Charlotte-Mecklenburg County, North Carolina, school system. The decision upheld the constitutionality of busing, racial quotas, pairing, and gerrymandering of attendance zones and other devices as a means to "dismantle the dual school systems" of the South.) Of vital importance is the course of the war in Vietnam. An early end to the war would advance the cause of civil rights.

As the world becomes smaller and human interdependence grows greater, as people everywhere begin to demand recognition of their worth and dignity, segregation and discrimination become ever more outworn, to be discarded as the relics of a barbarous age.

SUGGESTED READINGS

ASHMORE, HARRY. *An Epitaph for Dixie*. New York: W. W. Norton & Co., 1958.

CARMICHAEL, STOKELY and HAMILTON, CHARLES. *Black Power: The Politics of Liberation in America*. New York: Vintage Books, 1967.

CLEAVER, ELDRIDGE. *Soul on Ice*. New York: Delta Books, 1968.

DRAPER, THEODORE. *The Rediscovery of Black Nationalism*. New York: Viking Press, 1970.

FONER, PHILIP S. *The Black Panthers Speak*. Philadelphia: J. B. Lippincott Co., 1970.

GOLDEN, HARRY. *Mr. Kennedy and the Negroes*. Cleveland: World Publishing Co., 1964

GREENBERG, JACK. *Race Relations and American Law*. New York: Columbia University Press, 1961.

KONVITZ, MILTON R. *A Century of Civil Rights*. New York: Columbia University Press, 1961.

LOMAX, LOUIS E. *The Negro Revolt*. New York: Harper & Bros., 1962.

MALCOLM X. *The Autobiography of Malcolm X*. New York: Grove Press, 1964.

MILLER, LOREN E *The Petitioners: The Story of the Supreme Court of the United States and the Negro*. New York: Pantheon Books, 1966.

PARSONS, TALCOTT, and CLARK, KENNETH B. *The Negro American*. Boston: Houghton Mifflin Co., 1966.

QUINT, HOWARD H. *Profile in Black and White: A Frank Portrait of South Carolina*. Washington, D.C.: Public Affairs Press, 1958.

ROSS, ARTHUR M., and HILL, HERBERT. *Employment, Race, and Party*. New York: Harcourt, Brace & World, 197.

RUCHAMES, LOUIS. *Race, Jobs and Politics: The Story of FEPC*. New York: Columbia University Press, 1953.

WOODWARD, C. VANN. *The Strange Career of Jim Crow*. 2d Rev. ed. New York: Oxford University Press, 1966.

WORKMAN, WILLIAM D., JR. *The Case for the South*. New York: Devin-Adair Company, 1960.

DOCUMENT 34.1

The Doctrine of "Separate but Equal" Has No Place*

Reversing the "separate but equal" doctrine enunciated in *Plessy* v. *Ferguson* (1896), the Supreme Court, in 1954, established the principle that segregation in public education is unconstitutional. Defenders of white supremacy criticized the decision on the grounds that (1) it constituted an unwarranted interference with states' rights and (2) the court depended upon sociological data rather than upon legal precedent.

WARREN, C.J.: These cases come to us from the States of Kansas, South Carolina, Virginia, and Delaware. They are premised on different facts and different local conditions, but a common legal question justifies their consideration together in this consolidated opinion.

In each of the cases, minors of the Negro race, through their legal representatives, seek the aid of the courts in obtaining admission to the public schools of their community on a nonsegregated basis. In each instance, they had been denied admission to schools attended by white children under laws requiring or permitting segregation according to race. This segregation was alleged to deprive the plaintiffs of the equal protection of the

---

*Source: *Brown* v. *Board of Education Topeka*, 347 U.S. 483 (1954); 349 U.S. 294 (1955

laws under the Fourteenth Amendment. In each of the cases other than the Delaware case, a three-judge federal district court denied relief to the plaintiffs on the so-called "separate but equal" doctrine announced by this Court in *Plessy* v. *Ferguson*. . . . Under that doctrine, equality of treatment is accorded when the races are provided substantially equal facilities, even though these facilities be separate. In the Delaware case, the Supreme Court of Delaware adhered to that doctrine, but ordered that the plaintiffs be admitted to the white schools because of their superiority to the Negro schools.

The plaintiffs contend that segregated public schools are not "equal" and cannot be made "equal," and that hence they are deprived of the equal protection of the laws. Because of the obvious importance of the question presented, the Court took jurisdiction. Argument was heard in the 1952 Term, and reargument was heard this Term on certain questions propounded by the Court.

Reargument was largely devoted to the circumstances surrounding the adoption of the Fourteenth Amendment in 1868. It covered exhaustively consideration of the Amendment in Congress, ratification by the states, then existing practices in racial segregation, and the views of proponents and opponents of the Amendment. This discussion and our own investigation convince us that, although these sources cast some light, it is not enough to resolve the problem with which we are faced. At best, they are inconclusive. The most avid proponents of the post-War Amendments undoubtedly intended them to remove all legal distinctions among "all persons born or naturalized in the United States." Their opponents, just as certainly, were antagonistic to both the letter and the spirit of the Amendments and wished them to have the most limited effect. What others in Congress and the state legislature had in mind cannot be determined with any degree of certainty.

An additional reason for the inconclusive nature of the Amendment's history, with respect to segregated schools, is the status of public education at that time. In the South, the movement toward free common schools, supported by general taxation, had not yet taken hold. Education of white children was largely in the hands of private groups. Education of Negroes was almost nonexistent, and practically all of the race were illiterate. In fact, any education of Negroes was forbidden by law in some states. Today, in contrast, many Negroes have achieved outstanding success in the arts and sciences as well as in the business and professional world. It is true that public education had already advanced further in the North, but the effect of the Amendment on Northern States was generally ignored in the congressional debates. Even in the North, the conditions of public education did not approximate those existing today. The curriculum was usually rudimentary; ungraded schools were common in rural areas; the school term was but three months a year in many states; and compulsory school attendance was virtually unknown. As a consequence, it is not surprising that there should be so little in the history of the Fourteenth Amendment relating to its intended effect on public education.

In the first cases in this Court construing the Fourteenth Amendment, decided shortly after its adoption, the Court interpreted it as proscribing all state-imposed discriminations against the Negro race. The doctrine of "separate but equal" did not make its appearance in this Court until 1896 in the case of *Plessy* v. *Ferguson* . . . involving not education but transportation. American courts have since labored with the doctrine for over half a century. In this Court, there have been six cases involving the "separate but equal" doctrine in the field of public education. In *Cumming* v. *County Board of Education* . . . [1899], and *Gong Lum* v. *Rice* . . . [1927], the validity of the doctrine itself was not challenged. In more recent cases, all on the graduate school level, inequality was found in that specific benefits enjoyed by white students were denied to Negro students of the same educational qualifications.... [Gaines, Sipuel, Sweatt, McLaurin.] In none of these cases was it necessary to reexamine the doctrine to grant relief to the Negro plaintiff. And in *Sweatt* v. *Painter* ..., the Court expressly reserved decision on the questions whether *Plessy* v. *Ferguson* should be held inapplicable to public education.

In the instant cases, that question is directly presented. Here, unlike *Sweatt* v. *Painter*, there are findings below that the Negro and white schools involved have been equalized, or are being equalized, with respect to buildings, curricula, qualifications and salaries of teachers, and other "tangible" factors. Our decision, therefore, cannot turn on merely a comparison of these tangible factors in the Negro and white schools involved in each of the cases. We must look instead to the effect of segregation itself on public education.

In approaching this problem, we cannot turn the clock back to 1868 when the Amendment was adopted, or even to 1896 when *Plessy* v. *Ferguson* was written. We must consider public education in the light of its full development and its present place in American life throughout the Nation. Only in this way can it be determined if segregation in public schools deprives these plaintiffs of the equal protection of the laws.

Today, education is perhaps the most important function of state and local governments. Compulsory school attendance laws and the great expenditures for education both demonstrate our recognition of the importance of education to our democratic society. It is required in the performance of our most basic public responsibilities, even service in the armed forces. It is the very foundation of good citizenship. Today it is a principal instrument in awakening the child to cultural values, in preparing him for later professional training, and in helping him to adjust normally to his environment. In these days, it is doubtful that any child may reasonably be expected to succeed in life if he is denied the opportunity of an education. Such an opportunity, where the state has undertaken to provide it, is a right which must be made available to all on equal terms.

We come then to the question presented. Does segregation of children in public schools solely on the basis of race, even though the physical facilities and other "tangible" factors may be equal, deprive the children of the minority group of equal educational opportunities? We believe that it does.

In *Sweatt* v. *Painter*, ... in finding that a segregated law school for Negroes could not provide them equal educational opportunities, this Court relied in large part on "those qualities which are incapable of objective measurement but which make for greatness in a law school." In *McLaurin* v. *Oklahoma State Regents*, ... the Court, in requiring that a Negro admitted to a white graduate school be treated like all other students, again resorted to intangible considerations: "... his ability to study, to engage in discussions and exchange views with other students, and, in general, to learn his profession." Such considerations apply with added force to children in grade and high schools. To separate them from others of similar age and qualifications solely because of their race generates a feeling of inferiority as to their status in the community that may affect their hearts and minds in a way unlikely ever to be undone. The effect of this separation on their educational opportunities was well stated by a finding in the Kansas case by a court which nevertheless felt compelled to rule against the Negro plaintiffs:

Segregation of white and colored children in public schools has a detrimental effect upon the colored children. The impact is greater when it has the sanction of the law; for the policy of separating the races is usually in terpreted as denoting the inferiority of the Negro group. A sense of inferiority affects the motivation of a child to learn. Segregation with the sanction of law, therefore, has a tendency to retard the educational and mental development of Negro children and to deprive them of some of the benefits they would receive in a racially integrated school system.

Whatever may have been the extent of psychological knowledge at the time of *Plessy* v. *Ferguson,* this finding is amply supported by modern authority. Any language in *Plessy* v. *Ferguson* contrary to this finding is rejected.

We conclude that in the field of public education the doctrine of "separate but equal" has no place. Separate educational facilities are inherently unequal. Therefore, we hold that the plaintiffs and others similarly situated for whom the actions have been brought are, by reason of the segregation complained of, deprived of the equal protection of the laws guaranteed by the Fourteenth Amendment. This disposition makes unnecessary any discussion whether such segregation also violates the Due Process Clause of the Fourteenth Amendment.

Because these are class actions, because of the wide applicability of this decision, and because of the great variety of local conditions, the formulation of decrees in these cases presents problems of considerable complexity. On reargument, the consideration of appropriate relief was necessarily subordinated to the primary question—the constitutionality of segregation in public education. We have now announced that such segregation is a denial of the equal protection of the laws. In order that we may have the full assistance of the parties in formulating decrees, the cases will be restored to the docket, and the parties are requested to present further argument on Questions 4 and 5 previously propounded by the Court for the reargument this Term. The Attorney General of the United States is again invited to participate. The Attorneys General of the states requiring or permitting segregation

in public education will also be permitted to appear as *amici curiae* upon request to do so by September 15, 1954, and submission of briefs by October 1, 1954.

It is so ordered.

. . . . .

Mr. Chief Justice Warren delivered the opinion of the Court.

These cases were decided on May 17, 1954. The opinions of that date, declaring the fundamental principle that racial discrimination in public education is unconstitutional, are incorporated herein by reference. All provisions of federal, state, or local law requiring or permitting such discrimination must yield to this principle. There remains for consideration the manner in which relief is to be accorded.

Because these cases arose under different local conditions and their disposition will involve a variety of local problems, we requested further argument on the question of relief. In view of the nationwide importance of the decision, we invited the Attorney General of the United States and the Attorneys General of all states requiring or permitting racial discrimination in public education to present their views on that question. The parties, the United States, and the States of Florida, North Carolina, Arkansas, Oklahoma, Maryland, and Texas filed briefs and participated in the oral argument.

These presentations were informative and helpful to the Court in its consideration of the complexities arising from the transition to a system of public education freed of racial discrimination. The presentations also demonstrated that substantial steps to eliminate racial discrimination in public schools have already been taken, not only in some of the communities in which these cases arose, but in some of the states appearing as *amici curiae*, and in other states as well. Substantial progress has been made in the District of Columbia and in the communities in Kansas and Delaware involved in this litigation. The defendants in the cases coming to us from

South Carolina and Virginia are awaiting the decision of this Court concerning relief.

Full implementation of these constitutional principles may require solution of varied local school problems. School authorities have the primary responsibility for elucidating, assessing, and solving these problems; courts will have to consider whether the action of school authorities constitutes good faith implementation of the governing constitutional principles. Because of their proximity to local conditions and the possible need for further hearings, the courts which originally heard these cases can best perform this judicial appraisal. Accordingly, we believe it appropriate to remand the cases to those courts.

In fashioning and effectuating the decrees, the courts will be guided by equitable principles. Traditionally, equity has been characterized by a practical flexibility in shaping its remedies and by a facility for adjusting and reconciling public and private needs. These cases call for the exercise of these traditional attributes of equity power. At stake is the personal interest of the plaintiffs in admission to public schools as soon as practicable on a nondiscriminatory basis. To effectuate this interest may call for elimination of a variety of obstacles in making the transition to school systems operated in accordance with the constitutional principles set forth in our May 17, 1954, decision. Courts of equity may properly take into account the public interest in the elimination of such obstacles in a systematic and effective manner. But it should go without saying that the vitality of these constitutional principles cannot be allowed to yield simply because of disagreement with them.

While giving weight to these public and private considerations, the courts will require that the defendants make a prompt and reasonable start toward full compliance with our May 17, 1954, ruling. Once such a start has been made, the courts may find that additional time is necessary to carry out the ruling in an effective manner. The burden rests upon the defendants to establish that such time is necessary in the public interest and is consistent with good faith compliance at the earliest practicable date. To that end, the courts may consider problems related to administration, arising from the physical condition of the school plant, the school transportation system, personnel, revision of school districts and attendance areas into compact units to achieve a system of determining admission to the public schools on a nonracial basis, and revision of local laws and regulations which may be necessary in solving the foregoing problems. They will also consider the adequacy of any plans the defendants may propose to meet those problems and to effectuate a transition to a racially nondiscriminatory school system. During this period of transition, the courts will retain jurisdiction of these cases.

The judgments below, except that in the Delaware case, are accordingly reversed and remanded to the District Courts to take such proceedings and enter such orders and decrees consistent with this opinion as are necessary and proper to admit to public schools on a racially nondiscriminatory basis with all deliberate speed the parties to these cases. The judgment in the Delaware case—ordering the immediate admission of the plaintiffs to schools previously attended only by white children—is affirmed on the basis of the principles stated in our May 17, 1954, opinion, but the case is remanded to the Supreme Court of Delaware for such further proceedings as that court may deem necessary in light of this opinion.

It is so ordered.

DOCUMENT 34.2
Separate and Be Saved!*

The Black Muslim movement, although in existence for several years, has only recently gained national attention. Its program and objectives, as enunciated by its leader and theoretician, Elijah Muhammad, born Elijah Poole, a former Baptist clergyman, stand in open opposition to those of other Negro organizations.

The unwillingness of the slaves to leave their masters is due to their great love for the slave masters. If America is unwilling to grant her 20,000,000 ex-slaves freedom to go for self today, it is the same unwillingness of white America's forefathers in dealing with our parents less than 100 years ago.

During the time of the Emancipation Proclamation, we were scattered to the winds without any knowledge or ability to undertake the responsibilities of a half freedom. Our fathers, lacking the skills and the training of how to provide for themselves, were forced to remain with the masters in order to receive even the barest necessities of life.

Our former slave masters knowing of our dependence upon them, maliciously and hatefully adopted attitudes and social and educational systems that have deprived us of the opportunity to become free and independent right up to the present day.

But we, the black slaves, of this soil of bondage were not deprived of the freedom to fight in America's wars, but are deprived of the right to fight for our own freedom.

The opposition met by our forefathers who fought for their freedom is a chilled memory that history will not forget. The black people are given the freedom to give their lives for the American Cause of tyranny, but are not free to fight for their own freedom and independence.

*Source: *Muhammad Speaks*, August 2, 1963, pp. 1,9.

As long as my people are the blind lovers of their enemies, they will seek to forever return to the bosom of their masters in no better status or position than that of a slave.

Our foreparents' desire was to see us free indeed and not only are some of our people willing to betray those of our blood and kindred who died before us, but are now willing to betray the fruition of freedom to our generations to come. Allah will help us to get this freedom, justice, and equality and some of this earth that we can call our own.

．　．　．　．　．

We must have some of this earth that we can call our own! We and our fathers have been robbed of all that we originally possessed. And now we are left without anything to go for self like wealth and modern instruments to start a civilization as you have; though we helped you to get what you have. We, now, must have justice and some of this earth and its wealth that we can call our own.

HURRY AND JOIN UNTO YOUR OWN KIND! THE TIME OF THIS WORLD IS NOW AT HAND.

DOCUMENT 34.3
Can Negroes Afford to Be Pacifists?*

Robert F. Williams, a militant ex-marine from Monroe, North Carolina, was removed from his post as local NAACP leader by the national organization because of his alleged advocacy of violent Negro retaliation to white violence.

The State of Virginia is in open defiance of federal authority. States like my native state of North Carolina are submitting to token integration and openly

*Source: Robert F. Williams, "Can Negroes Afford to Be Pacifists?" *Liberation*, September 1959, pp. 4–7.

boasting that this is the solution to circumvention of the Supreme Court decisions. The officials of this state brazenly slap themselves on the back for being successful in depriving great numbers of their colored citizens of the rights of first-class citizenship. Yes, after having such great short-lived hope, I have become disillusioned about the prospect of a just, democratic-minded government motivated by politicians with high moral standards enforcing the Fourteenth Amendment without the pressure of expediency.

News Blackout

Since my release from the Marine Corps I could cite many cases of unprovoked violence that have been visited upon my people. Some, like the Emmett Till case, the Asbury Howard case and the Mack Parker incident, have been widely publicized. There are more, many many more, occurring daily in the South that never come to light of the press because of a news blackout sponsored by local racist officials.

Laws serve to deter crime and to protect the weak from the strong in civilized society. When there is a breakdown of law and the right of equal protection by constituted authority, where is the force of deterrent? It is the nature of people to respect law when it is just and strong. Only highly civilized and moral individuals respect the rights of others. The low-mentality bigots of the South have shown a wanton disregard for the well-being and rights of their fellowmen of color, but there is one thing that even the most savage beast respects, and that is force. Soft, polished words whispered into the ears of a brute make him all the more confused and rebellious against a society that is more than he can understand or feel secure in. The Southern brute respects only force. Nonviolence is a very potent weapon when the opponent is civilized, but nonviolence is no match or repellent for a sadist. I have great respect for the pacifist, that is, for the pure pacifist. I

think a pure pacifist is one who resents violence against nations as well as individuals and is courageous enough to speak out against jingoistic governments (including his own) without an air of self-righteousness and pious moral individuality. I am not a pacifist and I am sure that I may safely say that most of my people are not. Passive resistance is a powerful weapon in gaining concessions from oppressors, but I venture to say that if Mack Parker had had an automatic shotgun at his disposal, he could have served as a great deterrent against lynching.

"Turn-the-Other-Cheekism"

Rev. Martin Luther King is a great and successful leader of our race. The Montgomery bus boycott was a great victory for American democracy. However, most people have confused the issues facing the race. In Montgomery the issue was a matter of struggle for human dignity. Nonviolence is made to order for that type of conflict. While praising the actions of those courageous Negroes who participated in the Montgomery affair, we must not allow the complete aspects of the Negro struggle throughout the South to be taken out of their proper perspective. In a great many localities in the South Negroes are faced with the necessity of combating savage violence. The struggle is for mere existence. The Negro is in a position of begging for life. There is no lawful deterrent against those who would do him violence. An open declaration of nonviolence, or turn-the-other-cheekism is an invitation that the white racist brutes will certainly honor by brutal attack on cringing, submissive Negroes. It is time for the Negro in the South to reappraise his method of dealing with his ruthless oppressor.

In 1957 the Klan moved into Monroe and Union County. In the beginning we did not notice them much. Their numbers steadily increased to the point wherein the local press reported as many as seventy-five hundred racists massed at one rally They became so brazen that mile-long mo torcades started invading the Negro community. These hooded thugs fired pistols from car windows, screamed, and incessantly blew their automobile horns. On one occasion they caught a Negro woman on the street and tried to force her to dance for them at gun point. She escaped into the night, screaming and hysterical. They forced a Negro merchant to close down his business on direct orders from the Klan. Drivers of cars tried to run Negroes down when seen walking on the streets at night. Negro women were struck with missiles thrown from passing vehicles. Lawlessness was rampant. A Negro doctor was framed to jail on a charge of performing an abortion on a white woman. This doctor, who was vice-president of the N.A.A.C.P., was placed in a lonely cell in the basement of a jail, although men prisoners are usually confined upstairs. A crowd of white men started congregating around the jail. It is common knowledge that a lynching was averted. We have had the usual threats of the Klan here, but instead of cowing, we organized an armed guard and set up a defense force around the doctor's house. On one occasion, we had to exchange gunfire with the Klan. Each time the Klan came on a raid they were led by police cars. We appealed to the President of the United States to have the Justice Department investigate the police. We appealed to Governor Luther Hodges. All our appeals to constituted law were in vain. Governor Hodges, in an underhanded way, defended the Klan. He publicly made a statement, to the press, that I had exaggerated Klan activity in Union County—despite the fact that they were operating openly and had gone so far as to build a Klan clubhouse and advertise meetings in the local press and on the radio.

·   ·   ·   ·   ·

The Screams of the Innocent

I think there is enough latitude in the struggle for Negro liberation for the acceptance of diverse tactics and philosophies. There is need for pacifists and non-pacifists. I think each freedom fighter must unselfishly contribute what he has to offer. I have been a soldier and a Marine. I have been trained in the way of violence. I have been trained to defend myself. Self-defense to a Marine is a reflex action. People like Rev. Martin Luther King have been trained for the pulpit. I think they would be as out of place in a conflict that demanded real violent action as I would be in a pulpit praying for an indifferent God to come down from Heaven and rescue a screaming Mack Parker or Emmett Till from an ungodly howling mob. I believe if we are going to pray, we ought to pass the ammunition while we pray. If we are too pious to kill in our own self-defense, how can we have the heart to ask a Holy God to come down to this violent fray and smite down our enemies?

As a race, we have been praying for three hundred years. The N.A.A.C.P. boasts that it has fought against lynching for fifty years. A fifty-year fight without victory is not impressive to me. An unwritten anti-lynch law was initiated overnight in Monroe. It is strange that so-called Negro leaders have never stopped to think why a simple thing like an anti-lynch law in a supposedly democratic nation is next to impossible to get passed. Surely every citizen in a republic is entitled not to be lynched. To seek an anti-lynch law in the present situation is to seek charity. Individuals and governments are more inclined to do things that promote the general welfare and well-being of the populace. A prejudiced government and a prejudiced people are not going to throw a shield of protection around the very people in the South on whom they vent pent-up hatreds as scapegoats. When white people in the South start needing such a law, we will not even have to wait fifty days to get it.

·   ·   ·   ·   ·

King Cashes in on War

It is obvious that the Negro leadership is caught in a terrible dilemma. It is trying to appease both white liberals who want to see Negro liberation given to us in eye-dropper doses and the Negro masses, who are growing impatient and restive under brutal oppression. There is a new Negro coming into manhood on the American scene and an indifferent government must take cognizance of this fact. The Negro is becoming more militant, and pacifism will never be accepted wholeheartedly by the masses of Negroes so long as violence is rampant in Dixie. Even Negroes like King who profess to be pacifists are not pure pacifists and at times speak proudly of the Negro's role of violence in this violent nation's wars. In a speech at the N.A.A.C.P. convention, he said, "In spite of all of our oppression, we have never turned to a foreign ideology to solve our problems. Communism has never invaded our ranks. And now we are simply saying we want our freedom, we have stood with you in every crisis. For you, America, our sons died in the trenches of France, in the foxholes of Germany, on the beachheads of Italy and on the islands of Japan. And now, America, we are simply asking you to guarantee our freedom." King may not be willing to partake in expeditions of violence, but he has no compunction about cashing in on the spoils of war. There are too many Negro leaders who are afraid to talk violence against the violent racist and are too weak-kneed to protest the war-mongering of the atom-crazed politicians of Washington.

Some Negro leaders have cautioned me that if Negroes fight back, the racist will have cause to exterminate the race. How asinine can one get? This government is in no position to allow mass violence to erupt, let alone allow twenty million Negroes to be exterminated. I am not half so worried about being exterminated as I am about my children's growing up under oppression and being mentally twisted out of human proportions.

We live in perilous times in America, and especially in the South. Segregation is an expensive commodity, but liberty and democracy too, have their price. So often the purchase check of democracy must be signed in blood. Someone must be willing to pay the price, despite the scoffs from the Uncle Toms. I am told that patience is commendable and that we must never tire of waiting, yet it is instilled at an early age that men who violently and swiftly rise to oppose tyranny are virtuous examples to emulate. I have been taught by my government to fight, and if I find it necessary I shall do just that. All Negroes must learn to fight back, for nowhere in the annals of history does the record show a people delivered from bondage by patience alone.

DOCUMENT 34.4

A Plea for Nonviolent Resistance*

One of those who replied to Williams' article was the late Reverend Martin Luther King, Jr., who was generally accepted as the leading national spokesman for Negro nonviolent mass action.

Paradoxically, the struggle for civil rights has reached a stage of profound crisis, although its outward aspect is distinctly less turbulent and victories of token integration have been won in the hard-resistance areas of Virginia and Arkansas.

The crisis has its origin in a decision rendered by the Supreme Court more than a year ago which upheld the pupil placement law. Though little noticed then, this decision fundamentally weakened the historic 1954 ruling of the Court. It is imperceptibly becoming the basis of a *de facto* compromise between the powerful contending forces.

The 1954 decision required for effective implementation resolute Federal action

*Source: Martin Luther King, Jr., "The Social Organization of Nonviolence," *Liberation*, October 1959, pp. 5–6.

supported by mass action to undergird all necessary changes. It is obvious that Federal action by the legislative and executive branches was half-hearted and inadequate. The activity of Negro forces, while heroic in some instances, and impressive in other sporadic situations, lacked consistency and militancy sufficient to fill the void left by government default. The segregationists were swift to seize these advantages, and unrestrained by moral or social conscience, defied the law boldly and brazenly.

The net effect of this social equation has led to the present situation, which is without clearcut victory for either side. Token integration is a developing pattern. This type of integration is merely an affirmation of a principle without the substance of change.

It is, like the Supreme Court decision, a pronouncement of justice, but by itself does not insure that the millions of Negro children will be educated in conditions of equality. This is not to say that it is without value. It has substantial importance. However, it fundamentally changes the outlook of the whole movement, for it raises the prospect of long, slow change without a predictable end. As we have seen in Northern cities, token integration has become a pattern in many communities and remained frozen, even though environmental attitudes are substantially less hostile to full integration than in the South.

Three Views of Violence

This then is the danger. Full integration can easily become a distant or mythical goal—major integration may be long postponed, and in the quest for social calm a compromise firmly implanted in which the real goals are merely token integration for a long period to come.

The Negro was the tragic victim of another compromise in 1878, when his full equality was bargained away by the Federal Government and a condition somewhat above slave status but short of genuine citizenship became his social and political existence for nearly a century.

There is reason to believe that the Negro of 1959 will not accept supinely any such compromises in the contemporary struggle for integration. His struggle will continue, but the obstacles will determine its specific nature. It is axiomatic in social life that the imposition of frustration leads to two kinds of reactions. One is the development of a wholesome social organization to resist with effective, firm measures any efforts to impede progress. The other is a confused, anger-motivated drive to strike back violently, to inflict damage. Primarily, it seeks to cause injury to retaliate for wrongful suffering. Secondarily, it seeks real progress. It is punitive—not radical or constructive.

The current calls for violence have their roots in this latter tendency. Here one must be clear that there are three different views on the subject of violence. One is the approach of pure nonviolence, which cannot readily or easily attract large masses, for it requires extraordinary discipline and courage. The second is violence exercised in self-defense, which all societies, from the most primitive to the most cultured and civilized, accept as moral and legal. The principle of self-defense, even involving weapons and bloodshed, has never been condemned, even by Gandhi, who sanctioned it for those unable to master pure nonviolence. The third is the advocacy of violence as a tool of advancement, organized as in warfare, deliberately and consciously. To this tendency many Negroes are being tempted today. There are incalculable perils in this approach. It is not the danger or sacrifice of physical being which is primary, though it cannot be contemplated without a sense of deep concern for human life. The greatest danger is that it will fail to attract Negroes to a real collective struggle, and will confuse the large uncommitted middle group, which as yet has not supported either side. Further, it will mislead Negroes into the belief that this is the only path and place them as a minority in a position where they confront a far larger adversary than it is possible to defeat in this form of combat. When the Negro uses force in self-defense he does not forfeit support—he may even win it, by the courage and self-respect it reflects. When he seeks to initiate violence he provokes questions about the necessity for it, and inevitably is blamed for its consequences. It is unfortunately true that however the Negro acts, his struggle will not be free of violence initiated by his enemies, and he will need ample courage and willingness to sacrifice to defeat this manifestation of violence. But if he seeks it and organizes it, he cannot win. Does this leave the Negro without a positive method to advance? Mr. Robert Williams would have us believe that there is no effective and practical alternative. He argues that we must be cringing and submissive or take up arms. To so place the issue distorts the whole problem. There are other meaningful alternatives.

The Negro people can organize socially to initiate many forms of struggle which can drive their enemies back without resort to futile and harmful violence. In the history of the movement for racial advancement, many creative forms have been developed—the mass boycott, sit-down protests and strikes, sit-ins,—refusal to pay fines and bail for unjust arrests— mass marches—mass meetings—prayer pilgrimages, etc. Indeed, in Mr. Williams' own community of Monroe, North Carolina, a striking example of collective community action won a significant victory without use of arms or threats of violence. When the police incarcerated a Negro doctor unjustly, the aroused people of Monroe marched to the police station, crowded into its halls and corridors, and refused to leave until their colleague was released. Unable to arrest everyone, the authorities released the doctor and neither side attempted to unleash violence. This experience was related by the doctor who was the intended victim.

There is more power in socially organized masses on the march than there is in guns in the hands of a few desperate men. Our enemies would prefer to deal with a small armed group rather than with a huge, unarmed but resolute mass of people. However, it is necessary that the mass-action method be persistent and unyielding. Gandhi said the Indian people must "never let them rest," referring to the British. He urged them to keep protesting daily and weekly, in a variety of ways. This method inspired and organized the Indian masses and disorganized and demobilized the British. It educates its myriad participants, socially and morally. All history teaches us that like a turbulent ocean beating great cliffs into fragments of rock, the determined movement of people incessantly demanding their rights always disintegrates the old order.

It is this form of struggle—non-cooperation with evil through mass actions— "never letting them rest"—which offers the more effective road for those who have been tempted and goaded to violence. It needs the bold and the brave because it is not free of danger. It faces the vicious and evil enemies squarely. It requires dedicated people, because it is a backbreaking task to arouse, to organize, and to educate tens of thousands for disciplined, sustained action. From this form of struggle more emerges that is permanent and damaging to the enemy than from a few acts of organized violence.

Our present urgent necessity is to cease our internal fighting and turn outward to the enemy, using every form of mass action yet known—create new forms—and resolve never to let them rest. This is the social lever which will force open the door to freedom. Our powerful weapons are the voices, the feet, and the bodies of dedicated, united people, moving without rest toward a just goal. Greater tyrants than Southern segregationists have been subdued and defeated by this form of struggle. We have not yet used it, and it would be tragic if we spurn it because we have failed to perceive its dynamic strength and power.

CASHING IN ON WAR?

I am reluctant to inject a personal defense against charges by Mr. Williams that I am inconsistent in my struggle against war and too weak-kneed to protest nuclear war. Merely to set the record straight, may I state that repeatedly, in public addresses and in my writings, I have unequivocally declared my hatred for this most colossal of all evils and I have condemned any organizer of war, regardless of his rank or nationality. I have signed numerous statements with other Americans condemning nuclear testing and have authorized publication of my name in advertisements appearing in the largest circulation newspapers in the country, without concern that it was then "unpopular" to so speak out.

DOCUMENT 34.5

Strong Local Government Is the Foundation of Our System*

Alabama Governor George C. Wallace, in an official statement of June 1963, protested "federal coercion" of the state to force the admission of two Negroes into the University of Alabama. He argues here that such coercion is illegal.

As Governor and Chief Magistrate of the State of Alabama, I deem it to be my solemn obligation and duty to stand before you representing the rights and sovereignty of this state and its peoples.

The unwelcomed, unwanted, unwarranted and force-induced intrusion upon the campus of the University of Alabama today of the might of the Central Govern-

*Source: *The New York Times*, June 12, 1963. Copyright by the *The New York Times*; reprinted by permission.

ment offers frightful example of oppression of the rights, privileges and sovereignty of this state by officers of the Federal Government. This intrusion results solely from force, or threat of force, undignified by any reasonable application of the principle of law, reason and justice. It is important that the people of this state and nation understand that this action is in violation of rights reserved to the state by the Constitution of the United States and the Constitution of the State of Alabama. While some few may applaud these acts, millions of Americans will gaze in sorrow upon the situation existing at this great institution of learning.

Only the Congress makes the law of the United States. To this date no statutory authority can be cited to the people of this country which authorizes the Central Government to ignore the sovereignty of this state and attempt to subordinate the rights of Alabama and millions of Americans. There has been no legislative action by Congress justifying this intrusion.

When the Constitution of the United States was enacted, a Government was formed upon the premise that people, as individuals, are endowed with the rights of life, liberty and property, and with the right of local self-government. The people and their local self-governments formed a Central Government and conferred upon it certain stated and limited powers. All other powers were reserved to the states and to the people.

Strong local government is the foundation of our system and must be continually guarded and maintained. The 10th Amendment to the Constitution of the United States reads as follows:

"The powers not relegated to the United States by the Constitution, nor prohibited by it to the states, are reserved to the states respectively, or to the people." This amendment sustains the right of self-determination, and grants the state of Alabama the right to enforce its laws and regulate its internal affairs.

This nation was never meant to be a

unit of one but a united of the many—that is the exact reason our freedom-loving forefathers established the states, so as to divide the rights and powers among the many states, insuring that no central power could gain massive government control.

There can be no submission to the theory that the Central Government is anything but a servant of the people. We are God-fearing people—not Government-fearing people. We practice today the free heritage bequeathed to us by the founding fathers.

I stand here today, as Governor of this sovereign state, and refuse to willingly submit to illegal usurpation of power by the Central Government. I claim today for all the people of the state of Alabama those rights reserved to them under the Constitution of the United States. Among those powers so reserved and claimed is the right of state authority in the operation of the public schools, colleges and universities. My action does not constitute disobedience to legislative and constitutional provisions. It is not defiance for defiance sake, but for the purpose of raising basic and fundamental constitutional questions. My action is a call for strict adherence to the Constitution of the United States as it was written—for a cessation of usurpation and abuses. My action seeks to avoid having state sovereignty sacrificed on the altar of political expediency.

Further, as the Governor of the State of Alabama, I hold the supreme executive power of this state, and it is my duty to see that the laws are faithfully executed. The illegal and unwarranted actions of the Central Government on this day, contrary to the laws, customs and traditions of this state, is calculated to disturb the peace.

I stand before you today in place of thousands of other Alabamians whose presence would have confronted you had I been derelict and neglected to fulfill the responsibilities of my office. It is the right of every citizen, however humble he may be, through his chosen officials of representative government to stand courageously against whatever he believes to be the exercise of power beyond the constitutional rights conferred upon our Federal Government. It is this right which I assert for the people of Alabama by my presence here today.

Again I state—this is the exercise of the heritage of freedom and liberty under the law—coupled with responsible government.

Now, therefore, in consideration of the promises, and in my official capacity as Governor of the State of Alabama, I do hereby make the following solemn proclamation:

Whereas, the Constitution of Alabama vests the supreme executive powers of the state in the Governor as the chief magistrate, and said Constitution requires of the Governor that he take care that the laws be faithfully executed; and,

Whereas, the Constitution of the United States, Amendment 10, reserves to the states respectively or to the people, those powers not delegated to the United States, nor prohibited to the states; and,

Whereas, the operation of the public school system is a power reserved to the State of Alabama under the Constitution of the United States and Amendment 10 thereof; and,

Whereas, it is the duty of the Governor of the State of Alabama to preserve the peace under the circumstances now existing, which power is one reserved to the State of Alabama and the people thereof under the Constitution of the United States and Amendment 10 thereof:

Now, therefore, I, George C. Wallace, as Governor of the State of Alabama, have by my action raised issues between the Central Government and the sovereign State of Alabama, which said issues should be adjudicated in the manner prescribed by the Constitution of the United States and now being mindful of my duties and responsibilities under the Constitution of the United States, the Constitution of the

State of Alabama, and seeking to preserve and maintain the peace and dignity of this state, and the individual freedoms of the citizens thereof, do hereby denounce and forbid this illegal and unwarranted action by the Central Government.

DOCUMENT 34.6

I Have a Dream*

Perhaps nowhere have the aspirations of the American Negro been expressed so eloquently as by the Rev. Martin Luther King, Jr., at the great civil rights rally sponsored by the National Association for the Advancement of Colored People and held in Washinton, D.C., on August 28, 1963.

Now is the time to make the real promises of democracy. Now is the time to rise from the dark and desolate valley of segregation to the sunlit path of racial justice. Now is the time to lift our nation from the quicksands of racial injustice to the solid rock of brotherhood. Now is the time to make justice a reality for all of God's children.

There will be neither rest nor tranquility in America until the Negro is granted his citizenship rights. The whirlwinds of revolt will continue to shake the foundations of our nation until the bright day of justice emerges.

And that is something that I must say to my people who stand on the threshold which leads to the palace of justice. In the process of gaining our rightful place we must not be guilty of wrongful deeds.

Again and again, we must rise to the majestic heights of meeting physical force with soul force. The marvelous new militancy which has engulfed the Negro community must not lead us to a distrust of all white people, for many of our white brothers as evidenced by their presence

*Source: *The New York Times*, August 28, 1963. Copyright by *The New York Times*; reprinted by permission.

here today have come to realize that their destiny is tied up with our destiny!

"NEVER BE SATISFIED"

There are those who are asking the devotees of civil rights, "When will you be satisfied?" We can never be satisfied as long as the Negro is the victim of the unspeakable horrors of police brutality. We can never be satisfied as long as our bodies, heavy with the fatigue of travel, cannot gain lodging in the motels of the highways and the hotels of the cities.

We can never be satisfied as long as our children are stripped of their selfhood and robbed of their dignity by signs stating "for whites only." We cannot be satisfied as long as the Negro in Mississippi cannot vote and the Negro in New York believes he has nothing for which to vote.

No, we are not satisfied and we will not be satisfied until justice rolls down like water and righteousness like a mighty stream.

Now, I am not unmindful that some of you have come here out of great trials and tribulations. Some of you have come fresh from narrow jail cells.

Continue to work with the faith that honor in suffering is redemptive. Go back to Mississippi, go back to Alabama, go back to South Carolina, go back to Georgia, go back to Louisiana, go back to the slums and ghettoes of our Northern cities, knowing that somehow this situation can and will be changed. Let us not wallow in the valley of despair.

Now, I say to you today, my friends, so even though we face the difficulties of today and tomorrow, I still have a dream. It is a dream deeply rooted in the American dream. I have a dream that one day this nation will rise up and live out the true meaning of its creed: "We hold these truths to be self-evident, that all men are created equal."

I have a dream that one day on the red hills of Georgia the sons of former slaveowners and slaves will be able to sit down together at the table of brotherhood.

I have a dream that one day even the state of Mississippi, a state sweltering with the people's injustice, sweltering with the heat of oppression, will be transformed into an oasis of freedom and justice.

I have a dream that my four little children will one day live in a nation where they will not be judged by the color of their skin, but by the content of their character.

This is our home. This is the faith that I go back to the South with—with this faith we will be able to hew out of the mountain of despair a stone of hope.

DOCUMENT 34.7

Position Paper on "Black Power"*

Stokely Carmichael and the Student Nonviolent Coordinating Committee are the two names most closely associated with the philosophy of "Black Power." In the following essay, which consists of excerpts from a position paper written in 1966 by members of SNCC, with Carmichael playing a leading part in its formulation, the philosophy of Black Power receives one of its earliest formulations.

CHICAGO, Aug. 4—*Following are excerpts from a position paper, written by members of the Student Nonviolent Coordinating Committee, that serves as the basis for the organization's "black power" philosophy:*

The myth that the Negro is somehow incapable of liberating himself, is lazy, etc., came out of the American experience. In the books that children read, whites are always "good" (good symbols are white), blacks are "evil" or seen as savages in movies, their language is referred to as a

*Source: *The New York Times,* August 5, 1966, p. 10. © 1966 by The New York Times Company; reprinted by permission.

"dialect," and black people in this country are supposedly descended from savages.

Any white person who comes into the movement has these concepts in his mind about black people if only subconsciously. He cannot escape them because the whole society has geared his subconscious in that direction.

Miss America coming from Mississippi has a chance to represent all of America, but a black person from either Mississippi or New York will never represent America. So that white people coming into the movement cannot relate to the black experience, cannot relate to the word "black," cannot relate to the "nitty gritty," cannot relate to the experience that brought such a word into being, cannot relate to chitterlings, hog's head cheese, pig feet, hamhocks, and cannot relate to slavery, because these things are not a part of their experience. They also cannot relate to the black religious experience, nor to the black church unless, of course, this church has taken on white manifestations.

STEREOTYPE REINFORCED

Negroes in this country have never been allowed to organize themselves because of white interference. As a result of this, the stereotype has been reinforced that blacks cannot organize themselves. The white psychology that blacks have to be watched, also reinforces this stereotype. Blacks, in fact, feel intimidated by the presence of whites, because of their knowledge of the power that whites have over their lives. One white person can come into a meeting of black people and change the complexion of that meeting, whereas one black person would not change the complexion of that meeting unless he was an obvious Uncle Tom. People would immediately start talking about "brotherhood," "love," etc.; race would not be discussed.

If people must express themselves freely, there has to be a climate in which they can do this. If blacks feel intimidated by whites, then they are not liable to vent the rage that they feel about whites in the presence of whites—especially not the black people whom we are trying to organize; i.e., the broad masses of black people. A climate has to be created whereby blacks can express themselves. The reason that whites must be excluded is not that one is anti-white, but because the efforts that one is trying to achieve cannot succeed because whites have an intimidating effect. Offtimes the intimidating effect is in direct proportion to the amount of degradation that black people have suffered at the hands of white people.

Role in Movement

It must be offered that white people who desire change in this country should go where that problem (of racism) is most manifest. The problem is not in the black community. The white people should go into white communities where the whites have created power for the express [purpose] of denying blacks human dignity had self-determination. Whites who come into the black community with ideas of change seem to want to absolve the power structure of its responsibility of what it is doing, and saying that change can come only through black unity, which is only the worst kind of paternalism. This is not to say that whites have not had an important role in the movement. In the case of Mississippi, their role was very key in that they helped give blacks the right to organize, but that role is now over, and it should be.

People now have the right to picket, the right to give out leaflets, the right to vote, the right to demonstrate, the right to print.

These things which revolve around the right to organize have been accomplished mainly because of the entrance of white people into Mississippi, in the summer of '64. Since these goals have now been accomplished, their (whites') role in the movement has now ended. What does it mean if black people, once having the

right to organize, are not allowed to organize themselves? It means that blacks' ideas about inferiority are being reinforced. Shouldn't people be able to organize themselves? Blacks should be given this right. Further (white participation) means in the eyes of the black community that whites are the "brains," behind the movement and blacks cannot function without whites. This only serves to perpetuate existing attitudes within the existing society, i.e., blacks are "dumb," unable to take care of business," etc. Whites are "smart," the "brains" behind everything.

How do blacks relate to other blacks as such? How do we react to Willie Mays as against Mickey Mantle? What is our response to Mays hitting a home run against Mantle performing the same deed? One has to come to the conclusion that it is because of black participation in baseball Negroes still identify with the Dodgers because of Jackie Robinson's efforts with the Dodgers. Negroes would instinctively champion all-black teams if they opposed all-white or predominantly white teams. The same principle operates for the movement as it does for baseball: a mystique must be created whereby Negroes can identify with the movement.

Thus an all-black project is needed in order for the people to free themselves. This has to exist from the beginning. This relates to what can be called "coalition politics." There is no doubt in our minds that some whites are just as disgusted with this system as we are. But it is meaningless to talk about coalition if there is no one to align ourselves with, because of the lack of organization in the white communities. There can be no talk of "hooking up" unless black people organize blacks and white people organize whites. If these conditions are met then perhaps at some later date—and if we are going in the same direction—talks about exchange of personnel, coalition, and other meaningful alliances can be discussed.

In the beginning of the movement, we had fallen into a trap whereby we thought that our problems revolved around the right to eat at certain lunch counters or the right to vote, or to organize our communities. We have seen, however, that the problem is much deeper. The problem of this country, as we had seen it, concerned all blacks and all whites (and therefore) if decisions were left to the young people, then solutions would be arrived at. But this negates the history of black people and whites. We have dealt stringently with the problems of "Uncle Tom," but we have not yet gotten around to Simon Legree. We must ask ourselves who is the real villain? Uncle Tom or Simon Legree? Everybody knows Uncle Tom but who knows Simon Legree?

So what we have now (in S.N.C.C.) is a closed society. A clique. Black people cannot relate to S.N.C.C., because of its unrealistic, nonracial atmosphere; denying their experiences of America as a racist society. In contrast, S.C.L.C. [the Rev. Dr. Martin Luther King Jr.'s Southern Christian Leadership Conference] has a staff that at least maintains a black facade. The front office is virtually all-black, but nobody accuses S.C.L.C. of being racist.

If we are to proceed toward true liberation, we must cut ourselves off from white people. We must form our own institutions, credit unions, coops, political parties, write our own histories.

To proceed further, let us make some comparisons between the Black Movement of the (early) 1900s and the movement of the 1960s—the N.A.A.C.P. [the National Association for the Advancement of Colored People] with S.N.C.C. Whites subverted the Niagara movement [the forerunner of the N.A.A.C.P.] which, at the outset, was an all-black movement. The name of the new organization was also very revealing, in that it presupposed blacks have to be advanced to the level of whites. We are now aware that the N.A.A.C.P. has grown reactionary, is controlled by the black power structure itself, and stands as one of the main roadblocks

to black freedom. S.N.C.C., by allowing the whites to remain in the organization, can have its efforts subverted in the same manner, i.e., through having them play important roles such as community organizers, etc. Indigenous leadership cannot be built with whites in the positions they now hold.

These facts do not mean that whites cannot help. They can participate on a voluntary basis. We can contract work out to them, but in no way can they participate on a policy-making level.

The charge may be made that we are "racists," but whites who are sensitive to our problems will realize that we must determine our own destiny.

To Find a Solution

In an attempt to find a solution to our dilemma, we propose that our organization (S.N.C.C.) should be black-staffed, black-controlled, and black-financed. We do not want to fall into a similar dilemma that other civil rights organizations have fallen. If we continue to rely upon white financial support we will find ourselves entwined in the tentacles of the white power complex that controls this country. It is also important that a black organization (devoid of cultism) be projected to our people so that it can be demonstrated that such organizations are viable.

More and more we see black people in this country being used as a tool of the white liberal establishment. Liberal whites have not begun to address themselves to the real problem of black people in this country; witness this bewilderment, fear and anxiety when nationalism is mentioned concerning black people. An analysis of their (white liberal) reaction to the word alone (nationalism) reveals a very meaningful attitude of whites of any ideological persuasion toward blacks in this country. It means previous solutions to black problems in this country have been made in the interests of those whites dealing with these problems and not in the best interests of black people in this country. Whites can only subvert our true search and struggle for self-determination, self-identification, and liberation in this country. Re-evaluation of the white and black roles must NOW take place so that whites no longer designate roles that black people play but rather black people define white people's roles.

Too long have we allowed white people to interpret the importance and meaning of the cultural aspects of our society. We have allowed them to tell us what was good about our Afro-American music, art and literature. How many black critics do we have on the "jazz" scene? How can a white person who is not a part of the black psyche (except in the oppressor's role) interpret the meaning of the blues to us who are manifestations of the songs themselves?

It must also be pointed out that on whatever level of contact that blacks and whites come together, that meeting or confrontation is not on the level of the blacks but always on the level of the whites. This only means that our everyday contact with whites is a reinforcement of the myth of white supremacy. Whites are the ones who must try to raise themselves to our humanistic level. We are not, after all, the ones who are responsible for a genocidal war in Vietnam; we are not the ones who are responsible for neocolonialism in Africa and Latin America; we are not the ones who held a people in animalistic bondage over 400 years. We reject the American dream as defined by white people and must work to construct an American reality defined by Afro-Americans.

One of the criticisms of white militants and radicals is that when we view the masses of white people we view the over-all reality of America, we view the racism, the bigotry, and the distortion of personality, we view man's inhumanity to man; we view in reality 180 million racists. The sensitive white intellectual and radical who is fighting to bring about change is conscious of this fact, but does not have

the courage to admit this. When he admits this reality, then he must also admit his involvement because he is a part of the collective white America. It is only to the extent that he recognizes this that he will be able to change this reality.

Another concern is how does the white radical view the black community and how does he view the poor white community in terms of organizing. So far, we have found that most white radicals have sought to escape the horrible reality of America by going into the black community and attempting to organize black people while neglecting the organization of their own people's racist communities. How can one clean up someone else's yard when one's own yard is untidy? Again we feel that S.N.C.C. and the civil rights movement in general is in many aspects similar to the anti-colonial situations in the African and Asian countries. We have the whites in the movement corresponding to the white civil servants and missionaries in the colonial countries who have worked with the colonial people for a long period of time and have developed a paternalistic attitude toward them. The reality of the colonial people taking over their own lives and controlling their own destiny must be faced. Having to move aside and letting this natural process of growth and development take place must be faced.

These views should not be equated with outside influence or outside agitation but should be viewed as the natural process of growth and development within a movement; so that the move by the black militants and S.N.C.C. in this direction should be viewed as a turn toward self-determination.

It is very ironic and curious how aware whites in this country can champion anticolonialism in other countries in Africa, Asia, and Latin America, but when black people move toward similar goals of self-determination in this country they are viewed as racists and anti-white by these same progressive whites. In proceeding further, it can be said that this attitude derives from the overall point of view of the white psyche as it concerns the black people. This attitude stems from the era of the slave revolts when every white man was a potential deputy or sheriff or guardian of the state. Because when black people got together among themselves to work out their problems, it became a threat to white people, because such meetings were potential slave revolts.

It can be maintained that this attitude or way of thinking has perpetuated itself to this current period and that it is part of the psyche of white people in this country whatever their political persuasion might be. It is part of the white fear-guilt complex resulting from the slave revolts. There have been examples of whites who stated that they can deal with black fellows on an individual basis but become threatened or menaced by the presence of groups of blacks. It can be maintained that this attitude is held by the majority of progressive whites in this country.

A thorough re-examination must be made by black people concerning the contributions that we have made in shaping this country. If this re-examination and re-evaluation is not made, and black people are not given their proper due and respect, then the antagonisms and contradictions are going to become more and more glaring, more and more intense until a national explosion may result.

When people attempt to move from these conclusions it would be faulty reasoning to say they are ordered by racism, because, in this country and in the West, racism has functioned has [sic] a type of white nationalism when dealing with black people. We all know the habit that this has created throughout the world and particularly among nonwhite people in this country.

Therefore any re-evaluation that we must make will, for the most part, deal with identification. Who are black people, what are black people; what is their relationship to America and the world?

It must be repeated that the whole myth of "Negro citizenship," perpetuated by the white elite, has confused the thinking of radical and progressive blacks and whites in this country. The broad masses of black people react to American society in the same manner as colonial peoples react to the West in Africa, and Latin America, and had the same relationship—that of the colonized toward the colonizer.

DOCUMENT 34.8
The Ideology of the Black Panthers*

The Black Panthers are possibly the most influential and formidable purely nationalist movement in the United States. Their party was formed in Oakland, California, in October 1966, by two black nationalists, Huey Newton and Bobby Seale, and it became the heart of the Black Power movement. It represented a cry from the depths, a cry for humanity. It was also a conscious attempt to harness the rhetorical and emotional power of black nationalism to a practical program for the elimination of racial oppression in America. Rejecting acculturation, the Panthers believed it meant identification with the values of a society that had oppressed and degraded all Black people and, consequently, they sought their own national identity. Their ideology is revealed below, in the Black Panther 10-Point Platform and Program. At its heart is a call for "national liberation" of the "black colony" from what Cleaver (possibly out of Frantz Fanon) has called the "white mother country." This invocation of black nationalism was, however, at least in this early stage, not fully conceived since, in deciding to "dissolve the political bands" connecting the "black colony" to the existing United States, the platform did not seem to have any further steps in mind.

*Source: *The Black Panther*. This statement appears in every issue.

What We Want, What We Believe

1. *We want freedom. We want power to determine the destiny of our Black Community.*

We believe that black people will not be free until we are able to determine our destiny.

2. *We want full employment for our people.*

We believe that the federal government is responsible and obligated to give every man employment or a guaranteed income. We believe that if the white American businessmen will not give full employment, then the means of production should be taken from the businessmen and placed in the community so that the people of the community can organize and employ all of its people and give a high standard of living.

3. *We want an end to the robbery by the white man of our Black Community.*

We believe that this racist government has robbed us and now we are demanding the overdue debt of forty acres and two mules. Forty acres and two mules was promised 100 years ago as restitution for slave labor and mass murder of black people. We will accept the payment in currency which will be distributed to our many communities. The Germans are now aiding the Jews in Israel for the genocide of the Jewish people. The Germans murdered six million Jews. The American racist has taken part in the slaughter of over fifty million black people; therefore, we feel that this is a modest demand that we make.

4. *We want decent housing, fit for shelter of human beings.*

We believe that if the white landlords will not give decent housing to our black community, then the housing and the land should be made into cooperatives so that our community, with government aid, can build and make decent housing for its people.

5. *We want education for our people that exposes the true nature of this decadent American society. We want educa-*

tion that teaches us our true history and our role in the present-day society.

We believe in an educational system that will give to our people a knowledge of self. If a man does not have knowledge of himself and his position in society and the world, then he has little chance to relate to anything else.

6. *We want all black men to be exempt from military service.*

We believe that Black people should not be forced to fight in the military service to defend a racist government that does not protect us. We will not fight and kill other people of color in the world who, like black people, are being victimized by the white racist government of America. We will protect ourselves from the force and violence of the racist police and the racist military, by whatever means necessary.

7. *We want an immediate end to POLICE BRUTALITY and MURDER of black people.*

We believe we can end police brutality in our black community by organizing black self-defense groups that are dedicated to defending our black community from racist police oppression and brutality. The Second Amendment to the Constitution of the United States gives a right to bear arms. We therefore believe that all black people should arm themselves for self-defense.

8. *We want freedom for all black men held in federal, state, county and city prisons and jails.*

We believe that all black people should be released from the many jails and prisons because they have not received a fair and impartial trial.

9. *We want all black people when brought to trial to be tried in court by a jury of their peer group or people from their black communities, as defined by the Constitution of the United States.*

We believe that the courts should follow the United States Constitution so that black people will receive fair trials. The 14th Amendment of the U.S. Constitution gives a man a right to be tried by his peer group. A peer is a person from a similar economic, social, religious, geographical, environmental, historical and racial background. To do this the court will be forced to select a jury from the black community from which the black defendant came. We have been, and are being tried by all white juries that have no understanding of the "average reasoning man" of the black community.

10. *We want land, bread, housing, education, clothing, justice and peace. And as our major political objective, a United Nations supervised plebiscite to be held throughout the black colony in which only black colonial subjects will be allowed to participate, for the prupose of determining the will of black people as to their national destiny.*

When, in the course of human events, it becomes necessary for one people to dissolve the political bands which have connected them with another, and to assume, among the powers of the earth, the separate and equal station to which the laws of nature and nature's God entitle them, a decent respect to the opinions of mankind requires that they should declare the causes which impel them to the separation.

We hold these truths to be self-evident, that all men are created equal; that they are endowed by their Creator with certain unalienable rights; that among these are life, liberty, and the pursuit of happiness. *That, to secure these rights, governments are instituted among men, deriving their just powers from the consent of the governed; that, whenever any form of government becomes destructive of these ends, it is the right of the people to alter or to abolish it, and to institute a new government, laying its foundation on such principles, and organizing its powers in such form, as to them shall seem most likely to effect their safety and happiness.* Prudence, indeed, will dictate that governments long established should not be changed for light and transient causes;

and, accordingly, all experience hath shown, that mankind are more disposed to suffer, while evils are sufferable, than to right themselves by abolishing the forms to which they are accustomed. *But, when a long train of abuses and usurpations, pursuing invariably the same object, evinces a design to reduce them under absolute despotism, it is their right, it is their duty, to throw off such government, and to provide new guards for their future security.*

DOCUMENT 34.9

Disenchantment with President Nixon*

Bishop Stephen Spottswood of the National Association for the Advancement of Colored People was representative of the increasing disenchantment of blacks with the administration of Richard Nixon. His statement below indicates that the ties between the President and the black community, tenuous at best from the outset, had become gravely strained, owing to what Negroes interpreted as a series of measures and developments which suggested executive indifference to the Negro plight, even to his vote.

Mr. Chairman, President Kaplan, distinguished platform guests, members of the National Board of Directors, members of the National staff, officers of the regions, state conference and branches, youth councils and college chapters, members and friends, of the National Association for the Advancement of Colored People, the oldest, largest, most effective, most successful, most consulted, most respected, most feared of all the civil rights organizations in the world, I greet you to-

*Source: Bishop Stephen G. Spottswood, "Blacks Disenchantment with President Nixon." Reprinted with the permission of the National Association for the Advancement of Colored People, June 29, 1970, Cincinnati, Ohio.

night in the name of freedom and hail you as the protagonists of the fulfillment of the American Dream!

We are glad to meet again in Cincinnati, the city of seven hills, like ancient Rome, where we met 24 years ago—where the foundation for the development of our system of geographical regions was born, where Walter White denounced the political and economic oligarchies which were throttling liberty and destroying democracy by keeping the Negro "in his place." Then, as now, your Association expressed unequivocal opposition to all forms of segregation in American life; called for extension of the Emergency Price Control Act (OPA) (how we could use price controls today); urged the United Nations to proceed with all speed toward implementing the trusteeship and non-self governing territories provisions of the charter; called upon President Truman to integrate qualified Negro personnel in the Veteran's Administration; urged adoption of the Wagner-Ellender-Taft Housing Bill; urged support for the CIO and AFL organizing efforts in the South; urged abolition of discrimination in trade unions and called for enactment of a Federal Fair Employment Practices Act with adequate enforcement powers.

We are glad to note that in the intervening years, largely as a result of our efforts through legislative enactments and Supreme Court decisions, the Negro has reached a new plateau in American life.

Two years ago, former Attorney General Ramsey Clark, speaking for the Kerner Commission, called for "the reaffirmation of our faith in one society" and the Commission itself sounded a warning that the nation is moving in the direction of two societies—one black, one white—separate and unequal. Today, the signs are even more ominous. On every hand, the commentators and the politicians—the faint-hearted liberals and the tragically misguided black separatists, are announcing the end of integration, especially in the schools.

For the first time since Woodrow Wilson, we have a National Administration that can be rightly characterized as anti-Negro. This is the first time since 1920 that the National Administration has made it a matter of calculated policy to work against the needs and aspirations of the largest minority of its citizens.

Here are a few instances supporting our contention of the Administration's anti-Negro policy:

1. Signing of defense contracts with textile companies long in violation of contract requirements versus our recommendations that these contracts be cancelled.

2. The pull-back on school desegregation. The Administration went into court to secure delays in already ordered desegregation. Thank God, the Supreme Court struck down these attempts.

3. The nominations of Clement Haynsworth and G. Harrold Carswell to the United States Supreme Court (which nominations were defeated by the leadership of the NAACP, along with other organizations, including the leadership Conference on Civil Rights, of which Roy Wilkins is Chairman and in which fight our Clarence Mitchell demonstrated his superb skills on Capitol Hill as truly, the one hundred first senator!).

4. The Administration at Washington weakened our hard-won Voting Rights Act in the House.

5. The Administration opposed the cease and desist order power of the Equal Employment Opportunities Commission.

6. The Administration supported the Senate Amendment on the School Appropriation Bill.

7. The Administration produced the Moynihan Memorandum calling for "benign neglect."

8. The Administration supports tax exemption for white, separate private schools, designed to avert desegregation of the public schools.

9. On April 9th, after the rejection of his nominee, Judge Carswell, for the Supreme Court, the President described the

ideal judge as "someone who believes in the strict construction of the Constitution, as I do—A judge who will not use the power of the court to seek social change by freely interpreting the law or Constitutional clauses." This is the Administration's expressed opposition to the Equal Protection clauses of the 14th Amendment.

The effect of this has been exactly what was predicted. It has given encouragement to the Southern racists whose full page advertisements have exposed their radical retreat to the calendar level of the 1870's, such as produced by Senator Stennis of Mississippi and Governor McKeithan of Louisiana, to say nothing of the melodramatic pose of Florida's Governor Kirk in defying the Federal Court's orders to desegregate the public schools of the Everglades state.

Before us today, in the solution of the problem of a single society are the issues arising from what seems to many, the futility of our effort toward integration. There is a tremendous white backlash as we have forged a difficult path thru the metallic barriers in housing, employment and politics. A small but vociferous number of Negroes has effected the *black retreat* as indicated in the black college students' demands for separate dormitories, separate cafeterias, separate curricula and separate facilities. Incidentally, we should sympathize—even as we disagree—with young black youth whose bitter and bloody experiences on white college campuses have driven them to "the black retreat."

The white blacklash on the one hand and the black retreat on the other hand have combined to accentuate the racial polarity of which the Kerner Commission warned.

At this juncture in our national life, we of the NAACP, recalling Abraham Lincoln's declaration that "this nation cannot endure half free and half slave," emphatically paraphrase Mr. Lincoln and declare "this country cannot endure, half white

and half black!" If American democracy is to survive, we shall be one society, as the Declaration of Independence visioned and the Constitution declares!

Ours is a national problem affecting all Americans and no matter where we live, the problem of one society is before us. For instance, it is easy for Northern Negroes to forget the South because local needs are urgent and desperate but they do so at their own peril. Fifty-two percent of black Americans still live in the South, mostly in cities, where the problems of overcrowding, housing, crime, discrimination, poor education are the same as the North's. In addition, they have the Southern segregation traditions, white supremacy ideology and wanton murderousness.

Let us be reminded that the origins of the Northern ghetto problems are, to a great extent, the product of original Southern neglect. We will not win in the North unless we win in the South also. The Southern racist is a die-hard. Despite progress in race relations, despite defeat after defeat in seeking to solve segregation and discrimination he clings to his racism. For instance, Governor John Bell Williams, in the face of testimony of experts from the Department of Justice stating that there was no evidence of gunfire or attack by the students at Jackson State College, openly declared that snipers had fired on the State Police before they opened fire, killing two young Negroes and seriously wounding nine others.

Even as lynching was the Roman-holiday sport of 19th-Century America, killing black Americans promiscuously has been the 20th-Century pastime of our police whose primary duty is law enforcement and keeping the peace. I'm thinking of the six Negroes killed in Augusta, Georgia, all shot in the back; of the Panthers slain in their beds in Chicago; of the students slain at Jackson State College; of the almost daily news stories of the indiscriminate, ruthless slaying of black Americans by police and civilians, under the guise of "law and order" but actually fulfilling the guidelines of a bitter, white majority, whose vain effort to keep us "in our place" leads them to resort to the policeman's pistol and kangaroo court trials.

The white liberals and the churches have not been conspicuous in the fight for freedom lately. No one questions the demand for an immediate end of the Vietnam War. We ask again, why is it that white people always manage to find some issue, other than *race* to which they give their priority attention, the latest of which is pollution and the ecology? If racial justice and civil rights had commanded just ten percent of the attention that white liberals have given to the Vietnam War, we would not be in the position we are in today—and it is unlikely that we would have Nixon in the White House either!

The mid-century sarcasm on the white church was: "The 11 o'clock hour on Sundays is the most segregated hour in the United States!" Now the white church is trying to bring about token integration within its congregation while it should be engaged in the total task of integrating our society. When the latter is accomplished, the former objective would be an accomplished fact.

The NAACP has a vital role to play in the drama of democracy in the seventies. Many of our liberals have withdrawn from the lists because the battle is not merely a crusade in faraway Alabama, Mississippi or Louisiana but they have discovered that it is a fight in one's own state, own city, own neighborhood. Thru the efforts of the NAACP, the Supreme Court has agreed to hear the case on zoning in the suburbs to keep out low-income housing. We shall have to fight intellectuals like Professor Alexander Bickel of the Yale University Law School, who wrote in the *New Republic*, "The vanguard of black opinion—is oriented more toward the achievement of group identity and group autonomy than toward the use of public schools as assimilation agencies." Who asked Professor Bickell to determine the

vanguard of black opinion? We intend to integrate the public schools in order to give Black children equality of education —not for purposes of assimilation!

We must counteract some black authors who have tried to show that bad English grammar and slurred consonants and special terminology found among poorly educated Negroes (and poorly educated white people) are really a different language which should be learned and used in ghetto school teaching. Recently a black architect has been working on the theory that Negroes should have distinctive type housing—one which adequately accommodates their tribal instincts, inherited from our African past—*reductio ad absurdum*!

Then, after the long series of suggestions of self-imposed apartheid, we must beware of those who once stood on the solid ground of full freedom for all Americans and have now retreated to the wabbling field of compromise and the sinking sands of surrender. For example, Roy Innis, National Director of CORE recently made a Deep South visit where he was warmly received by Governors John Bell Williams of Mississippi, John J. McKeithan of Louisiana, Albert Brewer of Alabama and Lester (Ax-Handle) Maddox of Georgia. He was there to solicit their interest and support of the Innis plan to reestablish a dual school system. His scheme is not to have separate black and white systems by race, O No!—But to split the city in half along residential lines with the white half under its school system, and the black half under its system. You can just imagine how the governors were delighted with the Innis proposal, and Governor Kirk of Florida, must have felt slighted by the failure of Mr. Innis to visit him.

There are others who advocate a separate nation, to be set up *somewhere*, or for autonomous neighborhoods or districts in the cities—to run our own police, fire department, hospitals, schools and everything else. But they always make it clear that they expect to get the money from the rest of the community. *There is no such thing as autonomy on someone else's money.*

No major problem afflicting black Americans can be solved except by solving them for all Americans.

We have worked too long and too hard, made too many sacrifices, spent too much money, shed too much blood, lost too many lives fighting to vindicate our manhood as full participants in the American system to allow our victories to be nullified by phony liberals, diehard racists, discouraged and demoralized Negroes, and power-seeking politicians.

More and more the pieces fall into their places and more and more it looks like 1877—when the South made the deal with the Republican Party—and arranged to turn back the clock and to nullify the 13th, 14th, and 15th Amendments. The Wallace victory in Alabama was won by wooing the racial hatreds of the racist whites and the exaggerated threat of the rise of the black voter into power politics. Never doubt for a moment that they don't have hopes of doing it all over again—of nullifying the Civil Rights Laws of 1964, 1965, and 1968!

One of the loud hues and cries of the enemy is his opposition to busing in the school integration issue. The real issue is: What is the best, most practical, most economical way of ending racial imbalance or reducing it to a minimum? Is it pairing? Is it educational parks? Is it rearranging feeder patterns and school zone lines? If some bus transport of pupils is required, this is part of the plan.

Everyday, more than 20,000,000 children go to school by bus. Everyday, for scores of years, children in the South were bussed to long distances to segregated schools. Bussing was all right then because it sustained the dual system.

A recent survey in some 300 Southern school districts which had been desegregated showed that in 290 of them there was less bussing than there was under segregation. Hence, there is no other way

to interpret opposition to bussing for integration than as opposition to integration or inexcusable ignorance.

At this point let me insert a word of warning. When black students were beaten or killed by the police and state troopers on the campuses of Texas Southern University and South Carolina State College, we issued the age-old warning that if the police were permitted to shoot black students promiscuously, that sooner or later they would do the same to white students—Kent University was the fulfillment!

Right now we have a Board Committee wrestling with the problems of black students on college campuses, and we pledge our resources to see to it that their every right as American college students shall be protected.

Just a few days ago black high school students from the South told Government officials in Washington that they expected full student rights in the desegregation of the schools. Mrs. Ruby Martin, former Civil Rights Chief for HEW said, "No longer are black students willing to take slights and rebuffs, large and small, that Negro youngsters entering formerly all white schools have encountered in earlier years. Black kids are just not going to put up with it any longer." . . .

To cite the achievements of the NAACP during the last year would require a 24-hour speaking period. Let me point out a few of our great achievements since we met in Jackson.

First of all, let me extend to Charles Evers our hearty congratulations on being elected Mayor of Fayette! His election highlights the fact that 45 black Mayors are in as many city halls across the country and hundreds upon hundreds of black men and women have been elected to office, from the Congress down to ward Magistrate. Most recent is the magnificent victory for good government won by Kenneth Gibson in Newark, New Jersey. All this is due, in a large part, to the year-round voter registration campaigns of the

NAACP, fulfilling our original determination to make the American Negro free from disfranchisement.

Our General Counsel, Nathaniel R. Jones, has already—in less than a year—made his and the Association's weight felt in victories for black servicemen at Goose Bay, Labrador and Memphis, Tennessee. Our lawyers argued the defense of 21 San Fernando Valley College students, all of whom seemed to have a hopeless cause when we undertook their cases. Though we could not stave off convictions, it is good to report that all the defendants are today free on parole or probation.

Our Chicago Branch filed the first protest against the wanton killing of the Black Panthers in the windy city and Roy Wilkins and Arthur Goldberg are co-chairmen of the civilian Commission of Inquiry into the killings.

Roy Wilkins and Gloster Current made an immediate trip to Jackson following the killing in this city.

Our Branches, all around the country, are in the forefront of the school desegregation fight in our nationwide effort to bring quality education to all our children, white and black.

When the hurricane struck along the coasts of Mississippi and Louisiana, NAACP was there with food, money and led the fight against discrimination in flood relief. Let us hail the food-stamp program of the NAACP in Alabama, extended there recently from Mississippi, where within a 30-day period we purchased some $17,368 worth of food stamps for people in a starvation ridden county and gave direct assistance to 912 hopeless persons.

Housing, under the leadership of William Morris, had gone forward by a series of constructive steps in our housing division. We are supporting and stimulating the activities of Negro contractors; we are supplying nonprofit housing assistance to branches; we have conducted a nation-wide survey of Negro contractors and have developed guidelines for correlations of building programs. We have made a forthright attack on lily-white suburbia and we sponsored (but did not finance) a European trip to investigate the background for government-sponsored, low-cost housing for the millions in the cities of Western Europe.

NAACP led in the successful programs to bring about fair employment practices in the building trades in Pittsburgh and Chicago, to say nothing of the hundreds of other cities where we are constantly attacking the bugaboo of employment differentials.

NAACP will carry on the fight—we will grow stronger—we will rebuild the coalition of 1963 into something bigger, stronger, and more effective than it ever was!

We are dedicated to bringing the American Dream to reality for all our citizens—in the ghettos, the suburbs, in business, in Government, on the college campus, and in every neighborhood in these United States.

There must be a fusion of these ideas in the minds of all Americans. There must be a fusion of all the people of our country in the fight for freedom. We must merge on the constitutional ideal of one society. We must redeem the commitment in whose service Harry T. Moore, Medgar Evers, and Martin Luther King gave their lives. We will be worthy of them—or keep shamefully silent when their names are spoken. And we shall win!